MW00998629

Learning About Sociology and the Sociological Imagination

Edited by Daniel Bart Swann

University of Maryland

cognella®
SAN DIEGO

LIBRARY OF
CONGRESS
SURPLUS
DUPLICATE

Bassim Hamadeh, CEO and Publisher

Mieka Portier, Field Acquisitions Editor

Tony Paese, Project Editor

Casey Hands, Production Editor

Emely Villavicencio, Senior Graphic Designer

Stephanie Kohl, Licensing Coordinator

Natalie Piccotti, Director of Marketing

Kassie Graves, Vice President of Editorial

Jamie Giganti, Director of Academic Publishing

Copyright © 2021 by Cognella, Inc. All rights reserved. No part of this publication may be reprinted, reproduced, transmitted, or utilized in any form or by any electronic, mechanical, or other means, now known
or hereafter invented, including photocopying, microfilming, and recording, or in any information retrieval
system without the written permission of Cognella, Inc. For inquiries regarding permissions, translations,
foreign rights, audio rights, and any other forms of reproduction, please contact the Cognella Licensing
Department at rights@cognella.com.

Trademark Notice: Product or corporate names may be trademarks or registered trademarks and are used
only for identification and explanation without intent to infringe.

Cover image copyright © 2018 iStockphoto LP/RyanJLane.

Printed in the United States of America.

cognella® | ACADEMIC PUBLISHING

3970 Sorrento Valley Blvd., Ste. 500, San Diego, CA 92121

Brief Contents

Table of Contents

Introduction

WHAT IS SOCIOLOGY?

THE SOCIOLOGICAL PERSPECTIVE focuses on the link between individual experience, the current social context, and the past. Exploration of this link and examination of cultural variations in social interaction and the development of self, the formation of families and communities, the processes that produce conformity or deviance, and the conditions that lead to conflict and social change through selected readings, case studies, novels, and films—these sorts of exercises are practical applications of your sociological imagination, which we will aim to both understand conceptually as well as develop. Tracing changes in work, marital relationships, religious practices, and political participation, we will use theories and methods of sociology to explore the influence of race, class, gender, ethnicity, and age on the human experience.

This book focuses on social problems. There are innumerous issues in the world, and many of them relate to social structure, socialization processes, or a social issue. Many of these issues will be illuminated in this text, as will the ways in which these issues are received and dealt with by society.

Take time to discuss how wonderful some aspects of American society and humanity are. This book and your course (most likely) will necessarily focus more often than not on negative or problematic aspects of society.

SOCIAL PROBLEMS

- A **social problem** is a social condition or pattern of behavior that has negative consequences for individuals, our social world, and/or our physical world.
- Many more problems today as compared to the past are related to globalization; the increase of flows (and the ease of these flows) of ideas and products across boundaries. Problems are increasingly more global as compared to regional.
  - This course is, however, designed to focus more on domestic problems. When we can we will often use Maryland or the DC area.
- Can we think of some international social problems?

Development of a Social Problem

1. The transformation of a private trouble into a public issue (the recognition that a particular problem is shared collectively by many in society) can be done in both a top-down manner (rich are taxed too much) or through grass roots (women's suffrage).

2. The manner in which the social problems or complaints generated by people are dealt with formally.

3. In the event stage 2 does not solve the problem, activists, victims, proponents, and so on begin to distrust the structures of stage 2.

4. When a group of advocates no longer believe their issue can be addressed by the structures of stage 2, they must decide either to work outside of the current existing system or change it enough so that it will accommodate their interests.

THINKING SOCIOLOGICALLY

Basic Vocabulary

- **Structure**: The organized relationships between the basic components of a social system. Karl Mannheim believes social structure refers to the web of interacting social forces from which the various modes of observation and thinking have arisen. We are constrained by structure.
- **Power**: "The ability to control others, events, or resources; to make happen what one wants to happen in spite of obstacles, resistance, or opposition."[1]
- **Agency**: The capacity or ability of individuals to act independently and to make their own free choices. The freedom to operate independently or unconstrained by structure.
- **Intersectionality**: The intersection of two or more social problems; most often refers to forms of discrimination or oppression. The idea that structures that allow/promote discrimination are interconnected.
- **Objective reality**: Acknowledging there is a phenomenon happening through data or other forms of empirical evidence.
- **Social construction of reality**: Refers to how the world is a largely (if not entirely) a social creation, originating and evolving through everyday thoughts and actions. Most meanings and constructs in society are contested and fluid.

---

1   Max Weber, *The Theory of Social and Economic Organization* (New York: Oxford University Press, 1947).

- Through values (which are largely subjective), we label some of the phenomenon we examine in objective reality as social problems.
- **Macro**: Societal-level analysis
- **Micro**: Individual-level analysis

Reading 1.1.

How to Think Sociologically

by Steven M. Buechler

People have always tried to make sense of the world around them. Myths, fables, and religion provided traditional ways of making sense. More recently, science has provided additional ways of understanding the world. Sociology is part of the rise of science as a means of making sense of the world.

As we know in our own time, there can be tension between religious and scientific views. Contemporary disputes over evolution, sexuality, marriage, and even the age of our planet often pit religious values against scientific interpretations. More broadly speaking, both at home and abroad, religious fundamentalisms rest uneasily alongside modern, secular worldviews. These familiar tensions have a history that takes us back to the origins of sociology itself.

SOCIOLOGY AND MODERNITY

The rise of sociology is part of a much larger story about the emergence of the modern world itself. Modernity emerged in European societies through a long process of social change that unfolded from the sixteenth to the nineteenth centuries. During this time, virtually everything about organized social life in Europe was fundamentally transformed. In our day, we speak of globalization as a force that is changing the world in the most basic ways. But current patterns of globalization can be traced back to the rise of modernity itself; in many respects, they are a continuation of the changes that ushered in the modern world.

Economically, modernity transformed most people from peasants to workers in a complex division of labor. Politically, modernity created distinct nation-states with clear boundaries. Technologically, modernity applied scientific knowledge to producing everything from consumer goods to lethal weapons. Demographically, modernity triggered population growth and massive migration from small, familiar, rural communities to large, urban, anonymous cities.

When social worlds change like this, some people benefit while others are harmed. In addition, most people find rapid change and its inevitable conflict to be unsettling,

Steven M. Buechler, "How to Think Sociologically," *Critical Sociology*, pp. 3-15, 281-290. Copyright © 2014 by Taylor & Francis Group. Reprinted with permission.

and they seek to understand what is happening. It was this moment that gave rise to sociology. Explaining modernity became sociology's task at the same time that modernity was making sociology possible in the first place.

The link between modernity and sociology was the Enlightenment. This intellectual revolution accompanied other revolutionary changes occurring throughout Europe. In the broadest terms, the Enlightenment challenged religious belief, dogma, and authority. It sought to replace them with scientific reason, logic, and knowledge.

Four basic themes pervaded Enlightenment thought (Zeitlin 1987). First, human reason was the best guide to knowledge, even if it meant that scientific skepticism displaced religious certainty. Second, reason must be paired with careful, scientific observation. Third, Enlightenment thought insisted that social arrangements be rationally justified; if not, they must be changed until they could be rationally defended. Finally, Enlightenment thought assumed that with the systematic application of reason, the perfectibility of people and the progress of society were all but inevitable.

Enlightenment thought contained some potentially fatal flaws. It was a Eurocentric worldview, created by privileged white men, that made universal pronouncements about all people in all times and places. While applauding Europe's progress, it ignored the colonial domination of the rest of the world that provided the labor, goods, and wealth that underwrote that progress. Generalizations about "humanity" meant "males," to the exclusion of women, and pronouncements on the "human race" meant white Europeans, to the exclusion of darker people, who were viewed as subhuman.

The Enlightenment was much more than a justification of imperialism, sexism, and racism, but it could become that as well. More than two centuries later, the jury is still out on whether Enlightenment biases can be overcome and its promises be fulfilled. Some postmodernists see little hope for this to happen. Others, myself included, think that the critical spirit of the Enlightenment can help uproot its biases. The project is already under way as feminists, people of color, and postcolonial writers find their way into contemporary sociological discourses (Lemert 2013).

In its own day, the Enlightenment provoked a "romantic conservative reaction" (Zeitlin 1987) that rejected the elevation of reason and science over faith and tradition. It defended traditional customs, institutions, and ways of life from the new standard of critical reason. The debate between Enlightenment progress and conservative reaction set the agenda for sociology as the social science of modernity. Progress or order? Change or stability? Reason or tradition? Science or religion? Individual or group? Innovation or authority? Such dichotomies framed the subject matter of the new science of sociology.

The classical era of sociology refers to European thinkers whose ideas brought this new discipline to maturity from the late eighteenth to the early twentieth centuries.

The very different sociologies of Auguste Comte, Herbert Spencer, Ferdinand Toennies, Karl Marx, Max Weber, Georg Simmel, Emile Durkheim, and others are variations on sociology's main theme: How do we understand modern society? Given these efforts, we might think of sociology as the ongoing effort of human beings to understand the worlds they are simultaneously inheriting from earlier generations and maintaining and transforming for future generations.

This approach has been described as the "sociological imagination." It arises when people realize that they can only know themselves by understanding their historical period and by examining others in the same situation as themselves. We think sociologically when we grasp how our historical moment differs from previous ones and how the situations of various groups of people differ from each other (Mills 1959).

The sociological imagination is guided by three related questions. The first concerns the social structure of society. How is it organized, what are its major institutions, and how are they linked together? The second concerns the historical location of society. How has it emerged from past social forms, what mechanisms promote change, and what futures are possible based on this historical path? The third concerns individual biography within society. What kinds of character traits are called forth by this society, and what kinds of people come to prevail? The sociological imagination is thus about grasping the relations between history and biography within society.

The sociological imagination sensitizes us to the difference between "personal troubles" and "public issues." A personal trouble is a difficulty in someone's life that is largely a result of individual circumstances. A public issue is a difficulty that is largely owing to social arrangements beyond the individual's control. The distinction is crucial because common sense often interprets events as personal troubles; we explain someone's difficulties as springing from individual shortcomings. The sociological imagination recognizes that such difficulties are rarely unique to one person; they rather happen to many people in similar situations. The underlying causes derive more from social structures and historical developments than the individual alone. If our goal is "diagnosis," the sociological imagination locates problems in a larger social context. If our goal is "treatment," it implies changing the structure of society rather than the behavior of individuals.

This applies to success as well. Common sense often attributes success to individual qualities. The sociological imagination asks what social and historical preconditions were necessary for an individual to become a success. Many successful people, in Jim Hightower's memorable phrase, "were born on third base but thought they hit a triple." The point is that whereas common sense sees the world in individual terms, sociological thinking sees it in structural terms. Only by seeing the connections between structure, history, and biography can we understand the world in a sociological way.

This discussion implies that professional sociologists and ordinary people see the world differently. This is often true, but the issue is more complicated. Modernity has also led ordinary people to develop a practical sociology in their everyday lives. Think about it this way. Sociology sees the world as a social construction that could follow various blueprints. Indeed, social worlds *are* constructed in very different ways in different times and places.

In our time, an awareness of the socially constructed nature of social worlds is no longer the privileged insight of scholars, but has become part of everyday understanding. Whether owing to rapid change, frequent travel, cultural diffusion, or media images, many people understand that we live in socially constructed worlds. Some people are distressed by this fact, and others rejoice in it, but few can escape it. Thus, an idea that was initially associated with professional sociology has become part of the everyday consciousness of ordinary people today.

The result is that many people without formal sociological training understand social processes quite well. Put differently, the objects of sociological analysis are people who are quite capable of becoming the subjects of the sociological knowledge created by that analysis. Although few people can explain how quantum mechanics governs the physical world, many can describe sociological processes that shape the social world.

Certain circumstances prompt people to think sociologically. Perhaps the key stimulant is when familiar ways of doing and thinking no longer work. It is when people are surprised, puzzled, challenged, or damaged that they are most likely to think sociologically (Lemert 2008). People then develop sociological competence as they try to make sense out of specific, individual circumstances by linking them to broader social patterns. In this way, sociological awareness begins to understand bigger things as a by-product of wrestling with the practical challenges of everyday life.

Circumstances do not inevitably provoke sociological consciousness. Some people redouble their faith or retreat into ritualism. So perhaps we can conclude this way. Societies confront people with problems. These problems have always had the potential to promote a sociological awareness. In our times, there is a greater awareness of the socially constructed nature of the world. This makes it even more likely that when people in this society are confronted with practical challenges, they will develop sociological competence as a practical life skill. In late modernity, everyone can become a practical sociologist.

THINKING SOCIOLOGICALLY

The sociological perspective involves several themes. They overlap with one another, and some may be found in other social sciences as well as everyday consciousness. Taken together, they comprise a distinctive lens for viewing the social world. Here are some of those themes.

Society Is a Social Construction

People construct social order. Sociology does not see society as God-given, as biologically determined, or as following any predetermined plan beyond human intervention. At the same time, this does not mean that everyone plays an equal role in the process or that the final product looks like what people intended.

Social construction begins with intentions that motivate people to act in certain ways. When many people have similar goals and act in concert, larger social patterns or institutions are created. Goal-driven action is essential to the creation of institutions, and it remains equally important to their maintenance and transformation over time. Put succinctly, society is a human product (Berger and Luckmann 1966).

Basic human needs ensure some similarities in the goals that people pursue in all times and places. But these pursuits also unfold in specific historical circumstances and cultural contexts that have led to a dazzling variety of social worlds. This variety is itself the best evidence of the socially constructed nature of social worlds. If biology or genetics were the determining force behind social worlds, wouldn't they look a lot more similar than what we actually see around the globe?

Social constructionists thus insist that society arises from the goal-driven action of people. But they also recognize that the institutions created by such actions take on a life of their own. They appear to exist independently of the people who create and sustain them. They are experienced by people as a powerful external force that weighs down on them. When this external force becomes severe enough, people are likely to lose sight of the fact that society is a social product in the first place.

The value of the social constructionist premise is this dual recognition. On one hand, society is a subjective reality originating in the intentions of social actors. On the other hand, it becomes an objective reality that confronts subsequent generations as a social fact that inevitably shapes *their* intentional actions—and so it goes. Understood this way, the idea that society is a social construction is at the heart of the sociological perspective.

Society Is an Emergent Reality

Another premise of sociology is emergentism. This reveals sociology's distinctive level of analysis. For psychology, the level of analysis is the individual, even if it is acknowledged that individuals belong to groups. For sociology, the level of analysis is social ties rather than individual elements. Emergentism recognizes that certain realities only appear when individual elements are combined in particular ways. When they are, qualitatively new realities emerge through these combinations.

Take a simple example. Imagine a random pile of ten paper clips. Now imagine linking these paper clips together to form a chain. There are still ten paper clips, but a new emergent reality has appeared that is qualitatively different from the random pile because of how the elements are related to one another. Or consider human reproduction. Neither sperm nor egg is capable of producing human life on its own; in combination, qualitatively new life begins to emerge from a particular combination of elements.

Sociology specializes in the social level of analysis that emerges when elements are combined to create new, larger realities. Emergentism also implies that when we try to understand elements outside of their context, it is at best a simplification and at worst a distortion. The parts derive meaning from their relationship with other parts, and the sociological perspective is fundamentally attuned to such relationships.

Society Is a Historical Product

Thinking historically is a crucial part of the sociological imagination (Mills 1959). Classical sociologists thought historically because they lived in times of rapid social change and it was a major challenge to understand such change. Modern sociology tends to be more static, and modern people tend to be very present-oriented. Both professional and practical sociologists would benefit from a more historical perspective on the social world.

Seeing society as a historical product means recognizing that we cannot understand the present without understanding the past. Historical knowledge of past social conditions provides crucial comparisons. Without such benchmarks, it is impossible to understand what is genuinely new in the present day. Without a historical referent for comparison, sociology is clueless when it comes to understanding social change. Historical knowledge also provides the raw material for categories, comparisons, typologies, and analogies that are crucial to understanding both the present and possible future worlds.

The concept of emergentism applies here because the importance of seeing relationships between elements also works chronologically. If we look at society at only one point in time, we sever it from its past and its potential futures. Its very meaning arises from these relationships; to ignore them is to distort even the static understanding of society at one point in time. Consider the difference between a photograph and a film that presents a succession of images. We can learn something from the still photo, but its meaning often changes dramatically when we see it as one of a series of interrelated images.

Society Consists of Social Structures

Sociologists use the term *structure* to refer to the emergent products of individual elements. Structure implies that the social world has certain patterns or regularities that recur over time. Put differently, sociologists are keenly interested in social organization.

Structures are products of human purposes, but they acquire an objective reality and become a powerful influence on human action. Think about how physical structures like buildings shape action. We almost always enter buildings through doors; in rare cases we might do so through windows, but walking through walls is not an option. Social structures are less visible and more flexible than buildings, but they also channel people's actions, because they make some actions routine and expected, others possible but unlikely, and still others all but impossible.

Like buildings, social structures often have a vertical dimension. Social structures ensure that some people are better off than others and that some are not very well off at all. Some residential buildings have penthouses at the top, premium suites near the top, standard accommodations below them, and housekeeping staff in the basement. Social structures are also stratified, granting power, privilege, and opportunity to some while limiting or denying them to others. Sociologists are especially interested in the hierarchical dimension of social structures.

Sociologists traditionally thought of social structures as powerful forces weighing down upon the individual. In this image, structures constrain freedom of choice and behavior. But this is a one-sided view. Structures are constraining, but they are also enabling. These established patterns of social organization also make many actions possible in the first place or easier in the second place. Without preexisting social structures, we would have to do everything "from scratch," and the challenge of sheer survival might overwhelm us. The trick is thus to see social structures as simultaneously constraining and enabling social action (Giddens 1984).

Society Consists of Reflexive Actors

People in society are aware of themselves, of others, and of their relationships with others. As reflexive actors, we monitor our action and its effects on others. We continue, modify, or halt actions, depending on whether they are achieving their intended effects. According to one school of thought, we are literally actors, because social life is like a theatrical performance in which we try to convince others that we are a certain kind of person (Goffman 1959). To stage effective performances, we must constantly be our own critic, judging and refining our performances. Reflexivity thus means that when we act, we are conscious of our action, we monitor its course, and we make adjustments over time.

To stage such performances, we must undergo socialization. Along the way, we acquire a language that provides us with tools for reflexive thinking. We also acquire a self. Oddly enough, to have a self requires that we first have relationships with others. Through those relationships, we imaginatively see the world from their perspective, which includes seeing ourselves as we imagine we appear to them. It is this ability to see ourselves through the perspective of others—to see ourselves as an object—that defines the self. Reflexive action only becomes possible with a self.

Reflexivity makes ordinary people into practical sociologists. To be a competent person is to be a practical sociologist. We cannot help being sociologists every time we ponder a potential relationship, reconsider a hasty action, or adopt someone else's viewpoint. All such situations call upon and refine the reflexivity that is the hallmark of social action as well as a defining characteristic of the sociological perspective.

Society Is an Interaction of Agency and Structure

Social structures and reflexive actors are intimately connected. Unfortunately, much sociology emphasizes one side of this connection at the expense of the other. Agency-centered views stress the ability of people to make choices out of a range of alternatives in almost any situation. The emphasis on choice implies that people control their own destiny, at least within broad limits. Structure-centered views stress the extent to which people's choices are limited by social structures. The emphasis on structures implies that people's options—if not their lives—are essentially determined by larger social forces over which they have little control. Both approaches have merit, but the challenge is to see structure and agency in a more interconnected way.

Marx once said that people make their own history (acknowledging agency), but under circumstances they do not choose but rather inherit from the past (acknowledging structure). Here's an analogy from the game of pool. Each time you approach the table, you "inherit" a structure left by your opponent when they missed their last shot. Yet, for every layout of balls on the table, there is always a shot that you can attempt, and that action will alter the structure of the table for subsequent shots. In this analogy, structure (the position of balls on the table) both limits and creates opportunities for agency (taking a shot), which in turn alters the structure for the next round of shooting. If pool is not your game, chess is also a good analogy. The point is that agency and structure are two sides of the same coin; each conditions the possibilities of the other as we make our own history in circumstances we don't choose.

The close connection between structure and agency has led one theorist to reject the notion of structure altogether, because it implies something that exists apart from agency. Anthony Giddens (1984) talks about a *process* of structuration. In this view, actors use preexisting structures to accomplish their goals, but they also re-create them as a by-product of their actions. Consider a wedding ceremony. It is a preexisting cultural ritual people use to accomplish the goal of getting married. The by-product of all these individual marriages is the perpetuation of the cultural ritual itself. Generalize this to any situation in which we draw upon an established part of our social world to achieve a goal; in using this part we also sustain (and perhaps transform) it as a part of social structure.

Society Has Multiple Levels

Although society has multiple levels, sociologists often focus on one level at a time. Think about using Google Maps to locate a destination. You can zoom out to get the big picture at the expense of not seeing some important details. Alternatively, you can zoom in on some key details at the expense of not seeing the big picture. Combining these differing views will orient you to your destination, but we must remember it is ultimately all one interconnected landscape.

Sociologists nevertheless distinguish between macro and micro levels of society. When we look at the macro level, we typically include millions of people organized into large categories, groups, or institutions. The macro level is the "big picture" or "high altitude" perspective in which society's largest patterns are evident and individuals are invisible. When we look at the micro level, we might inspect no more than a dozen people interacting in a small group setting. Here, the role of particular individuals is very prominent, and larger social patterns fade into the background.

Some of the best sociology involves understanding not only structure-agency connections but also micro-macro links. Every macro-structure rests on micro-interaction, and every micro-interaction is shaped by macro-structures. The previous example of a wedding also illustrates this point. On the macro level, weddings are a cultural ritual that inducts people into the institution of marriage and the family. However, weddings, marriage, and the family would not exist on the macro level without countless, micro-level interactions. The macro-level institution depends on micro-level actions to sustain it. At the same time, anyone who has ever gotten married will tell you that macro-level, cultural expectations about weddings impose themselves on people as they plan for this supposedly personal event. Every micro-level wedding depends on a macro-level, cultural blueprint for its social significance. The micro and macro levels of society are one interdependent reality rather than two separate things.

SOCIETY INVOLVES UNINTENDED CONSEQUENCES

One of the more profound insights of the sociological perspective concerns unintended and unanticipated consequences of action. Much human action is purposive or goal-directed. People act because they want to accomplish something. Despite this, they sometimes fail to achieve their goals. But whether people achieve their goals or not, their actions always create other consequences that they don't intend or even anticipate. Shakespeare made a profoundly sociological point when he had Juliet fake her own suicide to dramatize her love for Romeo. Unfortunately, the plan never reached Romeo. Juliet neither intended nor anticipated that Romeo would find her unconscious, believe that she was really dead, and take his own life in response. Nor did he intend (or even realize) that she would awaken, discover his real death, and really take her life in response. Talk about unintended consequences!

This principle acknowledges the complexity of the social world and the limits on our ability to control it. It says that despite our best efforts, the effects of social action cannot be confined to one intended path; they always spill over into unexpected areas. The principle is also a cautionary message for those seeking to solve social problems. Such efforts might succeed, but they often bring other consequences that are neither positive nor intended.

Efforts to control crime provide an example. Consider policies to "get tough" on crime through harsher treatment like capital punishment and mandatory sentencing. Because the human beings who serve as judges and juries are reflexive actors who take these facts into account, they are often less likely to convict suspects without overwhelming evidence because of the harshness of the sentence. Thus, the unintended consequence of an attempt to "get tough" on crime might be the opposite, because fewer suspects are convicted than before.

A related idea is the distinction between manifest and latent functions. A manifest function is an outcome that people intend. A latent function is an outcome that people are not aware of; it can complement, but it often contradicts, the manifest function. Crime and punishment provide yet another example. The manifest function of imprisonment is punishment or rehabilitation. The latent function is to bring criminals together where they can meet one another, exchange crime techniques, and become better criminals upon their return to society.

The concept of latent functions is crucial to sociological analysis. Sometimes we observe behavior or rituals that seem irrational, pointless, or self-defeating. This is the time to begin looking for latent functions. What we will often find is that such "irrational" behavior reinforces the identity and sustains the cohesion of the group that performs it. Thus, before we dismiss the tribal rain dance (because "rain gods" don't exist), we must explore its latent function. Even when people don't (manifestly) know what they are (latently) doing, their behavior can be crucial to group cohesion.

Recognizing unintended consequences and latent functions is not just for professional sociologists. Daily living requires managing risk, and ordinary people in everyday life recognize the tricky nature of goal-directed action. The folk wisdom that "the road to hell is paved with good intentions" acknowledges the potential disconnect between goals and outcomes. Such recognition, however, never completely prevents outcomes we neither intend nor expect. These principles give social life some of its most surprising twists, and sociology some of its most fascinating challenges.

No attempt to capture the sociological perspective in a small number of themes can be complete. Other sociologists would doubtless modify this list. But most would recognize these themes as central to thinking sociologically. As such, they provide a foundation for the more detailed investigations to follow.

SOCIOLOGY'S DOUBLE CRITIQUE

This final theme deserves special emphasis as the foundation of this book. Last but not least, thinking sociologically means looking at the social world in a critical way.

In everyday language, *critical* implies something negative. Being critical is often seen as being harsh, unfair, or judgmental. When we say someone is "critical," we often mean that their behavior is inappropriately mean-spirited. This is a perfectly reasonable use of everyday language, and the point it makes about how people should treat one another is also perfectly reasonable.

In sociological language, *critical* means something else. Doing sociology in a critical way means looking beyond appearances, understanding root causes, and asking who benefits. Being critical is what links knowledge to action and the potential of building a better society. Being critical in the sociological sense rests on the profoundly *positive* belief that we can use knowledge to understand the flaws of the social world and act to correct them.

The sociological perspective contains a double critique. First, mainstream sociology brings an inherently critical angle of vision to its subject. Second, some particular approaches in sociology carry this critique further by building on values that make sociological analysis especially critical of power and domination.

The critical dimension of mainstream sociology derives from the Enlightenment. Despite the flaws noted earlier, the Enlightenment advocated the use of reason, science, and evidence to critically examine religious truth, established doctrine, and political authority. Given its Enlightenment roots, sociology has always cast a critical eye on all types of claims, forms of knowledge, and exercises of power.

It is this quality that Peter Berger (1963) called the "debunking" tendency of sociological consciousness. Debunking means that the sociological perspective never takes the social world at face value and never assumes that it is what it appears to be. The sociological perspective rather looks at familiar phenomena in new ways to get beyond the immediately obvious, publicly approved, or officially sanctioned view. In this way, sociology sees through the facades of social structures to their unintended consequences and latent functions. Sociologically speaking, the problem might not be crime but laws, not revolution but government. Berger concludes that sociology is not compatible with totalitarianism, because the debunking quality of sociology will always be in tension with authoritarian claims to knowledge and power.

Although the world has changed since Berger wrote, the need for debunking is greater than ever. The political fundamentalisms of Cold War and rival superpowers have been replaced by other fundamentalisms that are logical targets for sociology's debunking insights. A world in which more and more people feel they know things with absolute certainty is a world that drastically needs the sociological perspective.

At the same time that some people embrace fundamentalist beliefs, others become suspicious and cynical about everything. This stance ("debunking on steroids") is too much of a good thing. For the ultra-cynical poser, all ideas, values, and beliefs are suspect, and none deserve support. Against this stance, sociology offers nuance and judgment. The sociological perspective recognizes that some ideas, values, and beliefs have more merit, logic, or evidence than others. Careful sociological thinkers make such distinctions. Indeed, the ultra-cynical mind-set itself needs debunking. Cynicism helps people avoid action or evade responsibility. A sociological perspective suggests that such inaction, or evasion, *is* action that tacitly supports dominant powers by refusing to challenge them in any way.

Mainstream sociology does not take the world for granted. Just when we think we have the answers, it poses another level of questions. For all these reasons, sociology in its most generic form has always included a critical angle of vision.

Although mainstream sociology is inherently critical, some versions of sociology take critique to another level by adopting certain values as the basis for their critique. In contrast to mainstream sociology, these approaches are devoted to a critical analysis of how social structures create relations of domination.

This fully critical sociology is best understood in contrast to mainstream sociology. Although mainstream sociology is critical because of its debunking tendency, it also adopts a scientific posture of detachment. Mainstream sociology seeks to be value-free, value-neutral, or objective. Put differently, mainstream sociology deliberately refrains from taking sides that would jeopardize its scientific neutrality. Mainstream sociology recognizes that *as citizens*, sociologists can be political actors. But it insists that in their role as scientific sociologists, they must maintain their objectivity.

Critical sociology differs from mainstream sociology on these issues. It emphasizes that in social science, humans are both the subjects and the objects of study. Notions of objectivity derived from the natural sciences don't necessarily translate into social science. But even if sociology could approximate objectivity, critical sociologists reject such a stance. It is not desirable, because the quest for objectivity diverts sociologists from asking the most important questions and from taking a more active role in the resolution of social problems.

Think of the contrast in this way. Mainstream sociology is primarily committed to one set of Enlightenment values having to do with science and objectivity. Critical sociology is primarily committed to another set of Enlightenment values having to do with freedom and equality. The latter values demand critical scrutiny of any social order that imposes unnecessary inequalities or restrictions on people's ability to organize their lives as they wish. These values require critical analysis of social arrangements that create conflicting interests between people and allow one group to benefit at the expense of another.

Critical sociologists deliberately focus on relations of domination, oppression, or exploitation, because these actions so obviously violate the values of freedom and equality. Critical sociologists are willing to advocate for groups who are victimized by such arrangements. Good critical sociologists realize they cannot speak for such groups. But they can explore how social arrangements make it difficult for some to speak for themselves, and they can underscore the importance of changing those arrangements.

Other issues distinguish mainstream from critical sociology. Mainstream sociology's commitment to science means it maintains a strict divide between scientific questions of what *is* and normative questions of what *ought* to be. Critical sociology wants to transcend this divide by linking critical analysis of how the world is organized now with normative arguments for how the world should be organized in the future. Behind such arguments are hopeful, or even utopian assumptions about alternative worlds that might be constructed. Critical sociology is simultaneously pessimistic about the current state of the world and optimistic about its possible futures. It examines our potential for living humanely, the social obstacles that block this potential, and the means to change from a problematic present to a preferable future.

The debate between mainstream and critical sociology is important and complex, and it will not be resolved by anything said here. But what can be said is that sociology is better because of the debate. Each side provides a corrective to the faults of the other. At the extreme, mainstream sociology becomes an inhumane, sterile approach that reduces human beings to objects of scientific curiosity; it needs a course correction through the humane values of critical sociology. At the extreme, critical sociology becomes an empty, ideological stance that denies the complexities of its own value commitments; it needs a course correction through the scientific caution of mainstream sociology.

Sociology's double critique thus derives from mainstream and critical sociology, respectively. My primary goal in this book is to illustrate critical sociology, but I also include the critical insights of mainstream sociology. I do so because these approaches sometimes speak to different issues, because neither seems adequate on its own, because they are often complementary, and because this best conveys the richness of our discipline itself. In the end, it is less important which side is "right" than that both sides coexist and continually provoke us to be reflexive about our role as sociologists and as actors in the world.

Sociology's double critique is also crucial to rethinking the flaws of the Enlightenment itself. Mainstream sociology's notion of debunking accepted truths grew out of the Enlightenment struggle against religion, but there is no reason it can't also foster critical examination of the Enlightenment itself. Critical sociology's challenge to domination also seems tailor-made to examining and overturning those forms of domination that the Enlightenment ignored, accepted, or promoted. Thus, for all its flaws, the Enlightenment provides tools for its own examination, critique, and transformation.

REFERENCES

Berger, Peter. 1963. *Invitation to Sociology*. New York: Doubleday.

Berger, Peter, and Thomas Luckmann. 1966. *The Social Construction of Reality*. Garden City, NY: Anchor.

Giddens, Anthony. 1984. *The Constitution of Society*. Berkeley: University of California Press.

Goffman, Erving. 1959. *The Presentation of Self in Everyday Life*. Garden City, NY: Anchor.

Lemert, Charles. 2008. *Social Things*. 4th ed. Lanham, MD: Rowman & Littlefield.

———. 2013. *Social Theory: The Multicultural and Classic Readings*. 5th ed. Boulder, CO: Westview Press.

Mills, C. Wright. 1959. *The Sociological Imagination*. New York: Oxford University Press.

Zeitlin, Irving. 1987. *Ideology and the Development of Sociological Theory*. Englewood Cliffs, NJ: Prentice Hall.

THE SCIENCE OF SOCIOLOGY

The American Sociological Association says that "[s]ociology is the scientific study of society, including patterns of social relationships, social interaction, and culture."[2]

---

2   "Sociology," in *Dictionary of the Social Sciences*, edited by Craig Calhoun (New York: Oxford University Press, 2002), XX–XX.

What Do Sociologists Study?

Sociologists study all things human, from the interactions between two people to the complex relationships between nations or multinational corporations. While sociology assumes that human actions are patterned, individuals still have room for choices. Becoming aware of the social processes that influence the way humans think, feel, and behave plus having the will to act can help individuals to shape the social forces they face.[3]

- **Basic research**: Expands general understanding.
- **Applied research**: Aims to inform policy.
- **Quantitative methods**: Emphasize methods that allow the study and analysis of data through numbers and figures. These methods often lend themselves to a statistical analysis.
- **Survey research**: Data collected through a designed set of questions. One of many forms of quantitative research, but a particularly common one.
- **Qualitative methods**: Usually emphasize data collected in the field: observation, interviews, ethnography, and netnography. In this method data is more likely to be interpreted or defined by the researcher (i.e., If l am using observation to research deviance on campus, l as the researcher define what it is that l will consider deviance). Then l must evaluate/decide which acts l'm observing meet the scope of the definition that l as the researcher have set.
- **Historical and comparative methods**: Focuses on understanding the past or tracing events over time.
- **Secondary data analysis**: Re-examining or analyzing previously collected data (i.e., using the census to find a relationship between zip code health and unemployment).
- **Mixed methods**: Using two or more sociological methods in conjunction with one another. This has become increasingly popular.

APPLYING SOCIOLOGY TO EVERYDAY LIFE

CRITICAL THINKING: How might understanding sociology help us better understand our own lives?

---

3 Craig Calhoun, ed., *Dictionary of the Social Sciences* (New York: Oxford University Press, 2002); Anthony Giddens, *Sociology: A Brief but Critical Introduction* (Stanford, CA: Stanford University Press, 1987); Robert A. Nisbet, *The Sociological Tradition* (New York: Basic Books, 1966); Caroline Hodges Persell, *Understanding Society: An Introduction to Sociology*, 3rd edition (New York: Harper & Row, 1990).

One of the great things about sociology is how applicable it is to everyday life. It is a discipline that can be used to think about one's place in the world, social issues, behaviors, and/or outcomes and inequalities. A mastery of sociology, social concepts, and the sociological imagination allows individuals to situate themselves in a larger social context and have a much better gauge of their own fate in the world. While earlier scholars focused more on the nation-state as the unit of analysis, by the twentieth century many sociologists (like Mills) began to gear their research and work more toward the manner in which individuals are affected by social structure and institutions, constrained by social structure, and so on. Through this focus, sociologists are better able to understand lived experiences of people in society, and individuals who develop skills of social analysis (sociological toolbelt) are also able to gain understanding and insight into their everyday lives.

Reading 1.2.

The Sociology of Everyday Life

by Steven M. Buechler

Symbolic interactionism provides our best answers to questions about self and society, but other approaches broaden the questions and enrich the answers. This chapter examines sociologies of everyday life, including phenomenological sociology, the social construction of reality, ethnomethodology, and dramaturgical sociology. It concludes with final reflections about the self in a postmodern social world.

PHENOMENOLOGICAL SOCIOLOGY

Philosophers have long debated *ontology* and *epistemology*. Those are fancy words for questions about what really exists in the world and how we can have reliable knowledge of it.

Here's a real-life example: Imagine driving on a winding, two-lane road late at night. Just beyond your headlights, you see an ambiguous shape at the side of the road. In an instant, you convince yourself that it is a deer about to jump into the road. As you brake and approach, you realize there's no deer. It's simply a bush, backlit by the moon. Your mind tricked you into seeing a deer and believing it was real—but only for an instant. Philosophers ask whether such mind tricks occur more often and last longer. If so, how do we know what is real and that our knowledge is reliable?

Opposing answers may be found in the philosophies of John Locke (1632–1704) and Immanuel Kant (1724–1804). Locke maintained that an external, objective world exists independently of all observers. Moreover, that objective world has an inherent

Steven M. Buechler, "The Sociology of Everyday Life," *Critical Sociology*, pp. 207-221, 281-290. Copyright © 2014 by Taylor & Francis Group. Reprinted with permission.

order to it. Finally, people are blank slates, or passive observers of that world. We perceive an orderly world because we use our senses to grasp the objective world and its inherent order. For empiricism, order is *out there* and people learn about it as they interact with the world.

Kant took a rationalist or idealist position. He agreed that we have perceptions of the world around us, but thought they are chaotic and fragmented. They only become orderly because *we* organize them into meaningful patterns. Rather than blank slates, we are born with innate categories like time, space, motion, and causality. We use these categories to impose order on fragmentary sense impressions of the world. This is why we "see" a deer that isn't really there.

In contrast to empiricism, Kant argued that we can never know for sure about the external world and whether it is orderly. People might believe they live in an orderly world, but only because their mental categories create order for them. For rationalism, order is *in here* because people impose meaning on otherwise-chaotic perceptions.

Edmund Husserl (1859–1938) elaborated this position at the end of the nineteenth century by developing phenomenology. Like Kant, Husserl emphasized how mind creates order. Everything we know about the world is filtered through mind and consciousness. Our mind is the source of intentions, which in turn create a meaningful world. It is our purposes or goals that impose order on the world.

Like Kant, Husserl believed that an orderly world is an accomplishment of our minds. However, we are not necessarily aware of this accomplishment. In everyday life (what Husserl called the lifeworld), we rely on a natural attitude of taken-for-granted assumptions. Here's the interesting twist. The natural attitude makes us into naive empiricists who take an orderly world for granted. The natural attitude provides a sense of order, but obscures how it comes from us rather than existing "out there."

The natural attitude means we assume that an objective world exists, that it has meaning and order, and that it is intersubjectively shared with others who experience it in much the same way we do. The natural attitude just seems like common sense. In reality, it tricks us into thinking that order is in the world instead of in our minds. Based on these misguided assumptions, we plan, act, and find our way in the world.

This philosophical detour has taken us from Locke's empiricism through Kant's rationalism to Husserl's phenomenology. Let's get back on the main road of sociology with the guidance of Alfred Schutz (1932–1967). In the mid-twentieth century, he developed a phenomenological sociology indebted to Kant's emphasis on mental categories, Husserl's idea of intentionality, and Weber's emphasis on subjective meanings.

Schutz agrees with Husserl that the natural attitude is crucial in everyday life. Schutz, however, sees this common sense perspective as a fragile and delicate construction. He asks how we maintain this attitude in the first place. We return to sociology by examining how social interactions sustain the natural attitude. Put differently, how do we convince ourselves and others that we live in an objective, orderly, shared world?

The most basic way we do this is by *assuming* reciprocity of perspectives. We assume that "the experiences I am having here and now are similar or identical to the experiences you are having here and now; if we traded places, our experiences would be essentially the same."

This assumption is like the default setting for social interaction. It gets it started. However, even though we assume reciprocity of perspectives all the time, it is not necessarily true. The room we experience as cold might be warm to others; the poem that brings us to tears might leave others untouched; the music we find jarring could be someone else's favorite song. So it sometimes turns out that our perspectives are *not* so reciprocal after all.

When interaction breaks down in this way, the focus often shifts to consciously creating the reciprocity that people have just realized is missing. When we question others, express feelings, share impressions, or argue positions, it can narrow the gap between perspectives. Reciprocity is thus the unstated assumption of all social interaction, and it often becomes its explicit goal when people realize it is lacking.

The impression that we live in an orderly world is also maintained by stock knowledge. This is the commonsense stuff "everybody knows." Stock knowledge becomes so familiar that we forget we once had to learn it. Once we do so, it becomes "second nature" and unquestioned. This knowledge and the way it gets embedded in everyday life make our world appear natural, normal, logical, and inevitable. It makes it easy to see the world as an orderly place and hard to see how we create our impression of an orderly world.

Much the same may be said for recipes, or cultural knowledge of "standard operating procedures" for accomplishing everyday goals. The metaphor of a recipe suggests a basic set of ingredients while allowing for variations once people learn the recipe. Like stock knowledge, recipes are learned but eventually become second nature. As in the "habitus" discussed in the previous chapter, everybody struggles the first time they drive a car, use a computer, or play a musical instrument. As they become more skilled, they take that learning for granted and it becomes second nature. Thus as we unthinkingly resort to familiar routines to accomplish things, our skilled activities reinforce our sense of a naturally ordered world.

We also sustain a sense of order in the world through typifications. Like Kant, Schutz claims that we use mental categories to organize our experiences into coherent patterns. Unlike Kant, Schutz's typifications are not innate but learned.

Typifications are essential to everyday life. Here's why. Every person and situation we encounter is unique, at least in the details. If we were constantly attuned to the unique aspects of each person or situation, we would be mentally overwhelmed. Life would be an endless series of new events, and lessons from the past would not apply to the present. We manage this potentially dizzying complexity through typifications. We understand unique people or situations as instances of broader types of people or situations that we already know.

We grasp a complex world by sorting it into typifications and using them to understand particular people and situations. Typifications are like the definition of the situation. Once we know the definition of the situation—or once we find appropriate typifications through which to understand a situation—we know what to expect, what norms are in effect, how to behave, and the like.

Like stock knowledge and recipes, typifications are learned. They are a bit like stereotypes. We have typifications of corporate CEOs, movie stars, truck drivers, welfare recipients, lawyers, plumbers, and soccer moms. We have typifications about fraternity parties, funerals, weddings, football games, and jury trials. When we impose these typifications on people or events, it frames who or what they are. It also sustains a belief that the world is already organized along certain lines when the organization actually derives from typifications in our minds.

These ideas reinforce each other. The assumption about reciprocity of perspectives includes the assumption that other people share our stock knowledge, recipes, and typifications. The cumulative effect is to create the impression that we live in an "objective reality." Put differently, we convince ourselves that the order we detect in the world really exists out there rather than being the product of our minds. This is how we sustain the natural attitude.

Whenever these beliefs guide interaction to a smooth conclusion, it becomes easier to believe in an objectively ordered, intersubjectively shared world. Even so, the natural attitude remains a fragile construction. Its assumptions are not necessarily true. Every life contains moments when they break down. We might learn in the most unpleasant ways that others don't share our perspective, that our stock knowledge is no help, that our recipes led to unintended and unwanted outcomes, or that our typifications don't fit and have left us clueless.

As a final illustration, consider what happens when people have an existential crisis and fundamentally question their world. Others typically provide reassurances through Schutz's techniques. We tell people in a crisis that we once went through the same thing—invoking reciprocity of perspectives. We use typifications by saying they're going through a phase, or they're in the third stage of grief, or any other cultural category that draws the person back into a world of reciprocal meanings. And if we can't rescue them, we use yet another typification of "mental illness" that allows us (and perhaps them) to understand their lack of reciprocity with us. Such moments reveal how the natural attitude is a mere hypothesis and how the order in our world is socially constructed rather than objectively given.

THE SOCIAL CONSTRUCTION OF REALITY

Schutz's phenomenological sociology inspired the social constructionist theory of Peter Berger and Thomas Luckmann (1966). People construct many realities, but the reality of everyday life is fundamental. Although arbitrary and relative, we experience it as certain and absolute because of our assumptions about it. Through stock knowledge, typifications, and recipes, we define subjective experiences, intersubjective meanings, and objective structures as fundamentally real.

Language is central here. It is a repository of shared meanings and cultural typifications. Relevance structures are also central. Combining typifications and intentionality, relevance structures orient us and provide meaning in given situations.

Relevance structures mean people in the same objective space often live in different subjective worlds. Every day people gather in hospital emergency rooms, but they bring different relevance structures to it as accident victims, overworked surgeons, medical residents, claims adjustors, anxious relatives, triage nurses, and janitorial staff. What is "real" about the situation depends on whose relevance structure is in play. Relevance structures impose different meanings for different people.

The social construction of reality occurs through three interrelated processes. Externalization means that human purposes and intentions motivate actions that create a particular social world. Externalization means society is a human product.

Objectivation means that these externalizations seem to become independent, freestanding realities. They appear to have a life of their own and to exist without the intervention of people. Objectivation means that society is an objective reality.

Internalization means that this seemingly objective world is retrojected into our consciousness. Through socialization, we acquire an internalized understanding of this socially constructed world. Internalization means people are also a social product.

All three processes occur simultaneously. Consider any organization, school, church, business, or other enterprise. Trace its history back to its origin. Before that point, it had no reality outside the intentions of people who created it. As they did so, the organization took on a life of its own. It now might seem like a self-sustaining entity. People encountering the organization now are likely to do so in objectified ways that make it appear to stand apart from human action. Through socialization, moreover, they internalize an understanding of this seemingly objective organization, but they also become competent to act on their own intentions and relevance structures with regard to it. Multiply this example across all social organizations, and you get a sense of how reality is socially constructed.

This perspective seems to imply that people are the "authors" of their social worlds, but this metaphor invites further examination. In everyday life, many people feel as if they can't even control their personal lives, much less be the authors of the social world around them. Moreover, power differences mean that some people are in a much better position to construct social reality than other people. And finally, even if the world is the product of our intentions, it is also filled with unintended and unanticipated consequences. So the metaphor requires several caveats. Most basically, no one "authors" the world with a blank sheet of paper. Everyone inherits a preexisting world; through internalization that world becomes theirs before they can even have the tools to write their own world.

The world we inherit is institutionalized. Institutions emerge when people do habitual, repeated actions over a long time. Through habit and repetition, shared and reciprocal typifications emerge that become people's stock knowledge and recipes. By the time someone new comes along (and we were all new once), this world appears to exist on its own despite its creation by social actors.

Take a small but revealing example. On the first day of a college class, people make a decision about where to sit in the classroom. On the second day, there might be some reshuffling, but many people return to their original seat. By the fourth or fifth meeting, such decisions become routinized; people arrive and sit in "their" seats without even thinking about it. If people don't claim familiar seats, it feels awkward; it might even be seen as deviant if someone takes "someone else's" seat. In this mundane example, a type of social reality has been externalized from people's intentions, objectified as an external order, and internalized back into people as normative expectations. If you were there at the beginning, you know this "reality" is the collective product of intentional decisions. But by the end of the semester, it will feel like a taken-for-granted, natural order of things.

Society as an objective reality thus emerges through institutionalization. Over time, institutions also acquire legitimations that provide rationales for why things are the way they are. Such legitimations can draw on tradition, mythology, theology, philosophy, or science. When the power of legitimations is added to that of institutions, it is remarkable that we are able to see society as anything other than an objective reality that imposes itself on us from "out there."

If there is any circumstance that might help us see that reality is socially constructed, it is when realities collide. If people only live in one culture, they are especially likely to see it as objectively real. But when people are exposed to several cultures with different institutions and legitimations, they are more likely to see them as relative, socially constructed realities.

Modernity and relativism are thus intimately connected (Berger and Luckmann 1966). Modernity involves the conscious coexistence of multiple societies, cultures, institutions, and legitimations. Reality has always been socially constructed, but it might be easier for more people to see it that way since the dawn of the modern era.

THE ETHNOMETHODOLOGICAL TURN

The second offshoot of phenomenological sociology is ethnomethodology. Most closely associated with Harold Garfinkel (1967), ethnomethodology refers to the practical methods ordinary people use in everyday life to make sense of the social world around them. Whereas Schutz was interested in how people sustain the natural attitude, ethnomethodology explores the actual techniques people use to convince themselves and others that they live in an objectively ordered world.

People use procedures to produce interaction. These procedures can be directly observed, but they can also be accessed through people's descriptions of their interactions with others. Ethnomethodologists are interested in accounts people give of encounters with others, because they reveal how people collectively construct order.

Studying accounts and procedures reveals the indexicality of meanings or the importance of context. Meanings don't derive from words or gestures alone, because virtually all words and gestures carry multiple meanings. If all we had was the word or gesture, we wouldn't know which meanings are in effect. We decide among multiple meanings by considering words and gestures in the context in which they are used.

This is another version of the argument that order is not "out there" but rather "in here" as actors judge context to find meaning. Put differently, the explicit parts of communication are just the tip of the iceberg; what is literally said indexes an implicit context of understandings that is crucial to finding meaning.

Meaning also derives from reflexivity in social interaction. Consider again that social life is a sequence of unique events. No two situations are exactly alike. To the extent this is true, it poses a challenge for people. How do we make sense out of an unending sequence of new situations?

This is where reflexivity comes to the rescue. When we enter a situation, we interpret it as a particular instance of a more general category. Because we know about the category, we know what meanings to transpose from the category to the situation. Yet again, we find the experience meaningful not because order is "out there" but rather because we impose order on it using such categories.

Reflexivity resembles Kant's innate categories that impose structure on ambiguous perceptions and Schutz's typifications that place experience in familiar categories. What is crucial is that these mental categories do not have any objective reality; they are not "out there." They are rather tools that help convince us that there is an objective world out there, and that we understand it.

The belief that we live in an orderly world is an artful accomplishment of social actors rather than a passive recognition of external reality. Another way ethnomethodologists make this point is through conversation analysis. Careful scrutiny of the tiniest conversational details reveals how meaning only emerges from people's active search for it.

Consider how much of what people "understand" in a conversation is not actually said. We often "read between the lines," interpret the context, and attend to tone to form an understanding. Indeed, what is not said might be more significant than what is said. Moreover, understanding often depends on sequence. Two statements can mean different things when presented in different order, so we attend to sequence to determine meaning. We also rely on people's biographies to interpret what they say. Even so, we sometimes find no meaning until something "clicks" that allows us to retrospectively understand previously meaningless comments. Each aspect of conversation reveals the importance of context in finding meaning and how meanings are socially constructed.

Ethnomethodological analysis is challenging because these techniques are largely unconscious and taken for granted by skilled social actors. When we are good at using them, we create meaning without even realizing it. To expose these processes requires some clever inerventions into everyday life.

Consider an experiment that college students were told was designed to explore the value of brief therapy (McHugh 1968). Student volunteers were asked to describe a problem they were having and then ask questions of a therapist who would only respond with a "yes" or a "no." Students were then asked how they interpreted the advice and whether it was helpful. Unbeknownst to the students, the therapist's "answers" were randomly predetermined in a deliberately meaningless sequence. Although somewhat artificial, the experimental design ensured that there was absolutely no "meaning" on one side of the exchange.

Despite the therapist's meaningless input, students constructed "meaningful" interpretations out of the therapist's responses. Indeed, the experimenters were surprised by how many students completed all the questions and even claimed to have benefited from the therapy. Some became quite angry when they were debriefed and told that the "advice" they had just received was meaningless. Although this situation is contrived, it illustrates how people enter interaction with such a strong expectation of meaning that they often find it even when it isn't there.

Another way to see these practices is by "making trouble." You can make trouble in any situation by simply challenging things everybody takes for granted. The typical result is that the interaction quickly breaks down and people become upset and angry. The fact that social reality can be disrupted so readily is further evidence that it is a delicate, collaborative social construction. When we act in ways that undermine social reality, it proves to be not very real after all.

The ease with which social order can be disrupted underscores the importance of the techniques people routinely use to create and maintain it. A basic technique is *doing* reciprocity of perspectives. Schutz claimed this is something we assume; Garfinkel sees it as something we *do*. Indeed, we do it every time we nod or otherwise indicate understanding or agreement with someone in everyday interaction. Here's the interesting part. Sometimes we do reciprocity of perspectives even when we don't understand or agree with the other party. We thereby use techniques that imply reciprocity and a shared world even when they do not exist.

The same is true of the "et cetera principle." This refers to situations where people begin a story or an explanation but don't complete it on the assumption that the other person has enough information to do so on their own. When we rely on this principle, we rarely learn whether their version would actually match our own. But we are likely to assume it would, especially if they do reciprocity of perspectives by indicating that they know exactly where this story is going and there's no need for us to spell out every detail.

Despite such techniques, there are times when social order breaks down in obvious ways. Additional techniques are then used to repair the damage. These involve apologizing, explaining that we didn't mean to do something, or otherwise providing a rationale for disruptive actions. When others respond with empathy and reciprocity of perspectives (saying they've made the same mistake, etc.), the breach in social order has been repaired. In all these ways, ethnomethodology understands society as something social actors accomplish by using "folk" methods in everyday life.

SOCIAL LIFE AS DRAMA

Phenomenological sociology views people as agents who actively construct social worlds and their meanings. The same is true of dramaturgical sociology. The metaphor here is that the world is a stage and that people are players on it. Dramaturgical sociology literally sees people as actors in social life.

This approach is well summarized in *The Presentation of Self in Everyday Life* (Goffman 1959). The starting assumption is that people deliberately create and enact a certain type of self in every situation. Like all good acting, we try to create a *persona*, or an image of ourselves, as a certain kind of person. A major goal of self-presentation is impression management. When done successfully, performances are believable. The combination of self-presentation and audience validation means that we become the self that we are performing.

Ordinary people recognize this. We don't have to be trained sociologists to know that people try to make a good impression, that how they appear and who they really are might be different, and so on. So in everyday life, we are both performers and audiences for other performers. In both cases, we are keenly interested in authenticity.

When a performance seems authentic, we might say that "what you see is what you get" or that someone is "for real." We sense no gap between their performance and who they really are. We might conclude that there is no performance here and that we are seeing the "real person." These are the most effective performances of all.

This underscores the importance of judging performances. Doing so involves distinguishing between two kinds of expressions. Expressions *given* are aspects of a performance that are intended by the performer. Expressions *given off* are harder to control and slip through the performance. When there are contradictions between expressions consciously given and unconsciously given off, we tend to believe the latter and to judge the performance as unconvincing.

When a defense attorney has her client get a haircut and wear a suit to court, this is an attempt to control expressions given and create a good impression of the defendant. If the defendant leers at women jurors and uses obscenities on the witness stand, these expressions given off contradict those given by the suit and the haircut. Jurors are likely to conclude that the leering and obscenity are better clues to who this person is than the suit and haircut.

Many performances involve idealizations, where people present themselves in the best possible light or in socially desirable ways. To be effective, they can require tight control to prevent damaging information from slipping through and undermining the performance. Other performances might involve misrepresentation, where actors deliberately present themselves in a deceptive manner ("I'm your friend first and an insurance salesman second"). Still other performances involve mystification that creates social distance between the performer and audience, generating a feeling of awe. There are also demystified performances, as when rock stars, politicians, or celebrities wade into the audience to mingle with ordinary people.

Certain generic elements like fronts and props are found in many performances. Some fronts are spatial. The location of people in a suite of offices is a front supporting a performance about who's in charge: the person in the corner office farthest from the door you entered. I don't have a corner office, but my office is filled with thousands of books that support my performance as a professor (whether I've actually read them or not). The deliberate disorder of a teenager's bedroom is yet another front that supports the performance of a rebellious self.

Fronts can also be personally embodied. Clothing, grooming, and adornment are always crucial to self-presentation. As different as they might be, the suits and skirts of the business world and the piercings and tattoos of youth culture are both fronts supporting certain performances. Some fronts make explicit identity claims; slogans on clothing, buttons on backpacks, stickers on bumpers, and customized license plates are common examples.

Some performances involve teams and require the cooperation of several performers. When doctors and nurses do surgery or the staff of a formal restaurant opens for business, they are staging a collective presentation. Even if most team members hit their marks, the performance can still be undermined by the missteps of one or two team members.

Teams must therefore maintain loyalty. Anything that heightens the boundaries between insiders and outsiders can do the trick. One of the more interesting strategies is deprecating the audience. Team members can enhance their solidarity by making nasty comments about the bodies of patients or the preferences of diners. If the whole team participates in deprecating the audience, it heightens team loyalty and ensures a more effective performance.

Deprecating the audience will obviously backfire if it is done in their presence; it must occur out of view. This suggests another part of everyday performances. In the theater, we know that performances happen front stage while being assembled and supported backstage. We also know that audiences aren't supposed to go backstage, because it will undermine the illusion of the front-stage performance.

The same is true of social life and its performances. Front regions are places where performances occur, and back regions are places where they are prepared. Sometimes the distinction has more to do with time than space. When a band sets up and sound-checks their instruments before the club opens, it is a back region; when the doors open and the music begins, the same physical space is now a front region.

However defined, front regions are where performers and audiences interact, and back regions are where performers can retreat from the audience and drop out of their roles. But it's all relative. If the set designer also has designs on the lead actress, a second performance is occurring in the back region of the main performance.

As noted earlier, people are aware of the dramaturgical aspect of social life. At some level, we know people are engaged in performances. Consider how audiences typically support performances through tactfulness. Take an extreme case of audience support: the grade-school play. When the play inevitably goes awry, the audience will go out of its way to ignore the mishaps and maintain the illusion the play is trying to create. Such audience tact applies to a much broader range of performances.

Audiences exercise tact when they respect boundaries between front and back regions. If they must enter a back region, they announce their intention by knocking on a door, coughing loudly, or otherwise alerting performers so they can reassemble their fronts. Audiences also exercise tact when they symbolically isolate themselves from intimate performances not meant for them; if we are trapped on a long elevator ride with a bickering couple, we signal detachment and disinterest (while secretly listening in). Audiences are tactful whenever they overlook or excuse mistakes that could otherwise undermine a performance.

Audiences thus recognize that it is crucial for people to save face and maintain integrity. Because a discredited performance undermines integrity, audiences can be surprisingly supportive and gentle in their reception of flawed performances. Even though we routinely monitor authenticity, we seem inclined to support performances within rather broad limits. In accepting even flawed performances, we help construct a social world that we take to be orderly and meaningful.

THE SELF AS PROJECT, COMMODITY, AND STORY

Selves involve phenomenological and dramaturgical elements, but they also exist in sociohistorical contexts. For instance, societies like the United States have been described as late modernity, advanced capitalism, or postmodern societies. Each description poses distinct challenges to the self.

Anthony Giddens (1991) has described a late modern age that alters the nature of personal identity. As modern institutions undercut traditional customs, "self-identity becomes a reflexively organized endeavor" and "the notion of lifestyle takes on a particular significance" (Giddens 1991, 5). People now select lifestyles in a self-consciously deliberate way. The notion of "choosing" a lifestyle would strike most people throughout human history as bizarre. For better and worse, their identity was determined by birth, whereas ours is increasingly a matter of choice. The expansion of such choices typifies the self in late modern society.

The terms *ontological security* and *existential anxiety* refer to our degree of certainty about who we are and how we cope with life's uncertainties. Traditional societies relied upon myth, religion, and custom to establish ontological security and manage existential anxiety. Late modern societies undermine traditional knowledge and replace it with uncertainty, risk, and relativism. This leaves many people less certain about who they are or how to cope with life's unknowns. The "good news" is that modern selves have more options for dealing with these issues; the "bad news" is that the burden falls on us as individuals to find solutions, as custom and tradition lose their relevance.

These dynamics enlarge "space" for the self in modern life and turn us into self-therapists. We see the self as having a certain trajectory. We plan this trajectory from a menu of life options that might include going to a particular college, starting a certain career, moving to a new city, finding a partner, beginning a family, having children, and achieving particular goals by certain stages in the life cycle. To see the self as a reflexive project means we design our life out of the choices before us.

Such lifestyle planning extends to the body as well. In making choices about nutrition, exercise, muscle toning, bodybuilding, or cosmetic surgery, we construct a physical self as part of a chosen lifestyle.

Late modern selves also experience a new type of relationship. A "pure relationship" is one whose only rationale is the satisfactions or rewards that are generic to the relationship itself. It contrasts with more traditional societies where relationships served broader social purposes. Thus, marriage was historically an economic, political, or kinship exchange, in which the partners were less individuals than representatives of larger groups and interests.

The rise of "romantic love" began to detach marriage from larger social purposes and reframe it as an individual choice based on an emotional connection. "Pure relationships" extend this pattern. Whether marriage or friendship, a pure relationship exists for intrinsic satisfactions as opposed to larger social obligations. Such relationships are double-edged. On one hand, people have more choices about relationships and can enter into them based on what they (not others) see as fulfilling. On the other hand, such relations are fragile; when the parties no longer experience them as fulfilling, the relationship has no further justification and is likely to end. Given how we invest our modern selves in such relationships, their fragility can undermine ontological security and increase existential anxiety.

The reflexive self also involves "life politics." Whereas emancipatory politics meant fighting oppression as members of groups, life politics is more personalized. In life politics, daily activities become politicized. At the same time, late modernity has collapsed distinctions between the global and the personal, so that life politics involves planetary questions. Whether the issues are biology, sexuality, and reproduction or food, consumption, and environment, life politics has global implications.

This view of the late modern self as a reflexive project emphasizes choices. This emphasis, however, can be overdone. Another view of the self accentuates the power of large social forces over relatively defenseless individuals.

The commodified self has been a theme in both classical and contemporary sociology. Recall Marx's theory of alienation, whose starting premise is that labor is central to human beings. Labor means self-directed, creative, productive activity. When people do such labor, they create a material world through externalization (Berger and Luckmann 1966). Equally important, labor creates the person, because productive activity engages our senses, reveals our aptitudes, develops our skills, and fosters our humanity. We build a world but also become human through labor.

This, at least, is the ideal. Alienation means people cannot direct their own labor. The most basic way this occurs is through commodification. Capitalism reduces people to the commodity of labor-power, because it is only interested in how labor creates profits. As people are reduced to commodities, they are forced to sell themselves—or at least their labor-power—to the highest bidder. Marx likened wage-labor to prostitution. In both cases, a human capacity for self-expression (labor and sexuality) becomes a commodity sold to someone else. In both cases, people are valued only as means to ends defined by the purchaser.

Once labor becomes a commodity, people become alienated from the process and the product of their labor, as both are dictated by the boss. People become alienated from what makes them human in the first place. Labor's potential is denied and used for others' benefit. Alienation means that rather than living to work, we must work to live. As a final result, people become alienated from each other.

Contemporary commodified selves involve consumption more than production. In an advanced capitalist society shaped by compulsive consumerism and relentless advertising, meaning and identity become intertwined with the consumption of commodities. The philosopher René Descartes once said "I think, therefore I am"; bumper stickers now proclaim "I shop, therefore I am." A self that becomes real through consumption perfectly symbolizes a consumer culture in which public spaces are displaced by shopping malls.

Perhaps the pleasures of consumption compensate for the alienation of labor. Perhaps the modern bargain is that if we can't realize ourselves through producing things, we'll do it through consuming things. Despite rising consumer debt and personal bankruptcies, we seem cheerfully resigned to these circumstances, as expressed in another bumper sticker: "I owe, I owe, so off to work I go." Or maybe not. The image of a treadmill also comes to mind, and how many people have you seen on a treadmill who looked really happy?

Advertisers know they are not selling products as much as lifestyles and identities. The seemingly simple act of buying a product symbolically means identifying with a lifestyle and identity. Advanced capitalism provides do-it-yourself identity kits consumers can use for a customized self. "The advantage of market-promoted identities is that they come complete with elements of social approval ... [which] does not need to be negotiated for it has been, so to speak, built into the marketed product from the start" (Bauman and May 2001, 88).

The built-in approval of market-tested identities might explain their seductive appeal, but there is a downside. Planned obsolescence and fashion cycles guarantee that this year's hot product (and identity) will be painfully out of fashion next year. In entering the marketplace of identity, we commit to continually buying new or trading up to maintain the social approval such identities provide. It sounds like we're back on that treadmill again.

In Marx's day, labor-power became a commodity. Now the self and the body become commodities. To fetch the highest price in the marketplace of bodies, women (and now men) must approximate impossibly narrow standards of how their bodies should look. If we "choose" to pursue this goal, however, there are multibillion-dollar industries waiting to "serve" our "needs." One might question whether the benefits of the body industry outweigh its costs and risks to consumers, but there is no doubt about its profitability for those who control it.

Anthony Giddens's (1991) reflexive self emphasizes agency, control, and self-direction. The commodified self reminds us that in a consumer society, powerful forces colonize how this reflexive project of the self is carried out. Seen this way, the self is less a reflexive project than just another site of social control.

For still others, selves now exist in a postmodern world that undermines the very idea of a self. Imagine a continuum with modernism at one end. It has always emphasized a core self. Even modernism, however, recognized dangers to the self. Other-directedness could become overconformity, organizational identification could lead to selling out, and emotional control could promote the commercialization of feeling. Although recognizing such dangers, modernism still assumes that a core self develops.

An intermediate position on the continuum retains the possibility of an integrated self, although acknowledging it has become more problematic. With the compression of time and space and a flood of media images, the self becomes saturated (Gergen 1991) by forces that make an integrated self more difficult to sustain.

At the postmodern end of the continuum, the very idea of an integrated self is abandoned. Postmodernism questions whether things have a clear existence apart from how they are represented. Put differently, postmodernism collapses the distance between reality and images to the point where we can no longer tell which is which. Applied to the self, this implies that core selves and integrated identities are no longer possible.

An alternative is the "narrative self" (Holstein and Gubrium 2000). This arises out of people's subjectivity, their situational circumstances, and others' influence. In contrast to the modern, unitary self, the postmodern, narrative self contains multiple identities in different locations and circumstances. Each one is "authentic" in context, but none is the "real" self, because none transcend particular situations. To use dramaturgical language, it's as if we play many supporting roles in different scenes, but there is no leading role that gives our self a single, clear meaning.

This self is still a social construction, but the building relies heavily on language to construct selves through narratives we tell about who we are. These stories don't represent a "real" self as much as they create a situational self in the telling. Because we tell different stories about ourselves in different times and places, we create many "self-stories" rather than a singular identity. Our stories and our selves are different for diverse audiences or when viewed from different angles.

The materials for building a narrative self are found in everyday conversation. As we tell our stories and narrate our selves, we are like editors. We continually revise, modify, add, and delete pieces from our stories. Stories are also set in circumstances we neither choose nor control, but that inevitably shape them. It is within those limits that we talk ourselves into existence as narrative selves.

Consider the construction of an alcoholic self in the context of the support group Alcoholics Anonymous (Denzin 1987). The context provides a standard script of how people introduce themselves to the group and proceed to construct a narrative self as an alcoholic. In the telling of their lives, people revise, edit, and modify their story to arrange the elements in ways that tell the story of an alcoholic self. But these same people narrate different stories and selves in other circumstances. Although other examples are not as transparent, we are all engaged in constructing narrative selves through the stories we tell about who we are.

When the self is located in a specific historical context—whether late modernity, advanced capitalism, or postmodernism—we get new insights into how identities are socially shaped. These accounts build on phenomenological and dramaturgical approaches, interactionist theory, and the premise that we are social before we are individual. Durkhiem demonstrated that individuals only emerged with modern society. These accounts of individuals, selves, and identities are thus crucial to understanding modern society and its postmodern trajectories.

REFERENCES

Bauman, Zygmunt, and Tim May. 2001. *Thinking Sociologically*. Malden, MA: Blackwell.

Berger, Peter, and Thomas Luckmann. 1966. *The Social Construction of Reality*. Garden City, NY: Anchor.

Denzin, Norman. 1987. *The Alcoholic Self*. Newbury Park, CA: Sage.

Garfinkel, Harold. 1967. *Studies in Ethnomethodology*. Englewood Cliffs, NJ: Prentice Hall.

Gergen, Kenneth. 1991. *The Saturated Self*. New York: Basic Books.

Giddens, Anthony. 1991. *Modernity and Self-Identity*. Stanford, CA: Stanford University Press.

Goffman, Erving. 1959. *The Presentation of Self in Everyday Life*. Garden City, NY: Anchor.

Holstein, James, and Jaber Gubrium. 2000. *The Self We Live By*. New York: Oxford University Press.

McHugh, Peter. 1968. *Defining the Situation*. Indianapolis, IN: Bobbs-Merill.

CHAPTER 2

Sociological Perspectives and the Sociological Imagination

THEORIES IN SOCIOLOGY provide us with different perspectives with which to view our social world. A perspective is simply a way of looking at the world. A theory is a set of interrelated propositions or principles designed to answer a question or explain a particular phenomenon; it provides us with a perspective. Sociological theories help us to explain and predict the social world in which we live. Sociology includes three major theoretical perspectives: the functionalist perspective, the conflict perspective, and the symbolic interactionist perspective (sometimes called the interactionist perspective, or simply the micro view). Each perspective offers a variety of explanations about the social world and human behavior.

FUNCTIONALIST PERSPECTIVE

The functionalist perspective is based largely on the works of Herbert Spencer, Emile Durkheim, Talcott Parsons, and Robert Merton. According to functionalism, society is a system of interconnected parts that work together in harmony to maintain a state of balance and social equilibrium for the whole. For example, each of the social institutions contributes important functions for society: Family provides a context for reproducing, nurturing, and socializing children; education offers a way to transmit a society's skills, knowledge, and culture to its youth; politics provides a means of governing members of society; economics provides for the production, distribution, and consumption of goods and services; and religion provides moral guidance and an outlet for worship of a higher power.

The functionalist perspective emphasizes the interconnectedness of society by focusing on how each part influences and is influenced by other parts. For example, the increase in single-parent and dual-earner families has contributed to the number of children who are failing in school because parents have become less available to supervise their children's homework. As a result of changes in technology, colleges are offering more technical programs, and many adults are returning to school to learn new skills that are required in the workplace. The increasing number of women in the workforce has contributed to the formulation of policies against sexual harassment and job discrimination.

Functionalists use the terms *functional* and *dysfunctional* to describe the effects of social elements on society. Elements of society are functional if they contribute to social stability and dysfunctional if they disrupt social stability. Some aspects of society can be both functional and dysfunctional. For example, crime is dysfunctional in that it is associated with physical violence, loss of property, and fear. But according to Durkheim and other functionalists, crime is also functional for society because it leads to heightened awareness of shared moral bonds and increased social cohesion.

Sociologists have identified two types of functions: **manifest** and **latent**.[1] Manifest functions are consequences that are intended and commonly recognized. Latent functions are consequences that are unintended and often hidden. For example, the manifest function of education is to transmit knowledge and skills to society's youth. But public elementary schools also serve as babysitters for employed parents, and colleges offer a place for young adults to meet potential mates. The babysitting and mate-selection functions are not the intended or commonly recognized functions of education; hence, they are latent functions.

CONFLICT PERSPECTIVE

The functionalist perspective views society as composed of different parts working together. In contrast, the conflict perspective views society as composed of different groups and interests competing for power and resources. The conflict perspective explains various aspects of our social world by looking at which groups have power and benefit from a particular social arrangement. For example, feminist theory argues that we live in a patriarchal society—a hierarchical system of organization controlled by men. Although there are many varieties of feminist theory, most would hold that feminism "demands that existing economic, political, and social structures be changed."[2]

The origins of the conflict perspective can be traced to the classic works of Karl Marx. Marx suggested that all societies go through stages of economic development. As societies evolve from agricultural to industrial, concern over meeting survival needs is replaced by concern over making a profit, the hallmark of a capitalist system. Industrialization leads to the development of two classes of people: the bourgeoisie, or the owners of the means of production (e.g., factories, farms, businesses), and the proletariat, or the workers who earn wages.

The division of society into two broad classes of people—the "haves" and the "havenots"— is beneficial to the owners of the means of production. The workers, who may earn only

---

1   Robert King Merton, *Social Theory and Social Structure* (1968).

2   Sara Weir and Constance Faulkner, *Voices of a New Generation: A Feminist Anthology* (Boston: Pearson/ Allyn and Bacon, 2004), xii.

subsistence wages, are denied access to the many resources available to the wealthy owners. According to Marx, the bourgeoisie use their power to control the institutions of society to their advantage.[3] For example, Marx suggested that religion serves as an "opiate of the masses" in that it soothes the distress and suffering associated with the working-class lifestyle and focuses the workers' attention on spirituality, God, and the afterlife rather than on such worldly concerns as living conditions. In essence, religion diverts the workers so that they concentrate on being rewarded in heaven for living a moral life rather than on questioning their exploitation.

SYMBOLIC INTERACTIONIST PERSPECTIVE

Both the functionalist and the conflict perspectives are concerned with how broad aspects of society, such as institutions and large social groups, influence the social world. This level of sociological analysis is called macro sociology: It looks at the big picture of society and suggests how social problems are affected at the institutional level.

Micro sociology, another level of sociological analysis, is concerned with the social psychological dynamics of individuals interacting in small groups. Symbolic interactionism reflects the micro-sociological perspective and was largely influenced by the work of early sociologists and philosophers, such as Georg Simmel, Charles Cooley, George Herbert Mead, and Erving Goffman. Symbolic interactionism emphasizes that human behavior is influenced by definitions and meanings that are created and maintained through symbolic interaction with others. Sociologist W.l. Thomas[4] emphasized the importance of definitions and meanings in social behavior and its consequences. He suggested that humans respond to their definition of a situation rather than to the objective situation itself. Hence, Thomas noted that situations that we define as real become real in their consequences.

Symbolic interactionism also suggests that our identity or sense of self is shaped by social interaction. We develop our self-concept by observing how others interact with us and label us. By observing how others view us, we see a reflection ourselves that Cooley calls the "looking glass self."[5]

---

3   Karl Marx, *The Communist Manifesto* (Chicago: Pluto Press, 1996).

4   William l. Thomas and Morris Janowitz (eds.), *W.I. Thomas on Social Organization and Social Personality: Selected Papers* (Chicago: University of Chicago Press, 1966).

5   Charles Horton Cooley, *Human Nature and the Social Order* (New York: Scribner, 1922).

Functionalism (Durkheim)

- Examines functions or consequences of the structure of society
- Focuses mainly on social order and the way that social problems either serve or disrupt said order; operates under the assumption that everything is beneficial to at least some people else such structures would not exist.
- **Dysfunctions**: The negative consequences of social structures

Conflict Theory (Marx)

- Focuses on where power exists and how it operates and coerces (presumably for those already with power)
- In much of Marx's writing "control of the Means of Production = Power"[6]
- **Proletariat**: Workers
- **Bourgeoisie**: Owners
- **Alienation**: Separation from one's labor as well as coworkers and finished products. Marx's term *species being* refers to man's true self.
- **Exploitation**: The difference between the value of labor put in and the wages paid for the labor; equates to profit.
- **Class consciousness**: Awareness of social position and the resulting exploitation/ oppression.
- **Feminism**: Related to conflict theory and discusses women's oppression through patriarchy.

Symbolic Interactionism (Mead)

- Focuses on how we use symbols, words, and language to create and maintain our social reality.
- Emphasizes how the existence of mind, self, and society emerges from everyday interaction and the use of symbols.
  - Emphasizes roles and dramaturgy. We are all acting out roles in the best way we can.
- Social problems exist only when defined as such.

---

6   Karl Marx, *Das Kapital, a Critique of Political Economy* (Chicago: H. Regnery, 1959).

SOCIOLOGICAL CANON AND IMPORTANT THEORISTS

Karl Marx

- Sociologist's task is to analyze and explain conflict.
- Conflict is shaped by the means of production.
- Industrialization resulted in two classes: owners and laborers.

Emile Durkheim

- Provided insights into the social forces that contributed to the rise of a "global village."
- As division of labor becomes more specialized, and as sources of material become more geographically diverse, a new kind of solidarity emerges.
- Explores the relationship between social facts (facts, concepts, expectations that come not from individual responses and preferences but from the social community that socializes each of its members). **In other words, even the most personal of decisions is social.**
- Suicide is largely a function of social circumstances, social relations, and social structures.

C.W. Mills

- Come down from the ivory tower (deal more with people's lives).
- Coined and defined the sociological imagination.
- Proposed public sociology and linking macro with micro analysis.

Max Weber

- Focused on how the Industrial Revolution changed thoughts and action and how it brought about a process called rationalization.
- Rationalization refers to the way daily life is organized so as to accommodate large groups of people.
- Wrote *The Protestant Ethic and Spirit of Capitalism,* linking the development of capitalism with social and religious changes in parts of western Europe.

Harriet Martineau

- Wanted to communicate her observations without expressing her judgments.

- Gave a focus to her observations by asking the reader to compare the workings of society with the principles on which thought was founded, thus testing the state of affairs against an ideal standard.

W.E.B. Du Bois

- Contributed the idea of the double consciousness.
- Focused on the strange meaning of being black.
- One of the first prominent African American sociologists.

MILLS AND THE SOCIOLOGICAL IMAGINATION

- "The Sociological Imagination enables us to grasp history and biography and the relations between the two within society. That is its task and its promise."[7]
- The idea that the individual can understand his own experience and gauge his own fate only by locating himself within his period, that he can know his own chances in life only by becoming aware of those of all individuals in his circumstances.
  - Links our personal lives and experiences with those of our social world.
- Personal troubles occur within the character of the individual and within the range of his immediate relations with others; they have to do with his self and with those limited areas of social life of which he is directly and personally aware.
- Public issues have to do with matters that transcend these local environments of the individual and the range of his inner life.[8]
- Relating the social imagination to social problems

SOCIAL PROBLEMS: PATHS TO SOLUTIONS

- **Social policy**: The enactment of a course of action through laws or statutes.
- **Social innovation**: May take the form of policy but often features an untested, unique, or informal approach (i.e., partnership housing).
- **Cultural change/paradigm shift**: A large-scale change in belief or value systems, or social norms. May or may not be tied to policy.
- **Revolution**: Radically changing large structures in society.

---

7 C. Wright Mills, *The Sociological Imagination* (New York: Oxford University Press, 1959).

8 LaToya Egwuekwe-Smith, "Updated 04.08.11 – The Decline: The Geography of a Recession by LaToya Egwuekwe (OFFICIAL)," April 8, 2011, https://www.youtube.com/watch?v=hwWGzQ_FUtQ.

Fulfilling the Promise: Infusing Curiosity, Concern, and Passion with Sociological Imagination

by Devereaux Kennedy

It is not theoretical questions that first interest people in social study. It is curiosity about social life and how it works; concern for social problems and how to solve them; passion against social injustices and a desire to right them. If social study dampens this curiosity, concern, and passion, it betrays you. If social study shows you how to harness and employ that curiosity, concern, and passion, it does you a service.

CURIOSITY

When you study social life in a systematic and disciplined manner, it's important to periodically remind yourself why you do so. How did your journey start, and why do you continue it? Such journeys usually begin with curiosity. Why are things the way they are? Have they always been that way? Are they this way everywhere? How might they be different? Peter Berger (1963, 19), in his classic *Invitation to Sociology*, points to "the curiosity that grips any sociologist in front of a closed door behind which there are human voices. If he [or she] is a good sociologist, [she or] he will want to open that door, to understand these voices. Behind each closed door he [or she] will anticipate some new facet of human life not yet perceived and understood."

The limits of all of our experiences are such that the recognition of changes in our life and that of those around us don't necessarily tell us about what's happening to people outside our immediate vicinity. Are the changes happening to us peculiar to our neighborhood, region, class, ethnic or racial grouping, nation, or area of the world? When did these changes begin? How long have they been going on? Where will they lead? This is the curiosity out of which an interest in social study begins.

Margaret Kovach's interest in social life began with curiosity about her own origins. Her education was a portal to self-discovery. Her birth parents were Plains Cree and Salteaux. Her adopted parents were Eastern European. "I was a native kid who grew up round and about a small rural Saskatchewan town. I was loved but conflicted, questioning where I belonged, trying to stay at distances yet needing connection" (2009, 5).

Alison Wolf's upbringing was very different from that of Margaret Kovach, but of course for her, as for all of us, it was "normal." She "grew up in prosperous, peaceful southern England ... where it was simply taken for granted that we would all go on to college ... because it was normal for my school and for my friends, only years later did I realize how few women, even in our baby-boomer generations, did academic,

Devereaux Kennedy, "Fulfilling the Promise: Infusing Curiosity, Concern, and Passion with Sociological Imagination," *Exploring the Roots of Social Theory and Inquiry: Making Sense of Social Life*, pp. 1-8, 181-187. Copyright © 2018 by Cognella, Inc. Reprinted with permission.

let alone post-graduate degrees or how few had done so previously" (2013, xi). It was only later that she realized that hers was a "hinge generation." "My generation didn't see this coming. But then, as students or young professionals, we didn't or couldn't survey what society as a whole was doing. What was normal was what we, as privileged sub-group, did" (xii). It is only now that she is able to put what was happening to her and women like her into a global social context. It is only now that she realizes that hers was a hinge generation (xv).

The curiosity that initiates our interest in social life is usually mixed with an "unhealthy" dose of skepticism. Again, Peter Berger: "The first wisdom of sociology is this—things are not what they seem" (1963, 23). I say "unhealthy" because such curiosity and skepticism isn't always helpful in everyday situations. Much of our everyday interactions with others is based on routine. We do the same things in same way, every day. We rarely think about what is involved in taking the bus, buying groceries, riding the elevator, or hanging out with our friends. We don't have to think about how these things happen or what it takes to make them happen. We just do them.

Indeed, for everyday encounters with others to come off successfully, it is important not to think too carefully or deeply about what is really going on. We accept that the people we interact with are who they appear to be. They, in turn, accept the self we present to them as the real us. Irving Goffman (1967) tells us that this kind of mutual acceptance seems to be a basic structural feature of interaction, especially the interaction of face-to-face talk. Think too carefully about our routines as we perform them, question them too deeply, and they will be hard to do.

What might be unhealthy and destructive in everyday life can be important for the student of social life. The surface of social life is rarely, if ever, all there is. Beneath that surface are layers and layers of social meaning. Our everyday routines are rarely as simple as they appear. They are often not as secure as they seem. The tacit knowledge, practical consciousness, and unreflective negotiation that goes into riding the bus, having a meal in a restaurant, riding the elevator, buying groceries, or hanging out with our friends is the object of study of a whole branch of sociology known as **ethnomethodology**.

Ethnomethodology

Study of how everyday life interactions happen.
Endomethodologists view everyday life interactions like going to the grocery store, eating at a restaurant, taking a bus ride as artful accomplishments involving shared background knowledge, tacit understandings and negotiation between the participants in such interactions.

FIGURE 2.1　**Ethnomethodology**

Often our curiosity is piqued by something that seems out of the ordinary in our routine. As a civil rights attorney, Michelle Alexander saw her job as resisting attacks on affirmative action. One day she was rushing to catch a bus when she "noticed a sign stapled to a telephone pole that screamed in large bold print: 'The Drug War is the New Jim Crow'" (2012, 3). Her first reaction was that the comparison was absurd. Yet it made her curious.

Concern

Oh—something ain't right
Oh—something ain't right

—"Something Ain't Right," David Byrnes

Sometimes the desire to systematically study social life begins with the feeling or conviction that "something ain't right." The charge for riding the bus doubles and the service is reduced. The price of groceries rises dramatically. Our eyes fix on the people busing tables and washing dishes at the restaurant where we are having a meal. Thinking about their lives spoils the meal. Rowdy kids cut in front of an elderly woman in line for the elevator. When she complains, they push her down and laugh. Everyone else in line pretends not to notice. Our routines are interrupted. Things don't seem to be working the way we think they should or the way they used to. We wonder what has gone wrong, why things cost so much, why some people make so little, and why other people behave so badly.

Charles Murray (2012, 288) remembers that when he was growing up in the 1940s and 1950s there was a code governing the behavior of "gentlemen":

> I understood the code for males to go something like this: To be a man means that you are brave, loyal and true. When you are in the wrong you own up and take your punishment. You don't take advantage of women. As a husband, you support and protect your wife and children. You are gracious in victory and a good sport in defeat. Your word is your bond. It's not whether you win or lose but how you play the game. When the ship goes down, you put the women and children in the lifeboats and wave good-bye with a smile.

Murray admits that the above is crammed with clichés. But, he argues, "they were clichés precisely because boys understood that this was the way they were supposed to behave. ... The code of the American gentleman has collapsed, just as the parallel code of the American lady has collapsed" (2012, 288–89). He thinks the collapse of this code is a bad thing. He's concerned about why it has collapsed and what the consequences of its collapse will be.

PASSION

Something about the way things are doesn't seem just or fair. Parents sometimes rhetorically ask their kids, "Who said that life was fair?" They add, "When you get older you'll understand." For some of us, our parents' words aren't enough. Just because things aren't fair doesn't mean that we have to accept that unfairness. When we get older we still don't understand why social injustice has to exist. We want to know how social injustices can be addressed. Just because life isn't fair doesn't mean it can't be made fairer and more just.

In the Prologue of *Indigenous Methodologies*, Margaret Kovach says, "I get angry about the racism that Indigenous people experience. I am writing this here because it drives my work. ... The writing comes from the heart, it comes from who I am and all that I am. ... It comes from my own need and longing to engage with my Nehiyaw and Salteaux ancestry, and to say to my academic world that my culture counts" (2009, 5–8).

In the Preface to *The New Jim Crow*, Michelle Alexander (2012) identifies the readers for whom she has written her book:

> People who care deeply about racial justice but who, for any number of reasons, do not yet appreciate the magnitude of the crisis faced by communities of color as a result of mass incarceration. In other words, I am writing this book for people like me—the person I was ten years ago. I am also writing it for another audience—those who have been struggling to persuade their friends, neighbors, relatives, teachers, coworkers, or political representatives that something is eerily familiar about the way our criminal justice system operates, something that looks and feels a lot like an era that we supposedly left behind, but who have lacked the facts and data to back up their claims. It is my hope and prayer that this book empowers you and allows you to speak with greater conviction, credibility and courage.

Charles Murray directs his book *Coming Apart* at a very different audience, and has very different things to say than does Michelle Alexander. But he too is passionate about what he perceives as prevailing social wrongs, including the dysfunctionality and irresponsibility of the new American upper class:

> Personally and as families its members are successful. But they have abrogated their responsibility to set and promulgate standards. The most powerful and successful members of their class increasingly trade on the perks of their privileged positions without regard to the seemliness of that behavior. The members of the new upper class are active politically, but when it comes

to using their positions to help sustain the republic in day-to-day life, they are AWOL. (2012, 294)

USING YOUR SOCIOLOGICAL IMAGINATION TO MAKE CONNECTIONS

If interest in the systematic study of social life begins with curiosity, skepticism, concern, and passion, it doesn't end there. Curiosity needs to be sated; skepticism and suspicion justified or allayed; social wrongs righted. This requires the acquisition of particular kinds of knowledge and the use of a particular form of imagination—what C. Wright Mills (1959) called the **sociological imagination**.

By the sociological imagination, Mills meant that quality of mind which enables people who possess it to make connections between personal troubles and social issues. Troubles occur within or between individuals sharing the same immediate social environment. Losing a job; doing badly at school; failing at marriage or a relationship; even committing a crime, getting arrested, and being put in prison can certainly be understood in very immediate and personal terms. People lose jobs all the time because they screw up at work or can't get along with their bosses and coworkers. We sometimes do badly at school because we are too lazy to study or would rather party. People sometimes treat their partners with a lack of respect and fail to put the time and attention into a relationship necessary to make it work. Sometimes it really is our fault.

Often, however, it isn't—or isn't completely. When businesses close or stop hiring, when millions of people get laid off and you lose your job, that isn't your fault. When the dropout rates in urban public schools rise and the academic performance of the students who remain drops precipitately, something more is at work than student laziness. When the divorce rate rises dramatically, clearly more is at work than couples failing to make the compromises necessary for a successful marriage. When people decide to drive while drunk or stoned, they place themselves and others at risk. Surely, they should be held accountable for their actions. Yet the need for accountability doesn't explain why some people are held more accountable than others. While people of all races appear to use and sell illegal drugs at about the same rate, black men are imprisoned for drug offenses at rates twenty to fifty times greater than those of white men (Alexander 2012, 7). Sometimes personal problems are connected to public issues.

"An issue is a public matter: some value cherished by publics is felt to be threatened. Often there is a debate about what that value really is and about what it is that really threatens it" (Mills 1959, 8). Murray thinks that the core values, the "founding virtues" that made America great, indeed exceptional—industriousness, honesty, marriage, and religiosity—are being threatened (2012, 130). Alexander thinks that the incarceration of poor African American males for drug offenses is not about an increase in crime or drug abuse. It is rather the result of "a stunningly comprehensive and well-disguised system of racialized social control that functions in a manner strikingly similar to Jim Crow" (2012, 4).

Certainly, making connections between personal troubles and social issues requires gathering the relevant facts, and exercising our reasoning capacity to make sense of those facts. But making sense of the social world requires more than facts and reasoning. It requires a quality of mind that will help us "to use information and develop reason in order to achieve lucid summations of what is going on in the world and of what is happening in [ourselves]" (Mills 1959, 5). When we do this, we use our sociological imagination to theorize.

THEORY AND THEORIZING: A DIFFERENT WAY OF LOOKING AT SOCIAL THEORY

Too often, in my view, social theories and the work of social theorists are separated from both what the theories are about, and how social theorists employ those theories to make sense of the social world. In an important sense, all thoughtful students of social life are theorists. They create and present theoretical constructions, pictures of social reality, as explanations for social problems. These problems, they argue, exist because the social world looks and works like this. To solve these problems, they argue, the social world needs to look different and to work differently.

EXAMPLES OF THEORIZING

Here I have selected four works as examples of theorizing. I don't assume that the readers of this book will have read the studies analyzed in it, only that they could read and understand them, and works like them. The studies analyzed here focus on key contemporary social phenomena—history, race, culture, class, gender, and indigenous peoples. They do so, however, from widely different perspectives. Charles Murray is an unabashed man of the right and his book has been influential in conservative circles. Michelle Alexander is a proud woman of the left and her book is very influential in the liberal-left community. Alison Wolf is an accomplished British economist, educator, and journalist. Her book does one of the things important books on social life should do—examines the unexpected and potentially negative consequences of positive social developments. The subtitle of her well-reviewed book is "How the Rise of Working Women Has Created a Far Less Equal World." Margaret Kovach is a member of the Plains Cree and Salteaux peoples of the Great Plains in southern Saskatchewan. Hers is the only book of the four which could be considered a work of theory, but the indigenous theories and methods she discusses are not ones ordinarily covered in books or courses on theory.

I will try to show that each of these works involves theorizing. Each work is an attempt to address a particular social or intellectual problem. Each author begins by identifying something that they believe is out of order in the social world. They then present a picture of a social life that illustrates the nature of the problem they have identified. Finally, they show how that picture would have to be changed for the problem to be successfully addressed.

In this book, I will attempt to uncover, describe, and evaluate the theorizing that underlies these studies. **While you're reading this book, you should do two things. First, in conjunction with your instructor, select a study, reading, or readings that stimulate your curiosity, concern, and passion. Uncover, describe, and evaluate the theorizing that underlies the study you have chosen as you read this book. Second, use your curiosity, concern, passion, and sociological imagination to show how you might do your own theorizing. I don't ask that you construct a study; only that you write a proposal describing the kind of study you would like to do, had you the time and resources.**

At the end of each chapter I will give short assignments which will allow you to gradually uncover, describe, and evaluate the theorizing in the study you have chosen, and to demonstrate how you might do your own theorizing. If you complete the assignments at the end of each chapter, and use the explanation and analysis of the studies I provide here as examples of how to uncover, describe, analyze, and perform social theorizing, I think you will have accomplished a great deal.

STUDY QUESTIONS

1   What is the sociological imagination? What do I mean by the term "social theorizing?"
2   Identify something in social life about which you are curious.
3   Identify a social problem about which you are concerned.
4   Identify a form of social injustice that troubles you, and about which you are passionate.
5   Describe how these curiosities, concerns, and passions are linked to your life and the lives of those around you.

SUGGESTED ASSIGNMENT

1   Write a short essay (500 to 750 words) identifying one aspect of social life about which you are curious, one social problem about which you are concerned, and one form of social injustice about which you are passionate. Describe how these curiosities, concerns, and passions are related to your own life experiences.

SUGGESTED FURTHER READINGS

Berger, Peter. 1963. *Invitation to Sociology*, 164–177 (Sociology as a Humanistic Discipline). Garden City, New York: Doubleday Anchor Books.

Mills, C. Wright. 1959. *The Sociological Imagination*, 3–25 (The Promise). New York: Oxford University Press.

BIBLIOGRAPHY

Alexander, Michelle. 2012. *The New Jim Crow: Mass Incarceration in the Age of Colorblindness*, rev. ed. New York: The New Press.

Berger, Peter L. 1963. *An Invitation to Sociology*. Garden City, NY: Doubleday Anchor Books.

Goffman, Irving. 1959. *The Presentation of Self in Everyday Life*. New York: Anchor Books.

Kovach, Margaret. 2009. *Indigenous Methodologies: Characteristics, Conversations, and Contexts*. Toronto: University of Toronto Press.

Mills, C. Wright. 1959. *The Sociological Imagination*. New York: Oxford University Press.

Murray, Charles. 2012. *Coming Apart: The State of White America, 1960–2010*. New York: Crown Publishing.

Wolf, Alison. 2013. *The XX Factor: How the Rise of Working Women Has Created a Far Less Equal World*. New York: Crown Publishers.

Reading 2.2.

The Promise

by Mills

Nowadays men often feel that their private lives are a series of traps. They sense that within their everyday worlds, they cannot overcome their troubles, and in this feeling, they are often quite correct: What ordinary men are directly aware of and what they try to do are bounded by the private orbits in which they live; their visions and their powers are limited to the close-up scenes of job, family, neighborhood; in other milieux, they move vicariously and remain spectators. And the more aware they become, however vaguely, of ambitions and of threats which transcend their immediate locales, the more trapped they seem to feel.

Underlying this sense of being trapped are seemingly impersonal changes in the very structure of continent-wide societies. The facts of contemporary history are also facts about the success and the failure of individual men and women. When a society is industrialized, a peasant becomes a worker; a feudal lord is liquidated or becomes a businessman. When classes rise or fall, a man is employed or unemployed; when the rate of investment goes up or down, a man takes new heart or goes broke. When

C. Wright Mills, "The Promise," *The Sociological Imagination*, pp. 3-11. Copyright © 2000 by Oxford University Press. Reprinted with permission.

wars happen, an insurance salesman becomes a rocket launcher; a store clerk, a radar man; a wife lives alone; a child grows up without a father. Neither the life of an individual nor the history of a society can be understood without understanding both.

Yet men do not usually define the troubles they endure in terms of historical change and institutional contradiction. The well-being they enjoy, they do not usually impute to the big ups and downs of the societies in which they live. Seldom aware of the intricate connection between the patterns of their own lives and the course of world history, ordinary men do not usually know what this connection means for the kinds of men they are becoming and for the kinds of history-making in which they might take part. They do not possess the quality of mind essential to grasp the interplay of man and society, of biography and history, of self and world. They cannot cope with their personal troubles in such ways as to control the structural transformations that usually lie behind them.

Surely it is no wonder. In what period have so many men been so totally exposed at so fast a pace to such earthquakes of change? That Americans have not known such catastrophic changes as have the men and women of other societies is due to historical facts that are now quickly becoming 'merely history.' The history that now affects every man is world history. Within this scene and this period, in the course of a single generation, one sixth of mankind is transformed from all that is feudal and backward into all that is modern, advanced, and fearful. Political colonies are freed; new and less visible forms of imperialism installed. Revolutions occur; men feel the intimate grip of new kinds of authority. Totalitarian societies rise, and are smashed to bits—or succeed fabulously. After two centuries of ascendancy, capitalism is shown up as only one way to make society into an industrial apparatus. After two centuries of hope, even formal democracy is restricted to a quite small portion of mankind. Everywhere in the underdeveloped world, ancient ways of life are broken up and vague expectations become urgent demands. Everywhere in the overdeveloped world, the means of authority and of violence become total in scope and bureaucratic in form. Humanity itself now lies before us, the super-nation at either pole concentrating its most co-ordinated and massive efforts upon the preparation of World War Three.

The very shaping of history now outpaces the ability of men to orient themselves in accordance with cherished values. And which values? Even when they do not panic, men often sense that older ways of feeling and thinking have collapsed and that newer beginnings are ambiguous to the point of moral stasis. Is it any wonder that ordinary men feel they cannot cope with the larger worlds with which they are so suddenly confronted? That they cannot understand the meaning of their epoch for their own lives? That—in defense of selfhood—they become morally insensible, trying to remain altogether private men? Is it any wonder that they come to be possessed by a sense of the trap?

It is not only information that they need—in this Age of Fact, information often dominates their attention and overwhelms their capacities to assimilate it. It is not only the skills of reason that they need—although their struggles to acquire these often exhaust their limited moral energy.

What they need, and what they feel they need, is a quality of mind that will help them to use information and to develop reason in order to achieve lucid summations of what is going on in the world and of what may be happening within themselves. It is this quality, I am going to contend, that journalists and scholars, artists and publics, scientists and editors are coming to expect of what may be called the sociological imagination.

1

The sociological imagination enables its possessor to understand the larger historical scene in terms of its meaning for the inner life and the external career of a variety of individuals. It enables him to take into account how individuals, in the welter of their daily experience, often become falsely conscious of their social positions. Within that welter, the framework of modern society is sought, and within that framework the psychologies of a variety of men and women are formulated. By such means the personal uneasiness of individuals is focused upon explicit troubles and the indifference of publics is transformed into involvement with public issues.

The first fruit of this imagination—and the first lesson of the social science that embodies it—is the idea that the individual can understand his own experience and gauge his own fate only by locating himself within his period, that he can know his own hances in life only by becoming aware of those of all individuals in his circumstances. In many ways it is a terrible lesson; in many ways a magnificent one. We do not know the limits of man's capacities for supreme effort or willing degradation, for agony or glee, for pleasurable brutality or the sweetness of reason. But in our time we have come to know that the limits of 'human nature' are frighteningly broad. We have come to know that every individual lives, from one generation to the next, in some society; that he lives out a biography, and that he lives it out within some historical sequence. By the fact of his living he contributes, however minutely, to the shaping of this society and to the course of its history, even as he is made by society and by its historical push and shove.

The sociological imagination enables us to grasp history and biography and the relations between the two within society. That is its task and its promise. To recognize this task and this promise is the mark of the classic social analyst. It is characteristic of Herbert Spencer—turgid, polysyllabic, comprehensive; of E. A. Ross—graceful, muckraking, upright; of Auguste Comte and Emile Durkheim; of the intricate and subtle Karl Mannheim. It is the quality of all that is intellectually excellent in Karl Marx;

it is the clue to Thorstein Veblen's brilliant and ironic insight, to Joseph Schumpeter's many-sided constructions of reality; it is the basis of the psychological sweep of W. E. H. Lecky no less than of the profundity and clarity of Max Weber. And it is the signal of what is best in contemporary studies of man and society.

No social study that does not come back to the problems of biography, of history and of their intersections within a society has completed its intellectual journey. Whatever the specific problems of the classic social analysts, however limited or however broad the features of social reality they have examined, those who have been imaginatively aware of the promise of their work have consistently asked three sorts of questions:

1   What is the structure of this particular society as a whole? What are its essential components, and how are they related to one another? How does it differ from other varieties of social order? Within it, what is the meaning of any particular feature for its continuance and for its change?

2   Where does this society stand in human history? What are the mechanics by which it is changing? What is its place within and its meaning for the development of humanity as a whole? How does any particular feature we are examining affect, and how is it affected by, the historical period in which it moves? And this period—what are its essential features? How does it differ from other periods? What are its characteristic ways of history-making?

3   What varieties of men and women now prevail in this society and in this period? And what varieties are coming to prevail? In what ways are they selected and formed, liberated and repressed, made sensitive and blunted? What kinds of 'human nature' are revealed in the conduct and character we observe in this society in this period? And what is the meaning for 'human nature' of each and every feature of the society we are examining?

Whether the point of interest is a great power state or a minor literary mood, a family, a prison, a creed—these are the kinds of questions the best social analysts have asked. They are the intellectual pivots of classic studies of man in society—and they are the questions inevitably raised by any mind possessing the sociological imagination. For that imagination is the capacity to shift from one perspective to another—from the political to the psychological; from examination of a single family to comparative assessment of the national budgets of the world; from the theological school to the military establishment; from considerations of an oil industry to studies of contemporary poetry. It is the capacity to range from the most impersonal and remote transformations to the most intimate features of the human self—and to see the relations between the two. Back of its use there is always the urge to know the social and historical meaning of the individual in the society and in the period in which he has his quality and his being.

That, in brief, is why it is by means of the sociological imagination that men now hope to grasp what is going on in the world, and to understand what is happening in themselves as minute points of the intersections of biography and history within society. In large part, contemporary man's self-conscious view of himself as at least an outsider, if not a permanent stranger, rests upon an absorbed realization of social relativity and of the transformative power of history. The sociological imagination is the most fruitful form of this self-consciousness. By its use men whose mentalities have swept only a series of limited orbits often come to feel as if suddenly awakened in a house with which they had only supposed themselves to be familiar. Correctly or incorrectly, they often come to feel that they can now provide themselves with adequate summations, cohesive assessments, comprehensive orientations. Older decisions that once appeared sound now seem to them products of a mind unaccountably dense. Their capacity for astonishment is made lively again. They acquire a new way of thinking, they experience a transvaluation of values: in a word, by their reflection and by their sensibility, they realize the cultural meaning of the social sciences.

2

Perhaps the most fruitful distinction with which the sociological imagination works is between 'the personal troubles of milieu' and 'the public issues of social structure.' This distinction is an essential tool of the sociological imagination and a feature of all classic work in social science.

Troubles occur within the character of the individual and within the range of his immediate relations with others; they have to do with his self and with those limited areas of social life of which he is directly and personally aware. Accordingly, the statement and the resolution of troubles properly lie within the individual as a biographical entity and within the scope of his immediate milieu—the social setting that is directly open to his personal experience and to some extent his willful activity. A trouble is a private matter: values cherished by an individual are felt by him to be threatened.

Issues have to do with matters that transcend these local environments of the individual and the range of his inner life. They have to do with the organization of many such milieux into the institutions of an historical society as a whole, with the ways in which various milieux overlap and interpenetrate to form the larger structure of social and historical life. An issue is a public matter: some value cherished by publics is felt to be threatened. Often there is a debate about what that value really is and about what it is that really threatens it. This debate is often without focus if only because it is the very nature of an issue, unlike even widespread trouble, that it cannot very well be defined in terms of the immediate and everyday environments of ordinary men. An issue, in fact, often involves a crisis in institutional arrangements, and often too it involves what Marxists call 'contradictions' or 'antagonisms.'

In these terms, consider unemployment. When, in a city of 100,000, only one man is unemployed, that is his personal trouble, and for its relief we properly look to the character of the man, his skills, and his immediate opportunities. But when in a nation of 50 million employees, 15 million men are unemployed, that is an issue, and we may not hope to find its solution within the range of opportunities open to any one individual. The very structure of opportunities has collapsed. Both the correct statement of the problem and the range of possible solutions require us to consider the economic and political institutions of the society, and not merely the personal situation and character of a scatter of individuals.

Consider war. The personal problem of war, when it occurs, may be how to survive it or how to die in it with honor; how to make money out of it; how to climb into the higher safety of the military apparatus; or how to contribute to the war's termination. In short, according to one's values, to find a set of milieux and within it to survive the war or make one's death in it meaningful. But the structural issues of war have to do with its causes; with what types of men it throws up into command; with its effects upon economic and political, family and religious institutions, with the unorganized irresponsibility of a world of nation-states.

Consider marriage. Inside a marriage a man and a woman may experience personal troubles, but when the divorce rate during the first four years of marriage is 250 out of every 1,000 attempts, this is an indication of a structural issue having to do with the institutions of marriage and the family and other institutions that bear upon them.

Or consider the metropolis—the horrible, beautiful, ugly, magnificent sprawl of the great city. For many upper-class people, the personal solution to 'the problem of the city' is to have an apartment with private garage under it in the heart of the city, and forty miles out, a house by Henry Hill, garden by Garrett Eckbo, on a hundred acres of private land. In these two controlled environments—with a small staff at each end and a private helicopter connection—most people could solve many of the problems of personal milieux caused by the facts of the city. But all this, however splendid, does not solve the public issues that the structural fact of the city poses. What should be done with this wonderful monstrosity? Break it all up into scattered units, combining residence and work? Refurbish it as it stands? Or, after evacuation, dynamite it and build new cities according to new plans in new places? What should those plans be? And who is to decide and to accomplish whatever choice is made? These are structural issues; to confront them and to solve them requires us to consider political and economic issues that affect innumerable milieux.

In so far as an economy is so arranged that slumps occur, the problem of unemployment becomes incapable of personal solution. In so far as war is inherent in the nation-state system and in the uneven industrialization of the world, the ordinary individual in his restricted milieu will be powerless—with or without psychiatric aid—to solve the troubles this system or lack of system imposes upon him. In so far as the family as an institution turns women into darling little slaves and men into their chief providers and unweaned dependents, the problem of a satisfactory marriage remains incapable of purely private solution. In so far as the overdeveloped megalopolis and the overdeveloped automobile are built-in features of the overdeveloped society, the issues of urban living will not be solved by personal ingenuity and private wealth.

What we experience in various and specific milieux, I have noted, is often caused by structural changes. Accordingly, to understand the changes of many personal milieux we are required to look beyond them. And the number and variety of such structural changes increase as the institutions within which we live become more embracing and more intricately connected with one another. To be aware of the idea of social structure and to use it with sensibility is to be capable of tracing such linkages among a great variety of milieux. To be able to do that is to possess the sociological imagination.

3

What are the major issues for publics and the key troubles of private individuals in our time? To formulate issues and troubles, we must ask what values are cherished yet threatened, and what values are cherished and supported, by the characterizing trends of our period. In the case both of threat and of support we must ask what salient contradictions of structure may be involved.

When people cherish some set of values and do not feel any threat to them, they experience *well-being*. When they cherish values but *do* feel them to be threatened, they experience a crisis—either as a personal trouble or as a public issue. And if all their values seem involved, they feel the total threat of panic.

But suppose people are neither aware of any cherished values nor experience any threat? That is the experience of *indifference*, which, if it seems to involve all their values, becomes apathy. Suppose, finally, they are unaware of any cherished values, but still are very much aware of a threat? That is the experience of *uneasiness*, of anxiety, which, if it is total enough, becomes a deadly unspecified malaise.

Ours is a time of uneasiness and indifference—not yet formulated in such ways as to permit the work of reason and the play of sensibility. Instead of troubles—defined in terms of values and threats—there is often the misery of vague uneasiness; instead of explicit issues there is often merely the beat feeling that all is somehow not right. Neither the values threatened nor whatever threatens them has been stated; in short, they have not been carried to the point of decision. Much less have they been formulated as problems of social science.

What Fellow Citizens and Residents Think about Social Problems

UNDERSTANDING WHAT OTHER citizens and residents think is important in understanding social problems, especially since so many social problems are culturally situated. Understanding what people view as problems and how they prioritize social problems can tell us a lot about society, social institutions, and social structure. It is also important for politics and policies as these issues both map onto and are influenced by political rhetoric and debates, and ultimately the public's priorities are related to legislation and public policy.

Reading 3.1.

What is a Social Problem?

by Sara Towe Horsfall

SIX INGREDIENTS OF SOCIAL PROBLEMS

Everyone notices things in the world that need to be improved. But a social problem is more than a personal opinion about something. It has social components. For instance, those affected by a social problem will be a group (collectivity or category), not just one or two people. Also, a social problem is recognized as a problem by a group of people who feel strongly enough to take steps toward change.

Put another way, if people are suffering but no one recognizes it, there is no social problem. It becomes a social problem only when people agree that something is wrong and organize themselves to resolve it. That doesn't mean that people aren't suffering if no one recognizes it. But it does mean that their suffering hasn't filtered into social consciousness, so no one is willing to stop it.

Even those who are suffering may not consider their situation to be a social problem. They may conclude that it is due to their own failing—sin, lack of ability, bad luck, and so on. They may not be aware anyone else is suffering as they are. Or they may be resigned to their fate, believing that the effort to change things is too great and that no one cares about them. But what is defined as a social problem changes over time. Things that are not recognized as social

Sara Towe Horsfall, "What Is a Social Problem?" *Social Problems: An Advocate Group Approach*, pp. 3-26, 321-352. Copyright © 2012 by Taylor & Francis Group. Reprinted with permission.

problems today may be considered problems in the future. Recognizing something as a problem is the first step in the social change process.

How can it be that something is not a social problem if no one recognizes it? Consider child abuse. There is evidence that large numbers of children were battered in the eighteenth century and earlier. Yet it was not until the twentieth century that child abuse became a public issue. In 1962 a medical journal published a report by a pediatric radiologist stating that multiple injuries at different stages of healing indicate abuse. Almost immediately professional organizations began to campaign, and twelve years later legislation outlawing child abuse was passed (Kadushin and Martin 1980; Pfohl 1977). Today child abuse is a public issue addressed by social agencies and law enforcement.

Sociologists believe that we create society. We organize ourselves, establish the rules and regulations necessary to make things work, and collectively identify goals. An early sociologist, Emile Durkheim, said that these social norms are as important as, or more important than, instinct. These consensual beliefs tell us what to do and guide our daily lives. Collective recognition and resolution of social problems is part of that creative social process.

To understand the process of defining and resolving issues, we need to know the six ingredients of social problems. First, there are those who are suffering. This is the *target group*: a collection of individuals who are treated unfairly, don't get their fair share of social and/or material resources, or face serious threats to their well-being. In short, their personal well-being (life chances, e.g., satisfaction or emotional happiness) or their social well-being (equality, representation, and other social situations) is threatened. People in the target group may not know each other, so it is more correct to call them a target category or collectivity. For simplicity's sake, I use the term *target group* to mean collectivity, category, or group.

The second ingredient is the *adverse social situation* that affects the target group. It can be changed by human effort and probably has a human or social cause. A physical disaster—a tornado or a tsunami—is not in itself a social problem but can quickly develop into one. The tsunami in Southeast Asia in 2004 created many social problems. In the immediate aftermath, large numbers of people needed food, shelter, and medical assistance. Others suffered long-term needs, such as children without parents, unemployed persons, and persons unable to locate their relatives. These and other problems were addressed by local and international governments (Korf 2007; Tang 2007). Similarly, the 9.0 earthquake that hit Japan in 2011 affected a nuclear power plant. Residents in a nearby farming community were evacuated and, because of high levels of radioactivity, will not be able to return to live there for many years, if ever.

In contrast, several tornados blew through the Fort Worth, Texas, area in 2000 and 2001. There was substantial damage but surprisingly little loss of life (Letchford, Norville, and Bilello 2000). The only real social problem that developed was concern to create a better warning system in the future.

A preventable disaster is almost always a social problem. In 1984 in Bhopal, India, a Union Carbide pesticide factory leaked forty tons of methyl isocyanate gas into the air, killing an estimated 4,000 people, many of whom lived in makeshift houses next to the power plant.[1] There had been little public recognition of the danger to these people before the disaster. Afterward, individuals, groups, and governments debated the risks of dangerous engineering defects and human error in such factories (Perrow 1984; Jasanoff 1994; Hatvalne 2010). The original event was only one part of the problem. There was also concern about the potential for future leaks and the suffering they would cause.

The third ingredient is the group of people who recognize a social problem: the *advocate group*. These individuals are motivated for different reasons, including self-interest, altruism, and idealism. If their own social or physical well-being is threatened, they are heavily invested in the solution. Or they may be moved by the suffering of others. Or they may believe that something about the situation is wrong or sinful and needs to be changed because it offends their belief system. Whatever the reason, they decide that the target group's situation should be changed. They organize themselves to bring the issue into the public arena for discussion and action. They become claims makers (more about that later).

The fourth ingredient of a social problem is the *ameliorating action*—the proposed change—and the fifth ingredient is the *action group*—the group that puts the proposed change into effect.[2] After the Fort Worth tornado in 2000, neighborhood groups (advocate groups) complained that the warning sirens were not sufficient. The complaints were persistent enough and numerous enough that the city governments (action groups) in the surrounding communities took action. The sirens were tested and upgraded, and in some cases new ones were installed (ameliorating action).

A sixth ingredient is a *will to act* to solve the social problem. Social problems often arise because people find it easier not to act. There is usually a cost attached to the action—if not a monetary cost, then a cost in personal effort or sacrifice of personal interest. To bring change, people must be willing to bear the cost. Replacing the warning sirens was relatively inexpensive, and the will to act was sufficient. Within a few weeks they were replaced or repaired. But in the case of the fertilizer factory in Bhopal, India, there was less will to act. One question that arose was, Who is responsible? When no group or agency is willing to take responsibility or has the necessary resources, the will to act falls to the government.

In sum, then, the six ingredients of a social problem are (1) an advocate group that identifies the problem, (2) an adverse social situation, (3) a victim or target group or target category, (4) an ameliorating action, (5) an action group (organization or institution), and (6) the will to act. Subsequently we can define a social problem as *a situation judged by an advocate group to be adversely affecting the personal or social well-being of a target group (or collectivity) to the extent that it needs to be redressed by means of an ameliorating action to be taken by an action group/organization or institution.* An action group will take such action once there is sufficient will to act.

HOW DO SOCIAL PROBLEMS OCCUR?

Looking to the cause, it is easy to blame social problems on people who are irresponsible, selfish, immoral, or deviant in some way—the "nuts, sluts, and perverts" (Liazos 1972). This is the tendency to blame the powerless. Legal offenders are often held to blame. Although innocent people are sometimes convicted, offenders in the criminal justice system are generally assumed to be guilty. And crime is one of the most prominent and important social problems.[3]

But criminal activity is only one of many causes. Social problems arise because a society is developing or there is general ignorance of a particular situation. Some social problems arise because people pursue their own self-interest at the expense of others. Or there are competing interests. Serious social problems are associated with racism and group discrimination. There are unresolved problems whenever there is a long history of enmity and conflict between groups. This list of causes is not exhaustive, but it is diverse enough to be representative. We will examine each of these possible causes separately.

Development

Chudacoff and Smith's (2000) fascinating account of U.S. urban growth at the turn of the last century highlights problems caused by *development*. Fear of disease (unprotected water supplies were becoming contaminated by seepage from privies and graves) and fear of fire spurred city officials to protect public water supplies. Congestion and dangerous transportation issues in nineteenth-century cities led to complaints that drivers were intentionally reckless; thus traffic regulations and fines were devised for everyone's safety and comfort. Creative solutions to these and other social problems led to the development of the modern urban infrastructure, and the early twentieth century saw "the highest standards of mass urban living in the world" (Chudacoff and Smith 2000, 136, 87, 50). Sometimes developmental problems persist, indicating the existence of factors that erode the social will, such as lack of resources, an inadequate infrastructure, or an insufficient political structure.

Technological advances also bring problems. They create new conditions and issues not addressed by existing regulations or conventions. The rapid and amorphous growth of computers and the Internet during the late twentieth century illustrates this point. Issues of censorship and control are still being discussed—nationally and worldwide.

Aftermath of a Natural Event

A very different kind of social problem comes after a *natural event*. Hurricane Katrina in 2005 was one of the worst natural disasters to hit the United States during the twentieth century. Half a million people were evacuated, 1,600 people lost their lives, and more than 1,000 went missing (Kessler et al. 2006). From a social problems perspective, what is of interest is the way people organize themselves to respond to the possibility of disaster and the human needs arising from it. In the case of Katrina, the most publicized situation involved the low-income, primarily black residents who survived the hurricane but lacked food and shelter (Brodie et al. 2006). Many groups responded with assistance, including the local police, firemen, and Coast Guard, as well as federal agencies—FEMA (Federal Emergency Management Agency) and the Department of Homeland Security. A host of church groups, nonprofits such as the Red Cross, local organizations, and individuals in other cities also helped with shelter, basic necessities, and financial assistance during the subsequent evacuation.

The immediate outpouring of assistance was followed by several years of effort to rebuild the neighborhoods, the city, and the lives of those affected: home owners (Elliott and Pais 2006), those with increased mental health issues (Kessler et al. 2006), those who lost confidence in government officials, especially regarding issues surrounding waste disposal (Allen 2007). Other concerns focused on how the public was informed about environmental and public health threats, as well as preparedness at the local, state, and federal levels (Frickel and Vincent 2007).

Inequality

The most prominent *inequality* is poverty, which affects close to 13 percent of the U.S. population. People who are poor suffer from a lack of basic necessities and from their relationships within the social structure (Myers-Lipton 2006). Minorities are disproportionately affected by poverty and often have reduced access to social resources because of discrimination.[4] Personal, societal, and structural factors are compounded by the underlying ideological beliefs that perpetuate the inequality. A minority child from a low-income family is less likely to attend college or university than a nonminority child from a wealthy family—even if he or she has the intelligence to succeed academically. Sociologists call this *stratification*—organization of people according to differential access to resources and the consequent social positions in society. Problems associated with stratification have to do with health care, high rates of drug abuse, high crime areas, educational issues, political representation, and many others (Myers-Lipton 2006).

Self-interest

Self-interest is a major reason that stratification develops in the first place, and an important source of other social problems. The problem is that economic theories today stress self-interest and commonly assume that "individuals in a society always act according to their self-interest or private economic incentive" (Sen 1977). Rational choice theories used by social scientists and economists also assume self-interest. This view of human nature became acceptable around the time of the Industrial Revolution, when rational self-interest for men in the business world was legitimized. The eighteenth-century doctrine of "separate spheres" had women as keepers of religion and morality, whereas men managed the political, legal, and economic affairs outside the home (Coontz 2005). These two sets of values—the moral, "feminine" values inside the home and the rational, self-oriented "masculine" values outside the home—are in conflict. The popular character Tom Sawyer highlights this discrepancy.

> The late 19th century cliché of the mischievous boy was, like the sentimental-ization of women and children, an attempt to deal with one aspect of the era's central discomfiture. The very attributes that would make a man occupationally successful were unwelcome in the domestic environment of his own creation. In a situation of conflict, especially when resolution is not forthcoming, a common human response is to try to laugh; hence the mischievous boy and his exasperated female "superior." The image allowed just enough caricature of the rule-breaker and the rule maker to afford the populace a laugh, but few, it appears, truly understood the joke. The final effect of this phenomenon was perhaps its most subversive: the perception of boys' mischievous antics as masculine behavior invited reversal, so that immature or illicit activities of men could, in time, be construed as mischief that is natural and harmless. (Heininger 1984, 27–28)

Self-interest is widespread. It is the norm in a for-profit business world. There is nothing natural or harmless about the activities of senior officials at the Enron Corporation, who created a network of offshore companies to make the company look more profitable than it actually was. After the company collapsed, it became apparent who benefited at the expense of shareholders, employees, pensioners, customers, and suppliers. Even though it is generally accepted that top executives work to perpetuate their own interests (Egeberg 1995), there was an outcry about the actions of Enron officials who became a "visible symbol of the dangers of excessive self-interest" (Finkelstein et al. 2008). Dangerous self-interest, *greed* to Marxists, is a major reason for Marxist opposition to the capitalist system (Walker 2008).

Racism and Discrimination

Racism is the belief that people with different biological traits (e.g., skin color) have different social value. Discrimination is the differential treatment of categories of people. *Racism and discrimination* involve both personal and group self-interest in noncommercial areas. After the U.S. Civil War, the South was associated with white supremacy—local residents believed that theirs was and should be a "white man's country." Fears that the newly freed slaves would upset the balance of political power were supported by theories of scientific racism and "survival of the fittest" Social Darwinism—ideas popular in the late nineteenth century.[5] When Northerners did not react to court decisions that denied protection to blacks (between 1873 and 1898), disaffected Southerners pursued their own ends (McMillen 1990). The so-called Jim Crow laws created a segregated society, depriving African Americans of the right to vote (unless they owned property), the right to be educated in the same schools as whites, and free access to public facilities. Enforcement of the Jim Crow laws was supported by an atmosphere of fear created by lynching.

Let's analyze this situation using the social problems theory presented here. Disaffected whites in the South after the Civil War considered themselves victims. In their eyes, they were the *target group*. The *adverse situation* they faced was the loss of their way of life, as well as social and political power, to people who had once been their social inferiors. During Reconstruction, in addition to having the right to vote, 2,000 blacks served in federal, state, and local offices (Foner 1993). A racist *advocate group*, the Ku Klux Klan, was formed in Pulaski, Tennessee, in 1866 to oppose the social and political changes (Martinez 2007). It soon spread to other states.

> Fear convinces Klansmen that others, somehow different from them, have negatively affected their lives. They yearn for halcyon days when no one questioned their unbridled authority. Anything or anybody challenging the status quo threatens the established order, and threats must be handled through extra legal means, if necessary. (Martinez 2007, x)

As Martinez noted, the *ameliorating action* of the KKK was to handle the threat by any means that worked. The Jim Crow laws were intended to restrict the social and political power of southern blacks and keep them disadvantaged. Fear was a means of preventing blacks from reasserting themselves. The white supremacists' *will to act* came from the political threat and economic competition they felt from African Americans and fueled their desire to maintain caste boundaries (Beck and Tolnay 1990).

The KKK is uniquely a *target group* (according to its own assessment), an *advocate group,* and an *action group*—all at the same time. They saw themselves as the victim. They worked to draw attention to their situation among others in the South and worked out a solution themselves, rather than turn to the government to resolve the issue. From their point of view, they were successful—at least for a while.

From an African American point of view—and from the view of most people today—the actions of those associated with the KKK created a segregated society that was not legally redressed until the 1960s. It took that length of time for another *advocate group* (or movement, as it turned out) to form and to develop the *will to act* on a national scale. We will revisit this problem later in the section on opposition groups.

Stratification problems (stemming from inequality or discrimination) created by self-interest usually require government intervention, since those in power do not easily give up their position of advantage. Whether they are forced to reevaluate the situation by law or they choose to do so of their own free will, the concerned parties in power often lack a global perspective of the issue. Putting their own well-being on the same level as the other parties involved is one part of a solution. This usually requires relinquishing resources, potential resources, position, or prestige.

Competing Interests

Competing interests may technically be self-interest on a group level but can have other dimensions as well. Territorial claims are an important aspect of political interests, especially when natural resources such as water, energy, and minerals, geostrategic claims, and/or control of a population within territorial boundaries are at stake (Diehl 1999).

Competing territorial claims lie at the core of the Arab-Israeli conflict. In the late nineteenth century, Jews from Russia and eastern Europe began to conceive of the idea of a Jewish homeland to resolve their centuries-long existence as an oppressed minority scattered through many different countries (the diaspora). They began purchasing land in the Middle East—land that they thought, perhaps erroneously, was more or less unoccupied. Their secret intention was to become so numerous in the area that they could eventually claim the country as theirs. The conflict, then, came not from misunderstanding, but from the "conflicting interests and goals of the two populations. The Arabs sought instinctively to retain the Arab and Muslim character of the region and to maintain their position as the rightful inhabitants; the Zionists sought radically to change the status quo, buy as much land as possible, settle on it, and eventually turn an Arab populated country into a Jewish homeland" (Morris 2001, 49). The Jewish people received support from western forces in the region, and ultimately the modern state of Israel was born.

From a social problems perspective, Jewish and Arab *advocate groups* differ in terms of who is the victim. They propose different solutions that involve different organizations or countries to be part of the solution. In short, there are two different social problems here rather than one. Of course, most of us see it as one issue—not two. Part of the difficulty in resolving the conflict is agreeing on who is the victim, and why, and subsequently what kind of action should be taken, by whom.

Northern Ireland is another example of competing claims. Historically the roots of the problem go back to the sixteenth and seventeenth centuries, when Britain sought to reassert its control over Ireland by sending officers, soldiers, administrators, and clergy to settle and establish the country as a self-supporting contributor. The native Catholic population resisted this intrusion. The resulting conflict between the Protestant Unionists and the Catholic Nationalists has continued until today (Ruane and Todd 2000).

Yet another example of competing claims is Cyprus, where Turkish Cypriots and Greek Cypriots claim dominance of the island. The result is that the 3,571-square-mile island (approximately 40 miles across) has been divided since 1974. In 1983 the northern 1,300 square miles became the Turkish Republic of Northern Cyprus, whereas the southern part of the island is the Greek Cypriot Republic of Cyprus. A thin green line crosses the island and divides the capitol of Nicosia and has been patrolled by UN forces since 1964.

History of Enmity and Conflict

Sometimes problems between two peoples continue long after the specific issues have been resolved. Once people have been killed, the grief of the families and friends deepens hostility to the point where even the mention of the other side stirs up animosity and suspicion. After years of conflict in the Middle East, this is true for many Jews and Arabs. It has also been true in Northern Ireland, where there has been enmity between the two sides for hundreds of years—although currently there have been several years of relative peace. It was true in Cyprus, although happily here too the situation has vastly improved.

But there are other places where a history of enmity and conflict has not been resolved. As the former Yugoslavia was breaking apart in the 1990s, Serbs, Kosovar Albanians, Croats, and Bosnian Muslims "each claimed to be defending themselves against annihilation" (MacDonald 2002, 2). Yet a century earlier, they had worked together to form the Kingdom of Serbs, Croats, and Slovenes. They were rebelling against the centuries of domination by the Byzantines, the Ottomans, and the Hapsburg Empire. And in modern times the domination continued. The Germans occupied the area during World War II, and then the communist state of Yugoslavia was formed. The Balkan saying that behind every hero stands a traitor is understandable considering the area's history. Today there are separate countries of Croatia, Slovenia, Republic of Macedonia, Bosnia and Herzegovina, Serbia, Montenegro, and Kosovo. Some conclude that the enmity between the different peoples during the 1990s was a strategy to establish independence (MacDonald 2002). Such claims only highlight the complexities involved in resolving this kind of problem.

Yet another area of historic conflict is in Rwanda, where the Tutsi and Hutu have fought each other for many years. In 1994 an estimated 800,000 Tutsis and moderate Hutus were killed by the Hutus in power, in what is now called *genocide* (BBC 2008). One version of this story was told in the movie *Hotel Rwanda*.

Ignorance

Sometimes problems develop because of *ignorance*. When severe acute respiratory syndrome (SARS) developed in Hong Kong at the end of 2003, it was a new disease. The means of transmission was unknown, and there was no known cure; the reported death rate was 10 percent (Ap 2003; Tam et al. 2004). The epidemic highlighted the importance of understanding health factors among the population (Loh et al. 2004).

Similarly, few people realized the cause of AIDS when it appeared, or its serious consequences. In the early 1980s, when the public and medical professionals were largely silent about the disease, an estimated 100,000 to 300,000 persons on five continents became infected (Mann 1990). The disease continues to spread in countries such as India, where up to 30 percent of those exposed have never heard of it (Chatterjee 1999). As U.S. medical professionals learned more about the disease, the information was disseminated throughout the population, giving individuals an opportunity to take precautions and reduce its spread.

In sum, common causes of social problems include development, natural disasters, inequality, self-interest, racism and discrimination, competing interests, history of enmity and conflict, and ignorance. Social problems are difficulties that need to be "taken care of," or irritations that need our attention, to be fixed as quickly as possible. Social problems also offer an opportunity to improve our collective social life. They highlight areas that need to be addressed, expanded, and developed. They point to areas that require new and imaginative thinking to create adequate structures, regulations, and governance for the well-being of everyone. They are frequently a sign of healthy growth rather than something to hide and be embarrassed about. They always lead to change, and because people frequently resist change, solutions are not always welcomed or sought out. But in the end, addressing social problems today can help shape the world that we live in tomorrow. The better the solutions, the better tomorrow's world.

LEVELS OF SOCIAL PROBLEMS

When analyzing social problems, we need to identify the level of the problem. This is determined primarily by the target group and the action group. Are the people in the target group from one place, or are they scattered across the country or the world? Is the action group (institution or government) local, state, national, or international? In general, widespread problems require more coordination among institutions, agencies, and governments.

A *local level* social problem will fall primarily to local authorities. Several communities may have similar problems, but each resolves its own situation. For instance, consider the problem that developed after the Fort Worth tornado in 2000. The Bank One building, a popular landmark, was effectively destroyed. This was a social problem because it occupied a complete city block in the middle of the downtown area and sat virtually empty for close to five years, raising concerns of safety, crime, and ambiance. Asbestos was discovered, which made rebuilding expensive. For two years, owners, developers, city and state officials argued. The only business that reoccupied the building was a popular restaurant on the top floor, which was forced to relocate when the building was to be imploded. Implosion was finally abandoned due to safety fears and associated costs. Three years after the tornado, concerned parties finally agreed to redevelop the building into residences, retail spaces, and public parking. Two years later the first residents moved in (Whiteley 2002; Metro code 2009).

Other cities have faced similar problems after natural disasters. Local authorities assess the issues and resolve them—and perhaps consult others with similar issues.

State level problems fall under the jurisdiction of state authorities. States that have similar problems do not necessarily address them in the same way. For example, the Amish live in religious communities separated from others. Because of their preference for horse-drawn buggies instead of cars, they present a special challenge. Their simple lifestyle puts them at risk of fatal accidents on the highways (NBC4i 2009). Since close to 80 percent of the Amish live in Ohio, Pennsylvania, and Indiana, this problem is addressed by those states but is not of concern elsewhere.

Sometimes it is not clear which authority should address a problem. Illegal immigration, for instance, is a federal issue (although a 1996 bill allowed Immigration and Customs Enforcement, or ICE, to certify state and local law enforcement officers; Carafano and Keith 2006). But people in border communities or states, or in the smaller communities where illegal immigrants settle, feel that the federal government isn't doing a good job.

For instance, in Farmers Branch, a small community in Texas, the Hispanic population has increased to 37 percent in recent years, with illegal immigrants making up a large portion of the increase. This has put a severe strain on public services in the city of only 30,000 residents. City officials passed an ordinance making it an offense to rent to undocumented persons. This was seen as a controversial action in the state and elsewhere in the country.

In 2010, after a local resident was murdered, Arizona farmers living along the Mexican border complained that the flow of illegal immigrants defaces their property and puts them at risk. Claiming that the federal government had neglected "its constitutional duty to secure the border" (CNN 2011), Governor Jan Brewer introduced a bill requiring Arizona police to verify the legal status of anyone they apprehend. The U.S. Justice Department sued, claiming that only it had that authority. The dispute has gained national attention.

At a *national level*, social problems concern all citizens in some way. Federal authorities are involved in attempts at resolution. National level issues include immigration, certain crimes, drugs, moral issues, cultural violence, and wars, such as the war in Iraq.

Sometimes actions taken by state or local level authorities are seen as part of a national identity. This is the case with the death penalty for non–U.S. citizens. Although people in the United States realize that the penalty varies from state to state, others do not. On the other hand, legalizing marijuana and euthanasia has given the Netherlands an interesting international reputation.

Last, there are problems that affect everyone on our planet. Many governments cooperate to resolve these kinds of *international level* problems. Pollution, protection of national resources, trade agreements, terrorism, extradition, and crime are some examples.

INFORMATION AND CLAIMS MAKING

Informed citizens, advocate groups, action groups, and social researchers are all interested in information about social problems. Some professional groups, such as doctors, lawyers, teachers, social workers, and police, address social problems as part of their job, so they regularly collect information about those they serve. Action groups look to these sources and collect their own information in order to carry out the mandate they are given. The data of the federal government, one of the largest action groups (or organization), is a major resource for everyone.

Collecting and analyzing data is a topic in and of itself. There are established procedures to ensure accuracy and reliability.[6] Since most advocate groups use data that has already been collected and analyzed, it is important for us to understand how to evaluate presentations of data by claims makers.

Claims making is the process by which a person (or persons) tries to convince others of the truth and importance of an issue. In terms of social problems, it is an advocate group's efforts to convince the public and government officials (or other action groups, organizations or institutions) that there is a problem and that it needs attention. Advocate groups are the main claims makers, but action groups, social researchers, and, in fact, everyone engages in claims making at some time or another.[7] The researcher needs to know what goes into a claim.

Social Construction and Bracketing

The first step in evaluating a claim is to understand the advocate group's reality or worldview. Everyone sees things differently, and consequently one group's solution can be another group's problem (the KKK example above). Different worldviews are possible because we, together with our friends, determine what is important and real. This is what sociologists call *social construction*—arranging the factors of one's experience into a coherent worldview. If we can understand what members of an advocate group have experienced, we will better understand their worldview. But to truly understand another worldview, researchers must set aside their own beliefs and political views and examine values, beliefs, and threats without judgment.

Setting aside one's own ideas does not mean embracing another view. Nor does it imply carelessness with details. But it does allow enough space to look carefully at the implicit and underlying motivations without dismissing them as silly, irrelevant, or wrong. Judgment is reserved for a later time. This method of setting aside one's own ideas of reality to study another reality is called "bracketing."

Once the researcher understands the group's worldview, he or she will be able to appreciate its proposed action. In some ways, the W. I. Thomas theorem is relevant here: if you think that something is real, it will be real in its consequences. The social researcher does not have to believe in the same reality as the advocate group in order to study and understand it.

A UFO study illustrates the usefulness of this approach. The researcher was not interested in whether UFOs are real or not. But he was very interested in how a belief in UFOs affects someone's actions and attitudes. The social researcher "bracketed" his own beliefs so that he could understand, without judgment, the worldview of someone who does believe in UFOs.

Approaching scientific studies in this way has become more common in recent years. Even the most objective scientists have come to accept that it is not possible to be completely objective, since everyone is influenced by his or her own worldview.

If the issue is one that the social researchers feel strongly about, it may be appropriate at a certain point for them to inform others that they are switching from the role of a social researcher to that of a claims maker. Researchers should realize that by taking on the role of a claims maker, they forfeit some authority and their claims will be evaluated along with all the others.

Author Bias

The second step in evaluating a claim is to look for *author bias*—a distorted or misleading interpretation of the information of which the author may or may not be aware. Many advocate groups have well-known positions or political affiliations, which are reflected in the language and arguments of their claims. But knowing they have a position doesn't necessarily mean that their claim is distorted or misleading.

If the position of an advocate group is not known, the researcher should ask a series of questions about the presentation of information. Has the situation been overstated? Can known positions be recognized in the argument? What experiences in the author's background led to this view? What does the author hope to achieve from presenting this information? How does this view compare to what others think on this subject? Sometimes the author wants nothing more than to inform the reader. But at other times the author clearly wants to motivate the reader to act in a particular way. Perhaps the author wants to persuade the reader to his own worldview. Or perhaps the author wants the reader to be more sympathetic to an unpopular cause.

There is nothing wrong with listening to all sides of an issue. The conscientious researcher should understand the reasons why people have different worldviews and their interpretation of the facts. In some respects, no truly "objective" viewpoint exists. Each person looks at the world from his or her own perspective and will present facts and arguments accordingly or risk being viewed as insincere or incoherent. The researcher might even find it valuable to "walk in the shoes" of the other person—look at the situation from that perspective, in order to better understand the viewpoint being presented. ("Walking in the shoes of the other" is an opportunity to understand what the social construction process is about.)

The researcher needs to be wary of the author who, in an attempt to win over the reader, is guilty of distorting the facts or presenting the arguments in a misleading way.

If the information appears evenhanded, the researcher might want to look for other signs of a claims maker's intentions. Are there any indications of affiliation to a group or category that has a known position? Certain organizations that are referred to repeatedly may offer a clue. An article on evolution that refers to a fundamentalist Christian organization would be suspect, since most fundamentalist Christians oppose Darwinian evolution.

Identifying who published the article might give another clue. An article on science in the public school system published by the American Association for the Advancement of Science (AAAS) is likely to promote a different view than one published by the American Baptist Association (ABA). Ideally, the two sources would agree on essential points. Failing that, the researcher should weigh the data and arguments of the respective organizations while being alert to potential bias.

The social researcher should not be fooled by reputation. Just because a group has a well-known position doesn't mean it is always unreliable. For instance, one might expect a certain bias when a religious organization reports the news. But despite its religious affiliation, the *Christian Science Monitor* has been highly respected for a hundred years.

On the other hand, advocate group members who are well respected may be biased. Persons with a reputation for accuracy may nonetheless mistake their point of view for objectivity. This is apparently the case with the respected scientists Isaac Asimov, Carl Sagan, and Paul Kurtz, who cofounded the Committee for the Scientific Investigation of Claims of the Paranormal.[8] The group claims to "promote scientific inquiry" when "examining controversial and extraordinary claims." But an examination of these men's views reveals they discount the reality of spiritual phenomena.[9] Hence anyone reading articles in their publication, the *Skeptical Inquirer*, should beware of an antispiritual bias.

It is not uncommon for scientists to have a bias against religion or spiritual affairs. After all, there has been a "war" between science and religion for approximately five hundred years (Turrell 2004).

Another example of scientists who are biased against spiritual phenomena occurred more than a century ago. In the mid-1800s, the British Association for the Advancement of Science refused to hear papers on hypnotism or mesmerism, on the basis they were insignificant to scientific research. A few years later the British Royal Society of Science refused to hear a paper on spiritualism by physicist Sir William Crookes on similar grounds (Palfreman 1979; Doyle 1975). These incidents do not reflect the image that most people have of scientists objectively examining the data. Thus we can say that even scientists claiming objectivity are subject to bias. But again, the researcher must be careful not to assume that all scientists have a similar bias.

Last, the researcher should ask if the author has something to gain from the action he or she proposes. If a ketchup manufacturer advertised that its product helped prevent cancer, it obviously stands to benefit from all the people who believe the claim and rush out to buy ketchup to prevent cancer. The claim may be completely false or only partially true (more likely in a sophisticated world). The ketchup company may be using a study that found cooked tomatoes had a particularly healthful effect on participants. But it would be difficult to consume enough ketchup to approximate the required results. Thus the statement that ketchup can help reduce cancer is not technically false, but it is misleading.

Argument Bias

The third step in evaluating a claim is to look for *argument bias*—an attempt to convince by means other than use of data or information. Any argument made by an advocate group publication needs to be examined carefully. The researcher should be on the lookout for arguments that are intended to convince by means other than a careful weighing of the data. How specific is the argument? Does the author give details of the incidents, actions, or persons? Are the details left for the reader to figure out? Look for coherence and appropriateness. Are the claims that the author is making relevant to the question? Does the author stick to the point, going from one aspect to the next? Or does the author throw in a lot of unrelated points to stir the reader's emotions or give the impression of being knowledgeable?

An argument that uses glittering generalities will sound convincing until it is applied to a specific situation. Then the components of the argument break down. Other known tactics that are commonly used to sway someone include name-calling, plain Jane ("I'm just a simple boy"), testimonial, card stacking, bandwagon ("everyone knows"), and lies about the dead ("Before he died …").

Data Bias

Evaluating *data bias* in a claim can be difficult, and the researcher should ask the following questions: What data is used to substantiate the claim? Is it verifiable? Do the facts that are presented agree with reports from other reputable sources? Are the statistics exaggerated to make the claim more dramatic? Is there too much data included? Is it up-to-date?

The researcher is like a detective, sorting through all the available evidence, deciding which is credible and which is not, who to believe, and what arguments to take with a grain of salt. The social problems expert should never dismiss a source of information as invalid because the source does not seem reliable. On the other hand, giving an unreliable source undue weight could cause the conclusions to be biased.

It is impossible for sociologists and researchers to personally verify all the data and other information presented by advocate groups, action groups, or anyone making a claim. Most of the time a quick look at the way in which data is presented will reveal a lot about any misuse of data. Beyond that, to check specific claims, the social researcher can compare the advocate group claims with other claims about the same topic. If there is general agreement among the different claims, the data is probably correct.

Think tanks are advocate groups that study social situations and provide the public with reliable information.[10] Some of these groups have a better reputation for accuracy than others and most have a political leaning. It is important to know which sources are reliable. A researcher needs to know where to go for data, and how to verify its accuracy. There are large areas of agreement about data among the best think tanks, regardless of their worldview. If there is a discrepancy that the researcher feels needs to be checked, the most authoritative sources of information are the Census Bureau, or known national survey organizations such as General Social Survey, the Gallup Organization, and the Inter-university Consortium for Political and Social Research (ICPSR). Other government agencies sometimes provide reliable data.

Government agencies are generally careful to collect accurate data, but occasionally there are errors. Other organizations vary in the accuracy of their data and its availability to public inquiry. Sociological studies published in peer-reviewed journals can be taken as authoritative, unless there is a particular reason for questioning the way that the study was done.

Delineating all the ways to check for data bias is beyond the scope of this chapter. But we will consider, briefly, some things to watch for. In general, bias in the data means that a conclusion is not supported as claimed.

Wording

Look for exact meanings of the words and their implications. Scientific presentation of data is as precise as possible. A common mistake, for instance, is mixing up percentages. For instance, "The majority of the students taking the exam scored 80 percent or better" is easily misconstrued as "The majority scored above 80 percent." The word "majority," in this case, refers to the students taking the exam, not the majority of the whole class (or "population"). It is possible that only a small percentage took the exam. In that case, those who scored above 80 percent would be less than half.

Numbers Versus Percentages

Another way statistics are used inappropriately (some say, to "lie" with statistics) is to confuse numbers and percentages. For instance, the percentage of African Americans who live in poverty is higher than the percentage of white Americans who live in poverty, yet by far the majority (in terms of numbers) of those living in poverty are white.

Graphs

Exaggeration in graphic representation is not uncommon. A line going from 15 to 20 will appear more dramatic on a graph with a range of 10 to 25 than on a graph with a range of 0 to 50, particularly if the *x* axis markers are compressed. Someone reporting on the number of rapes in the United States could claim a dramatic increase using the first graph, while opponents could claim a slight increase using the second graph.

Errors in Conducting Studies

Usually evaluation of data bias will not include examining how a study was done. But occasionally nonscientific studies are given as evidence to support an advocate group claim. It is helpful to be able to recognize this when it happens.

Advocate group reports that cite data from specific studies should include enough information for the reader to find the study or the data. Census data should include the appropriate year and other pertinent information. Journal articles should include the author's name, the publication, and a date. If this information is missing, the data becomes suspect, and the researcher should not rely on it too heavily without verification.

Data that is public knowledge needs no reference. Election of U.S. presidents is a matter of public record, as are notable events such as that of September 11, 2001. At other times the datum is not public record but agrees with known facts; hence, it is believable. If it seems correct, and there is no reason not to trust the data, the researcher may decide to do so until it is discredited.

Additional Things to Watch For

Conceptualization: Did the authors of the study conceptualize the study correctly? Is the concept they claim to have studied really captured in their data? For many years church attendance was used as a measure of religiosity, whereas a person could be very religious and not go to church.

Sample and Generalization: To make generalizations about a larger population, the sample studied must be drawn statistically (randomly). If a researcher uses a convenience sample—stopping the first ten people he sees, for instance—the results tell you nothing beyond those ten people.

Significance: When statistics are used, significance tells the researcher if the results are by chance. The smaller the number, the less likely the results are by chance. However, results can be statistically significant but not substantively significant, meaning the difference is not important. A study comparing grades may find that a difference between 3.15 and 3.14 is highly significant. But how much difference does .01 make? Not much.

Cause Versus Correlation: Most social research only points to correlation. However, correlation is often interpreted as cause. If being hungry and eating is correlated, one is tempted to say feeling hungry causes eating. But what about the times when you visit someone's home and you eat the piece of cake your host offers? In other words, the cause and correlation are not so straightforward as they seemed at first.

CONCLUSION

The concepts in this chapter help clarify what is meant by social problems. Six ingredients help us know what to look for. By identifying the *advocate group* as a minimal public to recognize a social problem, we can track the ebb and flow of particular social problems. Identifying the *action group* and the *will to act* gives us insight into the inner dynamics of the situation. Examining the way in which the advocate group makes its claims and its proposed *ameliorating action* helps us spot other aspects of the problem that are not being addressed.

In the next chapter we will examine patterns of growth and development of advocate groups. Why do people organize themselves? How do they organize? What stages of development lead to successful advocating? What kind of action will a group think is appropriate? What kind of change is the advocate group seeking? To whom will it turn to take action? What motivates the group, and what will motivate others to go along with its proposed action? What are the likely consequences of the proposed action? There are no ready-made answers to these questions. Instead, conclusions will be drawn about each advocate group based on the information presented.

In the following chapters, we will consider specific solutions to particular social problems. Some problems are very complex, with many diverse advocate groups. In each case a summary is included to help sort these out.

Government action is not the only solution, although it is important. Some problems can be addressed with government programs or legislation. Other problems are addressed successfully by nongovernmental programs and actions. There are also educational campaigns and apologies—on the part of government officials or others. And of course there are actions of individuals. It is also important to look at how people react to advocate groups, and the consequences of actions that are taken. Not all consequences are positive or intended.

Later chapters discuss several models of change, drawn from the different assumptions that people have of human nature. In addition to the well-known models of human interaction, there are models having to do with structure, and models that emphasize resources.

It is always good to take a step back and look at the situation from a broader perspective. The social researcher who examines a social problem using these analytical concepts will surely have something worthwhile to contribute to any discussion.

QUESTIONS FOR REVIEW

1   What are the six ingredients of a social problem?

2   What are eight common reasons social problems develop?

3   Explain author bias, argument bias, and data bias.

QUESTIONS FOR FURTHER THOUGHT

1 How do social problems make society better?

2 How would you evaluate the claims of Arizona governor Jan Brewer regarding illegal immigration?

3 Is the news objective? Examine the news you listen to or read on a regular basis. Is there an argument bias?

4 In what situations might government data be biased?

NOTES

1 Subsequently 11,000 more died from aftereffects of the substance. According to the Indian government some 500,000 people were affected, including thousands of babies born with defects. In June 2010, seven former employees were convicted by an Indian court for their role in the incident.

2 Again, the terminology of "group" is not strictly correct here. The action group is usually an organization or an institution. But for simplicity's sake, when the term *action group* is used, it will mean group, organization, institution, or collectivity—whichever is appropriate.

3 The Innocence Project is an organization of lawyers, students, and others who work to assist prisoners who can be proven innocent by means not available at the time of sentencing—DNA testing. Since 1992, a total of 242 people, who served an average of twelve years in prison, have been exonerated and released. For more information, go to www.innocenceproject.org.

4 According to the U.S. Census Bureau, 8.3 percent of non-Hispanic whites lived in poverty, as compared with 24.9 percent of African Americans, 24.7 percent of American Indians, and 21.8 percent of Hispanics.

5 Ideology contributes to racism and discrimination. Nineteenth-century eugenicists concluded that Caucasians (in particular Caucasian males, since females weren't included in the top rank) were the most developed of all the races. In *Mismeasure of Man* Stephen J. Gould documents the bias in their "scientific" studies of intelligence used to support their theories. A less obvious ideology of racism today is the common impression that Hispanic children are less likely to do well at school than white children.

6 The main ways that sociologists and other social researchers collect data are surveys, interviews and field research, case studies, and experimentation. Sociologists also use secondary data sources, including government or other known organizations such as GSS, or others, and of course the U.S. Census.

7 Because of the focus of this book, most of the discussion centers on the claims making of advocate groups. Everything that is said about claims making and claims makers can apply to all other claims-making groups or individuals.

8 Changed to Committee for Skeptical Inquiry, or CSI in 2006. www.csicop.org.

9   Paul Kurtz is professor emeritus of both the CSI organization and the Council for Secular Humanism. A statement from the latter organization reads: "We are generally skeptical about supernatural claims. We recognize the importance of religious experience; we deny, however, that such experiences have anything to do with the supernatural. We have found no convincing evidence that there is a separable 'soul' or that it exists before birth or survives death. We must therefore conclude that the ethical life can be lived without the illusions of immortality or reincarnation."

10   To name just a few: the Brookings Institution, American Enterprise Institute, Urban Institute, Cato Institute, Tellus Institute, Heritage Foundation, American Civil Liberties Union, and Pew Research Center.

SOURCES

Allen, Barbara L. 2007. "Environmental Justice, Local Knowledge, and After-Disaster Planning in New Orleans." *Technology in Society*. Vol 29 no 2, pp 153–159.

Ap, John. 2003. "Encountering SARS: Perspective from an Infected Area." eReview of Tourism Research. Vol 1 no 1.

BBC. 2008. "Rwanda: How the Genocide Happened," December 18. http://news.bbc.co.uk/2/hi/1288230.stm. Accessed September 29, 2009.

Beck, E. M., and Steward E. Tolnay. 1990. "The Killing Fields of the Deep South: The Market for Cotton and the Lynching of Blacks, 1882–1930." *American Sociological Review*. Vol 55 no 4, pp 526–539.

Brodie, Mollyann, et al. 2006. "Experiences of Hurricane Katrina Evacuees in Houston Shelters: Implications for Future Planning." *American Journal of Public Health*. Vol 96 no 8, pp 1402–1408.

Carafano, James Jay, and Laura Keith. 2006. "The Solution for Immigration Enforcement at the State and Local Level." Heritage Foundation, Web Memo 1096, May 25.

Chatterjee, N. 1999. "They Have Not Heard of AIDS: HIV/AIDS Awareness Among Married Women in Bombay." *Public Health*. Vol 113 no 3, pp 137–140.

Chudacoff, Howard, and Judith Smith. 2000. *The Evolution of American Urban Society*. Upper Saddle River, NJ: Prentice Hall.

CNN. 2011. "Arizona Takes Controversial Immigration Law to Supreme Court," May 9. www.cnn.com/2011/US/05/09/arizona.immigration. Accessed June 6, 2011.

Coontz, Stephanie. 2005. *Marriage: A History*. New York: Viking.

Diehl, Paul Francis. 1999. *A Road Map to War: Territorial Dimensions of International Conflict*. Nashville, TN: Vanderbilt University Press.

Doyle, Arthur Conan. 1975 (1926). *The History of Spiritualism*. Vol 1. New York: Arno.

Egeberg, Morten. 1995. "Bureaucrats as Public Policy-Makers and Their Self-Interests." *Journal of Theoretical Politics*. Vol 7 no 2, pp 157–167.

Elliott, James R., and Jeremy Pais. 2006. "Race, Class, and Hurricane Katrina: Social Differences in Human Responses to Disaster." *Social Science Research*. Vol 35 no 2, pp 295–321.

Finkelstein, Sydney, Jo Whitehead, and Andres Campbell. 2008. *Think Again: Why Good Leaders Make Bad Decisions and How to Keep It From Happening to You*. Watertown, MA: Harvard Business Press.

Foner, Eric. 1993. *Freedom's Lawmakers: A Directory of Black Officeholders During Reconstruction*. New York: Oxford University Press.

Frickel, Scott, and Bess Vincent. 2007. "Hurricane Katrina, Contamination, and the Unintended Organization of Ignorance." *Technology in Society*. Vol 29 no 2, pp 181–188.

Gould, Stephen Jay. 1981. *The Mismeasure of Man*. New York: Norton.

Hatvalne, Prakash. 2010. "Seven Guilty in Toxic Gas Leak in 1984." *Arlington Star-Telegram*, June 8, sec A.

Heininger, Mary Lynn Stevens. 1984. "Children, Childhood, and Change in America, 1820–1920." In *A Century of Childhood, 1820–1920*. Rochester, NY: Margaret Woodbury Strong Museum.

Jasanoff, Sheila. 1994. *Learning from Disaster: Risk Management After Bhopal*. Philadelphia: University of Pennsylvania Press.

Kadushin, Alfred, and Judith A Martin. 1980. *Child Abuse: An Interactional Event*. Irvington, NY: Columbia University Press.

Kessler, Ronald C., and Hurricane Katrina Community Advisory Group et al. 2006. "Mental Illness and Suicidality After Hurricane Katrina." *Bull World Health Organ*. Vol 84 no 12, pp. 930–939.

Korf, Benedikt. 2007. "Antinomies of Generosity: Moral Geographies, and Post-Tsunami Aid in Southeast Asia." *Geoforum*. Vol 38 no 2, pp 366–378.

Letchford, C. W., H. S. Norville, and J. Bilello, 2000. "Damage Survey and Assessment of Fort Worth Tornado, 28 March 2000." www.depts.ttu.edu/weweb/Pubs/pdfs/D3-28-00%20Tor%20FtWorth. pdf. Accessed September 25, 2009.

Liazos, Alexander. 1972. "The Poverty of the Sociology of Deviance: Nuts, Sluts, and Perverts." *Social Problems*. Vol 20, pp 403–420.

Loh, L. C., et al. 2004. "Change in Infection Control Practices and Awareness of Hospital Medical Staff in the Aftermath of SARS." *Medical Journal of Malaysia*. Vol 59 no 5, pp 659–664.

MacDonald, David Bruce. 2002. *Balkan Holocausts? Serbian and Croatian Victim-Centered Propaganda and the War in Yugoslavia*. Manchester, UK: Manchester University Press.

Mann, J. 1990. "AIDS: A Worldwide Pandemic." *Current Topics in AIDS*. Vol 2. Edited by D. J. Jeffries et al. Hoboken, NJ: John Wiley.

Martinez, James Michael. 2007. *Carpetbaggers, Cavalry, and the Ku Klux Klan: Exposing the Invisible Empire*. Lanham, MD: Rowman & Littlefield.

McMillen, Neil R. 1990. *Dark Journey: Black Mississippians in the Age of Jim Crow*. Chicago: University of Illinois Press.

Metrocode. 2009. "Architecture in Fort Worth: The Tower." www.fortwortharchitecture.com/bankone. htm. Accessed October 2, 2009.

Morris, Benny. 2001. *Righteous Victims: A History of the Zionist-Arab Conflict, 1881–1999*. New York: Vintage.

Myers-Lipton, Scott J. 2006. *Social Solutions to Poverty: America's Struggle to Build a Just Society*. Boulder: Paradigm.

NBC4i. 2009. "Third Person Dies After Ohio Buggy Accident," September 6. http://www2.nbc4i.com/cmh/news/local/article/third_person_dies_after_ohio_buggy_accident/22728. Accessed September 30, 2009.

Palfreman, Jon. 1979. "Between Skepticism and Credulity: A Study of Victorian Attitudes to Modern Spiritualism." In *On the Margins of Science: The Social Construction of Rejected Knowledge*. Edited by Roy Wallis. Keele, Canada: University of Keele, pp 201–236.

Perrow, Charles. 1984. *Normal Accidents*. New York: Basic Books.

Pfohl, Stephen J. 1977. "The Discovery of Child Abuse." *Social Problems*. Vol 24, pp 310–323.

Ruane, Joseph, and Jennifer Todd. 2000. *The Dynamics of Conflict in Northern Ireland: Power, Conflict, and Emancipation*. Cambridge, UK: Cambridge University Press.

Sen, Amartya K. 1977. "Rational Fools: A Critique of the Behavioral Foundations of Economic Theory." *Philosophy and Public Affairs*. Vol 6 no 4, pp 317–344.

Tam, Kim-Pong, Ivy Yee-Man Lau, and Chi-Yue Chiu. 2004. "Biases in the Perceived Prevalence and Motives of Severe Acute Respiratory Syndrome Prevention Behaviors Among Chinese High School Students in Hong Kong." *Asian Journal of Social Psychology*. Vol 7 no 1, pp 67–81.

Tang, Catherine So-kum. 2007. "Trajectory of Traumatic Stress Symptoms in the Aftermath of Extreme Natural Disaster: A Study of Adult Thai Survivors of the 2004 Southeast Asian Earthquake and Tsunami." *Journal of Nervous and Mental Disease*. Vol 195 no 1, pp 54–59.

Turrell, David J. 2004. *Science vs. Religion: The 500 Year War Finding God in the Heat of the Battle*. Baltimore: Publish America.

Walker, C. 2008. "Marxism 101: Are People Too Greedy for Socialism?" *Dynamic*. Vol 19. www.yclusa.org/article/articleprint/1864/-1/341. Accessed September 27, 2009.

Whiteley, Michael. 2002. "Owners, Fort Worth in Standoff with State Over 'Plank One' Tower." *Dallas Business Journal*, July 19.

It is important to note that the problems that members of society find pressing can change over time. What people cite as problems has many cultural, historical, social, political, and technological factors. The degree to which a social phenomenon is considered a social problem or social issue also correlates with social factors like race, class, gender, socioeconomic status, and education. Like gender and race, social problems themselves are also social constructions. The following chapter from the book *Contemporary Social Constructionism: Key Themes* provides a contemporary look at how social problems themselves are social constructions and how this construction tends to manifest.

Reading 3.2.

The Social Construction of Social Problems

by Darin Weinberg

This [reading] moves on from the social construction of our external and internal, material and immaterial worlds to consider in depth the contribution social constructionism might make to critical theory—that is, those forms of social thought directly concerned not only with understanding the social world but also with critiquing it in the interest of progressive social change. It does so through an examination of the social construction of social problems. As is well known, John Kitsuse played a prominent and indispensable role in both founding and advancing the social constructionist approach to social problems. He did so in explicit opposition to structural functionalist approaches to theorizing social problems (Schneider 1985b; Spector and Kitsuse 2001). Whereas functionalist theorists have tended to regard social problems more or less as Durkheimian social facts that occur independently of the ways in which they are perceived by members of society, Kitsuse insisted that social problems cannot be separated from the perceptions and practical activities undertaken by members of the social worlds menaced by those problems. In observing that the very reality of social problems depends on how they are perceived and managed by members of historically and culturally specific constituencies, Kitsuse brought social problems research to an unprecedented level of epistemological depth and subtlety. Furthermore, through the use of constructionist insights, he and his social constructionist students and colleagues have illuminated an extensive domain of hitherto unexplored directions for sociological research. For example, constructionist theory has enabled social problems researchers to examine more effectively the social processes through which phenomena are construed as problematic, through which they are constituted as public rather than private problems, and through which prospective remedies for them are socially produced, implemented, evaluated, revised, combined, replaced, forgotten, and so on.

In each of these ways, constructionists have taken important theoretical strides beyond the limitations that had attended prior approaches to theorizing social problems. Attention to what Spector and Kitsuse (2001) once called the "subjective component" of social problems production and amelioration has indeed yielded a vast catalogue of empirical studies that demonstrate how social problems as various as AIDS (Epstein 1996), alcoholism (Schneider 1978; Wiener 1981), battered women (Loseke 1992), child abuse (Pfohl 1977), hate crimes (Jenness 1995), infertility (Scritchfield 1995), and stalking (Lowney and Best 1995), to name just a handful, acquired their characteristic features as problematic phenomena

Darin Weinberg, "The Social Construction of Social Problems," *Contemporary Social Constructionism: Key Themes*, pp. 113-133, 164-165, 167-183. Copyright © 2015 by Temple University Press. Reprinted with permission.

and as problematic phenomena worthy of particular types of public consideration and concern. But beyond demonstrating that by their very existence social problems entail the exercise and promotion of historically and culturally specific judgments that are themselves appropriate topics of empirical research, Kitsuse also proffered a still more radical claim, an ontological claim, regarding the relationship between the practices through which people construct social problems as meaningful phenomena and the worldly reality and repercussions of the problems so constructed.

In their classic formulation of the constructionist position, Spector and Kitsuse (2001, 76) admonished social problems researchers to studiously disattend whatever objective conditions claims makers presumed their activities to concern in favor of attending exclusively to the claims-making activities of those who propound or contest the nature of alleged social problems. This methodological advice deflected analytic attention away from how putatively problematic conditions, once assembled as meaningful objects of discourse and practice, might become dialectically related to the discursive claims made about them (Weinberg 1997, 2005). It thereby inaugurated a tradition in constructionist analysis of rendering the ostensive objects of claims-making activities *entirely* epiphenomenal to claims-making activities. Since the 1970s, a good deal of ink has been spilled in efforts to resolve the proper relationship of putatively objective conditions to constructionist analyses. While some argue for a "strict" constructionism that attends exclusively to claims-making activities and insists on their "symbol and language bound character" (Ibarra and Kitsuse 1993, 31), others advise a more tempered, "contextual" constructionism wherein the analyst might go beyond our research subjects' discursive claims to address the worldly practical circumstances that occasion those claims (Best 1993; Gubrium 1993; Holstein and Miller 1993). Advocates of both positions emphasize the importance of studying the activities by which people construct social problems, but a stable consensus has not yet been achieved as to whether putatively objective conditions might be legitimately invoked to understand and explain those activities.

In this [reading], I trace a brief genealogy of the debate Kitsuse inaugurated over objectivism in constructionist social problems theorizing and propose a solution to the dilemmas to which this debate has given rise. The proposed solution draws from post-foundationalist philosophers, sociologists, and historians of science who have radically reformulated the nature of empirical research such that the antinomy between subjectivism and objectivism is largely dissolved and the conceptual chasm between interpretive understanding and causal explanation is all but eliminated. Building on this literature, I describe and defend a middle road between Kitsusian constructionists' principled denials of any causal relationship between claims-making activities and the conditions those activities presumably concern and the theoretically moribund brands of objectivism that Kitsuse and his constructionist colleagues have been properly concerned to overcome.

ON THE IRRELEVANCE OF PUTATIVE CONDITIONS

Building on Kitsuse's earlier work in the sociology of deviance (see Holstein 2009), Spector and Kitsuse (2001) galvanized a movement among social problems theorists to develop a thoroughly constructionist approach to the study of social problems. While acknowledging their debt to the earlier work of Fuller and Myers (1941a, 1941b), Blumer (1971), Becker (1966) and others affiliated with the value-conflict and labeling schools, Spector and Kitsuse (2001) were concerned that these researchers had not yet fully abandoned what they viewed as a problematic tendency to privilege certain accounts of social reality over others. This privileging took place when some accounts of a putatively problematic social condition were consecrated as objective while others were regarded as merely subjective. Schneider (1985b, 211) has written in this regard, "Kitsuse and Spector ... argue that these authors compromised a distinct theory of social problems by their continued attention to objective conditions as a necessary part of the conceptualization." And Spector and Kitsuse (2001, 76) wrote: "We are interested in constructing a theory of claims-making activities, not a theory of conditions. Thus the significance of objective conditions for us is the assertions made about them, not the validity of those assertions as judged from some independent standpoint, as for example that of a scientist. To guard against the tendency to slip back into an analysis of the condition, we assert that even the condition itself is irrelevant to and outside of our analysis."

In place of attention to the conditions claims-making activities are ostensibly about, Spector and Kitsuse (2001) advised attending exclusively to the manner in which claims are formulated, promoted, contested, amended, defeated, or otherwise socially engaged. Social problems analysts were counseled to completely disregard any causal effect objective conditions might be held to exert on claims-making activities in favor of looking to a putative realm of purely symbolic interaction within which all claims making was held to be contained, confined, and, apparently, sealed off from so-called objective causal forces. This recommendation was quite clearly made in the interest of highlighting the enormous amount of strategic work and politicking that is involved in promoting and contesting claims about social problems. It was also intended to remedy what Spector and Kitsuse incisively noted was the disturbingly pervasive tendency of social scientists to uncritically endorse, legitimate, and indeed reify, the verity of accounts proffered of social problems by plainly interested parties. By radically dissociating their own research program from the agendas of those with obvious political, economic, and moral stakes in the outcomes of social problems debates, Spector and Kitsuse seemed to be offering a more scientific tack. Social problems researchers were to forsake the role of intellectual mercenary and stake out a disinterested, purely analytic ground of their own from which to scientifically assess the play of social forces that give rise to the symbolic identities of social problems (Gusfield 1984).

In the wake of Spector and Kitsuse's (2001) seminal contribution, most constructionist social problems theorists came to agree that, in principle, a very wide variety of social actors and actions might influence the symbolic identities of social problems and thus were proper subjects of social problems research. Most also insisted that, as a matter of theoretical principle, no one symbolic rendering of a putative social problem was to be given greater legitimacy than any other. In this way, the ascendance and demise of social problems claims came to be understood solely as products of people's symbolic interactions and perceptions. In other words, the empirical field of constructionist social problems research was strictly circumscribed as follows: *only the symbolic interactions of human individuals or human collectives were given credence as either causes or constitutive features of social problems*. For the purposes of constructionist analysis, the putatively nonsymbolic conditions people claim as problematic were to be understood as nonexistent, wholly irrelevant to, or mere epiphenomena of claims-making practices that are caused and constituted *only* by symbolic interaction.

ON FORMULATING RADICALLY CONSTRUCTIONIST EMPIRICAL ANALYSES OF SOCIAL PROBLEMS

For several years before Spector and Kitsuse published *Constructing Social Problems*, they, and a group of like-minded social problems researchers, had already been busy working out the methodological details of rendering radically constructionist empirical analyses of social problems (Conrad 1975; Gusfield 1975; Pfohl 1977; Schneider 1978). Specifically what kinds of data might be used to empirically demonstrate the total irrelevance of putative conditions to claims-making activities regarding them? Specifically how might those data be used to accomplish such empirical demonstrations? These questions posed challenging analytic puzzles for would be constructionists. As David Bloor (1976) famously noted, demonstrations of distance between descriptive activities and the things those descriptions are presumed to describe are usually intended to discredit those descriptive activities. Kitsusian constructionists, though, were not interested in simply debunking certain claims makers they did not find to their liking. They were concerned with devising analytic techniques that might be applied with equal vigor to the analysis of meritorious as well as erroneous claims-making activities. Ultimately, something of a working consensus was, in fact, forged regarding the proper conduct of radically constructionist empirical analyses.

One particular technique emerged during the 1970s to become the preeminent exemplar for radically constructionist empirical analyses of social problems. This analytic technique entailed empirically demonstrating that a condition had remained invariant while claims-making activities regarding it had changed. Thus, for example, in his classic study of the discovery of hyperkinesis, Peter Conrad (1975, 16) writes: "We assume that before the discovery of hyperkinesis this type of deviance was seen as disruptive, disobedient, rebellious, anti-social or deviant behavior. Perhaps the label 'emotionally disturbed' was sometimes used, when it was in vogue in the early sixties, and the child was usually managed in the context of the family or the school or in extreme cases, the child guidance clinic. How then did this constellation of deviant behaviors become a medical disorder?"

In this passage, Conrad refers to a "type of deviance" that earlier was regarded in one way and then, later, came to be regarded otherwise. By textually demonstrating that conditions remained invariant, radically constructionist social problems analysts also rendered them causally inert with respect to their explanations of changing claims-making activities. They thereby justified placing their explanatory focus on other matters (e.g., the clashing and confluence of rhetorical idioms, the practical interests of claims makers and their adversaries, power differentials between claims makers, or the historical and cultural circumstances under which claims are produced and promoted). Thus, as a matter of empirical analysis, it came to appear that if one was willing and able to demonstrate such a schism between claims-making activities and the putative conditions they concerned, even *changes* in the putative conditions that are the topic of claims-making activities could be construed as totally unrelated to changes in claims making regarding them. Spector and Kitsuse's classic theoretical assertion that such changes (if and when they might occur) are "irrelevant to, and outside of" constructionist analyses of claims-making activities thus appeared amenable to effective empirical defense.

Demonstrations that claims-making activities regarding a putatively problematic condition are unrelated to the objective status of that condition have been, and continue to be, invoked throughout the constructionist social problems literature. Thus, for example, in their study of the widespread alarm regarding crack use in the United States, Craig Reinarman and Harry Levine (1997) contrast various public claims made by politicians and news media personnel regarding the gravity of the American crack problem with official statistics regarding the prevalence of crack use and crack related problems in the United States. They show that while public claims making regarding crack is filled with hyperbole and doom saying, official government statistics provide evidence that the American crack problem is far less serious than public claims suggest. By way of this contrast, Reinarman and Levine (1997) make a strong case for finding the causes of public claims primarily in the political interests of claims makers, secondarily in the mass media's appetite for spectacle, and finally (and least significantly) in the objective prevalence of crack-related problems.

Properly accomplished, this type of empirical demonstration is powerful and no doubt will continue as a robust and significant resource in constructionist social problems research. Nonetheless, a nagging theoretical problem hovers over this analytic practice in constructionist studies. In an article that is now justly famous, Steve Woolgar and Dorothy Pawluch (1985) suggested there is an analytic difficulty in empirically demonstrating difference between changes in claims-making activities regarding a putatively problematic condition and changes (or stasis) in the objective status of that condition. If such demonstrations are held up as exemplars for radically social constructionist social problems theory, then they seem to entail espousing both a universal agnosticism regarding the objective existence of any putative conditions and, at the same time, telling how in specific cases the invariance of their manner of objective existence demonstrates their causal irrelevance to the dynamics of claims-making activities. Woolgar and Pawluch (1985) dubbed this analytic technique "ontological gerrymandering" because it appears to employ a strategically selective commitment to both radical constructionism and orthodox objectivism. By ontologically gerrymandering, one privileges one symbolic rendering of a particular condition as objectively superior to other renderings to first distinguish the condition from people's symbolic renderings and activities regarding it and then, ultimately, defend a systematically anti-objectivist theoretical program. Woolgar and Pawluch (1985) argued that such an analytic move is somewhat disingenuous because it requires that one trade on orthodox objectivist claims in particular empirical studies to defend a universal rejection of the legitimacy of objectivism in general social problems theorizing.

Woolgar and Pawluch (1985) sparked a great deal of debate in social problems theory. Disputants, by and large, either have accepted their critique and endeavored to formulate ways to banish ontological gerrymandering from constructionist analysis (Ibarra and Kitsuse 1993) or have argued against Woolgar and Pawluch's assessment of constructionist theorizing and insisted either that the best constructionists are not guilty of ontological gerrymandering (Schneider 1985a) or that ontological gerrymandering does not violate the principles of sound sociological theorizing (Best 1995; Gusfield 1985). For my part, I would like to suggest that despite the enlivened character of debate in constructionist social problems theorizing, we have not yet fully succeeded in emancipating ourselves from the hopelessly untenable forms of naïve objectivism that were the original impetus for constructionist theorizing. While it is surely inadequate to blithely presume the objective characteristics of putative conditions in our accounts of claims-making processes, there remain serious analytic difficulties that continue to attend our efforts as constructionists to ensure that putative conditions remain, in Spector and Kitsuse's (2001) words, "irrelevant to, and outside of" our analyses.

BEYOND ONTOLOGICAL GERRYMANDERING

In probably the best known, and certainly the most theoretically sophisticated, effort to banish ontological gerrymandering from constructionist theorizing regarding the nature of social problems, Peter Ibarra and John Kitsuse (1993) proposed that constructionists make references to their research subjects' *condition categories* in place of the older constructionist convention of referring to the *putative conditions* their discourse and practice are presumed to concern. References to people's condition categories, they argue, highlight more emphatically than did references to putative conditions the fact that it is "they" (as members of the settings we are studying) and not "us" (as analysts) who do the work of realizing the characteristics of the worlds in which they live. This terminology is also meant to underscore another aspect of Ibarra and Kitsuse's (1993) argument. It is meant "to highlight the symbol- and language-bound character of claims-making," and, further, that "the strict constructionist never leaves language" (Ibarra and Kitsuse 1993, 31).

After proposing several revisions to the classic formulations, Ibarra and Kitsuse (1993) go on to advocate a program of constructionist research that includes greater attention to the rhetorical assemblages through which social problems processes occur and the dialogical processes through which claims and counterclaims, rhetoric and counter-rhetoric are played off each other in the social construction of social problems. Theirs is a formulation that grants causal influence over the social problems process to human claimants and counterclaimants, as when they note, "The 'war on drugs' *initiated* under the Reagan and Bush administrations was itself rendered problematic when civil libertarians *cited* the intrusiveness of such measures as drug testing in the work place" (Ibarra and Kitsuse 1993, 42; emphasis added); to rhetorical idioms and counter-rhetoric, as when they note, "Each rhetorical idiom *encourages* participants to structure their claims along particular lines and not others" (Ibarra and Kitsuse 1993, 36; emphasis added); and to social settings, as when they ask, "How do the formal qualities of particular settings *structure* the ways in which claims can be formulated, delivered, and received?" (Ibarra and Kitsuse 1993, 53; emphasis added). In a deliberate effort to avoid ontological gerrymandering, however, they stop short of granting causal influence to the objective sociohistorical conditions under which claims are made. Apparently, Ibarra and Kitsuse are not averse to characterizing agents, assemblages of resources, and social environments or their specific causal influences on the manner in which social problems are constructed. Their effort, however, is to do so without invoking privileged renderings of either social problems themselves or the sociohistorical conditions that influence how people's claims-making activities take place. Although their effort to attend to how people's claims-making activities constitute the meaningful substance of social problems for them—and, above all, to do so without irony—is certainly a laudable one (and one that will surely continue to yield sociological benefits), their effort to do so without objectivist invocations of the sociohistorical contexts of claims-making processes is, in my view, less promising. My difficulty is that I cannot imagine how we might speak to the "agents," "assemblages of resources," and "social environments" in and through which claims-making activities take place such that (at least provisionally) objectivist construals of specific sociohistorical contexts are not inevitably implicated in our accounts.

I therefore cannot help but agree with Joel Best's (1995) suggestion of a more tempered approach to social problems theorizing, one that allows the constructionist to leave language and not only attend to research subjects' communicative action but also to interpret their various other practical activities, how they do them, even why they do them—and to do so by the lights provided by our own social scientific knowledge of their interactional, cultural, and historical contexts. As Best (1993, 141) writes, "The language of claims does not exist independently of the social world; it is a product of—and influence on—that world." James Holstein and Gale Miller (1993, 152) have similarly noted that what they call "social problems work" is intrinsically embedded in the routines of practice constitutive of the organizational settings in which that work is accomplished (see also Holstein and Gubrium 1994). These theorists contend that all activities concerning putatively problematic conditions are embedded in historical, cultural, and interactional contexts that are themselves empirically discoverable, available, and, I would argue, absolutely indispensable for use both by our research subjects and by ourselves (in our own distinctly social scientific efforts) to better understand those activities. But what, if anything, might distinguish our own efforts from the efforts of those who are not social scientists to interpret the link between social contexts and claims making?

WHAT IS THE DIFFERENCE BETWEEN SOCIAL SCIENTIFIC AND MUNDANE INTERPRETATION?

Ibarra and Kitsuse trade on the well-known ethnomethodological admonition not to confuse the "topics" of our research with the "resources" we adopt for accomplishing that research. Moreover, they also invoke a distinction between our research subjects' *practical* project wherein they seek to "alter or defend some aspect of social life" from the sociologist's *theoretical* project wherein sociologists seek to produce a "theoretical reconstruction of the vernacular features of social problems as moral discourse" (Ibarra and Kitsuse 1993, 29). As David Bogen and Michael Lynch (1993, 222) have noted, this distinction seems to reflect a supposition that the "analyst can somehow stand outside the commonsense world when investigating its constitutive organization. Somehow, it would seem, the analyst must conduct an activity that is not itself practical, vernacular, conventional, mundane, or informed by intuitive categories."

As Bogen and Lynch also note, Ibarra and Kitsuse's contrast between the "natural attitude" inhabited by members of society and the attitude of researchers that is presumed possible by theoretically, scientifically, analytically, or phenomenologically "bracketing" or "suspending" the natural attitude has a long pedigree that moves through many of the classic texts of ethnomethodology (Garfinkel and Sacks 1970; Zimmerman and Pollner 1970) and is obviously evident in the phenomenology of both Alfred Schutz (1964, 1966) and Edmund Husserl (1970). I would suggest tracing this pedigree even further afield to include the early efforts of Ludwig Wittgenstein (1922) and the logical positivists to cleanse serious analysis of any reliance on conceptual resources that are not drawn from either immediate empirical observation or formal logic. The efforts of Husserl and Schutz to draw absolute, or principled, contrasts between the "natural attitude" and the ideal attitude of the theorist are closely akin to the young Wittgenstein's efforts to draw principled contrasts between "ordinary" or "natural" language and the ideal language of logic and thereby to more effectively ground knowledge production. Despite its very distinguished legacy, for reasons I discuss below, I am doubtful that this project can be successful and do not think social constructionism benefits from remaining committed to it.

To the extent that we invoke principled distinctions between theory and practice and between analytical and mundane reason, or seek to develop formal methodological procedures (such as "bracketing the natural attitude") with which to ascend to a space of putatively detached theoretical reason, we must, I think, inevitably count ourselves as members of the Kantian tradition of seeking universal philosophical foundations for knowledge. Indeed, it must be acknowledged that the analytic presumption to "bracket" the natural attitude has, in fact, never had any purpose other than to provide philosophically principled grounds for the claim to have overcome the intrinsic biases of the natural attitude and thereby to claim a transcendental position of epistemological authority.[1] Moreover, notwithstanding their stated aim to avoid privileging any account of the social world as more objective than any other, I cannot see how Ibarra and Kitsuse are employing this gesture in any other way. While they clearly refuse to privilege scientific interventions into the social problems claims-making that constitutes their empirical research domain, they seem nonetheless quite committed to claiming their own transcendence of the natural attitude and, hence, their own detachment from the mundane practical concerns that systematically bias people's understandings of the world. This can be interpreted only as a claim to have transcended mundane biases and to have thereby achieved a higher epistemological authority as general theorists of mundane claims-making processes.

If as social constructionists we are committed to understanding how social life regulates and, indeed, constitutes the production of social problems (or anything else), I do not think we are well served by arguments like these that seek to erect principled conceptual partitions between the purely theoretical reason of the analyst and the mundane and practically interested reason of those we study (see also Bourdieu and Wacquant 1992; Lynch 1988, 1993). We must accept that we, no less than those we study, are forever ensconced in the mundane world and allow that our own claims-making practices as social scientists are no less implicated by worldly practical interests or the contingencies of history than are anyone else's (though these interests and contingencies may sometimes be quite different from those at work in the worlds we study). In answer to the question "What is the difference between social scientific and mundane interpretation?" we can offer no absolute, or principled, reply. We must instead answer, "It depends." It depends on what particular people mean by these terms, the practical interests of those who seek to construct differences between them, the practical conditions under which they feel compelled to do so, and the felicitousness of those conditions to the realization of those interests. Speaking more broadly, we must renounce the scientistic myth of wholly detached and disinterested inquiry and acknowledge that neither we as researchers nor those we study can ever intelligibly leave the domain of embodied, invested, and fully purposeful practical action.

BEYOND THE THEORY-PRACTICE DISTINCTION IN THE SOCIOLOGY OF SOCIAL PROBLEMS

As we saw above, Ibarra and Kitsuse (1993, 29) draw a contrast between their research subjects' *practical* project and sociologist's *theoretical* project. They do this on the grounds that while members of society seek to "alter or defend some aspect of social life," sociologists seek to produce a "theoretical reconstruction of the vernacular features of moral discourse." While I have no qualms about the claim that the work of social problems claims makers and the work of sociologists who study them may be variously empirically distinguishable, I am uncomfortable with Ibarra and Kitsuse's apparent claim that sociological analysts of the claims-making process have no interest in "alter[ing] or defend[ing] some aspect of social life." The methodological decision to refrain from actively campaigning alongside some and against others in any particular social problems arena does not spare us from taking sides in social scientific debates regarding the nature of what transpires in that arena. Put more plainly, social scientific work is no less concerned with altering or defending that aspect of social life known as [the-received-wisdom-in-one's-field] than social problems claims makers are concerned with altering or defending the aspect of social life on which their own work is focused. The present state of theoretical development in social problems research is every bit as much an aspect of social life as anything social problems claims makers seek to address. And to the extent that our theorizing is publicly expressed, it is, without exception, undertaken to alter or defend some aspect of the received wisdom.

To argue otherwise, one must trade on a seemingly otherworldly, disembodied, wholly contemplative, and ultimately asocial understanding of the work of social problems theorizing that is, to my mind, quite seriously at odds with the best social constructionist research on the nature of theoretical work. At least since Marx published his "Theses on Feuerbach" (see Marx 1983), we have had good cause to gravely doubt the legitimacy of research that fails to recognize that theoretical contemplation (including social theoretical contemplation) is decidedly not an otherworldly endeavor. It is, for better or for worse, an integral part of the world. Beyond Marx himself, American pragmatists from John Dewey to Richard Rorty have also provided an assortment of incisive arguments in favor of rejecting what Dewey called the "spectator theory" of knowledge, or the view that theorizing can somehow be detached from and disinterested in the worlds it considers. Theory is not merely concerned with producing, in Rorty's (1980) memorable phrase, an acausal "mirror of nature." It inevitably partakes—as feature, cause, and consequence—of the worlds it seeks to reveal. Moreover, as critical theorists of all stripes have long argued, our theoretical work is never amoral or "value-free." As noted above, to the extent that social problems theories are given expression, they are inevitably intended to produce an effect in the world. To precisely that extent, we can infer that the theorist has judged that this effect will be somehow beneficial or valuable.

In addition to the post-foundationalist philosophical efforts of Marxists, pragmatists, and other critical theorists, the theory-practice distinction also has been effectively critiqued by an extensive catalogue of sociological and historical studies of science. [T]hese studies have shown that scientific theorizing is founded less on a uniform logic or "method" (such as bracketing the natural attitude) than a heterogeneous collection of social institutions, social organizational contexts, and particular types of collective action. Inspired by Thomas Kuhn's seminal *The Structure of Scientific Revolutions* (1970), the Edinburgh School and then the Bath School produced finely grained empirical studies of various notable scientific controversies and the processes through which they were resolved. These studies demonstrated the disunity of even natural scientific rationality and the insinuation of broader social interests, dispositions, and processes into the very heart of scientific theory development. Contestation, competition, and controversy are endemic to the work of determining what will and will not be consecrated as a legitimate and valuable contribution to our scientific understanding of the world (Barnes 1977; Bourdieu 1975; H. Collins 1985; Shapin and Schaffer 1985).

And if this is true of the natural sciences, how much more so must it be acknowledged to be true among the social sciences, which are so obviously more abundant with theoretical pluralism and division? In place of images of scientific work that suggest a unity of epistemological standards and theoretical concerns, we are confronted with the obdurate social reality of differences among ourselves and of the unavoidable necessity for dialogue across these lines of difference. If we are to learn from them, participation in such dialogues requires that we continuously strive to make sense of our colleagues, always remaining attentive to one another's words for points of theoretical insight, agreement, controversy, or mistake. But it also requires that we remain vigilantly aware of the fact that we and our interlocutors may not share many, if any, presuppositions regarding the nature of valid and valuable social research. We must keep in mind the possibility that our theoretical differences reflect a broad spectrum of divergent practical interests and goals rather than, more parochially, our degrees of scholarly competence alone. Given this environment, we are all forced to ask ourselves continuously whether, and why, we wish to adopt, amend, critique, or simply ignore as irrelevant the accounts of the world proffered by our colleagues in the social sciences and beyond.

Hence, in the social world consisting of social problems researchers collaboratively engaged in scholarly dialogue and debate as to the most incisive, theoretically defensible, or empirically faithful renderings of people's claims-making activities, we, like anyone else, must inevitably engage in the ongoing, reflexively organized, practical work of formulating the meaning and significance of one another's scholarly activity in light of more inclusive formulations of our practical contexts, our relationships with one another, and our ongoing interaction. Moreover, as has long been abundantly evident throughout the scholarly literature pertaining to the social construction of social problems, our efforts to grasp the meaning of one another's theoretical undertakings are by no means confined to considerations of logic and evidence. Instead, we know that theoretical activities are always embedded in and bound up with wider social, economic, and political activities that not only influence the direction of their development but also inevitably contribute to the stability or instability of their epistemic legitimacy and theoretical meaning (Jasanoff 2005).

Thus, in interpreting the meaning and value of one another's scholarly work, we are continuously called on to provisionally assess not only our own and one another's scholarly objectives but also the objective characteristics of the wider social structural contexts within which our research takes place and the practical consequences (or causal effects) our work is likely to have on those contexts. Insofar as its intelligibility and practical relevance is inexplicable without reference to them, social problems theory must not be artificially divorced from the panoply of socio-historical and social interactional exigencies to which it is responsive. In short, we must acknowledge that provisionally objectivist efforts to identify the relevant social structural contexts of social problems theorizing is indispensable to the work of making sense of social problems theorizing. Social problems theorizing, then, cannot be understood as an ethereal, merely symbolic activity sealed off from the causal interactions that constitute objective social reality. It is, without remedy, a product, feature, and consequential producer of our objective social reality.

RELATIVISM, REFLEXIVITY, EVIDENCE, AND OBJECTIVISM

Rather than seeking to objectively identify and explain social problems, Kitsuse and his social constructionist colleagues turned to the identification and explanation of the claims made about them and properly insisted that the causes of those claims go well beyond the putatively determinant nature of their referents. For a variety of reasons, different people orient to prevailing social conditions in a variety of ways. What some see as problematic, others do not. What some see as worthy of public consideration and concern, others do not. For these reasons, we have been interested in discovering why and how different people have come to adopt their outlooks. And we have been concerned with discovering what accounts for the ascendance of some outlooks and the demise of others. These are critically important questions that any adequate sociology of social problems must address. However, I am convinced that our answers to these questions will inevitably remain insufficient if we confine our attention to either discursive structures or the communicative activity of social problems claims makers.

The difficulty is that neither the communicative activity of social problems claims makers nor the sociological interpretation of that communicative activity is possible without reference to the patterns of mutual accountability by which claims makers seek to influence one another. And as it turns out, these patterns are a good deal more complex than can be fully captured either with reference to shared discursive structures like the "vernacular resources" and "rhetorical dimensions" of claims making that Ibarra and Kitsuse (1993) incisively describe or even with reference to communicative activities construed more broadly. The crux of the problem is this: the theoretical payoff of analyzing the rhetorical dimensions of claims making is meant to be an understanding of the normative force these dimensions of rhetoric have over people's claims-making practices in real time. But, contra Ibarra and Kitsuse, when we get down to the work of empirically analyzing the various dimensions of social problems rhetoric or discourse in actual practice, we discover that neither the intensity nor the character of their normative force among members of society can be adequately understood in isolation from the nondiscursive, or structural, environments within which they occur (Rouse 2002). Why people are influenced and how they are influenced by particular rhetorical strategies are not questions that usually can be answered without a considerable amount of provisionally objectivist attention to the structural circumstances under which they are, in fact, influenced.[2]

This is not simply to argue that there is always more detail and contingency to real-time praxis than is captured by general theories. It is instead to argue that agnosticism regarding the structural contexts of human action comes at the cost of rendering that action normatively unaccountable—or, in other words, unintelligible. General social problems theory cannot succeed if it is confined to the comparative analysis of social problems discourse *in vacuo*. We must attend more inclusively to the myriad elements of context that observably influence the normative dynamics of claims makers' interactions, recognizing that for neither research subjects nor analysts can these elements always be reduced to the merely discursive interplay of symbolic structures or symbolic interactants (Goodwin 2000; Pickering 1995; Weinberg 1997). The patterns of accountability by which people seek to influence one another very plainly reflect not only their regard for one another's claims-making activity but also provisional assessments of the various nondiscursive structural resources available to one another and structural constraints that variously restrict one another's actions.

Although there is not enough space here to develop this point, I think this kind of more inclusive approach to general social problems theory expands rather than contracts the range of analytic axes for comparative constructionist research. And though I certainly abide by the notion that we ought to construct our analyses of the social construction of social problems by way of detailed investigations of what our research subjects themselves regard as the normative warrant for their own and one another's claims, I do not believe this can ever fully absolve us of scholarly responsibility for the specifically social scientific adequacy of our own interpretations of what they are doing and what they count as such warrants.[3] Though we might strive to grasp people's own understandings of their activities and circumstances in our efforts to analyze them, we are usually not interested in their activities and circumstances for the same reasons that they themselves are. Without returning to a principled philosophical contrast between analytic and mundane reason, we must keep in mind that claims makers generally interpret their own and one another's activities with an eye to their relevance to their own social problems claims-making activities, whereas we, as social scientists, interpret their activities (and the meaning they give those activities) with an eye to producing intellectually valuable contributions to specific dialogues in the social sciences.

Moreover, as was noted earlier, these social scientific dialogues are themselves diverse and entail attention to different aspects of both people's communicative activities and the contexts within which those activities occur. For example, some of us may attend to claims making about homelessness for what it reveals about broader claims-making struggles about poverty, while others may attend to it for its relevance to claims making about street crime or mental health care. What will count as evidence of the relevant categories, activities, and structural contexts will vary according to the scholarly interests governing our respective research agendas even though, in some sense, we may be looking at the exact same bits of social activity. In short, neither claims-making activities nor their contexts have unequivocal meanings either for members of society or for us as analysts. Their meanings are irremediably multiple and projected onto them by actors with any number of different interests in them. Although this is a kind of relativism, it by no means forecloses on the possibility of comparing different accounts of events as more or less helpful or astute, given the shared practical purposes for which these accounts are made. But such evaluations must involve ongoing reflexive efforts to identify just what those shared practical purposes happen to be.

Hence, in keeping with the social constructionist ethos Kitsuse did so much to establish and promote, we must acknowledge that the intellectual value of our accounts can be judged neither with respect to a fixed set of criteria for scientific excellence nor with respect to the myth of "brute social facts." Instead, it must be assessed with simultaneous regard for the available evidence pertaining to the research question(s) at hand and to the specific set of analytic outlooks that might be held to provide competing answers (Weinberg 2002, 2006). Social constructionists cannot avoid efforts to objectively identify the local activities that we deem relevant to our research questions. Neither can we avoid attempts to objectively identify the specific causal influences people have on one another's activities or that their structural contexts have on them. However, the kind of objectivity I am discussing here cannot be understood in the traditional senses of objectivity as consisting either in conformity with a universal standard of scientific rationality or striving to achieve direct correspondence between our theories and a world presumed to exist wholly independently of them.

Instead, as I define it, objectivity is simply a matter of answering questions in ways that account for the available evidence pertaining to those questions better than anyone else. By this definition, our objectivity must be viewed as provisional and thoroughly nested in the historically and culturally specific dispute domains within which it is achieved.[4] As noted above, this is a relativist and social constructionist position insofar as it insists that the achievement of objectivity cannot be meaningfully dissociated from the specific organizational circumstances within which it occurs.

But it is certainly not a relativist position in any of the baneful senses suggested by the critics of social constructionism. I am not exalting dogmatism, irrationality, or the idea that any analysis is as good as any other. And I do not by any means rule out the possibility of scientific progress or disconfirming evidence. I reject only the value of endorsing fixed, or socially invariant, measures of such things (see also Bourdieu 1975; Habermas 1987; Haraway 1991; Longino 2002; Rouse 2002). Once we have forsaken the philosophically foundationalist, and academically anachronistic, faith that all genuinely scientific research must be converging on a unified theory of everything in the cosmos, the bane of relativism arises only if and when we find ourselves incapable of assessing the comparative objectivity of incompatible answers to specific scientific questions. It emphatically does not arise simply by virtue of the fact that the same data can be described in different but equally valid ways.

CONCLUDING REMARKS

Kitsuse has profoundly and productively influenced contemporary social constructionism and social problems theory. More specifically, he has also had a profound and productive influence on my own thinking about these matters. This said, I do think there is value in constructive criticism and further development of the Kitsusian legacy. In this [reading], I have taken issue with his claim that social constructionists should sustain a blanket agnosticism with respect to the objective characteristics of the social world. Not only is this theoretical strategy unnecessarily limiting; it is, to my mind, simply untenable. Rather than seek to sustain this agnosticism, we should seek to build the best arguments—as determined, of course, from within our own historically and culturally specific dispute domains—as to the meaning and causes of the claims-making processes we have deemed most relevant to our research question(s). This will entail maximizing our attention and responsiveness to the available evidence concerning people's claims-making activities, their social contexts, and the nature of their influences on one another. Crucially, if we are to effectively develop our analytic sensibilities with respect to the various ways in which people influence one another, we will have to develop analytic resources with which to identify the ongoing dynamics of normative accountability that provide for the social coherence of any given domain of social problems claims making.

Perhaps the most urgent aspect of this task is to discriminate better between the more and less coercive—and, conversely, the more and less persuasive—claims making we discover in different social problems arenas (see Freedman 2005). No doubt, our research subjects themselves often exhibit their own ways of distinguishing coercive from persuasive claims making, but equally certainly, their expressions of these distinctions are colored primarily by their own interests as social problems claims makers rather than by our interests as social scientists. Although such expressions will certainly figure as data, I do not think they can, or should, stand in the place of social scientific analyses. The question we must ask ourselves as social scientists is how we might seek to justify our own social scientific orientations to this critically important matter, given the admitted absence of an Archimedean point of view. It is only if we are able to come up with such justifications that social scientists will ever constructively contribute to discussions of whether social problems claims making is oppressive or empowering in any given empirical case. Contributing to such discussions strikes me as a worthy candidate for inclusion in the Kitsusian legacy and, at the very least, a goal that we should aspire to fulfill.

NOTES

1   The presumption shared by the likes of Husserl, Schutz, and Ibarra and Kitsuse to "bracket" the natural attitude as a whole in favor of a purely theoretical regard for things must be clearly distinguished from the type of bracketing recommended in Holstein and Gubrium 2003. The former seek a principled distinction between ontologically invested, socially interested practical action and a wholly detached and disinterested form of theoretical contemplation. The latter seek only a systematic technique for prioritizing, foregrounding, and backgrounding aspects of social life, given our different practical and theoretical interests in them (see also Goffman 1959, 239–242). Unlike Husserl, Schutz, and Ibarra and Kitsuse, Holstein and Gubrium (2003) do not suggest that their constructionist analytics provide a technique with which the analyst might seek to completely emancipate herself from socially interested practice. They offer only a technique for methodically orchestrating our different interests.

2   A simple example would be the role played by the structural condition of their comparative material wealth and disposable income in dictating the degree to which people are responsive to the rhetorical pleas of political parties or organizations such as Oxfam and Amnesty International for financial support.

3   In a footnote to the revised version of their 1993 essay, Ibarra and Kitsuse (2003, 48) write that the interpretive approach they advocate "engages and implicates the analyst in how these processes are ultimately rendered." However, they continue, "We have no problem in assuming this responsibility; we merely insist that the raw materials of these analytic reconstructions originate with the categories and activities of the members." I agree with the gist of this advice, which I interpret as a call for claims making to remain the focus of social constructionist analyses. However, I am not sure it is possible for our analyses to originate exclusively with members' categories and activities insofar as working out what the relevant categories and activities actually are will inevitably be a product of our own interpretive work and not merely the self-evidently identifiable raw materials for it. I also suspect that identifying who is sufficiently salient in, or influential over, the process to warrant being categorized as a "member" in any given case will require considerably more scientific discretion than Ibarra and Kitsuse let on here.

4   The expression "dispute domain" is borrowed from Miller and Holstein (1995, 38), who define it as follows: "A dispute domain consists of the fundamental assumptions, vocabularies, orientations, concerns, and constraints that circumscribe conflictual interactions within particular organizational circumstances. ... [D]ispute domains provide the local conditions of possibility for disputing—the parameters for what disputes might become and the resources and orientations for their articulation." For a discussion of dispute domains within the context of social scientific method, see Weinberg 2002.

REFERENCES

Barnes, Barry. 1977. *Interests and the Growth of Knowledge*. London: Routledge and Kegan Paul.

Becker, Howard S., ed. 1966. *Social Problems*. New York: Wiley.

Best, Joel. 1993. "But Seriously Folks: The Limitations of the Strict Constructionist Interpretation of Social Problems." In *Reconsidering Social Constructionism*, ed. James A. Holstein and Gale Miller, 129–147. New York: Aldine de Gruyter.

———. 1995. "Constructionism in Context." In *Images of Issues*, 2d ed., ed. Joel Best, 337–354. New York: Aldine de Gruyter.

Bloor, David. 1976. *Knowledge and Social Imagery*. London: Routledge and Kegan Paul.

Blumer, Herbert. 1971. "Social Problems as Collective Behavior." *Social Problems*. 18:298–306.

Bogen, David, and Michael Lynch. 1993. "Do We Need a General Theory of Social Problems?" In *Reconsidering Social Constructionism*, ed. James A. Holstein and Gale Miller, 213–237. New York: Aldine de Gruyter.

Bourdieu, Pierre. 1975. "The Specificity of the Scientific Field and the Social Conditions for the Progress of Reason." *Social Science Information* 14 (5): 19–47.

Bourdieu, Pierre, and Loïc J. D. Wacquant. 1992. *An Invitation to Reflexive Sociology*. Chicago: University of Chicago Press.

Collins, Harry M. 1985. *Changing Order*. London: Sage.

Conrad, Peter. 1975. "The Discovery of Hyperkinesis: Notes on the Medicalization of Deviant Behavior." *Social Problems* 23:12–21.

Epstein, Steven. 1996. *Impure Science*. Berkeley: University of California Press.

Freedman, Karyn L. 2005. "Naturalized Epistemology, or What the Strong Programme Can't Explain." *Studies in the History and Philosophy of Science* 36:135–148.

Fuller, Richard C., and Richard R. Myers. 1941a. "The Natural History of a Social Problem." *American Sociological Review* 6:320–328.

———. 1941b. "Some Aspects of a Theory of Social Problems." *American Sociological Review* 6:24–32.

Garfinkel, Harold, and Harvey Sacks. 1970. "On Formal Structures of Practical Actions." In *Theoretical Sociology*, ed. J. C. McKinney and E. A. Tiryakian, 338–366. New York: Appleton Century Crofts.

Goffman, Erving. 1959. *The Presentation of Self in Everyday Life*. New York: Doubleday.

Goodwin, Charles. 2000. "Action and Embodiment within Situated Human Interaction." *Journal of Pragmatics* 32:1489–1522.

Gubrium, Jaber F. 1993. "For a Cautious Naturalism." In *Reconsidering Social Constructionism*, ed. James A. Holstein and Gale Miller, 89–101. New York: Aldine de Gruyter.

Gusfield, Joseph R. 1975. "Categories of Ownership and Responsibility in Social Issues: Alcohol Abuse and Automobile Use." *Journal of Drug Issues* 5:285–303.

———. 1984. "On the Side: Practical Action and Social Constructivism in Social Problems Theory." In *Studies in the Sociology of Social Problems*, ed. Joseph W. Schneider and John I. Kitsuse, 31–51. Norwood, NJ: Ablex.

———. 1985. "Theories and Hobgoblins." *SSSP Newsletter* 17 (Fall): 16–18.

Habermas, Jürgen. 1987. *The Philosophical Discourse of Modernity*. Cambridge, MA: MIT Press.

Haraway, Donna J. 1991. *Simians, Cyborgs, and Women*. London: Routledge.

Holstein, James A. 2009. "Defining Deviance: John Kitsuse's Modest Agenda." *American Sociologist* 40:51–60.

Holstein, James A., and Jaber F. Gubrium. 1994. "Phenomenology, Ethnomethodology, and Interpretive Practice." In *Handbook of Qualitative Research*, ed. Norman K. Denzin and Yvonna S. Lincoln, 262–271. Thousand Oaks, CA: Sage.

———. 2003. "A Constructionist Analytics for Social Problems." In *Challenges and Choices*, ed. James A. Holstein and Gale Miller, 187–208. New York: Aldine de Gruyter.

Holstein, James A., and Gale Miller. 1993. "Social Constructionism and Social Problems Work." In *Reconsidering Social Constructionism*, ed. James A. Holstein and Gale Miller, 151–172. New York: Aldine de Gruyter.

Husserl, Edmund. 1970. *The Crisis of European Sciences and Transcendental Philosophy*. Evanston, IL: Northwestern University Press.

Ibarra, Peter R., and John I. Kitsuse. 1993. "Vernacular Constituents of Moral Discourse: An Interactionist Proposal for the Study of Social Problems." In *Reconsidering Social Constructionism*, ed. James A. Holstein and Gale Miller, 25–58. New York: Aldine de Gruyter.

———. 2003. "Claimsmaking Discourse and Vernacular Resources." In *Challenges and Choices*, ed. James A. Holstein and Gale Miller, 17–50. New York: Aldine de Gruyter.

Jasanoff, Sheila. 2005. *Designs on Nature*. Princeton, NJ: Princeton University Press.

Jenness, Valerie. 1995. "Hate Crimes in the United States: The Transformation of Injured Persons into Victims and the Extension of Victim Status to Multiple Constituencies." In *Images of Issues*, 2d ed., ed. Joel Best, 213–237. New York: Aldine de Gruyter.

Kuhn, Thomas S. 1970. *The Structure of Scientific Revolutions*, 2d ed. Chicago: University of Chicago Press.

Longino, Helen E. 2002. *The Fate of Knowledge*. Princeton, NJ: Princeton University Press.

Loseke, Donileen R. 1992. *The Battered Woman and Shelters*. Albany: State University of New York Press.

Lowney, Kathleen S., and Joel Best. 1995. "Stalking Strangers and Lovers: Changing Media Typifications of a New Crime Problem." In *Images of Issues*, 2d ed., ed. Joel Best, 33–57. New York: Aldine de Gruyter.

Lynch, Michael. 1988. "Alfred Schutz and the Sociology of Science." In *Worldly Phenomenology*, ed. Lester Embree, 71–100. Washington DC: Center for Advanced Research in Phenomenology and University Press of America.

——. 1993. *Scientific Practice and Ordinary Action*. Cambridge: Cambridge University Press.

Marx, Karl. 1983. "Theses on Feuerbach." In *The Portable Karl Marx*, 155–158. London: Penguin.

Miller, Gale, and James A. Holstein. 1995. "Dispute Domains: Organizational Contexts and Dispute Processing." *Sociological Quarterly* 36 (1): 37–59.

Pfohl, Stephen J. 1977. "The Discovery of Child Abuse." *Social Problems* 24:310–323.

Pickering, Andrew. 1995. *The Mangle of Practice*. Chicago: University of Chicago Press.

Reinarman, Craig, and Harry G. Levine. 1997. "The Crack Attack: Politics and Media in the Crack Scare." In *Crack in America*, ed. Craig Reinarman and Harry G. Levine, 18–51. Berkeley: University of California Press.

Rorty, Richard. 1980. *Philosophy and the Mirror of Nature*. Oxford: Blackwell.

Rouse, Joseph. 2002. *How Scientific Practices Matter*. Chicago: University of Chicago Press.

Schneider, Joseph W. 1978. "Deviant Drinking as Disease: Alcoholism as Social Accomplishment." *Social Problems* 25 (4): 361–372.

——. 1985a. "Defining the Definitional Perspective on Social Problems." *Social Problems* 32 (3): 232–234.

——. 1985b. "Social Problems Theory: The Constructionist View." *American Review of Sociology* 11:209–229.

Schutz, Alfred. 1964. *Collected Papers II: Studies in Social Theory*, ed. Arvid Broderson. The Hague: Martinus Nijhoff.

——. 1966. *Collected Papers III: Studies in Phenomenological Philosophy*, ed. Ilse Schutz. The Hague: Martinus Nijhoff.

Scritchfield, Shirley A. 1995. "The Social Construction of Infertility: From Private Matter to Social Concern." In *Images of Issues*, 2d ed., ed. Joel Best, 131–164. New York: Aldine de Gruyter.

Shapin, Steven, and Simon Schaffer. 1985. *Leviathan and the Air Pump*. Princeton, NJ: Princeton University Press.

Spector, Malcolm, and John I. Kitsuse. 2001. *Constructing Social Problems*, 2d ed. London: Transaction.

Weinberg, Darin. 1997. "The Social Construction of Non-Human Agency: The Case of Mental Disorder." *Social Problems* 44 (2): 217–234.

——. 2002. "Qualitative Research Methods: An Overview." In *Qualitative Research Methods*, ed. Darin Weinberg, 1–22. Oxford: Blackwell.

——. 2005. *Of Others Inside: Insanity, Addiction, and Belonging in America*. Philadelphia: Temple University Press.

——. 2006. "Language, Dialogue, and Ethnographic Objectivity." In *Talk and Interaction in Social Research Methods*, ed. Paul Drew, Geoffrey Raymond, and Darin Weinberg, 97–112. London: Sage.

Wiener, Carolyn L. 1981. *The Politics of Alcoholism*. New Brunswick, NJ: Transaction.

Wittgenstein, Ludwig. 1922. *Tractatus Logico-Philosophicus*. London: Routledge.

Woolgar, Steve, and Dorothy Pawluch. 1985. "Ontological Gerrymandering: The Anatomy of Social Problems Explanations." *Social Problems* 32:214– 227.

Zimmerman, Don H., and Melvin Pollner. 1970. "The Everyday World as a Phenomenon." In *Understanding Everyday Life*, ed. Jack D. Douglas, 80–103. Chicago: Aldine de Gruyter.

CRITICAL THINKING:	What do you think are the top priorities/most pressing social issues of the American public?

The following narrative provides an example of how something can emerge as a widely recognized social problem. Telling this largely unknown story of how child abuse grew from a small, private-sector charity concern into a multimillion-dollar social welfare issue, Barbara Nelson provides important new perspectives on the process of public agenda setting. Using extensive personal interviews and detailed archival research, she reconstructs an invaluable history of child abuse policy in America. She shows how the mass media presented child abuse to the public, how government agencies acted and interacted, and how state and national legislatures were spurred to strong action on this issue. Nelson examines prevailing theories about agenda setting and introduces a new conceptual framework for understanding how a social issue becomes part of the public agenda. This issue of child abuse, she argues, clearly reveals the scope and limitations of social change initiated through interest group politics. Unfortunately, the process that transforms an issue into a popular cause, Nelson concludes, brings about programs that ultimately address only the symptoms and not the roots of such social problems.

Reading 3.3.

Child Abuse as a Social Problem

by Barbara J. Nelson

The date was March 26, 1973. The weather in Washington, D.C., was rainy and mild. On this typical early spring day a very atypical event was under way. Senator Walter F. Mondale (D., Minn.), an erstwhile presidential candidate, was holding the first day of hearings on his Child Abuse Prevention Act. Never before had Congress demonstrated so great a concern for child abuse. These hearings were proof to all who were interested that child abuse was firmly established on the congressional

Barbara J. Nelson, "Child Abuse as a Social Problem," *Making an Issue of Child Abuse: Political Agenda Setting for Social Problems*, pp. 1-19, 139-143. Copyright © 1986 by University of Chicago Press. Reprinted with permission.

agenda. The hearings began at 9:30 A.M. in the wood-paneled offices of the Dirksen Building. Second among the witnesses, and the most riveting, was "Jolly K.," founder of Parents Anonymous. Mondale asked her if she had abused her child:

"Yes, I did, to the point of almost causing death several times. ... It was extreme serious physical abuse. ... Once I threw a rather large kitchen knife at her and another time I strangled her because she lied to me. ... This was up to when she was 6V2 years old. ... It was ongoing. It was continuous.

"I had gone to 10 county and State facilities. Out of those, all but one were very realistic places to turn to. Six of them were social services, protective service units. ... Even the most ignorant listeners could have picked up what I was saying, that I was abusing [my daughter], and that I was directly asking for mental health services. ... I wanted to keep my child. I wanted to get rid of my problem. She wasn't the problem. She was the recipient of my behavior."[1]

Senator Jennings Randolph (D., W. Va.) turned the questioning to Jolly K.'s experience with Parents Anonymous, the self-help group for abusive parents styled after Alcoholics Anonymous (AA). Like AA, Parents Anonymous encourages abusive parents to talk about their fears and frustrations with child rearing, and their guilt and anguish over the harm members have caused their children. Randolph went straight to the political heart of the matter, asking how successful Parents Anonymous was in eliminating further abuse and keeping children at home. Happily, Randolph learned of the program's success:

"Most of them have the children in the home. Most of them have the symptomatic behavior of abuse now removed. ...

"We encourage parents to utilize us until they feel comfortable enough to go out and utilize other existing services. ... where they can work more deeply with internal problems.[2]

Jolly K. was the perfect witness, cutting through academic pieties to convince the assembled senators, witnesses, and journalists of the gravity of the problem. She was, figuratively, a sinner who had repented and been saved by her own hard work and the loving counsel of her friends. But more importantly, she embodied the American conception of a social problem: individually rooted, described as an illness, and solvable by occasional doses of therapeutic conversation.

Senator Mondale encouraged this conventional understanding of the problem. Any more elaborate view, especially one which focused on injustice as a source of social problems, threatened to scuttle his efforts to move this small piece of categorical legislation through Congress. With able maneuvering, Mondale's approach prevailed, and on January 31, 1974, President Richard M. Nixon signed the Child Abuse Prevention and Treatment Act (CAPTA) into law. The legislation authorized $86 million to be spent over the next three and a half years, mostly on research and demonstration projects, though some funds were earmarked for discretionary social service grants to the states.[3]

Eighty-six million dollars for child abuse, a problem which did not even warrant an entry in the *Readers' Guide to Periodical Literature* until 1968![4] How did this happen? Or, asked more elaborately, how did child abuse, a small, private-sector charity concern, become a multimillion-dollar public social welfare issue? This book tries to provide an answer. It is a study of the politics of child abuse and neglect, a history and analysis of political issue creation and agenda setting.

The book has three broad aims. *The first aim is, of course, to recount the history of child abuse policy-making over the last three decades.* The story begins in 1955 with the renewed efforts of the American Humane Association (AHA), a charitable organization engaged in research on child and animal maltreatment, to ascertain the extent of physical child abuse and the adequacy of governmental response. The AHA shared its findings with the U.S. Children's Bureau, which in 1963 proposed a model statute to encourage reporting of physical child abuse. Other organizations as diverse as the American Academy of Pediatrics and the Council of State Legislatures proposed different model reporting laws. Bombarded with model statutes and facing no opposition, state legislatures passed child abuse reporting laws with dizzying speed. The demand for services, or at least the demand for workable service models, encouraged Mondale to sponsor federal legislation in 1973; legislation which was successful despite opposition from the Nixon administration. That legislation appeared to be untouchable until President Ronald Reagan was elected and stripped social programs bare in an attempt to balance the budget and shift the initiative for solving social problems to the private sector.

But the history of child abuse policy making is also a vehicle for the discussion of political agenda setting more generally, this book's second aim. E. E. Schattschneider, the dean of agenda-setting studies by virtue of his classic work *The Semi-Sovereign People,* asserted that the most important decisions made in any polity were those determining which issues would become part of public discourse. "Some issues are organized into politics while others are organized out," Schattschneider said with economy.[5] This book tries to elaborate the process by which issues get "organized into politics." It is an attempt to advance our understanding of the first step of the policy process, the step where those issues which *will* receive governmental attention are chosen from among those issues which *could* receive governmental attention.

The third aim of the book is to discuss what I call "the public use of private deviance." My interest here is to link child abuse with other issues dealing with violence and personal autonomy (e.g., rape, domestic violence, incest, sexual abuse, and attacks on the elderly) which have recently become part of the governmental agenda. Like child abuse, each of these issues was accepted as a proper concern of government in part because it was represented as deviance improperly protected by the privacy of the family. But the focus on deviance—and medical deviance at that—turned policy makers away from considering the social-structural and social-psychological underpinnings of abuse and neglect. The advantages and limitations of the deviance approach, which are essentially the advantages and limitations of liberal reform, constitute the third theme.

The book focuses on decision making in governmental organizations. I am most interested in the process whereby public officials learn about new problems, decide to give them their personal attention, and mobilize their organizations to respond to them. Of course, this process is influenced by the type of problems considered and the organizational and political milieux in which officials work. Thus the book will give particular attention to the fact that during the agenda-setting process child abuse was vigorously portrayed as a noncontroversial issue. Disagreements about how best to respond to abuse were suppressed, along with the great debate over the extent to which government ought properly to intervene in family matters. These conflicts became much more apparent as the political climate grew more conservative in the late 1970s and early 1980s. Indeed, government's attention to child abuse in the post World War II period must be understood as part of a larger concern with equity and social justice. So too the movement away from governmental responsibility for child protection should be viewed as part of a larger concern with governmental efficiency and traditional patterns of family authority.

The book is organized chronologically, presenting three case studies of agenda setting in governmental institutions, and an analysis of the role of the mass and professional media. Chapter 2 discusses the theoretical approaches to agenda setting, expanding and linking the organizational, interest group, and economic literature. Chapter 3 shows how the first contemporary governmental interest in child abuse arose through communication between the American Humane Association and the U.S. Children's Bureau. Chapter 4 makes the connection between governmental response to child abuse and popular awareness of the problem, and illuminates the varying roles played by the professional and mass media in making the public aware of child abuse. Chapter 5 presents the states' response to child abuse. Here we shall discuss the rapid adoption of child abuse reporting laws—all fifty states passed legislation in only five years—as well as present a case study of the passage of New Jersey's first reporting law. Chapter 6 considers how Congress became aware of popular and professional interest in abuse and chose to do something about it. Chapter 7, the last chapter, reviews the findings about agenda setting and concludes with an assessment of the future of the public use of private deviance. The remainder of this chapter sets the stage by defining social problems, discussing the invention of child abuse as a social problem, presenting the difficulties in defining and measuring abuse, and elaborating on the theme of the public use of private deviance.

THE INVENTION OF CHILD ABUSE

Defining Social Problems

Examples of the brutal or neglectful treatment of children are found as far back as records have been kept. But the mere existence of a condition like cruelty to children does not mean that every society which witnessed abuse condemned it, although some individuals may have.[6] A social problem goes beyond what a few, or even many, individuals feel privately: a social problem is a social construct. Its "creation" requires not only that a number of individuals feel a conflict of value over what is and what ought to be, but also that individuals organize to change the condition, and achieve at least a modicum of recognition for their efforts from the wider public.[7]

The social problem we know as child abuse is a product of America's Gilded Era. Until the 1870s maltreatment of white children was not a part of public debate. Extreme brutality was handled by the court on a case-by-case basis. Less severe cases may have upset the neighbors, but child-rearing decisions were considered the prerogative of parents, particularly fathers.

What happened, then, to make the public think of abuse as a social problem? The answer rests in part with the "Mary Ellen" case, a rather grisly instance of abuse which received widespread publicity in New York City in 1874. A "friendly visitor" discovered that the girl had regularly been bound and beaten by her step-mother. Outrage over the incident precipitated the forming of the New York Society for the Prevention of Cruelty to Children, the first child protection association in the country.

A single incident, however momentous, does not guarantee that concerned individuals will view the event as an example of a larger problem, and organize to solve it. To bring a problem to light requires leadership to create the groups necessary to act, and a cultural willingness to accept the problem as defined. Sociologist Neil Smelser calls this latter requirement "structural readiness for change."[8] The requirement of structural readiness does not mean, of course, that if certain conditions are not defined as problems the time is simply not right for recognition. Repression keeps certain conditions from being defined as problems. Nonetheless, the creation of a social problem does require some public receptivity.[9]

The ideal of a "protected childhood" provided the cultural backdrop necessary for the acceptance of abuse as a social problem. Cruelty to children, especially by parents, appeared much more troublesome when contrasted with the "modern" image of childhood as a safe and sheltered period of life. Scholars have offered a number of rather different explanations for the creation of the modern family and its reverence for childhood.[10] Phillipe Aries suggests that the transformation of formal education under the Scholastics, the idea of privacy, and the rise of a partly urban, commercial society, conjoined to initiate the affective family and attention to childhood as a separate time of life deserving of protection. Lawrence Stone proposes another explanation. The rise of "affective individualism" in the West produced a bourgeois family based on friendship and sentiment. Both Aries and Stone locate the origins of the modern family in the bourgeoisie. In contrast, Edward Shorter locates the origin of the modern family in changes in village culture. Technological innovations which allowed capital surplus freed villagers from patriarchal village mores and permitted the development of "familial empathy."

Though they disagree on many points, these explanations all concur with the idea that in the modern family, normal, correct child rearing excludes excessive violence or gross inattention. In America, belief in a protected childhood was the product of three forces-natural rights ideology, commitment to civic education, and the increasing number of bourgeois families—which converged in the post—Civil War period. During Radical Reconstruction natural rights ideology, with its commitment to equality, drew a growing number of supporters. Its rhetoric frequently extended natural rights to animals and children. Elbridge T. Gerry, one of the founders of the New York Society for the Prevention of Cruelty to Children, was an advocate of this position. In 1882 he wrote that "at the present day in this country, children have *some* rights, which even parents are bound to respect," sentiments much less evident a century earlier.[11]

Those who might not fully support the notion of the natural rights of children could still see the wisdom of educating children for citizenship. Indeed, America's experiment in republican government produced a long-standing commitment to civic education.[12] But after the Civil War the support for civic education in part superceded older, more traditional educational concerns. Childhood was no longer seen only as the time to form a moral adult, but also the time to forge a separate citizen of the republic. Historian Stanley N. Katz nicely summarizes this transformation:

Philip Greven has graphically described how evangelical and even moderate colonial Americans self-consciously set out to subdue their children's independence and to make them conform to the dictates of divine law and parental wisdom. So long as salvation was generally perceived as dependent upon conversion, it was obviously the parents' highest duty so to treat their children. For the Rousseauian modern parent, however, precisely the opposite was indicated. For them the child was a fragile flower to be cultivated, nourished and appreciated so that its finest qualities could realize their potential. The discovery of childhood and an optimistic view of child psychology thus transformed child-parent relations.[13]

The increasing number of bourgeois families, where the wife and children did not work for wages, gave substance to this view. A protected childhood became a standard by which well-to-do families could measure the social adequacy and integration of less fortunate families. Well-to-do activists, who could afford to provide such protection for their children, organized child protective societies beginning in the 1870s. But as we shall see later, they were immediately confronted by the unsettling observation that economic conditions constrained many parents from providing such protection for their children.

The Mary Ellen Case

The first child protection society was formed in 1874 in response to the notorious Mary Ellen Wilson case. Mary Ellen's plight was crushingly Victorian. She lived in the home of Francis and Mary Connolly, but she was not the blood relative of either, being the illegitimate daughter of Mrs. Connolly's first husband, Thomas McCormack, and Fanny Wilson.[14] A neighbor noticed that Mrs. Connolly treated the child brutally, beating her with a leather thong and allowing her to go ill-clothed in bad weather. The neighbor told Mrs. Etta Angell Wheeler, a "friendly visitor," who then went to Henry Bergh, the founder of the American Society for the Prevention of Cruelty to Animals (ASPCA) to ask if the ASPCA could help the child.[15]

The popular version of Bergh's response reports that Bergh successfully argued in court that Mary Ellen ought to be removed from her cruel guardians because she, as a member of the animal kingdom, deserved the same protection as abused animals. Actually, the case was argued by Bergh's friend and counsel, Elbridge T. Gerry, who had Mary Ellen removed from her unwholesome surroundings by a petition for a writ *de homine replegando,* an old English writ for removing a person from the custody of another. The case was a staple in New York newspapers for months, no doubt aided by the fact that Mrs. Wheeler's husband was a journalist. In December 1874 the New York Society for the Prevention of Cruelty to Children (New York SPCC) was formed, with Gerry, who had successfully removed Mary Ellen from her home and won a prison sentence for her stepmother, as the moving force.[16]

Gerry and his friends had a ready model for action when the Mary Ellen case came to their attention: the British and American animal protection societies. Animal protection societies were first formed in England in 1824. Henry Bergh, who founded the American SPCA in 1866, explicitly used the Royal British SPCA as his guide. When not ignored, both the English and American SPCAs were the objects of laughter and scorn. Only the meat-packing industry, whose un-sanitary and cruel practices were often attacked, ever paid them much attention. Indeed, the important role of the animal protective societies in promoting sanitary meat and milk processing has largely been forgotten today, when we remember the SPCAs only as the perfect example of frivolous Victorian do-gooding.

In 1870, at Bergh's invitation, Gerry became counsel for the ASPCA. Though fourteen years separated them, Bergh and Gerry had similar careers. Both came from prominent Protestant families which provided them with private incomes, both attended Columbia University, both practiced law, and both were devoted to a vision of rational Christian social improvement. Their friends and acquaintances included the political and social leaders of New York City and State. It is no wonder, then, that when Mary Ellen's plight became known to them, one of their responses was to call a meeting.

The Rise of Protective Societies

The objective of the New York SPCC was to rescue children from situations which imperiled their morals, safety, health, or welfare-pretty much in that order. The New York Society's emphasis was on child rescue rather than family rehabilitation. It created for itself a police and placement function whereby it identified and prosecuted abusers, referring the children it "saved" to large child-minding institutions. It is often assumed that the New York SPCC usurped the policelike powers it wielded, but this is completely untrue. Rather, the cruelty and neglect statute passed by the New York legislature in 1881 at the Society's request made it a misdemeanor to interfere with the work of designated child protection agents. As a consequence the Society had enormous power over the poor families it monitored, even if it did help many children out of dangerous situations.

The New York SPCC's emphasis on controlling the poor is perhaps best portrayed by the engravings (and later photographs) depicting children "before" and "after" the Society's intervention. The *Annual Report* of 1876 shows two engravings of Ellen Conners. In the "before" picture, the child is portrayed as wild, ragged, badly cut about the face, and rather suspiciously scratching her genitals. In the "after" picture, Ellen is sweetly dressed in layer upon layer of fashionable clothes, and her hands, far from being anywhere near her crotch, are decorously hidden in a rabbit-fur muff. The emphasis on personal control in the engraving reflects the social goals of the organization: "These little waifs of society were destined to become the fathers and mothers of this Republic. If they were neglected the permanent interest of the Republic would be neglected."[17]

Not all SPCCs ran on the child rescue model favored by the New York Society. The Philadelphia and Illinois (Chicago) SPCCs responded more to problems of drunkenness, desertion, or neglect than to physical abuse of children. These SPCCs (as well as the New York Society) ran temporary shelters where women and children could find a brief respite from violence or economic distress.[18] The Massachusetts (Boston) SPCC was among the first of the protective societies to emphasize "family rehabilitation." Its members worked to bring about the social, political, and economic changes necessary to relieve "destitution." The child rescue and family rehabilitation approaches were at war for almost forty years. The oldline Scientific Charity advocates favored child rescue, which often separated parents and children. The Progressives, on the other hand, promoted the family rehabilitation view, which kept the child at home or in a homelike setting.

The Decline of Protective Societies

The family rehabilitation approach ultimately won. Many reasons are offered for its victory, most centering on the philosophical tenets of the Progressives. The Progressives, with their commitment to childhood as a stage of physical and civic development, felt that normal childhood was childhood in a home and thus the breakup of the family was not favored. To implement their beliefs, the Progressives encouraged the creation of a familylike setting in the juvenile courts and argued that the state had a positive duty to protect women and children. Progressives dismantled the poor-house, fought against child labor, and encouraged mothers' pensions.

The power of the family-centered response to child welfare was best demonstrated at the first White House Conference on Dependent Children in 1909, whose report stated unequivocally that

> home life is the highest and finest product of civilization. It is the great molding force of mind and of character. Children should not be deprived of it except for urgent and compelling reasons. Children of parents of worthy character, suffering from temporary misfortune and children of reasonably efficient and deserving mothers who are without the support of the normal breadwinner, should, as a rule, be kept with their parents, such aid being given as may be necessary to maintain suitable homes for the rearing of the children.[19]

The Conference also supported the establishment of a federal Children's Bureau, a proposal first introduced in Congress in 1906. The Progressives further urged that child protection become a responsibility of public child welfare departments, and in this they were often supported by socially minded SPCCs like the Massachusetts Society.[20] In 1923, C. C. Carstens, once the secretary of the Massachusetts SPCC and later director of the Child Welfare League of America, wrote that only half of the more than 800 humane societies formed since 1874 had survived, and many of them were only limping along.[21]

But the decline of SPCCs and the eclipse of cruelty as a separate problem of child welfare can be explained by the operation of large institutions as much as by the philosophical beliefs of the Progressives. These organizational reasons have gone largely unnoticed until now. The child rescue approach was made possible by the previous existence of large, asylumlike institutions which would accept the rescued child. But in the 1870s and 1880s the "placing out" system (i.e., foster care), which assigned children to willing and interested families, began competing with orphanages.

The increasing popularity of the "placing out" method had enormous consequences for the SPCCs, whose special function originally had been to identify and refer children. When one more child was added to an orphanage, the personality or characteristics of that child were not terribly important to the functioning of the institution. To say the least, institutional care in the late nineteenth century did not promote individualism among children. But when a child was referred for placing out, the characteristics of the child were very important. The family which took the child had to deal with him or her as an individual. "Placing out" agencies thus wanted desperately to control the composition of their clientele.

As public agencies began taking over such functions, they too wanted to do their own casefinding. Programmatic success required that public child welfare agencies pick which clients they would serve. In this light the reasons for the decline of SPCCs become clearer. For organizational as well as philosophical reasons, other agencies were opposed to the SPCCs' avowed function of casefinding. Only in places like New York City, with its firmly entrenched child-minding institutions, did the traditional SPCCs survive. Elsewhere their work was incorporated into public child welfare agencies.

The longevity of the New York SPCC was also aided by a well-established contract system which dispensed public money to private institutions for the care of poor, abused, neglected, or wayward children. Homer Folks estimated that in 1890 the New York SPCC "practically controlled the lives of an average number of about fifteen thousand children, and an average annual expenditure for their support of more than one and one half million dollars. Its influence has done more to strengthen and perpetuate the subsidy or contract system, as it existed prior to 1894, than any other one factor."[22] The large institutions and the New York SPCC formed a partnership wherein the SPCC found children, the orphanages provided the care, and the state supplied a constant stream of funds. Opposition to this arrangement came from the fact that it encouraged institutional care, not that it lacked accountability for the spending of public monies. The potential exploitation of a per capita billing system went largely unrecognized. The main management problem, as seen by Josephine Shaw Lowell, was access by the State Board of Charities for inspection of the institutions for health code violations.[23]

The experience of the New York SPCC was unusual, however, and even its power declined with the Great Depression. By World War II, the SPCC movement was completely enervated nationwide. The pressing needs of children displaced by war drove protective work even further into the social services backwater.

The Rediscovery of Child Abuse

By the 1950s, public interest in abuse and neglect was practically nonexistent, and even social workers did not rate it highly as a professional concern. How were these issues rediscovered and ultimately adopted as problems which government should help to solve? The specific answers to these questions need to be understood in their historical context.

The rediscovery of child abuse occurred in an era when issues of equity and social responsibility dominated public discourse. A long period of concern with a variety of equity issues began with the civil rights movement in the mid and late 1950s. The 1962 amendments to the Social Security Act urging child welfare services in every county demonstrated that the interests of children were part of the equity cycle. The child welfare amendments were followed by the "War on Poverty," which emphasized the importance of services to children as a method of eliminating poverty. In 1967 the equity cycle was given tremendous impetus by the Supreme Court's *In re Gault* opinion, which extended Bill of Rights protection to children. Later, the months spent crafting the Comprehensive Child Development Act (ultimately vetoed by President Nixon) educated members of Congress to the centrality (and difficulty) of providing adequately for the needs of all children.

Not unimportantly, this equity cycle coincided with years of great economic prosperity. Real GNP doubled between 1950 and 1970. Consequently, the material gains of one group did not appear to threaten the gains of others. It was a time when politics seemed to exist without trade-offs.

The concern for children was not limited to government. Pediatricians, the most prestigious group dealing with youngsters, enjoyed two decades of notable success in conquering deadly childhood diseases. With the ability to cure or prevent many children's diseases, pediatricians had the status, skills, and the slack resources to invest in research on problems which were at least partly behavioral in origin.

But it was the work of radiologists like John Caffey, P. V. Woolley, and W. A. Evans which alerted pediatricians to the specific problem of abuse. In 1946 Caffey first reported a number of cases in which infants had multiple long bone fractures and subdural hematomas. He did not, however, speculate on the causes of trauma. In 1953, Woolley and Evans suggested that similar injuries might be caused by the children's caretakers. In 1957, Caffey reexamined his original data and concluded that the trauma might well have been willfully perpetrated by parents. It took almost a decade for physicians to conclude that some parents were violently assaulting their children, a delay caused by professional cautiousness and a profound psychological resistance to recognizing that some parental behavior departed so radically from the ideal.[24]

This research, as well as the early work done by social workers,[25] was well known to pediatricians like C. Henry Kempe and his colleagues, who were investigating the causes as well as the appropriate responses to physical abuse. In 1962 they published their famous article "The Battered-Child Syndrome" in the prestigious *Journal of the American Medical Association*.[26] Within weeks of its publication, stories on child abuse were featured in popular magazines like *Time* and the *Saturday Evening Post*. The publication of the Kempe article is often used to date the rediscovery of child abuse as a social problem. But in point of fact, the popular articles based on Kempe's research were equally important in creating the sense of an urgent national problem.

DEFINING AND MEASURING CHILD ABUSE AND NEGLECT

Problems of Definition

The first people to identify a problem often shape how others will perceive it. Nowhere is this truer than with the issue of child abuse. In "The Battered-Child Syndrome" Kempe and his associates define the problem as "a clinical condition in young children who received serious physical abuse, generally from a parent or foster parent."[27] Based on a survey of the literature and an examination of 302 cases reported in 71 hospitals, the authors suggested that abusers had serious psychological problems but were not psychopaths:

> Psychiatric factors are probably of prime importance in the pathogenesis of the disorder, but our knowledge of these factors is limited. Parents who inflict abuse on their children do not necessarily have psychopathic or sociopathic personalities or come from borderline socioeconomic groups, although most published cases have been in these categories. *In most cases some defect of character structure is probably present; often parents may be repeating the type of child care practiced on them.*[28]

The individually centered psychological construction of the problem made it seem very self-contained. Governmental response to a self-contained, serious, but noncontroversial issue ought to be easy to obtain. And easy it was. Once alerted to the problem, the U.S. Children's Bureau and other organizations drafted model child abuse reporting laws which were rapidly passed by all state legislatures. The speed of adoption rested largely on this narrow construction of the problem. The early California reporting statute reflected this view. Child abuse was defined as "physical injuries or injury which appear to have been inflicted upon [the child] by other than accidental means."[29]

Almost as quickly as this narrow view took substance in the law, it was replaced by a more comprehensive construction of the problem. As scholars in a number of fields examined the problem, the socioeconomic considerations of child abuse—its connection to job-lessness, inadequate housing, and other chronic social ills—became evident and popular. (Interestingly, gender and power considerations were absent from most of this analysis.) In 1974, the federal Child Abuse Prevention and Treatment Act (CAPTA) incorporated a fairly comprehensive definition of the problem. CAPTA defines child abuse and neglect together:

> "Child Abuse and Neglect" means the physical or mental injury, sexual abuse, negligent treatment, or maltreatment of any child under the age of eighteen by a person who is responsible for the child's welfare under circumstances which indicate the child's health or welfare is harmed or threatened thereby.[30]

The definition of child abuse found in CAPTA provides a more comprehensive statement of the problem than one might expect after reading the transcripts of the legislative hearings. In the public debate over the congressional legislation, comprehensive definitions were actively suppressed in order to enhance the noncontroversial nature of the issue.

In fact, at each point when child abuse achieved a governmental agenda, the narrow definition was emphasized. The narrow definition predominated during agenda setting for three related reasons. First, agenda setting by the Children's Bureau and state legislatures occurred while the narrow definition was still quite popular. Second, physicians preferred the narrow definition because it best fit their experiences in hospital emergency rooms, and physicians, by virtue of their high status, had easy and early access to officials. Third and most important, a narrow definition of abuse reduced conflict, particularly from right-wing critics. The use of a narrow definition thwarted a potential conservative challenge to what might be seen as governmental action against normal parental discipline.

Favoring the narrow definition during agenda setting had important, long-lasting effects on the shape of child abuse policy. By ignoring neglect, the connection between poverty and maltreatment was purposely blurred. In fact, strenuous efforts were made to popularize abuse as a problem knowing no barriers of class, race, or culture. For some politicians, particularly Mondale, this was part of a conscious strategy to dissociate efforts against abuse from unpopular poverty programs. The purpose was to describe abuse as an all-American affliction, not one found solely among low-income people. While acknowledging that abuse and neglect were found in all strata of society, a number of scholars severely criticized this approach and maintained that the larger number of cases found among the poor was not only a function of reporting biases, but was present because poor people actually abused or neglected their children more. The message of the research was not that poor people were bad people or bad parents, but that the deprivations of poverty were real and encouraged abuse. These findings were very unpopular, however, and the "myth of classlessness" promoted during agenda setting was very difficult to counter.[31]

Measuring Child Abuse

No one actually knows the extent of child abuse and neglect, or whether their incidence is increasing or decreasing. At the National Conference for Family Violence Researchers, Professor Richard Gelles summed up the difficulties in measuring abuse and neglect: "We don't know a *damn* thing about whether child abuse is increasing, decreasing or staying the same."[32] It is not merely the lack of a commonly agreed-upon definition which hinders counting but also problems of methodology—of criteria, applications, and evidence—which make the task so difficult. Not surprisingly, the numbers vary widely. One of the lowest estimates comes from a *Pediatric News* (1975) report suggesting that one child dies of abuse every day, yielding a yearly incidence of 365 deaths. Using national survey data, David Gil (1970) offers a much higher figure, but for a different phenomenon. Gil suggests that for the year ending in October 1965, between 2.53 and 4.07 million American adults *knew* of physically abusive families, figures which Richard Light (1974) statistically adjusted to reach his estimate of approximately 500,000 cases of physical abuse during the year under study.[33]

From a public policy perspective, two estimates have been more important than all the others: one "guess" in an early medical article and the official reporting statistics gathered over the last several years. In fact, this early medical "guess" did not even mention statistics. Instead child abuse was described as possibly more lifethreatening than a host of well-known and feared childhood diseases. The story of this nonnumerical estimate bears telling because it shows how powerful a credible source can be in defining the extent of a social problem, even when that source offers no figures whatsoever.

In 1962, Dr. C. Henry Kempe and his associates published their famous article "The Battered-Child Syndrome" in the *Journal of the American Medical Association*.[34] In an accompanying editorial, the country's most powerful arbiters of medical knowledge wrote that "it is likely that [the battered child syndrome] will be found to be a more frequent cause of death than such well recognized and thoroughly studied diseases as leukemia, cystic fibrosis, and muscular dystrophy."[35] The editors were merely speculating about the extent of abuse and qualified all their comparisons. Politicians and journalists were not always as careful. Official after official and article after article repeated the comparison as though it were fact.

The consistency with which the AMA *Journal's* editorial was cited was probably more important than its accuracy. Gilbert Y. Steiner suggests that where estimates of problem size differ substantially, it is difficult to establish the legitimacy of the problem. He noted that the differing estimates of the size of the problem of domestic violence (ranging from 7.5 million to 526,000 episodes a year) allowed detractors to chip away at congressional support.[36] Modest and consistent estimates seem to inspire the most confidence, especially in cases of the public response to private deviance. Deviance can only exist as such if there is not too much of it.

The official reporting statistics, the second important measure of child abuse, do not indicate a modest problem at all. In 1979, the Child Protection Division of the American Humane Association compiled all the official abuse and neglect reports made in the fifty states and the territories. Nationwide there were 711,142 official reports of maltreatment, but the type of maltreatment could only be discerned in 234,000 of the reports. Of these, 25.1% were designated solely as abuse. Of course, there is a certain amount of comparing apples and oranges in the compilation of these figures. No uniform legal definition exists, and case-counting procedures differ markedly from state to state. Nonetheless, these figures give us some sense of the magnitude of the problem as understood by officials, regardless of how many or what kind of cases are not reported.[37]

These official figures have been used to promote and maintain interest in the problem. Similar figures were paraded during the first CAPTA reauthorization hearings in 1977 and again in 1981 to show the magnitude of the problem. These numbers are susceptible to political manipulation in an era of social service cutbacks. If reporting is lax and service positions go unstaffed, the number of cases will eventually fall off as concerned individuals concede the futility of reporting. If the numbers decline, then the problem can be described as waning, perhaps even as disappearing because of the application of a measured dose of governmental intervention.

Lower numbers, in turn, can be used to justify lower expenditures, in a widening circle of verbal deceit and programmatic despair.

THE PUBLIC USE OF PRIVATE DEVIANCE

Neglect and abuse are so common that it ought to be hard to maintain the image that they are rare, deviant behaviors. But the construction of this problem as one of medical deviance has proven extraordinarily durable. Because physicians played such a large role in setting governmental and media agendas, the first public presentation of the problem was as a social illness.[38] The considerations of power politics are rarely added to the discussion, perhaps because "power" is a public word and "child abuse" is understood to be a private problem.

Many behaviors with significantly aggressive or violent components have been similarly "medicalized." In addition to child abuse, examples include alcoholism, drug abuse, hyperkinesis, and to a lesser degree rape and domestic violence.[39] Earlier in this century alcoholism was variously considered a sin, a crime, or a labor discipline problem, but now it is most often described as a disease. Similar transformations have overtaken drug abuse and hyperkinesis. Rape and domestic violence have been more resistant to this reconstruction, however. Their obvious power connotations limit the applicability of medical metaphors, and thus limit the likelihood of government's adopting the issues. This is not to say that governmental action is necessarily the best way to respond to rape and domestic violence. Instead, the point is that government more readily adopts issues which are constructed as social illness than issues which confront long-established power arrangements.

There are two explanations of the trend toward constructing social problems concerning aggression and violence in terms of medical deviance. The first reason—little discussed in the social policy literature—is that one model of conventional illnesses is constructed on statistical deviation from population norms. In describing this approach to illness David Mechanic writes:

> Doctors frequently can recognize disease because it becomes apparent that in various ways the patient deviates from 'normal values.' In many cases the range of normal values has been established through observations of community populations over a period of time and thus marked deviations can easily be determined.[40]

In the case of behaviors rather than physical functioning, it is quite easy to assert that particular actions diverge from the measured—or even assumed—norm, With the rise of the concept of mental illness in this century, practically any disvalued behavior can be defined as medical deviance. In fact, merely by its being statistically rare a behavior can become disvalued and subject to medical response.[41]

The second reason for constructing some problems in terms of medical deviance is that medicine offers solutions to these problems, solutions which in the short run appear to be—and often are-humane and caring. Medicine professes to have solutions—ranging from psychotropic drugs, to therapy, to the mental hospital—which are supposed to treat rather than punish the sick person. Medical solutions both maintain and promote the power of medicine and medical professionals while simultaneously reassuring us that we live in a humanitarian rather than a punitive or repressive society.[42]

The political advantages of the construction of social problems as medical deviance are easy to see. Medicine views illness as individual in location if not cause, so a medical construction is consonant with the American individualistic approach to solving problems. By defining problems in terms of medical deviance, the status quo is maintained, at least in the short run.

The political limitations of the medical deviance approach are also obvious. Individualizing problems turns policy makers away from considering their structural causes. Policies which "treat" medical deviance no doubt help thousands of people, but they do so at the cost of expanding state intervention without increasing the state's ability to redress the fundamental inequities which underlie, say, abuse and neglect. Conservative critics then bemoan the loss of family autonomy and liberal critics bemoan the band-aid quality of public efforts, particularly the fact that public monies are not targeted where the problem is most severe and pressing. Socialist critics add that individually centered responses to social problems are designed to maintain existing power relations.

The people who promoted governmental interest in child abuse were mostly social welfare liberals, although the construction of the problem encouraged support across the political spectrum. They saw child abuse as a public health matter, with implications much like those of venereal disease. The case for state action was made on the grounds that child abuse was a social illness which had been improperly protected by the private status of the family. The government used the notion of medical deviance as the rationale for intervening in the family—hence the phrase "the public use of private deviance." At the same time government reaffirmed the essential split between the public and private spheres. Theorists like Zillah Eisenstein suggest that such actions eventually destabilize the liberal state and work to break down the public-private distinction which such policies intend to uphold.[43] The bureaucrats and legislators who promoted an interest in child abuse did not take such a long-sighted view, however. They believed that governmental action would aid the afflicted even if only modestly. They gave child abuse their professional attention, and then went about their jobs.

NOTES

1   "Child Abuse Prevention Act, S.1191" *Hearings before the Subcommittee on Children and Youth of the Committee on Labor and Public Welfare,* U.S. Senate, Ninety-third Congress, First Session, March 23, 1973, pp. 49–51; hereafter cited as Senate Hearings, March 1973.

2   Senate Hearings, March 1973, p. 52.

3   With the extensions of CAPTA in 1978 and 1981 a total of $160 million was authorized to fight abuse, neglect, and later to promote adoption reform, not all of which was appropriated as budget trimming became more important.

4   The entry "cruelty to children," with its somewhat old-fashioned connotation, appeared intermittently before this time, and early articles on the battered-child syndrome, child abuse, physical abuse of children, etc., were indexed under this heading. The Library of Congress changed its primary index entry to "child abuse" in 1968 and most of the major indexes followed suit.

5   E. E. Schattschneider, *The Semi-Sovereign People* (New York: Holt, Rinehart and Winston, 1960), p. 71.

6   By stating that a culture does not view a particular set of actions as a social problem, I do not mean to imply that the actions are necessarily ethically acceptable, or even that the only standard for ethical judgment is one which is specific to the situation or the time period. What I am arguing for is the realization that cultures *vary* in their recognition and definition of problems.

7   For an elaboration of these points see Malcolm Spector and John I. Kitsuse, "Social Problems: A Re-Formulation," *Social Problems* 21, no. 2 (Fall 1973): 145–159; Armand L. Mauss, "Introduction: Promises and Problems in American Society," in Armand L. Mauss and Julie Camille Wolfe, eds., *This Land of Promises: The Rise and Fall of Social Problems in America* (New York: J. B. Lippincott Co., 1977), pp. 1–23; and Barbara J. Nelson, "Helpseeking from Public Authorities: Who Arrives at the Agency Door?" *Policy Sciences* 12, no. 1 (August 1980): 175–192.

8   Neil Smelser, *Theory of Collective Behavior* (New York: Free Press, 1962).

9   For a discussion of a similar phenomenon, public response to social movements, see John D. McCarthy and Mayer N. Zald, "Resource Mobilization and Social Movements: A Partial Theory," *American Journal of Sociology* 82, no. 6 (May 1977): 1212–1241. McCarthy and Zald divide the public into constituents, adherents, bystanders, and opponents (p. 1221).

10 Phillipe Aries, *Centuries of Childhood: A Social History of Family Life,* trans. Robert Baldick, (New York: Vintage Books, 1962); Lawrence Stone, *The Family, Sex and Marriage*

in England, 1500–1800 (New York: Harper and Row, 1977), pp. 147–81; and Edward Shorter, *The Making of the Modern Family* (New York: Basic Books, 1975), pp. 255–268.

11   Elbridge T. Gerry, "The Relation of Societies for the Prevention of Cruelty to Children to Child-Saving Work," *Proceedings* of the National Conference of Charities and Corrections 1882, pp. 129–130, in Robert H. Bremner, ed., *Children and Youth in America: A Documentary History,* vol. 2, (Cambridge, Mass.: Harvard University Press, 1970), p. 196.

12   See, for example, "The 'New Education' and The Old Ideals" in Bernard Wishy, *The Child and the Republic: The Dawn of Modern American Child Nurture* (Philadelphia: University of Pennsylvania Press, 1968), pp. 136–158; Robert H. Wiebe, *The Search For Order: 1877–1920* (New York: Hill and Wang, 1967); Ellen DuBois, *Feminism and Suffrage: The Emergence of an Independent Women 's Movement in America, 1848–1869* (Ithaca, New York: Cornell University Press, 1978); and David Montgomery, *Beyond Equality: Labor and Radical Republicans, 1862–1872* (New York: Vintage, 1967).

13   Stanley N. Katz, "Legal History and Family History: The Child, the Family, and the State," address to the Boston College Law School, April 25, 1980, p. 7. See also Philip Greven, *The Protestant Temperament: Patterns of Child-Rearing, Religious Experience and the Self in Early America* (New York: Alfred A. Knopf, 1977).

14   The *New York Times,* April 22, 1874, p. 8.

15   Sydney H. Coleman, *Humane Society Leaders in America* (Albany, N.Y.: the American Humane Association, 1924), pp. 65–89: "Elbridge T. Gerry and the Prevention of Cruelty to Children."

16   The legal details are based on Mason P. Thomas, Jr., "Child Abuse and Neglect Part I: Historical Overview, Legal Matrix, and Social Perspectives," *North Carolina Law Review* 50 (February 1972): 293–349. The details of the case were reassembled through newspaper accounts. See the *New York Times* on the following dates in 1874: April 10 (p. 8), April 11 (p. 2), April 22 (p. 8), June 2 (p. 8), December 7 (pp. 3–4), December 27 (p. 12), and December 29 (p. 2).

17   The *New York Times,* December 29, 1874, p. 2. Two engravings of Ellen Conners can be found in the New York Society for the Prevention of Cruelty to Children's (unpublished) *Annual Report,* 1876, p. 73. See also Catherine J. Ross, "The Lessons of the Past: Defining and Controlling Child Abuse in the United States," in George Gerbner, Catherine J. Ross, and Edward Zigler, eds., *Child Abuse: An Agenda for Action* (New York: Oxford University Press, 1980), pp. 63–81.

18   Elizabeth Pleck, "Policing the Violent Family: The Humane Societies," unpublished paper given at the Bunting Institute, Radcliffe College, 1980, pp. 3–7.

19   "Proceedings of the Conference on the Care of Dependent Children Held at Washington, D.C.; January 25, 1909," U.S. Senate, Sixtieth Congress, Second Session, Document no. 721, (Washington, D.C.: United States Government Printing Office, 1909), p. 9.

20   William Schultz, *The Humane Movement in the United States, 1910–1922* (New York: Columbia University Press, 1924), pp. 223–228, in Bremner, ed., *Children and Youth* 2, pp. 217–219.

21   C. C. Carstens, "Who Shall Protect the Children?" *Survey* 51 (1923–24): 93.

22   Homer Folks, *Care of Destitute, Dependent, and Delinquent Children* (New York: J. B. Lyon Co., 1902), pp. 173–175, in Bremner, ed., *Children and Youth* 2, p. 213.

23   Josephine Shaw Lowell, "Report on the Institutions for the Care of Destitute Children of the City of New York," reprinted from the *New York State Board of Charities Annual Report for the Year 1885* (Albany, N.Y., 1886), pp. 167–243, in *Care of Dependent Children in the Late Nineteenth and Early Twentieth Centuries* (New York: Arno Press, 1974). The New York SPCC refused to be inspected by the State Board of Charities, and went to court to establish the fact that it was not charity but an arm of the police department. It won. See The People of the State of New York, *ex. rel.* The State Board of Charities *v.* the New York Society of the Prevention of Cruelty to Children, 161 NY, pp. 239–240, 248, in Bremner, ed., *Children and Youth* 2, p. 197, and Coleman, *Humane Society Leaders,* p. 83.

24   John Caffey, "Multiple Fractures in the Long Bones of Infants Suffering from Chronic Subdural Hematoma," *American Journal of Roentgenology* 56 (August 1946): 163–173; F. N. Silverman, "The Roentgen Manifestations of Unrecognized Skeletal Trauma in Infants," *American Journal of Roentgenology, Radium Therapy and Nuclear Medicine* 69 (March 1953): 413–426; John Caffey, "Some Traumatic Lesions in Growing Bones Other Than Fractures and Dislocation–Clinical and Radiological Features," *British Journal of Radiology* 30 (May 1957): 225–238.

25   For a review of the early social work research on physical child abuse, see David G. Gil, *Violence against Children: Physical Child Abuse in the United States* (Cambridge, Mass.: Harvard University Press, 1973), pp. 20–21.

26   C. Henry Kempe et al., "The Battered-Child Syndrome," *The Journal of the American Medical Association* 181, 1 (July 7, 1962): 17–24.

27   Ibid., p. 17.

28   Ibid., p. 24, my emphasis.

29   California Penal Code, Sec. 11161.5, in Jeanne M. Giovannoni and Rosina M. Becerra, *Defining Child Abuse* (New York: The Free Press, 1979), p. 6.

30   PL 93-247, 1974, Sec. 2.

31   See Leroy H. Pelton, "Child Abuse and Neglect: The Myth of Classlessness," in Leroy H. Pelton, ed., *The Social Context of Child Abuse and Neglect* (New York: Human Sciences Press, 1981), pp. 23–38; and Gil, *Violence against Children,* pp. 133–198.

32   National Conference for Family Violence Researchers, University of New Hampshire, Durham, N.H., July 21, 1981. Professor Gelles is a coauthor with Murray A. Straus and Suzanne K. Steinmetz of *Beyond Closed Doors: Violence in the American Family* (New York: Anchor Books, 1980).

33   For a good summary of the attempts at measuring and estimating child abuse, see Richard J. Gelles, "Violence toward Children in the United States," in Richard Bourne and Eli H. Newberger, eds., *Critical Perspectives on Child Abuse* (Lexington, Mass.: D. C. Heath and Company, 1979), pp. 53–68. The studies cited here are "One Child

Dies Daily from Abuse: Parent Probably Was Abuser," *Pediatric News* 9 (April 1975): 3; Gil, *Violence against Children,* pp. 58–60; and Richard Light,"Abused and Neglected Children in America: A Study of Alternative Policies," *Harvard Educational Review* 43 (November 1973): 556–598.

34 Kempe et al., "The Battered-Child Syndrome," pp. 17–24.

35 "The Battered-Child Syndrome" editorial in the *Journal of the American Medical Association* 181, no. 1 (July 7, 1962): 42.

36 Gilbert Y. Steiner, *The Futility of Family Policy* (Washington, D.C.: The Brookings Institution, 1980), pp. 167–170.

37 "The National Study on Child Neglect and Abuse Reporting" (Denver: The Child Protection Division, the American Humane Association, 1981), pp. 6–7.

38 Stephen J. Pfoll, "The 'Discovery' of Child Abuse," *Social Problems* 24, no. 3 (February 1977): 310–323; and Steven Antler, "Child Abuse: An Emerging Social Priority," *Social Work* 23 (January 1978): 58–61.

39 See, for example, Peter Conrad, "The Discovery of Hyperkinesis: Notes on the Medicalization of Deviant Behavior," *Social Problems* 23 (October 1975): 12–21; Russell P. Dobash and R. Emerson Dobash, "Community Response to Violence against Wives: Charivari, Abstract Justice and Patriarchy," *Social Problems* 28 (June 1981): 564–581; Michel Foucault, *Discipline and Punish: The Birth of the Prison* (London: Allen Lane, 1977).

40 David Mechanic, *Medical Sociology* (New York: Free Press, 1978, second edition), p. 44.

41 Edward Sagarin, *Deviants and Deviance: An Introduction to the Study of Disvalued People and Behavior* (New York: Praeger, 1975), pp. 221–225.

42 John A. Denton, *Medical Sociology* (Boston: Houghton Mifflin Co., 1978), pp. 21–22.

43 Zillah Eisenstein, *The Radical Future of Liberal Feminism* (New York: Longman, 1981).

The following charts illuminate what Americans currently label or prioritize as the most important/pressing social issues. Be sure to note the charts that address the social problems of younger Americans, in which the data encompasses many of the birth cohorts you all may belong to. The latter charts also demonstrate how the degree to which different social issues are conceived as social problems. You will see that health care, the economy, the government, immigration, and race relations have all tended to be toward the top of the list of "most important social problems facing the country today."

% who say ____ should be a top priority for Trump and Congress this year

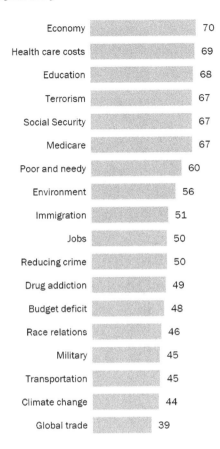

Economy	70
Health care costs	69
Education	68
Terrorism	67
Social Security	67
Medicare	67
Poor and needy	60
Environment	56
Immigration	51
Jobs	50
Reducing crime	50
Drug addiction	49
Budget deficit	48
Race relations	46
Military	45
Transportation	45
Climate change	44
Global trade	39

Source: Survey of U.S. adults conducted Jan. 9-14, 2019.

PEW RESEARCH CENTER

FIGURE 3.1   **Public's policy priorities for 2019.**

% of registered voters who say each is a 'very big' problem in the country today ...

	Support Rep candidate	Support Dem candidate
The way racial and ethnic minorities are treated by the criminal justice system	10	71
Climate change	11	72
Gun violence	25	81
The gap between the rich and the poor	22	77
Racism	19	63
The way immigrants who are in the country illegally are treated	15	57
Wages and the cost of living	27	67
Sexism	12	50
The affordability of health care	56	83
Job opportunities for all Americans	8	33
The affordability of a college education	47	71
The way the U.S. political system operates	49	68
Ethics in government	62	80
Violent crime	47	49
Drug addiction	64	67
The federal budget deficit	56	61
Terrorism	27	41
Illegal immigration	19	75

Note: Based on registered voters.
Source: Survey of U.S. adults conducted Sept. 24-Oct. 7, 2018.

PEW RESEARCH CENTER

FIGURE 3.2   **With few exceptions, wide partisan differences over the seriousness of problems facing the United States.**

% of teens saying each of the following is a ____ among people their age in the community where they live

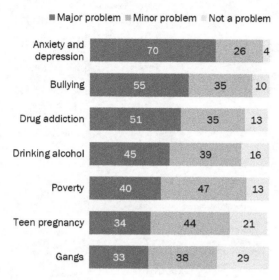

■ Major problem ■ Minor problem ▢ Not a problem

	Major problem	Minor problem	Not a problem
Anxiety and depression	70	26	4
Bullying	55	35	10
Drug addiction	51	35	13
Drinking alcohol	45	39	16
Poverty	40	47	13
Teen pregnancy	34	44	21
Gangs	33	38	29

Note: Share of respondents who didn't offer an answer not shown.
Source: Survey of U.S. teens ages 13 to 17 conducted Sept. 17-Nov. 25, 2018.
"Most U.S. Teens See Anxiety and Depression as a Major Problem Among Their Peers"

PEW RESEARCH CENTER

FIGURE 3.3   **Anxiety and depression top list of problems teens see among their peers.**

% of teens saying they personally feel ____ pressure to ...

■ A lot   ■ Some   ▢ Not too much   ■ None at all

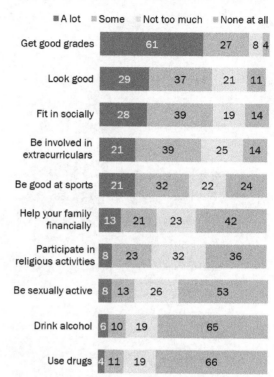

	A lot	Some	Not too much	None at all
Get good grades	61	27	8	4
Look good	29	37	21	11
Fit in socially	28	39	19	14
Be involved in extracurriculars	21	39	25	14
Be good at sports	21	32	22	24
Help your family financially	13	21	23	42
Participate in religious activities	8	23	32	36
Be sexually active	8	13	26	53
Drink alcohol	6	10	19	65
Use drugs	4	11	19	66

Note: Share of respondents who didn't offer an answer not shown.
Source: Survey of U.S. teens ages 13 to 17 conducted Sept. 17-Nov. 25, 2018.
"Most U.S. Teens See Anxiety and Depression as a Major Problem Among Their Peers"

PEW RESEARCH CENTER

FIGURE 3.4   **About six in ten teens say they feel a lot of pressure to get good grades.**

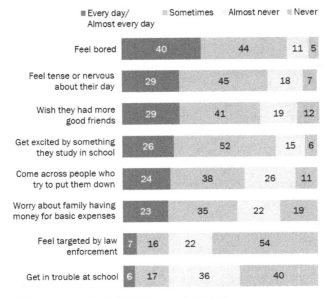

% of teens saying they experience each of the following ...

■ Every day/ ▪ Sometimes ▪ Almost never ▪ Never
Almost every day

	Every day/Almost every day	Sometimes	Almost never	Never
Feel bored	40	44	11	5
Feel tense or nervous about their day	29	45	18	7
Wish they had more good friends	29	41	19	12
Get excited by something they study in school	26	52	15	6
Come across people who try to put them down	24	38	26	11
Worry about family having money for basic expenses	23	35	22	19
Feel targeted by law enforcement	7	16	22	54
Get in trouble at school	6	17	36	40

Note: Share of respondents who didn't offer an answer not shown
Source: Survey of U.S. teens ages 13 to 17 conducted Sept. 17–Nov. 25, 2018
"Most U.S. Teens See Anxiety and Depression as a Major Problem Among Their Peers"

PEW RESEARCH CENTER

FIGURE 3.5 **About three in ten teens feel tense or nervous and wish they had more good friends almost daily.**

Problems mentioned by at least % of respondents in February

	Feb. 1-10, 2019 %
The government/Poor leadership	35
Immigration	19
Healthcare	6
Race relations/Racism	5
Unifying the country	4
Poverty/Hunger/Homelessness	4
Environment/Pollution	3
Ethics/Moral/Religious/Family decline	3
Federal budget deficit/Federal debt	3
Economy in general	3
Unemployment/Jobs	3
Lack of respect for each other	2
Education	2

GALLUP, FEB. 1-10, 2019

FIGURE 3.6 **Americans' views of the top problem facing the US.**

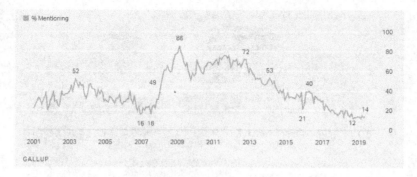

FIGURE 3.7 Percentage of Americans who mention economic issues as the nation's most important problem.

	May 2019	Apr 2019	Mar 2019	Feb 2019	Jan 2019	Dec 2018	Nov 2018
	%	%	%	%	%	%	%
ECONOMIC PROBLEMS (NET)	14	13	15	12	14	14	13
Economy in general	4	5	4	3	3	3	4
Unemployment/Jobs	3	2	3	3	1	3	3
Gap between rich and poor	2	2	*	1	2	2	1
Federal budget deficit/Federal debt	2	2	4	3	2	2	2
Lack of money	1	1	--	1	1	1	*
Wage issues	1	*	2	1	1	*	*
Taxes	*	1	1	1	1	1	1
High cost of living/Inflation	*	1	*	*	*	*	*
Corporate corruption	*	--	1	*	1	1	1
Fuel/Oil prices	--	*	--	*	*	*	*
Foreign trade/Trade deficit	--	--	*	*	*	1	*
NON-ECONOMIC PROBLEMS (NET)	83	83	83	87	83	84	86
The government/Poor leadership	23	23	29	35	29	19	18
Immigration	19	21	16	19	21	16	21
Healthcare	7	7	7	6	7	5	11
Race relations/Racism	6	6	7	5	8	7	9
Unifying the country	4	5	3	4	5	8	9
Environment/Pollution/Climate change	4	3	4	3	3	5	2
Education	4	3	3	2	2	2	3
Poverty/Hunger/Homelessness	3	5	3	4	3	6	2
Lack of respect for each other	3	4	3	2	3	5	6
Ethics/moral/religious/family decline	3	3	5	3	2	3	4
Crime/Violence	2	2	2	1	2	4	1
Judicial system/Courts/Laws	2	2	1	1	2	2	2
Drugs	2	1	2	1	1	2	1
Guns/Gun control	1	1	1	1	1	3	2
National security	1	1	2	1	*	1	1
Welfare	1	*	1	1	*	--	2
Abortion	1	*	1	*	*	*	*
The media	1	1	1	1	1	1	1
International issues, problems	1	1	*	1	*	1	1
Lack of military defense	1	1	1	*	*	*	--
Care for the elderly/Medicare	1	*	*	*	*	*	1
Foreign policy/Foreign aid/Focus overseas	1	*	1	1	2	*	*
Situation with China	1	*	--	*	--	*	*
Elections/Election reform	1	*	1	1	*	*	*
Wars/War (nonspecific)/Fear of war	1	*	*	1	*	*	1
Social Security	*	*	*	*	*	1	*
Terrorism	*	*	*	*	*	*	1
Gay/Lesbian rights	*	*	--	*	*	*	*
Situation with Russia	*	*	--	1	*	*	--
School shootings	*	*	--	*	--	1	1
Advancement of Computers/Technology	*	--	*	*	--	*	--
Situation in Iraq/ISIS	*	*	--	*	--	*	--
Situation with North Korea	*	--	*	--	--	*	*
Children's behavior/Way they are raised	--	*	*	*	*	*	1
War/conflict between Middle East nations	--	--	--	*	*	*	*
Other non-economic	4	7	6	4	7	6	4
No opinion	4	3	2	3	4	3	4
Total	119%	119%	120%	119%	121%	120%	125%

* Less than 0.5%. Percentages total more than 100% due to multiple mentions.

GALLUP

FIGURE 3.8 What do you think is the most important problem facing the country today?

Reading 3.4.

Social Change, Social Problems, and Demands for Knowledge

by Neil J. Smelser and John S. Reed

Why, we might ask, should human history ever have produced a situation in which society might find it necessary, valuable, and desirable that groups of specialists calling themselves social scientists should specialize in the production of knowledge that might be regarded as useful? The answer to that question is not self-evident, and any intelligible answer calls for reflection on many levels.

THE LONG HAUL THE SOCIAL SCIENCES AS CULTURALLY POSSIBLE AND SOCIALLY NECESSARY

The Broad Cultural Background

At the broadest level, it is essential to underscore that, historically, the social sciences did not simply "happen," but have been the outgrowth of cumulative cultural changes that have revolutionized western civilization in the past few millennia: changes in cosmological views of the world; changes in assumptions about nature, man, and society; changes in notions of causality; and changes in the nature of individual, legal, and social responsibility.

Prior to such developments, the world and its workings were conceived mainly but variously in ways dictated by the religions and superstitions of peoples: as products of fate; as anthropomorphically conceived forces of nature; as whimsical but powerful wishes and actions of deities or a divine God; or as covenants between the divine and the human. These worldviews, some of which survive in evolved form, have differed greatly, but above all they have tended to locate—or diffuse—the notions of causality, individuality, and human responsibility in *extrahuman* sources, thus diminishing or tempering the framing of humanity, social relations, society, and culture as *independent, objectified forces*.

In the evolution and ultimate modernization of the West, however, a number of fundamental cultural changes transformed these kinds of worldviews into a cultural milieu that has permitted and ultimately facilitated the principle idea of the *scientific* study of humans, society, and culture. Without attempting to exhaust or weigh the development of these changes, we mention the following:

- the revitalization of classical Greek thinking in the Middle Ages, especially Aristotelian philosophy, which included natural and quasiscientific ingredients of economics, politics, and psychology, and objective treatments of special social topics such as friendship.

Neil J. Smelser and John S. Reed, "Social Change, Social Problems, and Demands for Knowledge," *Usable Social Science*, pp. 293-314, 355-409. Copyright © 2012 by University of California Press. Reprinted with permission.

- the establishment and development of the great medieval universities, first as off-shoots of the Church and monasteries, but gradually evolving into seats of learning for all varieties of knowledge, many secular.

- the ramifications of the Renaissance and the Protestant Reformation, especially the accentuation of human potential and the importance of human agency.

- developments in philosophy, especially epistemological schools of skepticism and empiricism, and substantive areas of epistemology, moral philosophy, political philosophy, and philosophy of religion.

- revolutions in the physical and biological sciences, which not only furthered the objectification of nature, but also developed theories, laws, and methods that furthered human understanding and mastery of the laws of the universe and the relief of disease and suffering. These scientific revolutions were decisive because they supplied many of the elements of the assumption that human affairs and human society are also objects for scientific investigation and the establishment of scientific laws [...].

- the Enlightenment, which moved thinking about human nature and society decisively away from the dominant theological viewpoints it rejected.

- the development of certain secular worldviews, especially the idea of progress, which also accentuated human agency and optimism.

None of these developments alone determined the conception and rise of the social sciences as enterprises in the development of knowledge, but together they set the stage for the views that human affairs were "objective" and subject to study as such, that these affairs were subject to scientific laws, and that these laws could point the way to human betterment. It was in such a fertile intellectual field that the scientific manifestos and projects of the "founding fathers"—figures such as Adam Smith, Auguste Comte, Karl Marx, and Wilhelm Wundt—became culturally possible.

The Broad Structural Background

Standing alongside the broad cultural contours of change—and determined partially by them—has been a social-structural evolution of western societies during the past several hundred years that has both produced the need for systematic knowledge about society and shaped the disciplined modes of inquiry (the social sciences) that have been called upon to produce that knowledge. We review these social changes under two headings: the principal types of change and the emergence of institutional structures.

The Ubiquity of Change Some still maintain a distinction between modern (technology-based, industrial, urban) societies and traditional (primarily agricultural, small-community) societies. Social scientists themselves have been mainly responsible for this distinction [...]. The evolutionary schemata of nineteenth- and early-twentieth-century evolutionary anthropology contrasted various stages of primitive societies (e.g., savagery, barbarianism) with different stages of civilized society. While challenged by theoretical arguments, by evidence of significant innovation in "traditional" societies, and by sociocultural transformations in the colonial, postcolonial, and recent globalizing eras, the distinction has had a certain sticking power, sometimes accompanied by a tendency to romanticize the simpler societies.

One ingredient of this partially outmoded distinction is that modern societies are characterized by rapid and continuous change and traditional societies are stable, in part because they are characterized by primitive technology, old customs, superstitions, and customary social relations that defy change. That stereotype has proved to be only a partial truth. The march of history reveals the deterioration and collapse of many "primitive" societies, such as the Anasazi culture of the North American Southwest in the late thirteenth century. (Many possible causes have been advanced, the most likely of which is a combination of population growth, exhaustion of resources, and a long and deadly season of drought.) Treatises have been written on the rise and decline of many civilizations, most of them premodern (Toynbee, 1935; Kroeber, 1944). In western history, the received notions of stability and order of medieval civilization have been undermined by research on wars, the changing relations among the social orders, and the impacts of trade, commerce, and urbanization. The half-truth of the myth of stability is that in societies in existence prior to modern Europe, the pace of change was, in general, *comparatively* slow (with exceptions), but this generalization remains a relative, not an absolute one.

The more nearly correct side of the story is the view that in the past several centuries, the pace of change in all facets of society has been qualitatively new, massive, and accelerating. It has affected all facets of society and culture. We indicate its scope by detailing a number of "revolutions" that historians and other scholars have identified and detailed. In all cases, the revolutions' origins and precursors can be traced back centuries earlier, but modern acceleration and impact are indubitable. In listing the following revolutions, we also acknowledge irregularities and fits and starts. We list them to preview the kinds of consequences they have generated, including massive changes in scale and differentiation in society, failures of integration, tensions, social problems, injustices, group conflicts, and violations of the natural environment. Derivatively, our purpose in detailing these consequences is to indicate the explosion in the requirements for systematic knowledge to deal with these consequences. That, finally, is where the social sciences enter the scene.

- The agricultural revolution. Originating with new methods of cultivation, new crops, changing patterns of ownership and labor, and displacement of peasant populations, the march of agricultural productivity has generated increases in scale of agricultural enterprises, large-scale farm machinery, chemical fertilization and pesticides, agribusiness, the green revolution, a long-term decrease of agricultural workers in the labor force, and, by now, a globalization of agricultural production.

- The commercial revolution. Originating with the penetration of lesser-known regions of the world by those in search of precious metals, and the improvement of navigational technology and ocean transport, this revolution generated an expansion of markets, an accumulation of great wealth, and new configurations of power among the European nations. It also pointed toward the development of commercial enterprises such as the protected colonial company, the limited liability partnership, and the modern corporation, as well as banking and financial systems that have in the long run become fully internationalized.

- The industrial revolution. Originating in the British textile industry in the late eighteenth century (Ashton, 1969), this revolution was marked by the application of nonhuman power (water, coal and steam, electricity), the invention of machinery, and the gathering of wage laborers into centralized manufactories. Over time it has spread from power source to power source, product to product, and country to country, culminating in its recent dispersion from the industrialized countries to previously less-developed areas of the world and its expression in the multinational corporation [...].

- The scientific revolution. This refers especially to dramatic historical advances in the natural sciences, in part as a result of autonomous forces within science, and in part facilitated by the agricultural, commercial, and industrial revolutions, which continuously required new knowledge. The interaction among science, technology, and new forms of economic and social organization resulted in a number of economic "ages," such as the steamship age, the railway age, the chemical age, the electricity age, the aeronautical age, the information age, the green revolution, and the space age.

- The service revolution. This refers to the relative expansion of the tertiary sector of economies, especially in developed countries. It is a by-product of the need to coordinate complex societies and is driven by the technical needs of the economy, by larger and more complex systems of government, by the development of the media and advertising, by the rise and consolidation of the professions, by the information revolution, and by the need for ancillary personnel in all these arenas. The growth of services is typically at the expense of agriculture and manufacturing. Systematic psychological and social knowledge is necessary for informed decisions in all sectors, but clearly so in the service sector, which in its essence involves person-to-person and organization-to-organization interaction.

- The urban revolution. In many respects, the movement of populations into concentrated centers has been a by-product of the several revolutions already mentioned. It has involved both the economic push from agricultural sectors by displacement and low wages and the pull of centralized manufacturing and service industries. Some countertendencies have appeared, such as the dispersion of industry, suburbanization and exurbanization, and the possibilities of virtual occupations and organizations, but the movement into populated places still continues.

- The population revolution. The rapid increase of the world's populations has been made possible by the agricultural, commercial, and industrial revolutions, as well as the health revolution that has produced improvements in public health (e.g., sanitation, vaccination) and increases in longevity. Two additional facets of the population revolution have been increases in international migration as labor has become more globalized, and increases in diversity and multiculturalism as international migrations generate minority, creole, and diaspora populations.

- The nationalist revolution. Spreading irregularly and varying in form, this has nonetheless resulted in the consolidation of the nation-state as the principal mode of political integration and domination in the contemporary world. The evolution of nationalism also includes the creation and multiplication of nation-states in the postcolonial world. The state persists despite inroads on sovereignty made by globalization […].

- The democratic revolution, forwarded dramatically by the American Revolutionary War and the French Revolution, spreading irregularly throughout Europe, and including the wave of democratization late in the twentieth century. Diverse forms of democracy have been attempted, and many of these have failed, but the democratic impulse continues alive and strong. Closely associated with the spread of democracy has been the intensification of demands for political participation, social justice, humanitarianism, and, most recently, human rights—all of which, we argue, provide new bases for generating social problems and placing them on the political agenda.

- The education revolution, referring to the continuous spread of primary, secondary, and postsecondary education in the world. The impulse has been a product of diverse forces, including socialization and control of the lower classes in evolving industrial societies; as an adjunct to cultural aspects of nationalism and "nation-building"; as an instrument to impart skills to labor markets in countries that demand higher levels of skills, especially in the service sectors; and as an instrument of economic and cultural competition. The impulse to expand education has been almost universal.

- The secularization revolution, characterized by the long-term decline in religious beliefs and the cultural-political hegemony of established religious traditions. This revolution has been complicated and qualified by the emergence of new religions and the resurgence of secular religions, quasireligions, and fundamentalism in the twentieth and twenty-first centuries.

- Civil unrest, political revolutions, wars among nations, genocides, and, more recently, terrorism in an unending parade. Taken together, they have added a dimension of political uncertainty and instability to the experiences of all affected nations and populations.

- The organization revolution, involving a proliferation of specialized jobs and occupations and their combination into many formal and informal organizations: armies, business organizations, governmental organizations, quasi-governmental organizations, voluntary associations, and social-movement organizations. The revolution's growth spurs new requirements for ancillary service personnel, technical workers, managers, and coordinating personnel.

- The information revolution. Although it is traceable to the invention of the printing press, the sequential development of available news media, and the gradual spread of literacy, the term *information revolution* itself refers to the dawn of the computer and related information technology such as e-mail and the Web.

- The colonial revolution. Part of the globalization process, this revolution involved (1) colonialism proper, the imperial expansion of the great European powers (and to some extent the United States) associated in large part with economic and political competition; (2) anticolonialism, ever-present wherever colonialism was present but reaching a climax in nationalist independence movements after World War II; (3) postcolonialism, involving state-building efforts of nations emerging from colonial domination, efforts to develop economically, and struggles against continued domination by the great powers of the world.

- The globalization revolution. Again traceable back through centuries of internationalization of trade and economic and political domination (Wallerstein, 1974), globalization has accelerated through the vast increases in trade and finance and the growth of multinational corporations since World War II. Global capitalism was given further impetus in the 1990s with the decline of Marxism, the collapse of communism in the Soviet Union and its satellites, the end of the Cold War, and the end of any formidable ideological opposition to neoliberalism and the free market (Kurth, 2001). We have traced some of its multiple ramifications and creation of social problems [...].

So much for cataloging the changes that have shaped and continue to shape the contemporary world. All continue, some at an accelerating pace. They are, moreover, interrelated. All stand as both causes and effects of one another in evolving sequences of causal interdependency. The onset and development of each, however, is irregular, and as a result the world of change is forever producing leads and lags, accelerations, irregularities, diversions, tensions, resistances, and new unmet needs. From the standpoint of the structure of society, the cumulative effect of the revolutions has been greater *specialization and differentiation* of roles, organizations, and groups from one another on the one hand, and the requirement to find new forms of *coordinating and integrating* them on the other. In one of the last essays produced by Herbert Simon (2001) before his death, he endorsed a major theme in all the social sciences by remarking that the two great historical engines driving us toward productivity in organizations have been the specialization of roles and their coordination. His point can be generalized to society as a whole, and can be said to merge the principles enunciated separately by Adam Smith (on division of labor) (1937 [1776]) and Émile Durkheim (on integration) (1997 [1893]).

The Social Sciences as Reflections of Structural Change The social-science disciplines have developed since the eighteenth century. Many of them, it can be argued, reflected the broadest contours of the differentiation of the phenomena they were meant to study. The "dismal science" of economics arose in the context of the spread of markets, highlighting the difference between producers and consumers (and distinctions within both of these groups). Early political economy also became an ideological basis for the struggle of the commercial and industrial classes to shake free from the constraints of mercantilism and to find a political place in societies long dominated by aristocratic privilege and hegemony. But, above all, it was the differentiation of the economy as a visible institutional form that both permitted and demanded its study. This observation also suggests why—as economic anthropologists have argued interminably—formal economic assumptions about tastes, institutions, and rationality do not apply well to primitive and traditional societies, in which economic processes are less differentiated and more embedded in non-market dynamics of kinship, status, and community (see Malinowski, 1922; Firth, 1971; Dalton, 1971).

Similarly, the rise of political science reflected the differentiation of the nation-state and its institutions, as well as the distinctive political impetus to understanding the politics of democracy created in Europe and America after the great revolutions of the late eighteenth century. A preoccupation with democracy still dominates inquiry in political science. Among the items that appeared on the agenda of that developing field were parliaments and legislatures, the separation of powers, extension of the franchise, political parties, and the rise of political bureaucracies and civil service systems. As with economics, modern political science was born in the time of, and partly as a result of, the differentiation of modern states and political systems.

Sociology expressed the differentiation between polity and society as well as the rapid transformation of various institutions—economic, political, legal, family, and others—in the nineteenth century. As indicated, most of the great sociologists of that century were preoccupied with the transition from traditional to modern societies occasioned by the commercial, industrial, and scientific revolutions. As part of that agenda, sociologists also concentrated on the apparent pathologies of the industrializing world (social disorganization, poverty, crime, anomie, depersonalization, conditions of labor, economic exploitation, and class conflict). The social-reform impulse has been a dominant motif in sociological investigations up to the present.

Anthropology developed in the context of European colonialism and imperialism, which involved economic exploitation, political domination, religious proselytization, and cultural subordination of colonized regions. The process exposed colonies to western culture and exposed westerners to theirs. Anthropologists focused on these societies, and in their early investigations asked how these "savage" or "barbarian" societies fit into the evolution of human society and which forces drove the march toward higher civilization. Early anthropology also developed biological and temperamental theories of race, some of which served to justify western domination. Some have argued that early anthropology was an intellectual handmaiden of colonialism (a recent example is Tilley and Gordon, 2007). At the very least, it provided raw material for an ideology of domination, and perhaps set the stage for a more positive identification with nonwestern cultures as the field subsequently developed.

More Specific Historical Challenges and Preoccupations

Examining the correspondences among economic, political, and social differentiation on the one hand and the rise of the social-science specialties on the other yields only very general connections. Intensification of social-science interest also parallels more specific changes and crises. Among these are the study of the economic causes and social and psychological effects of unemployment in the 1930s; the study of propaganda during World War II; the postwar emergence of studies of "the authoritarian personality," in large part a reaction to fascism in Europe; the rise and consolidation of development studies among economists, political scientists, sociologists, and anthropologists during the surges of anticolonialism, independence, and nation-building after World War II; preoccupation with youth, generational relations, and counterculture as a response to the turbulence of the 1960s; the creation of gender studies as a response to the acceleration of feminism in the 1960s and 1970s; the new salience of race relations as a response to urban violence and the civil rights movements in the same decades; the economics of stagflation as a response to the economic conditions generated by the OPEC crisis of 1973 and other economic trends; identity movements and identity politics in response to the more general "cultural turn" in the social sciences in the 1980s; the preoccupation with total quality management and other Japanese methods of management in organizational studies during the period of heady economic competition with the Japanese in the 1980s; and the burst of research on terrorism after September 11, 2001.

As often as not, these seasons of crisis also stimulate funding from foundations and governments that encourages directions of research in the social sciences. Research on behavior in extreme situations, including disaster, for example, was largely the product of government funding of civil defense studies in the 1960s; external funding helped to stimulate research on many of the historical situations reviewed in the preceding paragraph. In addition, the National Research Council (a research and policy arm of the National Academies) is the frequent target of requests for inquiries from Congress and agencies in the executive branch. Some private foundations commission, request, and conduct reviews of knowledge in specific areas of concern. Many of the resulting reports deal with technical topics calling for the expertise of natural scientists (such as global warming), but many rely on social-science expertise. Examples of the latter are the investigations of racial factors in the delivery of healthcare services, the sources and significance of medical errors, drug practices and policies, the effects of free needle distribution on AIDS transmission, the origins of psychological compulsions to gamble, the effects of uncapping the age of retirement on the labor force in higher education, the institutional effectiveness of advanced certification of teachers, and the social and psychological origins of school shootings and related violence.

The combination of economic, political, and social developments, periodic inputs of research funds from governmental and private agencies, and studies by the National Research Council and other bodies together assign priority to and stimulate research in specific areas of the social sciences. Sometimes the call is for research in a general area, for which it is hoped that usable (policy-relevant) knowledge will be forthcoming. In other cases, the foci are more specific with respect to problems and the kinds of knowledge wanted. These forces constitute important demands for social-science knowledge. On their part, social scientists themselves also turn to the designated areas, partly as an expression of their own increased interest in the social conditions in question, partly out of motives of public service, partly to exert influence, and partly in response to increased opportunities for funding (dubbed the "pigs-to-the-trough" syndrome). Cynical humor about these effects appears, to the effect that academic entrepreneurs do what they want to do anyway and call it something else because that something else is being funded. In the 1960s, one heard remarks that social scientists were striking it rich by studying poverty.

By virtue of their involvement in pressing social issues, social scientists have become important voices in that vaguely demarcated subclass of society that specializes in identifying, describing, demonstrating the effects of, bemoaning, and suggesting reforms of social conditions. Other groups that read and interpret social conditions and trends are "intellectuals," media newspersons and commentators, politicians, religious and educational leaders, and spokespersons for social movements. Being drawn into that group, academic and applied social scientists become one of the many voices in the "new priestly classes" of contemporary society. This also means that they become competitors among themselves and with other voices. This circumstance constitutes a further basis for their interest in usability—that is, to appeal to their own expertise as a basis for exerting political influence. Some social scientists believe that they have special insights and special things to say about those issues that perplex societies, and this draws them into the competitive realm as they debate which of the competing varieties of knowledge is the most usable. Whether they wish to or not, they become a motivated political constituency.

SOCIAL CHANGE, NEW CONDITIONS, AND THE PRODUCTION OF SOCIAL PROBLEMS

New Situations, New Environments

The first corollary of change is that the combined effects of the noted revolutions create new ranges of scale and complexity in decision-making. In the world of business, one principle is economies of scale—the larger the enterprise, the more efficient the operation—a principle realized in both agricultural and manufacturing. Several complications accompany this principle, however. First, increased organizational size involves increased differentiation of activities and creates new requirements for their coordination, increased potential for individual alienation and group conflict, a more complex authority system, and perhaps less control over the execution of decisions, to such an extent that expansion alone can create diminished rates of return and inefficiencies. In a word, size and scale assume a more problematic status (see above, pp. 186–87).

By the same token, the environment for business has become more complex as multiorganization systems have evolved and new constituencies have grown historically: competitors, stockholders, consumers, workers and labor unions, insurance companies, and government regulators. One significant shift in the scholarly study of organizations in the late twentieth century has been less focus on internal dynamics and more on the environments and systemic involvements of organizations. As is the case with size, the increasing complexity of a business's environment complicates the decision-making process for those involved.

Similar points can be made with respect to spheres of governmental and professional life. Governmental agencies and bureaucracies have proliferated wherever societies have developed and as the need for coordination and the need to solve social problems have increased, giving the lie to hopes for smaller government as societies become more prosperous and complex. Patterns of accountability to political and organizational superiors and relationships to the constituencies they serve have likewise become more complex. For example, the migration of medical practice into organizational settings such as governments, hospitals, and medical groups has made it more complicated, more bureaucratized, and more complex in governance, with more parties involved in decision-making (see chapter 6, pp. 177–78). Similar arguments could be evoked in the academic world as well, as simpler collegiate forms have evolved into giant bureaucratic universities and systems of universities embedded in still more complex systems of constituencies, requiring more of those in decision-making capacities and making their lives more embattled (Smelser, 2010).

The rise and consolidation of formal organizations in industry resulted historically in the generalization of wage (including salary) labor as the basis for the economic survival and welfare of the family. Among other things, wage labor in organizations removed economic production from and separated the worker from his or her family. The wage package, moreover, often became the sole source of family income and created a new and more encompassing meaning of *unemployment*. Wage labor, furthermore, redefined social class relations in all societies that have industrialized or become dependent on wage-paying organizations; this fundamentally reshaped the array of political constituencies and the patterns of conflict in affected societies. Wage labor itself has undergone many vicissitudes, the latest connected with the evolution of more decentralized, flexible, and network-dominated organizations, as expressed in the terms *reorganization, downsizing, outsourcing, flattening the pyramid,* and *teaming.* This has meant that workers must have a more transferable portfolio of skills and must maintain those skills; it has also brought them interorganizational employability, increased capacity for teamwork, serial rather than continuous links to specific organizations, and, as a result, a new kind of career insecurity (Weinart, 2001).

As a final illustration of the transformations associated with increasing complexity, we point to the precipitation of countless new types of politically significant *groups.* Differentiation has been accompanied by diversification. New occupational roles—agricultural laborers, industrial laborers, businessmen, engineers, and other professionals—create new bases for collective interests. Within medicine, new bases of group interest have emerged; in addition to physicians (in all their specialties), we note the emergence of nurses, paramedics, hospital administrators, and patients (even patients with specific afflictions), as well as patients' relatives and loved ones, all of whom constitute actual or potential interest groups. Changing demographic and life-course patterns have yielded political groups based on age and life stage—youth, parents of young children, retired elderly. International migration generates new and politically significant groups organized around cultural identities and loyalties, as well as indigenous groups opposing migration and migrants. Social movements generate new political forces and constituencies, as well as countermovements (pro-choice versus right to life, McCarthyism versus anti-McCarthyism, environmentalism versus business interests). The consolidation of old and the generation of new political groups are endless and impose a group rather than an individual basis for governing polities; in the process this renders political decision-making more complex and contingent.

The Generation and Flux of Social Problems

So much for examples—which could be proliferated—of new conditions generated by the march of social change. A special, overlapping case of this principle is the continuous generation of social *problems,* which demand attention, create conflict, and demand new knowledge to attack them. Again, we will be illustrative:

- Market failures and business cycles generate and aggravate problems of unemployment and poverty.
- New occupational roles generate new forms of occupational risk and stress.
- The increasingly complex couplings of systems such as nuclear power plants, aircraft transport systems, weapons systems, banking systems, and hospitals have led to a preoccupation with catastrophes stemming from systemic failures of operation and coordination [...]. The side effects of new medications constitute a constant source of risk, despite the widespread use of clinical trials.

Two additional postulates may be enunciated. The first is that new technologies generate new and distinctive forms of deviance, which grow into social problems. Thievery is as old as the history of humankind, but the invention and consolidation of complex forms of bookkeeping made possible sophisticated forms such as embezzlement. The invention of ships and their presence on the high seas created the possibility of piracy. Skyjacking is not possible without the presence of aircraft. Automatic tellers create locations for obtaining and exchanging cash, but also provide new sites for robbery, especially at night. The invention of Social Security numbers, credit cards, and systems of computer storage have made identity theft a more serious and endemic crime. A closely related postulate is that any new rule presents new opportunities to circumvent that rule, sometimes generating new crimes and other problems. New tax codes provide new loopholes and opportunities for evasion. Crackdowns on drunken driving, gang activity, and prostitution in one community often move those activities into adjacent communities. Sometimes technology can be used to fight such social problems. Shoplifting as a form of thievery is the child of the institutionalization of stores as economic units. In the future, shoplifting may well disappear with the development of increasingly sophisticated systems of bar-code identification and other security systems. Technologically based security devices have also reduced rates of automobile theft in the past two decades.

The most recent manifestations of the generation of social problems via social change are found in the process of globalization, a multidimensional phenomenon involving the increasing internationalization of production, finance, organizations, regulation, culture, and the polity. Many of the problems generated by globalization are not entirely new, but have become more salient as a result of these processes. We mention a few from a larger catalogue:

- An increase in the environmental problems of exhaustion, degradation, and pollution, generated by the increasing scale of the exploitation of nature, plus the fact that much international activity that generates these problems is still locally and nationally regulated. An array of environmental movements (promoting, e.g., sustainability) has matched the march of environmental problems and generated political conflicts.

- Changing patterns of income distribution among and within nations that have accompanied economic globalization, the most important facets of which are the continued generation of poverty and the social problems that accompany it.

- The international spread of diseases, largely via the increased international movement of persons.

- International sex tourism, general but concentrated in areas such as Eastern Europe, South Asia, and the Philippines. The ease of international travel for customers who can afford the travel and the sex services has aggravated this problem. Few international mechanisms are available for its regulation, which remains primarily national and local in character.

- Resistance to globalization, taking the form of local movements such as locavorism (regional self-sufficiency in food). The revitalization of regional, local, and religious identities and sensitivities—all of which are arrayed, whether correctly or incorrectly, against "globalism"—also creates new forms of political conflict. Especially salient are movements of religious fundamentalism, concentrated in but not exclusive to less-developed regions of the world.

- An apparent homogenization of culture, especially mass culture, through the international influence of a few western (especially American) mass media firms. This includes the spread of values of materialism, consumer culture, and democracy. Student exchange programs, the offering of standard computer courses by universities, and international travel supplement these effects. The effects are equivocal, however, because of continuous local adaptation to and modification of foreign cultural influences and some reverse flows of culture, such as the export of aboriginal art.

- Closely related to global cultural penetration are new patterns of conflict between "globalized" youth culture, influenced by international flows of music, films, and advertisements on the one hand and traditional local and national cultures on the other.

- Increasing diversity of local populations, fostered especially by international migration, referred to variously as hybridization, creolization, diversification, pluralism, and multiculturalism. New political tensions and conflicts are created, especially in regions and cities that have not previously been targets of immigration.

- Intensification of old and creation of new legal problems, "from international [labor contracts], international marriages, adoption of foreign children, legal protection of tourists, and cross-border consumer rights, to civil, political, and social rights of legal and illegal foreign migrant workers, refugees, and asylum seekers" (Santos, 2001: 6281).

- New problems for nation-states, whose fortunes are increasingly influenced by international economic, political, and cultural forces over which they have less control, but for which their domestic governments are often held accountable [...].

All these illustrations establish the basic link between social change and the rise of social problems.

HOW SOCIAL SITUATIONS BECOME SOCIAL PROBLEMS

We cannot be content with any implication of the concept that social problems arise in an automatic way from social changes. In the process of emerging, these problems run a course and produce a dynamic of their own. The essentials of this dynamic must be laid out, in part because they raise issues about the role of knowledge in attacking social problems.

The following can be said to be the necessary ingredients of a social problem, if it is to be characterized as such:

- Empirical assertions that a state of affairs exists. One prerequisite for asserting that white-collar crime or child abuse or homelessness or spouse battering is a social problem is that those who claim it is must demonstrate that it exists, and that it must have a sufficiently strong presence to make it problematical. A social problem is thus necessarily based on empirical assertions. Debates among groups over the reality and validity of these assertions are a further ingredient of a social problem. On the one side, partisans claim a situation is a problem because it exists—and is likely spreading—while on the other side, partisans claim that it does not exist or is incidental or trivial, and therefore a nonproblem. (Already we see the relevance of social-science knowledge, in the form of accurate and independent empirical—including statistical—investigation and interpretation of asserted states of affairs.)

- Closely related, empirical assertions that the posited state of affairs has damaging consequences for some group or for society at large. Sometimes these assertions are explicitly advanced (for example, that those who were abused as children become abusers later; that homelessness breeds crime). Sometimes they are advanced in terms of economic or social costs—the costs of crime, apprehension, and incarceration; the costs of pregnancy and birth outside marriage; the costs of welfare dependency. In other cases, such claims of harm are regarded as self-evident or remain implicit.

- Less obvious, the invocation of certain normative or value standards, which give legitimacy to the claim that a state of affairs is a problem. Those who decried the slavery trade in Great Britain and those abolitionists who decried slavery in the United States did so in the name of humanitarian standards. Without such standards, the empirical assertions about the existence and consequences of slavery would have lost their bite. In some cases, social problems become social problems because the legitimizing standards—not social reality—change. Through much of human history, child labor has been deemed to be a positive because of its contribution to the family economy, especially in agricultural settings. Indeed, child abuse in many settings has also been considered a virtue ("Spare the rod and spoil the child"). It was only in the nineteenth and twentieth centuries, when new standards of humanitarianism were brought to bear in new social settings, that child labor and child abuse came to be regarded as social problems rather than mere social facts or social virtues. In the past half century, the intensification of international concern with the standards of democracy and human rights has given higher salience to phenomena not previously considered as problematic—political disenfranchisement, genocide, torture, the economic exploitation of women, and highly specific practices such as female circumcision. In a word, a social problem expresses a *relationship* between an empirical state of affairs and invoked value standards.

- Additional assumptions that something effective can be done to alleviate the problem—passing and enforcing legislation against it, reforming those responsible for it, devoting resources to its cure. Furthermore, if this component of potential improvement is not present, the problem loses much of its problematical status. Consider stress as an example. Is stress or "being stressed out" a social problem? If it is defined as the product of some incidental biological rhythm, or the collective inability of large numbers of people to cope psychologically, it is likely to be regarded as an individual problem or a nonproblem. If, however, it is regarded as the inhumane consequence of stressful occupational roles or harmful organizational practices, then it is more likely to be defined as a social problem because, it is believed, we can attack its presumed causes. As a general rule, people of conservative political persuasion are more likely to define states of affairs as nonproblems about which little or nothing can be done; those of liberal persuasion are quicker to identify social problems and propose social solutions.

- Causal assumptions and assertions. The element of causality enters the concern with social problems at two junctures. The first is in the diagnosis of the problem: what gave rise to or is responsible for the social problem is known, is asserted to be known, or is assumed. This involves causal knowledge or causal assumptions. Second, claims are made about what will cure or ameliorate the problem. These are causal claims as well, and usually take the form of counterfactual statements [...]: if we intervene in a certain way, we may expect certain results; and if we do not intervene, conditions will continue or worsen.

- Political dimensions. A repeated feature of concern with a social problem is the necessity to persuade others that it is serious and that it should be attacked. Those responsible for dealing with social problems (typically political leaders) have to be persuaded that the problem exists, that it is serious, that it violates values and norms that we hold to be sacred or important, that it urgently demands attention, and that attention to will bring amelioration. The agents in this political process are often "moral entrepreneurs" who promote the social definition of a phenomenon as problematic, preferably outrageous. Religious organizations, voluntary organizations, political lobbies, social movement organizations, and blocs of politicians all play a role in this political process.

- Some or all of the foregoing ingredients are often "prepackaged" in group ideologies, which contain general worldviews, complaints about what is both right and wrong in the world, proposed ways to reform the world, and political strategies and tactics. Ideologies are thus selective and predispose groups to seek out and highlight social problems.

The interplay among all these ingredients determines the identification of social problems, the attention paid to them, and their ultimate fate. Our account contrasts with a more positivistic approach that treats social problems as objective things that appear on the social horizon. It is too much to claim that social problems are made, not born, because part of the determination of social problems is, as we have seen, the appearance of real situations bred by social conditions and social changes. It is, however, important to grasp that social problems also are the results of a social and political "process," above and beyond their status as "products" of objective circumstances. Treating them in this way, moreover, stresses the importance of knowledge claims involved in identifying social problems and in pressing for social reforms.

IMPLICATIONS OF THE FOREGOING FOR THE USABILITY OF KNOWLEDGE

As indicated, this chapter concerns, above all, the broadest consideration of the "demand side" for systematic knowledge in society. The results of the chapter can be summarized in three basic propositions:

1   Knowledge and knowledge approximations are *universal concomitants and requirements* for all decision-making, policy determination, and problem-solving.

2   The appearance of qualitatively new settings for decision-making has increased the need for *systematic, scientifically based knowledge* because the uncertainties and contingencies involved in decision-making are greater.

3   The accumulation of new situations, conditions, and social problems means that knowledge generated in the context of—and relevant to—previous circumstances is continuously being *outmoded,* with new kinds of knowledge required to suit novel contexts.

We conclude this chapter by elaborating on these propositions.

Knowledge, Decision-Making, and Purposeful Action

In the nature of the human condition, some level of cognitive knowledge accompanies all purposeful human action. In most cases, that knowledge is incomplete, consisting of personal experience, hunches, a sense of relevant environmental and situational features, some (often unconscious) sense of purpose, some (also often unconscious) sense of anticipatory and anticipated emotions, and some sense of constraints on one's actions—uncertainties, dangers, barriers, lack of power. It is also true that purposeful action is taken in the context of the actor's larger worldviews, for example, a conviction that larger religious forces are at work, that one should have faith in a deity, or that one is an agent in the world. These general principles apply comparatively and historically.

The Evolving Contemporary Situation

The changes wrought by revolutions and trends in modern history have not altered the general principles of decision-making and purposeful action, but both the *contexts* of that decision-making and the *types of knowledge available* have been revolutionized. The continuing scientific and technological revolutions have meant that much of the requisite knowledge for decision-making is often beyond the expertise of those who decide, who must rely on others for that knowledge and advice based on it. The organizational revolution has meant that decisions are made in more specialized contexts and must take account of more and different kinds of actors. The environments of organizations have also become more tenuous with the appearance of other significant organizations and new constituencies. The proliferation of politically significant groups has rendered the life of political and civil authorities more complex, both in maintaining their own authority and in dealing with the myriad political issues before them. The globalization revolution assures that many forces lie beyond the traditionally understood environments of actors and organizations. Social problems multiply, and the politics as well as the effectiveness of attempted solutions grow more complex. The signature features of contemporary life are continuing *specialization* and *complexity,* increased *uncertainty* about the environment in which decisions are made, and, derivatively, a greater degree of unknown *risks*. Among the needs generated by these conditions is the requirement for new knowledge of many sorts—about what has created the issue at hand, which factors to take into account, whose cooperation to secure, how to contend with competitors and enemies, and the consequences of decisions, once made, for all strategies crafted to deal with those consequences in the future.

The Behavioral and Social Sciences and the Generation of Knowledge

Two further postulates inform our understanding of the relations between knowledge on the one hand and decision-making and problem-solving on the other. The first is that no matter what we say about systematization of knowledge via research and its applications, much of the knowledge available to decision-makers will still be generated from other sources—ad hoc assessments of the immediate environment; personal experience of past successes and failures; general informing assumptions; rules of thumb; hunches; and gut feelings. The second postulate is that decision-making will continue to be based on a combination of types of knowledge, only some of which can be generated by systematic, disciplined, and reliable research; from this we assume that human decision-making will never be a matter of automatic application of valid knowledge—no matter how much that might be hoped for or how many formulae are designed. It will always incomplete and imperfect.

That being said, it is also true that one of the many revolutionary changes of modern history has been the development of the social sciences—those enterprises that are dedicated in large part to generating scientifically reliable and valid knowledge, applicable to many of the arenas in which decision-makers and their organizations are involved. Psychologists specialize in discovering regularities and contingencies in individual behavior, and the social sciences cover the relevant social situations and environments in which decision-makers and their organizations are implicated. The main disciplines concentrate on economic, political, social, and cultural dimensions. History makes use of all these disciplines—among other sources of knowledge—to reveal, interpret, and understand the past. In addition, these sciences produce much knowledge that is *relevant* to decision-making: how to understand the limitations of one's own decision-making and decisions; how actors and groups join in networks and influence one another; how individual decisions aggregate into more general outcomes; how organizations succeed and fail; and how conflicts develop, unfold, remain endemic, or are resolved. Social scientists try to isolate causes, systems of causal relations, feedbacks, and interrelationships. [M]uch of the work of social scientists has been driven by their concern with the very conditions and problems that the contemporary world has generated. The resulting knowledge is the "supply side" of the knowledge-decision-action relationship. However, as we will also demonstrate, social scientists have been preoccupied with things other than applying knowledge. As a result, much of the knowledge they produce is neither relevant nor applicable. This circumstance produces the irregularity of fit between much knowledge produced and the requirements of those implicated in decision-making worlds.

Outmoding and Catch-Up

We conclude this chapter by describing a constant dynamic between knowledge produced and knowledge required, a dynamic that produces simultaneously (1) the need for new knowledge generated by the appearance of new social conditions and new social problems; and (2) the selective but continuous outmoding of existing social-science knowledge. We demonstrate by a few examples:

- By the mid-twentieth century, a body of knowledge about labor and labor management relations was generated by economists, sociologists, industrial psychologists, students of management, and historians. Much of this knowledge assumed the presence of labor unions, the dominance of business unionism as a major form of interaction, the importance of strikes, the effect of unions on wages and productivity, and the legal and contractual aspects of labor-management practices such as mediation and arbitration. Much relevant knowledge was generated. In the past several decades, a number of decisive institutional changes have transpired: expansion of service occupations, only some of which are organized along traditional industrial-union lines, and some of which are not organized at all; increases in female labor-force participation and in immigrant labor; decline of union-member numbers as well as the decline of the economic and political power of unions; the decline of the strike as a weapon; new patterns of relations between management and labor resulting from the penetration of multinational corporations into other countries; outsourcing and downsizing; and the dispersion of labor through the development of virtual corporations (Shostak, 1998). Most of these developments were neither evident nor foreseen in the industrial relations era. Yet whole new lines of social-scientific inquiry and knowledge are required to understand and fashion policies relating to the new and different patterns of labor-management relations.

- One subfield of economics, known as location theory, has come from the work of regional economists and economic geographers. It is the study of the optimum market location of firms in different industries and the actual patterns of location that emerge as a result of business decisions. Traditional factors in determining industrial location, such as distance from the supply of raw materials, the location of producers of needed resources, proximity to markets, and the location of available labor, were combined—sometimes in mathematical form—to determine the optimal location of a firm (see Lösch, 1954). Residential location of workers was calculated to be based on a tradeoff between living near work (high housing, low transportation costs) and living far from work (low housing, high transportation costs). The determination of location on the basis of these primarily spatial factors, however, no matter how finely developed and sophisticated, has been rendered inadequate in some respects by changing patterns of commerce and distribution. Among these are the worldwide dispersion of markets through globalization, the tendencies to decentralize firms in the interests of efficiency, the rise of the "virtual firm," e-commerce of all forms (which defy space in fundamental ways), and the increasing possibility of a new pattern of cottage industries wherein workers spend most of their time working at home and maintaining electronic communication with headquarters. These developments appear to have simultaneously redefined space and given firms greater discretion with respect to location. Furthermore, they dictate the need for new knowledge about how to take these changes into account in decisions to locate.

- The appearance and development of the HIV/AIDS epidemic since the 1980s obviously required new biological and medical knowledge about means of transmission, the deterioration of the immune system, and the discovery of means to counter the effects of the virus. In addition, new psychological and social knowledge is evidently required to understand, treat, and perhaps someday cure the disease. This includes better knowledge of the social relationships and networks involved in both homosexual and heterosexual contacts; knowledge of the dynamics of needle using and needle sharing in the world of drugs; understanding effective means to minimize risk; understanding public attitudes toward victims of HIV/AIDS; and comparative-historical knowledge about similar patterns of stigmatization of those thought to be polluted. Existing knowledge does not provide adequate answers.

- In an earlier era, dispersion of families in work roles and through increased migration was thought to constitute a threat to, if not the demise of, extended kinship in modern societies (Ogburn and Nimkoff, 1955). Studies by social scientists, however, took the edge off these gloomy predictions by pointing out that changes in transportation and communication (plane travel, the telephone, efficient ways to transfer money) operated to counter these geographical tendencies and permit new, albeit different, forms of relationships among extended kin, despite their geographical dispersion [...]. More recently, radical changes in communication, especially e-mail, the cellular phone, and text messaging, have arrived on the scene. These have implications for more frequent but more superficial contact among intimates, new patterns of cliquing among the young, new ways to assert and achieve status, and more secretive gossiping and teenage scapegoating, to say nothing about new possibilities for psychological dependency on the gadgetry among those so inclined [...]. We do not have adequate knowledge about the psychological and social dimensions of these new technologies, and new knowledge is required.

- Terrorism is not new in the world, as historians of the phenomenon have reminded us (Laqueur, 1977). However, its internationalization since the 1960s has created a political situation that commands the attention of many nations, if not the entire world. International terrorism is a form of war, but the understanding and rules of the game of traditional wars between armies and nations do not apply. Nor do the principles involved in understanding crime, political protest, or even guerrilla warfare. International terrorism is a mix of these, but not any single one of them. As such, this phenomenon has generated the need for new knowledge regarding recruitment, the role of extremist ideologies, the maintenance of secrecy, the possible use of weapons of mass destruction, the psychology and politics of mass fear, and the multiplicity of psychological, social, and political reactions to terrorist attacks. Some of this knowledge is beginning to appear, but it is far from adequate and certainly has not informed the decision-making of those responsible for dealing with terrorism, who have tended to rely on technological solutions and ad hoc political responses (Smelser, 2007).

- In the previous section, we observed that the appearance of any social problem—or any situation argued to be a social problem—involves a number of claims of empirical evidence and causation, relating to how and where the problem came about, who is responsible for it, what might be done about it, and what the effects of reform efforts might be. Both advocates and opponents of reform advance conflicting empirical claims, and, in so doing, "invent" their own psychological and social theories. It is apparent, moreover, that such knowledge claims touch on and overlap with social-science studies of conflict, social movements, and social change. Social scientists can contribute by studying the formation and attempted solutions of social problems, estimating their extent and salience, and identifying and establishing their imputed causal relations, thus playing the roles of more nearly neutral arbiters of these empirical claims. Yet this process, too, involves continuing research and the production of new knowledge.

  This interplay among social conditions, social change, social problems, and social knowledge has been a recurring topic in this volume. In concluding this discussion, we may venture two general observations.

1   One characteristic of the social sciences is that they are forever catching up to social changes in the world. New situations require new knowledge and new ways of bringing that knowledge to bear.

2   Early and periodically in the development of the social sciences, it was assumed and argued that they could establish general "laws" of psychology (e.g., learning), economics (the law of supply and demand), politics (the law of oligarchy), and society (social evolution) that were analogous to the laws of the natural and life sciences [...]. The history of investigation in these fields has revealed the naïveté of these expectations, and has led to more modest views. It can still be claimed that some processes, mechanisms, and patterns of behavior and social organization are general in their application, but it is also true that new parameters for those generalizations are forever evolving and creating needs to qualify and extend them accordingly. We are thus dealing with sciences that are simultaneously general and situationally specific.

These two observations point directly to the "supply side" of the production of knowledge, and invite inquiry into social sciences themselves, with special emphasis on modes of inquiry, their internal dynamics, and the distinctive kinds of usable and nonusable knowledge they produce.

REFERENCES

Ashton, Thomas S. 1969. *The Industrial Revolution, 1760–1830*. London: Oxford University Press.

Dalton, George. 1971. *Economic Anthropology and Development: Essays in Tribal and Peasant Economies*. New York: Basic Books.

Durkheim, Émile. 1997. [1893] *The Division of Labor in Society*. Trans. W. D. Halls, with an introduction by Lewis A. Coser. New York: Free Press.

Firth, Raymond. 1971. *Elements of Social Organization,* 3rd ed. London: Tavistock Publications.

Kroeber, Alfred Louis. 1944. *Configurations of Culture Growth*. Berkeley: University of California Press.

Kurth, James R. 2001. Globalization: Political Aspects. In *International Encyclopedia of the Social and Behavioral Sciences,* eds. Neil J. Smelser and Paul B. Baltes. Oxford: Elsevier. Vol. 9, 6284–87.

Laqueur, Walter. 1977. *Terrorism*. London: Weidenfeld and Nicolson.

Lösch, August. 1954. *The Economics of Location*. New Haven, CT: Yale University Press.

Malinowski, Bronislaw. 1922. *Argonauts of the Western Pacific*. London: Routledge and Kegan Paul.

Ogburn, William F., and Meyer F. Nimkoff. 1955. *Technology and the Changing Family*. Boston: Houghton Mifflin.

Santos, Boaventura de Sousa. 2001. Globalization: Legal Aspects. In *International Encyclopedia of the Social and Behavioral Sciences,* eds. Neil J. Smelser and Paul B. Baltes. Oxford: Elsevier. Vol. 9, 6277–84.

Shostak, Arthur B. 1998. Virtual Corporations and American Labor Unions: So Many Unknowns, So Much Potential. In *The Virtual Workplace,* eds. Magid Igbaria and Margaret Tan. Hershey, PA: Idea Group Publishing, 360–67.

Simon, Herbert A. 2001. Rationality in Society. In *International Encyclopedia of the Social and Behavioral Sciences*, eds. Neil J. Smelser and Paul B. Baltes. Oxford: Elsevier. Vol. 19, 12782–86.

Smelser, Neil J. 2007. *The Faces of Terrorism: Social and Psychological Dimensions*. Princeton: Princeton University Press.

——. 2010 *Reflections on the University of California: From the Free Speech Movement to a Global University*. Berkeley: University of California Press.

Smith, Adam. 1937. [1776] *The Wealth of Nations*. New York: Modern Library.

Tilley, Helley, with Robert J. Gordon. 2007. *Ordering Africa: Anthropology, European Imperialism, and the Politics of Knowledge*. Manchester: Manchester University Press.

Toynbee, Arnold J. 1935. *A Study of History*. London: Oxford University Press.

Wallerstein, Immanuel. 1974. *The Modern World System*. New York: Academic Press.

Weinart, A. B. 2001. Career Development, Psychology of. In *International Encyclopedia of the Social and Behavioral Sciences*, eds. Neil J. Smelser and Paul B. Baltes. Oxford: Elsevier. Vol. 3, 1471–76.

SUMMARY

Through examining what American citizens and residents consider important social problems we are able to learn a great deal about the nature of social problems, though over time the degree to which social problems are considered important is quite dynamic. Recently health care, the economy, the government, climate change, immigration, and race relations are the issues that are most consistently cited as being important. We've also seen that social factors like political affiliation, race, and age also affect what sorts of things are seen as important social issues. These factors as well as cultural norms, social structures, and the kind of governments that exist within a given society also effect the manner in which solutions to social problems are conceived of and implemented. Lastly, we have established that social problems themselves are social constructions and that the scope of a social problem, definitions and meanings of a social problem, and whether something is labeled as a social problem is contested in society.

Image Credits

Fig. 3.1: Source: https://www.pewresearch.org/fact-tank/2019/02/04/state-of-the-union-2019-how-americans-see-major-national-issues/.
Fig. 3.2: Source: https://www.people-press.org/2018/10/15/little-partisan-agreement-on-the-pressing-problems-facing-the-u-s/.
Fig. 3.3: Source: https://www.pewsocialtrends.org/2019/02/20/most-u-s-teens-see-anxiety-and-depression-as-a-major-problem-among-their-peers/psdt_02-20-19_teens-00-00/.
Fig. 3.4: Source: https://www.pewsocialtrends.org/2019/02/20/most-u-s-teens-see-anxiety-and-depression-as-a-major-problem-among-their-peers/psdt_02-20-19_teens-00-08/.
Fig. 3.5: Source: https://www.pewsocialtrends.org/2019/02/20/most-u-s-teens-see-anxiety-and-depression-as-a-major-problem-among-their-peers/.
Fig. 3.6: Source: https://news.gallup.com/poll/246800/record-high-name-government-important-problem.aspx.
Fig. 3.7: Source: https://news.gallup.com/poll/1675/most-important-problem.aspx.
Fig. 3.8: Source: https://news.gallup.com/poll/1675/most-important-problem.aspx.

CHAPTER 4

Race

IN AMERICA RACE has played a distinctively significant part in the development of the country and is uniquely important in understanding both the history of America and contemporary America. It is imbued in politics, can be controversial, and can be quite uncomfortable to talk about or discuss. In fact, there are many pressures not to directly discuss race or even make direct appeals to race when talking about things like inequality (*see colorblindness*). However, as will be discussed in this chapter, race is one of (and arguably the most) impactful aspect of American society. In fact, almost every important metric social scientists use to analyze society correlates with race. From living arrangements, to income, to public opinion a wide variety of social factors show a racial component that sociologists must factor in.

Particularly, race holds a unique place in American sociology in the amount of study that was devoted to it, as it was one of the earliest areas of formal study and one of the first academic arenas to include prominent black voices (e.g., W.E.B. Du Bois). It has remained an integral part of sociological, and many disciplines like critical race theory, and African American studies have sprung at least in part from this lineage tree.

WHAT IS RACE?

In short, race is a social construct based around physical features. Ideas about race, as well as a standardized definition, are fluid over time and in different societies. Sociologists have sought, often with input from biology and other disciplines, to define race as it relates to its operation in human society(ies). Many of these definitions are societally or culturally specific, while some are broader in nature.

Classical Definitions
The most influential and cited definitions of race in contemporary times mention that race does indeed often point to perceived physical differences, but also point to the idea that race is socially constructed. For instance, The American Sociological

Association says that "'[r]ace' refers to physical differences that groups and cultures consider socially significant."[1]

The Conservation of Races

by W. E. B. Du Bois

The American Negro has always felt an intense personal interest in discussions as to the origins and destinies of races: primarily because back of most discussion of race with which he is familiar, have lurked certain assumptions as to his natural abilities, as to his political, intellectual and moral status, which he felt were wrong. He has, consequently, been led to deprecate and minimize race distinctions, to believe intensely that out of one blood God created all nations, and to speak of human brotherhood as though it were the possibility of an already dawning to-morrow.

Nevertheless, in our calmer moments we must acknowledge that human beings are divided into races; that in this country the two most extreme types of the world's races have met, and the resulting problem as to the future relations of these types is not only of intense and living interest to us, but forms an epoch in the history of mankind.

It is necessary, therefore, in planning our movements, in guiding our future development, that at times we rise above the pressing, but smaller questions of separate schools and cars, wage discrimination and lynch law, to survey the whole question of race in human philosophy and to lay, on a basis of broad knowledge and careful insight, those large lines of policy and higher ideals which may form our guiding lines and boundaries in the practical difficulties of every day. For it is certain that all human striving must recognize the hard limits of natural law, and that any striving, no matter how intense and earnest, which is against the constitution of the world, is vain. The question, then, which we must seriously consider is this: What is the real meaning of Race; what has, in the past, been the law of race development, and what lessons has the past history of race development to teach the rising Negro people?

When we thus come to inquire into the essential difference of races we find it hard to come at once to any definite conclusion. Many criteria of race differences have in the past been proposed, as color, hair, cranial measurements and language. And manifestly, in each of these respects, human beings differ widely. They vary in

---

[1] "Race and Ethnicity," American Sociological Assocation, 2020, http://www.asanet.org/topics/race-and-ethnicity.

W. E. B. DuBois, "The Conservation of Races," *Theories of Race and Racism: A Reader.* Copyright © 2000 by Taylor & Francis Group. Reprinted with permission.

color, for instance, from the marble-like pallor of the Scandinavian to the rich, dark brown of the Zulu, passing by the creamy Slav, the yellow Chinese, the light brown Sicilian and the brown Egyptian. Men vary, too, in the texture of hair from the obstinately straight hair of the Chinese to the obstinately tufted and frizzled hair of the Bushman. In measurement of heads, again, men vary; from the broad-headed Tartar to the medium-headed European and the narrow-headed Hottentot; or, again in language, from the highly-inflected roman tongue to the monosyllabic Chinese. All these physical characteristics are patent enough, and if they agreed with each other it would be very easy to classify mankind. Unfortunately for scientists, however, these criteria of race are most exasperatingly intermingled. Color does not agree with texture of hair, for many of the dark races have straight hair; nor does color agree with the breadth of the head, for the yellow Tartar has a broader head than the German; nor, again, has the science of language as yet succeeded in clearing up the relative authority of these various and contradictory criteria. The final word of science, so far, is that we have at least two, perhaps three, great families of human beings—the whites and Negroes, possibly the yellow race. That other races have arisen from the intermingling of the blood of these two. This broad division of the world's races which men like Huxley and Raetzel have introduced as more nearly true than the old five-race scheme of Blumenbach, is nothing more than an acknowledgement that, so far as purely physical characteristics are concerned, the differences between men do not explain all the differences of their history. It declares, as Darwin himself said, that great as is the physical unlikeness of the various races of men their likenesses are greater, and upon this rests the whole scientific doctrine of Human Brotherhood.

Although the wonderful developments of human history teach that the grosser physical differences of color, hair and bone go but a short way toward explaining the different roles which groups of men have played in Human Progress, yet there are differences—subtle, delicate and elusive, though they may be—which have silently but definitely separated men into groups. While these subtle forces have generally followed the natural cleavage of common blood, descent and physical peculiarities, they have at other times swept across and ignored these. At all times, however, they have divided human beings into races, which, while they perhaps transcend scientific definition, nevertheless, are clearly defined to the eye of the Historian and Sociologist.

If this be true, then the history of the world is the history, not of individuals, but of groups, not of nations, but of races, and he who ignores or seeks to override the race idea in human history ignores and overrides the central thought of all history. What, then, is a race? It is a vast family of human beings, generally of common blood and language, always of common history, traditions and impulses, who are both voluntarily and involuntarily striving together for the accomplishment of certain more or less vividly conceived ideals of life.

Turning to real history, there can be no doubt, first, as to the widespread, nay, universal, prevalence of the race idea, the race spirit, the race ideal, and as to its efficiency as the vastest and most ingenious invention for human progress. We, who have been reared and trained under the individualistic philosophy of the Declaration of Independence and the laisser-faire [sic] philosophy of Adam Smith, are loath to see and loath to acknowledge this patent fact of human history. We see the Pharaohs, Caesars, Toussaints and Napoleons of history and forget the vast races of which they were but epitomized expressions. We are apt to think in our American impatience, that while it may have been true in the past that closed race groups made history, that here in conglomerate America nous avons changer tout cela—we have changed all that, and have no need of this ancient instrument of progress. This assumption of which the Negro people are especially fond, cannot be established by a careful consideration of history.

We find upon the world's stage today eight distinctly differentiated races, in the sense in which History tells us the word must be used. They are, the Slavs of eastern Europe, the Teutons of middle Europe, the English of Great Britain and America, the Romance nations of Southern and Western Europe, the Negroes of Africa and America, the Semitic people of Western Asia and Northern Africa, the Hindoos of Central Asia and the Mongolians of Eastern Asia. There are, of course, other minor race groups, as the American Indians, the Esquimaux and the South Sea Islanders; these larger races, too, are far from homogeneous; the Slav includes the Czech, the Magyar, the Pole and the Russian; the Teuton includes the German, the Scandinavian and the Dutch; the English include the Scotch, the Irish and the conglomerate American. Under Romance nations the widely-differing Frenchman, Italian, Sicilian and Spaniard are comprehended. The term Negro is, perhaps, the most indefinite of all, combining the Mulattoes and Zamboes of America and the Egyptians, Bantus and Bushmen of Africa. Among the Hindoos are traces of widely differing nations, while the great Chinese, Tartar, Corean and Japanese families fall under the one designation—Mongolian.

The question now is: What is the real distinction between these nations? Is it the physical differences of blood, color and cranial measurements? Certainly we must all acknowledge that physical differences play a great part, and that, with wide exceptions and qualifications, these eight great races of to-day follow the cleavage of physical race distinctions; the English and Teuton represent the white variety of mankind; the Mongolian, the yellow; the Negroes, the black. Between these are many crosses and mixtures, where Mongolian and Teuton have blended into the Slav, and other mixtures have produced the Romance nations and the Semites. But while race differences have followed mainly physical race lines, yet no mere physical distinctions would really define or explain the deeper differences—the cohesiveness and continuity of these groups. The deeper differences are spiritual, psychical, differences—undoubtedly based on the physical, but infinitely transcending them. The forces that bind together the Teuton nations are, then, first, their race identity and common blood; secondly, and more important, a common history, common laws and religion, similar habits of thought and a conscious striving together for certain ideals of life. The whole process which has brought about these race differentiations has been a growth, and the great characteristic of this growth has been the differentiation of spiritual and mental differences between great races of mankind and the integration of physical differences.

The age of nomadic tribes of closely related individuals represents the maximum of physical differences. They were practically vast families, and there were as many groups as families. As the families came together to form cities the physical differences lessened, purity of blood was replaced by the requirement of comicile, and all who lived within the city bound became gradually to be regarded as members of the group; i.e., there was a slight and slow breaking down of physical barriers. This, however, was accompanied by an increase of the spiritual and social differences between cities. This city became husbandmen, this, merchant, another warriors, and so on. The ideals of life for which the different cities struggled were different. When at last cities began to coalesce into nations there was another breaking down of barriers which separated groups of men. The larger and broader differences of color, hair and physical proportions were not by any means ignored, but myriads of minor differences disappeared, and the sociological and historical races of men began to approximate the present division of races as indicated by physical researches. At the same time the spiritual and physical differences of race groups which constituted the nations became deep and decisive. The English nation stood for constitutional liberty and commercial freedom; the German nation for science and philosophy; the Romance nations stood for literature and art, and the other race groups are striving, each in its own way, to develop for civilization its particular message, its particular ideal, which shall help to guide the world nearer and nearer that perfection of human life for which we all long, that "one far off Divine event."

This has been the function of race differences up to the present time. What shall be its function in the future? Manifestly some of the great races of today—particularly the Negro race—have not as yet given to civilization the full spiritual message which they are capable of giving. I will not say that the Negro race has yet given no message to the world, for it is still a mooted question among scientists as to just how far Egyptian civilization was Negro in its origin; if it was not wholly Negro, it was certainly very closely allied. Be that as it may, however, the fact still remains that the full, complete Negro message of the whole Negro race has not as yet been given to the world: that the messages and ideal of the yellow race have not been completed, and that the striving of the mighty Slavs has but begun. The question is, then: How shall this message be delivered; how shall these various ideals be realized? The answer is plain: By the development of these race groups, not as individuals, but as races. For the development of Japanese genius, Japanese literature and art, Japanese spirit, only Japanese, bound and welded together, Japanese inspired by one vast ideal, can work out in its fullness the wonderful message which Japan has for the nations of the earth. For the development of Negro genius, of Negro literature and art, of Negro spirit, only Negroes bound and welded together, Negroes inspired by one vast ideal, can work out in its fullness the great message we have for humanity. We cannot reverse history; we are subject to the same natural laws as other races and if the Negro is ever to be a factor in the world's history—if among the gaily-colored banners that deck the broad ramparts of civilization is to hang one uncompromising black, then it must be placed there by black hands, fashioned by black heads and hallowed by the travail of 200,000,000 black hearts beating in one glad song of jubilee.

For this reason, the advance guard of the Negro people—the 8,000,000 people of Negro blood in the United States of America—must soon come to realize that if they are to take their just place in the van of Pan-Negroism, then their destiny is not absorption by the white Americans. That if in America it is to be proven for the first time in the modern world that not only Negroes are capable of evolving individual men like Toussaint, the Saviour, but are a nation stored with wonderful possibilities of culture, then their destiny is not a servile imitation of Anglo-Saxon culture, but a stalwart originality which shall unswervingly follow Negro ideals.

It may, however, be objected here that the situation of our race in America renders this attitude impossible; that our sole hope of salvation lies in our being able to lose our race identity in the commingled blood of the nation; and that any other course would merely increase the friction of races which we call race prejudice, and against which we have so long and so earnestly fought.

Here, then, is the dilemma, and it is puzzling one, I admit. No Negro who has given earnest thought to the situation of his people in America has failed, at some time in life, to find himself at these cross-roads; has failed to ask himself at some time: What, after all, am I? Am I an American or am I a Negro? Can I be both? Or is it my duty to cease to be a Negro as soon as possible and be an American? If I strive as a Negro, am I not perpetuating the very cleft that threatens and separates Black and White America? Is not my only possible practical aim the subduction of all that is Negro in me to the American? Does my black blood place upon me any more obligation to assert my nationality than German, or Irish or Italian blood would?

It is such incessant self-questioning and the hesitation that arises from it, that is making the present period a time of vacillation and contradiction for the American Negro; combined race action is stifled, race responsibility is shirked, race enterprises languish, and the best blood, the best talent, the best energy of the Negro people cannot be marshalled to do the bidding of the race. They stand back to make room for every rascal and demagogue who chooses to cloak his selfish deviltry under the veil of race pride.

Is this right? Is it rational? Is it good policy? Have we in America a distinct mission as a race—a distinct sphere of action and an opportunity for race development, or is self-obliteration the highest end to which Negro blood dare aspire?

If we carefully consider what race prejudice really is, we find it, historically, to be nothing but the friction between different groups of people; it is the difference in aim, in feeling, in ideals of two different races; if, now, this difference exists touching territory, laws, language, or even religion, it is manifest that these people cannot live in the same territory without fatal collision; but if, on the other hand, there is substantial agreement in laws, language and religion; if there is a satisfactory adjustment of economic life, then there is no reason why, in the same country and on the same street, two or three great national ideals might not thrive and develop, that men of different races might not strive together for their race ideals as well, perhaps even better, than in isolation. Here, it seems to me, is the reading of the riddle that puzzles so many of us. We are Americans, not only by birth and by citizenship, but by our political ideals, our language, our religion. Farther than that, our Americanism does not go. At that point, we are Negroes, members of a vast historic race that from the very dawn of creation has slept, but half awakening in the dark forests of its African fatherland. We are the first fruits of this new nation, the harbinger of that black to-morrow which is yet destined to soften the whiteness of the Teutonic to-day. We are that people whose subtle sense of song has given America its only American music, its only American fairy tales, its only touch of pathos and humor amid its mad money-getting plutocracy. As such, it is our duty to conserve our physical powers, our intellectual endowments, our spiritual ideals; as a race we must strive by race organization, by race solidarity, by race unity to the realization of that broader humanity which freely recognizes differences in men, but sternly deprecates inequality in their opportunities of development.

For the accomplishment of these ends we need race organizations: Negro colleges, Negro newspapers, Negro business organizations, a Negro school of literature and art, and an intellectual clearing house, for all these products of the Negro mind, which we may call a Negro Academy. Not only is all this necessary for positive advance, it is absolutely imperative for negative defense. Let us not deceive ourselves at our situation in this country. Weighted with a heritage of moral iniquity from our past history, hard pressed in the economic world by foreign immigrants and native prejudice, hated here, despised there and pitied everywhere; our one haven of refuge is ourselves, and but one means of advance, our own belief in our great destiny, our own implicit trust in our ability and worth. There is no power under God's high heaven that can stop the advance of eight thousand thousand honest, earnest, inspired and united people. But—and here is the rub—they must be honest, fearlessly criticizing their own faults, zealously correcting them; they must be earnest. No people that laughs at itself, and ridicules itself, and washes to God it was anything but itself ever wrote its name in history; it must be inspired with the Divine faith of our black mothers, that out of the blood and dust of battle will march a victorious host, a mighty nation, a peculiar people, to speak to the nations of earth a Divine truth that shall make them free. And such a people must be united; not merely united for the organized theft of political spoils, not united to disgrace religion with whoremongers and wardheelers; not united merely to protest and pass resolutions, but united to stop the ravages of consumption among the Negro people, united to keep black boys from loafing, gambling and crime; united to guard the purity of black women and to reduce that vast army of black prostitutes that is today marching to hell; and united in serious organizations, to determine by careful conference and thoughtful interchange of opinion the broad lines of policy and action for the American Negro. This, is the reason for being which the American Negro Academy has. It aims at once to be the epitome and expression of the intellect of the black-blooded people of America, the exponent of the race ideals of one of the world's great races. As such, the Academy must, if successful, be

  (a) Representative in character.
  (b) Impartial in conduct.
  (c) Firm in leadership.

It must be representative in character; not in that it represents all interests or all factions, but in that it seeks to comprise something of the best thought, the most unselfish striving and the highest ideals. There are scattered in forgotten nooks and corners throughout the land, Negroes of some considerable training, of high minds, and high motives, who are unknown to their fellows, who exert far too little influence. These the Negro Academy should strive to bring into touch with each other and to give them a common mouthpiece.

The Academy should be impartial in conduct; while it aims to exalt the people it should aim to do so by truth—not by lies, by honesty—not by flattery. It should continually impress the fact upon the Negro people that they must not expect to have things done for them—they MUST DO FOR THEMSELVES; that they have on their hands a vast work of self-reformation to do, and that a little less complaint and whining, and a little more dogged work and manly striving would do us more credit and benefit than a thousand Force or Civil Rights bills.

Finally, the American Negro Academy must point out a practical path of advance to the Negro people; there lie before every Negro today hundreds of questions of policy and right which must be settled and which each one settles now, not in accordance with any rule, but by impulse or individual preference; for instance: What should be the attitude of Negroes toward the educational qualification for voters? What should be our attitude toward separate schools? How should we meet discriminations on railways and in hotels? Such questions need not so much specific answers for each part as a general expression of policy, and nobody should be better fitted to announce such a policy than a representative honest Negro Academy.

All this, however, must come in time after careful organization and long conference. The immediate work before us should be practical and have direct bearing upon the situation of the Negro. The historical work of collecting the laws of the United States and of the various States of the Union with regard to the Negro is a work of such magnitude and importance that no body but one like this could think of undertaking it. If we could accomplish that one task we would justify our existence.

In the field of Sociology an appalling work lies before us. First, we must unflinchingly and bravely face the truth, not with apologies, but with solemn earnestness. The Negro Academy ought to sound a note of warning that would echo in every black cabin in the land: Unless we conquer our present vices they will conquer us; we are diseased, we are developing criminal tendencies, and an alarmingly large percentage of our men and women are sexually impure. The Negro Academy should stand and proclaim this over the housetops, crying with Garrison: I will not equivocate, I will not retreat a single inch, and I will be heard. The Academy should seek to gather about it the talented, unselfish men, the pure and noble-minded women, to fight an army of devils that disgraces our manhood and our womanhood. There does not stand today upon God's earth a race more capable in muscle, in intellect, in morals, than the American Negro, if he will bend his energies in the right direction; if he will

Burst his birth's invidious bar

And grasp the skirts of happy chance, And breast the blows of circumstance, And grapple with his evil star.

In science and morals, I have indicated two fields of work for the Academy. Finally, in practical policy, I wish to suggest the following Academy Creed:

1   We believe that the Negro people, as a race, have a contribution to make to civilization and humanity, which no other race can make.

2 We believe it the duty of the Americans of Negro descent, as a body, to maintain their race identity until this mission of the Negro people is accomplished and the ideal of human brotherhood has become a practical possibility.

3 We believe that, unless modern civilization is a failure, it is entirely feasible and practicable for two races in such essential political, economic and religious harmony as the white and colored people of America, to develop side by side in peace and mutual happiness, the peculiar contribution which each has to make to the culture of their common country.

4 As a means to this end we advocate, not such social equality between these races as would disregard human likes and dislikes, but such a social equilibrium as would, throughout all the complicated relations of life, give due and just consideration to culture, ability, and moral worth whether they be found under white or black skins

5 We believe that the first and greatest step toward the settlement of the present friction between the races—commonly called the Negro problem—lies in the correction of the immorality, crime and laziness among the Negroes themselves, which still remains as a heritage from slavery. We believe that only earnest and long continued efforts on our own part can cure these social ills.

6 We believe that the second great step toward a better adjustment of the relations between the races, should be a more impartial selection of ability in the economic and intellectual world, and a greater respect for personal liberty and worth, regardless of race. We believe that only earnest efforts on the part of the white people of this country will bring much needed reform in these matters.

7 On the basis of the foregoing declaration, and firmly believing in our high destiny, we, as American Negroes, are resolved to strive in every honorable way for the realization of the best and highest aims, for the development of strong manhood and pure womanhood, and for the rearing of a race ideal in America and Africa, to the glory of God and the uplifting of the Negro people.

DISCUSSION QUESTIONS

1 How does Du Bois characterize African Americans' response to the question of race in his day? And what response does he advocate in its place? Why?

2 How does the author define race, and how does this differ from commonplace or even not-so-commonplace definitions of race today?

3 What is the rationale for the American Negro Academy, and how does that rationale and the American Negro Academy's mission mesh with recent arguments for and against affirmative action policies?

Racial Formation

There are literally hundreds of definitions of race and/or different frameworks from which to analyze race since Du Bois began writing on the subject. And certainly, along the way, we've had several paradigm shifts in how race is viewed as well as challenges and changes to racial categories. One of the most important recent developments in sociology is the concept of *racial formation*, put forward by Michael Omni and Howard Winant.

Reading 4.2.

Racial Formation: Understanding Race and Racism in the Post-Civil Rights Era

by Michael Omi and Howard Winant

In 1982–83, Susie Guillory Phipps unsuccessfully sued the Louisiana Bureau of Vital Records to change her racial classification from black to white. The descendent of an 18th century white planter and a black slave, Phipps was designated "black" in her birth certificate in accordance with a 1970 state law which declared anyone with at least 1/32nd "Negro blood" to be black.

The Phipps case raised intriguing questions about the concept of race, its meaning in contemporary society, and its use (and abuse) in public policy. Assistant Attorney General Ron Davis defended the law by pointing out that some type of racial classification was necessary to comply with federal record-keeping requirements and to facilitate programs for the prevention of genetic diseases. Phipps's attorney, Brian Begue, argued that the assignment of racial categories on birth certificates was unconstitutional and that the 1/32nd designation was inaccurate. He called on a retired Tulane University professor who cited research indicating that most Louisiana whites have at least 1/20th "Negro" ancestry.

In the end, Phipps lost. The court upheld the state's right to classify and quantify racial identity.[1]

Phipps's problematic racial identity, and her effort to resolve it through state action, is in many ways a parable of America's unsolved racial dilemma. It illustrates the difficulties of defining race and assigning individuals or groups to racial categories. It shows how the racial legacies of the past—slavery and bigotry—continue to shape the present. It reveals both the deep involvement of the state in the organization and interpretation of race, and the inadequacy of state institutions to carry out these functions. It demonstrates how deeply Americans both as individuals and as a civilization are shaped, and indeed haunted, by race.

Having lived her whole life thinking that she was white, Phipps suddenly discovers that by legal definition she is not. In U.S. society, such an event is indeed catastrophic.[2] But if she is not white, of what race is she? The state claims that she is black, based on its rules of classification,[3] and another state agency, the court, up-

Michael Omi and Howard Winant, "Racial Formation: Understanding Race and Racism In the Post-Civil Rights Era," *Racial Formation in the United States: From the 1960s to the 1990s.* Copyright © 1994 by Taylor & Francis Group. Reprinted with permission.

holds this judgment. Despite the classificatory standards that have imposed an either-or logic on racial identity, Phipps will not in fact "change color." Unlike what would have happened during slavery times if one's claim to whiteness was successfully challenged, we can assume that despite the outcome of her legal challenge, Phipps will remain in most of the social relationships she had occupied before the trial. Her socialization, her familial and friendship networks, her cultural orientation, will not change. She will simply have to wrestle with her newly acquired "hybridized" condition. She will have to confront the "other" within.

The designation of racial categories and the assignment of race is no simple task. For centuries, this question has precipitated intense debates and conflicts, particularly in the U.S.—disputes over natural and legal rights, over the distribution of resources, and indeed, over who shall live and who shall die.

A crucial dimension of the Phipps case is that it illustrates the inadequacy of claims that race is a mere matter of variations in human physiognomy, that it is simply a matter of skin "color." But if race cannot be understood in this manner, how can it be understood? We cannot fully hope to address this topic—no less than the meaning of race, its role in society, and the forces that shape it—in one chapter, nor indeed in one book. Our goal in this chapter, however, is far from modest: we wish to offer at least the outlines of a theory of race and racism.

WHAT IS RACE?

There is a continuous temptation to think of race as an essence, as something fixed, concrete and objective. And there is also an opposite temptation: to imagine race as a mere illusion, a purely ideological construct that some ideal non-racist social order would eliminate. It is necessary to challenge both these positions, to disrupt and reframe the rigid and bipolar manner in which they are posed and debated, and to transcend the presumably irreconcilable relationship between them.

The effort must be made to understand race as an unstable and "decentered" complex of social meanings constantly being transformed by political struggle. With this in mind, let us propose a definition: race is a concept that signifies and symbolizes social conflicts and interests by referring to different types of human bodies. Although the concept of race invokes biologically-based human characteristics (so-called "phenotypes"), selection of these particular human features for purposes of racial signification is always and necessarily a social and historical process. In contrast to the other major distinction of this type, that of gender, there is no biological basis for distinguishing among human groups along the lines of race.[4] Indeed, the categories employed to differentiate among human groups along racial lines reveal themselves, upon serious examination, to be at best imprecise, and at worst completely arbitrary.

If the concept of race is so nebulous, can we not dispense with it? Can we not "do without" race, at least in the "enlightened" present? This question has been posed often, and with greater frequency in recent years.[5] An affirmative answer would of course present obvious practical difficulties: it is rather difficult to jettison widely held beliefs, beliefs which moreover are central to everyone's identity and understanding of the social world. So the attempt to banish the concept as an archaism is at best counterintuitive. But a deeper difficulty, we believe, is inherent in the very formulation of this schema, in its way of posing race as a problem, a misconception left over from the past, and suitable now only for the dustbin of history.

A more effective starting point is the recognition that despite its uncertainties and contradictions, the concept of race continues to play a fundamental role in structuring and representing the social world. The task for theory is to explain this situation. It is to avoid both the utopian framework that sees race as an illusion we can somehow "get beyond," and also the essentialist formulation that sees race as something objective and fixed, a biological datum.[6] Thus we should think of race as an element of social structure rather than as an irregularity within it; we should see race as a dimension of human representation rather than an illusion. These perspectives inform the theoretical approach we call racial formation.

RACIAL FORMATION

We define racial formation as <u>the sociohistorical process by which racial categories are created, lived out, transformed, and destroyed</u>. Our attempt to elaborate a theory of racial formation will proceed in two steps. First, we argue that racial formation is a process of historically situated projects in which human bodies and social structures are represented and organized. Next we link racial formation to the evolution of hegemony, the way in which society is organized and ruled. Such an approach, we believe, can facilitate understanding of a whole range of contemporary controversies and dilemmas involving race, including the nature of racism, the relationship of race to other forms of differences, inequalities, and oppression such as sexism and nationalism, and the dilemmas of racial identity today.

From a racial formation perspective, race is a matter of both social structure and cultural representation. Too often, the attempt is made to understand race simply or primarily in terms of only one of these two analytical dimensions.[7] For example, efforts to explain racial inequality as a purely social structural phenomenon are unable to account for the origins, patterning, and transformation of racial difference. Conversely, many examinations of racial difference—understood as a matter of cultural attributes a la ethnicity theory, or as a society-wide signification system, a la some poststructuralist accounts—cannot comprehend such structural phenomena as racial stratification in the labor market or patterns of residential segregation.

An alternative approach is to think of racial formation processes as occurring through a linkage between structure and representation. Racial projects do the ideological "work" of making these links. A racial project is simultaneously an interpretation, representation, or explanation of racial dynamics, and an effort to reorganize and redistribute resources along particular racial lines. Racial projects connect what race means in a particular discursive practice and the ways in which both social structures and everyday experiences are racially organized, based upon that meaning. Let us consider this proposition, first in terms of large-scale or macro-level social processes, and then in terms of other dimensions of the racial formation process.

RACIAL FORMATION AS A MACRO-LEVEL SOCIAL PROCESS

To interpret the meaning of race is to frame it social structurally. Consider for example, this statement by Charles Murray on welfare reform:

> My proposal for dealing with the racial issue in social welfare is to repeal every bit of legislation and reverse every court decision that in any way requires, recommends, or awards differential treatment according to race, and thereby put us back onto the track that we left in 1965. We may argue about the appropriate limits of government intervention in trying to enforce the ideal, but at least it should be possible to identify the ideal: Race is not a morally admissible reason for treating one person differently from another. Period.[8]

Here there is a partial but significant analysis of the meaning of race: it is not a morally valid basis upon which to treat people "differently from one another." We may notice someone's race, but we cannot act upon that awareness. We must act in a "color-blind" fashion. This analysis of the meaning of race is immediately linked to a specific conception of the role of race in the social structure: it can play no part in government action, save in "the enforcement of the ideal." No state policy can legitimately require, recommend, or award different status according to race. This example can be classified as a particular type of racial project in the present-day U.S.—a "neoconservative" one.

Conversely, to recognize the racial dimension in social structure is to interpret the meaning of race. Consider the following statement by the late Supreme Court Justice Thurgood Marshall on minority "set-aside" programs:

> A profound difference separates governmental actions that themselves are racist, and governmental actions that seek to remedy the effects of prior racism or to prevent neutral government activity from perpetuating the effects of such racism.[9]

Here the focus is on the racial dimensions of social structure—in this case of state activity and policy. The argument is that state actions in the past and present have treated people in very different ways according to their race, and thus the government cannot retreat from its policy responsibilities in this area. It cannot suddenly declare itself "color-blind" without in fact perpetuating the same type of differential, racist treatment.[10] Thus, race continues to signify difference and structure inequality. Here, racialized social structure is immediately linked to an interpretation of the meaning of race. This example too can be classified as a particular type of racial project in the present-day U.S.—a "liberal" one.

These two examples of contemporary racial projects are drawn from mainstream political debate; they may be characterized as center-right and center-left expressions of contemporary racial politics.[11] We can, however, expand the discussion of racial formation processes far beyond these familiar examples. In fact, we can identify racial projects in at least three other analytical dimensions: first, the political spectrum can be broadened to include radical projects, on both the left and right, as well as along other political axes. Second, analysis of racial projects can take place not only at the macro-level of racial policy-making, state activity, and collective action, but also at the level of everyday experience. Third, the concept of racial projects can be applied across historical time, to identify racial formation dynamics in the past. We shall now offer examples of each of these types of racial projects.

THE POLITICAL SPECTRUM OF RACIAL FORMATION

We have encountered examples of a neoconservative racial project, in which the significance of race is denied, leading to a "color-blind" racial politics and "hands off" policy orientation; and of a "liberal" racial project, in which the significance of race is affirmed, leading to an egalitarian and "activist" state policy. But these by no means exhaust the political possibilities. Other racial projects can be readily identified on the contemporary U.S. scene. For example, "far right" projects, which uphold biologistic and racist views of difference, explicitly argue for white supremacist policies. "New right" projects overtly claim to hold "color-blind" views, but covertly manipulate racial fears in order to achieve political gains.[12] On the left, "radical democratic" projects invoke notions of racial "difference" in combination with egalitarian politics and policy.

Further variations can also be noted. For example, "nationalist" projects, both conservative and radical, stress the incompatibility of racially-defined group identity with the legacy of white supremacy, and therefore advocate a social structural solution of separation, either complete or partial.[13] [N]ationalist currents represent a profound legacy of the centuries of racial absolutism that initially defined the meaning of race in the U.S. Nationalist concerns continue to influence racial debate in the form of Afrocentrism and other expressions of identity politics.

Taking the range of politically organized racial projects as a whole, we can "map" the current pattern of racial formation at the level of the public sphere, the "macro-level" in which public debate and mobilization takes place.[14] But important as this is, the terrain on which racial formation occurs is broader yet.

RACIAL FORMATION AS EVERYDAY EXPERIENCE

Here too racial projects link signification and structure, not so much as efforts to shape policy or define large-scale meaning, but as the applications of "common sense." To see racial projects operating at the level of everyday life, we have only to examine the many ways in which, often unconsciously, we "notice" race.

One of the first things we notice about people when we meet them (along with their sex) is their race. We utilize race to provide clues about who a person is. This fact is made painfully obvious when we encounter someone whom we cannot conveniently racially categorize—someone who is, for example, racially "mixed" or of an ethnic/racial group we are not familiar with. Such an encounter becomes a source of discomfort and momentarily a crisis of racial meaning.

Our ability to interpret racial meanings depends on preconceived notions of a racialized social structure. Comments such as, "Funny, you don't look black," betray an underlying image of what black should be. We expect people to act out their apparent racial identities; indeed we become disoriented when they do not. The black banker harassed by police while walking in casual clothes through his own well-off neighborhood, the Latino or white kid rapping in perfect Afro patois, the unending faux pas committed by whites who assume that the nonwhites they encounter are servants or tradespeople, the belief that nonwhite colleagues are less qualified persons hired to fulfill affirmative action guidelines, indeed the whole gamut of racial stereotypes—that "white men can't jump," that Asians can't dance, etc. etc.— all testify to the way a racialized social structure shapes racial experience and conditions meaning. Analysis of such stereotypes reveals the always present, already active link between our view of the social structure—its demography, its laws, its customs, its threats—and our conception of what race means.

Conversely, our ongoing interpretation of our experience in racial terms shapes our relations to the institutions and organizations through which we are imbedded in social structure. Thus we expect differences in skin color, or other racially coded characteristics, to explain social differences. Temperament, sexuality, intelligence, athletic ability, aesthetic preferences, and so on are presumed to be fixed and discernible from the palpable mark of race. Such diverse questions as our confidence and trust in others (for example, clerks or salespeople, media figures, neighbors), our sexual preferences and romantic images, our tastes in music, films, dance, or sports, and our very ways of talking, walking, eating, and dreaming become racially coded simply because we live in a society where racial awareness is so pervasive. Thus in ways too comprehensive even to monitor consciously, and despite periodic calls—neoconservative and otherwise—for us to ignore race and adopt "color-blind" racial attitudes, skin color "differences" continue to rationalize distinct treatment of racially-identified individuals and groups.

To summarize the argument so far: the theory of racial formation suggests that society is suffused with racial projects, large and small, to which all are subjected. This racial "subjection" is quintessentially ideological. Everybody learns some combination, some version, of the rules of racial classification, and of her own racial identity, often without obvious teaching or conscious inculcation. Thus are we inserted in a comprehensively racialized social structure. Race becomes "common sense"—a way of comprehending, explaining, and acting in the world. A vast web of racial projects mediates between the discursive or representational means in which race is identified and signified on the one hand, and the institutional and organizational forms in which it is routinized and standardized on the other. These projects are the heart of the racial formation process.

Under such circumstances, it is not possible to represent race discursively without simultaneously locating it, explicitly or implicitly, in a social structural (and historical) context. Nor is it possible to organize, maintain, or transform social structures without simultaneously engaging, once more either explicitly or implicitly, in racial signification. Racial formation, therefore, is a kind of synthesis, an outcome, of the interaction of racial projects on a society-wide level. These projects are, of course, vastly different in scope and effect. They include large-scale public action, state activities, and interpretations of racial conditions in artistic, journalistic, or academic fora,[15] as well as the seemingly infinite number of racial judgments and practices we carry out at the level of individual experience.

Since racial formation is always historically situated, our understanding of the significance of race, and of the way race structures society, has changed enormously over time. The processes of racial formation we encounter today, the racial projects large and small which structure U.S. society in so many ways, are merely the present-day outcomes of a complex historical evolution. The contemporary racial order remains transient. By knowing something of how it evolved, we can perhaps better discern where it is heading. We therefore turn next to a historical survey of the racial formation process, and the conflicts and debates it has engendered.

THE EVOLUTION OF MODERN RACIAL AWARENESS

The identification of distinctive human groups, and their association with differences in physical appearance, goes back to prehistory, and can be found in the earliest documents—in the Bible, for example, or in Herodotus. But the emergence of a modern conception of race does not occur until the rise of Europe and the arrival of Europeans in the Americas. Even the hostility and suspicion with which Christian Europe viewed its two significant non-Christian "others"—the Muslims and the Jews—cannot be viewed as more than a rehearsal for racial formation, since these antagonisms, for all their bloodletting and chauvinism, were always and everywhere religiously interpreted.[16]

It was only when European explorers reached the Western Hemisphere, when the oceanic seal separating the "old" and the "new" worlds was breached, that the distinctions and categorizations fundamental to a racialized social structure, and to a discourse of race, began to appear. The European explorers were the advance guard of merchant capitalism, which sought new openings for trade. What they found exceeded their wildest dreams, for never before and never again in human history has an opportunity for the appropriation of wealth remotely approached that presented by the "discovery."[17]

But the Europeans also "discovered" people, people who looked and acted differently. These "natives" challenged their "discoverers'" preexisting conceptions of the origins and possibilities of the human species.[18] The representation and interpretation of the meaning of the indigenous peoples' existence became a crucial matter, one which would affect the outcome of the enterprise of conquest. For the "discovery" raised disturbing questions as to whether all could be considered part of the same "family of man," and more practically, the extent to which native peoples could be exploited and enslaved. Thus religious debates flared over the attempt to reconcile the various Christian metaphysics with the existence of peoples who were more "different" than any whom Europe had previously known.[19]

In practice, of course, the seizure of territories and goods, the introduction of slavery through the encomienda and other forms of coerced native labor, and then through the organization of the African slave trade—not to mention the practice of outright extermination—all presupposed a worldview which distinguished Europeans, as children of God, full-fledged human beings, etc., from "others." Given the dimensions and the ineluctability of the European onslaught, given the conquerors' determination to appropriate both labor and goods, and given the presence of an axiomatic and unquestioned Christianity among them, the ferocious division of society into Europeans and "others" soon coalesced. This was true despite the famous 16th-century theological and philosophical debates about the identity of indigenous peoples.[20]

Indeed debates about the nature of the "others" reached their practical limits with a certain dispatch. Plainly they would never touch the essential: nothing, after all, would induce the Europeans to pack up and go home. We cannot examine here the early controversies over the status of American souls. We simply wish to emphasize that the "discovery" signaled a break from the previous proto-racial awareness by which Europe contemplated its "others" in a relatively disorganized fashion. In other words, we argue that the "conquest of America" was not simply an epochal historical event—however unparalleled in its importance. It was also the advent of a consolidated social structure of exploitation, appropriation, domination. Its representation, first in religious terms, but soon enough in scientific and political ones, initiated modern racial awareness.

The conquest, therefore, was the first—and given the dramatic nature of the case, perhaps the greatest—racial formation project. Its significance was by no means limited to the Western Hemisphere, for it began the work of constituting Europe as the metropole, the center, of a series of empires which could take, as Marx would later write, "the globe for a theater."[21] It represented this new imperial structure as a struggle between civilization and barbarism, and implicated in this representation all the great European philosophies, literary traditions, and social theories of the modern age.[22] In short, just as the noise of the "big bang" still resonates through the universe, so the overdetermined construction of world "civilization" as a product of the rise of Europe and the subjugation of the rest of us, still defines the race concept.

FROM RELIGION TO SCIENCE

After the initial depredations of conquest, religious justifications for racial difference gradually gave way to scientific ones. By the time of the Enlightenment, a general awareness of race was pervasive, and most of the great philosophers of Europe, such as Hegel, Kant, Hume, and Locke, had issued virulently racist opinions.

The problem posed by race during the late 18th century was markedly different than it had been in the age of conquest, expropriation, and slaughter. The social structures in which race operated were no longer primarily those of military conquest and plunder, nor of the establishment of thin beachheads of colonization on the edge of what had once seemed a limitless wilderness. Now the issues were much more complicated: nation-building, establishment of national economies in the world trading system, resistance to the arbitrary authority of monarchs, and the assertion of the "natural rights" of "man," including the right of revolution.[23] In such a situation, racially organized exploitation, in the form of slavery, the expansion of colonies, and the continuing expulsion of native peoples, was both necessary and newly difficult to justify.

The invocation of scientific criteria to demonstrate the "natural" basis of racial hierarchy was both a logical consequence of the rise of this form of knowledge, and an attempt to provide a more subtle and nuanced account of human complexity in the new, "enlightened" age. Spurred on by the classificatory scheme of living organisms devised by Linnaeus in Systema Naturae (1735), many scholars in the eighteenth and nineteenth centuries dedicated themselves to the identification and ranking of variations in humankind. Race was conceived as a biological concept, a matter of species. Voltaire wrote that "The negro race is a species of men (sic) as different from ours … as the breed of spaniels is from that of greyhounds," and in a formulation echoing down from his century to our own, declared that "If their understanding is not of a different nature from ours …, it is at least greatly inferior. They are not capable of any great application or association of ideas, and seem formed neither for the advantages nor the abuses of philosophy".[24]

Jefferson, the preeminent exponent of the Enlightenment doctrine of "the rights of man" on North American shores, echoed these sentiments:

> In general their existence appears to participate more of sensation than reflection. … [I]n memory they are equal to whites, in reason much inferior … [and] in imagination they are dull, tasteless, and anomalous. … I advance it therefore … that the blacks, whether originally a different race, or made distinct by time and circumstances, are inferior to the whites. … Will not a lover of natural history, then, one who views the gradations in all the animals with the eye of philosophy, excuse an effort to keep those in the department of Man (sic) as distinct as nature has formed them?[25]

Such claims of species distinctiveness among humans justified the inequitable allocation of political and social rights, while still upholding the doctrine of "the rights of man." The quest to obtain a precise scientific definition of race sustained debates that continue to rage today. Yet despite efforts ranging from Dr. Samuel Morton's studies of cranial capacity[26] to contemporary attempts to base racial classification on shared gene pools,[27] the concept of race has defied biological definition.

In the 19th century, Count Joseph Arthur de Gobineau drew upon the most respected scientific studies of his day to compose his four-volume Essay on the Inequality of Races (1853–1855).[28] He not only greatly influenced the racial thinking of the period, but his themes would be echoed in the racist ideologies of the next one hundred years: beliefs that superior races produced superior cultures and that racial intermixtures resulted in the degradation of the superior racial stock. These ideas found expression, for instance, in the eugenics movement launched by Darwin's cousin, Francis Galton, which had an immense impact on scientific and sociopolitical thought in Europe and the United States.[29] In the wake of civil war and emancipation, and with immigration from southern and Eastern Europe as well as East Asia running high, the U.S. was particularly fertile ground for notions such as social darwinism and eugenics.

Attempts to discern the scientific meaning of race continue to the present day. For instance, an essay by Arthur Jensen that argued that hereditary factors shape intelligence not only revived the "nature or nurture" controversy, but also raised highly volatile questions about racial equality itself.[30] All such attempts seek to remove the concept of race from the historical context in which it arose and developed. They employ an essentialist approach that suggests instead that the truth of race is a matter of innate characteristics, of which skin color and other physical attributes provide only the most obvious, and in some respects most superficial, indicators.

FROM SCIENCE TO POLITICS

It has taken scholars more than a century to reject biologistic notions of race in favor of an approach that regards race as a social concept. This trend has been slow and uneven, and even today remains somewhat embattled, but its overall direction seems clear. At the turn of the century Max Weber discounted biological explanations for racial conflict and instead highlighted the social and political factors that engendered such conflict.[31] W. E. B. DuBois argued for a sociopolitical definition of race by identifying "the color line" as "the problem of the 20th century."[32] Pioneering cultural anthropologist Franz Boas rejected attempts to link racial identifications and cultural traits, labeling as pseudoscientific any assumption of a continuum of "higher" and "lower" cultural groups.[33] Other early exponents of social, as opposed to biological, views of race included Robert E. Park, founder of the "Chicago school" of sociology, and Alain Leroy Locke, philosopher and theorist of the Harlem renaissance.[34]

Perhaps more important than these and subsequent intellectual efforts, however, were the political struggles of racially defined groups themselves. Waged all around the globe under a variety of banners such as anti-colonialism and civil rights, these battles to challenge various structural and cultural racisms have been a major feature of 20th century politics. The racial horrors of the 20th century—colonial slaughter and apartheid, the genocide of the holocaust, and the massive bloodlettings required to end these evils—have also indelibly marked the theme of race as a political issue par excellence.

As a result of prior efforts and struggles, we have now reached the point of fairly general agreement that race is not a biologically given but rather a socially constructed way of differentiating human beings. While a tremendous achievement, the transcendence of biologistic conceptions of race does not provide any reprieve from the dilemmas of racial injustice and conflict, nor from controversies over the significance of race in the present. Views of race as socially constructed simply recognize the fact that these conflicts and controversies are now more properly framed on the terrain of politics. By privileging politics in the analysis that follows we do not mean to suggest that race has been displaced as a concern of scientific inquiry, or that struggles over cultural representation are no longer important. We do argue, however, that race is now a preeminently political phenomenon. Such an assertion invites examination of the evolving role of racial politics in the U.S. This is the subject to which we now turn.

DICTATORSHIP, DEMOCRACY, HEGEMONY

For most of its existence both as a European colony and as an independent nation, the U.S. was a racial dictatorship. From 1607 to 1865—258 years—most nonwhites were firmly eliminated from the sphere of politics.[35] After the civil war there was the brief egalitarian experiment of Reconstruction which terminated ignominiously in 1877. In its wake followed almost a century of legally sanctioned segregation and denial of the vote, nearly absolute in the South and much of the Southwest, less effective in the North and far West, but formidable in any case.[36] These barriers fell only in the mid-1960s, a mere quarter-century ago. Nor did the successes of the black movement and its allies mean that all obstacles to their political participation had now been abolished. Patterns of racial inequality have proven, unfortunately, to be quite stubborn and persistent.

It is important, therefore, to recognize that in many respects, racial dictatorship is the norm against which all U.S. politics must be measured. The centuries of racial dictatorship have had three very large consequences: first, they defined "American" identity as white, as the negation of racialized "otherness"—at first largely African and indigenous, later Latin American and Asian as well.[37] This negation took shape in both law and custom, in public institutions and in forms of cultural representation. It became the archetype of hegemonic rule in the U.S. It was the successor to the conquest as the "master" racial project.

Second, racial dictatorship organized (albeit sometimes in an incoherent and contradictory fashion) the "color line," rendering it the fundamental division in U.S. society. The dictatorship elaborated, articulated, and drove racial divisions not only through institutions, but also through psyches, extending up to our own time the racial obsessions of the conquest and slavery periods.

Third, racial dictatorship consolidated the oppositional racial consciousness and organization originally framed by marronage[38] and slave revolts, by indigenous resistance, and by nationalisms of various sorts. Just as the conquest created the "native" where once there had been Pequot, Iroquois, or Tutelo, so too it created the "black" where once there had been Asante or Ovimbundu, Yoruba or Bakongo.

The transition from a racial dictatorship to a racial democracy has been a slow, painful, and contentious one; it remains far from complete. A recognition of the abiding presence of racial dictatorship, we contend, is crucial for the development of a theory of racial formation in the U.S. It is also crucial to the task of relating racial formation to the broader context of political practice, organization, and change.

In this context, a key question arises: In what way is racial formation related to politics as a whole? How, for example, does race articulate with other axes of oppression and difference—most importantly class and gender—along which politics is organized today?

The answer, we believe, lies in the concept of hegemony. Antonio Gramsci—the Italian communist who placed this concept at the center of his life's work—understood it as the conditions necessary, in a given society, for the achievement and consolidation of rule. He argued that hegemony was always constituted by a combination of coercion and consent. Although rule can be obtained by force, it cannot be secured and maintained, especially in modern society, without the element of consent. Gramsci conceived of consent as far more than merely the legitimation of authority. In his view, consent extended to the incorporation by the ruling group of many of the key interests of subordinated groups, often to the explicit disadvantage of the rulers themselves.[39] Gramsci's treatment of hegemony went even farther: he argued that in order to consolidate their hegemony, ruling groups must elaborate and maintain a popular system of ideas and practices—through education, the media, religion, folk wisdom, etc.—which he called "common sense." It is through its production and its adherence to this "common sense," this ideology (in the broadest sense of the term), that a society gives its consent to the way in which it is ruled.[40]

These provocative concepts can be extended and applied to an understanding of racial rule. In the Americas, the conquest represented the violent introduction of a new form of rule whose relationship with those it subjugated was almost entirely coercive. In the U.S., the origins of racial division, and of racial signification and identity formation, lie in a system of rule that was extremely dictatorial. The mass murders and expulsions of indigenous people, and the enslavement of Africans, surely evoked and inspired little consent in their founding moments.

Over time, however, the balance of coercion and consent began to change. It is possible to locate the origins of hegemony right within the heart of racial dictatorship, for the effort to possess the oppressor's tools—religion and philosophy in this case—was crucial to emancipation (the effort to possess oneself). As Ralph Ellison reminds us, "The slaves often took the essence of the aristocratic ideal (as they took Christianity) with far more seriousness than their masters."[41] In their language, in their religion with its focus on the Exodus theme and on Jesus's tribulations, in their music with its figuring of suffering, resistance, perseverance, and transcendence, in their interrogation of a political philosophy that sought perpetually to rationalize their bondage in a supposedly "free" society, the slaves incorporated elements of racial rule into their thought and practice, turning them against their original bearers.

Racial rule can be understood as a slow and uneven historical process that has moved from dictatorship to democracy, from domination to hegemony. In this transition, hegemonic forms of racial rule—those based on consent—eventually came to supplant those based on coercion. Of course, before this assertion can be accepted, it must be qualified in important ways. By no means has the U.S. established racial democracy at the end of the century, and by no means is coercion a thing of the past. But the sheer complexity of the racial questions U.S. society confronts today, the welter of competing racial projects and contradictory racial experiences that Americans undergo, suggests that hegemony is a useful and appropriate term with which to characterize contemporary racial rule.

RACE, RACISM, AND HEGEMONY

Parallel to the debates on the concept of race, recent academic and political controversies about the nature of racism have centered on whether it is primarily an ideological or structural phenomenon. Proponents of the former position argue that racism is first and foremost a matter of beliefs and attitudes, doctrines and discourse, which only then give rise to unequal and unjust practices and structures.[42] Advocates of the latter view see racism as primarily a matter of economic stratification, residential segregation, and other institutionalized forms of inequality that then give rise to ideologies of privilege.[43]

From the standpoint of racial formation, these debates are fundamentally misguided. They discuss the problem of racism in a rigid "either-or" manner. We believe it is crucial to disrupt the fixity of these positions by simultaneously arguing that ideological beliefs have structural consequences, and that social structures give rise to beliefs. Racial ideology and social structure, therefore, mutually shape the nature of racism in a complex, dialectical, and overdetermined manner.

Even those racist projects that at first glance appear chiefly ideological turn out upon closer examination to have significant institutional and social structural dimensions. For example, what we have called "far right" projects appear at first glance to be centrally ideological. They are rooted in biologistic doctrine, after all. The same seems to hold for certain conservative black nationalist projects that have deep commitments to biologism.[44] But the unending stream of racist assaults initiated by the far right, the apparently increasing presence of skinheads in high schools, the proliferation of neo-Nazi websites on the Internet, and the appearance of racist talk shows on cable access channels, all suggest that the organizational manifestations of the far right racial projects exist and will endure.[45]

By contrast, even those racisms that at first glance appear to be chiefly structural upon closer examination reveal a deeply ideological component. For example, since the racial right abandoned its explicit advocacy of segregation, it has not seemed to uphold—in the main—an ideologically racist project, but more primarily a structurally racist one. Yet this very transformation required tremendous efforts of ideological production. It demanded the rearticulation of civil rights doctrines of equality in suitably conservative form, and indeed the defense of continuing large-scale racial inequality as an outcome preferable to (what its advocates have seen as) the threat to democracy that affirmative action, busing, and large-scale "race-specific" social spending would entail.[46] Even more tellingly, this project took shape through a deeply manipulative coding of subtextual appeals to white racism, notably in a series of political campaigns for high office that have occurred over recent decades. The retreat of social policy from any practical commitment to racial justice, and the relentless reproduction and divulgation of this theme at the level of everyday life—where whites are now "fed up" with all the "special treatment" received by nonwhites, etc.—constitutes the hegemonic racial project at this time. It therefore exhibits an unabashed structural racism all the more brazen because on the ideological or signification level it adheres to a principle to "treat everyone alike."

In summary, the racism of today is no longer a virtual monolith, as was the racism of yore. Today, racial hegemony is "messy." The complexity of the present situation is the product of a vast historical legacy of structural inequality and invidious racial representation, which has been confronted during the post-World War II period with an opposition more serious and effective than any it had faced before. The result is a deeply ambiguous and contradictory spectrum of racial projects, unremittingly conflictual racial politics, and confused and ambivalent racial identities of all sorts.

DISCUSSION QUESTIONS

1 In recent years civil rights advocates have brought suit against companies like CSX railroad and Fleet Bank on the grounds that they profited from from African slavery in their early years. For example, the lawsuits alleged that corporate ancestors of CSX used slave labor to lay railroad track and to build railroad facilities; they charged that corporate ancestors of Fleet Bank (which merged with Bank of America in 2004) insured plantation owners' "property" (the slaves themselves) in the antebellum South against the risk of slaves running away.

In your view what merit do these lawsuits have? Should contemporary corporations be liable for their predecessors' collaboration with slavery? Are the descendents of slaves entitled to compensation because their ancestors' labor was (allegedly) coerced by CSX's antecedents or because their ancestors' bodies were (allegedly) insured by Fleet's corporate founders against loss to their slavemasters? Is the black community as a whole entitled to such compensation?

2 The United States is becoming a lot less white. Projecting current population (and immigration) trends forward to the year 2050, the US Census Bureau predicts that in 2050, the population will be about 25% Latino/Hispanic, 17% black, and 9% Asian

American. In many of the largest cities in the US, whites are already a minority. The state of California, which was about 75% white in 1975, was only about 42% white in 2007.

What are the implications of these population trends for racial formation in the United States? How in your view will the country adapt to these patterns? For example, do you foresee a greater acceptance among whites of their minority status? Or do you think there will be greater hostility to members of "other" groups? What racial projects do you expect whites to be carrying out as a result of their declining proportion of the US population?

3   In 2005 white families' average net worth (the monetary value of investments savings, and property belong to these families) was approximately 11X the average net worth of black families. This inequality in wealth distribution had grown significantly over the four decades since the passage of civil rights legislation in the 1960s.

In your view what accounts for the continuing (and in some ways increasing) gap between blacks and whites in the present, supposedly "color-blind" era?

4   In 1997 golf star Tiger Woods referred to himself as "Cablinasian" on the Oprah Winfrey TV program. He said that it bothered him when people referred to him as black, since he is one-fourth black, one-fourth Thai, one-fourth Chinese, one-eighth white and one-eighth American Indian.

Discuss Woods's self-identification as a racial project. In what ways is he situating himself in the US racial mosaic? What are the implications for him (and for other Americans) of his invention of a "Cablinasian" identity?

5   Starting in the 1970s, and more intensively since then, many politicians, academics, and public figures have argued that the United States is becoming a "color-blind" society. (The term actually goes back to Justice Harlan's dissent in the landmark *Plessy v. Ferguson* decision of 1896.) Yet survey results continue to show persistent beliefs in black inferiority, laziness, and criminality.

Is there a discrepancy here, or can these two trends be reconciled? Discuss these views on race as conflicting or overlapping racial projects.

NOTES

1   San Francisco Chronicle, September 14, 1982, May 19, 1983. Ironically, the 1970 Louisiana law was enacted to supersede an old Jim Crow statute which relied on the idea of "common report" in determining an infant's race. Following Phipps' unsuccessful attempt to change her classification and have the law declared unconstitutional, a legislative effort arose which culminated in the repeal of the law. See San Francisco Chronicle, June 23, 1983.

2   Compare the Phipps case to Andrew Hacker's well-known "parable" in which a white person is informed by a mysterious official that "the organization he represents has made a mistake" and that "... [a]ccording to their records ..., you were to have been born black: to another set of parents, far from where you were raised." How much

compensation, Hacker's official asks, would "you" require to undo the damage of this unfortunate error? See Hacker, <u>Two Nations: Black and White, Separate, Hostile, Unequal</u> (New York: Charles Scribner's Sons, 1992), pp. 31–32.

3   On the evolution of Louisiana's racial classification system, see Virginia Dominguez, <u>White By Definition: Social Classification in Creole Louisiana</u> (New Brunswick: Rutgers University Press, 1986).

4   This is not to suggest that gender is a biological category while race is not. Gender, like race, is a social construct. However, the biological division of humans into sexes—two at least, and possibly intermediate ones as well—is not in dispute. This provides a basis for argument over gender divisions—how natural?" etc.—which does not exist with regard to race. To ground an argument for the "natural" existence of race, one must resort to philosophical anthropology.

5   "The truth is that there are no races; there is nothing in the world that can do all we ask race to do for us. ... The evil that is done is done by the concept, and by easy—yet impossible—assumptions as to its application." (Kwame Anthony Appiah, <u>In My Father's House: Africa in the Philosophy of Culture</u> (New York: Oxford University Press, 1992.) Appiah's eloquent and learned book fails, in our view, to dispense with the race concept, despite its anguished attempt to do so; this indeed is the source of its author's anguish. We agree with him as to the non-objective character of race, but fail to see how this recognition justifies its abandonment. This argument is developed below.

6   We understand essentialism as *belief in real, true human essences, existing outside or impervious to social and historical context*. We draw this definition, with some small modifications, from Diana Fuss, <u>Essentially Speaking: Feminism, Nature, & Difference</u> (New York: Routledge, 1989), p. xi.

7   Michael Omi and Howard Winant, "On the Theoretical Status of the Concept of Race," in Warren Crichlow and Cameron McCarthy, eds., <u>Race, Identity, and Representation in Education</u> (New York: Routledge, 1993).

8   Charles Murray, <u>Losing Ground: American Social Policy, 1950–1980</u> (New York: Basic Books, 1984), p. 223.

9   Justice Thurgood Marshall, dissenting in *City of Richmond v. J.A. Croson Co.*, 488 U.S. 469 (1989).

10 See, for example, Derrick Bell, "Remembrances of Racism Past: Getting Past the Civil Rights Decline," in Herbert Hill and James E. Jones, Jr., eds., <u>Race in America: The Struggle for Equality</u> (Madison: The University of Wisconsin Press, 1993), pp. 75–76; Gertrude Ezorsky, <u>Racism and Justice: The Case for Affirmative Action</u> (Ithaca: Cornell University Press, 1991), pp. 109–111; David Kairys, <u>With Liberty and Justice for Some: A Critique of the Conservative Supreme Court</u> (New York: The New Press, 1993), pp. 138–41.

11 Howard Winant has developed a tentative "map" of the system of racial hegemony in the U.S. circa 1990, which focuses on the spectrum of racial projects running from the political right to the political left. See Winant, "Where Culture Meets Structure:

Race in the 1990s," in idem, <u>Racial Conditions: Theories, Politics, Comparisons</u> (Minneapolis: University of Minnesota Press, 1994).

12   A familiar example is use of racial "code words." Recall George Bush's manipulations of racial fear in the 1988 "Willie Horton" ads, or Jesse Helms's use of the coded term "quota" in his 1990 campaign against Harvey Gantt.

13   From this perspective, far right racial projects can also be interpreted as "nationalist." See Ronald Walters, "White Racial Nationalism in the United States," <u>Without Prejudice</u> I, 1 (Fall, 1987).

14   Howard Winant has offered such a "map" in "Race: Theory, Culture, and Politics in the United States Today," in Marcy Darnovsky et al., eds., <u>Contemporary Social Movements and Cultural Politics</u> (Philadelphia: Temple University Press, 1994).

15   We are not unaware, for example, that publishing this work is in itself a racial project.

16   Although the Inquisition pioneered racial anti-semitism with its doctrine of "limpieza de sangre" (the claim that Jews could not be accepted as converts because their blood was "unclean"), anti-semitism only began to be seriously racialized in the 18th century, as George L. Mosse shows in <u>Toward the Final Solution: A History of European Racism</u> (New York: Howard Fertig, 1978).

17   As Marx put it:

> The discovery of gold and silver in America, the extirpation, enslavement, and entombment in mines of the aboriginal population, the beginning of the conquest and looting of the East Indies, the turning of Africa into a warren for the commercial hunting of blackskins, signalized the rosy dawn of the era of capitalist production. These idyllic proceedings are the chief momenta of primitive accumulation. (Karl Marx, <u>Capital</u>, Vol. I (New York: International Publishers, 1967), p. 751.)

> David E. Stannard argues that the wholesale slaughter perpetrated upon the native peoples of the Western hemisphere is unequalled in history, even in our own bloody century. See his <u>American Holocaust: Columbus and the Conquest of the New World</u> (New York: Oxford University Press, 1992).

18   Winthrop Jordan provides a detailed account of the sources of European attitudes about color and race in <u>White Over Black: American Attitudes Toward the Negro, 1550–1812</u> (New York: Norton, 1977 [1968]), pp. 3–43.

19   In a famous instance, a 1550 debate in Valladolid pitted the philosopher and translator of Aristotle, Gines de Sepulveda, against the Dominican Bishop of the Mexican state of Chiapas, Bartolome de Las Casas. Discussing the native peoples, Sepulveda argued that

> In wisdom, skill, virtue and humanity, these people are as inferior to the Spaniards as children are to adults and women to men; there is as great a difference between them as there is between savagery and forbearance, between violence and moderation, almost—I am inclined to say, as between monkeys and men (Sepulveda, "Democrates Alter," quoted in Tsvetan Todorov, <u>The Conquest of America: The Question of the Other</u> (New York: Harper and Row, 1984), p. 153).

In contrast, Las Casas defended the humanity and equality of the native peoples, both in terms of their way of life—which he idealized as one of innocence, gentleness, and generosity—and in terms of their readiness for conversion to Catholicism, which for him as for Sepulveda was the true and universal religion (Las Casas, "Letter to the Council of the Indies," quoted ibid, p. 163). William E. Connolly interrogates the linkages proposed by Todorov between early Spanish colonialism and contemporary conceptions of identity and difference in <u>Identity/Difference: Democratic Negotiations of Political Paradox</u> (Ithaca: Cornell University Press, 1991), pp. 40–48).

20   In Virginia, for example, it took about two decades after the establishment of European colonies to extirpate the indigenous people of the greater vicinity; 50 years after the establishment of the first colonies, the elaboration of slave codes establishing race as prima facie evidence for enslaved status was well under way. See Jordan, <u>White Over Black</u>.

21   <u>Capital</u>, P. 751.

22   Edward W. Said, <u>Culture and Imperialism</u> (New York: Alfred A. Knopf, 1993).

23   David Brion Davis, <u>The Problem of Slavery in The Age of Revolution</u> (Ithaca: Cornell University Press, 1975).

24   Quoted in Thomas F. Gossett, <u>Race: The History of an Idea in America</u> (New York: Schocken Books, 1965), p. 45.

25   Thomas Jefferson, "Notes on Virginia" [1787], in Merrill D. Peterson, <u>Writings of Thomas Jefferson</u> (New York: The Library of America, 1984), pp. 264–66, 270. Thanks to Prof. Kimberly Benston for drawing our attention to this passage.

26   Proslavery physician Samuel George Morton (1799–1851) compiled a collection of 800 crania from all parts of the world which formed the sample for his studies of race. Assuming that the larger the size of the cranium translated into greater intelligence, Morton established a relationship between race and skull capacity. Gossett reports that "In 1849, one of his studies included the following results: the English skulls in his collection proved to be the largest, with an average cranial capacity of 96 cubic inches. The Americans and Germans were rather poor seconds, both with cranial capacities of 90 cubic inches. At the bottom of the list were the Negroes with 83 cubic inches, the Chinese with 82, and the Indians with 79." Gossett, <u>Race: The History of an Idea in America</u>, p. 74. More recently, Steven Jay Gould has reexamined Morton's data, and shown that his research data were deeply, though unconsciously, manipulated to agree with his "a priori conviction about racial ranking." Gould, <u>The Mismeasure of Man</u> (New York: W. W. Norton, 1981), pp. 50–69.

27   Definitions of race founded upon a common pool of genes have not held up when confronted by scientific research which suggests that the differences *within* a given human population are every bit as great as those *between* populations. See L. L. Cavalli-Sforza, "The Genetics of Human Populations," <u>Scientific American</u>, (September 1974), pp. 81–89.

28   A fascinating summary critique of Gobineau is provided in Tsvetan Todorov, On Human Diversity: Nationalism, Racism, and Exoticism in French Thought, trans. Catherine Porter (Cambridge, MA: Harvard University Press, 1993), esp. pp. 129–40.

29   Two good histories of eugenics are Allen Chase, The Legacy of Malthus (New York: Knopf, 1977); Daniel J. Kelves, In the Name of Eugenics: Genetics and the Uses of Human Heredity (New York: Knopf, 1985).

30   Arthur Jensen, "How Much Can We Boost IQ and Scholastic Achievement?" Harvard Educational Review, 39 (1969), pp. 1–123.

31   See Weber, Economy and Society, Vol. I (Berkeley: University of California Press, 1978), pp. 385–87; Ernst Moritz Manasse, "Max Weber on Race," Social Research, Vol. 14 (1947), pp. 191–221.

32   DuBois, The The Souls of Black Folk (New York: Penguin, 1989 [1903]), p. 13. Du Bois himself wrestled heavily with the conflict between a fully sociohistorical conception of race, and the more essentialized and deterministic vision he encountered as a student in Berlin. In "The Conservation of Races" (1897) we can see his first mature effort to resolve this conflict in a vision which combined racial solidarity and a commitment to social equality. See Du Bois, "The Conservation of Races," in Dan S. Green and Edwin D. Driver, eds., W. E. B. Du Bois On Sociology and the Black Community (Chicago: University of Chicago Press, 1978), pp. 238–49; Manning Marable, W. E. B. Du Bois: Black Radical Democrat (Boston: Twayne, 1986), pp. 35–38. For a contrary, and we believe incorrect reading, see Appiah, In My Father's House, pp. 28–46.

33   A good collection of Boas's work is George W. Stocking, ed., The Shaping of American Anthropology, 1883–1911: A Franz Boas Reader (Chicago: University of Chicago Press, 1974).

34   Robert E. Park's Race and Culture (Glencoe, IL: Free Press, 1950) can still provide insight; see also Stanford H. Lyman, Militarism, Imperialism, and Racial Accommodation: An Analysis and Interpretation of the Early Writings of Robert E. Park (Fayetteville: University of Arkansas Press, 1992); Locke's views are concisely expressed in Alain Leroy Locke, Race Contacts and Interracial Relations, ed. Jeffrey C. Stewart (Washington, DC: Howard University Press, 1992), originally a series of lectures given at Howard University.

35   Japanese, for example, could not become naturalized citizens until passage of the 1952 McCarran-Walter Act. It took over 160 years, since the passage of the Naturalization Law of 1790, to allow all "races" to be eligible for naturalization.

36   Especially when we recall that until around 1960, the majority of blacks, the largest racially-defined minority group, lived in the South.

37   The construction of whiteness and its tropes of identity is explored in numerous studies, far too many to cite here. Some outstanding examples are Toni Morrison, Playing In The Dark: Whiteness and the Literary Imagination (Cambridge, MA: Harvard University Press, 1992); Michael Paul Rogin, Fathers and Children: Andrew Jackson and the Subjugation of the American Indian (New York: Knopf, 1975; Richard Drinnon,

<u>Facing West: The Metaphysics of Indian-hating and Empire-building</u> (Minneapolis: University of Minnesota Press, 1980).

38   This term refers to the practice, widespread throughout the Americas, whereby runaway slaves formed communities in remote areas, such as swamps, mountains, or forests, often in alliance with dispossessed indigenous peoples.

39   Antonio Gramsci, <u>Selections from the Prison Notebooks</u>, edited and translated by Quintin Hoare and Geoffrey Nowell Smith (New York: International Publishers, 1971), p. 182.

40   Anne Showstack Sassoon, <u>Gramsci's Politics</u>, 2nd. ed. (London: Hutchinson, 1987); Sue Golding, <u>Gramsci's Democratic Theory: Contributions to Post-Liberal Democracy</u> (Toronto: University of Toronto Press, 1992).

41   Ralph Ellison, <u>Shadow and Act</u> (New York: New American Library, 1966), p. xiv.

42   See Miles, <u>Racism</u>, p. 77. Much of the current debate over the advisability and legality of banning racist hate speech seems to us to adopt the dubious position that racism is primarily an ideological phenomenon. See Mari J. Matsuda et al, <u>Words That Wound: Critical Race Theory, Assaultive Speech, and the First Amendment</u> (Boulder, CO: Westview Press, 1993).

43   Or ideologies which mask privilege by falsely claiming that inequality and injustice have been eliminated. See Wellman, <u>Portraits of White Racism</u>.

44   Racial teachings of the Nation of Islam, for example, maintain that whites are the product of a failed experiment by a mad scientist.

45   Elinor Langer, "The American Neo-Nazi Movement Today," <u>The Nation</u>, July 16/23, 1990.

46   Such arguments can be found in Nathan Glazer, <u>Affirmative Discrimination</u>, Charles Murray, <u>Losing Ground</u>, and Arthur M. Schlesinger, Jr., <u>The Disuniting of America</u>, among others.

Racial Narratives

Since race operates so fluidly across a wide range of variable factors, it can be valuable to hear people's personal experiences or narratives. When listening to these narratives it is important to remember that there is no one or true "Asian experience," or "white experience" and that there are a nearly infinite number of racial identities and corresponding experiences. The following narratives come from a cross section of society, from plumbers to academics, speaking about race in their own words.

Reading 4.3.

The Coming of Age of a Chinese-Vietnamese American

by Sucheng Chan

The author came from a large, well-to-do ethnic Chinese family in South Vietnam. The seventh child in a family of eleven children, she recalls how government officials "visited" them, took an "inventory" of the family members, and confiscated their car, bicycles, and television set after three of her older sisters and oldest brother escaped in 1977. The second batch of family members to escape, in 1978, included the narrator, another brother, two sisters, an aunt, and a cousin. The narrator was only seven years old at the time but she has vivid recollections of the journey, their shipwreck, and the harsh living conditions in the refugee camp at Pulau Bidong, Malaysia. A little later, when her parents and three younger siblings tried to escape, their boat capsized and her mother's body was never recovered. Pinning her hopes on the fact that her mother might not have perished after all, the author began a poignant, futile search for her. This richly textured account also chronicles the tensions that surfaced after the author's father and surviving younger sibling finally rejoined the rest of the family in California. Written in 1990, this reflexive autobiography of a strong-willed young woman concludes with a discussion of her determined efforts to express her individuality.

Our family came to this country to escape from the inequality and differential treatment that we had experienced under the Communists in Vietnam who regarded us Chinese-Vietnamese as people with too much wealth and whose properties should be confiscated. In 1977, two years after the fall of Saigon, I was sitting on the stairs eavesdropping on a conversation between my mother and our maid, Mai. Mom told Mai that our family was deeply grateful for her service through the years but now we had no choice except to let her go because the new government had reduced the value of the currency. Mai protested and insisted that she be allowed to remain with us even if we could not pay her. However, my mother ordered Mai to take the money my mother gave her and use it to buy her way out of the country. I could not understand what my mother meant by "leave the country." Why should Mai leave? Where would she go? I knew of only one country—Vietnam. Later, when I questioned my mother, all she said was, "You're too young to understand."

A few days later, I saw a scene that was even more confusing. Even though I asked, no one told me what was happening. My parents, oldest brother, and three oldest sisters were standing before the Buddhist altar that we had in our house

Sucheng Chan, "The Coming of Age of a Chinese-Vietnamese American," *The Vietnamese American 1.5 Generation: Stories of War, Revolution, Flight and New Beginnings*, pp. 158-170. Copyright © 2006 by Temple University Press. Reprinted with permission.

and praying. Their eyes were red and wet from crying. My father gave some money to my brother and told him to use it as needed. He emphasized the importance of remaining alive and instructed my brother and sisters to give "them" the money and jewelry if "they" demanded it. My mother, who was kneeling before the altar with joss sticks between her palms, sobbed so hard that she could not say a word. Finally, they all hugged and my brother and sisters left. I thought they must be going to visit our grandparents. I did not realize they were leaving the country forever.

A year passed. In 1978, I entered first grade at an elementary school but I hated school because we were required to wear a red scarf around our neck as part of our school uniform. One day, when I took the scarf off during recess, I was sent to the principal's office. He wanted to know why I had taken my scarf off and who had taught me to do so. He asked whether my parents had told me to do that. I answered, "I took it off because it is ugly." He sent me home and told me I would remain on detention for two days. To my surprise, my parents did not punish me but only advised me to keep my mouth shut from then on. I did not understand why.

In the spring of 1978, two "visitors" from the government came to our house to take an inventory of my family members. They asked me for the names of all my brothers and sisters. My response was, "I don't know." It was an honest answer because I did not, in fact, know their names as I always called them "older brother" or "older sister." When my mother smiled at me, I realized I must have given the correct answer. I overheard my dad tell the visitors that there were only seven children in the family. I was puzzled because I thought there were eleven of us. What about the other four? I asked myself. Fortunately, I did not ask that question out loud in front of the visitors or my father would have had a lot of explaining to do. The visitors searched every room in the house—the living room, dining room, four bedrooms, bathrooms, sewing room, storage room, and garage. I noticed they paid special attention to the bicycles, the car, and the television. They came back the next day and confiscated those items. They told us we no longer needed those things because there was no time for leisure in the new society. My little brother cried for days afterward because he loved watching television. I was afraid they would visit us again in the future. Who knows? Maybe they would take my dolls and picture books next.

One foggy morning, my mother woke up my older brother, sister, me, and my younger sister. Silently, she bundled us up in long pants, shirts, sweaters, and jackets. I felt like a stuffed turkey. One by one, my dad took each of us on his motorcycle to the port. Everything was happening so fast that my head was spinning. My aunt and one of my cousins met us at the port and led us to a wooden boat. We all got in. Only when the motor began to roar did my aunt tell us that we were going to visit my grandparents. I believed her. As the boat moved into deeper waters, I looked out of the window in the ship's cabin and saw my mom with her face buried in my dad's chest. His arms were wrapped tightly around her. At that instant, I realized we were probably not going to visit my grandparents, but instead, to someplace far away. Suddenly, I wept because I feared I would never see my parents and other brothers and sisters again. Could this be our last farewell?

The boat moved into the endless sea. For three days, huge waves splashed violently against our boat and soaked my body. I recall crying constantly, craving water, and vomiting. My mouth was dry as a rice cake. I tried to swallow my own saliva but there wasn't any in my mouth. My older sister scooped up saltwater for us. It was most inviting at first but the salt left in my mouth and throat made my weak stomach feel worse. I vomited even more until there was nothing left in my stomach. All I could do was groan.

On the fourth night, a loud crash woke us up. People started screaming as the boat tilted to one side. Everyone rushed up the stairs, pushing their way out of the cabin. People pulled each other's hair and fistfights broke out. As the water rose up to my neck, someone grabbed my wrist and pulled me out. I thought my arm was being yanked off. It was pitch dark but somehow I managed to climb on to the rocks that had punctured our boat. I was so relieved when I found my brother, sisters, aunt, and cousin. We realized we had just experienced a shipwreck and might have lost everybody. By the time everyone had climbed on to the rocks, the fuel tanks were leaking rapidly. Soon, the sea was a shimmering black. A dead baby was still lying on the deck. Two women wrapped their arms around the bawling mother and held her back as she cried, "Just let me be with my baby!" Tears came to my eyes as I remembered my younger brother and sisters who were back in Vietnam with my parents.

We sat on the rocks for a day until a fishing boat found us. The fishermen contacted a large ship that came to pick us up. It took us to an island housing Vietnamese prisoners who had tried to escape from the country. We stayed there for about a month until the government decided to let us go. My aunt told us we were lucky because we had left Vietnam as Chinese who had obtained legal permits to depart. So, after a month in prison, we were allowed to leave in a boat that the government provided us. This time, we had more water and more food on board. I vomited and cried less but every time I closed my eyes my mind flashed back to our kitchen at home. The image was so real and vivid that I was surprised that my mother, who was cooking, did not seem to see me or speak to me. I was invisible to her. When I opened my eyes, I realized I was still on the boat.

Five days later, we found land. It was a rocky island called Pulau Bidong in Malaysia. The fishermen we had met at sea advised us to destroy our boat once we got near the island. Otherwise, they said, the Malaysian authorities would tow us back to sea. The captain headed directly to shore and some men punctured a large hole in the bottom of the boat with an ax. We all jumped into the water and waited for further instructions. The Malaysian officials led us to a camping area. There were no built structures and we had to sleep under the stars until we could construct our own shelter. Unfortunately for us, a harsh wind howled all night as needlelike rain pelted us. I thought there was no God to answer our prayers. It was up to us to make the best of everything. My belief in God ceased to exist.

For months, all we had to eat were noodles and watery congee [rice porridge] for both lunch and dinner. We were not given any breakfast. Worse, millions of black flies settled on everything we ate and drank. Diarrhea was a common illness. As for our shelter, the brilliant sun was our cover. My once pale complexion transformed into dark brown skin and my once straight hair turned into an entwined bird's nest where hundreds of lice made their home. Only three months later were we supplied with metal sheeting that enabled us to construct a long building to house fifty families. The building had only a roof and no walls. Our "home" reminded me of a swap meet in Saigon.

While living on this small island, I learned to behave like an adult. My daily chores included cooking, washing clothes, and sprouting green beans. When I was sick, I went to the doctor myself. The sick people could not simply walk in or make appointments. Rather, we had to line up starting at 2:00 or 3:00 A.M. and wait until the doctor's office opened, usually around 9:00 A.M. The line was always as long as a dragon. Another duty I had was to guard all the new boats that arrived. Some friends who arrived after us told us that most of my relatives, including my grandmother, had also managed to leave the country. Since they never showed up at Pulau Bidong, we figured they must have gone to another island.

Dying was a common event on Pulau Bidong. Each day, numerous people died of various diseases or accidents. A few were killed when falling coconuts struck them on the head. Others slipped off rocks while trying to fish. Nothing was a surprise anymore. One day, we received a letter from my dad. As my aunt read the letter, her hands shook violently and after she finished reading, she screamed. Tears flooded her eyes, rolling down her hollow cheeks, dropping to the ground. Everyone gathered around us and demanded to know what was in the letter. When my aunt did not respond, a woman picked up the letter that my aunt had thrown on the ground and read it to us. My dad wrote that the boat that he, my mother, my younger brother, and two sisters were on sank before it even left port. More than half of the passengers died. The Communists did not allow my dad to return to the boat until three days after the accident. He found the bodies of two of my siblings and buried them, but he never found my mother's body. He did not know where it had drifted. The woman could not continue reading because she was sobbing so hard. However, no tears poured out of my eyes. I pinched myself to cry, but because I had cried so much since I left Vietnam, there were no more tears left. Although I felt as if a sharp needle was stabbing my chest, my eyes were dry.

My aunt wept for one long week; she did enough crying for all of us. She could not eat and drank only a few sips of water. She cursed the Communists and my mother's stupidity. She said my mother would not have died had she left with us. But, no, my mother had insisted that she would only leave with my dad. At times, my aunt screamed and begged Buddha to take her life so that she could reunite with her mother. Later, however, she changed her mind and asked Buddha not to take her life because she was stuck on this island with the son and daughters of her brother. I felt as though she hated us and was blaming us for her misfortunes.

After eight months on the island, we were informed that we would be admitted into the United States where my oldest brother and sisters already were. As my aunt prepared for our departure, she wanted to take the pots and pans we had accumulated to the United States but my cousin talked her out of doing so. She managed to grab only a soup pot to take with her. I explored the island one last time and found more graves than I had expected. I was grateful that none of the graves belonged to the people I knew.

While waiting for a 747 jet to transport us to our destination, I mentally rehearsed the little bit of English I had learned on the island. "How are you?" "I am fine." "Thank you." "You're welcome." "I don't know." Even though I sounded alien and funny, I hoped that I would soon be able to speak English fluently. In May 1979 we arrived in Texas. During the reunification with my older brother and sisters, I felt overwhelmed with excitement. For the first time, I learned their names and found out how old they were. They told me I was the seventh child in a family of thirteen people and that only my dad and our baby sister were still in Vietnam. While we ate dinner, we shared our experiences on our respective journeys to the United States. Since I left Vietnam, I had never felt so complete. Now, there need be no more worries about dying of starvation or disease.

Having heard how warm the weather is in California and how many Asians live in that state, we decided to move there. After three months in Texas, we packed our bags again, climbed aboard a Greyhound bus, and headed to the Golden State. When we arrived in Glendale in southern California, I expected to see lots of Asians but, instead, most of our neighbors were White. I did not feel comfortable among them because they often stared or frowned at us. At times, I heard "they're Vietnamese" whispered behind my back. A Spanish-speaker called me "China." Those remarks made me feel like a dirty kid who lived in a trash dump and smelled like shit. Although I was upset, I could not defend myself. This feeling of helplessness was most depressing.

When fall arrived, I entered second grade. I was terrified by the language barrier and the fact that I had never encountered people of other races. What if they hated me because I was an alien? On the first day of class, the teacher did a roll call. I felt my heart pumping a thousand times faster than normal. When the Caucasian teacher called my name, I could not recognize it because I had never heard my name pronounced in English before. I glanced around the classroom: all eyes were on me. My cheeks became flushed as I stood up and shrieked feebly, "he-e-e-re," which caused a few giggles. The teacher smiled at me. Unsure of myself, I did not know whether to smile back or to ignore her. Back in Vietnam, teachers do not smile at their students during roll call, which was performed in a very strict and formal way.

During lunchtime, everyone ate sandwiches and drank milk. I was reluctant to take out my rice but my hunger could not wait. So, I got my container and removed the lid. The smell of rice and spicy fish sauce wafted across the lunch area. A couple of students covered their noses while others moved away. I was embarrassed and desperately wished the earth would swallow me up. Instead, I pretended not to notice and waited until everyone had left the lunch area to dump my container and its contents into the trash can. Even though I was very hungry, I felt I had to get rid of all the evidence for the crime I had committed.

I gradually adjusted to my new life by trial and error. I learned from observing my classmates and by enduring the laughter of those who thought I was stupid. By the end of the school year I knew how to eat burritos and drink cold milk. My English had improved to such an extent that I could ask directions to the library or the restroom. My sister and I tried speaking English to each other but the language still sounded strange to us. We laughed at our own accents. After a while, we unconsciously got into the habit of slipping a few English words and phrases into our conversations in Vietnamese. I tried to forget about the past—until the night my father flew to the United States.

It was eight o'clock in the evening when the phone rang. One of my brothers picked it up. The call was from my father who said he would arrive in the United States the next morning. Our family was so excited. One of my sisters went to the supermarket to buy food for the celebration and my aunt kept thanking Buddha as she knelt in front of the altar. Later that night, my aunt warned us not to mention the dreadful past. I could not sleep at all that night as I began to feel guilty. I felt I was a terrible person because I had not been able to cry when I heard about my mother's death. I was not excited like everyone else about the reunion with my father. One half of me was afraid of him while the other half wanted to see him again. I feared that members of my family would have difficulties readjusting to one another. I also worried that I would not be able to have a conversation with my dad since I was now speaking mostly English. I was afraid I might upset him.

My father and my youngest surviving sister arrived the next morning. We had a grand dinner that evening. Everyone was cautious of what he or she said. Finally, my dad broke the ice as he retold the shipwreck story, except this time it was more detailed. The only sentence I remember was, "Your mother's body was never found." This suddenly gave me hope that she might have been saved by someone. From then on, I commenced a secret investigation to find my mother. During the search, I encountered many difficulties, but because I had a deep faith that she had somehow survived, I was extremely upset when my aunt insisted I go to a Buddhist temple with her to pray for my mother's soul so that she could enter heaven. I refused to go. My aunt thought I had become too Americanized and she told my father how disobedient I was. My dad, who is not as religious as my aunt, let her remark pass. However, he did begin to worry that his children were becoming too Americanized. So, he set down regulations. We were not allowed to speak English at home and could speak only Vietnamese or Cantonese. We were not allowed to participate in extracurricular activities after school. The only thing we could do was to go to the library to study. He also enrolled the younger children in a Chinese-language school that held classes on the weekends.

These rules hampered my search for my mother as I could no longer go to Chinatown by myself to peer at the women there to see if one of them might be my mother. I also could not buy newspapers to look through all the ads for announcements of women who survived their escapes. Almost every night, I dreamed that my mother had come back to us. Sometimes she appeared very distant while at other times I could almost touch her. Some nights she talked to me, telling me to give up my search and crying before her image faded. These dreams continued on and off for at least a year.

Then, things suddenly changed. One night, my father announced his decision to remarry. Everyone in the family was shocked but we did not dare object. We felt we had no right to interfere with his personal life. Moreover, it had already been three years since our mother's disappearance. We hoped his new wife would make his life merrier. Although I did not dare voice an objection, I was afraid that my dad would not love us anymore. It was bad enough that I was the number-seven child—a middle child who had received little attention. Now, I would have to compete with another person for my father's love. I was scared. That night, I saw my mother again in my dreams. I remember vividly how I watched her sitting in a tree, crying. Then another dream overlapped with the first dream. I saw another of my aunts who had also died in the shipwreck. She advised me to forget about my mother because she had already reached heaven and was happy there. This was the last time I saw my mother in a dream. From then on, I gave up all hope of her survival.

I finally graduated from the sixth grade. Elementary school was over. As I entered junior high school, I became more aware of my appearance, especially the clothes I wore and the cosmetics other girls my age used. My Caucasian friends wore the latest fashions and started using makeup. I wanted to be like them but my older brothers and sisters forbade me to use lipstick, eye shadow, or eyeliner. My clothes were hand-me-downs from my older sisters. Unable to keep up with my white friends, I switched to Asian, mainly Chinese-Vietnamese, friends. I found I could relate to them better because we had the same experiences as "boat people" and their parents were similarly strict and stubborn. We also shared the same difficulties in terms of the language barrier, our taste in food and music, and values.

By 1987, Glendale had become more densely populated and our rent rose rapidly. The landlady suggested that we move because she wanted to remodel the house. My father was angry with her because he thought she was discriminating against us. The house, from his point of view, was not that old. We were the only Asian family in that neighborhood; our neighbors on both sides were old Caucasian ladies who often complained about the noise we made. They accused us of playing our music too loudly even though the biggest "stereo" we could afford at that time was a Walkman that could not possibly have produced the loud music they complained about. As we felt more and more unwelcome, my father decided we should move to Los Angeles in order to be close to its Chinatown that has a large Chinese community. He said that living among White people was too frustrating because they did not respect us. I objected to the move because I was finally feeling that I had adapted to American life. I could communicate better in English than in Cantonese or Vietnamese. Moreover, moving meant I would have to make new friends. The thought of another move brought painful memories of my departure from Vietnam.

My dad insisted we move and we did so in the summer of 1987 after I completed ninth grade. When school started in September, I encountered culture shock. I had not seen so many Asians since I left Vietnam. Although I had visited Chinatown, I had never lived among Chinese or Vietnamese in the United States. As my dad was satisfied with our new environment, I did not dare to complain. I feared my dad would get angry at all his children. Whenever one of us did something wrong, all of us got into trouble. He never saw us as individuals. So, I kept quiet for the sake of my brothers and sisters.

Upon entering high school, I decided I could no longer attend the Chinese-language school because even after four years of study, I still had not learned the language. I could not concentrate on what the teachers were saying and kept wishing I could skip class. I went to class only because I was afraid my dad would find out if I played hooky. Sometimes, I brought my homework from public school to do while I was sitting in the Chinese class. Finally, going to Chinese school became so intolerable that I got up the courage to tell my dad I no longer wanted to attend. My aunt, who was listening in on the conversation, started lecturing me harshly. She blamed my dad for being too lenient with me and my siblings. She reminded us that there are important traditional values we should treasure and that we could retain those values only if we knew the language. She accused me of wanting to be an American and of abandoning my roots. Then she blamed my dad for not watching over us and for allowing us to do too many things freely. The bottom line, in her eyes, was that my dad did not know how to be a proper father. She said she regretted taking some of his children, including me, out of Vietnam. She declared she would never have done so if she had known we would become so disobedient and disrespectful.

That night, our house was filled with tension. We all went to bed early. I crawled into my only private space—my bed—and cried in anger and confusion. I felt completely alone. Half of me wanted to give up the fight and follow all of my dad's and aunt's expectations, while the other half wanted to find the inner me, to do the things I wanted to do and not what others expected of me. Up to that point, all my actions had been directed by other members of my family. Whatever I wanted to do had to be approved by the entire family. That was really difficult because there was always at least one person who opposed my desires. It was so frustrating to try to please everyone. I asked myself, if I were to disobey them, would I then be considered a selfish person?

As I lay in bed, I thought of something one of my dad's friends had confided to him: this friend was afraid that his children would send him to an old folks home as they went on with their lives. He thought they would probably visit him only on weekends. He warned my dad how easily Chinese or Vietnamese children became Americanized and once they did, they would no longer care for their parents. They would become totally selfish, he said.

Despite my father's and my aunt's objections, I discontinued Chinese school. I felt I was mature enough to make such a decision. At age fourteen, I felt like an adult because of all I had been through. Not only was I working at a part-time job, but I had also long ago learned to go see the dentist or the doctor by myself. I cooked for my family, studied hard, and did not socialize. I did not feel like a normal teenager who still needed her parents' guidance. Thus, I thought I should be allowed to make decisions because I understood their consequences. The sentence, "You're too young to know or understand" no longer existed in my world.

During high school, I rebelled against all the expectations that my family and friends placed on me. After being on the tennis team for a year, I developed a new interest and enrolled in the Junior Reserved Officers' Training Corps (JROTC), which caused countless objections from the people who tried to shape my life. I joined JROTC to avoid going to physical education classes, which I despised because there were so many unmotivated students who hated to exercise. I soon became committed to JROTC, which inspired and motivated me to participate in all its extracurricular activities. I was on the exhibition drill team and the staff team. It is difficult to explain the satisfaction I derived from this program. At home, I had no space I could call my own: every corner of the house belonged to everyone. There was no space in which I could recognize myself as an individual. JROTC gave me an opportunity to gain insight into myself, my likes and dislikes, my hidden skills and talents, and my real personality.

From my family's perspective, JROTC reminded them of the Communists who had forced us to leave our country. My green uniform especially troubled them. My father strongly discouraged my participation because he felt ashamed and disturbed as I proudly wore my neatly pressed uniform in public. He could not understand why I wanted to show my patriotism when the United States is not our "original" country. He also objected because I was a young woman. Even though my father is not an overly dominating male who believes women belong only in the kitchen, he felt the army is not the right place for women. I also sensed that my military uniform brought back painful memories of the war and of my mother's death. Because of my inability to express myself well in Chinese, I did not succeed in explaining to him what JROTC meant to me.

Some of my friends also disapproved of my participation in JROTC. They even accused me of becoming a violent person because I was learning to spin rifles while not shooting them. They thought I was too gung-ho for war. Others felt I was trying to imitate Americans by participating in an American program. The proof they offered was that I was not active in ethnic cultural organizations.

All these objections forced me to reconsider my priorities. Although I managed to remain in JROTC for three years—until I graduated from high school—I often wondered if I was being too selfish. I felt ashamed about my father's displeasure; at the same time, my ability to stick it out gave me a sense of accomplishment and victory. I had proven to my father that JROTC did not automatically lead to my joining the "real" army and that I was simply educating myself through an uncommon venue. Following my example, both my younger sisters are also in JROTC. The pressure that other members of my family impose on them is not as great as what they inflicted on me. I presume it is because my family is slowly accepting the fact that their most strenuous objections will not always make us change our minds.

The next step I took toward independence was in my choice of which college to attend. I wanted to go to a college that would not be too close to Los Angeles, which would require me to live at home, but at the same time was not too far away so that I could visit my family on holidays. My father wanted me to live at home and attend a local college, possibly the same one that all my older siblings were attending, California State Polytechnic University in Pomona. But I was determined to be "unlike" any other member of my family. I also wanted to be a role model for my younger sisters. I wanted to prove to my father that I could get admitted into a

University of California campus, which is harder to get into than a California State University campus. As for my intended major, recalling my experience as a junior counselor and a teacher's aide, I thought that I would like to major in psychology.

When I was accepted at this university, the only members of my family who supported my decision to enroll here were one of my older sisters and my two younger sisters. They agreed with me that it was best to go away to college so that I would not have to worry about family problems all the time. My sisters and I feel that we can become more independent if we move away from our huge family. By doing so, we will have a chance to learn to rely on ourselves. However, my father and older brothers and sisters thought I had gone insane. They claimed that the campus I chose was not the right college for me because so many of its students are European Americans and it is famous as a "party school." They thought if I wanted to attend a University of California campus, I should go to UCLA. They also opposed my desire to study psychology, telling me that I should study medicine or dentistry—more "practical" professions that ensure a high income—instead.

Since coming to this university, I have made many new discoveries about myself. At the beginning of the first quarter, I felt homesick and lonely because everywhere I saw unfamiliar faces and heard unfamiliar voices. Though I yearned to see the faces of my family members, I did not go home often because I could not allow them to assume that I had made a wrong decision. I did not want them to force me to return home. I also had trouble eating bland American food in the dormitory dining rooms. I even missed washing the dishes because I was so used to doing them. What frustrates me most now is the loss of my identity. I often feel as if I do not know who I am. When people ask me what kind of music I like, I have no answer because at home I always listened to whatever my brothers and sisters wanted to hear. Now I have to make decisions about even trivial matters. Although I fought for this freedom for many years, I am not sure I enjoy it now that I have it. In addition, there is no longer pressure to do anything I do not want to do, like go to a Buddhist temple to pray. It is devastating not knowing what I believe in. Now, when people ask me what religion I belong to, I tell them I am an agnostic.

When I visited my family in Los Angeles after being in this school for a few months, they told me I had changed radically. They complained that I had become too Americanized because I could not speak Chinese well and now ate pizza for dinner instead of rice, or angel cake instead of moon cakes as snacks. My father and older brothers and sisters still oppose my desire to major in psychology. They say it is a "useless" major that is full of "bullshit." They claim it is an "American" major, something inappropriate for a Chinese to study. My father and aunt want all of us to become doctors and engineers as those professions would bring honor to the family. So far, I have not yet succeeded in convincing them that I really enjoy what I am studying and that I cannot major in something they like but I don't. My plan is to continue studying psychology. My family needs to realize that psychology is *my* major.

My closest friends, who are Chinese and Vietnamese, tell me I have matured too quickly and that I am becoming too "liberal." Yet, they still support my decision to go away to college. I guess this is what makes us close friends. Having gone through some of the same experiences, they understand where I am coming from.

On this campus, I feel more Chinese than American. Although I do things most Americans do, such as go to football and basketball games, I still interact mainly with Asian Americans. Sometimes I yearn for Chinese food and miss the Chinese holidays. Many of my values are still traditional. For example, I do not believe in premarital sex, but at the same time, I think it is fine for young people of both sexes to live together without having to marry or even to date each other. Whenever my "old" and "new" values conflict, I choose what makes the most sense to me. Therefore, I classify myself as a Chinese-Vietnamese American: I live in between not two, but three worlds.

Reading 4.4.

"I Don't Mind My Light Shining,"
Speech Delivered at a Freedom Vote Rally in Greenwood, Mississippi, Fall 1963

by Fannie Lou Hamer

Of the many strategic innovations introduced in Mississippi by the Student Nonviolent Coordinating Committee and the Council of Federated Organizations, perhaps none was more consequential than the Freedom Vote of fall 1963. The joint creation of Allard Lowenstein and Bob Moses, the Freedom Vote was a "mock election" designed to dramatize, especially to the federal government, that disenfranchised black Mississippians would cast a ballot if given the opportunity. In addition, in order to vote for meaningful racial progress in the state, black Clarksdale pharmacist Aaron Henry and white Tougaloo College chaplain Reverend Edwin King were recruited to run as an integrated ticket for governor and lieutenant governor, respectively.

As the campaign gathered momentum and publicity by late October, Freedom Vote rallies were held across the state. At one such rally, held in the SNCC-headquartered town of Greenwood in the Delta, Fannie Lou Hamer delivered a brief but impassioned address to her fellow black Deltans. In this, the earliest

Maegan Parker Brooks and Davis W. Houck, ""I Don't Mind My Light Shining" Speech Delivered at a Freedom Vote Rally in Greenwood, Mississippi, Fall 1963," *The Speeches of Fannie Lou Hamer: To Tell It Like It Is*, pp. 3-4. Copyright © 2010 by University Press of Mississippi and Fannie Lou Hamer. Reprinted with permission.

known recording of Hamer's speechmaking, she borrows extensively from the Old and New Testaments not only to legitimize her role of rhetorical leadership—Jesus had answered her prayer and opened a way for her to speak—but to have Scripture also function as something of a cudgel: if Mississippi blacks did not take action and vote at this defining hour, they would go "straight to hell" with their oppressors.

This opening salvo in Hamer's rhetorical ministry foreshadows many of the themes she would address during the next thirteen years: the intimidation and violence she had faced immediately upon attempting to register to vote on August 31, 1962; her brutal beating on June 9, 1963, in a Winona, Mississippi, jail; the extent to which the black church was often an insular house of hypocrisy rather than a house of meaningful political action; the relationship among poverty, race, and social justice; and always the impassioned righteousness that sprang from the unswerving knowledge that she was doing God's will.

The Mississippi Freedom Vote was a stunning success: nearly eighty thousand ballots were cast between November 2 and 4; the arrival of white Yale University undergraduates to assist in the campaign generated local, state, and national publicity; the Henry-King political ticket foreshadowed the creation six months later of the Mississippi Freedom Democratic Party; and the influx of northern college students proved so successful that Freedom Summer of 1964 was modeled after such domestic missionary work.

* * *

From the fourth chapter of St. Luke beginning at the eighteenth verse: "The Spirit of the Lord is upon me because he has anointed me to preach the gospel to the poor. He has sent me to heal the brokenhearted, to preach deliverance to the captive, and recover the sight to the blind, to set at liberty to them who are bruised, to preach the acceptable year of the Lord."

Now the time have come that was Christ's purpose on earth. And we only been getting by, by paying our way to Hell. But the time is out. When Simon [of] Cyrene was helping Christ to bear his cross up the hill, he said, "Must Jesus bear this cross alone? And all the world go free?" He said, "No, there's a cross for everyone and there's a cross for me. This consecrated cross I'll bear, till death shall set me free. And then go home a crown to wear, for there's a crown for me."

And it's no easy way out. We just got to wake up and face it, folks. And if I can face the issue, you can too. You see, the thing, what's so pitiful now about it, the men been wanting to be the boss all of these years, and the ones that ain't up under the house is under the bed.

But you see, it's poison; it's poison for us not to speak what we know is right. As Christ said from the seventeenth chapter of Acts and the twenty-sixth verse, says: "Has made of one blood all nations, for to dwell on the face of the earth." Then it's no different, we just have different colors.

And, brother, you can believe this or not: I been sick of this system as long as I can remember. I heard some people speak of depression in the '30s. In the '20s, it was 'pression with me! De-pression. I been as hungry—it's a funny thing since I started working for Christ—it's kind of like in the twenty-third of Psalms when he says, "Thou prepareth a table before me in the presence of my enemies. Thou anointed my head with oil and my cup runneth over."

And I have walked through the shadows of death because it was on the tenth of September in '62 when they shot sixteen times in a house and it wasn't a foot over the bed where my head was. But that night I wasn't there—don't you see what God can do? Quit running around trying to dodge death because this book said, "He that seeketh to save his life, he's going to lose it anyhow!"

So as long as you know you going for something, you put up a life. That it can be like Paul, say, "I fought a good fight." And I've "kept the faith." You know, it had been a long time—people, I have worked, I have worked as hard as anybody. I have been picking cotton and would be so hungry—and one of the poison things about it—wondering what I was going to cook that night. But you see all of them things was wrong, you see? And I have asked God, I said, "Now Lord"—and you have too—ain't no need to lie and say that you ain't. Said, "Open a way for us." Said, "Please make a way for us, Jesus." Said, "Where I can stand up and speak for my race and speak for these hungry children." And he opened a way and all of them mostly backing out.

You see, he made it so plain for us. He sent a man in Mississippi with the same name that Moses had to go to Egypt. And tell him to go down in Mississippi and tell Ross Barnett to let my people go. And you know I feel good, I feel good. I never know today what's going to happen to me tonight, but I do know as I walk alone, I walk with my hand in God's hand.

And, you see, you know the ballot is good. If it wasn't good how come he trying to keep you from it and he still using it? Don't be foolish, folks: they going in there by the droves and droves and they had guards to keep us out of there the other day. And dogs. Now if that's good enough for them, I want some of it too.

You see, as I said, it was on the tenth of September when they shot in the house for me sixteen times, but I didn't stop. Now some of the time since then I got hungry, but I got consolation because I had got hungry before I got in it. Wasn't going to be no more hungry now than I was then. Then, on the ninth of June, this year,

I was beat in a jailhouse until I was hard as metal. And I told the policeman, I said, "It's going to be miserable when you have to face God." I said, "Because one day you going to pay up for the things you have done." I said, because, as the Scripture says, "Has made of one blood all nations." He said, "It's a damn lie," said, "Abraham Lincoln said that." So that's pitiful—I'm telling you the truth, but it's pitiful, you see—that people can have so much hate that will make them beat a person and don't know they doing wrong.

But open your New Testament when you get home and read from the twenty-sixth chapter of Proverbs and the twenty-seventh verse: "Who so diggeth a pit shall fall down in it." Pits have been dug for us for ages. But they didn't know, when they was digging pits for us, they had some pits dug for themselves. And the Bible had said, "Before one jot of my word would fail, Heaven and earth would pass away. Be not deceived for God is not mocked. For whatsoever a man soweth, that shall he also reap."

All we got to do—that's why I love the song "This Little Light of Mine"—from the fifth chapter of Matthew, He said, "A city that's set on a hill cannot be hid." And I don't mind my light shining; I don't hide that I'm fighting for freedom because Christ died to set us free. And he stayed here until he got thirty-three years old, letting us know how we would have to walk.

And we can come to this church and we can shout till we look foolish, because that's what we're doing. And we can come out here and live a lie and like the lie and we going just as straight to hell, if we don't do something. Because we got a charge to keep too. Until we can sing this song of Dr. Watts: "Should earth against my soul engage and fiery darts be hurled, but when I can smile at Satan's rage and face the frowning world." Thank you.

From these narratives you can see that how people feel about race and racial identities (even very similar ones) changes over time. Of course, they are but a slice of the racial identities and realities that exist. Though at times more or less in the foreground, race has consistently been meaningful for individual identities, interpersonal relations, and society at large.

WHAT IS THE SIGNIFICANCE OF RACE?

The significance of race varies from society to society, and it is constantly contested in both macro- and micro-level structures. Race has had varying degrees of significance depending on the particular time and the society that is the subject of focus. In sociology we say that race is "real," meaning that there are real impacts of racial constructs, racial experiences, racial stereotypes, and racial/racialized policies. While these impacts are very real, sociologists accept the findings of biologists, geneticists, anthropologists, and fellow sociologists that there is no such thing as biological race.

More resources:

How Science and Genetics are Reshaping the Race Debate of the 21st Century: http://sitn.hms.harvard.edu/flash/2017/science-genetics-reshaping-race-debate-21st-century/

A More Personal Perspective on Race

There has been significant contact between different populations, ethnic groups, and what we would like to call races throughout all of written history. New developments in genetic testing demonstrate this as well. The likelihood of an individual having ancestry from multiple regions of the world is very high. Biological notions about race—that one can use regional ancestry to determine racial categories and racial characteristics—are seriously challenged (if not rendered nonsensical) by the ways in which human societies have historically reproduced.

That's young Dr. Swann on the left!

FIGURE 4.1   **Me, my father, mother, and brother.**

Allow this picture of my family to serve as an example. That's me all the way on the left (well before being a dad added 20 pounds to my frame), my mother (yes, my biological mother), my father, and my brother. There are several ways in which this picture can help us explore the social construction of race. One is the idea that there are pure biological-based racial categories.

Another is that race is a *social construct* situated in a specific time, cultural context, and social context. While I am clearly equally related to both my mother and father (50%), in America I am considered the same race as my father and brother, "black." This is the way I was raised, the way in which I was treated by society at large, and the way in which I identify myself. And it was constantly reinforced by society; for instance, institutional forms did not include a category of "mixed" in my formative years. When I was five my mother's old hair salon refused to cut my hair saying, "We don't cut that kind of hair." Along with parents' understandings of such matters, these sorts of experiences and the available recognized institutional categories go a long way in establishing one's racial identity. In the future it's possible that a kid in America with a very similar background to mine grows up with the racial identity of "mixed race," "black-white," or any number of yet-to-be-recognized categories. In other societies there are a variety of categories for people of mixed racial or ethnic descent such as Pardo in Brazil or Mestizo in Central America.

Further reading:

www.dailymail.co.uk/news/article-2123050/Look-The-black-white-twins-turn-seven.html

www.dailymail.co.uk/news/article-2974869/The-twins-tell-apart-Striking-sisters-couldn-t-different-quirk-mixed-raced-parentage.html

Skin color is simply a phenotype, just like eye color and earlobe length. While there are other traits aside from skin color that go into our conception of race, they too are merely phenotypic expressions (we'll explain more later). Figure 4.2 is of my family and serves to drive home the same point. I had two sons with a black woman with two black parents, who have three black grandparents. What about their future kids? You can see how the idea of race mapping onto some sort of biological reality starts to become a bit silly.

Historically

The most dominant racial frame across the world and in America has been a biological racial frame. That is, race is an objective characteristic about an individual that carries with it meaningful corollaries to some character traits. As noted, sociologists cast this notion aside some time ago in favor of a social construction model. American society has also cast this belief aside in many ways, although some remnants do remain.

Contemporary

Contemporary notions of race, like historical ones, vary across the globe. In America, since the end of the civil rights movement the dominant societal paradigm is that of a colorblind frame. While there are differences in the way it is conceived, generally it means that one does not overtly tend to race and that one cannot use race as an explanatory mechanism. This is very good in that this paradigm sees overt racism and racist language as deviant; however, it comes with the downside of often classifying the recognition and discussion of racial disparities as similarly deviant. It is also important to note that contemporary understandings of race cannot be completely untwined from historical understandings and conceptions of race.

Embodying the White Racial Frame:
The (In)Significance of Barack Obama

by Wendy Leo Moore and Joyce M. Bell

INTRODUCTION

The victory of Barack Obama in the 2008 presidential election marked a significant historic moment in the United States. In a nation founded upon, and owing much of its economic growth and prosperity to the institution of racialized slavery, the election of the first African American president was a powerful symbolic challenge to a long and violent history of racial oppression and white supremacy. Immediately after Obama's election, within both popular and scholarly discourse, claims that his election signified a "post-racial" America emerged. Even among commentators who didn't go so far as to suggest that racial inequality or racism were now a thing of the past, Barack Obama's election was hailed as evidence of the decreasing relevance of racism in the fabric of our society. In support of this assertion, many commentators pointed to the fact that Obama received widespread support from whites, without which his victory would not have been possible. Yet the systemic racial inequality that characterized the United States social structure on November 4th 2008, did not disappear, or even lessen because of the election results. How then, as social scientists and public policy analysts, do we reconcile a symbolic racial victory in American politics and the resulting rhetoric surrounding it, which declares this victory as indicative of racial progress, with the persistent and deep structural racial inequalities that characterize the United States? Herein we suggest that, in fact, these phenomenon are not incompatible, but are instead deeply, and dangerously connected.

As Joe Feagin (2000) has documented, the United States, in all its major institutions, is characterized by racism and racial inequality. As a result of a history and legacy of legally-constructed and -enforced racial oppression, deep structural inequalities permeate U.S. society today (Bell, 2000; Harris, 1993; Haney López, 2006; Moore, 2008). The United States is the most residentially racially segregated country in the world, and this geographical segregation (which is the result of historical and contemporary legal, political and economic racist practices) corresponds to severe structural economic inequality (Conley, 2009; Jargowsky, 1997; Massey and Denton, 1993; Bell, 2000; Oliver and Shapiro, 2006). The history of racism, combined with contemporary structural inequalities affects nearly every facet of American society. Education in the K-12 system is as segregated and unequal in many instances as it was pre-*Brown v. Board of Education*[1] (Kozol, 1992; Lewis, 2003; Orfield and Eaton,

Wendy Leo Moore and Joyce M. Bell, "Embodying the White Racial Frame: The (In)Significance of Barack Obama," *The Journal of Race and Policy*, vol. 6, no. 1, pp. 122-137. Copyright © 2010 by Old Dominion University. Reprinted with permission. Provided by ProQuest LLC. All rights reserved.

1996). People of color are under-represented in higher education and historically white educational institutions remain demographically disparate and ideologically organized around white norms, making them fundamentally white institutional spaces in which students of color struggle to perform to their full capabilities (Feagin, Vera and Imani, 1997; Moore, 2008). Furthermore African Americans are vastly over-represented in jails and prisons and under the authority of the ever expanding criminal justice system (Davis, 2003; Glover, 2009; Tonry, 1995). Within such a clearly structurally unequal society, where does the suggestion of "post-racialism" or a declining significance of racial inequality come from?

At least part of the answer to this question lies, we suggest, within a changing terrain of racial politics and ideology that emerged as dominant in the post-civil rights era. In reaction to the dramatic challenges of the Civil Rights Movement to the explicitly white racist structure and ideology of the United States, a new ideological framing of race emerged as dominant. The new post-civil rights ideological and discursive frame seemingly incorporates civil rights conceptions of color-blindness, equality and democracy, yet covertly protects white privilege, power, and wealth by rhetorically divorcing these concepts from the structural realities of racial inequality (Bell, 1987, 1992). Rhetorical manipulations of civil rights language makes it possible for individuals to assert, for example, an opposition to racial segregation in schools, and a simultaneous opposition to having their own children bussed in a desegregation plan (see Wellman, 1993). This is accomplished through color-blind and abstract liberalist discursive tactics which recognize race as a superficial set of cultural differences, which should be accepted and celebrated, but simultaneously denies that race has any real effect on the life chances of individuals or that race shapes social life in any significant way (see Bonilla-Silva, 2001, 2003; Carr, 1997; Crenshaw, 1997; DiTamaso, et al. 2003; Doane, 2003; Gallagher, 2003). The notion of post-raciality as an outcome of the election of an African American president fits neatly within the cultural and political context of a society characterized by a major disjuncture in the dominant ideological narrative of racial inequality and the structural actualities of this inequality.

Thus the political atmosphere that enabled the election of Barack Obama is one that is connected to a broader politics of race—which is more nuanced and less obvious than that of previous historical eras. With color-blindness and abstract liberalism at the center of the dominant post-civil rights discourse, the overt racial hostilities of the Jim Crow era were transformed into a seemingly kinder, gentler form of racism, and one which is often less easy to articulate (see, for example Bonilla-Silva, 2001, 2003; Bell and Hartmann, 2007; Feagin, 2009; Moore, 2008; Wellman, 1993). Within this ideological framing, there is room for people of color to occupy positions of power as long as they espouse the central tenets of the color-blind, abstract liberalist position. In fact, this racial "diversity" secures credibility for the broader ideological frame precisely because it provides the appearance that color-blindness and abstract liberalism lead to the dismantling of white supremacy. Yet—and this is why 'diversity' here must remain in quotations—the strategy by which individuals like Barack Obama gain mass white support takes place through the incorporation and presentation of the dominant white framed ideology (see Harvey Wingfield and Feagin, 2009); an ideology that actually functions to secure the reproduction of white privilege, power and wealth. Moreover, the symbolic power of the espousal of the tenets of a white-framed ideology by an African American man is dangerous to real racial progress in that it provides an illustrative tool to those who would assert that the United States is now a post-racial society.

The election of Barack Obama did nothing to dismantle the deeply embedded structural mechanisms that function to maintain racial inequality, yet immediately following his election the media declared his election an indication of racial progress. We suggest that this move is the natural extension of a color-blind, abstract liberalist white racial frame (see Feagin, 2009); one which has been damaging to policies designed to remedy racial inequality, and which functions to protect and preserve structures of inequality. We argue that this sense that we have "arrived" in terms of racial progress in the United States as a result of Barack Obama's presidency is a natural extension of a color-blind, abstract liberalist white racial frame (see Feagin, 2009). Here, we look to the development of affirmative action, one of the most widely recognized racially remedial policies to come out of the Civil Rights Movement to illustrate the dangerous possibility of this frame to impair the development of policy that is racially progressive. It is our contention that while affirmative action was ideologically born in the executive branch, it has been constructed and bounded by the judiciary in a manner that has nearly completely stalled its remedial efficacy. The rhetorical framing of the Court with regard to affirmative action illustrates the power of color-blindness, abstract liberalism, and a white normative conception of "diversity," to retrench the legal protection of white interests. The following analysis of affirmative action, then, illuminates the power of white racial framing as a protective mechanism for white power, privilege and wealth. More than that, it helps to illustrate how color-blindness, abstract liberalism, and the corresponding conception of "diversity" can lead to the election of Barack Obama to the presidency, facilitate the corresponding discursive celebration of racial progress, and at the same time further embed structural racial inequality. We begin with a discussion of the politics of race, move on to establish the role of African Americans in the larger racialized structure and end with an examination of the implications of affirmative action in this context.

THE CHANGING TERRAIN OF THE POLITICS OF RACE

Since the mid- to late 1970s the political landscape has gradually morphed into one deeply connected to the politics of identity and the connection between identity and social structure. The affirmations of identity expressed by oppressed racial groups, as well as women of all races, and the challenges to structural inequalities that was fundamental to the Civil Rights Movement resulted in shifts in political discourse, and in particular in the politics of race (Marable, 1991; Omi and Winant, 1994). Michael Omi and Howard Winant (1994) note that the challenges to racial inequality during the Civil Rights Movement result in a white backlash, one aspect of which was the development of the "new right." The new right, unable to draw upon the old political narrative of natural (or biological) racial inferiority, needed to create new mechanisms by which to protect the racial status quo from further challenge from communities of color (Omi and Winant, 1994, 123). One of the central mechanisms employed by the new right was a new language of race, one which drew upon racially coded language. Thus we see conservative politicians decrying the rise in crime, often voiced over the face of a black man, and calling for a return to law and order; we see challenges to social welfare policies presented with the image of the African American woman portrayed as a "welfare queen" (Hill Collins, 2000), and we find a new rhetorical fervor concerning the dangers of a culture of poverty which deliberately signifies the poverty endemic in African American communities—in other words, a shift towards what has been called a "culture of poverty racism" (Bonilla Silva, 2001).

The tactics of the new right were remarkably successful, ushering in 12 consecutive years of Republican administration during the Reagan and Bush Eras from 1981 to 1993 (and a total of 20 out of 28 years when including the George W. Bush terms) and opening space for a successful Republican takeover of Congress in the 1994 mid-term elections. The broad support for this conservative Republican leadership came from a neo-conservative constituency which effectively co-opted the language of the Civil Rights Movement so that calls for "equality of opportunity" and "color-blindness," which had previously served to illuminate the disjuncture between the rhetorical ideals of democracy and the fact of structural racial inequality, were re-worked in such a way to stall further challenges to white privilege, power, and wealth (Crenshaw, 2007; Lipsitz, 2006). As Omi and Winant (1994, 131) note, "racial discrimination and racial equality—in the neo-conservative model—were problems to be confronted *only* [authors' emphasis] at the individual level, once legal systems of discrimination, ... *de jure* segregation had been eliminated." Through political maneuvers like this, neo-conservatives were able to turn color-blindness from a concept meant to challenge both individual and structural racial oppression into a rhetorical tool of abstract liberalism by asserting concepts like "reverse discrimination" aimed at stalling affirmative action.

The political tactics of neo-conservatives ushered in an era of what Eduardo Bonilla-Silva (2003) has called "color-blind racism." In other words, the post-civil rights discourse has come to be dominated by an ideological framework that minimizes the relevance of race and racism, and discursively divorces structural racial inequality from historical and present day racism (Carr, 1997; Crenshaw, 1998). As Ian Haney Lopez argues, "the perversity of colorblindness [is that it] redoubles the hegemony of race by targeting efforts to combat racism while leaving race and its effects unchallenged and embedded in society, seemingly natural rather than the product of social choice" (2006, 125).

Yet while the post-civil rights politics of race, with its color-blind racist underpinnings, may have had its origins in new right political strategy, its effect was much broader. The discourse of abstract liberalism and color-blind racism spread well beyond the political constituencies of neo-conservatives (Omi and Winant, 1994). In fact, this discourse has come to operate as a central aspect of what Harvey Wingfield and Feagin term the "soft white racial frame" (2009, 19). The white racial frame can be defined as "an organized set of racialized ideas, emotions, and inclinations, as well as recurring or habitual discriminatory actions, that are consciously or unconsciously expressed in, and constitutive of, the routine operation and racist institutions of U.S. society" (Feagin, 2006, 23). With regard to understanding race in the United States there has always existed a master frame, a powerfully dominant framework that centers on whiteness and a white perspective, thereby normalizing and justifying both white superiority and black inferiority. The master frame is cognitive and ideological, but also emotional and visual, and is often implicit so that it does the work of normalizing white privilege and white perspectives on the unconscious level as well as the conscious level. Furthermore, this master frame has been resilient, remaining dominant through centuries of challenge from communities of color, sometimes morphing and shifting, but remaining the pervasive organizing racial logic (Bell, 1987, 1992). While aspects of the white racial frame can be openly racially antagonistic and hostile—what Harvey Wingfield and Feagin (2009,19) term "hard racial framing"—the racial coding and co-optation of the language of equality of abstract liberalism and color-blind racism represents a softer version of the white racial frame. In this way, the rhetorical frames of abstract liberalism and color-blindness can be viewed as discursive mechanisms in the broader white racial frame which ideologically (as well as emotionally and visually) organizes and justifies white racial supremacy.

In the political sphere, the white racial frame found its mirror in the Democratic party in what Omi and Winant (1994) have called neo-liberalism. They note that "neo-liberalism ... does not claim to be color-blind; indeed it argues that any effort to reduce overall inequality ... will disproportionately benefit those concentrated at the bottom of the socio-economic ladder, where racial discrimination has its most damaging effects" (1994, 148). However, they go on to note that "the neoliberal project avoids (as far as possible) framing issues or identities racially" (1994, 148). Here, Omi and Winant (1994) suggest that it was only by avoiding a direct claim of color-blindness, but identifying race only in the most abstract ways, and only in connection with a broader liberal social and economic agenda that will directly benefit whites, that Bill Clinton was able to secure victory after 12 years of Republican administration. This illustrates the pervasive, if subtle, influence of abstract liberalism and the white racial frame in U.S. politics. In the current political landscape, discussions of racial inequality that are not couched within the dominant frame are certainly outside the boundaries of polite conversation and would likely have negative impacts for politicians and political campaigns that engage them.

BLACK BODIES AND THE WHITE RACIAL FRAME

Even before the election of Bill Clinton in 1992, Republicans and their neo-conservative constituency recognized a need to distance themselves from allegations of racism. One of the central ways in which neo-conservatives did this was to engage in the exploitation of Black bodies in the proliferation of an abstract liberalist and color-blind racist ideology. Conservative strategists recognized the power in placing extremely conservative token African Americans into positions of power (Bell, 1994). This tactic provided legitimacy to claims that conservative ideology and discourse were non-racial *political* positions thereby turning the tables on liberal calls for affirmative action in employment, education and politics. This political project was illustrated, for example, when George Bush nominated Clarence Thomas, an African American man, to replace Thurgood Marshall, the first African American Supreme Court Justice to the United States Supreme Court calling into stark question the importance of descriptive versus substantive representation for African Americans.[2] Clarence Thomas, had been appointed as Head of the Equal Employment Opportunity Commission (EEOC) in 1982 by then President Ronald Reagan, specifically for the purpose of changing and limiting the reach of the Commission with regard to racial discrimination in employment. As head of the EEOC, Thomas dramatically shifted the work of the Commission by taking an extremely individualistic view of racial discrimination, and limiting the action of the EEOC to only those cases where individual bad actors could be identified (Greene, 1989, 5). Class action suits and suits that were based upon alleged "pattern and practice" discrimination were no longer investigated by the EEOC (Greene, 1989 5, 54). Having shown himself to be committed to an extremely limited view of discrimination, one which ignored entirely the present day structural consequences of the long history of racial oppression in the United States, Thomas became a natural choice for ultra-conservative President George Bush. It was clear in this move to replace an African American man who had articulated an expansive Constitutional construction in his race jurisprudence which recognized the structural realities of white supremacy, with an African American man who was politically and ideologically the polar opposite, particularly with regard to issues of race, that President Bush was engaged in both denying the realities of race, and using those realities as a political tool to protect white racial privilege, power, and wealth.

Conservatives garnered power by using African Americans who engaged in the discourse of the White Racial Frame to proliferate their message. As Derrick Bell (1994) has noted, the placement of extremely conservative African Americans in positions of power provides an easy retort for allegations of racism: a Black person says these things, so it cannot be racist. Thus, conservative African Americans acquired an authority *never* granted to progressive or critical African Americans (Bell, 1992, 1994). And when the Republicans came back into executive power, with the election of George W. Bush after Bill Clinton's tenure, their strategists seemed even more aware of the power of such exploitation of the bodies of people of color. Hence *Time* magazine made George W. Bush its 2004 Person of the Year, in part by show-casing his appointment of the most "diverse" cabinet in presidential history, proclaiming his "The Benetton-Ad Presidency"[3] (referring to television and print advertisements of the time that showed a wide variety of racial and ethnic types).

To be clear, this political racial project was one that simultaneously ignored *and* participated in the political construction of race. In other words, as Chris Iijima (1997) has noted, race is not only a social and historical construct, but is also fundamentally a *politically* constructed identity. The social location of racial groups, the subordination and oppression of African Americans and people of color and the privileging and empowerment of whites, is one that was created and enforced by the state through force of law and politics (see also Harris, 1993 and Powell, 1997). United States "politics" has always been racialized and the political machinery of the U.S. government has been utilized in the construction of racial groups and the simultaneous construction of racial domination and subordination (Bell, 2000; Omi and Winant, 1994; Urofsky, 2001). Race is not, and has never been, an apolitical construct nor can political constructions in the United States be non-racial (Marable, 1991; Iijima, 1997). Understanding the political nature of race, it becomes clear that from a structural vantage point the effort among conservative whites to find and promote African Americans who espoused conservative political discourse was clearly an exploitation of Black bodies in the service of a broader political project that operated to maintain racial inequality in the midst of a changed social situation. There is no doubt that black conservative politicians believe in their political positions and are certainly responsible for their own politics and ideas. However, here we want to call attention to the crucial symbolic function that black espousers of white racial rhetoric play in the larger political and policy atmosphere.

The exploitation of Black bodies in the service of white supremacist positions is not a new phenomenon in United States racial history (see, for example Hill Collins, 2000; Fanon, 1967). But the post-civil rights neo-conservative political project employed by neo-conservatives utilized the political gains achieved by people of color through the Civil Rights Movement to create a new form of black exploitation—one in which black political officials who espouse and symbolize the dominant white racial frame are put on display in such a way that validates this position on race relations. And though this tactic has been most extreme and obvious when practiced by political conservatives, it is not an uncommon tactic among white liberals (see Bell, 1994). We suggest that Barack Obama serves this same function within white liberal racial discourse by serving as a symbolic or token Black body who espouses soft white racial framing.

Barack Obama, White Liberals, and Post-Civil Rights Politics of Race.

As noted above, the white racial frame is a cognitive, emotional and visual master frame that structures understandings of race and racial equality broadly in the United States. We are arguing that the white racial frame has been employed not only in neo-conservative politics, but is also central to white liberalism. As Omi and Winant note, the election of Bill Clinton was largely a result of a movement of what they term "neoliberals" to put forward a message of abstract liberalism (1994, 152–158). In this political framing, Democratic strategists downplayed continuing significance of racism and structural racial inequality, promoted the idea of universalist and abstractly constructed liberal ideologies of equality, and emphasized the need for individual or "personal" responsibility. The power of these aspects of the white racial frame, and of color-blind racist ideologies, is that they give white liberals the ability to disassociate themselves from explicit racial hostility and animosity while simultaneously benefiting from structural white supremacy and white privilege. These rhetorical and ideological moves appease white liberal guilt over racial oppression while at the same functioning to reproduce structural racial inequality. As we will discuss in the following sections, these discursive frames distort and ultimately stifle progressive racial policies aimed at dismantling structural racial inequality. First, however, it is important to situate the election or Barack Obama to the presidency within this ideological and political project.

As Harvey Wingfield and Feagin (2009) have noted in their analysis of Barack Obama's political campaign, Obama and his campaign staff framed their campaign, and Obama's ideological position, in much the same vein as Bill Clinton had. Obama's campaign manager David Plouffe continually explicitly noted that he did not want race to be a defining aspect of the campaign, and he counseled Obama to avoid making public statements explicitly about race (Harvey Winfield and Feagin, 2009, 40). Despite the clear and obvious fact that Barack Obama would be the first African American president in a country in which African Americans had been violently and systematically oppressed, the campaign downplayed race at every turn. Obama himself downplayed the issue of race by emphasizing his mixed racial heritage, and focusing on appeals to so-called universalistic ideologies of equality of opportunity.

What the election of an African American man who espouses the tenets of the white racial frame does for the frame is key; in the same way that extremely conservative African Americans are supported and utilized in key positions of power by white neo-conservatives in order to claim that their politics are non-racial, having an African American man who centers his political ideology in an abstract liberalist white racial frame enables and lends authority to the white liberal claim of "post-racialism." Furthermore, when the language and the ideological tenets of the white racial frame come from the mouth of an African American, it relieves white people of the perception that they are implicated in contemporary racial inequality or are accountable for past racial harms (Bonilla-Silva, 2003). It is not surprising, then, that Obama received significant support from white voters. As Eduardo Bonilla-Silva has argued about Obama, "the white left and right ... are willing to rally around any minority willing to deny collective and systemic racialized problems" (Bonilla Silva, 2009). It is our claim that Obama's presidency serves as a politically racialized symbol of authority for the white racial frame. With this in mind, we turn to the example of affirmative action as a potentially progressive racial policy, to explicate the implications of this connection between the election of an African American president, abstract liberalism and color-blind ideology, and the potential danger to policy makers interested in dismantling continuing racial inequality.

AFFIRMATIVE ACTION: ABSTRACT LIBERALISM, COLOR-BLIND IDEOLOGY AND DIVERSITY

Affirmative action as it is currently known was born out of the executive branch when, in 1965, President Lyndon B. Johnson signed Executive Order 11246, which required that federal contractors and subcontractors take "affirmative action to ensure that applicants are employed, and that employees are treated during employment, without regard to their race, color, religion, sex, or national origin."[4] This executive call for affirmative steps in remedying racial inequality and disparity in government employment was eventually incorporated into Title VII of the 1964 Civil Rights Act (see Greene, 1989). However, the meaning of "affirmative action," and the parameters of its function as a remedial policy ultimately came from the United

States Supreme Court. In order to understand how affirmative action was legally constructed and defined, and how this relates to Barack Obama and his presidency, it is necessary to examine the manner in which the Court utilizes abstract liberalism and color-blind framing in its racial jurisprudence.

As noted above, a key element of abstract liberalism and color-blindness includes the assertion that "formal legal equality" already exists in the United States as a result of the legal changes coming out of the Civil Rights Movement. That assumption in place, group-based remedial policies like affirmative action were almost immediately challenged by whites who suggested that they were unfairly harmed by these policies and that affirmative action constituted "reverse discrimination." This was precisely the situation in the first Supreme Court case to examine affirmative action. The 1978 case of *Regents of the University of California v Bakke*[5] dealt with the University of California, Davis, School of Medicines decision to implement a policy to set aside seats each year in its admissions process for under-represented minority applicants. A white student, Mr. Bakke, challenged this policy suggesting that it violated his Fourteenth Amendment right to Equal Protection under the law, and constituted Constitutionally impermissible reverse discrimination.

There was no opinion with respect to the constitutionality of affirmative action in the Bakke case because the Court was widely divided on the several issues involved in the case; however the plurality of Justices supporting various aspects of Justice Powell's decision lead to a judgment in the case and Justice Powell's decision became extremely influential in future cases. The reasoning in Justice Powell's decision in *Bakke* was firmly embedded within an abstract liberal and color-blind analysis (as were, the concurring and dissenting opinions). The Court (through Justice Powell and the plurality) said,

> The guarantee of equal protection cannot mean one thing when applied to one individual and something ... else when ... applied to a person of another color. If both are not accorded the same protection, then it is not equal (1978, 289–290).

With this case the Court revealed that it would judge affirmative action policies, as well as other government policies, based upon an *abstract* notion of equality which did not situate that principle within the context of a society and social structure that was racially-constructed andy ordered based explicitly upon the concept of white legal, political, material, moral and ideological supremacy (Thomas, 1990; Harris, 1993; Williams, 1997). Instead, the notion of equality, and "equal protection of the law" would mean like treatment for all individuals, without regard for individuals' differential social location resulting from historical racism, or contemporary structural inequality. The system of setting aside admission seats for under-represented minority applicants was determined to be the equivalent of a "quota" system, which the Court ruled violated the equal protection guaranteed by the Constitution.

The Court in *Bakke* did recognize, however, that there were *limited* circumstances in which race could be considered. Justice Powell stressed that "racial and ethnic distinctions of any sort are inherently suspect and thus call for the most exacting judicial examination." [6] Given this strict construction, it remained a question as to what kind of situation would allow even limitd, consideration of race; the answer was to be found in Justice Powell's construction of the concept of "diversity." Justice Powell suggested that in the context of higher education, a center of knowledge construction and learning, universities had a compelling interest in having diversity in their student body, as this would enhance and increase the learning. As a result of Powell's decision in *Bakke*, "diversity" was legally defined, in the context of education, as a compelling governmental interest. It is important to note, however, the manner in which Powell constructed diversity. Not only was Powell's concept of diversity divorced from any broader construction of systemic or structural racism, but the concept, in a clearly abstract liberal and color-blind fashion, is de-racialized in the sense that diversity is about all characteristics that may add value to knowledge production and learning in education.

Justice Powell explicitly notes in *Bakke* that, "preferring members of any one group for no reason other than race or ethnic origin is discrimination for its own sake" (307). This is true no matter the motivation for the racial consideration (i.e. whether it is for purposes of invidious or malicious discrimination, or to remedy racial inequality resulting from systemic racism). However, Justice Powell notes, "race or ethnic background may be ... deemed a 'plus' in a particular applicant's file ... [such that] the file of a particular black applicant [can] be examined for his potential contribution to diversity without the factor of race being decisive when compared, for example, with that of an applicant identified as an Italian-American if the latter is thought to exhibit qualities more likely to promote beneficial educational pluralism" (1978, 317). The use of race here, in the context of an affirmative action policy to create diversity, may *only* be used as a 'plus' factor and furthermore it must be, "flexible enough to consider *all pertinent elements of diversity* (our emphasis)" (1978, 317). As we discuss in more detail below, Justice Powell's decision in *Bakke* lay the groundwork for both a fundamentally individualistic (as opposed to structural) analysis of race and racial inequality, and an extremely watered down definition of "diversity" which equates race to culture (without structural contextualization) or talent. This conception of diversity becomes important as the affirmative action case law develops after *Bakke*.

After *Bakke*, an important question that remained: What, if anything, would constitute a "compelling" reason to take race into consideration in a remedial project besides the concept of diversity? The Supreme Court would speak on this issue in the 1980 case of *Fullilove v. Klutznick* (1980).[7] The *Fullilove* case came out of a provision to the Public Works Employment Act of 1977 which set aside 10% of the federal grant lunds for public works for services or supplies from "minority business enterprises," an action which was viewed as a statutory articulation of Johnson's executive order concerning affirmative action in government contracts. As in *Bakke,* the Court again divided and produced no conclusive opinion, so that the legal principles had to be gleaned from looking at the plurality opinions. Justice Powell and the plurality remained true to a commitment to the highest level of scrutiny in the case of policies including a racial classification, even for purposes of remedial action; but Justice Powell stated in his opinion, this time speaking only for himself: "I believe that [the 10% set aside of Rinds] is justified as a remedy that serves the *compelling governmental interest in* eradicating the continuing effects of past discrimination identified by Congress (our emphasis)."[8] It seemed, then, that the Court had identified a new compelling interest of the federal government, one based upon the consequences of historical and structural inequality.

It was merely five years later, however, in the case of *Wygant v. Jackson Board of Education,*[9] that the Court began a line of reasoning that explicitly rejected historical or structural racism as a sufficiently compelling reason to enact race conscious remedies like affirmative action. *Wygant* concerned the temporary suspension of a seniority system in the Jackson school system in order to prevent lay-offs that would have a greater effect on more recently hired African American school officials. Although there appeared to be a clear connection to historical discrimination in this case, the Court, this time in an opinion supported by a clear majority noted explicitly that for race based affirmative action policies, "[f]indings of *societal* discrimination will not suffice; the findings must concern 'prior discrimination *by the government unit involved* '(italics in original)."[10] The Court employed an extremely individualistic reasoning; societal, or systemic structural patterns of racial inequality was not a compelling enough reason to allow the government to explicitly account for race. And furthermore, according to the *Wygant* Court, the clearly connected present day affects of historical discrimination would only become compelling when it was proved that the specific agency involved in the case had done the previous discriminating. With this analysis the Court thus attached itself to a narrow abstract individualistic logic which was completely divorced from the explicit historical discrimination which had created the deeply structured racial inequality that policies like affirmative action were designed to remedy.

In the years that followed *Wygant* the Court furthered their abstract individualistic legal analysis, all but decimating the very affirmative action initiative begun by President Johnson: government public works contracts. In the 1989 case of

Richmond v. J.A. Croson Co.[11] involving a public works set-aside program created by the city of Richmond, Virginia (which set aside 30% of the city's contracts to minority owned businesses, based upon the fact that the city population was over 50% African American), the Court held that state and local government agencies could not employ set-asides in public works contracting. In the *Croson* opinion, written by Justice O'Connor, the Court applied an extremely stringent color-blind analysis of this affirmative action policy. Justice O'Connoidwrote, "the standard of review under the Equal Protection Clause is not dependent on the race of those burdened or benefited by a particular classification."[12] In other words, the Court confirmed that it would apply "strict scrutiny" to any government consideration of race whether for purposes of invidious discriminatin, *or* remedial policy. And furthermore the *Croson* Court stated conclusively that remedying widespread racial disparities or inequality did not provide a "compelling" enough government interest to allow use of race-conscious affirmative action; thus striking down the city of Richmond's public works set-aside program as unconstitutional.[13]

The message of *Croson* and made it clear that the Court had moved to a position of extreme abstract liberalist individualism and color-blindness. And in the 1995 *Adarand v. Pena*[14] the Court utilized this color-blind frame to nullify the federal government's 10% government contracts set-asides, and in doing so both explicitly rejected the analysis put forth by Justice Powell in *Fullilove* and ended the initiative beguf by President Johnson in 1964. Yet in *Adarand,* Justice O'Connor noted that the decision did not signal the end of any and all affirmative action policis., despite Justice Thurgood Marshall's statement that strict scrutiny of affirmative action is fatal in fac."[15] Her assurances that, despite the abstract individualistic application of strict scrutiny, there were some forms of affirmative action that would not violate the constitution left an open question as to what, in fact, would provide a compelling enough interest as to allow the government to consider race in a remedial manner. The answer came in the 2003 cases, once again involving affirmative action policies in institutions of higher education, of *Gratz v. Bollinger* and *Grutter v. Bollinger:* diversity.[16] As might be expected, it was once again Justice O'Connor whose opinion explained the framing of the Court in both *Gratz* and *Grutter,* and her opinion relied heavily upon Justice Powell's conception of diversity in the Bakke case. The conclusion of the two cases was that diversity in education is a compelling enough interest that some consideration of race might be used for affirmative action admissions policies by colleges and universities. Securing the Court's adherence to the abstract liberal principle of individualism, as opposed to a recognition of group-based consequences resulting from societal racism and discrimination, past and present. However, she rejected any mechanical formulation in the method of considering race in admissions (see e.g. *Gratz)* and limited consideration of race to those that only considered race on an individual basis as part of an examination of the whole person (see e.g. *Grutter*). Quoting at length from Justice Powell's decision in the Bakke case, Justice O'Connor said, "a university may consider race or ethnicity only as a '""plus' in a particular applicant's file," without "insulating the individual from comparison with all other candidates for the available seats. ..." In other words, an admissions program must be "flexible enough to consider all pertinent elements of diversity in light of the particular qualifications of each applicant, and to place them on the same footing for consideration, although not necessarily according them the same weight" (citations removed).[17]

As we have already noted, this conception of diversity is grounded in an abstract liberalism, color-blind ideology and the white racial frame—an "assumption of a white center to which color is harmoniously added" (Bell and Hartmann, 2007, 909). This construction of diversity, which is central to U.S. affirmative action jurisprudence, dilutes and minimizes the political relevance of race and racism (both historical and contemporary) at the same time that it purports to recognize the politics of race. The Court's conception of diversity echoes, and is echoed back by the same white racial framing employed in white liberal discourse, and the political discursive frame of Barack Obama. The consequence of this framing with regard to affirmative action policies has been all but fatal.

We note that many of the decisions we have discussed have been written by, and supported by, conservative Justices of the Supreme Court, nearly all of whom were appointed to the Court by conservative and Republican Presidents. Some might argue that Barack Obama has already influenced this frame by appointing Sonia Sotomayor, someone who has shown a commitment to liberal framing in her jurisprudence, to the Supreme Court. We argue that this appointment has limited ability to shape the Courts framing of affirmative action policy for three important reasons. First, Justice Sotomayor does not have structural power on the Court, given that she replaced a similarly liberal Justice Souter, and the majority of the Court remains clearly committed to the principles set forth in the cases discussed herein (in fact, the current Court majority may be even more committed to color-blind, abstract liberalism and the white racial frame). Second, even were Barack Obama able to recompose the Court, a possibility that seems highly unlikely, the principle of *stare decisis*, which requires the Court to recognize and remain consistent with the dictates of past legal decisions, would bind the hands of a liberal Court without a serious departure from and rejection of the current legal frame in all its abstract liberal and color-blind positioning. And this brings us to our third, and most crucial point, the dominant liberal ideological rhetoric, relying as it does on principles of abstract liberalism, color-blindness, and conceptions of diversity as happy-talk, *cannot* dismantle the deeply embedded white racial framing of race and affirmative action in the law.

BARACK OBAMA, ABSTRACT LIBERALISM AND DIVERSITY

Responding to his own victory Barack Obama proclaimed:

> If there is anyone out there who doubts that America is a place where anything is possible, who still wonders if the dream of our founders is alive in our time, who still questions the power of our democracy, tonight is your answer. Young and old, rich and poor, Democrat and Republican, black, white, Hispanic, Asian, Native American, gay, straight, disabled and not disabled … We have been and always will be the United States of America.

In this emotionally powerful historical moment, President-elect Obama, by virtue of his words as well as his own racial identity, affirmed the color-blind notion that equality of opportunity is real in the United States, and that there are universalistic normative American values that transcend race (as well as age, class, political affiliation, sexuality, and ability). Here Obama utilizes the diversity element of the white racial frame as well as tacitly utilizing his own racial status in such a way to decry the universalist and abstract liberalist idea that upward mobility, even to the U.S. presidency, is an equally attainable possibility for all U.S. citizens (see Bonilla-Silva, 2009). Unfortunately, this statement blithely ignores the realities of the racial social structure, and in doing so Obama feeds directly into an already existing racialized legal frame.

As we illustrate in our examination of affirmative action above, a central way in which color-blindness gets articulated in both ideology and action in the institutional contexts of American life is through the notion of diversity. Diversity as a racial project fits nicely into the dominant white racial frame because it simultaneously recognizes racial difference and avoids discussions of power, privilege and inequality. Part of the way that diversity works is to encourage the celebration of symbolic elements of difference that are in-line with a feel-good conception of race, which Joyce Bell and Doug Hartmann (2007) have called "happy talk." Harmony, then, is central to the diversity project in such a way that any discussion of discord among the "different" doesn't fit in the confines of the discourse.

In some ways Barack Obama is a central figurehead in the diversity project. Beyond his strategic framing of his "multi-cultural" heritage as post-racial, Obama's racial message has been very much in-line with diversity's "happy talk" tenor (see Eduardo Bonilla-Silva, 2009). In his famous single speech on the subject of race during the 2008 campaign, *A More Perfect Union,* Obama certainly focuses on racial inequality.

But the speech is constructed in such a way to suggest that despite all of the racial disparities we see, that he is convinced that we are fundamentally a society that is not divided by race. For example, in that speech he talks about his decision to run for president, saying,

> ... I believe deeply that we cannot solve the challenges of our time unless we solve them together, unless we perfect our union by understanding that we may have different stories, but we hold common hopes; that we may not look the same and we may not have come from the same place, but we all want to move in the same direction—towards a better future for of children and our grandchildren.

This "vague promise of racial reconciliation," as Adolph Reed (2008) termed it, holds fast to a notion that racial harmony is possible, desirable, indeed on its way, without ever offering new or validating existing solutions for addressing past or present racial injustices.

This rhetoric is particularly troubling because of that way that his racial identity shapes how people receive these messages. A black man, whose set of racial ideas is packaged in such a way to minimize our discomfort about racial inequality, thus works to validate the white racial frame. Regardless of the reasons behind his employment of the frame, the outcome is to reinforce a conception of race that, at its core, holds that there may be racial problems, but that we each, individually need to address our role in reaching our "common hopes." This is a conception that most often precludes structural remedies.

CONCLUSION

We suggest that the notion that the election of the U.S.'s first black president has transformed our society into one that is "post-racial" is much more insidious than being merely a troublesome liberal discursive move. Rather, we suggest that the combination of the symbolic significance of Obama's election, combined with the discursive assertion of post-racialism has the potential to further entrench the severe and serious structural racial inequalities in U.S. society that continue to limit the life chances of people of color, especially African Americans.

We need only consult the legal history of affirmative action policy to understand the potential of the white racial frame to stall or even regress potentially progressive racial policies. Our analysis of affirmative action case law reveals that the court's reliance on the frames of color-blindness has resulted in a turning back of the clock on affirmative action as a remedy for unequal access to education and jobs for people of color. The idea that race is no more than a set of individual characteristics and that racism is purely an individual disorder creates a policy atmosphere that is hostile to projects that seek to redress racial inequality on a structural level.

We fear that we are in a dangerous moment in U.S. history with regards to racial policy. The fact that we have a black man as president who is politically situated squarely within the white racial frame creates the ultimate justification for failing to create policy that promotes racial equality on a structural level. The very fact of his black body occupying the most powerful office in the country, indeed, the world, could be reason enough to claim that we have arrived—the ultimate proof of equality of opportunity. Combine this with Obama's espousal of a set of ideas that encourages that line of thinking, and his election, a truly exceptional event, becomes the grounds for claiming the end of racism—an idea that the millions of people of color in the United States who suffer because of racism cannot afford.

Lastly, then, we must note the structural insignificance of the election of Barack Obama. He is the only president of the U.S. to not be a white man. In a statistical analysis he would be an outlier—potentially an interesting case, but irrelevant in the sense of representativeness. In our estimation, the importance of Obama's election, from the standpoint of race scholars and policy-makers, must be to interrogate the manner in which his race gets utilized in discursive racial moves (explicitly or tacitly), in connection with his politics, to further a white liberalistic agenda which entrenches racial structural inequality.

NOTES

1   *Brown v. Board of Education,* 347 U.S. 483 (1954).

2   See Guinier 1994; Swain 1995, 1993; Thernstrom 1987; and Tate 2004 on the subject of descriptive and symbolic versus substantive representation. These authors take up the long standing debate in black politics about whether black bodies are necessary for black political representation or if white politicians can represent black interests, calling into question whether descriptive representation is the same as substantive representation. We certainly argue here that descriptive representation isn't enough to remedy racial inequality, but take a more nuanced perspective that claims that the very presence of black politicians who espouse the dominant racial frame reinforces the existing racial order in a way that is detrimental to progressive racial policy.

3   http://www.time.com/time/subscriber/personoftheyear/2004/poyklein.html

4   3 C.F.R. Sect. 340 (1965).

5   *Regents of the University of California v. Bakke,* 438 U.S.265 (1978).

6   *Regents of California v. Bakke,* 438 U.S. at 291 (1978).

7   *Fullilove v. Klutznick,* 448 U.S. 448 (1980).

8   *Fillilove v. Kltznick,* J. Powell concurring, 448 U.S. at 496 (1980).

9   *Wygant v. Jackson Board of Education*, 476 U.S. 267 (1985).

10 *Wygant v. Jackson Board of Education*, 476 U.S. at 274 (1985). Note that in the *Wygant case,* the Court discusses Title VII of the 1964 Civil Rights Act, and its specific protection of seniority systems (a clear protection for white workers that served to structurally embed white privilege power and wealth even as Congress attempted to address racial inequality). We do not discuss the line of cases that deal only with Title VII and its amendments; these are cases which discuss the boundaries of affirmative action for private employers. We make this decision for the sake of brevity, because this case law is lengthy and is tied to principles of employment law, as well as employment discrimination law more broadly, which would make an adequate handling of these cases impossible for this article. In addition, our focus here is upon government action, and specifically the ability of elected officials, particularly Barack Obama as president, to affect racial change. We do note, however, that the case law involving Title VII does employ a abstract liberalist and color-blind framing very similar to that articulated in the Equal Protection cases we review herein. See for example, *Ward's Cove Packing Co. v. Antonio,* 109 S. Ct. 2115 (1989) and *Ricci v. DeStafano, 557* U.S. _____ (2009).

11 *Richmond v. J. A. Croson Co.,* 488 U.S. 469 (1989).

12 *Richmond v. J. A. Croson Co.,* 488 U.S at 493–4 (1989).

13 *Id.* at 485.

14 *Adarand* v. *Pena,* 515 U.S. 200 (1995).

15 Justice O' Connor was responding to the allegation by Justice Thurgood Marshall that in the case of affirmative action strict scrutiny was "strict in theory, fatal in feet" stated in his opinion in the *Fullilove* case. See *Fullilove v. Klutznick,* 448 U.S. at 519 (1989).

16 Gratz v. Bollinger, 539 U.S. 234 (2003); *Grutter v Bollinger,* 539 U.S. 306 (2003).

17 *Grutter v Bollinger,* 539 U.S. at 336 (2003).

REFERENCES

Andersen, Margaret. 1999. "Diversity Without Oppression: Race, Ethnicity, Identity and Power. In *Critical Ethnicity: Countering the Waves of Identity Politics,* Mary Kenyatta and Robert Tai, eds. Totowa, NJ: Rowman and Littlefield.

Bell, Derrick. 1987. *And We are Not Saved: The Elusive Quest for Racial Justice.* New York: Basic Books.

——. 1992. *Faces at the Bottom of the Well: The Permanence of Racism.* New York: Basic Books.

——. 1994. *Confronting Authority: Reflections of an Ardent Protester.* Boston: Beacon Press.

——. 2000. *Race, Racism and American Law.* Fourth Edition. New York: Aspen Press.

Bell, Joyce and Douglas Hartmann. 2007. "Diversity in Everyday Discourse: The Cultural Ambiguities and Consequences of 'Happy Talk'." *American Sociological Review* 72. 895–914.

Bobo, Lawrence, James R. Kluegel, and Ryan Smith. 1997. "Laissez-Faire Racism: The Crystallization of a Kinder, Gentler Antiblack Ideology," in *Racial Attitudes in the 1990s, Continuity and Change,* Steven A. Tuch and Jack K. Martin, eds. Westport, Connecticut: Praeger.

Bonilla-Silva, Eduardo and Victor Ray. 2008. "When Whites Love a Black Leader: Race Matters in Obamamerica." *Journal of African American Studies* 13: 176–183.

———. 1997. "Rethinking racism: Toward a Structural Interpretation." *American Sociological Review* 62. 465–480.

———. 2001. *White Supremacy and Racism in the Post-Civil Rights Era* Boulder, CO: Lynne Rienner Publishers, Inc.

———. 2003. *Racism without Racists: Colorblind Racism and the Persistence of Racial Inequality in the United States.* Lanham, MD: Rowman & Littlefield

Carr, Leslie. 1997. *Colorblind Racism.* Thousand Oaks, CA: Sage.

Crenshaw, Kimberle W. 1997. "Colorblind Dreams and Racial Nightmares: Reconfiguring Racism in the Post-Civil Rights Era." In *Birth of a Nation'hood,* Toni Morrison and Claudia Brodsky Lacour, eds. New York: Pantheon Books.

Crenshaw, Kimberle. 1998. "Race, Reform, and Retrenchment: Transformation and Legitimation in Antidiscrimination Law." *Harvard Law Review* 101: 1331–1383.

Conley, Dalton. 2009. *Being Black, Living in the Red: Race, Wealth and Social Policy in America.* Berkeley: University of California Press.

Crenshaw, Kimberle W. 2007. *"Framing Affirmative Action,"* Michigan Law Review 105: 123–133. Retrieved from http://www.michiganlawreview.org/firstimpressions/voll05/crenshaw.pdf.

Davis, Angela. 1993. *Are Prisons Obsolete?* New York: Seven Stories Press.

DiTamaso, Nancy, Rochelle Parks-Yancy, and Corinne Post. 2003. "White Views of Civil Rights: Color Blindness and Equal Opportunity." In *White Out: The Continuing Significance of Racism,* Ashley Doane and Eduardo Bonilla-Silva, eds. New York: Routledge.

Doane, Ashley W. and Eduardo Bonilla-Silva. 2003. *White Out: The Continuing Significance of Racism.* New York: Routledge.

Estrada, Kelly and Peter McLaren. 1993. "A Dialogue on Multiculturalism and Democratic Culture." *Educational Researcher,* 22(3): 27–33.

Fanon, Frantz. 1967. *Black Skin White Mask.* New York: Grove Press.

Feagin, Joe. 2000. *Racist America.* New York: Routledge.

———. 2006. *Systemic Racism.* New York: Routledge.

———. 2009. *The White Racial Frame.* New York: Routledge.

Feagin, Joe, Heman Vera, and Nikitah Imani. 1997. *The Agony of Education.* New York: Routledge.

Flagg, Barbara J. 1993. "'Was Blind But Now I See': White Race Consciousness and the Requirement of Discriminatory Intent." *Michigan Law Review* 91: 953–1017.

Gallagher, Charles A. 2003. "Color-Blind Privilege: The Social and Political Functions of Erasing the Color Line in Post Race America. *Race, Gender, and Class* 10(4): 22–37.

Glover, Karen S. 2009. *Racial Profiling: Research, Racism, and Resistance.* Lanham, MD: Rowman & Littlefield.

Greene, Kathanne. 1989. *Affirmative Action and Principles of Justice.* New York: Greenwood Press.

Guinier, Lani. 1994. *The Tyranny of the Majority: Fundamental Fairness in Representative Democracy.* New York: The Free Press.

Haney López, Ian. 2006. *White by Law.* New York: New York University Press.

Harris, Cheryl. 1993. "Whiteness as Property." *Harvard Law Review,* 106: 1709–1789.

Harvey Wingfield, Adia and Joe R. Feagin. 2009. *Yes We Can? White Racist Framing and the 2008 Presidential Campaign.* New York: Routledge.

Hill Collins, Patricia. 2000. *Black Feminist Thought.* New York: Routledge.

Iijima, Chris. 1997. "The Era of We-construction: Reclaiming the Politics of Asian Pacific Identity and Reflections on the Critique of the Black/Whitc Paradigm." *Columbia Human Rights Law Journal.* 15: 47–90.

Jackman, Mary. 1996. "Individualism, Self-interest, and White Racism." *Social Sciences Quarterly* 77:760–67.

Jargowsky, Paul A. 1997. *Poverty and Place: Ghettos, Barrios, and the American City.* New York: Russell Sage Foundation.

Kozol, Jonathan. 1991. *Savage Inequalities.* New York: Harper Collins.

Lewis, Amanda. 2003. *Race in the Schoolyard: Negotiating the Color Line in Classrooms and Communities.* New Brunswick, NJ: Rutgers University Press.

Lipsitz, George. 2006. *The Possessive Investment in Whiteness.* Philadelphia: Temple University Press.

Marable, Manning. 1991. *Race, Reform, and Rebellion.* Jackson: University Press of Mississippi.

Miller, Mark. 1995. *The High Priests of American Politics.* Knoxville: University of Tennessee Press.

Massey, Douglas S. and Nancy A. Denton. 1993. *American Apartheid; Segregation and the Making of the Underclass.* Cambridge: Harvard University Press.

Moore, Wendy Leo. 2008. *Reproducing Racism: White Space, Elite Law Schools, and Racial Inequality.* Lanham, MD: Rowman &C Littlefield.

Oliver, Melvin and Thomas Shapiro. 2006. *Black Wealth/White Wealth: A New Perspective on Racial Inequality.* New York: Routledge.

Omi, Michael and Howard Winant. 1994. *Racial Formation in the United States: From the 1960s to the 1990s.* New York: Routledge.

Orfield, Gary and Susan Eaton. 1996. *Dismantling Desegregation: The Quiet Reversal of Brown v. Board of Education.* New York: New Press.

Powell, John. 1997. "The "Racing" of American Society: Race Functioning as a Verb Before Signifying as a Noun." *The Journal of Law and Inequality,* Vol. 15: 99–147.

Reed, Adolph. 2008. Obama, no. *The Progressive.* May. Retrieved from http://www.progressive.org/mag_reed0508

Ross, Thomas. 1990. "Innocence and Affirmative Action." *Vanderbilt Law Review* 43:297–376

——. 1990. "The Rhetorical Tapestry of Race: White Innocence and Black Abstraction," *William & Mary Law Review.* 32: 1—42.

Swain, Carol. 1993. *Black Faces, Black Interests.* Cambridge: Harvard University Press.

——.1995. "Strategies for Increasing Black Representation in Congress." *The Politics of Race,* Theodore Rueter, ed. Annonk: M.E. Share.

Thernstrom, Abigail M. 1987. *Whose Votes Count?* Cambridge: Harvard University Press.

——. 1995. "More Notes from a Political Thicket." *Emory Law Journal* 44:911–941.

Tonry, Michael. 1995. *Malign Neglect.* New York: Oxford University Press.

Urofsky, Melvin I. 1988. *A March of Liberty; A Constitutional History of the United States Since 1865, volume II,*. New York: McGraw Hill.

Wellman, David T. 1993. *Portraits of White Racism.* **Second Edition. Cambridge: Cambridge University Press.**

Williams, Patricia. 1997. *Seeing a Color-Blind Future: The Paradox of Race.* **New York: The Noon Day Press.**

Reading 4.6.

Take the Ishihara Race Test
Stephen Is Race-blind (And So Can You!)

by John Jacobson And Jeffrey Gauthier

This is a test. Look closely at the following images. Your responses will determine whether you, like Stephen, are truly race-blind.

HERE'S HOW TO EVALUATE YOUR RESULTS

Figure 4.6.1. If you're oblivious to the big 'E', you may suffer from Colbertian Race Blindness. For Colbert, blacks and whites look the same. If you see the big 'E', but want to know how the race-blind would see *Figure 4.6.1,* then look at *Figure 4.6.2.*

Of course Colbert could be faking, just putting us on, and pretending he cannot see the big letter. So, the race-blindness test battery includes stimuli such as *Figure 4.6.3* in which normals see just bears and people who are race-blind can see a super-imposed figure; in this instance a lowercase letter 't' (*Figure 4.6.4*).

As far as we know, race-blindness only afflicts whites, and is associated with, among other things, the confounding of racial equality with racial indifference, the belief that Chinese and Japanese are the same, and, in the worst cases, schizoid identity disorder (witness Colbert's "People tell me I'm white, and I believe them because police call me 'sir.'"[1]).

John Jacobson and Jeffrey Gauthier, "Take the Ishihara Race Test: See if You Are Colorblind Like Stephen!," *Stephen Colbert and Philosophy: I Am Philosophy (And So Can You!),* pp. 259-262. Copyright © 2009 by Cricket Media. Reprinted with permission.

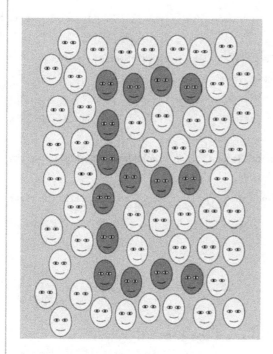

FIGURE 4.6.1   Stimulus A

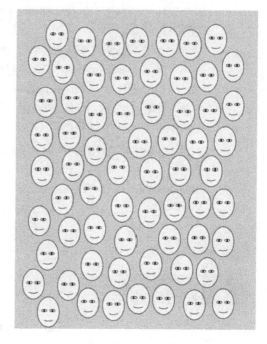

FIGURE 4.6.2   How Stephen Sees Stimulus A

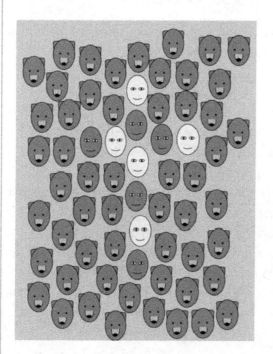

FIGURE 4.6.3   Stimulus B

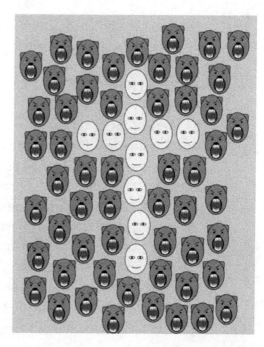

FIGURE 4.6.4   How Stephen Sees Stimulus B

To truly generate empathy for the race-blind and see the world from their eyes, it's useful to understand their view of the Civil Rights Movement (1954–1968). According to the race-blind, Civil Rights philosophy discovered that whites and blacks are the same, with the same histories, the same developmental environments, and perfectly identical cultures. And when the race-blind imagine Dr. King's vision of a colorblind society, all people are one color: white.[2]

NOTES

1   Episode 3016, originally aired February 1st, 2007.

2   Episode 5012, originally aired January 22nd, 2009. "Why not have everybody just be white? And then there's no racism. ... Why not dream, as I believe Dr. King did, that one day *everyone* would be the same color?"

Reading 4.7.

Black Males in the Green Mountains: Colorblindness and Cultural Competence in Vermont Public Schools

by Abimbola Akanni and Denise Helen Dunbar

Denis Helen Dunbar, scholar, advocate, consultant and anti-racist educationist could not have been ingenuously described. The startling boldness and clear-cut approach with which she unmasked racism and inequality in the educational system in Vermont public schools could not have better done other than someone who has lived in Vermont for more that thirty-one years. This is coupled with her 30 years of experience in the field of social justice education. Her choice of title for the book aptly reflects her concern for equal educational curriculum for both white as well as students of color. Living in Vermont has afforded her the privilege of observing the racist attitude of whites that has been institutionalized over a long period of time at the expense of students' of color aspirations for success.

Racism in public schools has been a theme that scholars and public analysts are often careful to openly talk about. But with her wealth of experience, the author professionally painted a fascinating description of Vermont spiced with Green Mountains with its alluring beauty to anyone visiting the place for the first time, in other to craftily present whites' color blindness to racism, against students of color. The book offers an explicit account of the deceptive picture of Vermont, which is quite "vocal in its antislavery rhetoric, as having "a documented history of racism". She acknowledged that the completing the book was by no means a solo endeavour,

Abimbola Akanni, "Black Males in the Green Mountains: Colorblindness and Cultural Competence in Vermont Public Schools," *The Journal of Pan African Studies*, vol. 6, no. 8, pp. 268-270. Copyright © 2014 by Itabari Zulu. Reprinted with permission. Provided by ProQuest LLC. All rights reserved.

but a shared process of many years of concerted efforts (p. 3). In the spirit of racial justice, the subject of the book shows how she moved from exposing the consequences of racism to creating the need to identify and respect cultural difference in the public schools.

In a professional manner, Dunbar uses a nuanced qualitative research method to specifically open a discussion on a sensitive but crucial concept—racism. Her presentations describe the synopsis of racism, its continued prevalence, and how to minimize its negative effects on students of color. The book is divided into two parts of five chapters. The first part consists of two chapters that reveal the serenity of Vermont in the picture of the Twenty-first century schools viz-a-viz the realities of the educational system that operate there. Looking through the lens of the critical race theory, a down-to-earth description of the Black males unpleasant experiences were presented.

In the acknowledgement section, the author succinctly describe the numerous sources upon which she relied, including the academic and social justice inspirations at various levels and phase of the write-up. The women of African Diaspora were also acknowledged. The "Bibliography" section concludes the book coupled with the index that serves as a quick link to both the key names and subjects for easy navigation through the book.

The titles of the chapters accurately reveal their contents. The first chapter "Don't Believe the Hype" exposes the concealed voice of the new face of Vermont, the race based bullying harassment that characterised the black mountains with dots of anti-slavery rhetoric, religious intolerance, bigotry and hatred contrary to the scenic splendour and beauty of the green mountains that seduced her from the very beginning. The next chapter, titled "Does Race Matters?," chronicles the genesis of racism that was meant to "create a sense of inferiority status in order to oppress and dehumanize blacks" (p. 44). The third chapter, titled "In the Field," presents testimonial accounts of adults as well as personal perspectives to bring lived experiences to the audiences who need to know. "Voices from the Field" identifies those needs that are still unmet as far as equal opportunity for the students of colour are concerned. She came up with 20 themes that aligned with the 20 domains in the critical race theory. The final chapter evidently admits that the colour line still exists and that "strategic plan to move the district forward in its efforts to making the schools socially equitable" be jointly pursued (p. 144).

My thoughtful sojourn through the pages of the book offered me a sense of deep appreciation of the expertise with which Dunbar pressed home her demand for social equity in Vermont public schools. The five-chaptered book systematically takes the reader through a ride from the deceptive picture of no racism to the appreciation of its existence in Vermont. Dunbar assiduously unearths the depth of racism through scientific technique. Using snowball sampling technique, she sampled the opinions of thirteen Black males who had in one time or the other suffered racism, unjust discipline over non-violent incidents (p. 57). The voice of and the will of the people has spoken by making it clear that racism is a problem in our schools (p. 144)

She convincingly argued that "there appeared to have been an overall lack of respect for students of color, especially related to teachers' and administrators' resistance to responding to racial issues" (p. 21). Staff and administrators were not responding timely and in a just manner to bullying and harassment that was racial in nature. This was as a result of "vested color blindness and unconscious internalized bias" that has been imprinted in the psychics of the whites (p. 132).

Besides frankly challenging racism, color blindness and cultural incompetence, Dr. Dunbar challenged the attitudes of administrators and educators even with her own "institutional racism". She did not limit the scope of her argument to Vermont but also to the entire district. Dunbar opined that educators must start with themselves, examining flawed perceptions, and choose to improve their teaching services. She thoughtfully quoted Murrell, 2002

"Teachers of African American students must be able to understand contemporary educational theory and apply it to their practice while integrating the historical, cultural, political and developmental considerations of the African American experience into a unified system of practice for educational achievement" (Murrell, 2002).

Considering the fact that racist's attitudes negatively impact on the self-worth and self-efficacy of Black males, the author suggests that strong school leadership that will take ownership of the work needed to get males on courses for success, male empowerment sessions, and culturally responsive schools will enable Black males overcome the dreadful outcomes of racism (p. 167). Having grown up in mixed neighbourhoods where she had white people as both her biological and extended family and was exposed to racism and whites color blindness, she is qualified to exquisitely write this book.

THE RESULTS OF RACE INEQUALITY (VALUE GAP)

- Eddie Glaude, professor of religion and African American studies at Princeton University introduces the value gap: "Put simply, it is the belief that white people matter more. And the extent to which that belief animates our habits, behavior, and racial practices."[2] He also says that the value gap is "an inherent barrier to democracy."

- Suggests the value gap is at the heart of the maintenance and acceptance of not just contemporary racial inequality but was also inscribed in the US nearly from its inception.

CRITICAL THINKING:	Do American ideals challenge the value gap? Or is the value gap an American ideal?

Reading 4.8.

The Challenge of Inequality

by Justin Steil

Economic inequality and mobility are increasingly recognized as defining issues for America's future. Between 2009 and 2012, 95% of all national income gains went to the very top 1% of earners. Extreme concentrations of income and wealth pose fundamental challenges to America's ideals of democracy and equal opportunity. Indeed, President Obama remarked in December that "increasing inequality ... challenges the very essence of who we are as a people." (Obama 2013) Evoking Eleanor Roosevelt and Harry Belafonte, New York City Mayor Bill de Blasio focused his inaugural remarks on the crisis of inequality faced by the city, resolving that he would not let inequality "define our future." (de Blasio 2014)

What do we actually know about the dynamics of income inequality over time? And what can be done about it? Recent economics research by some of our nation's leading scholars offers important insights into these profound challenges now facing American society. This article reviews some of this recent scholarship, including studies from scholars affiliated with the Economic Disparities research cluster of the Haas Institute for a Fair and Inclusive Society at U.C. Berkeley, on accelerating economic inequality, the stalled rate of economic mobility, and the shrinking of the middle class. It also describes several policy recommendations that emerge from this research to address either rising income inequality or rising poverty rates, including raising the

---

2   Eddie S. Glaude, *Democracy in Black: How Race Still Enslaves the American Soul* (New York: Crown, 2016); Moyers & Company, "The Value Gap in America Today," May 10, 2016, https://www.youtube.com/watch?v=A5R5966c7Ek.

Justin Steil, "The Challenge of Inequality," *Poverty and Race*, vol. 23, no. 2, pp. 1-2, 6-9. Copyright © 2014 by Poverty & Race Research Action Council. Reprinted with permission. Provided by ProQuest LLC. All rights reserved.

minimum wage, enhancing the Earned Income Tax Credit, taxing more progressively, extending investments in education, and addressing residential segregation.

ACCELERATING INEQUALITY

The share of the national income received by the top 1% of residents in the United States has more than doubled over the last 30 years, rising from 9% of the total in 1976 to more than 22.5% (including capital gains) in 2012. (Alvaredo et al. 2014) The average annual income for the top 1% of households in 2012 was about $1.3 million, as compared to the median household income of $51,371. (Alvaredo et al. 2014) The increasing share of income going to the top 1% of earners is not limited only to states that are centers of banking and finance (such as New York and Connecticut, where average incomes of the top 1% in 2011 were roughly 40 times those of the bottom 99%), but extends to every state in the nation. (Sommeiller & Price 2014)

The recent recession has only exacerbated this inequality because its effects were not evenly distributed. In terms of unemployment rates, the recession affected men more than women, African Americans and Latinos more than whites, and younger workers more than older workers. The recession's impact on unemployment for black men was almost double that for white men and the impact for black women was almost triple that for white women. (Hoynes, Miller & Schaller 2012) Overall, declining workforce participation rates have added a significant obstacle in the path of working- and middle-class families' efforts to move further up the economic ladder and have pushed many families into poverty. These challenges are reflected, for example, in an increase in the poverty rate from 12.5% in 2007 to 15.9% in 2012. More than 1 in 5 children currently live in poverty.

STALLED ECONOMIC MOBILITY

The growing economic inequality that the recession accentuated is of particular concern because that growing inequality has the effect of pulling the rungs on the ladder of class advancement farther apart, potentially affecting economic mobility. It is a long-standing pillar of faith in the United States that regardless of where one starts out, one has the opportunity to do better than one's parents. Yet recent research by Raj Chetty, Nathaniel Hendren, Patrick Kline & Emmanuel Saez (2014) finds that how much children are able to earn as adults is strongly correlated with how much their parents earned. While there is indeed still some mobility across classes, the majority of children retain an economic status similar to that of their parents—more than 60% of those children who grew up in families with incomes in the top fifth of income earners remain in the top two-fifths, while more than 60% of those children who grew up in families with incomes in the bottom fifth remain in the bottom two-fifths (Chetty et al. 2014).

One of the most surprising findings in this research is that intergenerational mobility varies substantially by metropolitan region. The probability that a child from the bottom fifth will end up in the top fifth of income earners is only 4.4% in Charlotte but nearly three times higher in San Jose—12.9%. (Chetty et al. 2014) A child whose parents' earnings were in the 20th percentile ends up, on average, in the 45th percentile in Salt Lake City, but only the 35th percentile in Indianapolis. (Chetty et al. 2014) In short, the geographic location where one grows up matters significantly for where one ends up economically as an adult.

"The middle class is shrinking."

A GROWING ECONOMY BUT A SHRINKING MIDDLE CLASS

At the same time as inequality is increasing and mobility seems stagnant, the middle class is shrinking. Between 1990 and 2012, the proportion of households with incomes between $40,000 and $100,000 (in 2012 constant dollars) fell from 43% to 39%, while the proportion of households with incomes less than $40,000 (in 2012 constant dollars) increased from 35% to 39%. The middle class is increasingly being pushed toward poverty. But it's not because the U.S. economy has failed to grow.

During the three decades following the Second World War, the United States witnessed rapid upward mobility because productivity and wages grew together and gains were relatively evenly distributed over the income scale. Since the 1980s, however, productivity has continued to grow (increasing by 78% between 1980 and 2009) yet median wages have stagnated. (Levy & Kochan 2012) In the 30 years between 1982 and 2012, the median household income increased only $5,289, from $46,082 to $51,371 (in 2012 constant dollars). Where, then, did the economic gains from increased productivity go? A growing share went to the top 1%.

From 1993 to 2012, the incomes of the top 1% grew by 86%, while the incomes of the remaining 99% grew by just 6.6% (an annual growth rate of only 0.34%). (Saez 2013) The top 1% captured over two-thirds of the overall income growth between 1993 and 2012. (Saez 2013) This disparity has only grown since the recession. Looking just at the time period since the economic recovery began in 2009, fully 95% of all of the national income gains went to the top 1%. (Saez 2013)

IS INEQUALITY INEVITABLE?

Some suggest that this widening gulf between the wealthiest few and the rest is inevitable (e.g., Cowen 2013). Broad historical and international trends suggest, however, that we have the capacity to reduce income inequality and increase economic mobility. First, incomes in the United States were much more equal from the 1940s through the 1970s, when the top 1% of earners took home roughly 9% of national income and the economy grew at a rapid pace. (Alvaredo et al. 2013) Indeed, the significant income gains of the immediate post-war period were generally equally shared across classes. (Alvaredo etal. 2013) Second, the fact that many other industrialized countries have not experienced the same rapid increase in inequality yet have continued to grow economically at a similar pace suggests that national policies can make a difference. (Alvaredo et al. 2013) Finally, the findings with regard to the wide gaps in economic mobility across metropolitan regions suggest that local policies can also influence access to opportunity. (Chetty et al. 2014)

Recent economic research suggests that it is possible to reduce inequality and address poverty without significantly slowing economic growth by, among other things, increasing the minimum wage, enhancing the Earned Income Tax Credit, taxing more progressively, investing in education, and addressing segregation.

MINIMUM WAGES

One approach to reducing income inequality is to raise wages for those workers at the bottom of the distribution, the nearly 4 million workers earning the minimum wage or below. (Bureau of Labor Statistics 2011) Congress and the White House are currently debating an increase in the federal minimum wage, but there is uncertainty about the impact any increase will have on employment rates, especially for the low-wage workers the increase is meant to help.

The primary argument against the minimum-wage increase is that it may lead to losses in low-wage jobs because: 1) higher wages will raise the cost to employers of producing goods and services and consumers will then reduce their consumption as prices rise; and 2) employers forced to pay higher wages will have more incentives to substitute more efficient technologies for low-wage workers. Any effects on employment rates are likely to fall disproportionately on those groups already hardest hit by the decline in employment during the recession, such as black low-wage workers. At the same time, however, a higher minimum wage shifts more income to low-wage workers who generally spend a greater proportion of their earnings than higher-wage workers, potentially leading to increased demand for goods and services that could boost employment.

The most accurate way to predict what will happen if the minimum wage is increased in the future is to examine what has actually happened when minimum wages have been increased in the past. Sylvia Allegretto, Arindrajit Dube, Michael Reich and Ben Zipperer (2013) have studied the effect of state minimum wage increases on the earnings and employment rates of two groups of low-wage workers—teenagers, who comprise more than one-quarter of all workers earning within 10% of the minimum wage, and workers in the restaurant industry, which is the largest employer of minimum-wage workers in the nation.

The findings suggest that many existing studies overestimate the negative impact of minimum wage increases on employment levels because they do not sufficiently take into account the economic and political differences between states with relatively high versus low minimum wages. Allegretto et al. (2013) controlled for these differences by comparing the effects of a minimum wage increase across neighboring counties where one county experienced an increase in the minimum wage while the neighboring county did not.

"Growing income inequality is contributing to increasing levels of segregation by income."

Allegretto et al. (2013) found no statistically significant evidence that an increase in the minimum wage reduced the growth of employment. What higher minimum wages did do was significantly lift the earnings of the teenagers and of restaurant workers studied. Higher minimum wages also reduced the high rates of employee turnover that are pervasive in low-wage industries, which is beneficial news for employers who waste significant resources in searching for and training new employees.

The research cannot rule out some effects on employment rates from increasing the minimum wage, even if their magnitude is significantly less than has traditionally been estimated.

Increases in the minimum wage also do not significantly address the declining fortunes of the middle class, but higher wages for the lowest-paid workers have the potential to lift nearly 1 million people out of poverty and add approximately $2 billion to the nation's overall real income. (Congressional Budget Office 2014)

THE EARNED INCOME TAX CREDIT

The largest federal program currently aimed at raising the incomes of working poor families in the United States is the Earned Income Tax Credit (EITC). Almost 1 out of 5 tax filers in the U.S. receive the EITC, resulting in an average credit of $2,194 in 2010. In recent years its impact on families has lifted roughly 4.7 million children above the poverty line annually.

Extensive research has shown that the EITC provides critical support to families who are working but still poor and also that it significantly increases labor force participation for single parents (e.g., Eissa & Hoynes 2006). The additional income it provides to working families has been correlated with improvements in maternal and infant health (Hoynes, Miller & Simon 2012) and with improvements in cognitive achievement in children. (Dahl & Lochner 2012)

The significance of the EITC is highlighted by the fact that at least 26 states have adopted their own earned income tax credit programs to add state benefits to the federal credit. The boost that these state programs provide for low-income families matters for economic mobility. Chetty et al. (2014) find larger earned income tax credits provided by states are associated with higher levels of upward mobility at the metropolitan level.

Recent research on participation in the EITC program during times of economic hardship, however, suggests that it may not serve as an effective safety net for some groups. (Bitler, Hoynes & Kuka 2014) Taking advantage of the differences among states in both the timing and severity of recent economic downturns, Bitler, Hoynes & Kuka (2014) find that the EITC significantly reduces the effect of an increase in unemployment on the increase in the poverty rate for two-parent households but has only minimal effects for single-parent households.

Together, this research suggests that the EITC is a critical program for raising the incomes of working families and especially for encouraging labor force participation by single-parent households, but that it could do more to provide an effective safety net for those single-parent households that experience employment losses during recessions.

TOP TAX RATES

The primary factor contributing to growing income inequality is the consistently rising share of income increases that go to the very top 1% of earners. Alvaredo et al. (2013) have noted that as the share of income going to the top 1% of earners has increased, the top income tax rates have declined. The federal income tax rates for the very highest earners fell from 70% or greater from 1936 to 1981 to 39.6% today for the top income category (i.e., an individual filer making more than $406,751). It is commonly argued that lower tax rates lead to economic growth, based on the idea that lower levels of taxation for the highest earners spur more work and greater entrepreneurship (e.g., Feldstein 1995; see also Mankiw 2013). But Alvaredo and his co-authors (2013) find no correlation between cuts in the top tax rates and growth in real per capita GDP. Between the late 1970s and the beginning of the recession, OECD countries such as the U.S. or the U.K. that cut top tax rates dramatically have not grown significantly faster than countries that did not reduce their top tax rate, such as Germany or Denmark.

Indeed, Alvaredo et al. (2013) suggest that lower top tax rates did not make top income earners more productive, but instead increased their incentives to bargain for higher compensation (see also Stiglitz 2012). And American chief executives have reaped salaries that are multiples higher than their counterparts at companies in similar sectors and of comparable sizes in continental Europe, where top tax rates have remained largely unchanged. Piketty, Saez & Stantcheva (2011) suggest accordingly that the top tax rate could be higher, providing more resources for investment in education and other priorities, without negatively affecting economic growth or productivity.

"Intergenerational mobility varies substantially by metropolitan region."

INVESTMENTS IN EDUCATION

Research on numerous fronts reinforces established findings regarding the significance of educational quality for future economic opportunity and mobility. Recent studies by Rucker Johnson (2010) confirm that differences in early education and school quality are among the most important components of the persistence in income disparities across generations. Johnson (2012) has also found that early childhood educational interventions, such as Head Start, have significant beneficial effects on educational attainment and earnings. The positive effects of these interventions are magnified when spending on those programs is higher and when children subsequently attend schools with higher per-pupil spending during their adolescent years. (Johnson 2012)

These findings are supported by those of Chetty et al. (2014) showing that areas with higher mean test scores in math and English from grades 3–8 (after controlling for income levels) and lower high-school dropout rates were highly correlated with economic mobility. The findings regarding school quality make sense, especially because differences in intergenerational mobility appear to emerge early in life, well before children actually enter the labor market. The findings are also consistent with earlier studies by Chetty and others that have found that kindergarten test scores are highly correlated with college attendance, homeownership, retirement savings, and later earnings (Chetty et al. 2011; see also Card & Krueger 1992). In short, investments in education beginning in early childhood can increase economic mobility, contribute to increased productivity, and decrease economic inequality.

RESIDENTIAL SEGREGATION

In analyzing the economic mobility data, Chetty et al. (2014) found that higher levels of racial residential segregation within a metropolitan region were strongly correlated with significantly reduced levels of intergenerational upward mobility for all residents of that zone. Segregation by income, particularly the isolation of low-income households, was also correlated with significantly reduced levels of upward mobility. These findings are especially worrisome, given that growing income inequality is contributing to increasing levels of segregation by income (see Reardon & Bischoff 2011) and the continuing concentration of poverty. (Jargowsky 2013)

"These policies could be enacted if there is the political will."

It is not the average income of commuting zones that matter—children in the commuting zones with the lowest mean incomes (around $21,900) reach the same percentile of the national income distribution at the same rate as those in the commuting zones with the highest incomes (around $47,600). What matters for the mobility of all residents of the metropolitan region is the level of economic and racial segregation within that region. Building on the insight that enduring neighborhood inequalities create a "durable spatial logic that mediates social life" (Sampson 2012), these findings suggest that residential segregation is a crucial mechanism in the reproduction of inequality (see Pattillo-McCoy 1999; Sharkey 2013).

These findings regarding the correlation between segregation and lack of economic mobility highlight the significance of local and national efforts to support fair housing enforcement, to invest in fostering greater opportunity in low-income neighborhoods, and to provide more pathways for housing mobility.

CONCLUSION

After reaching a high point in 1928 when the top 1% received 23% of national income, income inequality declined from the 1930s until the 1970s while the economy grew. Through this period of economic growth, there was support for government investment in programs like the New Deal and the G.I. Bill that were designed to create a safety net and to invest in educational and residential opportunities (at least for whites—see e.g. Katznelson 2005).

Income inequality has now reached levels not seen since the 1920s. Recent research suggests that policies such as investments in education, more progressive taxation, and efforts to address the racially and economically segregated structure of U.S. metropolitan areas could decrease inequality and increase economic mobility. Higher minimum wages and enhanced EITC, although addressing poverty, most directly also have the potential to affect inequality and mobility.

Policymakers must be attentive to the impacts universal approaches such as these can have on differently situated groups that could have the unintended impact of exacerbating existing disparities. Particularly low-wage workers could be hurt by a slight increase in minimum wages that could cause some reductions in employment, the reduction of some employment benefits, or additional costs passed on to workers. Nevertheless, each of these policies, if carefully implemented, has the potential to lift working households out of poverty, support greater economic mobility, or reduce the growth of income inequality. The inter-relatedness of these issues suggests that a strategy of focusing on both poverty and inequality is important, recognizing that, although related, poverty and inequality are not the same. To understand the impacts of such policies going forward requires disaggregating information on different populations and geographic areas, especially because the existing research has identified wide variations among each.

"Extreme concentrations of income and wealth challenge America's ideals of democracy and equal opportunity."

All of these policies could be enacted at local, state and federal levels—if there is the political will. On the one hand, the increasing concentration of income at the top of the income scale creates the possibility that inequality becomes ever harder to challenge, as that income can be used to influence the perception of its fairness through the media, and efforts to address it, through lobbying. (Alvaredo et al. 2013) On the other hand, the widening gulf between the top 1% and the remaining 99% creates momentum for creative policies that can bring together broad constituencies to address the structures that continue to pull us apart.

WORKS CITED

Allegretto, Sylvia, Dube, Arindrajit, Reich, Michael & Zipperer, Ben, 2013. "Credible Research Designs for Minimum Wage Studies." IZA Discussion Paper No. 7638. Available at SSRN: http://ssm.com/abstract=2336435

Alvaredo, Facundo, Anthony Atkinson, Thomas Piketty & Emmanuel Saez. 2013. "The Top 1 Percent in International and Historical Perspective." *Journal of Economic Perspectives,* 27(3): 3–20

Alvaredo, Facundo, Anthony Atkinson, Thomas Piketty & Emmanuel Saez. 2014. The World Top Incomes Database, http://topincomes.g-mond.parisschoolofeconomics.eu/, 2/21/2014

Bitler, Marianne, Hilary Hoynes & Elira Kuka. 2014. "Do In-Work Tax Credits Serve as a Safety Net?" NBER Working Papers 19785, National Bureau of Economic Research, Inc.

Bureau of Labor Statistics. 2011. Characteristics of Minimum Wage Workers: 2011

Card, David & Alan Krueger. 1992. "School Quality and Black-White Relative Earnings: A Direct Assessment" *The Quarterly Journal of Economics,* 107(1): 151–200

Chetty, Raj, John Friedman, Nathaniel Hilger, Emmanuel Saez, Diane Whitmore Schanzenbach & Danny Yagan. 2011. "How Does Your Kindergarten Classroom Affect Your Earnings? Evidence from Project Star" The *Quarterly Journal of Economics,* 126(4): 1593–1660

Chetty, Raj, Nathaniel Hendren, Patrick Kline & Emmanuel Saez. 2014. "Where is the Land of Opportunity? The Geography of Intergenerational Mobility in the United States," NBER Working Papers 19843, National Bureau of Economic Research, Inc.

Congressional Budget Office. 2014. The Effects of a Minimum-Wage Increase on Employment and Family Income. Available at: http://www.cbo.gov/publication/44995

Cowen, Tyler. 2013. *Average Is Over: Powering America Beyond the Age of the Great Stagnation.* New York: Dutton

Dahl, Gordon & Lance Lochner. 2012. "The Impact of Family Income on Child Achievement: Evidence from the Earned Income Tax Credit," *American Economic Review,* 102(5): 1927–56

de Blasio, William. 2014. Inaugural Address. Available at http://www1.nyc.gov/office-of-the-mayor/news/005-14/inaugural-address-mayor-bill-de-blasio-progress-new-york#/0

Eissa, Nada & Hilary Hoynes, 2006. "Behavioral Responses to Taxes: Lessons from the EITC and Labor Supply." *Tax Policy and the Economy,* 20: 73–110

Feldstein, Martin. 1995. "The Effect of Marginal Tax Rates on Taxable Income: A Paenl Study of the 1986 Tax Reform Act." *Journal of Political Economy* 103(3): 551–72

Hoynes, Hilary, Douglas Miller & Jessamyn Schaller. 2012. "Who Suffers during Recessions?" *Journal of Economic Perspectives,* 26(3): 27–48

Hoynes, Hilary, Douglas L. Miller & David Simon. 2012. "Income, the Earned Income Tax Credit, and Infant Health," NBER Working Papers 18206, National Bureau of Economic Research, Inc.

Jargowsky, Paul. 2013. *Concentration of Poverty in the New Millenium: Changes in Prevalence, Composition, and Location of High-Poverty Neighborhoods.* New York: The Century Foundation

Johnson, Rucker. 2012. "School Quality and the Long-Run Effects of Head Start." Working paper available at: http://socrates.berkeley.edu/~ruckerj/workingpapers.html

Johnson, Rucker. 2010. "Who's on the Bus? The Role of Schools as a Vehicle to Intergenerational Mobility." Working paper available at: http://socrates.berkeley.edu/~ruckerj/workingpapers.html

Katznelson, Ira. 2005. *When Affirmative Action Was White: An Untold History of Racial Inequality in Twentieth-Century America.* New York: W.W. Norton & Company

Levy, Frank & Thomas Kochan. 2012. "Addressing the Problem of Stagnant Wages." *Comparative Economic Studies* 54: 739–764

Mankiw, N. Gregory. 2013. "Defending the One Percent." *Journal of Economic Perspectives,* 27(3): 21–34

Obama, Barack. 2013. Remarks by the President on Economic Mobility. Available at http://www.whitehouse.gov/the-press-office/2013/12/04/remarks-president-economic-mobility

Pattillo-McCoy, Mary. 1999. *Black Picket Fences: Privilege and Peril among the Black Middle Class.* Chicago: Univ. of Chicago Press

Piketty, Thomas, Emmanuel Saez & Stefanie Stantcheva. 2011. Taxing the 1% Available at: http://www.voxeu.org/article/taxing-l-why-top-tax-rate-could-be-over-80

Reardon, Sean & Kendra Bischoff. 2011. "Income Inequality and Income Segregation." *American Journal of Sociology.* 116(4): 1092–1153

Saez, Emmanuel. 2013. Striking it Richer: The Evolution of Top Incomes in the United States. Available at: http://elsa.berkeley.edu/~saez/saez-UStopincomes-2012.pdf

Sampson, Robert. 2012. *Great American City: Chicago and the Enduring Neighborhood Effect.* Chicago, IL: Univ. of Chicago Press.

Sharkey, Patrick. 2013. *Stuck in Place: Urban Neighborhoods and the End of Progress Toward Racial Equality.* Chicago, IL: Univ. of Chicago Press

Sommeiller, Estelle & Mark Price. 2014. "The Increasingly Unequal States of America: Income Inequality by State, 1917 to 2011" Available at: http://www.epi.org/publication/unequal-states/

Stiglitz, Joseph. 2012. *The Price of Inequality.* New York: W.W. Norton & Company, Inc.

Economics (Income and Wealth)

Race correlates very highly with both median and average income, be it personal income or household income. It correlates even more highly with wealth than income but also correlates with things like poverty, liquid assets, and expendable income.

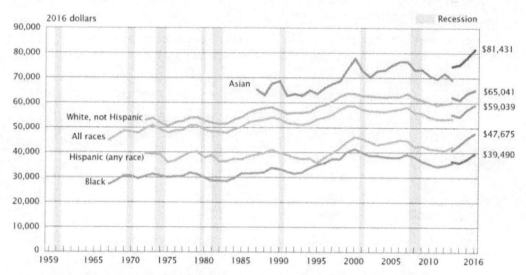

Note: The data for 2013 and beyond reflect the implementation of the redesigned income questions. The data points are placed at the midpoints of the respective years. Median household income data are not available prior to 1967. For more information on recessions, see Appendix A. For more information on confidentiality protection, sampling error, nonsampling error, and definitions, see <www2.census.gov/programs-surveys/cps/techdocs/cpsmar17.pdf>.

Source: U.S. Census Bureau, Current Population Survey, 1968 to 2017 Annual Social and Economic Supplements.

FIGURE 4.2   Real median household income by race and Hispanic origin: 1967 to 2016.

Average Family Wealth by Race/Ethnicity, 1963–2016

Source: Urban Institute calculations from Survey of Financial Characteristics of Consumers 1962 (December 31), Survey of Changes in Family Finances 1963, and Survey of Consumer Finances 1983-2016.

Notes: 2016 dollars. No comparable data are available between 1963 and 1983. Black/Hispanic distinction within nonwhite population available only in 1983 and later.

URBAN **INSTITUITE**

FIGURE 4.3   Notice that wealth disparities are quite a bit greater than income disparities.

CRITICAL THINKING: Wealth disparities are greater than income disparities. Why do you think that is the case?

Wealth adds in a factor of time, specifically inheritance over time.

Criminal Justice

Criminal justice has often been a flashpoint to discuss race, racism, and policing in the United States. Notable cases in the last decade, including the Trayvon Martin and George Zimmerman cases, the shooting of Michael Brown and resulting Ferguson protests, the death of Eric Garner, the death of Freddie Gray and resulting Baltimore protests, and the NFL National Anthem protests designed to bring attention to police brutality, have renewed levels of discussions of criminal justice and race, making them prominent social issues. The killing of George Floyd in May 2020 elevated these issues from prominent to preeminent, and may precipitate many changes on public opinion on issues of race. While there is an entire chapter of the book devoted to criminal justice, this chapter will focus on particular racial disparities in the criminal justice system and the explanations behind them. The following selections discuss race and prison in the United States.

Reading 4.9.

Race, Prison, and the Aesthetic Imagination

by Deborah E. McDowell, Claudrena N. Harold and Juan Battle

It's around midnight. The lights are out and the T.V.'s off. For the past hour some young bloods, huddled in the back of the cage, have been do/wopping some old songs. This is my best time; I just lie/back on my bunk and space out. Right now a dude in the cage behind me is singing, "I've seen fire, I've seen rain—I've seen sunny days. ..." This is the first time I've really listened to the lyrics; it's a heavy song. And the dude has a good solid voice—you can hear it leaving his throat. For some reason—perhaps it's the steel and the corridors—the acoustics in jail are extraordinary. Sounds carom down the corridors, reverberating and magnifying. You can lie in your cell and dig the whole joint with your ears: a man urinating, the toilet flushing, a man screaming in his sleep, another coughing and snoring and always—keys jingling and bells ringing steel doors slamming. Jail sounds, sounds of ice.

—Etheridge Knight

Deborah E. McDowell, Claudrena N. Harold and Juan Battle, "Race, Prison, and the Aesthetic Imagination," *The Punitive Turn: New Approaches to Race and Incarceration.* Published in 2013 by University of Virginia Press.

Sometimes I think this whole world is one big prison yard
Some of us are prisoners, the rest of us are guards.

—Bob Dylan, *"George Jackson"*

In a universe of cells—who is not in jail?

—Bob Kaufman, *"Jail Poems"*

Reading 4.10.

Punishment in Historical Perspective

by Deborah E. McDowell, Claudrena N. Harold and Juan Battle

A genealogy of the contemporary prison regime awakens both the historical memory
and the sociopolitical logic of the Middle Passage. The prison has come to form a
hauntingly similar spatial and temporal continuum between social and biological
notions of life and death, banal liberal civic freedom and totalizing unfreedom,
community and alienation, agency and liquidation, the "human" and subhuman/
nonhuman.

—Dylan Rodriquez

The overweening, defining event of the modern world is the mass movement of
raced populations, beginning with the largest forced transfer of people in the history of the world: slavery. ... The contemporary world's work has become policing,
halting, forming policy regarding, and trying to administer the movement of people.

—Toni Morrison

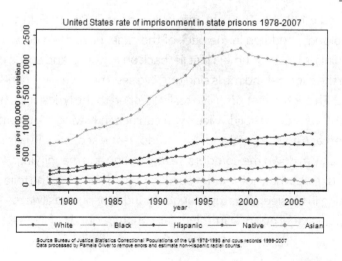

FIGURE 4.4 **US rate of imprisonment in state prisons, 1978–2007.**

Deborah E. McDowell, Claudrena N. Harold and Juan Battle, "Punishment in Historical Perspective," *The Punitive Turn: New Approaches to Race and Incarceration*. Published in 2013 by University of Virginia Press.

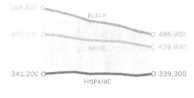

Sentenced federal and state prisoners by race and Hispanic origin, 2009–2016

584,800 — BLACK
490,000 — 486,900
439,800
WHITE
341,200 — 339,300
HISPANIC

2009 '10 '11 '12 '13 '14 '15 '16

Note: Whites and blacks include only those who are single-race, not Hispanic. Hispanics are of any race. Prison population is defined as inmates sentenced to more than a year in federal or state prison.
Source: Bureau of Justice Statistics

PEW RESEARCH CENTER

FIGURE 4.5 **Racial and ethnic gaps shrink in US prison population.**

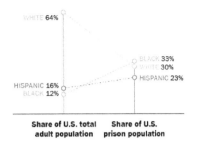

Total U.S. adult population and U.S. prison population by race and Hispanic origin, 2016

WHITE 64%
BLACK 33%
WHITE 30%
HISPANIC 23%
HISPANIC 16%
BLACK 12%

Share of U.S. total adult population   Share of U.S. prison population

Note: Whites and blacks include only those who are single-race, not Hispanic. Hispanics are of any race. Prison population is defined as inmates sentenced to more than a year in federal or state prison.
Source: Bureau of Justice Statistics

PEW RESEARCH CENTER

FIGURE 4.6 **Blacks and Hispanics are overrepresented in US prisons.**

Figures 4.5 and 4.6 demonstrate just how strongly race correlates with incarceration. While there does exist prevailing evidence that the crime rate among Blacks does tend to be higher than that of whites (almost exclusively as a function of poverty or some related economic factor, i.e., controlling for financial means makes the difference approach zero), this difference does not approach the disparity we see in incarceration rates.

It is important to note that the incarceration disparity is improving (we may not be able to say this as much as some of you might like) since peaking around 2009. Part of this is due to the decriminalization/legalization of marijuana, which was one of the most disparate offenses for which people were incarcerated. As an example of why crime rates alone do not explain the large gap in incarceration rate, consider the following charts.

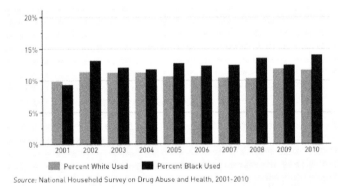

Source: National Household Survey on Drug Abuse and Health, 2001-2010

FIGURE 4.7 **Marijuana use by race: Used marijuana in past 12 months (2001–2010).**

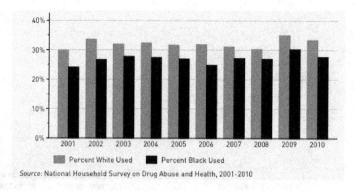

Source: National Household Survey on Drug Abuse and Health, 2001-2010

FIGURE 4.8 **Marijuana use among 18- to 25-year-olds by race: used marijuana in past 12 months (2001–2010).**

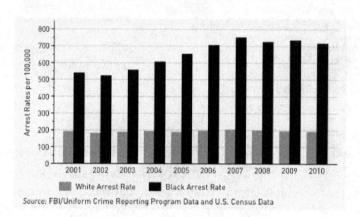

Source: FBI/Uniform Crime Reporting Program Data and U.S. Census Data

FIGURE 4.9 **Arrest rates for marijuana possession by race (2001–2010).**

That use rates were similar, but arrest rates so disparate indicate that there is some sort of bias operating as it relates to who is arrested for marijuana possession.

CRITICAL THINKING:	What might some of the biases related to the disparity in marijuana arrests be?

These differences are not universally recognized. In fact, note how there are meaningful racial differences that show measures of public opinion about policing. This further reinforces the idea that different experiences by race affects perspectives and opinions, often leading to racial differences in polling. This extends to polls about topics that are not explicitly about race (or ostensibly about race at all); these sorts of things include favorite sports, politics, and opinions about public schools.

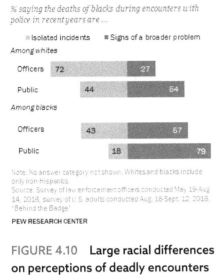

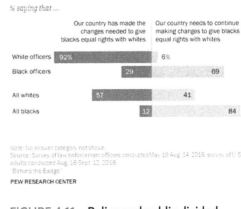

FIGURE 4.11   Police and public divided by race over whether attaining equality requires more changes.

FIGURE 4.10   Large racial differences on perceptions of deadly encounters between blacks and police among police and the public.

CRITICAL THINKING: In figures 4.10–4.11, why do we see a bigger gap among officers than the public as a whole?

Education

Race also correlates highly with many facets of education. The narratives that follow touch on stereotypes, how widely held they are, and what data can show us about the effect of these stereotypic beliefs. The disparities in income and wealth also affect the schools children attend and the push/pull factors that affect decisions about education. Additionally, as can be seen in the next section about segregation, racialized living patterns also play into some differences in educational outcomes.

As can be seen in the narratives, there are a number of biases about race that ultimate cause different children to have different experiences. Bias will be discussed as a concept in more detail shortly, but these sorts of biases (whether explicit or implicit) are pervasive enough in nature as to have a great deal of effect over time. When such biases are laid on top of historical realties, economic inequalities, and living arrangements they tend to reproduce historical inequalities. This can be seen in the graphs that follow the readings.

CRITICAL THINKING: What are some reasons this disparity might have shrunk over time?

Reading 4.11.

Do Black Families Value Education?
White Teachers, Institutional Cultural Narratives, & Beliefs about African Americans

by Laurel Puchner & Linda Markowitz

INTRODUCTION

...the value of education is different in a Black family than in a White family. And I think you gotta be aware of that...

The above quote is from an interview with an effective, caring, seventh grade math teacher in a racially and socio-economically diverse school in the Midwestern U.S. She was one of six White teachers who were participants in our study of the evolution of preservice teacher understandings about race. All six of the inservice and preservice teachers in the study expressed the belief that African American families do not place a high value on education.

The problem of negative beliefs about African American families in schools is not a new idea, and many educators, including Delpit (2012) and Ladson-Billings (2000), have written much about institutionally racist beliefs held by teachers about Black families. However, many people still don't realize it's a problem, and teacher education programs in particular need to continue to figure out how to expose the reality of racism in our schools. Also relatively little recognized is the thesis of this article: racism works via unconscious cultural narratives of which people are mostly unaware, even while those narratives have a major impact on their behavior within institutions.

Speaking recently about police shootings of unarmed Black men, FBI director James Comey (2015) acknowledged that law enforcement has a troubled history when it comes to race. Comey was speaking in relation to recent tragedies involving police officers killing unarmed Black men. In August 2014, not far from the Midwestern schools that provide the setting for this article, a White police officer killed an unarmed Black teenager in Ferguson, Missouri. In July 2014 in Staten Island a White police officer put an unarmed Black man in a chokehold and, despite the man's cries that he couldn't breathe, several New York Police Department officers continued to assault him until he died a few moments later. Grand juries failed to indict either of the police officers responsible for these deaths.

These are just two recent high profile cases, and we know the statistics are frightening. Comey attributed some of the trouble to unconscious racial biases that re-

Laurel Puchner and Linda Markowitz, "Do Black Families Value Education? White Teachers, Institutional Cultural Narratives, and Beliefs about African Americans," *Multicultural Education*, vol. 23, no. 1, pp. 9-16. Copyright © 2015 by Caddo Gap Press. Reprinted with permission. Provided by ProQuest LLC. All rights reserved.

search has shown are held by all people. He also said that cops are no more racist than people in other professions.

Teachers are an obvious example of another profession where unconscious bias can have profound effect on the lives of African Americans, as negative beliefs about Blacks held by school staff have very serious consequences. Schools are primarily in the hands of Whites right now in the U.S. (Boser, 2014). As we train new White teachers, they go out into schools where teachers tend to hold (mostly unconscious) racist beliefs about African American families, and where the preservice teachers themselves are predisposed to hold such beliefs. These beliefs have a negative impact on teacher expectations, school climate, and the quality of the educational experience of students of color, leading to enormous negative consequences for the lives of thousands of children and youth in the U.S.

The dynamics underlying the problems of teacher beliefs about the value of education in Black families and of police mistreatment of Black men and boys are the same, and the question in both cases is one that Michael Gerson of the *Washington Post* asked, in relation to the Ferguson events, in a recent editorial:

> How people who do not regard themselves as biased can be part of a system that inevitably results in bias. How men and women who view themselves as moral can comprise an immoral society. (Gerson, 2015)

Individual beliefs and actions such as those of the teachers in our study and the police officers in Ferguson and Staten Island are individual acts and beliefs that both maintain and are maintained by institutional racism. The negative beliefs are very resistant to change partly because teachers and others in the institution think the beliefs are a rational conclusion based on logic and personal experience.

In fact, however, the beliefs actually stem from unfounded and untested assumptions about the way the world works and comprise the individual narratives that are engrained in institutional culture. In this article we illustrate the racist background stories embedded within institutions and how those background stories become expressed in individual cultural scripts about race. We use Haney López's (2000) and Bonilla-Silva's (2003) theories and some of the data from our 2010–2011 study. Specifically, we use the six teachers' expressions of the belief that Blacks place a low value on education to explicate the relationship between institutional and individual racism in schools. We also argue that greater recognition of racism needs to be acknowledged by teacher educators and by society at large.

The examples and anecdotes we describe in this article emerged from a qualitative study that we carried out in 2010–2011 focused on evolution of beliefs about race of two preservice teachers, Amber and Michelle.[1] We conducted about six hours of interviews each with Amber and Michelle over an eight-month period, in addition to interviews with the four inservice teachers with whom Amber and Michelle were placed for field experiences. We also did about 38 total hours of observation in the inservice teachers' classrooms. However, this is not an empirical research report. This article uses study data to explore the intangible place where institutions and individuals meet in propagating and perpetuating racism.

We begin below by illustrating the first theme of our argument, that racism, largely unconscious and unintentional, gets embedded within institutional background stories and expressed in individual racist scripts. Then we illustrate the power of the cultural narratives that feed the racism. Finally, we explore the role played by social class in these unconscious cultural narratives.

BACKGROUND STORIES AND RACIST SCRIPTS

Our first illustration of White teacher beliefs about African American families comes from Amber's cooperating in-service teacher during her second field placement, Mrs. James. Mrs. James's school comprised mainly middle and upper middle income students and her 4th grade class contained about 20 White students and about five students of color, who were mainly African American. The teaching episode in question occurred while Laurel Puchner was observing alongside Amber in Mrs. James's classroom in November.

Once the students had settled into their seats after returning from physical education, Mrs. James said she was going to tell them a story, and that the story was about her recent opportunity to help at a "soup bus" in a neighboring town. The following excerpt from Puchner's fieldnotes describes what Mrs. James told her 4th graders. (The quotation marks indicate quotes that Puchner felt she had written down close to verbatim, though she did not audio record the event):

> She tells them that last night she went with some friends to [North City], to a "very very rough neighborhood called The Projects." And she got on a bus and they drove to the projects and served soup for a few hours to kids in this "very dangerous" neighborhood. Kids as young as three or four were there and the oldest was about 14 and they came out to the bus by themselves with no parents and it was their only meal. She stressed how these little kids were all by themselves. "We gave them food because they don't get food." "We had chili and hot dogs and buns we gave them. They don't have a family like yours that's fortunate enough. And every one of the kids said thank you and please..."
>
> White Girl raises hand: Do they go to school?

Teacher: Yes they do. It was really scary because there were seven or eight year old kids taking care of their little siblings.

Boy of Color in back of room raises hand: What happened to the families? ...

Teacher: Well they were at home ... or they didn't care about their kids. There were two moms who didn't eat bwcause they wanted to make sure their kids got food. But lots of kids were by themselves ...

Teacher: We gave them each a book, too, so hopefully some of them will read their books to their kids but probably not because they don't have parents that read to them.

Mrs. James appears to be very well-intentioned here. In fact, she seems to be going out of her way to replace a regular academic lesson with a moral one that she feels is important for the students. At the level that we believe she was intending to communicate to the children (and also likely to Puchner) she seems to be attempting to model moral behavior (devotion of time and perhaps money to those less fortunate) and to teach the students a lesson about gratefulness and politeness. (The full transcript shows her several times comparing the soup bus children's high level of politeness to the class's often low level of politeness).

However, she was also communicating several more subtle but very dangerous messages to the students about Black people who are poor. The town that Mrs. James visited is well-known locally for its poverty and majority African American population. It is safe to assume from the story that Mrs. James did not know the children or the families of the children to whom she served food. It appears that all she witnessed was children eating food she served them. Yet her story implies that in her brief experience "in the projects" (code for Black) with them she decided the children's families were neglectful.

She communicated that to the students by stating or implying the following: poor Black parents don't care about their children; poor Black children have to raise themselves; poor Black parents don't read to their children; poor Black children need White "saviors" such as herself to survive. Each of these messages is a racist assumption that is part of a large packet of racist assumptions that are dominant in U.S. society (Delpit, 2012; Markowitz & Puchner, 2014). According to Haney López (2000), a set of assumptions embedded in a communication like this is an example of the use of a "racist script."

When people like Mrs. James use such scripts, they are not intentionally or consciously racist. Rather, Haney López argues, contrary to what is posited in rational choice theory, behavior is not determined by individuals choosing the best option for maximizing self-interest among a range of choices. Instead, people follow established patterns of behavior that are based on accepted, unquestioned, background understandings of how the world works and about what's true and not true about the world. Thus we mostly go through life with unexamined assumptions about the way things are and the way things work, and these unexamined assumptions become normal and natural for us, and in effect become reality.

Unfortunately, the unexamined assumptions or background understandings under which we behave in the U.S. are generally racist (Haney López, 2000). Similar to King's (1991) notion of *"dysconscious racism,"* background understandings serve to rationalize discriminatory behavior and beliefs, hence most of the time individuals act in harmful and racist ways without realizing it or consciously intending to because they act according to these racist scripts.

Since these patterns are common within institutions, these background understandings are part of the culture of the institution, and to be a good member of our culture we act in accordance with them (Haney López, 2000). At times we are reflective and thoughtful to a degree, but our behavior is still heavily constrained by the background cultural understandings of the institution, which restricts our range of options (Haney López, 2000) and leads to the unintentional use of racist scripts.

There are several clues in the data from our study that support the idea that Mrs. James was not being intentionally racist in telling her story. First, Mrs. James admitted in a later interview with us that she was uncomfortable with the topic of race and believed in colorblindness:

> I try and stay away from the race factor. We don't mention it in the classroom ... I treat them as equal ... I don't know if there is a better way to do it. I know it is a problem but I really don't touch on it.

Further, she told the story while both the researcher and about five African American 4th graders were present. It seems unlikely that someone who tried to "stay away from race" and who was talking to such an audience would be conscious of how racist the story is. Rather, in telling that story she was likely unreflectively following a script. The background assumptions of that script, which made up reality for her, were racist, but she was not aware of it.

What makes this a particularly clear example of an individual following an unconscious script in Haney López's theory is that Mrs. James probably did not even know that she was talking about race in the story. She didn't mention race, and undoubtedly didn't realize how much her story was fueled by what Haney López (2000) calls "racial institutions" (p. 1806), or "any understanding of race that has come to be so widely shared within a community that it operates as an unexamined cognitive resource for understanding one's self, others, and the-way-the-world-is" (p. 1808). If you asked Mrs. James whether the families were Black, obviously she'd say yes. However, although she probably thinks the details in her story were shaped entirely by her experience on the soup bus, the shape the story took emerged in large part from unconscious assumptions about poor Black people that form a particular script that she was using in telling the story.

Importantly, Mrs. James is unintentionally *individually* expressing implicit racist beliefs even without mentioning race, but her individual expression of racist beliefs is a part of institutional racism because people "both inherit and remake racial institutions," and these beliefs need "group dynamics for their perpetuation" (Haney López, 2000, p. 1806). Following Haney López's theory we conclude that such beliefs are likely a part of the culture of her organization, the school, and with this soup bus story she contributed to the collective yet mainly unconscious project of the school to pass unconscious racist cultural understandings onto the students.

Finding that a single teacher such as Mrs. James holds racist beliefs might be considered an anomaly, but the fact that all six teachers in our study demonstrated racist beliefs is alarming. It's not inconsistent with past research, but it is inconsistent with most people's beliefs about teaching and teacher education. How can teacher education be effective if institutional racism pervades schools? Individual police officer and individual teacher beliefs and actions vary. But in both professions we need to recognize that racist background stories are the prevailing truth. And, as we'll focus on more later, we need to recognize that in schools (as in policing) the intersection of race and poverty magnify the problem.

THE POWER OF CULTURAL SCRIPTS

As mentioned earlier, all six teachers included in this study expressed views indicating that they believe African American families do not prioritize education. In the case of Mrs. James, as we've already seen, the view manifested during a story she told to her students while teaching. With the other teachers, these views came across in the individual interviews that we conducted.

In the case of the two preservice teachers (PTs), we have extensive interview evidence of their beliefs about race. In many respects, Amber and Michelle were similar. They fit the demographic of typical PTs nationally in being young, White women (both were 21 years old in Fall of 2010). They also fit the demographic of typical PTs at the university as they were both from working class families and grew up in small, homogeneous, White rural towns. Their parents had high school diplomas but did not have college degrees.

In talking about race, they both generally used racial discourse that fit within the *new racism* described by Bonilla-Silva (2003), characterized by minimization of racism, use of culturally based arguments, and blindness to structural racism. Their views were also consistent with prior research on typical White PT racial discourse (c.f., Levine-Rasky, 2000), including blindness to White privilege and a belief in "reverse racism."

However, interview data also showed important differences between the two. Michelle appeared to truly value diversity, and felt that her lack of exposure to diversity as a child had done her a disservice. She was also highly engaged in all of her courses, and particularly loved the multicultural course. Amber was less engaged in coursework, and her interview responses betrayed a very negative emotional reaction to African Americans that was not present in Michelle's discourse.

In the interest of space, we are focusing here on interview evidence that illustrates their beliefs about the specific issue of the value of education in African American families. Amber spoke to this issue in our very first interview with her. She had made a comment regarding a video about Japanese math teaching that she had seen in her math methods class, and stated that Japanese people valued education more than people in the U.S. Then Linda Markowitz asked her a follow up question:

Markowitz: So do you think that it's true here for different racial groups or class groups that there's certain groups that value education more than others or might make it easier to teach to?

Amber: I think the Asian population would be easy to teach to because you know their parents still kind of like instill that upon them and then I would probably say the White community would be the next you know and then probably the African American community would be lowest to teach, though I don't really know why [I think that]

As can be seen in the excerpt, Michelle stated that she thought African Americans valued education less than Whites and Asians, but then indicated uncertainty about why she believed that. A similar phenomenon occurred in our interview with Mrs. Lester, a kindergarten teacher who was Michelle's second mentor teacher of the year. As seen in the quote below, Mrs. Lester said that she believed that African American students struggle more and have less involved parents, but then indicated that she didn't know why she thought that. Mrs. Lester had no students of color in her class that year:

Markowitz: Have you thought about how it might be different to teach a class of students that was racially mixed?

Mrs. Lester: I don't want to be prejudice but I think there would be more behavioral problems if I had a class that was more racially mixed. Those kids tend to struggle more and it's harder to get hold of parents and I don't know why I think that. Because I know compared to the neighbor next door, the teacher next door, she has three [low performing] kids and hers are the African Americans...

... That's why I think that. Because I'm not racist. I think I would have more lower kids if I had more African Americans. And she's always talking about how parental involvement isn't high but I had an African American kid last year and her parents were involved. So it's not always across the board...

In the above quote Mrs. Lester says she'd have lower achievement, more behavior problems, and less parental involvement with a racially mixed class than she does with her all White class. Mrs. Lester's claim is not directly about value of education—rather, it's about the related topic of parent involvement. But as with Amber's quote, Mrs. Lester's statements fit with the culture of low expectations for African American students that is institutionalized in U.S. schools (Delpit, 2012). Interestingly, Mrs. Lester and Amber's statements about Black families/parents are followed by expressions of uncertainty about why they believed what they had just said. We contend that this uncertainty provides a particularly clear example of individuals making decisions based on unconscious and unexamined assumptions about the world. When answering the question about race, they didn't make a thoughtful, rational decision; rather, they followed a cultural script, and hence were not even sure why they'd said what they said.

Yet after making belief statements people don't usually express puzzlement about why they hold the beliefs, so why did Mrs. Lester and Amber wonder about their own beliefs? We speculate that the taboo nature of the topic of race meant that Mrs. Lester and Amber expressed ideas they were not even fully aware of. In other words, although people generally don't recognize the unconscious assumptions underlying their beliefs, they are usually accustomed to expressing their beliefs, so the beliefs don't come as a surprise. But since race is a taboo topic in much of U.S. society, Amber and Mrs. Lester probably very rarely, if ever, spoke directly about race, so some of their own racial ideas might not have been completely familiar to them.

Indeed, Amber's statement about values was in response to our first direct question about race in our very first interview with her. Likewise, Mrs. Lester's similar comment came in response to the interviewer's first question about race. Even though Amber and Mrs. Lester stated they did not know why they believed what they said they believed, they both quickly found a rationalization for their belief, with Amber saying "I think it's something I've seen in my [field placement] observations" (though in the next interview she claimed not to have noticed any racial differences in achievement or behavior), and Mrs. Lester deciding her belief came from reports from the teacher next door. Interestingly, Mrs. Lester appeared to place more stock in hearsay from next door than in her own personal experience with her actively involved African American parent from the year before, likely because she unknowingly held the beliefs she expressed long before she expressed them during the interview and long before she met the involved African American parent.

As Bonilla-Silva (2003) has argued, "cultural" arguments about deficiencies of African American families are currently relatively socially acceptable, and have replaced biological arguments about inferiority. So although many underlying assumptions that are part of the culture of institutions have no basis and are largely unconscious, we are not arguing that Whites are unaware of all of their negative beliefs about blacks. Indeed, Bonilla-Silva's research indicates that most are aware of their own cultural arguments about inferiority of Blacks (Bonilla-Silva, 2003). The unconscious part in many cases likely comes mainly in where they think the origin of those beliefs lies.

In other words, people believe their beliefs are based on evidence, when in fact they are simply part of an unconscious cultural narrative. Excerpts from two different interviews with Michelle provide a clear example of this phenomenon. In an excerpt from the April 2011 interview (at the very end of the study) Michelle told Markowitz that she felt the achievement gap between White and African American children was caused by family life in African American families and specifically the fact that African American parents are not as involved as White parents:

Markowitz: Why do you think there is an achievement gap?

Michelle: I don't know. I think going off of my experience I have seen in placements a lot of it has to do with family life. I don't know why it is. Why just because you are of a certain color your family is just, but that is what I have noticed in Ms. [Rain's] class.

Markowitz: What do you think families are doing differently, white families versus families of color?

Michelle: I don't think the parents are that involved as the parents that are white. ...I am basing this off of the parent conferences I had with Ms. [Rain]. Many of them [African American parents] she had to give packets for and say go over this at home and that is going to help your kid in the classroom and she didn't have to do that with a lot of the parents that were White.

Mrs. Rain was the teacher for Michelle's first field placement, several months earlier, and in this excerpt Michelle is referencing parent teacher conferences that she participated in during her time in that placement. In Mrs. Rain's third grade class 22 of 27 students (81%) were students of color, mostly African American. In the interview above, from April 2011, Michelle appears quite conscious of her belief that Black families are not involved in their children's education. She believes the reason she holds this belief comes from personal experience with the parent teacher conferences. However, we have good evidence that her belief does not come from the personal experience she cites. First of all, the Black/White student ratio in the class was such that even if the teacher had given homework packets to one White parent and six Black parents the proportion would be about the same, indicating that she wasn't using logic or rational thinking.

However, the clearest evidence that her belief about low involvement among the African American parents did not come from her observation of parent teacher conferences is that five months earlier she had used the same parent teacher conference experience, at that point much fresher in her memory, to argue that African American families did value education as much as Whites. Here is an excerpt from the November 2010 interview in which she is responding to a direct question about whether African American families value education less than White families:

> I'm going to relate back to the parent teacher conferences because that was really eye opening hearing how they [African American parents] think of their kid as a student and how they think of the homework and things like that. I don't think they value it any differently at all. I didn't see a difference the entire time I was there. All of them want their children to get good educations and learn.

The quote indicates that directly following the parent teacher conferences the experience had convinced Michelle that African American parents valued education as much as her White students. The quote betrays the fact that she held low expectations for the families prior to meeting them; yet, the experience had proven her wrong. By the April interview, however, five months later, the underlying cultural assumptions of the institution apparently proved stronger than her memory of the actual behavior of the African American parents.

As indicated earlier, the belief that African Americans don't value education is a prominent part of the institutional racism package experienced by African American children in schools. Since this belief is a focal point for the current analysis, here we describe prior research on the topic as well as the relationship between this focal issue and some of the related ideas that play important roles in institutional racism of U.S. schools and society.

Beliefs about the value of education are linked to beliefs about the heavily researched topic of parental involvement. Parent involvement is related to student achievement (Banerjee, Harrell, & Johnson, 2011; Kerbow & Bernhardt, 1993), and studies show that when people perceive low parental involvement, they assume parents are not motivated and don't value education (Kerbow & Bernhardt, 1993; Lee & Bowen, 2006; Wong & Hughes, 2006).

However, teacher perceptions are not always accurate, and teachers often assume low parental involvement when it is not the case (Msengi, 2007; Wong & Hughes, 2006). Empirical research indicates that the belief that African American families are less involved than White families simply isn't true. For example, Kerbow and Bernhardt (1993) analyzed data from the 1988 National Educational Longitudinal Study, which included a U.S. sample of 26,000 8th graders, their parents, teachers, and administrators. They found that controlling for SES, African American and Hispanic families were more involved than White families, and that especially with African American families, involvement was much higher.

Parental involvement can take many different forms, including parents' home interactions with children that tell them what the parents' expectations are and what they feel is important; parent-initiated contact with the school; and participation in parent-teacher organizations at the school (Kerbow & Bernhardt, 1993). The first type of parental involvement is generally invisible to teachers, and parents who communicate high levels of expectations and values toward school might not communicate with school. Hence even when teachers and administrators don't see involvement in school it does not necessarily mean it isn't happening (Kerbow & Bernhardt, 1993; Lee & Bowen, 2006).

A further complicating factor is that the relationship between visible school involvement and value of education is not always direct. For example, school personnel often don't consider the multiple factors other than "value of education" that influence school involvement. Especially with low income families, low involvement often means lack of time and resources, and lack of comfort with school personnel, rather than low value placed on education (Geenen, Powers, & López-Vazquez, 2005; Wong & Hughes, 2006).

Kerbow and Bernhardt (1993) found that single parenting, being low income, and working full-time were the most significant variables negatively impacting parental involvement. For poor parents who are less comfortable in a school environment, the difficulties are compounded. Structural barriers to school involvement, such as time and transportation, may lead teachers to believe the parents lack motivation and do not value school (Lee & Bowen, 2006). This perception may lead school personnel to treat those parents in a negative manner, thus exacerbating the lack of comfort those parents felt with school involvement to begin with (Lee & Bowen, 2006).

One of the best predictors of a child's achievement is teacher expectations for that student (Brown & Medway, 2007; Hauser-Cram, Sirin, & Stipek, 2003), and the perception on the part of schools that African Americans don't value education is closely linked to low expectations for Black student performance that characterize U.S. schools (Delpit, 2012; Ladson-Billings, 2007). Indeed, research indicates that the teacher's perception of the parental value of education influences teacher expectation of that student (Msengi, 2007; Tyler, Boelter, & Boykin, 2008).

Hauser-Cram et al (2003) found that when teachers perceived there to be a large difference between their own educational values and the values of students' parents, they had lower expectations for the students, even when students' actual skills were controlled. There was a trend toward greater discrepancy when children were African American as opposed to White or Hispanic (Hauser-Cram et al, 2003).

The research cited above indicates that the value of education is likely not lower among African American families than White families, but another question to consider is whether it would in fact be appropriate if it were. In other words, should African American children and families, especially if they are poor, value education as much as White families? Job discrimination, poverty in the community, and lack of models of individuals from the community who have used education to get ahead may mean that not valuing education would be an appropriate response to the life situation of many African Americans (Philipsen, 1993). Thus not only should teachers not assume a low value of education, but if they do perceive it to be true, it probably should be considered a rational and logical response to the reality of being poor and Black instead of as a character flaw or an aberration.

Another factor that may be linked to teacher beliefs about the value of education in Black families is student resistance. Resistance is "opposition with a social and political purpose" (Abowitz, 2000, 878). In the context of schools, resistance occurs when students struggle against the authority and organizing structures and norms of schools because of their own marginalization, lack of power, and poor treatment (Abowitz, 2000; Hendrickson, 2012; McLaren, 1985). Resistance theorists see resistance as a logical and often unconscious reaction to the recognition that instead of being the democratic institutions they are purported to be, schools are in fact places where social reproduction occurs.

In other words, contrary to dominant ideology, school is not a system that provides knowledge and opportunities equally to all, but rather a system in which higher social classes get what they need to maintain their position of power and lower classes are kept in their place (McLaren, 1985). Resistance can take active forms of misbehavior and overt defiance, but it also takes more passive forms such as sleeping in class, and failure to do assigned work. Either way, it is often interpreted by teachers and others "as their culture not valuing education" (Abowitz, 2000).

Unfortunately, while adults who think outside the box and challenge marginalization are sometimes considered heroic, students are not, and resistance tends to make it even less likely that they will get any benefit from school and education (Abowitz, 2000; Gilmore, 1985; Hendrickson, 2012).

RACE AND SOCIAL CLASS

One question that often comes up in discussions of racial bias is whether the bias is about race or social class. The comments and observations that have been discussed so far, as well as past research, indicate that the beliefs held by the teachers in this study are likely about both. In the U.S., negative beliefs (conscious and unconscious) about poor people abound, and negative beliefs (conscious and unconscious) about Black people abound—these beliefs and assumptions are part of the dominant narrative.

When these categories are combined, negative narratives stringing negative sets of beliefs and assumptions tend to be magnified. Thus, for example, in their study of special education Harry, Klingner, and Hart (2005) found that families who were victims of unwarranted negative assumptions and mistreatment by teachers and administrators were not those who were poor and White, or those who were Black and middle class, but those who were both poor and Black.

The families that were the subject of Mrs. James's soup bus story were both poor and Black, and the script she followed in talking about them was likely a script that combined the two characteristics in a way that would be difficult to untangle. However, although students in our university courses sometimes argue that claims of racism are entirely about social class and not race, research indicates that race does act independently of social class.

This is supported by research, as in Skiba et al (2014), who studied the discrepancy in suspension and expulsion rates in schools, and who wrote: "Multivariate analyses have consistently demonstrated that race remains a significant predictor of suspension and expulsion even after controlling for poverty" (p. 646). Interview responses of the remaining two teachers in our study also clearly illustrate the independent role of race above and beyond social class in their beliefs about families.

Mrs. Blair, Amber's first mentor teacher in Fall 2010, was a 7th grade math teacher. At Mrs. Blair's school, Whites made up almost two-thirds of the student body, and the rest were mainly African American, with Hispanic and Asian students each making up around 2% of the population. Fifty-four percent of the students qualified for Free or Reduced Lunch. A White teacher with 21 years of teaching experience, Mrs. Blair taught three regular and three honors sections of math each day. Our observations led us to believe she was a caring and effective teacher. Below Mrs. Blair was responding to a question about whether she believes one should try to ignore race as a teacher or to take it into account:

> Mrs. Blair: I try not to ignore [race], obviously fru fru White female and I try to stay up with the hip hop world, try to make sure I can at least relate some way. Obviously I don't fall in their same socioeconomic background either, I was raised by two parents that lived together, I raised my kids by two parents so that part of it, I think because there are so many single parents there, and that's something you have to pay attention to and it's not necessarily just the Black community, that's probably all of the kids, but then the value of education is different in a Black family than in a White family …

> Puchner: And why do you think there's that difference in education?

> Mrs. Blair: … I don't know why the parent won't say education is the best way to go and that you need to stay in school and that you need to get the education, not drop out and work …

In the excerpt above, Mrs. Blair begins by referencing cultural differences ("the hip hop world") between herself and her Black students that necessitate her effort to make sure she can "relate in some way" to the students in order to be a good teacher. Then she explores the social class and family configuration differences and notes that single parent families are not unique to the Black community. However, she finishes the response by emphasizing that although single parent families are White and Black, there is a White-Black difference in "value of education."

The comments indicate that Mrs. Blair sees social class as an issue, but that when it comes to the specific question of value of education, in her reality there is a Black-White difference that transcends social class. As with the previous examples of teacher statements, Mrs. Blair likely does not realize the extent to which that idea is an untested background assumption that permeates the institutional culture of the school.

Mrs. Rain's interview even more directly addresses the role of race above and beyond social class. Mrs. Rain was a 3rd grade teacher for Michelle's first field placement. Seventy-five percent of the students in the school qualified for free or reduced lunch, and, as indicated earlier, 81% of Mrs. Rain's students were students of color. Mrs. Rain had been teaching for eight years, and had a friendly, open personality. Our observations of her classes indicated that she had a very difficult time with behavior management, primarily due to weak teaching skills, a conclusion also expressed by Michelle in our interviews with her.

In our interview with her, Mrs. Rain did not directly say that African American families don't value education, but this belief underlay much of what she said. The views that she expressed in the interview were in general quite disturbing, and because of space we are sharing just a few very brief excerpts from a much larger narrative. During the interview she derided two nearby school districts that are almost 100% African American, she derided families "on public aid" who request not to pay textbook fees, and she derided children who spoke African American dialect. (Regarding student use of the phrase "that's mines" instead of "that's mine," among other things she said: "...you can't say words that aren't real. And he's like, 'but that's just my language', and I said, 'so your language is unreal words?'")

We speculate that Mrs. Rain was very frustrated by the difficulties she had with behavior management, and that one way that she dealt with the frustration was to denigrate and blame her students' parents and families. We also speculate that because of institutional racism and classism, even though she admitted during the interview that one of her most difficult students was White, she placed the blame entirely on the families of her Black students and by extension on Black families in general, who she implied were irresponsible, selfish, and neglectful in how they raised their children.

At one point she lamented the fact that when she was growing up, parents volunteered in school and in the classroom, but that it's different now.

I don't want to say that parents don't care, but sometimes it seems like that. Sometimes it seems like they have other priorities, and their kids aren't at the top of that priority list.

A little later Markowitz picked up on that statement:

Markowitz: You were saying you think parents have another, sometimes the kids aren't their first priority. Like what is their first priority, like in your experience?

Mrs. Rain: Themselves. They want to dress nice, they want to look nice, they have other kids, maybe one other kid, or multiple other kids, so there's just so many kids I've seen, it's like let the kids fend for themselves, and the oldest one can deal with everybody else, and I'm going to sit back and do what I want to do.

We see here a repeat of one of the salient themes in Mrs. James's story, cited earlier, about bad parenting in African American families, illustrating commonalities among institutions. Mrs. Rain's responses demonstrate an underlying belief that

African American students tended to have worse behavior and lower achievement than White students, and that it was due to family acceptance of bad behavior at home, selfishness of the parents, and low value placed on education. At one point Mrs. Rain acknowledged that since most of her students were African American, it's hard to tell whether race is the cause "…when the majority of your class is African American, it's hard to say." However, later in the interview this exchange occurred:

Markowitz: Like if this whole class was full of White kids who were just from a lower SES, do you think you'd see some of the same issues?

Mrs. Rain: I think I would see some but I think it plays part with race, I really do. Just because of, like I said, because of their background, because of what they grow up with, and what they see at home, and what their parents are saying at home …

Markowitz: So what else … do you think would be different in [an all-African American] classroom?

Mrs. Rain: Academics I think. I think that the way they perceive school would be different. I know that some kids come to school just because they have to, because their parents say they have to, because their parent brings them. It's like a daycare, here you go, keep my kid until you possibly can. I think that it would be different just because I think that the backgrounds of the people, or of those kids' families, really play a part of how they act here.

Mrs. Rain's interview responses show very negative beliefs about Black families in general, with the low value of education a prominent theme. Further, Mrs. Rain felt that the problems she experienced with some students were more likely to occur with lower income children, but she did not feel that being poor was the complete explanation.

Mrs. Rain also told us in the interview that parents have accused her of being racist, and although she denied that she is, it's not hard to understand why many parents would feel that way. Importantly, the fact that Mrs. Rain felt comfortable expressing the beliefs she did to the researcher is likely an indicator of the nature of the institutional culture.

IMPLICATIONS

The data we've provided from the six teachers portrayed in this article do not prove that schools are institutionally racist, but they show us the faces of institutional racism that we know exists from other research (Levine-Rasky, 2000; Sleeter, 1994; Vaught & Castagno, 2008). An important message from this material is that teacher education has a bigger challenge than most of us realize. Both preservice teachers and teacher educators need to understand better the institutional background stories of the schools we are sending our teacher education students to, and figure out how to wrestle with it.

In Ferguson Missouri, although the police officer who shot and killed Michael Brown in August 2014 was not charged, U.S. Justice Department investigations found widespread abuse of African American citizens. This abuse was not usually lethal, but it caused great harm. The context of teaching and the context of policing are very different, but the underlying institutional dynamics are not.

School cultures permeated by a belief that African American families do not value education have multiple negative effects on students of color. Two of the most commonly discussed problems are low teacher expectations for students of color and disproportionate punishment (Hauser-Cram et al, 2003; Lee & Bowen, 2006; Skiba et al, 2014).

Social trust, or the extent to which the students, teachers, administrators, and parents of a school maintain relationships with each other characterized by respect, personal regard, competence, and personal integrity (Bryk & Schneider, 2003, pp. 41–42), is also effected. Social trust has been found to be more important to school improvement than many other frequently-cited factors (Bryk & Schneider, 2003), and of course when teachers don't value or respect parents and their opinions or hold them in high regard, social trust is low. Preservice teachers who do field experiences in schools with institutional cultures characterized by low social trust are likely to have a harder time moving away from that pattern.

Although the unintentional racism causes great harm, and lack of intention does not equal lack of responsibility, understanding intent is important in planning anti-racist education. Haney López's theory helps us see the need to factor in the role of agency but in a way that also keeps in mind the institutionalized nature of the racism.

One avenue is helping people understand how all of our thinking in daily life relies on unexamined assumptions about the world, and that we act with unconscious patterns of cognition and scripts in all areas, not just race. Haney López (2000) cites examples from prior research of non-race related assumptions people hold as they go through life. One such assumption is that communication is always meaningful, and one experiment showed how people go to great lengths to create meaning out of communication that is actually entirely random (Garfinkel, 1967, as cited in Haney López 2000).

Relatedly, Haney López's theory helps us see the role of attempts to change individual beliefs. Although "group interaction generates racial institutions, and … such institutions influence individual behavior through widely shared cognitive process-es" (Haney López, 2000, p. 1808), not all individuals within an institution must act in accordance with the group.

Hence in the area of teacher education, educating individual teachers to resist a racist institutional culture could certainly change to a certain degree the experience of students within an individual teacher's classroom. The punishment for violating cultural norms often makes it very difficult to behave in ways outside of the norma-tive background stories, but the closed doors of U.S. classrooms make some devia-tion possible. Thus quality teacher education for diversity will be useful, since even mild disruptions made by individual teachers can make a difference to the students they are teaching (Khalifa, 2012; Marriott, 2003).

Further, a critical mass of individuals with background assumptions that are less racist or anti-racist will alter the institutional culture; obviously there are some schools that meet the needs of all students better than others. That being said, though, the theory also helps us understand the limitations of attempting to change beliefs.

CONCLUSION

In this article we illustrate a major problem in education and in teacher education, the underlying dynamics of which are a national problem. The Ferguson unrest has spurred a spate of newspaper editorials addressing unconscious racial bias. However, although the bias part is somewhat well-known, it is not well-accepted, and neither is institutional racism.

What Haney López's and Bonilla-Silva's theories show is how individual uncon-scious bias and institutional racism fit together to decrease the odds of African American students succeeding, especially if they are poor. In teacher education most people tend to think we are already doing what is necessary to deal with ra-cial issues by incorporating multicultural education into our courses. However, the current study shows what happens when you scratch the surface.

The national reform agenda for the past 20 years has focused on test scores and teacher evaluation, with no improvement in educational equity (Lee & Wong, 2004; Ravitch, 2010). Addressing the problem illustrated by the teachers profiled in this article would arguably have a greater positive impact on student learning and stu-dent achievement than recent or current major reform efforts.

In the case of policing, the very unfortunate recent events have placed a national spotlight on racial bias, which for the moment has the public's attention and might lead to some positive change. In teaching, negative beliefs about Black families don't directly kill people, and it's hard right now to get the public to pay attention to it. So we need to work harder to raise the alarm and take action.

NOTE

1   All names are pseudonyms to protect the privacy of study participants.

REFERENCES

Abowitz, K. K. (2000). A pragmatist revisioning of resistance theory. *American Educational Research Journal, 37*(4), 877–907.

Banerjee, M., Harrell, Z.A.T., & Johnson, D. J. (2011). Racial/ethnic socialization and parental involvement as predictors of cognitive ability and achievement in African American children. *Journal of Youth Adolescence, 40*, 595–605.

Bonilla-Silva, E. (2003). *Racism without racists: Color-blind racism and the persistence of racial inequality in the United States.* Lanham, NJ: Rowman & Littlefield.

Brown, K.E., & Medway, F.J. (2007). School climate and teacher beliefs in a school effectively serving poor South Carolina (USA) African-American students: A case study. *Teaching and Teacher Education, 23*, 529–540.

Boser, U. (2014). *Teacher diversity revisited.* Center for American Progress. Retrieved March 25, 2015. https://www.americanprogress.org/issues/race/report/2014/05/04/88962/teacher-diversity-revisited/

Bryk, A. S., & Schneider, B. (2003). Trust in Schools: A core resource for school reform. *Educational Leadership*, March, 40–44.

Comey, J. (2015, February). Hard truths: Law enforcement and race. Speech at Georgetown University, Washington, D.C. Retrieved March 23, 2015, for Federal Bureau of Investigation Website. http://www.fbi.gov/news/speeches/hard-truths-law-enforcement-and-race.

Delpit, L. (2012). *"Multiplication is for White people": Raising expectations for other people's children.* New York: The New Press.

Geenen, S., Powers, L.E., & López-Vazquez, A. (2005). Barriers against and strategies for promoting the involvement of culturally diverse parents in school-based transition planning. *The Journal for Vocational Special Needs Education, 27*(3), 4–14.

Gerson, M. (2015). Viewing Ferguson from Selma: Bloody Sunday anniversary. *St. Louis Post-Dispatch*, March 12, p. A15.

Gilmore, P. (1985). "Gimme room": School resistance, attitude, and access to literacy. *Journal of Education, 167*(1). 111–128.

Haney López, I. F. (2000). Institutional racism: Judicial conduct and a new theory of racial discrimination. *The Yale Law Journal, 109*, 1717–1884.

Harry, B., Klingner, J. K., & Hart, J. (2005). African American families under fire: Ethnographic views of family strengths. *Remedial and Special Education 26*, 101–112.

Hauser-Cram, P., Sirin, S. R., & Stipek, D. (2003). When teachers' and parents' values differ: Teachers' ratings of academic competence in children from low-income families. *Journal of Educational Psychology, 95*, 813–820.

Hendrickson, K. A. (2012). Student resistance to schooling: Disconnections with education in rural Appalachia. *The High School Journal*, Apr/May, 37–49.

Kerbow, D., & Bernhardt, A. (1993). Parental intervention in the school: The context of minority involvement. In B. Schneider & J. S. Coleman (Eds)., *Parents, their children, and schools* (pp. 115–146). Boulder, CO: Westview Press.

Khalifa, M. (2012). Caught between theory and reality: Positionality of a Black male teacher in urban Detroit. *Vitae Scholasticae, 29*(2), 5–31.

King, J. E. (1991). Dysconscious racism: Ideology, identity, and the miseducation of teachers. *Journal of Negro Education, 60*, 133–146.

Ladson-Billings, G. (2000). Fighting for our lives: Preparing teachers to teach African-American students. *Journal of Teacher Education*, 51(3), 206–214.

Ladson-Billings, G. (2007). Pushing past the achievement gap: An essay on the language of deficit. *Journal of Negro Education, 76*, 316–323.

Lee, J., & Bowen, N.K. (2006). Parent involvement, cultural capital, and the achievement gap among elementary school children. *American Educational Research Journal, 43*, 193–218.

Lee, J., & Wong, K. K. (2004). The impact of accountability on racial and socioeconomic equity: Considering both school resources and achievement outcomes. *American Educational Research Journal, 31*(4), 797–832.

Levine-Rasky, C. (2000). The practice of whiteness among teacher candidates. *International Studies in Sociology of Education 10*(3), 263–284.

Markowitz, L., & Puchner, L. (2014). Racial diversity in the schools: A necessary evil? *Multicultural Perspectives, 16*(2), 72–78.

Marriott, D. M. (2003). Ending the silence. *Phi Delta Kappan 84*(7), 496–501.

McLaren, P. L. (1985). The ritual dimensions of resistance: Clowning and symbolic inversion. *Journal of Education. 167*(2), 84–97.

Msengi, S. G. (2007). Family, child and teacher perceptions of African American adult assistance to young readers. *The School Community Journal, 17*, 33–60.

Philipsen, M.(1993). Values-spoken and values-lived: Female African Americans' educational experiences in rural North Carolina. *Journal of Negro Education, 62*(4). 419–426.

Ravitch, D. (2010). Why I changed My mind. *The Nation*, June, 20–24.

Skiba, R. J., Chung, C-G., Trachok, M., Baker, T. L., Sheya, A., & Hughes, R. L. (2014). Parsing disciplinary disproportionality: Contributions of infraction, student, and school characteristics to out-of-school suspension and expulsion. *American Educational Research Journal, 51*(4), 640–670.

Sleeter, C. (1994). White racism. *Multicultural Education, 1*(4), 5–8.

Tyler, K. M., Boelter, C. M., & Boykin, A. W. (2008). Linking teachers' perceptions of educational value discontinuity to low-income middle school students' academic engagement and self-efficacy. *Middle Grades Research Journal, 3*(4), 1–20.

Vaught, S., & Castagno, A. (2008). "I don't think I'm a racist": Critical Race Theory, teacher attitudes, and structural racism. *Race Ethnicity and Education, 11*, 95–113.

Wong, S. W., & Hughes, J. N. (2006). Ethnicity and language contributions to dimensions of parent involvement. *School Psychology Review, 35*, 645–662.

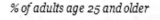

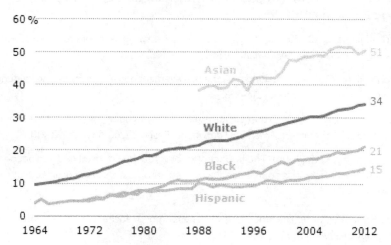

Note: White, black and Asian adults include only those who reported a single race. Native Americans and mixed-race groups not shown. Data for whites, blacks and Asians from 1971 to 2011 include only non-Hispanics. Data for whites and blacks prior to 1971 include Hispanics. Comparable data for Hispanics not available prior to 1971. Data for Asians not available prior to 1988. Asians include Pacific Islanders. Before 1992 refers to those who completed at least 16 years of school. For 1992-2012 refers to those who have at least a bachelor's degree.

Source: Pew Research Center tabulations of the Current Population Survey Annual Social and Economic Supplement (IPUMS)

PEW RESEARCH CENTER

FIGURE 4.12 **College completion by race/ethnicity, 1964–2012.**

Understanding that race is a social construct allows us to appeal to social structures, social practices, and social factors as explanations for these inequalities/social disparities rather than making the appeal that race itself is some sort of driving factor in outcomes. This is decidedly different than the consensus view through the mid-twentieth century, which often appealed to race itself or racial differences for explanatory power.

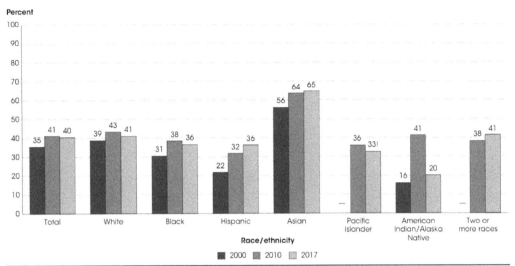

Percent

— Not available.
! Interpret data with caution. The coefficient of variation (CV) for this estimate is between 30 and 50 percent.
NOTE: Data are based on sample surveys of the civilian noninstitutionalized population. Separate data for young adults who were Pacific Islander and of Two or more races were not available in 2000. In 2000, data for individual race categories include persons of Two or more races. Prior to 2003, data for Asian young adults include Pacific Islander young adults. Race categories exclude persons of Hispanic ethnicity. Although rounded numbers are displayed, the figures are based on unrounded data.
SOURCE: U.S. Department of Commerce, Census Bureau, Current Population Survey (CPS), October Supplement, 2000, 2010, and 2017. See *Digest of Education Statistics 2018*, table 302.60.

FIGURE 4.13 **College enrollment rates of 18- to 24-year-olds by race/ethnicity: 2000, 2010, and 2017.**

SEGREGATION

Both a cause and a driver of racial inequality, living patterns reflect many different contemporary racial realities in the United States. As these disparate patterns have persisted for generations in many cases, it has resulted in the invisibility of these patterns. Alternatively, because there are no laws that allow housing discrimination on the basis of race, many argue that these patterns are mostly a result of choice. However, analyzing race as a social construct, and considering how historical notions of race and the history of legal segregation, sociologists argue that these patterns are largely a factor of how race has operated in American society.

Due to a variety of factors, including the aforementioned concepts of experiences varying by race, segregation, cultural narratives, and distributions of income, wealth, prestige, and ultimately power, opinions in society can vary widely across racial groups (and within them; see *intersectionality*). Public opinion polls show significant differences by race in regard to a number of important aspects of society, including political affiliation, policing, housing, education, and the legal system as well as racism/prevalence of discrimination and the historical and contemporary significance of race itself.

An Example

Figure 4.14 is a picture of a swath of Detroit, Michigan. If you have ever seen the film *8 Mile* starring Eminem, this is indeed the 8 Mile Road depicted in the film. Note how the road serves as a de facto line of segregation even though there are no segregation laws in Michigan.

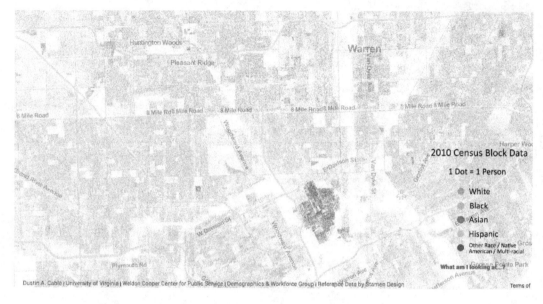

FIGURE 4.14   8 Mile Road racial divide.

CRITICAL THINKING:	1. If there are no longer what forces or phenomenon facilitate these living arrangements? 2. Discuss how you think this map compares to a map from 1960 in a couple of cities.

BIAS

Implicit bias refers to the attitudes or stereotypes that affect our understanding, actions, and decisions in an unconscious manner. These biases, which encompass both favorable and unfavorable assessments, are activated involuntarily and without an individual's awareness or intentional control. Residing deep in the subconscious, these biases are different from known biases that individuals may choose to conceal for the purposes of social and/or political correctness. Rather, implicit biases are not accessible through introspection.

The implicit associations we harbor in our subconscious cause us to have feelings and attitudes about other people based on characteristics such as race, ethnicity, age, and appearance. These associations develop over the course of a lifetime beginning at a very early age through exposure to direct and indirect messages. In addition to early life experiences, the media and news programming are often-cited origins of implicit associations.

- Implicit biases are pervasive. Everyone possesses them, even people with avowed commitments to impartiality such as judges.
- Implicit and explicit biases are related but distinct mental constructs. They are not mutually exclusive and may even reinforce each other.
- The implicit associations we hold do not necessarily align with our declared beliefs or even reflect stances we would explicitly endorse.
- We generally tend to hold implicit biases that favor our own ingroup, though research has shown that we can still hold implicit biases against our ingroup.
- *Implicit biases are malleable. Our brains are incredibly complex, and the implicit associations that we have formed can be gradually unlearned through a variety of debiasing techniques.*[3]

Explicit bias is the formalized expression of bias through language, action, or policy. In these cases race is typically overtly tended to. This includes things like having membership in a group like the Ku Klux Klan, making a statement that deems at least one racial (ethnic, religious, etc.) group as inferior or lesser, or suggesting that at least one racial group should be treated worse.

SUMMARY

We have just briefly explored the notion of race in the United States and the consequences that broadly emanate from such notions. We explored historical and modern notions of race and discussed how race can be real without being *real* through the socially constructed nature of the concept (how's that for nuance?!). Moreover, we discussed the importance of race and racial constructs and how they impact both the everyday lives of individuals and large-scale social life.

Race can be an uncomfortable subject to talk about, and open discourse about race is often discouraged in the "colorblind" society in which we currently live. The colorblind-era notion that "talking about race is racism," permeates much of society. It is something that many of you have been taught is correct, respectful, polite, politically correct, and

---

3   Cheryl Staats, Kelly Capatosto, Robin A. Wright, and Danya Contractor, *Kirwan Institute Research Report* (Columbus: The Ohio State University, 2015).

so on. This is a notion that must be put aside for your class discussions surrounding this chapter and other chapters that intersect with it. Even people who have the best of intentions and a genuine interest in having open and honest dialogue about race can often have uncomfortable feelings when engaging in such conversations.

More resources:

"Do White People Get Stressed Talking About Race?":
https://www.youtube.com/watch?v=YX-i11lGj5w

The following video from Buzzfeed helps illuminate that race and talking about race can affect how a person is thinking. It also demonstrates how these sorts of thoughts and the way they manifest themselves physiologically are often beyond our control.

It is also important to allow people to make mistakes. In most arenas of life, we give leeway and the benefit of the doubt to people who are learning or taking a genuine interest in learning or implementing something new. Yet when it comes to race (although certainly not limited to only this arena of society), partly due to lack of experience in having these conversations (in the same way you learn how to eat at a restaurant or board a plane, you learn to talk about race) due to the colorblind suggestion that talking about/acknowledging race contributes to the problem, it is not uncommon to see people shut down a conversation when a genuine learning opportunity presents itself.

Like most other topics we cover (and maybe even more so) race does not end with this chapter. It affects and influences other major arenas of social life like gender, social class, sexuality, and culture. For instance, as an intersection with gender it allows us to talk about a particular kind of "black masculinity," its development, and the effects that it has on people in this sphere of socialization.

Hopefully, this introduction has piqued your interest and will prompt you to investigate the myriad other material that is out there. This is but a fraction of the rigorous work that has been done on this issue for over a century, some of which has an important history of affecting social understandings, social policy, and laws. Additionally, there are many cross-disciplinary studies about race, as well as studies and theories postulated by other disciplines. There is no one perfect theory of race, and this chapter is but a brief foray into social thought and studies that increase our ability to understand racial dynamics in the United States and more broadly across the world.

GLOSSARY OF TERMS

- **Biologic notions of race**: A group or population that shares a specific set of features and is somehow genetically distinct (usually to the point of qualitative difference); sociologists, biologists, and geneticists reject this notion.

- **Social construct**: Something is a social construct when meanings are defined by social values and structure. *The meaning of race is defined and contested in society.*
- **Social construction of race**: Race is socially constructed to fit the narrative and structure of society (i.e., to justify slavery in the US, the idea that blacks were subhuman was propagated as a racial narrative).
- **Racial formation theory (Winant)**: The process by which social, economic, and political forces determine the content and importance of racial categories and by which they are in turn shaped by racial meanings.
    http://www.youtube.com/watch?v=_qaWp8_z81w
- **Ethnicity**: A shared set of cultural practices, language, religion, history, and usually geography.
- **Race**: A socially constructed way of categorizing people into groups based on perceived phenotypic and cultural traits, as well as historical perceptions. Racial categories have considerable variability from society to society and varying levels of importance.
- **Racism**: A belief that some races are inferior/superior to others or having different valuations of different races. Also often includes actions on behalf of such beliefs or speech that lends credence to such beliefs.
- **Structural racism**: Denotes racist practices that exist within the structural framework of a society, either codified into law or as a prevailing norm and often, but not necessarily, government sanctioned.
- **Segregation**: Living spaces and commercial districts are largely separated by race; Houston is the most segregated city in the US.
- **De facto segregation**: Subtle processes like redlining (a housing practice in which blacks are discouraged from buying houses in certain neighborhoods) and other policies that still result in segregated living.
- **Gentrification**: A systematic moving out of a poorer population and a reinvestment into those areas by wealthier people. Raises property values but displaces poor people.
- **Intersectionality**: The idea that the aggregation of multiple social constructs produces unique intersectional identities and that these identities often operate independently from their disaggregated forms.

Image Credits

Fig. 4.2: Source: https://www.census.gov/content/dam/Census/library/visualizations/2017/demo/p60-259/figure1.pdf.
Fig. 4.3: Source: https://apps.urban.org/features/wealth-inequality-charts/img/Nine%20Charts%20All%20Charts.pdf.
Fig. 4.4: Source: https://orgtheory.wordpress.com/2016/09/07/did-bill-clinton-accelerate-black-mass-incarceration-yes-he-did-but-he-put-a-bunch-of-white-people-in-prison-to-even-it-out/.
Fig. 4.5: Source: https://www.pewresearch.org/fact-tank/2019/04/30/shrinking-gap-between-number-of-blacks-and-whites-in-prison/.

Fig. 4.6: Source: https://www.pewresearch.org/fact-tank/2019/04/30/shrinking-gap-between-number-of-blacks-and-whites-in-prison/.

Fig. 4.7: Source: https://www.washingtonpost.com/news/wonk/wp/2013/06/04/the-blackwhite-marijuana-arrest-gap-in-nine-charts/?utm_term=.aa14aa455657.

Fig. 4.8: Source: https://www.washingtonpost.com/news/wonk/wp/2013/06/04/the-blackwhite-marijuana-arrest-gap-in-nine-charts/?utm_term=.aa14aa455657.

Fig. 4.9: Source: https://www.washingtonpost.com/news/wonk/wp/2013/06/04/the-blackwhite-marijuana-arrest-gap-in-nine-charts/?noredirect=on&utm_term=.90edbf8da3a0.

Fig. 4.10: Source: https://www.pewresearch.org/fact-tank/2017/01/12/black-and-white-officers-see-many-key-aspects-of-policing-differently/.

Fig. 4.11: Source: https://www.pewresearch.org/fact-tank/2017/01/12/black-and-white-officers-see-many-key-aspects-of-policing-differently/.

Fig. 4.12: Source: https://www.pewsocialtrends.org/2013/08/22/chapter-3-demographic-economic-data-by-race/.

Fig. 4.13: Source: https://nces.ed.gov/programs/coe/pdf/coe_cpb.pdf.

Fig. 4.14: Source: https://www.huffpost.com/entry/map-segregation-america-race_n_3824693.

Gender

Like most topics in sociology, gender can be controversial. However, unlike many sociological topics, gender is something we discuss quite often, and fairly openly in society. As a result, many people, including students and readers such as yourselves, tend to have more preconceived notions regarding gender than with most topics.

DEFINING GENDER

- **Biological notions of gender**: Male and female.
- **Gender binary**: The notion that there are only two genders, male and female, and every person fits one. Societies that operate on this paradigm institutionally only recognize two genders, and this often follows culturally and socially as well.
- **Sociological notions of gender**: Gender is defined by society; there are societies that incorporate more than two genders in both contemporary and historical times. Examining these societies suggests that gender is socially constructed.
- **Sex**: Typically thought to be given by biology (i.e., genitals, chromosomes, hormones).
- **Gender**: A socially constructed identity and category that organizes social life. Gender is created and recreated through social interaction. It is performed, and its performance is enforced. The way in which actors "do" their gender varies by context.

CRITICAL THINKING:	What are some traits/characteristics often associated with masculinity and what are some traits/characteristics associated with femininity?

CRITICAL THINKING:	Who is this?

FIGURE 5.1.

<table>
<tr><td>CRITICAL THINKING:</td><td>Why is FDR dressed like that as a young child?</td></tr>
</table>

GENDER SOCIALIZATION

From essentially the moment we are born, we are taught gender roles and norms. As with race, the roles, norms, and characteristics we learn to associate with gender are usually assigned different values. In most cases what is masculine or male is valued over what is feminine or female.

More resources:

Gender roles: Interviews with Kids:
https://www.youtube.com/watch?v=-VqsbvG40Ww
Addressing Gender Socialization and Masculinity Norms among Adolescent Boys:
https://www.ncbi.nlm.nih.gov/pmc/articles/PMC5817048/

GENDER IDENTITY

- **Identity theory**: The part of individual's self-concept derived from perceived membership in a relevant social group
- **Ascribed identities**: Identities that seem natural: race, sex, athletic, pretty, and so on.
- **Achieved identity**: Identities that seem merit based, based on social relations: gender, teacher, rich, college graduate, and so on.

Even though it may seem natural, gender is an achieved identity because it is a fluid social construct based on personal understandings. Much of gender identity, as well as perceptions of gender, relate to personal choices and methods of self-presentation and behaviors. Therefore, there are any number of gender identities, and these identities may indeed be fluid.

More resources:

More resources: Non-Binary Gender Identities: https://www.apadivisions.org/division-44/resources/advocacy/non-binary-facts.pdf

GENDER ROLES

- **Gender roles**: Through socialization we learn what "males" do and what "females" do; we use these typologies to make decisions about our own actions and behavior.

What are some gender roles?

- **Gender roles**: Sets of social and behavioral norms that are generally considered appropriate for either a man or a woman in a social or interpersonal relationship.

Gender role theory emphasizes the environmental causes of gender roles and the impact of socialization, or the process of transferring norms, values, beliefs, and behaviors to group members, in learning how to behave as a male or a female.

- **Boundaries**: The edge of what is socially acceptable.

Reading 5.1.

Gender: The Infinite Ocean

by Innis Sampson

SELF-CREATED, SELF-DEFINED, SELF-SUSTAINED

When gender is seen as binary, any deviations from these polar extremes are rendered invisible. In this silenced state, diversity suffers, which in turn negatively impacts individuals and community. A person's identity and individuality are robbed from them when gender becomes a binary label. This binary labeling demonstrates a lack of sensitivity and respect for a person's background, experiences, skills, and knowledge. Variety within community diminishes when this valuable information is not shared and diversity isn't valued and prioritized amongst members.

Innis Sampson, "Gender: The Infinite Ocean," *Communities*, vol. 162, pp. 35-37, 71. Copyright © 2014 by Fellowship for Intentional Community. Reprinted with permission. Provided by ProQuest LLC. All rights reserved.

When gender is self-created, self-defined, and self-sustained, existence within community becomes positive and allows people, as well as community, to flourish. Because one cannot exist without the other, it is the responsibility of both the individual and the community to maintain a healthy and safe environment for gender variant people. This ultimately creates a safe environment for everyone. Most people would not allow another to dictate their race, ability, sex, or other personal characteristics. Although sometimes these things may seem apparent, no one can truly know another person's realities or preferences. This ignorance often leads to the "isms" (ageism, racism, sexism, able-ism, etc.) and can become hurtful to individuals and community at large.

When speaking about the isms, genderism does not come up often. Genderism is the belief that gender is binary, and that only two genders—male and female—exist. Genderism marries gender and sex, concluding that they are one and the same. Many people make this mistake, but it's important, even crucial, to remember that "sex" refers to one's biological sex at birth: male, female, or intersex. Gender is a person's internal sense of self, role, expression, and behavior. Gender is also determined by society and others' perception. Misgendering can become very detrimental to the person who is being misidentified.

I have experienced genderism in many different types of communities. Even the most open communities which tout feminism, diversity, and queer inclusion have exhibited genderism towards me. These experiences have been in cities, towns, neighborhoods, intentional communities, group organizations, and friend circles. Often these experiences were due to a lack of information about gender politics and visibility of gender variant people within community. I do not believe that my gender and my sex are one and the same, and that has been difficult for many to understand and accept. For me, these experiences have been hurtful, awkward, scary, and painful. They have also been enlightening, positive, and have allowed me to work on my patience as well as develop my teaching skills.

For the purposes of this article, I feel that examining my own "gender work" is more valuable than focusing on the gender-based interactions I have had with others. Although my experiences with others have helped shape my understanding of gender, most of my work has been done within my self. Communities can become sensitive to gender variant people but I think they can benefit most from becoming sensitive to everyone's realities and preferences, because this story could be anyone's. Gender is something that is incredibly intimate, exceptional, and is often left unspoken

"Gender is incredibly intimate, exceptional and is often left unspoken until there is a safe space without judgment."

until there is a safe space without judgment. It is a community's responsibility to create these safe spaces.

For many years, the unfavorable gender-based experiences I have had within community affected my self-confidence negatively. When I found myself in a community that was understanding of gender issues, I valued that safe space and I made the decision to live my truth and let my true spirit show. I set off and embarked on a journey that has been perpetually changing the way I look at my life, relationships, and self as a whole.

Spiritual Gender

I am a storyteller. I am a spiritual body. I am a gender warrior. During my time on this Earth, I have been a conscious and unconscious warrior: fighting politics, disassembling stereotypes, and constructing (dis)comfort all in the name of freedom—my own name. There is an innate personal freedom inside everyone, one which is often denied. It is often absent-mindedly given to other people, institutions, or structures to determine and label. This act of surrender compromises respect and responsibility, and therein, the true self is relinquished. When the self is given up, you can envision this act as the conforming masses of society moving quickly down a voracious river, advancing towards an unforgiving sea without question. Some find that their eyes fill with water, splashed from another's desperate attempt to stay afloat. The vision is skewed, creating blurred forms and grandiose ideas. It becomes a sink-or-swim game and many who drown never dream of growing gills. There is a comfort in the darkness of the depths and there is always company just as nearsighted and comfortable.

A few years ago, I went through the painful process of growing my own gills. My new breath allowed me to explore all parts of the ocean: the beautiful and the terrifying. Then I grew legs and walked upon the shore. All in due time, I returned to the Earth, and thus became the rocks, the soil, the plants, and the animals. My name is Innis. My name means "an island with two rivers flowing through it." I am an island in the sea. These rivers flow through me as sentient representations of the sacred feminine and the sacred masculine. The sea surrounds me, steady and safe in my comfort. My fluid nature is muted, influenced by quiet balance of the creator and the nurturer. Great energies undulate; the Earth and the sky form the great coalescence. I have built and sustained myself in this sea. I have accepted that the rivers are an innate part of me. I am a spiritual body and I do not deny my presence on this Earth.

When I was denying my presence in the past, I was denying my spirit. I define my own gender as the seamless interrelationship between my physical self—my body, my outward presentation and behaviors—and my internal sense of self: my spirit. Ultimately, my gender is a mirror of my spirit. It has taken me years to even begin entertaining that idea, and even more energy for me to live it. There is an innate spiritual connection between how I present myself as a human being and who I am as one of the innumerable souls navigating the sea of the universe. I certainly did not always feel this sense of spiritual connection to who I have become.

A Mirror of the Soul

I have found, through my life experiences, that gender is not at all what it appears. It is in the presentation, expression, and actions of a person, so it is expressed internally and externally. It lives, grows, and sometimes hides within the heart. Sometimes it is swaddled and sometimes it is bare. Its appearance sometimes can feel like pure comfort; other times it is extremely raw.

My gender has been in a constant state of flux for my whole life. This fluidity has always been rooted in my being, and my journey has been about connecting to that base root. No matter how far I feel I have diverted off the path to understanding my true self, I always come back to center, pulled back in like the tides of the ocean. Sometimes this pull has been abrupt and painful, and sometimes it is nothing less than blissful.

I identify the ever-fluidity of my gender as genderqueer. For me, genderqueer is an umbrella term but it means that I am queering my relationships to gender and sexual orientation. For me they are intertwined. For me, queering is a deviation within the norm. Those who identify as queer as a sexuality often work beyond traditional labels to create space for those who are gender and sexually variant and who may have alternative views of sexual orientations. I also qualify my sexual orientation as "queer." My exploration of gender has certainly been a transition, but I am not trans-identified.

I think that some people who are unaware of gender politics perceive gender transitions, in whatever form they make take, to be a dualistic transition. It is seen as linear, beginning at one place and ending at another. In speaking about my journey, this can't be further from the truth. My ritual of identity and transition often feels akin to the cyclical energy of the moon, dictating the tides of the ocean and creating undulations and surges of self-discovery. My identity and transition are both conscious and unconscious. I exist as much as I live. I make conscious choices about how I present myself in certain communities. I try to examine and understand how that affects my self-confidence and others' understanding.

Duality and Triality

My spiritual journey is not a linear experience where I began at one place and ended in another. It is an ongoing process that moves beyond the perceived duality of nature. Duality is a polar expression where only realms of opposites exist. In the quality of being dual, or being made up of two things, energy is focused on contrast and the differences between those two points. The values of those opposing points are not celebrated; they are only pitted against each other. Male and female, black and white, night and day are common examples of duality. Duality can be seen visually as a line with two points at each end of the line. As humans, we are bombarded with examples of duality every day, and have become accustomed to absolute polar extremes. In my exploration of gender, duality has reared its two ugly heads time and time again in opposition of my journey.

With inhuman amounts of strength, my fight against duality turned into a peaceful battle. My spirit evolved with truthfulness and love. I began listening to myself more. With my intuition I was able to become more in touch with my true needs. I began to live my truth. It was certainly uncomfortable, but the more I changed my life to become the one that I wanted, the more I became happy, grounded, and proud of myself.

Spiritually, I searched for something that could help put some perspective on the work that I had been doing. One day I came across the idea of triality. From my understanding, triality is moving beyond duality by adding another point, or perspective that is virtually infinite. This other vantage point allows one to recognize the balance between the dualistic nature of things. There is a state of observation that is separate from emotion, which allows us to consciously balance out perceived opposites. This act creates an internal and external transition that in turn births openness and infinite possibility.

Triality is a limitless spectrum of points not married by a line or lines but connected in a universal nature. Think about the stars and how they are all connected and part of a common form but each has its own place in space. This model of triality feels like a community to me. There is a collective force to this group that is unified because of its sharing of space and relationship to each other, and its celebration of diversity.

My gender became reaffirmed in the idea of triality. My identity was not one (female) or the other (male) but something else. This something else is not entirely new, but birthed from these dualistic energies. I channel my masculinity through a feminine lens (specifically my body) to create a holistic otherness, a third gender that is infinite. It is everything those energies are, but everything they are not. It is in between and outside. It is a multi-colored spectrum. It is self-created, self-defined, and a true product of my soul's searching. The community sustains the self and allows for all to interact. It is that cosmic community and it is that ocean.

Empowerment in Community

As a gender variant person I have realized that not only is my honesty my most powerful tool, but it allows me to create truthful relationships with those in community. To me, community is my most powerful support system. I cannot compare anything to the feelings that I have had being involved in my community, the queer community. Queer community has granted me the space (physically and mentally) to express my true self. There is an understanding of sensitivity towards everyone's identity and journey, and there is an emphasis on respecting that. Respect in queer community breeds empowerment within me.

I cannot always be in queer community though. An overwhelming majority of my time is spent outside of queer community. When there is not a lot of LBGTQIA (lesbian, bisexual, gay, trans, queer, intersex, asexual) and gender variant visibility in a particular community, I often feel hyper aware of my environment and the way that people react to my identity and appearance. I have created internal and external safety tactics for myself to ease navigating through non-queer communities, as well as worked on ways to stay constant, sure, and comfortable in my gender and self-expression. I have recognized that when I exhibit these tactics, people become aware that I am pushing away fear, conformity, and self-restriction. My presence does not become about gender anymore but living my truth in an effort to be a positive example to others to simply be themselves.

I believe there are universal and humanistic tools communities can use in an effort to work towards becoming sensitive and more understanding to gender variant people. The most powerful implements of compassion are listening, having empathy, becoming allies, and respecting everyone regardless of internal or external identity. We truly have no idea of each others struggles until we open our hearts and shed all of our stereotypes, projections, and stubborn ideas of "this is the way it has always been."

When it comes to gender, I can only speak for myself and from my own experiences. I do not believe that everyone's gender journey is spiritual; mine just happened to be. I also believe that there is no such thing as coincidence, and I see all of my life's lessons as part of a bigger whole.

My journey is far from over but I have found myself grounded in that ocean I once feared. I remember that my transition is internal as well as external—and that it is as limitless as the communities that surround me. I remember that the best work that I can do in community is to simply be myself, watching the trickle-down theory form a vast ocean, ever wealthy with beautiful diversity.

PROBLEMS WITH THE GENDER BINARY

Women and men are harmed when they attempt to conform to gendered expectations. For instance, they are harmed by practices that seek to inscribe gender into the body (e.g., foot binding, genital cutting, breast implants). Women and men are often physically and emotionally harmed when they fail to conform to gendered expectations; there can be social, emotional, family, educational, and occupational consequences. Moreover, the attributes and stereotypes associated with men and women are not random. In most societies, including America, women are overwhelmingly stereotyped and paired with attributes that work to limit their personal and collective power. However, the traits associated with masculinity often lead to risky behavioral choices, which contribute in part to the five- to six-year difference in less of life expectancy among American men as compared to women. Traits like toughness and self-dependence lead men to ask for help less, including seeking less medical treatment, and traits like bold, daring, and fearless are linked with systematically riskier physical behaviors. As was mentioned by Sampson, trans individuals, and people who do not identify with the dominant paradigm of the gender binary are usually especially harmed.

Societies with Third Genders

It is important to recognize that the United States is not the only game in town. There are numerous societies across the world that as of 2018 either culturally or institutionally recognize and operate with more than two genders. Following is a discussion of the the Fa'afafines in Samoa.

Reading 5.2.

The Social Construction of Gender: Microfinance and fa'afafines in Samoa

by Guy Stuart, Regina Galang and Susie Margolin

WHAT IS A WOMAN? WHAT IS A MAN?

In 2003 Minh Lai, manager of the South Pacific Business Development Foundation (SPBD), a non-profit microfinance institution providing financial services to woman in Samoa, made a decision to lend to *fa'afafines*, after several asked whether SPBD would lend to them.

Fa'afafines are biologically men, but dress and behave like women. How boys become *fa'afafines* varies. It may be a matter of choice by a boy to take on a female role or it may be a role that they are raised to play by a family that has no or few daughters and needs someone to carry out female tasks within the household: cooking, cleaning and washing. Some *fa'afafines* are active in Samoan cultural life, performing on stage and in drag queen beauty contests, but others go about their everyday lives as women without calling much attention to their status. Regardless, *fa'afafines* perform the roles of women and remain a prevalent, integral and accepted part of Samoan society, a society in which homosexual acts are still illegal. *Fa'afafines* are widely regarded as valuable members of the community given the combination of their masculine and feminine traits. Within Samoa, there is a saying, "If you want something done, ask a *fa'afafine*."

When *fa'afafines* requested loans from SPBD, Lai had to consider this request in the context of SPBD's women-only policy. He recalled the controversy that surrounded his mandate to begin lending to them.

> The biggest resistance came from male staff members, but I overrode them. In order to calm some nerves, I left it to each loan officer to decide whether to admit *fa'afafines* in their respective regions or not. Only Penitito never admitted any *fa'afafines*.

Guy Stuart, Regina Galang and Susie Margolin, "The Social Construction of Gender: Microfinance and Fa'af-afines in Samoa," pp. 1-6. Copyright © 2005 by Kennedy School of Government. Reprinted with permission.

While all female loan officers were very accepting of the new policy, some male Center Managers said, 'They are men and we don't lend to men." Lai's response to them was, "But what is a man though? And how do *fa'afafinis* behave?" He elaborated:

If you act as a woman, you want to be a woman, you dress as a woman, you talk like a woman; therefore, you are woman and therefore, eligible. So for me, why can't *fa'afafines* being transvestite, join in the program? In many ways they are not men. They dress as a woman and they do women's duties. The *fa'afafines* are very accepted in society. You see them in government positions and they dress as women and they go to work. I think they [*fa'afafines*] expected a negative answer as the services are clearly marked for women only. For me, it was very simple.

By early 2005, approximately 20 *fa'afafines* had received loans from SPBD and, according to Lai, they had been good members. Dr. Viopapa Annadale, a medical doctor, a SPBD advisory board member and a woman that Lai called the Ms. Gender of Samoa, remarked of this management decision, "The literal translation of *fa'afafine* is "like women." They behave like women and in many ways they think like women. Well done, Minh! They fulfill a lot of the criteria apart from gender or in this case sex." Of SPBD's policy on *fa'afafines* Casagrande, an American businessman and Founder and President of SPBD, commented, "I delegated that decision to Minh. It's a Samoan cultural issue."

SPBD, Microfinance and Women

Microfinance is the provision of financial services to poor people. It is common in developing countries, especially in Asia, and it often targets women. Initially, SPBD had lent to both men and women, but in October 2000, about nine month after starting operations, it switched to lending to women only.

Greg Casagrande explained the decision by noting that women demonstrated better repayment rates, attendance, on-time payment at the meetings, a stronger willingness to enforce the group guarantee and did not "pull cultural rank over our female CMs."[1] He added, "... the men's poor repayment rate and the extra effort required by CMs to get payments from them, meant that the business decision to focus on women was also a good financial decision." Furthermore, Casagrande felt that SPBD could have a greater development impact by focusing on women. He explained:

SPBD Foundation began with a focus on women but not exclusively. My interest in working primarily with women was spurred on by international development literature which suggested that a dollar invested in a woman yields a bigger developmental impact than a dollar invested in a guy. At the end of the day, I started SPBD Foundation to make a positive impact upon the poor. If investing in women was going to yield the biggest impact, then that's where I wanted our limited resources to be focused. I was also mindful that I was not an expert on Samoan society and did not want to upset any locals, hence I thought that keeping it open to men, but focusing on women was the safest strategy ... [A]necdotal evidence suggested that women were passing on more benefits to their families than the men who tended to spend more money on drinking and smoking, socializing and gift-giving.

Both male and female Center Managers agreed that SPBD was more successful in lending only to women. Center Manager Ken commented:

If men are allowed in the program, they are tough. If a CM faced a man, they would be tough and not pay. If a CM faces a woman, it is very easy. She takes what I say. For example, if I'm a CM and I tell a man to pay his payment, he might fight me. But women understand. They will listen. Samoan men are tough guys. If a man cannot be in at the center, maybe he goes out drinking or smoking when the money is disbursed. But a woman always thinks first of family and kids. Men are spending too much. They don't think first this is for the kids. They're always drinking, smoking. When it's time for a payment, there's no money. But women thinking family first, kids first.

Male Center Manager Polevia observed, "When they give the money to the men, they do the business, and stop in two weeks. But the women do the business. It's the women's mentality. They're working hard. They don't give up early. Some men do." Tae Anasapi, an SPBD client and center chief of one of the centers in Vaimoso Uta added: "The women can do the program in the family. They buy clothes for the kids. It's different from the men. They share."

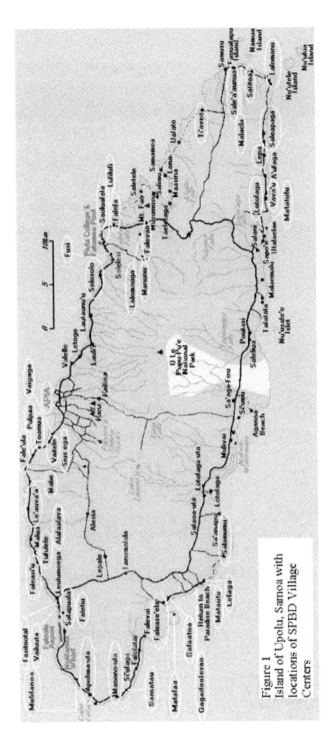

Figure 1
Island of Upolu, Samoa with
locations of SPBD Village
Centers

FIGURE 5.2.1

TABLE 5.2.1

CLIENT OUTREACH & LOAN ACTIVITY

ALL AMOUNTS IN SAMOAN TALA	2004	2003	2002	2001	2000
Number of active members	2,511	1,740	647	1,510	1,463
Number of loans issued in period	2,985	943	400	629	1,630
Cumulative # of loans issued since 2000	6,702	3,717	2,771	2,259	1,630
Value of loans issued in fiscal period	T$2,552,053	T$891,875	T$494,957	T$735,936	T$1,378,553
Cumul. value of loans issued since 2000 T$ = *tala*	T$6,007,194	T$3,455,191	T$2,563,266	T$2,114,489	T$1,378,553

TABLE 5.2.2

PORTFOLIO PERFORMANCE

	2004	2003	2002	2001	2000
Gross loans receivable (in NZD)	T$657,731	T$284,144	T$223,967	T$489,398	T$591,607
PAR* > 30 days	0.2%	1.7%	4.1%	49.9%	10.4%

*PAR: Portfolio-at-risk ratio using CGAP definitions

T$ = *tala*

TABLE 5.2.3

LOAN PRODUCTS OF COMMERCIAL BANKS

Bank	Amount	Interest Rate	Criteria/Conditions
ANZ	Up to 1,500 *tala*; 2,000 on during Independence weekend	12%	50% debt servicing ratio, minimum balance in bank; direct payment from paychecks where possible
WestPac	3,000 to 5,000 *tala*	16.5%	Maximum term: 3 yrs. Permanent employment, demonstrated surplus funds, minimum account balances

TABLE 5.2.4

SPBD FOUNDATION STAFF GENDER ANALYSIS

	31-Dec 2000	31-Dec 2001	31-Dec 2002	31-Dec 2003	31-Dec 2004
# of CM's					
Male	1	0	0	3	5
Female	2	6	3	3	3
Total	3	6	3	6	8
Other Staff					
Male	1	4	2	2	2
Female	2	2	3	4	4
Total	3	6	5	6	6
Total Staff					
Male	2	4	2	5	7
Female	4	8	6	7	7
Total	6	12	8	12	14

TABLE 5.2.5

COMPARISON OF 50-WEEK LOAN AND THE 4-MONTH LOAN PRODUCTS

Key Comparisons	4-Month Loan	50-Week Loan
Maximum 1st loan size	T$300	T$750
Subsequent loan increase	T$200	T$500
Interest rate	10%	21%
Fees	None	None
Repayment Term	17weeks	50 weeks
Security/Collateral	None	None

T$ =tala

TABLE 5.2.6

STAFF CAPACITY & PRODUCTIVITY

	2004	2003	2002	2001	2000
Number of active members	2,511	1,740	647	1,510	1,463
Number of full-time paid staff	13	13	10	12	8
Number of active members per staff	193	134	65	125	182
Institutional Sustainability					
As of December 31st	2004	2003	2002	2001	2000
Operating Revenues/Operating Costs	77.3%	44.6%	22.0%	46.1%	34.7%
Operating Revenues/Total Costs	66.5%	34.1%	19.1%	32.6%	19.6%
Total Revenues/Total Costs	85.6%	42.7%	42.1%	33.4%	20.4%

Note: 2004 data is being audited.

NOTES

1   CMs were Center Managers who were SPBD's loan officers. They were each in charge of managing about 20 centers composed of about 20 women each. The CMs collected payments from the women members of each center every week, and disbursed new loans at the same time. If a person was not able to pay their weekly installment, it was largely the responsibility of the CM to find out why they could not pay and find a way to get them to pay.

NARRATIVES

It is important to get a sense of people's lived experiences, and how societal norms (laws in some social contexts) and expectations help shape these experiences. Following is a piece that discusses the experiences of trans individuals' daily lives.

REVIEW

by ANGELA P. HARRIS

What is the relationship between the transgender movement and the feminist movement: are they allies, rivals, opponents, or a complex mix of all three? The two books under review offer some answers to this question.

Transgender Rights (hereafter *TR*) is a magisterial collection of essays covering cutting-edge legal developments, movement histories, and political theory, written by some of the most celebrated names in both trans activism and scholarship. In addition to the three editors—all national figures in the transgender movement—contributors include some of the leading lights in gay and lesbian legal scholarship, such as Kendall Thomas and Ruthann Robson. The collection even includes an essay by Judith Butler, whose pioneering work using the practices of drag to understand gendering makes her both celebrated and controversial. The essays are all relatively short and accessible to a wide audience, yet they are also uniformly theoretically challenging and conceptually rich, suggesting heroic labor on the part of the editors. This is an indispensable collection.

Whipping Girl (hereafter *WG*) is a collection of personal narratives, political polemics, academic exegeses, and media critiques, thrown at you at top speed with dark wit and a dizzying number of neologisms. Unlike *TR*, which mostly speaks in the dispassionate third person, *WG* takes the passionate, sardonic voice of a pissed-off trans woman who doesn't intend to take it anymore. Like *TR*, however, *WG* moves with facility across a wide terrain, addressing academics, nonacademics, trans people and nontrans people (or "cissexuals" as Serano names people whose subconscious sex has always been identical with their ascribed sex). One moment, Serano is speculating about the biological origins of gender dysphoria; the next she is penning a furious diatribe against all those creepy straight men who want to tell her how turned on they are by the idea of a "she-male." *TR* engages with a number of identity movements, including the disability rights movement, the intersex movement, and the gay and lesbian movement. *WG* also interrogates the gay and lesbian movement, but is particularly concerned with feminism.

Angela P. Harris, "Transgender Rights/Whipping Girl: A Transsexual Woman on Sexism and the Scapegoating of Femininity," *Women's Studies Quarterly*, vol. 36, no. 1-2, pp. 315-319. Copyright © 2008 by Feminist Press. Reprinted with permission. Provided by ProQuest LLC. All rights reserved.

These books revealed for me three issues common to feminist and trans agendas: identity politics, the relationship between "nature" and "culture," and the value of the feminine. Regarding identity politics, the essays in *TR* make clear that at least some trans scholars and activists have internalized the lesson that many feminists had to learn the hard way: race, class, sexuality, and gender are not severable. Trans activists and scholars come by antiessentialism honestly. As nearly every book on trans identity begins by acknowledging, the term is an umbrella that attempts to shelter very different kinds of folks. Proliferating terms vividly illustrate the diversity: transvestite, cross-dresser, trannie, trans, genderfuck, genderqueer, FMT, MtM, trans men, boyz, bois, bigendered, third sex, nellie, queer, eonist, invert, androgyne, butch, femme, she-male, he-she, boy-dyke, girlfag are all identities that have been claimed by (and sometimes inscribed upon) people who in some way violate the rigid gender-norm system enforced by United States heteropatriarchy. The trans movement has lacked a stable and homogenous subject position from the get-go, and so by necessity has avoided some (not all) of the painful internal "authenticity" purges that African American, lesbian, and other communities have endured.

As the trans movement has learned from feminism's failures, so feminism can learn from the trans movement's successes. Both *TR* and *WG* show how it is possible to acknowledge the heterogeneity of identity while still challenging subordination in politically potent ways. The co-constitutive nature of subordination means that the most far-reaching political work in an identity movement is not done on behalf of the "but-for" people—the people who "but for" a single stigma would be able to realize the American Dream—but on behalf of the queerest, those who live furthest from the norm. Accordingly, Dean Spade places trans issues in the context of the contradictions of capitalism and the legacy of white supremacy. Spade argues that the trans fight must be not for "non-discrimination"—which would leave race and class privilege intact—but for "gender self-determination," which necessitates, among other things, giving individuals the right to hormone and surgical therapies on demand. Gender self-determination thus requires class struggle.

A second intersection between feminism and the trans movement is the relationship between "nature" and "culture." Feminists, in their effort to counter the notion that "biology is destiny" (meaning, of course, that women do not make good mathematicians, physicists, artists, or orchestra conductors), have stressed the "social construction" of gender. This move tends to make "sex" a simple biological substrate with very little content and "gender" a complex cultural superstructure that does all the work. (There are also some who have attempted to understand "sex" itself as a product of gender politics, making it socially constructed turtles all the way down.) Serano, a biologist by training, wonderfully complicates this approach. She offers what she calls an "intrinsic inclination" model of sex/gender, under which subconscious sex, gender expression, and sexual orientation are separate "inclinations" that vary independently from one another. Each of these inclinations should, in her view, moreover be understood as "intrinsic"—that is, not the product of either conscious choice or social construction but rooted deep in the body, stubbornly resistant to attempts to purge, repress, or ignore them. Serano does not, however, turn to biological reductionism: for her, each of these inclinations is itself the product of a complicated interplay of genetic, hormonal, environmental, cultural, and psychological factors. Although at the scale of the population these inclinations correspond roughly with two types of genitalia, producing evidence for the view that there are two and only two "sexes" or "genders," at the level of the individual there are endless variations (PFG, 99–100).

This model produces an elegant and thought-provoking way to understand sex and gender: not in terms of norms and deviations, "choice" versus "immutability," or "nature" versus "nurture," but as a complex interaction producing, as Serano puts it, "naturally occurring examples of human variation" (100). In support of this model, Serano provides a nuanced account of her own transition from male to female sexed body, during which she experienced a complex give-and-take between the physical and the psychic. Serano also talks about what it feels like to have one's subconscious sex diverge from one's ascribed sex. The striking word Serano uses to describe this is "sadness": "a chronic and persistent grief over the fact that I felt so wrong in my body" (85). Serano portrays this grief as persistent, beyond the reach of either individual or social interventions, and eased only by her hormonal transition.

Feminists ought to be invested in the issue of how sex/gender arrives upon us, especially at this moment when genetic explanations for everything pervade scientific and popular culture. Serano makes a powerful case that some feminists have imposed their own version of "biology is destiny" upon trans women (as in the notorious exclusion of trans women from the Michigan Womyn's Festival), and that this position is foolish and destructive. At the same time, Serano does not embrace the idea to which Judith Butler's work is sometimes reduced: that gender is nothing but a set of cultural norms that can be thrown off with enough political will. To Serano gender is both given and chosen, persistent and plastic. Her model has much to offer feminist theorists.

A third intersection between the trans and feminist movements is the valuation of traditional femininity. Serano argues throughout her book that both male supremacists and feminists have spent a lot of time trashing femininity, and that much of what is usually thought of as "transphobia" directed at trans women is better described as pure misogyny. Here she distinguishes trans men from trans women, arguing that trans women come in for a unique stigmatization, sexualization, and denigration that has everything to do with our culture's devaluation of the feminine. As she puts it: "The idea that masculinity is strong, tough, and natural while femininity is weak, vulnerable, and artificial continues to proliferate even among people who believe that women and men are equals" (*WG*, 5). She calls upon us to find value in the "soft" qualities traditionally associated with femininity and to support those people who express those qualities in their daily lives, no matter in what kind of body or identity they find themselves—cissexual, trans, sissy, transsexual.

The essays in *TR* do not discuss femininity as such, but Kendall Thomas's brilliant and thought-provoking closing essay does articulate in its most attractive form a vision that Serano views as deeply problematic. Thomas wonders whether "human rights" is a capacious enough term to express the goals of the trans movement, given that some trans people claim identities that are beyond gender or outside gender. If in the dominant culture traditional gender is necessary for a recognizably human identity, trans people mark (trans-gress) the boundary between the human and the nonhuman. Thomas concludes, approvingly, that "the denizens of trans-gender publics are experimenting with a new art of the self and fashioning an insolent political aesthetics of affirmative inhuman being" (*TR*, 323).

How radical, we can imagine Serano responding; and how radically chic. Serano argues that the desire to "shatter the gender binary," though described by some as the ultimate aim of trans activism, is not, in fact, universally shared. In her view, the portrayal of people who reject gender as more trans-gressive and thus more politically progressive than other trans people gives rise to a dangerous internal contest over who's the most "gender-radical" and contributes to the denigration of people who find themselves comfortable within traditional genders.

As I read them, Thomas and the other TR authors do not mean to reject traditional genders by affirming support for what Thomas calls "the right to indetermination." Paisley Currah, for example, sees transgender activism as moving toward the elimination of "any legally prescribed relationship between biological sex, gender identity, and gender expression" (*TR*, 23). This is a vision of autonomy, not re-regulation: Currah hopes for a world in which we can argue about gender without putting child custody, employment, or lives at stake. Serano, however, fears the creep of a moral hierarchy in which identifying as "beyond gender" is cooler than identifying with a gender, and a traditionally feminine gender is the uncoolest identification of all.

More conversation between trans and feminist thinkers is overdue. Now and then one of my friends asks me in a whisper appropriate to respect for the passed, "So, whatever happened to feminism?" From now on I intend to recommend these books to them, and tell them, "Transgender happened. Check it out." Check it out.

ANGELA P. HARRIS is a professor at the University of California-Berkeley School of Law (Boalt Hall). She writes widely on questions of gender, race, sexuality, and class inequalities in American legal theory.

Gendered Outcomes

- On average, men and women tend to have different jobs.
  - Most jobs are either female dominated or male dominated.
  - Let's think of a hospital: Which jobs are female dominated versus male dominated?
- Two major sociological explanations:
  1. There are overt discrimination or stringent gendered qualifications.
  2. Through gendered socialization we come to have different selves and different values.
- These can cascade on themselves and intersect to further the gendering of certain occupations.[1]
- Either way, gender is not just an attribute that people bring with them to the job but is built into the workplace itself.
- It is also inarguable that we as a society systematically devalue what we think of as women's work.
  - "Women's work" is typically connected stereotypic domestic roles: watching and teaching children, cleaning, and organizational and secretarial support roles.
- Women make between $.80 and $.92 for every dollar a man makes for similar work, depending on how the calculation is done. This gap is shrinking, and in some fields among millennials and Generation Z these gaps have approached zero. Note that since the 1980s women have been receiving more college degrees than men on average.

More resources:

Non-Gender Binary in America: https://www.youtube.com/watch?v=RO-jtETLNknY

College Degrees	Class of 2012 Percentages Male	Female	Females per 100 Males	Class of 2021 (est.) Percentages Male	Female	Females per 100 Males
Associate's	37.7%	62.3%	165	35.8%	64.2%	179
Bachelor's	43.5%	56.5%	130	42.0%	58.0%	138
Master's	41.5%	58.5%	141	39.3%	60.7%	154
Doctor's	48.4%	51.6%	107	46.2%	53.8%	116
All Degrees	41.7%	58.3%	140	40.4%	59.6%	148

FIGURE 5.2. COLLEGE DEGREES: MALE VERSUS FEMALE.

1 Rice University, "Personal Values Impact Occupational Sex Segregation," May 22, 2014, https://www.youtube.com/watch?v=JrNDKPl_i2s.

How to Convince a Skeptic the Pay Gap is Real

https://www.cnbc.com/2018/04/10/6-ways-to-convince-a-skeptic-the-pay-gap-is-real.html

Median hourly earnings of U.S. women as percentage of men's median among ...

Note: Estimates are for civilian, non-institutionalized, full- or part-time employed workers with positive earnings. Self-employed workers are excluded.
Source: Pew Research Center analysis of Current Population Survey data.

PEW RESEARCH CENTER

FIGURE 5.3 **The gender pay gap is narrower among young adults than among workers overall.**

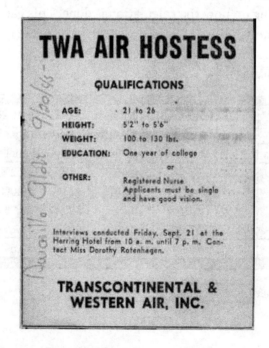

FIGURE 5.4 **TWA Air hostess.**

CONCLUSION

While gender may seem very natural, and the way most of us are socialized with gender serves to reinforce this idea, it is important to remember that it too is a social construct. Similarly, the gender roles and gender traits that are readily recognizable in American social life are also products of social decisions made in society more broadly. While gender can be personal and intimate, there is no doubt that a great deal of one's gender identity is related to the socially constructed nature of gender itself.

More resources:

Links between Family Gender Socialization Experiences in Childhood and Gendered Occupational Attainment in Young Adulthood: https://www.ncbi.nlm.nih.gov/pmc/articles/PMC4786944/

Image Credits

Fig. 5.1: Source: https://commons.wikimedia.org/wiki/File:Franklin-Roosevelt-1884.jpg.
Fig. 5.2: Source: https://www.aei.org/publication/huge-gender-college-degree-gap-for-class-of-2012-do-we-really-need-hundreds-of-womens-centers/.
Fig. 5.3: Source: https://www.pewresearch.org/fact-tank/2019/03/22/gender-pay-gap-facts/ft_18-04-06_wage_gap/.
Fig. 5.4: Source: https://repository.duke.edu/dc/adaccess/T1960.

CHAPTER 6

Sexuality

WHAT DO WE MEAN BY SEXUALITY?

Sexual Identity (Sexual Orientation)

Sexual identity is an identity that is organized by the gender(s) of the person(s) to whom we are sexually attracted. People may incorporate more specific characteristics into their sexual identity as well.

How Is sexuality social?

Like some of the previous topics that have been discussed, sexuality may seem very natural and biologically determined. Unlike race and gender, sociologists do leave quite a bit of explaining to biologists and psychologists. For example, concepts like how attraction or arousal work are best left explained by these fields of science. However, standards of beauty, what is considered "sexy," what is considered sexually appropriate, and a number of other aspects of sexuality, are very much determined by society, institutions, and the individuals who compose them. There is a very complex intersection of sexuality and gender, and in American society sexuality is closely linked to gender. The clip that follows explores that complex intersection in more detail.

More resources:

Understanding the Complexities of Gender, Sam Killermann at TEDxUo-fIChicago:
https://www.youtube.com/watch?v=NRcPXtqdKjE

Reading 6.1.

Connected Love and Relations?

An exploration of the technology of connectivity and College Students' Love and Sexuality

by Hsing-Chen Yang

I. INTRODUCTION

The occurrence and negotiation of love and all the behaviors and development in the interactions are all cultural activities which come with a lot of social significance, especially the relationship between gender and power issues. For example, a invitation or an acceptance of a invitation involves the implementation of gender norms and the corresponding of sex-gender relations, such as male/female, the pursuit/ pursuer, active/passive or demand/obedience (Kehily, 2002). This relationship and interaction tend to be highly gendered and imply structural inequality of power. In addition, the pursuit of love, sexual invitation or interaction, all are an exploration and practice of gender and sexual identity, but we rarely know when the moment of intimate relationship (such as a love announcement, the first date, a sex or love invitation. the first time of sex) should be, how to actually interact with him/her, and in such micro-processes personal encounters involved in which social and cultural significance and structural forces that affect both action?

In addition, the contemporary intimate relationship to a considerable extent by the impact of new technologies, the development and use of new technologies are gradually changing and shaping the intimate interactions between people, patterns and behaviors (Jamieson, 1998). Nowadays younger students are generally immersed in the new technology and network media (such as mobile phones, facebook, msn); they are to show the practices of masculinities and femininities than in the past is more complicated. Today, we cannot categorically celebrate the collapse and disappearing of heterosexual hegemony and the male-centered thoughts, but many studies also found that younger students were good at using new technology to express their love, or transform traditional masculinity or femininity into the pursuit of the opposite sex (Tseng & Yang, 2010; Hsieh & Yang, 2010; Donn & Sherman, 2002; Farier & Gavin, 2009). New technology, especially Internet technology, the students of the younger generation or LGBT, whether it is a new world of a gender? A new living space to provide people across gender order, arrangement and configuration, and to try the more intimate network selection, where s/he lives, interacts with people, feel intimate, and create and maintain the love?

Love is an important issue for young students in the college life. How does the development of new technologies make influences to students' love experiences?

Hsing-Chen Yang, "Connected Love and Relations? An Exploration of the Technology of Connectivity and College Students' Love and Sexuality," *International Conference on Political Science, Sociology and International Relations (PSSIR). Proceedings.* Copyright © 2012 by Global Science and Technology Forum. Reprinted with permission. Provided by ProQuest LLC. All rights reserved.

How do heterosexual discourses and love scripts influence students in their relationships, and to what extent they can create new love stories and actions? This study attempted to explore college students' love experiences to answer these questions, and based on the findings, it could provide insights to reform general education of gender education curriculum.

II. LITERATIRE REVIEW

Feminists argued that heterosexuality is an invisible political institution that makes women to the lack of choice, desire and power (Rich, 1983; Jackson, 1999, 2005). Holland, Ramazanoglu, Sharpe, and Thomson (2004) used the metaphor of "the male in the head" to explain how the ideology of heterosexual patriarchy embedded in social systems and stationed in being the head of the young men and women; "young men and women jointly engaged in constituting a single standard of heterosexuality and being regulated by it in differing ways" (10).

Recent studies have still found that men in the first appointment are usually active roles (active solicitation, escort girls, take the initiative to open the door, is responsible for the appointment overhead, and kiss goodnight on the sexual activity; girls take to respond, that is, they wait for men taking the initiative to begin the next move (Emmers-Sommer, et. al., 2010). Additionally, many studies have also found that both men and women are more equal in terms of courtship and interaction in relations; men and women are likely to take the initiative to refuse unwanted sexual relations. However, many studies still show positive discourses of female sexual pleasure is still lacking, and men still have more privilege than women to do sexual experiments (Ex: Seal & Ehrhardt, 2003; Ortiz-Torres, Williams, & Ehrhardt, 2003; Tsang & Young, 2010; Hsieh & Yang, 2010; Kennett, Humphreys, & Patchell, 2009; Maxwell & Aggleton, 2010).

Mobile phones, msn, facebook, social networking, instant messaging have been conceptualized as a technology of connectivity (Campbell, 2006; Green & the Singleton, 2009). Many studies have found that a technology of connectivity as well as mastery of a particular technology operating gradually transformed the intimate relationship and interaction between men and women, such as courtship, dating, and emotional expression (Ex: Donn & Sherman, 2002; Farrer & Gavin, 2009; Cooper, Mansson, Daneback, Tikkanen & Ross, 2003); to rewrite traditional gender order and romance narrative, the performances of self and intimate meaning, as well as loose or change power relations between men and women(Nice & Katzev, 1998; Hillier & Harrison, 2007).

Cooper et al (2003) pointed out that 45% of women in Sweden participated in web network activities. Through the Internet, these women found their partners and used the network to contact, flirt, and maintaining relationships with their partners. Especially, to flirt with a date is the main reason for women to participate in the sexual activities of the network. Hillier and Harrison (2007) found that web network is an importantly sexual space for those marginalized young people, such as gay men, lesbians and bisexuals; through the Internet, they could find other LGBT people like themselves, learned what was about sex, or increased their sex life and community activities, as well as improved their sexual identity.

In summary, intimate relationships and behaviors can not be independent of social context and gender relations. Although young people are still influenced by the "male-in-the head" (Holland, et. al, 2004), they have the capacity to develop different experiments in evading heteronormativity and go beyond the limitations of masculinity and femininity.

III. THE PARTICIPANTS

The six participants, five female and one male, are mainly from University M. There are three heterosexual students, two homosexuals, and 1 bisexual. University M is a well-known Medical University in southern Taiwan. It is conservative with the emphasis on discipline, and students carry heavy academic burdens. We interviewed the six college students at least four times and used a semi-structured interview format. The interviews typically lasted between two and three hours. We also took extensive notes and personal profiles in which we described our own thoughts about the students and reactions to the interactions that had taken place.

IV. FINDING AND DISCUSSION

The Connectivity Technology for Governing Love and Relationships

A technology of connectivity, especially the rise of social networks changed the construction of today's youth to self-awareness and identity (Beck & BeckGersheim, 2001; Furlong & Cartmel, 1997). The "Who am I" identity issues, in addition to the traditional social attributes, such as age, gender, sexual orientation, class, racial, ethnic and other outside, now including the "relationship status" to expose, and have become an important part for the young generations in the construction of the self. Young people need to undergo more choices and decisions, such as "Who are the 'friends', 'good friends' and 'family' and whom belonging to Plurk, MSN or FB, as well as more emotional and relational governance. Relationship governance means to use the technology of connectivity to declare the state of love, explain oneself, communicate, track each other or get rid of a third party. For example, Amy's ex-boyfriend by The FB hanging single state to let their friends know that he had broke up and Amy; Amy disguised by changing the status Lesbian, into stable contacts with female friends, to get rid of the suitors of entanglement.

Long-distance relationship was thought as a killer of love and relationship, but now a technology of connectivity closer the distance for each other, it uses including surveillance, care about each other's actions and words and doings. For example, Helen's experience with her girlfriend who was far away in a foreign country:

"I think 'seeing' the face is very important, through 'daily contact', she lets me know where she is, which makes it a lot easier"

"Sometimes she tells me where she is, lets me know that she is safe … I would find her by Google Location, and ask her why she being there … I will limit her activities, so that she won't get too close to some people."

"We usually fight in the afternoon or evening because we have more time to fight … when you apologize to her but she ignores you, then you must text to say you are sorry before going to bed at night. Do not just say 'I'm sorry, and I want to sleep. Good night.' It has to be at least one page long. One or two like this, and it usually soften her and she will usually return the three text messages saying what she was sad about and angry about. Then you have to return a text or call back to comfort her. After we have gone through this kind of process, it usually works."

This kind of "endless connection" changes the contact specification of the caring and bounding in a loving relationship. It blurs the boundaries of care, trust, and monitoring and increases the tensions of power dynamics and controlling desire in the relationship, thus adds new issues in negotiation and the meaning of caring. The concept of dominating male and submissive female has not much explanatory power to these new issues, because both men and women, heterosexual or homosexual, these young people are experiencing the contradictions of the new technology as a way to maintain love relationships, they have to face of more complex love interactions and practices and these experiences need further interpretation.

"Connectivity Technology" as a platform of homosexual knowledge and relational education

Living in a heterosexual patriarchy society, gay men do not have as many relationships and social resources as heterosexuals do, and the technology of connectivity thus provides resources and space for homosexual doing social network, conversation, and activities. Simon mentioned the breaking up of his first love. At that time, he attempted to talk to his roommate but was overlooked and not listened to. He said: "Once I told my roommate that I broke up with someone without saying it was with a man or woman, then I just said I broke up with my ex-girlfriend, he was like "ha ha ha ha" laughing at me, so how could I tell him about it?" The built-in social and cultural gender roles and discourse of masculinity/femininity not only deeply affect the interactions of men and women in love relationships but also affect the relationship between men with each other in sharing and emotional exchanges, and thus between male friends there can be gossips, but no inner feelings. And this "no" is not a natural born, and the by the impact of hegemonic masculinity.

Under the norms of heterosexual practices and scripts, it is harder for gay students to seek someone to talk, share the emotional plight because of the double constraints of gender and sexual identity. In particular, if gay or lesbian students faced multiple parties in sex and love exercises. Therefore, they might start to find information and a way out through internet. Simon said:

"In the beginning I was shocked. I like him, but why breaking up? And I was not able to accept it ... lately ... I do not know, I started to self adjust and read some articles on the net. ... there are a lot of good articles on the PTT Gay board ... three days or four days after the break up, I started to think this is not working so I went online and started to search what to after a break up ... I used yahoo to look for love consulting rooms. There were so many articles ... So that's how it is. I had to turn my mind around so not to trap myself in that situation."

"But I think inside yahoo search there were relatively few gay issues, so I will turn to look in the PTT gay forum ... There were people who faced the situation like me, how do they solve? How do they adjust? How to express? Others had situations that were even worse than I did ... People who were still in love with each other, but were forbidden by their family. The feeling that people were in love yet can not be together brought reflection on my own situation."

"Safer sex is very important. I began to visit PTT Gay board after this break up and got a little information to know the importance of safe sex and the likes. I think that this counts for a benefit from the break up. I started to think more or be inspired by someone else's story."

The public sexual stories have possibility to convert the meaning and practice of intimate relationships in the daily life. Public sex stories can be a resource of "intellectual empowerment" (Holland, et al, 2004). They help young gay students improve self-awareness and promote sexual and emotional knowledge. In Simon's experience, safe sex knowledge and skills of gay people as well as how to handle the breaking up for gay and lesbian couples, are information that are not easy to acquire in formal education courses or social and cultural scripts. Learning through the Internet platform, let Simon increase the knowledge and confidence and be ready for the next love or sexual relationship in the "real" world. As Hiller and Harrison (2007) stated, young gay men are by no means silly Internet users. They enter the Internet world and allow themselves to improve their self-consciousness and re-define the things they know, rather than by the prefixed definition.

REFERENCES

Beck, U., & Beck-Gernsheim, E. (2001). *Individualization*. London: Sage.

Campbell, R. (2006). Teenage girls and cellular phones: Discourses of independence, safety and rebellion. *Journal of Youth Studies, 9* (2), 195–212.

Cooper, A., Månsson, S.A., Daneback, K., Tikkanen, R., & Ross, M. (2003). Predicting the future of internet sex: Online sexual activities in Sweden. *Sexual and Relationship Therapy, 18*(3), 277–291.

Donn, J. E., & Sherman, R. C. (2002). Attitudes and practices regarding the formation of romantic relationships on the internet. *Cyber Psychology & Behavior, 5*(2), 107–122.

Emmers-Sommer, T. M., Farrell, J., Gentry, A., Stevens, S., Eckstein, J. Battocletti, J. & Gardener, C. (2010). First date sexual expectations: The effects of who asked, who paid, date location and gender. *Communication Studies, 61*(3), 339–355.

Farier, J., & Gavin, J. (2009). Online dating in Japan: A test of social information processing theory. *Cyber Psychology & Behavior, 12*(4), 407–412.

Furlong, A., & Cartmel, F. (1997). *Young people and social change: Individualisation and risk in late modernity*. Buckingham: Open University Press.

Green, E. & Singleton, C. (2009). Mobile connections: An exploration of the place of mobile phones in friendship relations. *The Sociological Review, 57*(1), 125–144.

Hillier, L. & Harrison, L (2007). Building realities less limited than own: Young people practicing same-sex attraction on the Internet. *Sexualities, 10,* 82–100.

Hsieh, K. L., & Yang, H. C. (2010). Dodging love: Making sense of the experiences when gay men facing the pursuit of heterosexual women. *Studies in Sexuality, 1*(1), 1–20.

Holland, J., Ramazanoglu, C., Sharpe, S. & Thomson, R. (2004). *The Male in the Head: Young people, heterosexuality and power*. London: The Tufnell Press.

Jamieson, L. (1998). *Personal relationships in modern societies*. Malden, MA: Blackwell.

Jackson, S. (1999). *Heterosexuality in question*. London: Sage.

Kehily, M. J. (2002). *Sexuality, gender and schooling: Shifting agendas in social learning*. London: Routledge.

Kennett, D.J., Humphreys, T.P., & Patchell, M. (2009). The role of learned resourcefulness in helping female undergraduates deal with unwanted sexual activity. *Sex Education, 9*(4), 341–353.

Maxwell, C., & Aggleton, P. (2010). Agency in action: Young women and their sexual relationships in a private school. *Gender and Education, 22*(3), 327–343.

Nice, M. L., & Katzev, R. (1998). Internet romance: The frequency and nature of romantic on-line relationships. *Cyberpsychology & Behavior, 1,* 217–223.

Ortiz-Torres, B., Williams, S. P., & Ehrhardt, A. A. (2003). Urban women's gender scripts: Implications for HIV prevention. *Culture, Health and Sexuality, 5*, 1–17.

Plummer, K. (1995). *Telling sexual stories: power, change and social worlds.* NewYork: Routledge.

Rich, A. (1983). Compulsory heterosexuality and lesbian

Ortiz-Torres, B., Williams, S. P., & Ehrhardt, A. A. (2003). Urban women's gender scripts: Implications for HIV prevention. *Culture, Health and Sexuality, 5*, 1–17.

Plummer, K. (1995). *Telling sexual stories: power, change and social worlds.* NewYork: Routledge.

Rich, A. (1983). Compulsory heterosexuality and lesbian existence. In E. Abel & E. K. Abel (Eds.), *The Signs reader: Women, gender and scholarship* (pp.177–205). London: University of Chicago press.

Seal, D.W., & Ehrhardt, A. A. (2003). Masculinity and urban men: Perceived scripts for courtship, romantic, and sexual interactions with women. Culture, *Health & Sexuality, 5*(4), 295–319.

Tseng, Y. C., & Yang, H. C. (2010). The exploration of methods and experiences from vocational higher school students' active pursuit of male. *Secondary Education, 61*(4), 84–101.

Trends in Modern American Society

There are a couple of notable trends in American sexuality. One notable trend is that younger people (Gen Z and millennials) are having less sex than previous generations at similar ages. Another is society more broadly is becoming increasingly more accepting of different kinds of sexual and romantic relationships. A third is that teen pregnancies are on the decline, and they are much less frequently cited as a social problem than in previous decades.

Gendered Sexual Inequality

There are a number of gendered sexual inequalities. Many of these relate to gender socialization and gender norms. Some of these inequalities are listed.

Men are judged significantly less for their sexual behaviors.

Women's most valuable asset is often seen as sex.

- In addition, women are seen as prey or objects.
- They are not seen for their brains or other mental abilities.
- Furthermore, men often discuss sexual behaviors in violent terms.

There are few if any analogous terms for "slut," "ho," or "bitch" to apply to men.

- Slut shaming
- The virgin/whore dichotomy

CRITICAL THINKING:	• Can you think of any more gendered sexual inequalities? Think double standards. • Why are these problematic?

Because of norms and social desirability, women on average underreport their number of sexual partners while men overreport. Even when controlled for, trends are skewed. The most likely answer is men consider more things sex than do women, which again relates to social desirability.

The following piece examines the intersection between sexual and gendered inequalities.

Queer Theory

A hybrid theory emerging from LGBT studies, feminist critiques, and postmodernism, queer[1] theory is based on the idea that there are no fixed and stable identities that determine who we are. Moreover, queer theorists view the attempt to categorize and essentialize people as having fixed and all-encompassing identities as a practice involved in marginalizing and discriminating. Its most famous proponent is probably Dr. Judith Butler.

Reading 6.2.

Structurelessness, Structure, and Queer Movements
by Darnell L. Moore

Queer political work might appear to be grounded in a theory of structurelessness, at least as it relates to the making of an imagined queer community/movement organized around the need to alleviate the unbending boundaries and centers of sexual identification. Yet it is also true that queer communities can be limited by the very ways they are structured by and constituted through race, class, ability, and other forms of social categorization. Critics have rightly asked, for example,

---

1   Note that the word *queer is often used in everyday speech as an all-inclusive umbrella term for gays, lesbians, bisexuals, transsexuals, transgendered, and intersexed people.*

Darnell L. Moore, "Structurelessness, Structure, and Queer Movements," *Women's Studies Quarterly*, vol. 41, no. 3-4, pp. 257-260. Copyright © 2013 by Feminist Press. Reprinted with permission. Provided by ProQuest LLC. All rights reserved.

what is at stake in the life of the queer who is not white, able bodied, cis-male, or "naturalized" as a U.S. citizen within a queer (mostly U.S. based) political movement organized around supposed visions of structurelessness? To what extent does this "structureless" politics of identity attend to the needs of those who exist within the margins—the structure of the other—of an already interstitial space? What is a stake for the *queers of the queers* within a movement that might easily establish centers even as it seeks to destabilize the same?

E. Patrick Johnson offers the following query in response to the failures of academic queer theory in the way that it attends to the material needs of the multiply marginalized: "What, for example, are the ethical and material implications of queer theory if its project is to dismantle all notions of identity and agency? The deconstructive turn in queer theory highlights the ways in which ideology functions to oppress and to proscribe ways of knowing, but what is the utility of queer theory on the front lines, in the trenches, on the street, or any place where the racialized and sexualized body is beaten, starved, fired, cursed—indeed, where the body is the site of trauma?" (2001, 5).

In what follows, I revisit Jo Freeman's essay "The Tyranny of Structurelessness," and complicate her specific turn to structure. More specifically, I offer thoughts on queer political work and the ways that the "queer" serves as a sign for structurelessness even while queer movements might easily prompt tacit and direct forms of remarginalization through a privileging of structurelessness. In other words, queerness seeks to raze some structures and fortify others. But what is the utility, if any, of structures within queer movement work when "structurelessness" is something of a byword for queer culture and politics? I argue that rethinking the development of structures helps to theorize forms of intervention, which allow for the naming and organizing against forms of remarginalization, in a queer theoretical project that is predominantly organized around whiteness.

QUEER THEORY AND QUEER POLITICAL WORK: AGAINST STRUCTURE

Queerness, in theory, is poststructural. Quite literally, queer theory is a theoretical project that is shaped by the critical insights of philosophers like Jacques Derrida, Michel Foucault, and Judith Butler (among others) who criticized structuralist paradigms by calling into question the limiting and rigid notion of *conceptual* structures (i.e., binary oppositions and its reinforcement of the sign/signifier/signified dynamic) imposed by and evidenced through language, discourse, and law.

Queer theory also illuminates the ways that ideology (and its structuring impulses) works itself out in the domain of the *material*. In the Derridean poststructuralist sense, queerness implies a theoretical process of deconstruction or, rather, a move to interrogate and unknot rigid hegemonic sexual logics and representations perpetuated by and sustained through discourse and state regulation. Indeed, queerness is antagonistic to processes of order and regulation. And in the ACT-UP protest model, queerness similarly guided counterhegemonic resistance—a move to protest against and destabilize structures of "normative" sexualities and relationality as they shape the ways we exist in the world as gendered beings. Queerness, in praxis, is antistructure.

Thus, queerness is a political posture that ostensibly seeks to redress, if not wholly resist, structure at the level of ideology as well as the level of the material, that is, human life. In this regard, Michael Warner notes, "The preference for 'queer' represents, among other things, an aggressive impulse generalization; it rejects a minoritizing logic of toleration or simple political interest-representation in favor of a more thorough resistance to regimes of the normal" (1993, xxvi). Yet, and again, even in its quests to resist structures, the "queer" exists as another space wherein structure is once again reconfigured and operationalized, particularly as it relates to the ways that some bodies and political interests are made visible in queer movements while others are not.

STRUCTURELESSNESS BEGETS STRUCTURE

What is the utility of a mostly white and cis-gendered (male?) U.S.-based queer movement for a queer who is black, or brown, or female? What is constructive about a movement that struggles to make connections between theories of disidentification and anti-identitarian politics, for instance, within a society that is very much organized around social determinants such as race, class, and gender, as well as their often violently consequential outcomes: racism, classism, and sexism/misogyny? What is the utility of disidentification and anti-identity for the lives of those whose white racial identities always enable their movement as unmarked and, therefore, always already privileged in their claim for an anti- and disidentity? Structures are necessary, I contend, to protect against the "tyranny" of a type of "structurelessness" that seeks to do away with those modes of power that in fact support the well-being for the lives of some queers.

Indeed, if multiply marginalized queers are to list the types of discriminations they face within queer spaces—spaces wherein oppressions like heteronormativity tend to be named and contested even as some other types of marginalization like white racism are often invisibilized and reinforced—structures are necessary to ensure accountability. In addition, organizing/theorizing within queer movements must be guided by an ethic of justice that centralizes the bodies and needs of those most marginalized even within queer movements. The organizing principles of whiteness, able-bodiedness, monolingual communication (English), cisgendered identification, and other forms of privilege have to be continually revised and reordered.

Structures are necessary, therefore, to secure a pragmatic set of political action for all queers. For example, my colleague Beryl Satter and I talked a few years back about the lack of visibility of black and brown, economically disenfranchised queer people in historical narratives that center on the lives of "the queer." Our critique, however, was not enough to correct the erasure. Instead, we developed the Queer Newark archive, a structure of documents and material culture, as a means to render visible the lives of queer subjects who have been *othered* out of queer histories by, often, other queers. The archive is a necessary structure developed in response to one of the problems of structurelessness associated with queer theory and politics; namely, it provides the framework for accountability—indeed, the responsibility to name and redress forms of marginalization of queers by queers—within queer movements and community. It seems to me, as Jo Freeman notes in her now-classic essay, "There is nothing inherently bad about structure itself—only its excessive use." And I would contend further that there is something inherently troubling about (queer) structurelessness when, in fact, it itself is excessive and ultimately reinforces another structure that privileges a few. To queerly disidentify is all well and good for those whose very claim to an identity carries significant economic and cultural effect. To eliminate structure in the name of a liberated structurelessness is to eliminate the possibilities for analyzing power relations and inequities while holding accountable those bodies and systems that multiply marginalize others.

WORKS CITED

Freeman, Jo. 1972. "The Tyranny of Structurelessness." *Second Wave 2* (1):20–33.

Johnson, E. Patrick. 2001. "'Quare' Studies, or (Almost) Everything I Know About Queer Studies I Learned from My Grandmother." In *Text and Performance Quarterly* 21(1):1–21.

Warner, Michael. 1993. Introduction to *Fear of a Queer Planet: Queer Politics and Social Theory*, ed. Michael Warner. Minneapolis: University of Minnesota Press.

Discrimination against LGBTQ Persons

Homophobia: An attitude or a socially approved dislike of gay men and lesbians; often includes the presumption that they are inferior to straight people or that their existence or sexuality is inherently immoral.

Heterosexism: *An institutionally as well as culturally based inequality that may derive from homophobia. As a set of practices, rather than an ideology, heterosexism may be more pervasive than homophobia. It is the privileging of heterosexual relationships over all other forms of relationship.*

American Views on Some Issues Are Changing Quickly

Note how in a 22-year span American views on gay marriage have nearly totally inversed, going from a 41-point gap against gay marriage in 1996 to a 38-point gap in favor of gay marriage in 2018. This is a very fast shift on a societal social view, and normative changes are almost certain to come with it.[2]

A great example of this quick sea change is former president Barack Obama. During his 2008 campaign candidate Obama was very explicit that he did not support same-sex marriage (though he did support civil unions), stating often that he believed that marriage was "between a man and a woman." By the time the Supreme Court legalized gay marriage in 2015, the Obama administration celebrated the ruling by illuminating the White House in the LGBTQ rainbow flag.

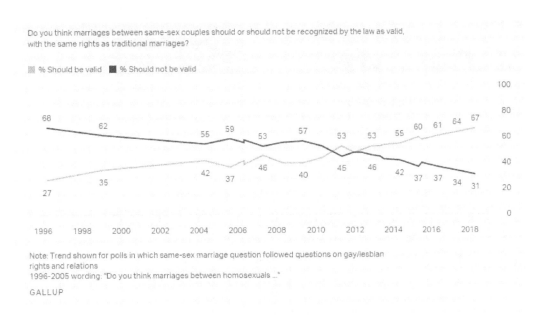

Do you think marriages between same-sex couples should or should not be recognized by the law as valid, with the same rights as traditional marriages?

▨ % Should be valid   ■ % Should not be valid

Note: Trend shown for polls in which same-sex marriage question followed questions on gay/lesbian rights and relations
1996–2005 wording: "Do you think marriages between homosexuals ..."

GALLUP

FIGURE 6.1   **Two in three Americans support gay marriage in 2018.**

_____

2   In fact, looking at pop culture and politics it is very easy to make the argument that these normative changes are already in the process of occurring.

FIGURE 6.2   **Rainbow White House.**

There Still Remain a Number of Arenas Where Discrimination Remains

- Like people at the bottom of the race and gender hierarchies, gay people suffer forms of discrimination. Like blacks and women, they initially had almost no rights. In addition, there is substantial implicit and explicit bias about them against them and directed toward them.
  - http://www.aei.org/publication/polls-on-attitudes-on-homosexuality-gay-marriage-march-2013/
  - www.huffingtonpost.com/2011/10/04/gay-resume-study_n_994098.html
  - www.businessinsider.com/hate-crimes-against-gays-in-america-2013-5
  - http://www.splcenter.org/the-anti-gay-lobby-the-family-research-council-the-american-family-association-the-demonization-of--3
- There is also a very large (though shrinking) group of people who view being gay as disgusting and/or immoral and are seeking to eradicate the "gay lifestyle."
- Homosexuality was also considered a mental disorder until 1974.

In over half of states, it is still legal to fire people based on their sexual orientation and/or gender identity.

State-wide employment non-discrimination
law covers sexual orientation and gender identity

State-wide employment non-discrimination law
covers only sexual orientation (not gender identity)

State-wide employment non-discrimination law
does not cover sexual orientation or gender identity

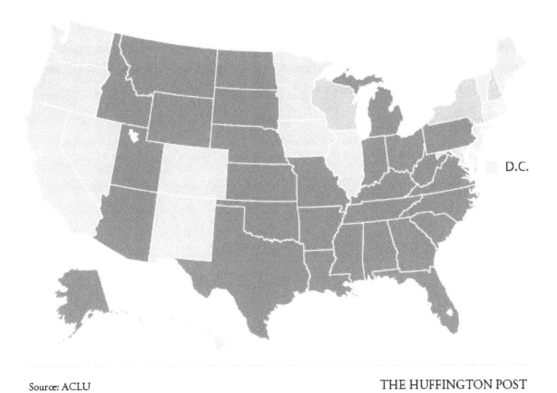

Source: ACLU   THE HUFFINGTON POST

FIGURE 6.3   **Where you can be fired for being LGBT.**

Trans Inequality

Many people do not fit into the gender binary, and there are in fact numerous contemporary and historical examples of societies that operate(d) with more than two genders. While becoming more visible in society, trans individuals are not recognized on federal forms in the United States and in very few states. Because the gender binary paradigm is so dominant, trans individuals are among the most commonly marginalized groups of Americans. This marginalization is related to a lack of legal protections and below average social outcomes on a number of dimensions, including life expectancy and SES.

CONCLUSION

There are a number of social problems related to sexuality and sexual identity. Many people in the United States and across the world face stigma, repression, and marginalization based on their sexual identities, sexual orientations, gender identities, and other social aspects that relate to sexuality. Furthermore, there are social issues that are related to the practices or assertion of sexuality, including sexually transmitted disease rates, harassment and sexual assault, and youth pregnancy. Many aspects of sexuality across a number of societies are gendered, often around male assertiveness and female passivity.

It is also important to remember that the US is not the only game in town. Many scholars including aesthetic anthropologists and cultural sociologists tell us beauty and "sexiness" are culturally defined.

Image Credits

Fig. 6.1: Source: https://news.gallup.com/poll/234866/two-three-americans-support-sex-marriage.aspx.
Fig. 6.2: Copyright © Nick Amoscato (CC by 2.0) at https://commons.wikimedia.org/wiki/File:Rainbow_White_House_(19485803955).jpg.
Fig. 6.3: Source: https://www.huffingtonpost.com/2014/10/30/fired-for-being-gay_n_6076492.html.

CHAPTER 7

Media and Public Discourse

MEDIA

- **Media**: Different technological processes that facilitate communication between sender and receiver.
- It is important to note that media does not just speak to us, but that we talk back to it.
- The media represents society to us, especially the parts with which we are unfamiliar or do not engage in often.
- The media also represents us (US) to the world.[1]
- **Mass media**: Media intended to reach a large audience; forms of communication designed to reach a vast audience without any personal contact between the senders and receivers. Examples include newspapers, magazines, video recordings, radio, and television.
- **Mainstream media**: Media owned and operated by one of the five major media corporations or its subsidiaries.
- **Independent media**: Media with ownership unconnected to the major five media corps. Some independent media is funded by donors. Has a stronger internet than TV or radio presence.
- **Social media**: Media based on the conversation and interaction with individuals or companies online.
- **Media literacy**: The ability to assess and analyze media messages.
- **Influencers:** An increasingly prominent form of media personality that is most ubiquitous on social media. The number of followers combined with personal branding and usually corporate sponsors allow this person to directly "influence" their immediate sphere as well as parts of the broader culture.

---

1   The Representation Project, "Cause and Effect: How the Media Can Change Your Life," March 7, 2012, https://www.youtube.com/watch?v=Hv5Z2Xv8iJU.

Types of Media

- **Press/news**: The sector of the media that engages in reporting current events, news, politics, and other stories of natural interest. The dominant form of media for the majority of American history.
- **Music and art**: Published musicians and artists and those who write about them (film critics, fashion bloggers, etc.).
- **Academia**: Papers, research, policy statements, press releases, and so on from institutions like colleges, universities, and think tanks.
- **Entertainment**: The sector of the media that creates sitcoms, dramas, movies, and so on.
- **Sports**: The sector of the media focusing on reporting sports and sports interest stories.
- **Tech media**: Those who write and publish about the world of technology, technological advances, and tech culture and tech subcultures.
- **Business media**: Those who produce content about business, economics, and the business world.

Media Sources

- Television
- Advertisements
- Internet
- Radio
- Social media
- Newspaper/magazines
- Physical representations; ad presence like billboards
- Video games and apps

Media Consumption

Media consumption is on the rise, having increased from about eight hours in 2005 to over twelve hours in 2018. Most of that increase has come from an increase in digital and mobile media, which has been facilitated by the rise (and now ubiquity) of smartphones. There are a finite number of hours in a day, and it is important to note that such an increase in media consumption must take collective social time away from other areas. Notably, reading (which is a source of media) and going out with friends are two such activities that are done less frequently in the last five to ten years.

hrs:mins

	2012	2013	2014	2015	2016	2017	2018
Digital	**4:10**	**4:48**	**5:09**	**5:28**	**5:43**	**5:53**	**6:01**
—Mobile (nonvoice)	**1:28**	**2:15**	**2:37**	**2:53**	**3:06**	**3:15**	**3:23**
——Radio	0:26	0:32	0:39	0:44	0:47	0:50	0:52
——Social networks	0:09	0:18	0:23	0:26	0:29	0:32	0:34
——Video	0:09	0:17	0:22	0:26	0:29	0:31	0:34
——Other	0:44	1:08	1:14	1:16	1:20	1:22	1:24
—Desktop/laptop*	**2:24**	**2:16**	**2:14**	**2:12**	**2:11**	**2:10**	**2:08**
——Video	0:20	0:22	0:23	0:24	0:25	0:25	0:24
——Social networks	0:22	0:17	0:16	0:15	0:14	0:13	0:13
——Radio	0:07	0:06	0:06	0:06	0:06	0:06	0:05
——Other	1:35	1:31	1:28	1:27	1:26	1:26	1:26
—Other connected devices	**0:18**	**0:17**	**0:19**	**0:23**	**0:26**	**0:28**	**0:30**
TV**	**4:38**	**4:31**	**4:22**	**4:11**	**4:05**	**4:00**	**3:55**
Radio**	**1:32**	**1:30**	**1:28**	**1:27**	**1:27**	**1:26**	**1:25**
Print**	**0:40**	**0:35**	**0:32**	**0:30**	**0:28**	**0:27**	**0:26**
—Newspapers	0:24	0:20	0:18	0:17	0:16	0:15	0:15
—Magazines	0:17	0:15	0:13	0:13	0:12	0:11	0:11
Other**	**0:38**	**0:31**	**0:26**	**0:24**	**0:22**	**0:21**	**0:20**
Total	11:39	11:55	11:57	12:00	12:05	12:07	12:08

Note: ages 18+; time spent with each medium includes all time spent with that medium, regardless of multitasking; for example, 1 hour of multitasking on desktop/laptop while watching TV is counted as 1 hour for TV and 1 hour for desktop/laptop; *includes all internet activities on desktop and laptop computers; **excludes digital
Source: eMarketer, April 2016

207855   www.eMarketer.com

FIGURE 7.1   **Average time spent per day with major media by US adults, 2012–2018.**

Media Consolidation

- **Media conglomeration** (also called "media consolidation"): The merging of media enterprises, which results in a shrinking number of media enterprises.[2]
- **Vertical integration**: Occurs when a company owns all levels of production (e.g., car company buying a steel mill and tire company).
- **Horizontal integration**: Occurs when a firm is being taken over by, or merged with, another firm in the same industry and in the same stage of production as the merged firm (e.g., car company buying another car company).
- **Monopoly**: When a specific person, company, or corporation is the only supplier of a product. Characterized by lack of competition and market domination. For all intents and purposes, monopolies are illegal in the United States.
- Media conglomeration has made many more issues national, while fewer remain local.

Media Bias

- The bias of journalists and news producers (who behind the scenes usually have more impact than hosts or journalists) in the mass media in the selection of events and stories that are reported (or not reported) and how they are covered (termed *spin*). Media bias implies a pervasive or widespread bias, compromising the standards of journalism, rather than the perspective of an individual journalist or article. The direction and degree of media bias in various countries is widely disputed.
- Sociology, as well as many other disciplines, view the role of the media as a watchdog. It is the fourth estate, a check outside of the official checks and balances of our government.
- **FCC**: The Federal Communications Commission regulates interstate and international communications.
- Fairness Doctrine: FCC Law passed in 1949 that required the holders of broadcast licenses to both present controversial issues of public importance and to do so in a manner that was, in the Commission's view, honest, equitable and balanced. The FCC decided to eliminate the doctrine in 1987, and in August 2011 the FCC formally removed the language that implemented the doctrine.
- Two basic elements: required broadcasters to devote some of their airtime to discussing controversial matters of public interest and to air contrasting views regarding those matters.

---

2   Ashley Lutz, "These 6 Corporations Control 90% of the Media in America," Business Insider, June 14, 2012, https://www.businessinsider.com/these-6-corporations-control-90-of-the-media-in-america-2012-6.

- Our media is also becoming more insular, allowing very different narratives about the same facts.

Conflict Perspective

- Conflict perspective especially asserts that the media cannot perform its job as a "watchdog" if they are run and owned by the same powerful people it is supposed to be watching.
- News executives are financially motivated, by ratings but also by ownership and large funders. Since news is "the result of what a news organization decides to show" most stories that would reflect badly on these powerful people are withheld.

CULTURE

- **Culture**: A sense of collectiveness that unifies a group of people through shared traits, boundaries, identities, and practices.
  - The values, norms and material goods shared by a given group.
  - Watercooler talk: What do we talk about? What do we collectively find important?
- Media and culture strongly influence each other. Media represents culture to us, and cultural norms are largely responsible for defining what is and is not acceptable in media.

Examining the Effects of Social Media and I-gen

Social media is having profound impacts on our societies, social worlds, relationships and personal lives. Few if any technologies have ever been so rapidly and so widely adopted.
The following resources can be used to explore social media use and its effects:

- http://www.pewinternet.org/files/old-media//Files/Reports/2013/PIP_SocialMediaUsers.pdf
- www.pewinternet.org/fact-sheets/social-networking-fact-sheet/
- **Digital divide**: Sociological term that refers to a large divide between those with internet access and those without.
  - Millennials are the first "digital generation."
- **Gender divide**: Overall, women have more of a presence on social media, but men spend more time on job and business sites.
- **Internet addiction**: Neglecting other parts of one's life to facilitate routine internet activities.

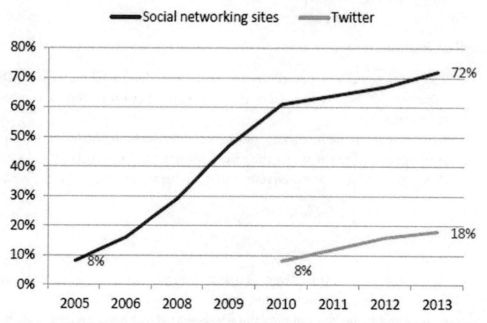

% of adult internet users who use social networking sites or Twitter, over time

Source: Pew Research Center's Internet & American Life Project tracking surveys 2005-2013. Spring Tracking Survey, April 17 – May 19, 2013. N=1,895 adult internet users ages 18+.

FIGURE 7.2   Adult use of social networking sites and Twitter: change over time.

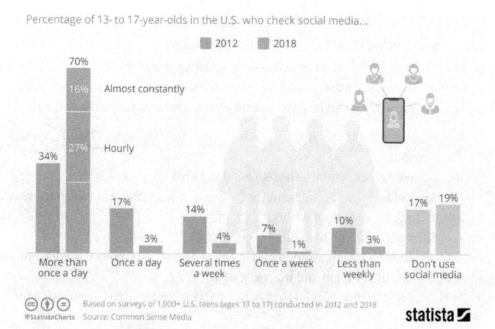

Percentage of 13- to 17-year-olds in the U.S. who check social media...

Based on surveys of 1,000+ U.S. teens (ages 13 to 17) conducted in 2012 and 2018
@StatistaCharts   Source: Common Sense Media

statista

FIGURE 7.3   Teens' social media usage is drastically increasing.

Reading 7.1.

Defining Social Media

by Joseph W. Barnes

Defining social media is like trying to define the Internet, in part, because the technology, platforms, and use of the platforms are in constant evolution. Who would have thought just 16 years ago that we would have powerful platforms such as Facebook, Twitter, YouTube, Instagram, Pinterest, LinkedIn, Google+, Vine, Tumblr, Flickr, and more?

We also have technology that has given us real-time sharing opportunities, through mobile apps.

Social media is by its very nature about **sharing, the creation of community, and interaction.** Social media is about being social, it is about **a participatory culture,** whether on a large scale or small scale. There are people who consume social media content, there are people who share, and there are people who create content. This results in an enormous amount of information being shared, some positive, some negative, some personal, some about businesses and organizations. Like it or not, social media is the future of communication.

Brian Solis, a digital analyst, anthropologist, and futurist studies the effects of disruptive technology on business and society. Solis (2012) believes we should think about social media in a broad perspective:

"We should think about social media and mobile behavior as it's related to psychology, anthropology, communication, economics, human geography, ethnography, et al. After all, everything comes down to people. Unfortunately, in new media, we tend to put technology ahead of people." (Solis 2012)

"Relationships are not a function or derivative of technology. At best, the definition of relationships when technology is at the center of connectivity, can mean nothing more than the way in which two or more concepts, objects, or people are connected, or the state of being connected. Relationships are not static. They are in fact dynamic and becoming more so every day." (Solis 2012)

We share both the good and the bad experiences online just as we do in person with family, friends, and coworkers.

"The connected evaluate shared experiences of those they trust, and expect businesses to respond to their socialized questions. As a consequence, they don't follow a linear approach through the classic 'interest to intent' funnel during their decision making process. Rather, they follow an elliptical pattern where their next steps are inspired by the insights of others, and their experiences are, in turn, fed back into the cycle to inform the decisions of others." (Solis 2012)

Joseph W. Barnes, "Defining Social Media," *Social Media Ethics Made Easy: How to Comply with FTC Guidelines*, pp. 9-11, 94-95. Copyright © 2016 by Business Expert Press. Reprinted with permission.

Social media is a force that has changed our lives. We keep in touch like never before through social media; we share pictures and videos at unprecedented rates; we post reviews of products we like and dislike for thousands to see; and if we are an unhappy consumer, we can tweet our dislike and even share a picture for thousands to read. As consumers, the power has shifted from a push mentality by marketers to interactivity requiring smart businesses to listen and respond. We also make mistakes, as individuals and as businesses. In part, that is why we need to study social media ethics, understand what is appropriate, what is not appropriate, and why every business and organization needs to have a social media ethics policy in place.

ENTER: THE POWER OF WORD-OF-MOUTH RECOMMENDATIONS AND ONLINE REVIEWS

How powerful are word-of-mouth recommendations and reviews in person and online?

"According to a study from marketing firm Lithium Technologies, one third of Americans said they don't trust advertising to give them information about a product or service they are interested in buying. More than two-thirds of the respondents in the U.S. said they were more receptive to recommendations from family and friends than to online advertising, the study found." (Wall Street Journal 2014)

"According to Nielsen, 92-percent of consumers believe recommendations from friends and family over all forms of advertising." (Whitler 2014)

This is an incredibly powerful statistic. Just think about this for a moment. Over 90 percent of us trust recommendations from family and friends over all forms of advertising. In addition, we trust online product and service reviews from people we don't even know, more than traditional advertising. This is why, it's so important to help businesses and organizations understand the importance of establishing social media ethical guidelines.

Consumers are evolving faster than businesses can keep up with them. Why? Because we live in a 24/7-connected world.

As we proceed in this book, let me quote from parts of NPR's code of ethics,

"The Internet and the social media communities it encompasses can be incredible resources. They offer both a remarkably robust amount of historical material and an incredible amount of 'real-time' reporting from people at the scenes of breaking news events. But they also present new and unfamiliar challenges, and they tend to amplify the effects of any ethical misjudgments you might make. So tread carefully. Conduct yourself online just as you would in any other public circumstances. Treat those you encounter online with fairness, honesty and respect, just as you would offline. Be honest about your intent." (ethics.npr.org n.d.)

SUMMARY

In this chapter, we have learned that the definition of social media is evolving based on new technologies, platforms, and applications. However, the constant is that social media is about sharing. As humans, we have a need to share the good, the bad, and the ugly. We do it in person, and now in greater numbers, we do it online.

We also learned that over 90 percent of consumers now trust recommendations from family and friends—and yes even from online reviewers we've never met—more than traditional advertising.

REFERENCES

Marsden, P. 2000. "Social Networks." In *Encyclopedia of Sociology*, 2nd ed., edited by E.F. Borgatta, and R.J.V. Montgomery. New York, NY: Macmillan, pp. 2727–35.

Wasserman, S., and K.B. Faust. 1994. *Social Network Analysis: Methods and Applications*. New York, NY: Cambridge University Press.

Pescosolido, B.A., and E.R. Wright. 2004. "The View from Two Worlds: The Convergence of Social Network Reports between Mental Health Clients and Their Ties." *Social Science & Medicine* 58, no. 9, pp. 1795–806.

Knoke, D. 1990. *Political Networks*. New York, NY: Cambridge University Press.

Scott, J., and P.J. Carrington. 2011. *The SAGE Handbook of Social Network Analysis*. Thousand Oaks, CA: SAGE Publications.

Solis, B. 2012. "Social Media Is About Social Science Not Technology." Retrieved from: www.briansolis.com/2012/03/social-mediais-about-social-science-not-technology/

Gallivan, R. 2014. "Amid Fake Reviews, Consumers Are Skeptical of Social Media Marketing." Retrieved from: http://blogs.wsj.com/digits/2014/06/03/amid-fake-reviews-consumers-skeptical-of-social-media-marketing/tab/print/?mg=blogs-wsj&url=http%253A%252F%252Fbl%E2%80%A6

Whitler, K.A. 2014. "Why Word of Mouth Marketing Is the Most Important Social Media." Retrieved from: www.forbes.com/sites/kimberlywhitler/2014/07/17/why-word-of-mouth-marketing-is-the-most-important-social-media/

Reading 7.2.

Towards a Sociological Understanding of Social Media: Theorizing Twitter

by Dhiraj Murthy

The first twitter of Spring, How melodious its ring
The first twitter of Spring, How melodious its ring, its ring
[...]
O'er the down and the dell [...]
Song birds that flit, Singing cheerily twit, twitter twit, tra la la, tra la
(Callcott, 1863: 1–7)
Two Tasks: to defend the new against the old and to link the old with the new
(Nietzsche, 1873, cited in Rabinow, 2008: 101)

In his late 18th-century play titled *The Telegraph, or, A New Way of Knowing Things* (1795), John Dent satirizes the effect of the telegraph at the time. As performed at the Theatre Royal in London, its protagonist, Sir Peter Curious, is dead set on getting a telegraph of his own so he can spy on his family and check if his wife, Lady Curious, is being unfaithful. Sir Peter describes the telegraph by saying it is 'an apparatus, by which you may find out what's doing in one's family, let it be ever so far off' (Dent, 1795: 9). The telegraph's ability to combine the immediacy of messages with interlocutors at great distances fascinates Sir Peter, leading him to add, 'if you say in Basinghall Street, "How d'ye do?" they'll answer you in five minutes, "Pretty well I thank you" in the blue mountains'(1795: 9). Sir Peter is particularly keen to spy on his family and eagerly awaits the arrival of the telegraph of his own so that 'I [Sir Peter] shall know to a certainty, what my Lady is about at Sydenham, and be convinced, whether I have any cause, or not, to suspect her of infidelity' (1795: 9–10). This notion that the telegraph will blur the boundaries of public and private culminates in a scene in which the coachman, gardener, butler and housekeeper begin confessing improprieties (including the butler stealing over a dozen bottles of champagne). They know that the days of raiding their boss's liquor cabinet are numbered as Sir Peter will, of course, find out about *everything* in the future through the telegraph (1795: 20–21).

Though Dent's play was written over 200 years ago, it is striking just how resonant it is with the contemporary reception to new media technologies which seek similarly to compress time and space (Harvey, 1989) as well as shrink or blur the boundaries between private and public. Modern-day Sir Peters snoop on loved ones or children through new web-based technologies including social networking sites (such as Facebook and Google+). In other words, Dent's play also highlights the

Dhiraj Murthy, "Towards a Sociological Understanding of Social Media: Theorizing Twitter," *Sociology*, vol. 46, no. 6, pp. 1059-1073. Copyright © 2012 by SAGE Publications. Reprinted with permission.

issue of surveillance and technology. The relevance of his play is, however, much deeper in that the telegraph, his object of interest, has many parallels to Twitter, a prominent social media website in which users send updates restricted in length to 140 characters (termed 'tweets') to a global public. Like the telegraph, it is used to send short messages. Like the telegraph, it is a controversial technology. In the 18th and indeed 19th centuries, most lauded the telegraph (with *The Times*, 1796, calling it an 'ingenious and useful contrivance' and *Scientific American* heralding it as the bringer of a 'kinship of humanity', cited in Fischer, 1992: 2). Others at the time viewed it as a means to dumb down society and the harbinger of letter writing's death. Indeed, even in the early 20th century, discussions of the telegraph's impact on letter writing continued (e.g. *The Times*, 1900). Although these early critics saw the telegraph's immediacy and brevity as a threat to letter writing, ironically, the telegraph highlighted the permanence of letter writing in that it remained an important medium. Similarly, when the telephone was seen as potentially replacing telegrams, the permanence of the telegram becomes highlighted; as Peggy Olson in her ad campaign during an episode of the television series *Mad Men* remarks, 'You can't frame a phone call. A telegram is forever.' And, today, critics of Twitter such as Keen (2010) view social media as threatening blogging and other longer-length electronic media. But will the immediacy and brevity of Twitter, on the other hand, give permanence to earlier, longer-length electronic media? Additionally, as tweets are being archived by the American Library of Congress, will the next communicative technology give permanence to tweets?

Though these broad historical arguments reveal similarities of emergent social media to older communication technologies, what makes Twitter distinct is also its departures from the telegraph. Specifically, it is free to use, public (or perhaps semi-public), multicast (i.e. many to many), interactive, and networked. The power of Twitter and other social media is also that they are designed to provoke and call forth regular updates from their users. Highlighting these differences is key to a critical, yet balanced, understanding of the potential uniqueness of social media like Twitter.

This article seeks to extend and innovate existing sociological theory to understand emergent social media. To do this, Twitter is explored in light of work by Erving Goffman and other theorists. However, before trying to form a theoretical understanding of Twitter and social media in general, the technology needs first to be introduced.

TWITTER AS SOCIAL MEDIA

Blair (1915) in his popular 20th-century stage song 'I hear a little Twitter and a Song' was, of course, referring to birdsong. However the website has become ubiquitous. For most internet-using adults, to hear a twitter today refers to one of the largest and most popular social media websites.[1] This section explains the medium itself and the ways in which it is organized. What this section does not do is provide a conclusive argument of how or why Twitter is different from other ways of interaction. Rather, like the rest of this article, this section intentionally aims to begin this conversation.

First, the distinction should be made between 'social network' and 'social media' technologies. The former, which encompass Facebook and LinkedIn amongst others, are defined by boyd and Ellison (2008: 211) as web services which facilitate users maintaining a 'public or semi-public profile within a bounded system' and through which they can 'articulate a list of other users with whom they share a connection'. Some elide social networking and social media together. Though the two are not mutually exclusive, it is more useful to make clear that social media are mainly conceived of as a medium wherein 'ordinary' people in ordinary social networks (as opposed to professional journalists) can create user-generated 'news' (in a broadly defined sense). The 'social' part of social media refer to its distinction from 'traditional' media (Murthy, 2011). This new medium is designed to facilitate social interaction, the sharing of digital media, and collaboration. Social networks are also important to social media—especially in their ability to disseminate. Twitter has been labelled a 'microblog' technology due to the medium's restriction of posts to 140 characters or fewer. Microblogging services, like Twitter, are one type of social media. For the sake of clarity, I define microblogging as an internet-based service in which (1) users have a public profile in which they broadcast short public messages or updates whether they are directed to specific user(s) or not, (2) messages become publicly aggregated together across users, and (3) users can decide whose messages they wish to receive, but not necessarily who can receive their messages; this is in distinction to most social networks where following each other is bi-directional (i.e. mutual).

Unlike social network sites where users often interact with people they know offline (boyd, 2007; Ellison et al., 2007), users of social media often consume media produced by people they have found of interest, leading to interactions with strangers and, albeit more rarely, celebrities. In my research on new media and a Muslim youth subculture (Murthy, 2010), a respondent of mine recounted how he posted a tweet disparaging Deepak Chopra only to find that Chopra himself responded and invited my respondent to have a meal with him (an offer which was taken up).[2] This phenomenon is, of course, part of a larger trend in which web-based spaces are becoming more interactive (e.g. comments on online news articles and professors responding to ratings on sites like ratemyprofessors.com). Whether instances like this one involving Chopra are the exception or the norm, social media are designed to facilitate interactive multicasting (i.e. the broadcasting of many to many). Twitter, for example, makes it very easy for tweets to be 'retweeted' (i.e. forwarded) to one's set of followers, people who have subscribed to read that individual's tweets.

Tweets are a public version of Facebook's now well-known status update function. Twitter is similar to chat rooms in that dialogue between Twitter users occurs through the at-sign (e.g. a user can direct tweets to another user by prefixing a post with an at-sign before the target user's name). However, unlike many chat rooms, Twitter is public. Anyone can post a tweet directed to @barackobama or @KatyPerry and many do (Murthy, 2011). The boundaries of public and private are critical to understanding microblogging as well as its predecessor technologies. Rosenthal (2008: 159) helps make this distinction by observing that '[n]ewsletters by e-mail are still newsletters, but blogs bring personalized and interpersonal communication into the public domain'. For those unfamiliar with Twitter (and microblogging in general), upon logging in, a user is presented with their profile page. On Twitter, this page is known as a timeline. Its purpose is to act as a live feed which displays tweets both by the user as well as anyone the user is 'following'.[3] Similarly, users who are 'following' you will receive tweets you post in their timeline.[4]

If someone is following you whom you do not want to be followed by, you can block them. However, this does not preclude anyone from pointing their browser to your public Twitter profile and reading all of your tweets. It just means they are not publicly associated as a 'follower' of you and will not receive your tweets in their timeline.

I TWEET, THEREFORE I AM

Like all social media, Twitter has everything to do with self-presentation. Though not reductively Cartesian, the act of tweeting is born from individual contributions and, sociologically speaking, is about self-production. Indeed, microblogging services depend on regular posting by users. Without this regularity, the utility of social media such as Twitter diminishes significantly. Like status updates on Facebook, users of social media continue to post regularly as the status updating practice becomes a meaningful part of their identities (Boon and Sinclair, 2009; Nosko et al., 2010). Daily posts which indicate what one had for breakfast or what one is wearing can easily be relegated to the merely banal. But, as sociologists, we should recall Bourdieu's (1984) argument that the daily, sometimes 'banal', is pregnant with meaning. In the case of Twitter, 'banal' social media posts serve as an important vehicle of self-affirmation. We can read tweets such as 'had too many espresso shots today' as a means by which individuals affirm their identities in a constantly shifting, 'liquid modern' (Bauman, 2000) world. The seemingly banal tweet becomes an important tool to say 'look at me' or 'I exist'. This need to confirm their identities keeps regular users invested in the act of posting on social media websites on a regular (sometimes daily or hourly basis). This is part of what Gackenbach (2007) calls 'inventing the self'.

Goffman (1981: 21) also notes how our daily communicative rituals have considerations of 'ego' and 'personal feelings'. It is useful to draw a comparison between mobile phone text messages and Twitter. Though the former is presumably a private bilateral communicative act, its content is often similar to Twitter. As Licoppe (2004: 143) found, mobile phone-mediated communication helps people tell each other about their days and this brought the communicating individuals 'closer'. And this feeling of 'closeness' is not lessened *per se* because of its mediated state. Rather, as Putnam (2000: 27) argues, internet-mediated communication presents a counterexample to the 'decline of connectedness' we see in many aspects of American community life. Shirky (2010) extends this argument by noting that in recent years the hours of television American youths watch has declined. Given the historical upward trend in their television consumption, this is noteworthy. Shirky (2010) attributes this to an increase in hours spent by these youth using social media and other internet applications.

Regardless, it is not difficult to make the argument that these forms of self-confirmation are redolent of the nihilism Heidegger associates with aspects of modernity. However, sociologically, it is critical that we recognize the importance of these posts to the identities of the posters. We can understand this through *Bildung*, which Herder (cited in Gadamer et al., 2004: 8) refers to as 'cultivating the human'. Gadamer et al. (2004: 8) explain *Bildung* as the 'concept of self-formation'. From the perspective of identity, Gadamer (2004: 10) sees *Bildung* as describing 'the result of the process of becoming' and, as such, 'constantly remains in a state of continual *Bildung*'. Though it is easy to view tweets merely as a crude mode of communication, doing so misses the impact tweets have on one's *Bildung*. For active users of Twitter, posting tweets is part of their identity maintenance and the constancy of active Twitter users confirms this relationship or, as a Cartesian aphorism: I tweet, therefore I am. Tying this back to Goffman, these changes in social communication are part of 'ego' and 'personal feelings' and are critical to understanding Twitter and, especially, its role in self-production. Though tweeting is part of becoming for its users, it departs from Cartesian dualism in that the former is contingent on a community of interactants, whereas the latter makes the argument that the individual mind is thinking and, as such, stands apart from community and, indeed, the body. Examining Twitter alongside Cartesian thought reveals that the former complicates the autonomous individuality of the latter. Specifically, Twitter seems to provide ways for individuals to assert and construct the self which are contingent on a larger dialogic community (Bakhtin and Holquist, 1981).

TWITTER AS DEMOCRATIZING?

One shortcoming of understanding social media through *Bildung* is that it does not capture the shift the medium has experienced from being an exclusively elite form to a more accessible one. An important question is whether the medium opened up access to the production of selves by tweeting. Turner (2010: 2) argues that contemporary media forms have experienced a 'demotic turn', which refers 'to the increasing visibility of the "ordinary person" as they have turned themselves into media content through celebrity culture, reality TV, DIY websites, talk radio and the like'. Turner (2010: 3) makes the key point that the media have perhaps experienced a shift from 'broadcaster of cultural identities' to 'a translator or even an author of identities'. George Gilder (1994), a dot-com cyber evangelist, extended this idea much further, arguing that new media would be 'moving authority from elites and establishments [and that these ...] new technologies [would] drastically change the cultural balance of power'. However, Turner is more cautious, pointing out that the 'demotic turn' seen in contemporary media should not be conflated with democratization and the end of the digital divide. Specifically, he argues against Hartley's (1999) notion of 'democratainment', arguing that, in neologisms such as this, the democratic is almost always secondary (Turner, 2010: 16). I agree with him when he argues that no 'amount of public participation in game shows, reality TV or DIY celebrity web-sites will alter the fact that, overall, the media industries still remain in control of the symbolic economy' (2010: 16). Furthermore, we should not underestimate the startling ability of states to pull the plug, as occurred in Egypt in 2011.

The natural question which arises is whether Twitter is different in any meaningful way. An argument can be made that, within Western society itself, Twitter and other microblogging sites do indeed represent a significant 'demotic turn' (i.e. ordinary people are able to break 'news', produce media content, or voice their opinions publicly). Microblogging, more than many web spaces, is event driven. Organizing social life by events presents opportunities for everyday people and traditional media industries to tweet side-by-side. One way to render this visible is through Twitter's 'trending topics' function, a list of the most popular subjects people are tweeting about. Interestingly, there are always 'demotic' trending topics such as what people are listening to, celebrities one hates, or the '#lesserbooks' trending topic which called for book titles which never made it to the shelf (e.g. 'Zen and the Art of Unicycle Maintenance'). Simultaneously, a significant number are based around breaking news events (e.g. the death of Michael Jackson or the BP Deepwater Horizon oil spill). Although traditional media industries usually determine what events become considered important, many trending topics come into being through a single tweet or a small group of individuals. Many tweets referring to breaking news events contain hyperlinks to full-length newspaper articles.

Therefore, it is perhaps more useful to see Twitter and other social media as part of what Therborn (2000: 42) calls the 'event society' (*Erlebnisgesellschaft*). And Huyssen (2000: 25) translates it as 'society of experience', a turn toward social communication being event-based. Seen as part of the larger cosmology of Twitter, this reflects a particular aspect of modernity in which events, however transient or superficial, are of importance to society. Huyssen's explanation of *Erlebnisgesellschaft* captures these elements well. He writes that the term 'refers to a society that privileges intense but superficial experiences oriented toward instant happening in the present and consumption of goods, cultural events, and mass-marketed lifestyles' (2000: 25). Through this reading of *Erlebnisgesellschaft*, the intriguing question of what constitutes an 'event' itself emerges (e.g. does Charlie Sheen mouthing off to a reporter constitute an 'event'?)

Erlebnisgesellschaft seems to draw from Kierkegaard and Dru's (1962: 35) argument that 'ours is the age of advertisement and publicity. Nothing ever happens but there is instant publicity everywhere.' Tempting as it is for some, applying Kierkegaard's 'nothing happens' argument to Twitter is a potentially dangerous one. Rather, as argued previously, our interpersonal interactions on Twitter and other new media such as Facebook and LinkedIn are part of our daily happenings. And, following Adorno and Bernstein (1991), our daily interaction with media is very much a part of our larger socioeconomic life. For Adorno, our interactions with any media are routed through what he calls the 'culture industry', institutions which control the production and consumption of culture. What we listen to or what we read are all mediated by the culture industries and, from his perspective, its 'commercial character' (Adorno and Bernstein, 1991: 61). Ultimately, relegating Twitter to a space where 'nothing happens' not only ignores the fact that the interactions we have on Twitter are a product of larger social, political, and economic process, but it also smacks of elitism (a charge which Waldman, 1977, argues was, ironically, often levelled at Adorno). The latter part of Kierkegaard's argument, however, is critically important to understanding Twitter. There is definitely an 'immediate publicity everywhere' (Kierkegaard and Dru: 35) in that everything from one's daily happenings or musings become part of a publicity-driven culture. In a sense, Twitter markets us through our tweets and, as such, shifts us more towards 'an age of advertisement', where we are not necessarily advertising products, but rather ourselves (and our self-commodification). As research has shown (e.g. Livingstone, 2008), the amount of followers or friends one has on social media websites factors into how we perceive ourselves. And, following the inverse, cyber-bullying has the real potential to harm or even destroy one's self-image (Li, 2006). Although beyond the scope of this introductory article, larger questions are posed throughout the following section to provide directions for future work.

TOWARDS A SOCIOLOGICAL UNDERSTANDING OF TWITTER

The study of social media is a new area of scholarship in the social sciences and humanities. Twitter, like any new communication technology, shapes our social world. As Raymond Williams (1974) famously cautioned, technology shaping our social world is different to determining it, or as Fischer (1992: 5), in reference to the telephone, puts it: 'fundamental' shifts in communication technology change 'the conditions of daily life, [but they...] do not determine the basic character of that life'. Specifically, Fischer (1992: 5) sees the telephone as not 'radically alter[ing] American ways of life'. Rather, Americans used the telephone 'to more vigorously pursue their characteristic ways of life'. In other words, the telephone facilitated the intensification of pre-existing characteristics of social life (Fischer, 1992: 5). In the case of Twitter, it may be intensifying pre-existing characteristics of an erosion of the private in which more quotidian aspects of our lives are publicly shared. These are some of the new messages made possible by the new medium. We learn about other people's daily rituals, habits, happenings, and the places they visit. Not only do we potentially get a certain level of richness which we do not get in other mediated communication, but we also are exposed to a certain candour. Following Habermas's (1970: 372) notion that 'all speech [...] is oriented towards the idea of truth', we are perhaps getting more truthful portrayals of some sides of people, which were previously kept in the private sphere or what Goffman (1959: 119) calls the 'backstage', which constitutes 'places where the camera is not focused at the moment'. Or, most likely, we are getting a posed view of the backstage: we see what people want us to/let us see. These are pressing questions to which sociologists can offer valuable insights. This article begins this conversation by specifically extending Goffman's theoretical work to better understand Twitter.

Goffman's corpus of interactionist work gives sociologists a set of tools which can be developed to understand social media, including Twitter. Specifically, recent work like that of Knorr Cetina (2009) has argued that Goffman's work can be useful for understanding mediated interactions. In the case of Twitter, the work of Goffman and his interactionist followers is helpful in understanding the concepts relating to self-production discussed earlier. For the benefit of those unfamiliar with his work, I first introduce some basics of Goffman in terms of face-to-face dialogic interaction before delving into Twitter. Goffman's (1981) approach places primacy on interaction and views our face-to-face social situations as critical. From one vantage point, to understand Twitter is to understand how we 'talk'. Goffman conceptualizes 'talk' through three themes: 'ritualization', 'participation framework', and 'embedding'. The first refers to his argument that the 'movements, looks, and vocal sounds we make as an unintended byproduct of speaking and listening never seem to remain innocent' (1981: 2). A key aspect of ritualization is that we acquire gestural conventions over our lifetime and that these gestures cannot be captured by the term 'expression' (1981: 3). Second, 'participation framework' refers to Goffman's theory that 'those who happen to be in perceptual range of the event will have some sort of participation status relative to it' and that these positions can be analysed (1981: 3). Lastly, 'embedding' refers to the 'insufficiently appreciated fact that words we speak are often not our own, at least our current "own"' and that 'who can speak is restricted to the parties present' (1981: 3). He adds that 'although who speaks is situationally circumscribed, in whose name words are spoken is certainly not'. Goffman (1981: 3) emphasizes that '[u]ttered words have utterers', but utterances 'have subjects (implied or explicit)'. He concludes that the subjects may ultimately point to the utterer, but 'there is nothing in the syntax of utterances to require this coincidence' (1981: 3).

I have intentionally outlined Goffman's three key themes surrounding 'talk' although he is referring to unmediated rather than mediated talk. The literature extending Goffman's ideas about talk to mediated communication is now established (Adkins and Nasarczyk, 2009; Bryant and Miron, 2004; Riva and Galimberti, 1998; Spitzberg, 2006; Walther, 1996). Indeed, in an issue of this journal, Rettie (2009) successfully extends Goffman to mobile phone communication. Knorr Cetina's (2009) work on stock market traders is particularly innovative in extending Goffman to interactive new media. She argues that their social interactions with other traders can be thought of as 'synthetic situations', which are 'entirely constituted by on-screen projections' (2009: 65). Knorr Cetina begins the process of extending the idea of 'synthetic' to Goffman's concept of 'situation', but stops at the 'synthetic situation'. To understand Twitter and other emerging media, we would be well served by extending Knorr Cetina's idea of the synthetic to Goffman's concepts of 'embedding' and 'encounters'. Building from this literature, I use Goffman's three key themes surrounding 'talk' (ritualization, participation framework, and embedding) to make some initial extensions of his work to the mediated space of Twitter.

Drawing from 'ritualization', tweets seem a-gestural and the term 'expression' seems perfectly able to capture what the tweeting individual is trying to 'express'. However, it is easy to forget that any computer-mediated communication has acquired gestural conventions which also 'never seem to remain innocent'. Though the gestural conventions may be mediated through graphical avatars, emoticons, or even unintended typed characters, these can be considered 'gestures' and they are laden with meaning. For example, on Twitter, one can decipher a sigh or pause through subtle and not-so-subtle textual cues (e.g. '...' for an explicit pause). This is a critical point and one supported by the literature that users 'compensate textually' in computer-mediated communication (Herring, 2008).

In terms of participation framework, computer-mediated communication which is public has a 'perceptual range' which cannot actually be fully perceived by the speaker of the word. That being said, there is a 'perceptual range' which is at least partially perceived by the sender of the tweet and those who receive the tweet in their Twitter timelines have a 'participation status relative' (Goffman, 1981: 3) to the tweets. What I mean by this is that the person sending the tweet knows that there is a potential audience for it and that the readers of the tweet have different participation statuses relative to the tweet. Specifically, a tweet by an individual or group may have triggered the tweet. Or it could be a more subtle relationship. Regardless, this participation status is important to understanding social communication on Twitter.

Lastly, and most importantly, is Goffman's idea of embedding. For him, embedding signifies the distinction between the situational circumscription of speaker and the fluidity of who 'owns' those utterances. Specifically, he argues that utterances have subjects, but the original utterer need not be preserved in the utterance itself. Additionally, Goffman (1981: 3) observes that this 'embedding capacity' is part of our general linguistic ability to embed utterances in 'any remove in time', rather than just in 'the situated present'. Goffman's theoretical perspective is particularly suited to understanding Twitter because of his development of embedding. Specifically, when they have been broadcasted to the Twitter universe ('Twitterverse') tweets become removed from the situational circumscription which face-to-face communication provides. Like the utterances Goffman is referring to, tweet utterances also have subjects. However, the circulation of tweets is more largely dependent on whose name the utterance is being attributed to, rather than who is the original utterer. Specifically, if an unknown person sends a fabulously interesting tweet, it is most likely destined never to be read. Of course, this is true of any communication in that reception depends on audience. However, the ability of Twitter to re-embed tweets into the situational space of another Twitter user (through retweets) generates wholly new audiences which feel the utterance to be originating from the retweeter. This is particularly interesting because the retweet most often bears reference to the original Twitterer (through an @ reference, e.g. @whitehouse). However, this part of the tweet is usually unconsciously or consciously ignored (see Figure 7.1). Of course, some recipients of retweets do pay particular attention to the original Twitterer (and decide to follow them, etc.) and future empirical research will no doubt shed more light on this.[5]

Furthermore, embedding is also particularly useful in theorizing Twitter as it also refers to our linguistic ability to temporalize utterances fluidly. Although Twitter, as a medium, can be synchronous in communicative interactions (if Twitterer and tweet recipient are both online at the same time), it most often has some element of asynchronicity. However, when tweets are retweeted, they become re-embedded into the situated present of the recipient. And if that recipient retweets, the new recipients also view the tweet utterance in their situated present. Because in virtual spaces 'the interacting parties meet in time rather than in a place' (Knorr Cetina, 2009: 79), it is useful to think of what I term 'synthetic embedding', which places primacy on 'response presence' (Goffman, 1983) rather than physical place. That being said, synthetic embedding, like physical embedding, reformulates the space it is embedded in, which happens to be a virtual space.

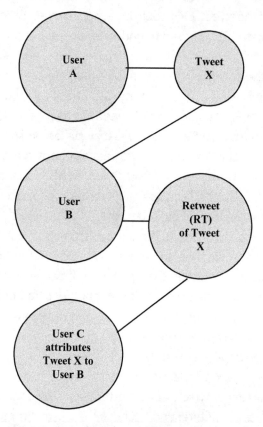

FIGURE 7.2.1   **Twitter attribution**

The difference with Twitter is that the audience range of tweets is not always in congruence with the perceptual range (or indeed intended range) of the original Twitterer. Specifically, the original Twitter poster intends the tweet to circulate to their immediate followers. They are not always consciously aware that their tweets have the potential to travel further. This is a key distinction between synthetic embedding and embedding. Kwak et al. (2010: 6) note that once a tweet is retweeted (regardless of the number of followers the original Twitterer has), it reaches an audience (mean) size of 1000. This is quite significant, as an 'everyday' tweet posted by an ordinary individual has a potentially large readership if it is retweeted. Therefore, like any utterances with intended audiences, tweets are not only synthetically embedded in some time frame, but also audience contexts. And if tweets do become retweeted, they experience synthetic reembedding in both a different temporal frame and potentially different social context.

The above does not take into account replies to tweets and the responses to these replies. Rather, it has been restricted to a single tweet utterance and the ways in which we can theorize its production, perception, and reproduction. However, a critical function of Twitter and reason for its popularity is the ability for users to reply to one another. When replying to a tweet or directing a tweet to a specific user, the site prefixes the reply with an '@' and the intended recipient sees this in their Twitter page when they log on. Like face-to-face communication, utterances on Twitter generate responses. Similarly, these responses are, following Goffman (1981: 5) 'realized at different points in "sequence time"'. Conversations on Twitter become marked by the exchange of responses which can be aggregated into a sequence (by time) and this forms a 'coherent' conversation. This assumes that the response exchanges can be paired into 'dialogic units' as Goffman (1981: 6) refers to them. However, having a conversation on Twitter can be more like sitting in a room with a door, not knowing who is going to pop their head around and respond or who is listening behind the door. Additionally, it could be several people coming through that door within seconds of each other. This is compounded by the fact that the number of other rooms grows larger every time someone retweets your tweets to their followers. Also, if the user identification of the originating Twitterer is retained (through an at-sign), the originating Twitterer has the ability to see who is retweeting and responding. They can choose to become a respondent to a retweeter, thereby opening the door to one or many of these other rooms.

Ultimately, there is a sense of boundedness of the retweet to the new utterer. However, anyone, not just the originating Twitterer, can open any of these doors or they can form a new room and 'own' the tweet. This type of computer-mediated communication does have a history in forms of copy and paste communication (e.g. if someone copied a discussion idea from one email list to another, they become considered the original utterer). However, within the etiquette of emailing lists, the original utterer is preserved and it is customary for an original poster (OP), even if on another site or mailing list, to be referred to or thanked (Hansen et al., 2010).

Of course, a distinguishing aspect of communication on Twitter is also its terseness. Trying to communicate in the restricted format of 140 characters seems unduly limited to some. And to Twitter's critics (e.g. Keen, 2010), it may even be considered a threat to our current modes of communication. Critics also argue that new media more generally are leading to the impoverishment of grammar, vocabulary, spelling, etc. (Tucker, 2009). However, one can make the argument that these types of communication on Twitter (sharing links to news stories, updates on where one is, what one is doing, etc.) are also expressed tersely not only in other mediated forms, but in face-to-face communication as well. Goffman refers to these as 'truncated verbal forms' (1981: 7). Specifically, not all communication needs to be verbose. If we are asking someone which direction a subway station is or how much a newspaper costs, a couple of words will satisfy the questioner. Those, such as Keen (2010), who argue that Twitter heralds the death of meaningful communication may be failing to appreciate this. The key to understanding 'talk' on Twitter is not to get drawn into a privileging of verbosity in speech acts. This is a slippery slope ending, more often than not, in stratified communication. Rather, the assumption needs to be made that the actors in Twitter are satisfied by the sub-140 character responses they receive. Following Goffman (1981: 10), perhaps the most important conclusion is that a 'basic normative assumption about talk is that, whatever else, it should be correctly interpretable in the special sense of conveying to the intended recipients what the sender more or less wanted to get across'. They need not 'agree' with the message, they just need to be in agreement 'as to what they have heard' (1981: 10). Or more concisely put: 'illocutionary force is at stake, not perlocutionary effect' (1981: 10). I would add though that the recipients of tweets may not be intended and that illocutionary force can be diminished as tweets become more and more removed from the original tweeting speaker. However, the medium ultimately tends towards the privileging of verbatim tweets rather than insuring the preservation of intended meaning (i.e. what the original speaker 'wanted to get across'). Additionally, the diminishing of the illocutionary force of tweets may be accelerated when non-native English speakers enter the predominantly English Twitterverse. But, paradoxically, Twitter may be increasing illocutionary force for non-native speakers of the global *lingua franca* who enter into this English-dominated media space because it may require less English-language competency.

CONCLUSION

Sir Peter, a character in the play mentioned at the start of this article, believes that once he gets hold of a telegraph, he 'shall then be acquainted with every thing, and find [his] Lady Curious out in all her tricks, and [his] servants too' (Dent, 1795: 10–11). Though not 'tricks', Twitter (and social media more generally) has enabled its users to become more acquainted with certain everyday aspects of fellow users' lives. For example, when people follow the tweets of those they have met at conferences, they will most likely be exposed to their daily music listening habits, sports interests, current location, and shopping wish-lists, amongst other things. Many see this as a means to get to know people at a more multidimensional level. Additionally, they see aspects of people's lives which are normally 'backstage' (Goffman, 1959). On the other hand, an argument can be made that Twitter represents Bauman's (2000) 'runaway world'; or, from Heidegger's (1977: 25) perspective, 'the fate of our age', 'the inevitableness of an unalterable course'. Granted, the boundaries of public and private have shifted remarkably in modernity (Murdock, 1993). However, speaking in the context of the telegraph and telephone, some emergent communication technologies have had the same effect historically. Rather than view Twitter as 'the fate of our age', another potential approach is to consider the power of Twitter to democratize consumption. Do Twitter and other social media give consumers greater choice by not having elite-centered broadcasting dominate? From this standpoint, Twitter users are individual consumers who make reflective decisions on what information they want coming up on their Twitter feeds.

Like the telegraph, a new and revolutionary technology in its time, Twitter, currently the most prominent social media site, is experiencing immense growth as well as harsh criticisms. Also like the telegraph, Twitter's users are ultimately trying to say something to each other. In his patent application, James Boaz (1802: 2) talks about one ship approaching another and using an optical telegraph to say, 'I wish to speak with you'. Though far less cumbersome than the 25 lamps of Boaz's telegraph signalling system, perhaps Twitter's millions of users are just trying to do the same: 'I wish to speak with you'.

This article has sought to start the conversation of sociological understandings of emergent social media including Twitter by extending interactionist and other sociological work. It is envisioned that future sociological work can help empirically answer some of the questions posed, which include if or how Twitter has changed self-production, how we communicate, interaction orders, the synchronicity of social interaction, the way people use language (including shifts in verbosity), and power relations between interactants. Ultimately, our uses of social media are products of larger social and economic forces and sociology as a discipline is well placed to answer these timely questions.

ACKNOWLEDGEMENTS
I would like to thank Susan Bell, Andrea Drugan, and Pamela Ballinger and the two anonymous reviewers for their invaluable comments on earlier versions of this article.

NOTES
1   Other sites include Blellow, Jaiku, Plurk, and Foursquare.
2   Personal interview.
3   To 'follow' on Twitter is akin to subscribing to another user's tweets.

4 They will also receive any retweets (tweets a user has forwarded to them) in their timeline.

5 My current research explores this question within the context of health messages on Twitter.

REFERENCES

Adkins BA and Nasarczyk J (2009) Asynchronicity and the 'time envelope' of on-line annotation: the case of the photosharing website, Flickr. *Australian Journal of Communication* 35(3): 115–40.

Adorno TW and Bernstein JM (1991) *The Culture Industry: Selected Essays on Mass Culture*. London: Routledge.

Bakhtin MM and Holquist M (1981) *The Dialogic Imagination: Four Essays*. Austin, TX: University of Texas Press.

Bauman Z (2000) *Liquid Modernity*. Cambridge: Polity.

Blair W (1915) *I Hear a Little Twitter and a Song*. Words by G Plass. Cincinnati, OH: J. Church Co.

Boaz J (1802) *A Few Particulars Respecting Mr. Boaz's Patent Telegraph*. London: Unknown.

Boon S and Sinclair C (2009) A world I don't inhabit: disquiet and identity in Second Life and Facebook. *Educational Media International* 46(2): 99–110.

Bourdieu P (1984) *Distinction: A Social Critique of the Judgement of Taste*. Cambridge, MA: Harvard University Press.

boyd dm (2007) Why youth ♥ social network sites: the role of networked publics in teenage social life. *The John D. and Catherine T. MacArthur Foundation Series on Digital Media and Learning*: 119–42.

boyd dm and Ellison NB (2008) Social network sites: definition, history, and scholarship. *Journal of Computer-Mediated Communication* 13(1): 210–30.

Bryant J and Miron D (2004) Theory and research in mass communication. *Journal of Communication* 54(4): 662–704.

Callcott JG (1863) *The First Twitter of Spring*. Part song, written by WS Passmore. London: Foster & King.

Dent JD (1795) *The Telegraph, or, a New Way of Knowing Things: A Comic Piece, as Performed at the Theatre Royal, Covent Garden, with Universal Applause*. London: J. Downes & Co.

Ellison NB, Steinfield C and Lampe C (2007) The benefits of Facebook 'friends': social capital and college students' use of online social network sites. *Journal of Computer-Mediated Communication* 12(4): 1143–68.

Fischer CS (1992) *America Calling: A Social History of the Telephone to 1940*. Berkeley, CA: University of California Press.

Gackenbach J (2007) *Psychology and the Internet: Intrapersonal, Interpersonal, and Transpersonal Implications*, 2nd edn. Amsterdam/Boston: Elsevier/Academic Press.

Gadamer HG, Weinsheimer J and Marshall DG (2004) *Truth and Method*, 2nd edn. London: Continuum.

Gilder G (1994) Life after television, updated. *Forbes ASAP*, 23 February.

Goffman E (1959) *The Presentation of Self in Everyday Life*. Garden City, NY: Doubleday.

Goffman E (1981) *Forms of Talk*. Oxford: Blackwell.

Goffman E (1983) The interaction order: American Sociological Association 1982 Presidential Address. *American Sociological Review* 48(1): 1–17.

Habermas J (1970) Towards a theory of communicative competence. *Inquiry: An Interdisciplinary Journal of Philosophy* 13(1): 360–75.

Hansen DL, Shneiderman B and Smith M (2010) Visualizing threaded conversation networks: mining message boards and email lists for actionable insights. In: An A, Lingras P, Petty S and Huang R (eds) *Active Media Technology*, Vol. 6335. Berlin: Springer.

Hartley J (1999) *Uses of Television*. London: Routledge.

Harvey D (1989) *The Condition of Postmodernity: An Enquiry into the Origins of Cultural Change*. Oxford: Basil Blackwell.

Heidegger M (1977) *The Question Concerning Technology, and Other Essays*, 1st ed. New York: Harper and Row.

Herring SC (2008) Computer-mediated discourse. In: Schiffrin D, Tannen D and Hamilton HE (eds) *The Handbook of Discourse Analysis*. London Blackwell.

Huyssen A (2000) Present pasts: Media, politics, amnesia. *Public Culture* 12(1): 21–38.

Keen A (2010) Reinventing the Luddite: an interview with Andrew Keen. *Futurist* 44(2), 1 March. World Future Society.

Kierkegaard S and Dru A (1962) *The Present Age and Of the Difference between a Genius and an Apostle*. Dru A (Transl. and introduction). London: Collins.

Knorr Cetina K (2009) The synthetic situation: interactionism for a global world. *Symbolic Interaction* 32(1): 61–87.

Kwak H, Lee C, Park H and Moon S (2010) What is Twitter, a social network or a news media? *Proceedings of the 19th International Conference on World Wide Web*. Raleigh, NC: ACM.

Li Q (2006) Cyberbullying in schools. *School Psychology International* 27(2): 157–70.

Licoppe C (2004) 'Connected' presence: the emergence of a new repertoire for managing social relationships in a changing communication technoscape. *Environment and Planning D: Society and Space* 22(1): 135–56.

Livingstone S (2008) Taking risky opportunities in youthful content creation: teenagers' use of social networking sites for intimacy, privacy and self-expression. *New Media & Society* 10(3): 393–411.

Murdock G (1993) Communications and the constitution of modernity. *Media, Culture & Society* 15(4): 521–39.

Murthy D (2010) Muslim punks online: a diasporic Pakistani music subculture on the internet. *South Asian Popular Culture* 8(2): 181–94.

Murthy D (2011) Twitter: Microphone for the masses? *Media, Culture & Society* 33(5): 779–89.

Nosko A, Wood E and Molema S (2010) All about me: disclosure in online social networking profiles: the case of Facebook. *Computers in Human Behavior* 26(3): 406–18.

Putnam RD (2000) *Bowling Alone: The Collapse and Revival of American Community.* New York: Simon & Schuster.

Rabinow P (2008) *Marking Time: On the Anthropology of the Contemporary.* Princeton, NJ: Princeton University Press.

Rettie R (2009) Mobile phone communication: extending Goffman to mediated interaction. *Sociology* 43(3): 421–38.

Riva G and Galimberti C (1998) Computer-mediated communication: identity and social interaction in an electronic environment. *Genetic, Social and General Psychology Monographs* 124: 434–64.

Rosenthal A (2008) Gerald M. Phillips as electronic tribal chief: socioforming cyberspace. In: Adams T and Smith SA (eds) *Electronic Tribes: The Virtual Worlds of Geeks, Gamers, Shamans, and Scammers*, 1st ed. Austin, TX: University of Texas Press.

Shirky C (2010) *Cognitive Surplus: Creativity and Generosity in a Connected Age.* New York: Penguin Press.

Spitzberg BH (2006) Preliminary development of a model and measure of computer-mediated communication (CMC) competence. *Journal of Computer-Mediated Communication* 11(2): 629–66.

The Times (1796) Yesterday a TELEGRAPH was erected over the Admiralty. Issue 3504.

The Times (1900) The Post Office (Letters to the Editor). Issue 36250.

Therborn G (2000) At the birth of second century sociology: times of reflexivity, spaces of identity, and nodes of knowledge. *British Journal of Sociology* 51(1): 37–57.

Tucker P (2009) The dawn of the postliterate age. *Futurist* 43(6): 41–5.

Turner G (2010) *Ordinary People and the Media: The Demotic Turn.* London: Sage.

Waldman D (1977) Critical theory and film: Adorno and 'The Culture Industry' revisited. *New German Critique* (12): 39–60.

Walther JB (1996) Computer-mediated communication. *Communication Research* 23(1): 3–43.

Williams R (1974) *Television: Technology and Cultural Form.* London: Fontana.

Dr. Jean Twenge and I-gen

Dr. Jean Twenge was one of the first American academics to rigorously study the potential effects of social media on Americans, particularly on young Americans. What she found is that using over 90 minutes of social media a day is correlated with all sorts of negative social outcomes. These included but were not limited to increased anxiety, increased rates of depression, increased rates of suicide and suicide attempts, being more likely to feel lonely, being more likely to feel left out, having negative self-worth, going out less, sleeping less, and doing worse in school. Since she wrote her book *I-Gen*, several studies have been done that suggest that there is not just a correlation between all the aforementioned negative social outcomes, but a significant level of causation.

Additional Resources:

https://www.youtube.com/watch?v=UA8kZZS_bzc
https://www.youtube.com/watch?v=MA8q88nEEwM&t=417s

SUMMARY

As a function of technology, media consumption is changing rapidly. Media consumption is both increasing exponentially and becoming more digital and mobile. Growing up in an increasingly digital world is going to have many effects on the lives of individuals and social life more broadly, some of which we have a good idea about, some which we are just beginning to understand, and some effects that require further study. And the increasing omnipresence of media and surge in media consumption will likely have similarly dramatic effects on society. Particularly, the increasing ubiquity of social media is having seemingly large effects on society as a whole, and on the individuals who use it. But it is very important to note just how much our social worlds are changing in relation to changes in media and technology.

Image Credits

Fig. 7.1: Source: https://heidicohen.com/us-daily-media-consumption/.
Fig. 7.2: Source: https://www.forbes.com/sites/steveolenski/2013/09/06/social-media-usage-up-800-for-us-online-adults-in-just-8-years/#95303bc42375.
Fig. 7.3: Source: https://www.statista.com/chart/15720/frequency-of-teenagers-social-media-use/.

Violence

WHAT DO WE KNOW AND THINK ABOUT VIOLENCE?

AT LEAST ON the surface the topic of violence seems less controversial than most. Very few people or public figures are overtly pro violence. Most people are against most forms of violence most of the time. There is also a threshold for violence if one wishes to maintain an ordered society, and on the extreme end a sustainable population. For instance, a society with a higher murder rate than birth rate is mathematically unsustainable over time.

What is and is not considered violent, what is and is not considered normative about violence, cultural representations of violence, and what types of violence are accepted or encouraged, are all culturally relative and can vary greatly from society to society.

TYPES OF VIOLENCE

- **Social violence** (generic term): Violence that can be boiled down to historical and social reasons: wars, riots, protests, gangs, etc. Excludes most interpersonal sociopathic and mental health related violence.
- **Symbolic violence**: Symbolic violence is the often unnoticed and mostly subconscious domination that everyday social habits maintain over the conscious subject (e.g., a tie and nice suit signal us to listen when that person talks as opposed to a person with holes in their jacket signals us to dismiss what is being said).
- **Structural violence**: A form of violence where some social structure or social institution purportedly harms people by preventing them from meeting their basic needs; this violence is institutionalized and often considered legitimate (e.g., police brutality against blacks).
- **Cultural violence**: Refers to aspects of culture that can be used to justify or legitimize direct or structural violence such as religion, ideology, or culture.
- **State violence**: Violence on behalf of a nation-state.
- **Interpersonal violence**: Violence between citizen actors.

CAUSES OF SOCIAL VIOLENCE

- Poverty and inequality
  - Both matter; one generally matters more—which one?
- Discrimination or perceived unfair treatment
- Changes in/contesting of borders or territory
- Migration
  - Especially forced migration
- Political differences
  - Revolutions and coups
  - Political beliefs
  - Dictators, authoritarians and others use strategically
- Religious differences
  - Religious beliefs
- Self-interest/advancement (e.g., criminal enterprises (a cause in SI perspectives, a symptom in others)).
- Other geopolitical grievances between nation states (war).

Pierre Bourdieu

- A French sociologist.
- Studied social positioning, capital, power, and the way in which the three interact.
- Saw violence as a form of power used mostly to dominate but occasionally to make change.
- Defined several types of violence, including social, symbolic, structural, and cultural.
- Symbolic power: Mostly tacit modes and forms of cultural/social domination occurring in everyday social habits.
  - Symbolic violence is the exercise of symbolic power.

TYPES OF VIOLENCE

- **Domestic violence:** Violence within the home, including spousal and child abuse.
- **Terrorism:** The unlawful use of force or violence against people or property to intimidate or coerce governments or people to take some sort of political action.
- **Riots:** A spontaneous outburst of violence that occurs usually because of perceived slights.[1]

---

1   GHSRArchives, "North America - US - Rodney King Riots - 19920430 - Los Angeles—Truck Driver on the Ground," August 18, 2011, https://www.youtube.com/watch?v=mZ1gwK0QBio.

FIGURE 8.1   U.S. Marines direct a concentration of fire at the enemy, Vietnam, May 8, 1968.

- **Criminal**: Unlawful violence committed in an attempt to gain resources; can be for either personal gain or to forward the goals of larger-scale criminal networks.
- **Rape**: Sexual actions against a person's will.
- **Capital punishment**: State-sanctioned killing of law certain violators (considered legitimate).
- **War**: A political instrument of states; conflict between two or more identified combatants (considered legitimate).
- **Suicide**: Purposeful, self-inflicted death.

CULTURE OF VIOLENCE

In large, complex, and pluralistic societies, subgroups learn and develop specialized norms and values through differential associations and organizations that emphasize and justify the use of physical force above and beyond that which is regarded as "normative" of the culture as a whole. Family and street violence, for example, are often viewed as the products of an exaggerated ethos of masculinity or of machismo, characteristic of "lower-class" society.

   Violent scripts: Culturally socialized actions/responses that tend to escalate interpersonal strife toward violence.

CRITICAL THINKING: Name one example of a violent script.

Durkheim and Suicide

- *Suicide*: A book written by Durkheim.
- Explores the relationship between social facts (facts, concepts, expectations that come not from individual responses and preferences but from the social community that socializes each of its members). **In other words, even the most personal of decisions is social.**
  - Suicide is largely a function of social circumstances, social relations, and social structures.
- Four types of suicide
  - **Anomic:** Related to moral confusion and lack of direction; a perceived inability to meet goals established by society (social facts) through the means that one has available to them.
  - **Fatalistic:** Sense of hopelessness (e.g., prison).
  - **Egoistic:** Not enough social integration (the degree to which one is intermeshed with society and individuals).
  - **Altruistic:** Too engrained in a group or movement.

Are We Becoming More Violent?

Though it may seem otherwise from watching YouTube or cable news, violent crime has been curbed significantly since the 1990s. In some respects, crime is at or near an all-time recorded low. The following chart and article both attest to this fact.

Number of victims per 1,000 population aged 12 or older

Source: Bureau of Justice Statistics

GALLUP

FIGURE 8.2 **Total violent crime in the United States, 1973–2009.**

Reading 8.1.

Less violence in 2014
Crime Declines, Again

by Jesse Walker

In September the FBI released its annual report on crime in America, bringing the publicly available data up to the end of 2014. While elements of both the left and the right speak as though we're in the midst of a crime surge—the former in discussions of gun control, the latter in discussions of criminal justice reform—the FBI paints a less fearful picture.

Overall, the agency found that the violent crime rate declined in 2014—by 1 percent from the previous year, by 9.6 percent from five years before, and by 22.1 percent from 10 years before. The rate for murder and non-negligent manslaughter was 1.2 percent lower than one year earlier, 6.1 percent lower than five years earlier, and 20.8 percent lower than 10 years earlier.

Robbery, burglary, larceny, and car theft all continued to drop as well. Motor vehicle thefts showed the biggest reduction from a decade before, with the rate sliding 48.1 percent.

The FBI's talliers recently revised their definition of rape, making cross-year comparisons difficult. But using the older definition, the crime increased slightly, by 1.6 percent, from 2013 to 20i4.The rate was still 17.2 percent lower than 10 years earlier. The one other major crime rate that increased since 2013 was aggravated assault, which went up 1.2 percent. But that too saw a dramatic decrease in the last decade, going down 20.1 percent

A school district in Okemah, Oklahoma, says it is investigating why a teacher told a 4-year-old student not to write with his left hand and then sent his mother, Alisha Sands, an article saying that in many cultures, left-handedness Is considered "unlucky, inauspicious and frankly evil."

Officials at Winslow Township School 4 in New Jersey suspended an 8 year-old girl for violating the dress code. The girl wore a kelly green shirt to school, and the rules allow only white, navy blue, or *dark* green shirts.

New Mexico's La Cueva High School has prohibited cheerleaders from wearing their uniforms on campus, saying the outfits are too revealing. The girls are still allowed to wear them at games.

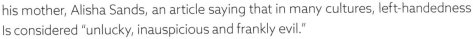

Jesse Walker, "Crime Declines, Again," *Reason*, vol. 47, no. 8, pp. 9-10. Copyright © 2016 by Reason Foundation. Reprinted with permission. Provided by ProQuest LLC. All rights reserved.

The Secret Service disrupted a planned vigil by forcing hundreds of children with cancer and their parents out of Lafayette Square Park in Washington, O.C. The park was barricaded for hours, and families were not allowed to get back in to retrieve their belongings. Parents say agents told them they closed the square because President Obama had left the White House from a nearby exit.

When Emma Gonzalez, 9, reached for her inhaler during a coughing fit at Utah's Columbia Elementary School, her teacher sent her to the principal's office. Though Emma was coughing so hard she vomited, staff confiscated the inhaler because the school had not received official notification she had a prescription for it. They say that policy is for student safety.

A German court has ordered Berlin cat breeder Jacqueline Linke to have her male Sphynx cat neutered, ruling that passing on Willie's hairless genes and lack of whiskers would amount to animal cruelty.

An Egyptian court has sentenced belly dancers Suha Mohammed Aliand Dalia Kamal Youssef to six months in jail each for inciting debauchery through music videos.

New Zealand has banned its first book in 22 years, following a complaint from a conservative group that Ted Dawe's award-winning novel *Into the River* contains sex and drug use.

Garbage men in Hull, England, are refusing to pick up trash unless the cans are pointed in the right direction. They say they could get injured turning the cans around.

Founders Brewing has been forced to change the label on its Breakfast Stout beer, which features a bibbed baby eating something from a bowl. Michigan law bans images of minors on alcoholic beverage labels. Bottles sold in the state will now feature the bowl and a note from the baby.

The student union at the University of East Anglia, a public university in England, ordered a Mexican restaurant to stop handing out sombreros during a student fair, saying this was racist "cultural appropriation." Members of the student union also took sombreros from those who had received them, to keep anyone from being offended.

Charles Oliver
2015 may turn out to be another story. But as of the last year for which we have the data crime was continuing its long decline.

However, America is uniquely violent among rich nations. In the following two charts it can be seen that the United States has significantly higher levels of violence than most similarly wealthy countries, which has held true even with the recent downturn in violence. It can also be seen that one of the drivers of America's high levels of violence are gun homicide and gun suicide rates that can only be considered as outliers.

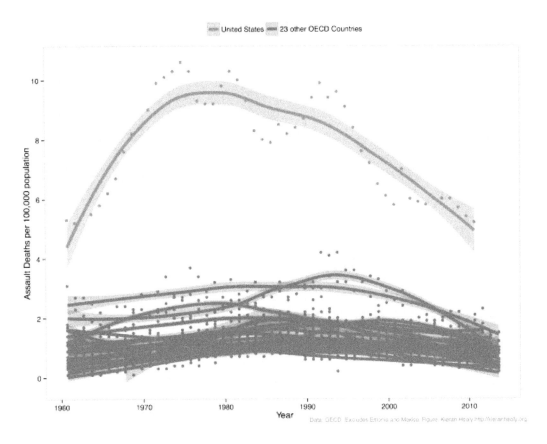

FIGURE 8.3 **Assault deaths over time.**

Country	Firearm Homicide Rate	Non-Firearm Homicide Rate	Total Homicide Rate	Firearm Suicide Rate	Non-Firearm Suicide Rate	Total Suicide Rate	Unintentional Firearm Death Rate	Undetermined Firearm Death Rate	Total Firearm Death Rate
Australia	0.2	0.9	1.1	0.8	10.2	11.0	0.0	0.1	1.0
Austria	0.2	0.4	0.5	2.7	12.4	15.1	0.0	0.1	3.0
Belgium	0.3	0.7	1.1	1.3	17.1	18.4	0.0	0.1	1.8
Canada	0.5	1.0	1.5	1.7	9.9	11.6	0.0	0.0	2.3
Czech Republic	0.1	2.4	2.6	1.4	11.2	12.5	0.1	0.2	1.8
Denmark	0.2	0.6	0.8	1.3	8.8	10.1	0.0	0.0	1.6
Finland	0.3	1.6	1.9	3.3	14.5	17.8	0.0	0.0	3.6
France	0.2	0.4	0.6	2.2	14.3	16.5	0.1	0.3	2.8
Germany	0.1	0.5	0.6	0.9	11.3	12.3	0.0	0.1	1.1
Hungary	0.1	1.4	1.5	0.8	24.1	24.9	0.0	0.0	0.9
Ireland	0.4	0.5	0.8	0.5	10.1	10.7	0.0	0.1	1.0
Italy	0.3	0.4	0.8	0.9	5.7	6.6	0.1	0.0	1.3
Japan	0.0	0.3	0.3	0.0	23.1	23.1	0.0	0.0	0.0
Netherlands	0.2	0.7	0.9	0.2	9.4	9.7	0.0	0.0	0.5
New Zealand	0.2	1.1	1.2	1.0	11.3	12.3	0.0	0.0	1.2
Norway	0.0	0.6	0.7	1.7	9.5	11.2	0.0	0.0	1.8
Portugal	0.5	0.5	1.0	1.1	9.3	10.4	0.0	0.2	1.8
Republic of Korea	0.0	1.3	1.3	0.0	31.5	31.5	0.0	0.0	0.0
Slovakia	0.2	1.0	1.2	0.9	10.8	11.7	0.4	0.2	1.8
Spain	0.1	0.6	0.7	0.4	6.4	6.9	0.1	0.0	0.6
Sweden	0.2	0.7	0.9	1.2	11.0	12.2	0.1	0.0	1.5
United Kingdom	0.0	0.3	0.3	0.2	6.6	6.8	0.0	0.0	0.2
United States	3.6	1.7	5.3	6.3	6.1	12.4	0.2	0.1	10.2

FIGURE 8.4 **Total death rates per 100,000 population by non-US high-income countries, 2010.**

Prevalence of Guns and American Gun Culture

There are nearly 400 million guns in America, which is about half of the privately owned guns in the world. As with a number of other social issues, this makes the United States an outlier among the rest of the world. Part of this is due to gun laws, but equally as impactful is the gun culture that was developed and has been strongly maintained in the United States. The following book excerpt touches on this American gun culture.

Reading 8.2.

Preface

by Jimmy D. Taylor

From previous books and research efforts, we know that there are a lot of guns in the United States of America. Guns are all around us. Not only is there a very real physical presence of guns in the United States, their symbolism permeates American culture in other ways, from heated political debates and landmark court cases to song references, television shows, popular movies, and even t-shirt slogans. But what do all of these guns really mean to their owners? This is an important area of gun ownership that has been overlooked by researchers and policy makers alike. This book explores the symbolic meaning of guns, and the ways in which the meaning of gun ownership, as well as the symbolic meaning imbued in individual guns influences aspects of social interaction.

This ethnographic research effort applies thick, descriptive methods of observation and grounded theoretical techniques to this largely unexplored aspect of U.S. gun culture. A total of 52 interviews of varying length were conducted with a range of gun owners in venues that included gun collectors' homes, shooting events, and public gun shows in the Midwest. Subjects were asked to share the stories of their guns, and explore the value and meaning of separate guns in their collections.

Some interesting findings are revealed, which are not limited to the following: 1) Guns, as an aspect of culture, or product of social interaction, are rich with symbolic values; 2) For many gun owners, the value placed on guns is far more emotional in nature than monetary; 3) The value assigned to guns by their owners appears to influence the way in which gun owners interact with their guns as well as their social audience; 4) Gun owners recognize a unique type of stigma associated with these cultural products, and respond through a complex series of stigma management techniques; and 5) U.S. gun culture involves a series of deference and demeanor-filled rituals; rituals pertaining to being the gun owner, the gun user, and possibly even the gun as an object of near-worship.

CONCLUSION

There are several social precursors that correlate with violence. At the level of the nation-state these include contestation of borders or resources, economic turmoil, and the persecution of ethnic, racial, or religious minorities. At the level of the individual, social aspects of one's life, such as experiencing violence, abuse, or trauma, drug and alcohol addiction, and anomic stress, are correlated with increased levels of violence.

Jimmy D. Taylor, "Preface," *American Gun Culture: Collectors, Shows, and the Story of the Gun.* Copyright © 2009 by LFB Scholarly Publishing. Reprinted with permission.

More resources:

Most Armed Man in America:
https://www.youtube.com/watch?v=b0vpz-pjKVsw

As discussed by Dr. Richard Wilkinson, "[V]iolence is reliably higher in more unequal societies."[2] This is partially due to cultural factors brought about by the way in which status operates as a marker of importance and respect. It is also related to the wide dissemination of cultural goals and the anomic stress systematically experienced by people lower in the social hierarchy as they have less structural and social access to legitimate pathways.

Although there are several nations with significantly more violence, America is uniquely violent among rich nations. Part of this relates to America being one of the most unequal rich countries, but there are cultural and structural issues that also contribute to the United States being such an outlier among rich countries.

Image Credits

Fig. 8.1: Source: https://commons.wikimedia.org/wiki/File:U.S._Marines_in_Operation_Allen_Brook_(Vietnam_War)_001_(colorized).jpg.
Fig. 8.2: Source: https://news.gallup.com/poll/150464/americans-believe-crime-worsening.aspx.
Fig. 8.3: Source: https://kieranhealy.org/blog/archives/2017/10/02/assault-deaths-to-2015/.
Fig. 8.4: Source: https://www.amjmed.com/article/S0002-9343(15)01030-X/fulltext.

---

2   Renegade Inc., "Richard Wilkinson - on Origins of Social Violence," June 19, 2011, https://www.youtube.com/watch?v=yYXOTpgWqPE.

CHAPTER 9

Drugs and Substance Abuse

DEFINITIONS

HERE ARE SOME important definitions to understand when studying drugs and society:

- **Illicit drugs**: Drugs that are illegal to possess or sell: cocaine, marijuana, heroin, ecstasy, and so on; street drugs.
- **Schedule 1**: The Controlled Substances Act for the United States. Required findings for drugs to be placed in this schedule include the following:
  - The drug or other substance has a high potential for abuse.
  - The drug or other substance has no currently accepted medical use in the United States.
  - There is a lack of accepted safety for use of the drug or other substance under medical supervision.
- Except as specifically authorized, it is illegal for any person
  - to manufacture, distribute, or dispense, or possess with intent to manufacture, distribute, or dispense, a controlled substance; or
  - to create, distribute, or dispense, or possess with intent to distribute or dispense, a counterfeit substance.
- **Drug abuse**: The use of any drug or medication for reasons other than its intended use, which can lead to impairment or distress.
- **Drug addiction**: Physical or psychological dependence on a substance.
- **Decriminalization**: A general policy position that while it should not be legal to sell or distribute drugs things like possession and personal use should not be seen as criminal offenses.
- **Legalization**: Often used interchangeably with decriminalization, but also pushes for the regulation and legal distribution of substances. Attitudes about both decriminalization and legalization are changing rapidly.

Do you think the use of marijuana should be made legal, or not? (%)

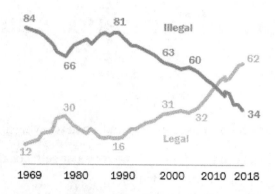

% who say marijuana should be made legal

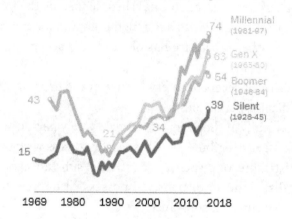

Note: Don't know responses not shown.
Source: Survey of U.S. adults conducted Sept. 18-24, 2018.

PEW RESEARCH CENTER

FIGURE 9.1.   **US public opinion on legalizing marijuana, 1969–2018.**

REASONS FOR USE

CRITICAL THINKING: What are some reasons people use drugs and alcohol?

- **Peer pressure:** In young cohorts especially, using is normative.
- **Social/cultural pressure:** The society or culture at large says that using (at least reasonably) is good.

- **Media portrayals**: Using is cool.
- **Use value**: People like to get drunk and high. Alcohol was historically one of few beverages safe to drink.
- Unemployment, financial, or other forms of stress:
  - **Acculturative stress**: Experienced by immigrants faced with adapting to a new culture.
  - **SES stress**: Experienced by ethnic minorities who feel disempowered.
  - **Minority stress**: The tension minorities encounter because of racism.
- **Increasing reflexivity**: An awareness of one's body and self. Peer pressure and media portrayals often lead to reflexive responses.
- **Inequality**: Reliably higher in more unequal countries.
- **Social cohesion**: Use designed to bind groups together (e.g., fraternity hazing).

Index of use of: opiates, cocaine, cannabis, ecstasy, amphetamines

Source: Wilkinson & Pickett, The Spirit Level (2009)

www.equalitytrust.org.uk   Equality Trust

FIGURE 9.2   **Drug use is more common in more unequal countries.**

SOCIOLOGICAL THEORIES ABOUT DRUG USE

The following sociological theories are often used to explain or predict drug usage. They are by no means perfect, nor are they the only available theories, but they are among the most commonly cited.

Strain Theory

- **Role strain**: The stress or strain experienced by an individual when incompatible behavior, expectations, or obligations are associated with a single social role.
- Very similar to anomie by Durkheim but is conceptualized as operating within spheres of society rather than simply as a function of a lack of resources. Brings in almost the entire population under the scope of analysis; relatively minimizes broad social goals.

Differential Association

An early symbolic interactionist theory, differential association was developed to apply to crime but was incidentally used to explain drug use and other deviant behavior.

1. Deviant behavior is <u>learned</u>
   a. in <u>interaction</u> with others in a process of communication;
   b. within intimate personal <u>groups</u>.
2. The learning includes (a) <u>techniques</u> and (b) <u>motives</u>, drives, rationalizations, and attitudes.
3. The specific direction is learned from <u>definitions</u> of the legal code as favorable and unfavorable.
4. One becomes deviant because of an <u>excess</u> of definitions favorable to law violation over definitions that are unfavorable.
5. <u>Differential associations</u> vary in frequency, duration, priority, and intensity.
6. This learning process involves the same mechanisms as any <u>other learning process</u>.
7. Criminal behavior is not explained by <u>general needs</u> ($) and values, since non-criminal behavior expresses the same needs and values.

In short, DA mainly uses culture and subcultures to explain deviance and has slowly come to be replaced by social disorganization theory.

Reading 9.1.

A Theory of Differential Association

by Edwin H. Sutherland and Donald R. Cressey

Before Sutherland developed his theory, crime was usually explained in terms of multiple factors—like social class, broken homes, age, race, urban or rural location, and mental disorder. Sutherland developed his theory of differential association in an effort to explain why these various factors were related to crime. In doing so, he hoped to organize and integrate the research on crime up to that point, as well as to guide future research.

Sutherland's theory is stated in the form of nine propositions. He argues that criminal behavior is learned by interacting with others, especially intimate others. Criminals learn both the techniques of committing crime and the definitions favorable to crime from these others. The sixth proposition, which forms the heart of the theory, states that "a person becomes delinquent because of an excess of definitions favorable to law violation over definitions unfavorable to violation of law." According to Sutherland, factors such as social class, race, and broken homes influence crime because they affect the likelihood that individuals will associate with others who present definitions favorable to crime.

Sutherland's theory has had a tremendous influence on crime research and it remains one of the dominant theories of crime. Studies on the causes of crime routinely attempt to determine whether individuals are associating with delinquent or criminal others. Although one can learn definitions favorable to crime from law-abiding individuals, one is most likely to learn such definitions from delinquent friends or criminal family members. These studies typically find that association with delinquent others is the best predictor of crime, and that these delinquent others partly influence crime by leading the individual to adopt beliefs conducive to crime (see Agnew, 2000; Akers, 1998; Akers and Sellers, 2004; Warr, 2001 for summaries of such studies).

Sutherland's theory has also inspired much additional theorizing in criminology. Theorists have attempted to better describe the nature of those definitions favorable to violation of the law. They have attempted to better describe the processes by which we learn criminal behavior from others. And they have drawn on Sutherland in an effort to explain group differences in crime rates. Sutherland's theory of differential association, then, is one of the enduring classics in criminology (for excellent discussions of the current state of differential association theory, see Matsueda, 1988, and Warr, 2001).

Edwin H. Sutherland and Donald R. Cressey, "A Theory of Differential Association," *Principles of Criminology*. Copyright © 1960 by Taylor & Francis Group. Reprinted with permission.

The following statement refers to the process by which a particular person comes to engage in criminal behavior:

1   *Criminal behavior is learned* Negatively, this means that criminal behavior is not inherited, as such; also, the person who is not already trained in crime does not invent criminal behavior, just as a person does not make mechanical inventions unless he has had training in mechanics.

2   *Criminal behavior is learned in interaction with other persons in a process of communication.* This communication is verbal in many respects but includes also "the communication of gestures."

3   *The principal part of the learning of criminal behavior occurs within intimate personal groups.* Negatively, this means that the impersonal agencies of communication, such as movies and newspapers, play a relatively unimportant part in the genesis of criminal behavior.

4   *When criminal behavior is learned, the learning includes (a) techniques of commit ting the crime, which are sometimes very complicated, sometimes very simple; (b) the specific direction of motives, drives, rationalizations, and attitudes.*

5   *The specific direction of motives and drives is learned from definitions of the legal codes as favorable or unfavorable.* In some societies an individual is surrounded by persons who invariably define the legal codes as rules to be observed, while in others he is surrounded by persons whose definitions are favorable to the violation of the legal codes. In our American society these definitions are almost always mixed, with the consequence that we have culture conflict in relation to the legal codes.

6   *A person becomes delinquent because of an excess of definitions favorable to violation of law over definitions unfavorable to violation of law.* This is the principle of differential association. It refers to both criminal and anti-criminal associations and has to do with counteracting forces. When persons become criminal, they do so because of contacts with criminal patterns and also because of isolation from anti-criminal patterns. Any person inevitably assimilates the surrounding culture unless other patterns are in conflict; a Southerner does not pronounce "r" because other Southerners do not pronounce "r." Negatively, this proposition of differential association means that associations which are neutral so far as crime is concerned have little or no effect on the genesis of criminal behavior. Much of the experience of a person is neutral in this sense, e.g., learning to brush one's teeth. This behavior has no negative or positive effect on criminal behavior except as it may be related to associations which are concerned with the legal codes. This neutral behavior is important especially as an occupier of the time of a child so that he is not in contact with criminal behavior during the time he is so engaged in the neutral behavior.

7   *Differential associations may vary in frequency, duration, priority, and intensity.* This means that associations with criminal behavior and also associations with anti-criminal behavior vary in those respects. "Frequency" and "duration" as modalities of associations are obvious and need no explanation. "Priority" is assumed to be important in the sense that lawful behavior developed in early childhood may persist

throughout life, and also that delinquent behavior developed in early childhood may persist throughout life. This tendency, however, has not been adequately demonstrated, and priority seems to be important principally through its selective influence. "Intensity" is not precisely defined but it has to do with such things as the prestige of the source of a criminal or anti-criminal pattern and with emotional reactions related to the associations. In a precise description of the criminal behavior of a person these modalities would be stated in quantitative form and a mathematical ratio be reached. A formula in this sense has not been developed, and the development of such a formula would be extremely difficult.

8   *The process of learning criminal behavior by association with criminal and anti-criminal patterns involves all of the mechanisms that are involved in any other learning.* Negatively, this means that the learning of criminal behavior is not restricted to the process of imitation. A person who is seduced, for instance, learns criminal behavior by association, but this process would not ordinarily be described as imitation.

9   *While criminal behavior is an expression of general needs and values, it is not explained by those general needs and values since non-criminal behavior is an expression of the same needs and values.* Thieves generally steal in order to secure money, but likewise honest laborers work in order to secure money. The attempts by many scholars to explain criminal behavior by general drives and values, such as the happiness principle, striving for social status, the money motive, or frustration, have been and must continue to be futile since they explain lawful behavior as completely as they explain criminal behavior. They are similar to respiration, which is necessary for any behavior but which does not differentiate criminal from non-criminal behavior.

It is not necessary, at this level of explanation, to explain why a person has the associations which he has; this certainly involves a complex of many things. In an area where the delinquency rate is high, a boy who is sociable, gregarious, active, and athletic is very likely to come in contact with the other boys in the neighborhood, learn delinquent behavior from them, and become a gangster; in the same neighborhood the psychopathic boy who is isolated, introverted, and inert may remain at home, not become acquainted with the other boys in the neighborhood, and not become delinquent. In another situation, the sociable, athletic, aggressive boy may become a member of a scout troop and not become involved in delinquent behavior. The person's associations are determined in a general context of social organization. A child is ordinarily reared in a family; the place of residence of the family is determined largely by family income; and the delinquency rate is in many respects related to the rental value of the houses. Many other aspects of social organization affect the kinds of associations a person has.

The preceding explanation of criminal behavior purports to explain the criminal and non-criminal behavior of individual persons. As indicated earlier, it is possible to state sociological theories of criminal behavior which explain the criminality of a community, nation, or other group. The problem, when thus stated, is to account for variations in crime rates and involves a comparison of the crime rates of various groups or the crime rates of a particular group at different times. The explanation of a crime rate must be consistent with the explanation of the criminal behavior of the person, since the crime rate is a summary statement of the number of persons in the group who commit crimes and the frequency with which they commit crimes. One of the best explanations of crime rates from this point of view is that a high crime rate is due to social disorganization. The term "social disorganization" is not entirely satisfactory and it seems preferable to substitute for it the term "differential social organization." The postulate on which this theory is based, regardless of the name, is that crime is rooted in the social organization and is an expression of that social organization. A group may be organized for criminal behavior or organized against criminal behavior. Most communities are organized both for criminal and anti-criminal behavior and in that sense the crime rate is an expression of the differential group organization. Differential group organization as an explanation of variations in crime rates is consistent with the differential association theory of the processes by which persons become criminals.

DISCUSSION QUESTIONS

1   What does Sutherland mean by "definitions favorable to violation of law"? Give examples of such definitions.

2   According to Sutherland, our associations do not carry equal weight; some are more influential than others. What types of associations carry the greatest weight in influencing our behavior?

3   Strain theorists [...] argue that frustration is a major cause of crime. How would Sutherland respond to this argument?

4   What policy recommendations might Sutherland have made for controlling crime?

REFERENCES

Agnew, Robert. 2000. "Sources of Criminality: Strain and Subcultural Theories." In Joseph F. Sheley (ed.), *Criminology: A Contemporary Handbook,* 3rd edition, pp. 349–371. Belmont, CA: Wadsworth.

Akers, Ronald L. 1998. *Social Learning and Social Structure: A General Theory of Crime and Deviance.* Boston: Northeastern University Press.

Akers, Ronald L. and Christine S. Sellers. 2004. *Criminological Theories: Introduction and Evaluation,* 4th edition. Los Angeles: Roxbury Publishing.

Matsueda, Ross L. 1988. "The Current State of Differential Association Theory." *Crime and Delinquency* 34: 277–306.

Warr, Mark. 2001. "The Social Origins of Crime: Edwin Sutherland and the Theory of Differential Association." In Raymond Paternoster and Ronet Bachman (ed.), *Explaining Criminals and Crime,* pp. 182–191. Los Angeles: Roxbury Publishing.

Frequency

The United States is among the biggest consumers of illicit drugs in the world. Americans lead the world in the consumption of several substances, including methadone and opioids. The percentage of Americans taking prescription drugs has also increased in the recent past.

More resources:

U.S. Leads the World in Illegal Drug Use: https://www.cbsnews.com/news/us-leads-the-world-in-illegal-drug-use/

Reading 9.2.

PRESCRIPTION DRUG USE IN THE PAST 30 DAYS, BY SEX, RACE AND HISPANIC ORIGIN, AND AGE: UNITED STATES, SELECTED YEARS 1988-1994 THROUGH 2011-2014

Excel version (with more data years and standard errors when available): https://www.cdc.gov/nchs/hus/contents2017.htm#079. [Data are based on a sample of the civilian noninstitutionalized population]

SEX, RACE AND HISPANIC ORIGIN,[1] AND AGE	AT LEAST ONE PRESCRIPTION DRUG IN PAST 30 DAYS				THREE OR MORE PRESCRIPTION DRUGS IN PAST 30 DAYS				FIVE OR MORE PRESCRIPTION DRUGS IN PAST 30 DAYS			
	1988-1994	1999-2002	2007-2010	2011-2014	1988-1994	1999-2002	2007-2010	2011-2014	1988-1994	1999-2002	2007-2010	2011-2014
All ages, age-adjusted[2]	**Percent of population**											
Both sexes[3]	39.1	45.2	47.5	46.9	11.8	17.8	20.8	21.5	4.0	7.5	10.1	10.9
Male	32.7	39.8	42.8	42.6	9.4	14.8	19.1	19.7	2.9	6.1	9.2	9.7
Female	45.0	50.3	52.0	51.2	13.9	20.4	22.5	23.2	4.9	8.7	11.0	12.0
Not Hispanic or Latino:												
White only	41.1	48.7	52.8	51.9	12.4	18.9	22.4	23.1	4.2	7.8	10.7	11.5
White only, male	34.2	43.0	47.5	46.8	9.9	15.9	20.6	21.1	3.1	6.3	9.8	10.2
White only, female	47.6	54.3	57.9	57.0	14.6	21.8	24.3	25.1	5.1	9.2	11.6	12.8
Black or African American only	36.9	40.1	42.3	44.2	12.6	16.5	20.7	22.5	3.8	7.7	10.8	12.1
Black or African American only, male	31.1	35.4	36.7	38.3	10.2	14.5	17.7	19.4	2.9	6.4	9.1	10.1

(Continued)

Source: https://www.cdc.gov/nchs/data/hus/2017/079.pdf.

PRESCRIPTION DRUG USE IN THE PAST 30 DAYS, BY SEX, RACE AND HISPANIC ORIGIN, AND AGE: UNITED STATES, SELECTED YEARS 1988–1994 THROUGH 2011–2014 (CONT'D)

Excel version (with more data years and standard errors when available): https://www.cdc.gov/nchs/hus/contents2017.htm#079. [Data are based on a sample of the civilian noninstitutionalized population]

SEX, RACE AND HISPANIC ORIGIN,[1] AND AGE	AT LEAST ONE PRESCRIPTION DRUG IN PAST 30 DAYS				THREE OR MORE PRESCRIPTION DRUGS IN PAST 30 DAYS				FIVE OR MORE PRESCRIPTION DRUGS IN PAST 30 DAYS			
	1988–1994	1999–2002	2007–2010	2011–2014	1988–1994	1999–2002	2007–2010	2011–2014	1988–1994	1999–2002	2007–2010	2011–2014
Black or African American only, female	41.4	43.8	46.8	49.0	14.3	18.1	22.9	24.9	4.5	8.7	12.0	13.7
Asian only	- - -	- - -	- - -	34.3	- - -	- - -	- - -	14.3	- - -	- - -	- - -	6.2
Asian only, male	- - -	- - -	- - -	31.9	- - -	- - -	- - -	14.1	- - -	- - -	- - -	6.2
Asian only, female	- - -	- - -	- - -	36.3	- - -	- - -	- - -	14.6	- - -	- - -	- - -	6.1
Hispanic or Latino	- - -	- - -	35.2	35.7	- - -	- - -	15.7	16.0	- - -	- - -	8.4	8.4
Hispanic or Latino, male	- - -	- - -	31.7	32.1	- - -	- - -	14.0	15.0	- - -	- - -	7.3	7.9
Hispanic or Latina, female	- - -	- - -	38.8	39.2	- - -	- - -	17.4	17.1	- - -	- - -	9.5	8.8
Mexican origin	31.7	31.7	33.9	34.2	9.0	11.2	15.0	15.9	2.9	4.4	7.9	8.7
Mexican origin, male	27.5	25.8	31.0	31.8	7.0	9.5	13.4	14.9	2.0	3.5	7.2	8.2
Mexican origin, female	36.0	37.8	37.0	36.9	11.0	12.8	16.6	17.0	3.7	5.2	8.7	9.2
All ages, crude												
Both sexes[3]	37.8	45.0	48.5	48.9	11.0	17.6	21.7	23.1	3.6	7.4	10.6	11.9
Male	30.6	38.6	43.0	43.7	8.3	13.9	19.0	20.4	2.5	5.6	9.1	10.0
Female	44.6	51.1	53.8	53.9	13.6	21.1	24.2	25.8	4.7	9.1	12.1	13.6
Not Hispanic or Latino:												
White only	41.4	50.7	56.2	57.0	12.5	20.6	25.8	27.7	4.2	8.7	12.6	14.3
White only, male	33.5	43.8	50.3	51.4	9.5	16.5	22.9	24.6	2.9	6.6	11.0	12.1
White only, female	48.9	57.5	61.8	62.4	15.4	24.5	28.6	30.7	5.4	10.8	14.2	16.4
Black or African American only	31.2	36.0	40.2	42.8	9.2	13.5	18.6	21.1	2.6	6.2	9.4	11.2

Black or African American only, male	25.5	30.7	33.9	36.3	7.0	10.9	15.0	17.5	1.8	4.8	7.5	8.9
Black or African American only, female	36.2	40.6	45.7	48.5	11.1	15.7	21.7	24.2	3.3	7.4	11.1	13.1
Asian only	- - -	- - -	- - -	34.0	- - -	- - -	- - -	13.6	- - -	- - -	- - -	5.7
Asian only, male	- - -	- - -	- - -	30.5	- - -	- - -	- - -	12.6	- - -	- - -	- - -	5.5
Asian only, female	- - -	- - -	- - -	37.1	- - -	- - -	- - -	14.5	- - -	- - -	- - -	6.0
Hispanic or Latino	- - -	- - -	28.6	29.5	- - -	- - -	10.3	10.9	- - -	- - -	5.0	5.3
Hispanic or Latino, male	- - -	- - -	24.9	25.4	- - -	- - -	8.4	9.3	- - -	- - -	3.8	4.6
Hispanic or Latina, female	- - -	- - -	32.5	33.5	- - -	- - -	12.3	12.6	- - -	- - -	6.2	6.0
Mexican origin	24.0	23.6	26.4	27.0	4.8	6.1	9.0	9.8	1.4	2.1	4.1	4.9
Mexican origin, male	20.1	18.8	23.7	24.9	3.4	4.8	7.6	9.0	0.9	1.6	3.4	4.6
Mexican origin, female	28.1	28.9	29.4	29.3	6.4	7.5	10.6	10.8	1.9	2.7	4.9	5.4
Both sexes	**Percent of population**											
Under 18 years	20.5	23.8	24.0	21.5	2.4	4.1	3.8	3.9 *	*	0.8	0.8	0.8
18–44 years	31.3	35.9	38.7	37.1	5.7	8.4	9.7	10.1	1.2	2.3	3.1	3.9
45–64 years	54.8	64.1	66.2	69.0	20.0	30.8	34.4	36.4	7.4	13.3	16.8	18.3
65 years and over	73.6	84.7	89.7	90.6	35.3	51.8	66.6	66.8	13.8	27.1	39.7	40.7
Male												
Under 18 years	20.4	25.7	24.5	21.1	2.6	4.3	4.4	4.3	*	*	0.8	0.9
18–44 years	21.5	27.1	29.5	28.8	3.6	6.7	7.1	7.5	*0.8	1.7	2.1	3.0
45–64 years	47.2	55.6	61.3	65.6	15.1	23.6	30.4	33.0	4.8	9.5	14.4	15.7
65 years and over	67.2	80.1	88.8	88.7	31.3	46.3	66.8	65.2	11.3	24.7	39.5	38.4
Female												
Under 18 years	20.6	21.7	23.5	22.0	2.3	3.9	3.1	3.5	*	*0.8	*0.7	*
18–44 years	40.7	44.6	47.6	45.3	7.6	10.2	12.2	12.6	1.7	2.8	4.0	4.8
45–64 years	62.0	72.0	70.8	72.1	24.7	37.5	38.1	39.4	9.7	16.8	19.1	20.7
65 years and over	78.3	88.1	90.4	92.1	38.2	55.9	66.4	68.1	15.6	28.9	39.8	42.6

— Data not available.

* Estimates are considered unreliable. Data preceded by an asterisk have a relative standard error (RSE) of 20%–30%. Data not shown have an RSE greater than 30%.

[1] Persons of Hispanic and Mexican origin may be of any race. Starting with 1999 data, race-specific estimates are tabulated according to the 1997 *Revisions to the Standards for the Classification of Federal Data on Race and Ethnicity* and are not strictly comparable with estimates for earlier years. The non-Hispanic race categories shown in the table conform to the 1997 Standards. Starting with 1999 data, race-specific estimates are for persons who reported only one racial group. Prior to data year 1999, estimates were

tabulated according to the 1977 Standards. Estimates for single-race categories prior to 1999 included persons who reported one race, or if they reported more than one race, identified one race as best representing their race.

See Appendix II, Hispanic origin; Race.

[2] Estimates are age-adjusted to the year 2000 standard population using four age groups: under 18 years, 18–44 years, 45–64 years, and 65 years and over. Age-adjusted estimates in this table may differ from other age-adjusted estimates based on the same data and presented elsewhere if different age groups are used in the adjustment procedure. See Appendix II, Age adjustment.

[3] Includes persons of all races and Hispanic origins, not just those shown separately.

NOTES: See Appendix II, Drug. Standard errors are available in the spreadsheet version of this table. Data for additional years are available. See the Excel spreadsheet on the *Health, United States* website at: https://www.cdc.gov/nchs/hus.htm.

SOURCE: NCHS, National Health and Nutrition Examination Survey. See Appendix I, National Health and Nutrition Examination Survey (NHANES).

DRUG OVERDOSES

The year 2017 marked a record high for drug overdoses in the United States, with over seventy thousand unintentional overdoses. Much of the recent increase has come from prescription drugs, synthetic narcotics like fentanyl, heroin, and methamphetamines.

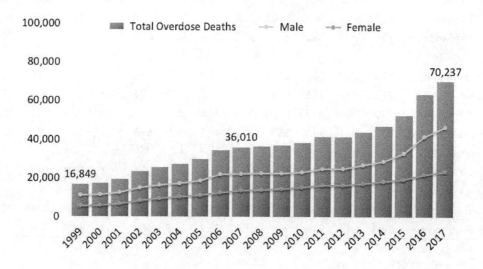

Source: : Centers for Disease Control and Prevention, National Center for Health Statistics. Multiple Cause of Death 1999-2017 on CDC WONDER Online Database, released December, 2018

FIGURE 9.3   National drug overdose deaths among all ages, by gender, 1999–2017 (bar graph).

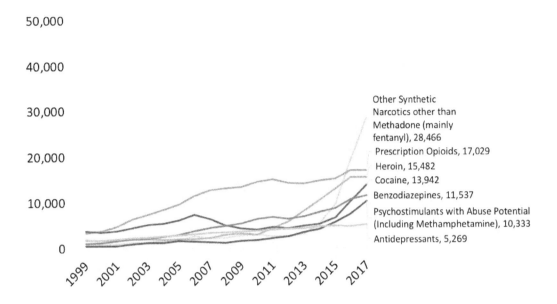

Source: : Centers for Disease Control and Prevention, National Center for Health Statistics. Multiple Cause of Death 1999-2017 on CDC WONDER Online Database, released December, 2018

FIGURE 9.4   **National drug overdose deaths among all ages, by gender, 1999–2017 (line graph).**

Harm Score

The harm score is a WHO (World Health Organization) measure of personal and societal harm done by a drug, quantified into one number.

| **CRITICAL THINKING:** | 1. Does harm matter for legality?
2. What makes a drug or substance harmful? |

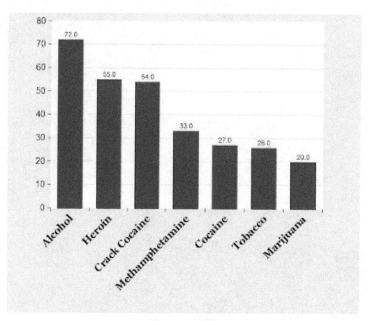

FIGURE 9.5   Total harm scores for various drugs.

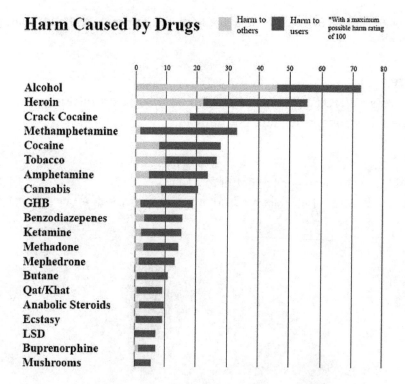

Adapted from "Drug harms in the UK: a multi-criteria decision analysis", by David Nutt, Leslie King and Lawrence Phillips, on behalf of the Independent Scientific Committee on Drugs. The Lancet.

FIGURE 9.6   Harm caused by drugs.

| CRITICAL THINKING: | 1. Why is alcohol the substance that is most harmful to others? |
| | 2. If it is not the harm principle that determines legality, what is it? |

Drug War and Intersection with Incarceration

Two of the explicit goals at the inception of the war on drugs were to reduce drug use and to reduce drug deaths. While the war on drugs has correlated with a dramatic rise in the prison population, along with some other consequences, neither of these main objectives has been achieved. More people use both illegal drugs and pharmaceuticals today, and the unintentional drug overdose rate has increased by nearly 20 times since President Nixon began the war on drugs in the 1970s.

Reading 9.3.

Social Consequences of the War on Drugs: The Legacy of Failed Policy

by Eric L. Jensen, Jurg Gerber and Clayton Mosher

In a previous article, we argued that "the 1986 War on Drugs has resulted in some of the most extensive changes in criminal justice policy and the operations of the justice system in the United States since the due process revolution of the 1960s" (Jensen & Gerber, 1996, p. 421). This most recent in a series of drug wars in the United States has now lasted almost 17 years. Although huge amounts of economic resources, $18.8 billion by the federal government in fiscal year 2002 alone, personnel, and massive prison construction have been hurled at the problem, the drug war has failed to eliminate illegal drug use. In fact, the Household Survey of Drug Abuse shows that illegal drug use was declining substantially in the 6 to 7 years before the drug war was declared by President Reagan and continued this downturn for the next 6 years with fluctuations occurring since the early 1990s (Jensen & Gerber, 1998; *Sourcebook of Criminal Justice Statistics*, 2001). Given this seemingly natural downturn—which was occurring in Canada also—the drug war seems to have had no effect on illegal drug use.

The war on drugs and its influences on the criminal justice system have received a great deal of attention from criminologists and other social scientists. Prison populations have exploded with persons convicted of drug offenses. Between 1980 and 2001, the number of persons in state and federal prisons for drug offenses increased by approximately 1,300% (www.ojp.usdoj.gov/bjs/prisons.htm). Incarceration and prison construction have become major industries; in part replacing the old rust

Eric L. Jensen, Jurg Gerber, and Clayton J. Mosher, "Social Consequences of the War on Drugs: the Legacy of Failed Policy," *Criminal Justice Policy Review*, vol. 15, no. 1, pp. 100-121. Copyright © 2004 by SAGE Publications. Reprinted with permission.

belt industries that were the economic backbone of America for decades (Christie, 2000). Law enforcement personnel are being redirected away from handling other types of crimes in favor of drug offenses (Mast, Benson, & Rasmussen, 2000). Criminal courts are so overloaded with drug cases that special drug courts have been created to more speedily handle the burdensome caseloads (Inciardi, McBride, & Rivers, 1996). For the first time in American history much harsher sentences are required for one form of an illegal drug (crack) than another form of the same substance (powder cocaine) (Belenko, 1993). Attempts have been made to criminalize the behavior of pregnant women by charging them with delivery of drugs to a minor (Beckett, 1995; Sagatun-Edwards, 1998). If these charges fail—as they most often do—child protection services have been used to remove the baby from its mother.

The drug war has also spread over into the civil arena. This pandemic spillover of state intrusion into the civil arena in the name of controlling crime represents a rapid and drastic slide down the slippery slope of reducing what heretofore were considered the due process rights of Americans. The most pervasive example of crime control absent due process is the civil forfeiture of assets in drug-related cases (Blumenson & Nilsen, 1998; Jensen, 2000). Law enforcement agencies seized nearly $7 billion in allegedly drug-related assets from fiscal year 1985 through 1999 (Jensen, 2000; *Sourcebook of Criminal Justice Statistics*, 2001). When law enforcement is partially self-financed, it becomes less accountable to the public.

Public school students are required to take drug tests in an increasing number of schools even when drugs have not been shown to be a serious problem in the school (see Crowley, 1998). Drug-sniffing dogs are frequently used in schools and school parking lots to uncover illegal drugs without search warrants.

The U.S. drug war is becoming global. The federal government is attempting to influence the governments of other nations throughout the world to deal with drug issues as the U.S. government sees fit. This international arm twisting and cajoling interferes with the sovereignty of foreign governments (Bouley, 2001; Bullington, Krebs & Rasmussen, 2000; del Olmo, 1993; Denq & Wang, 2001; Garcia, 1997; Ryan, 1998).

Although criminologists are aware of this multitude of problematic justice system outcomes associated with the War on Drugs, we must now begin to consider the widespread social, economic, health, political, and human costs of the current antidrug crusade. The objective of this article is to bring attention to these broader societal costs of the drug war. Drug policy has become a major force in the lives of millions of persons caught in the justice system; the same holds true for millions of their family members, relatives, and friends; and the inner-city communities that suffer as a result of the policies emanating from this state-constructed moral panic.

What does the future hold for the millions of young men—disproportionately African American—who will come out of prison to face a new life stigmatized as ex-convicts and drug addicts? Will they find living-wage jobs and form stable families or return to the destructive lifestyles of their youth? How is the legitimate political influence of African Americans being influenced by the loss of the right to vote of millions of young, Black men who are convicted felons? How have repressive policies regarding syringes led to the spread of HIV/AIDS? The prison construction boom of the 1980s and 1990s may lead to the need for continued, expanded wars on crime when the cohorts of young men are smaller in the future—capacity causes utilization. Crime control is now a basic industry in the United States. The benefits of medical cannabis use for the chronically ill may not be realized due to the active federal intervention to stop state initiatives that allow it. These are the broader issues that we will begin to draw attention to in this article.

PRISON CAPACITY: IF YOU BUILD IT, THEY MUST COME

It has been argued by some criminologists that the creation of prison capacity generates the prisoners to fill this capacity (see Coates, Miller, & Ohlin, 1978); others assert that limited prison capacity acts as a constraint on prison populations. In the late 1960s, criminologists and other analysts of criminal justice system trends, perhaps deluded by the increased use of alternative sanctions such as probation, predicted a leveling-off, or even declines in the overall level of imprisonment in the United States (e.g., Blumstein & Cohen, 1973; Rothman, 1971). The President's Commission on Law Enforcement and Administration of Justice (1967, pp. 4–5) predicted that the increased use of community programs would curtail institutional growth: "the population projection for the prison system shows the smallest aggregate increase of any of the correctional activities." In addition to the impact of alternative sanctions on prison populations, some held that judicial decisions on prison overcrowding in the 1970s, which prevented corrections officials in some states from receiving new inmates and even ordered some facilities closed, presaged a decline in the use of incarceration (Zimring & Hawkins, 1991).

As early as 1971, however, the American Friends Service Committee (1971, p. 172) argued that the result of providing new cell space was "inevitable: the coercive net of the justice system will be spread over a larger number of people, trapping them for longer periods of time." Similarly, a 1980 study sponsored by the National Institute of Justice (1980), while indicating that the data were only "suggestive," asserted that

> as a matter of history, this study has found that state prison populations were more likely to increase in years immediately following construction than at any other time, and that increases in the numbers of inmates closely approximates the change in capacity. (pp. 138–139)

Between 1990 and 1999, the total number of inmates in state and federal prisons increased 75%. State prisoners increased by 71% and federal prisoners by 127%. States with the largest increases in prison populations during this time were Texas (173%), Idaho (147%), West Virginia (126%), and Hawaii (124%) (Bureau of Justice Statistics, 2000b). California has built 21 new prisons in the last 20 years and increased its inmate population eightfold. As Schlosser (1998) has noted, the number of drug offenders imprisoned in California in 1997 was more than twice the number imprisoned for *all* crimes in 1978.

During the mid-1990s, an average of three 500-bed prison facilities have opened *each week* in the United States (Schlosser, 1998). Christie (2000), in his provocatively titled book *Crime Control as Industry*, refers to low-level offenders as the "raw material" for prison expansion. He suggests that the prison industry needs inmates just as the paper industry needs trees—the key difference, however, is that trees may well turn out to be a finite resource.

And of course, the war on drugs has led to unprecedented racial disproportions in our prison population. Donzinger (1996) estimated that if current growth rates continue for the next 10 years, by the year 2020 more than 6 in 10 African American males between the ages of 18 and 34 will be incarcerated, with the total prison population topping 10 million. And once built at an average cost of $100,000 per cell, these prison beds must be occupied.

Significant developments in the 1980s and into the 1990s would appear to indicate that the incredible recent growth rates in incarcerated populations will not soon abate; although the rate of growth in prison populations slowed somewhat from 1999 through 2001 (Bureau of Justice Statistics, n.d.). Consider, in this context, the rising rates of juvenile incarceration and the continual calls for transferring more juveniles to adult court. There is also the issue of the increasing involvement of private companies in the imprisonment business (Quittner, 1998); the globalization of the economy, whereby companies that are unwilling or unable to obtain cheap labor in Third World countries are making increased use of prison labor (Overbeck, 1997; Robinson, 1998; Wright, 1998), and the growing interest of rural communities in securing prisons as a means of economic development (McDonald, 1997). As a prison liaison group chair in a rural Michigan jurisdiction noted, "this is going to mean more jobs and more money to the community ... there's no possible way for those guys to get out, so we just reap the benefits" (as cited in Julien, 1998).

There is of course a very cruel irony in all these developments. As state governments take funds from education and social programs to expand their prison systems, citizens are less able to compete in an increasingly competitive marketplace. Skills will be low, employment opportunities limited, and more people will live in poverty. Such conditions are criminogenic, but instead of investing in programs to prevent criminal activity, "the government spends dollars on the final result of the poverty circle" (McDonald, 1997).

As Schlosser (1998) recently pointed out, there are several similarities between the emergent prison-industrial complex and the military-industrial complex that it appears to have superseded. Although crime has replaced communism as the external evil that can be exploited by politicians, the most striking similarity between the two is the need to create policies that are more concerned with the economic imperatives of the industry than the needs of the public it allegedly serves. In addition, the policies allegedly create significant employment opportunities in the communities where prisons locate, thereby tying the economic prosperity of literally millions of people to the growth of the crime control industry. Finally, both the military and prison industries have an internal logic that allows them to benefit regardless of whether their policies succeed or fail. As Donzinger (1998) notes,

> if we lose a war, we need more weapons to win the next one; if we win a war, we need more weapons so we can keep on winning; if crime is up, we need more prisons to lower crime, if crime is down, we need more prisons so it stays down.

The importance of labor market conditions was also emphasized by Sellin (1976, p. vii) who argued that "the demands of the labor market shape(d) the penal system and determined its transformation over the years, more or less unaffected by the theories of punishment in vogue." Similarly, Rusche and Kirchheimer (1939) in their classic historical-comparative study of prisons, noted that compared to European countries, the United States was characterized by a shortage of labor in the early industrial period, with the result that convict labor needed to be productive. However, this position has been critiqued for its tendency to economic reductionism (Greenberg, 1980; see also Zimring & Hawkins, 1991). In a recent comparative study of the influences on rates of imprisonment from 1955–1985, Sutton (2000) found that significant predictors of growth in prison populations in the United States were higher rates of unemployment, the right-party (Republican) domination of the cabinet, and declines in welfare spending.

DIMINISHED LIFE CHANCES: INCARCERATION, JOBLESSNESS, AND WEAK SOCIAL BONDS

Between 1980 and 2001, the number of persons incarcerated in state prisons in the United States grew by 316% (Bureau of Justice Statistics, n.d.a.). Furthermore, the number of incarcerated persons per 100,000 population rose from 139 in 1980 to 470 in 2001 (Bureau of Justice Statistics, n.d.a.). Interestingly, "tough on crime" policies implemented during the Clinton administration resulted in the largest increases in federal and state prison populations of any president in American history (Feldman, Schiraldi, & Ziedenberg, 2001).

Incarceration is concentrated among young, uneducated males; particularly African Americans. In 1999, over 44% of the number of inmates in state and federal prisons and local jails were Black, and 11% of Black males in their 20s and early 30s were either in prison or jail in 1999 (Bureau of Justice Statistics, 2000a). In the mid-1990s, one out of every three young Black males was under some form of state supervision (Western & Beckett, 1999).

A growing proportion of prison inmates has been convicted of nonviolent drug offenses. In 1979, 6% of state prison inmates were convicted of nonviolent drug offenses, whereas in 1998 the proportion had increased to nearly 21%, nearly a fourfold increase (Bureau of Justice Statistics, n.d.b; Western & Beckett, 1999). In 1985, before the declaration of a new war on drugs and the passage of harsh federal antidrug legislation, 34% of federal prisoners were incarcerated for drug offenses. By 1998, 58% of federal prisoners had been sentenced for drug offenses (Bureau of Justice Statistics, 2000a).

Furthermore, sentences for drug offenses are long in comparison to other crimes. In 2000, mean times served for selected federal offenses were as follows: drug offenses 41 months, violent crimes 54 months, fraudulent property crimes 15 months, and other property crimes 19 months (Sourcebook of Criminal Justice Statistics, 2001. Thus, average times served for drug offenses were closer to those for violent crimes than for property offenses.

It has also been found that African Americans are more likely than Whites to be in prison for drug offenses (Irwin & Austin, 2001; Maguire & Pastore, 1998, p. 505). This disproportionality of incarceration by race is exacerbated by the infamous 100:1 sentencing ratio for crack offenses. In 1996, 86% of federal convictions for crack offenses were Black whereas only 5% were White (Maguire & Pastore, 1998, p. 415). In addition, the median sentence for Blacks convicted of a federal drug offense was 84 months—2 years longer than the average sentence for a violent crime—whereas it was 46 months for Whites (Maguire & Pastore, 1998, p. 396). Thus, Blacks experience the brunt of these extremely harsh crack sanctions.

In sum, the end result of these changes in penalties and prosecution of drug offenses is a large number of young, Black males in prison for such offenses. Additionally, they are serving long prison terms in comparison to many other inmates. Although the effects of this change in patterns of imprisonment for the criminal justice system are intuitively obvious, we must turn our attention to the long-term effects on society, specifically the unemployment and further marginalization of these men once they are released from prison.

Research has clearly shown that the likelihood of unemployment increases as a result of incarceration (Sampson & Laub, 1993; Western & Beckett, 1999). Western and Beckett (1999, pp. 1048–1051) found that incarceration has large negative effects on the employment of ex-prisoners, which decay 3 to 4 years after release. Changes in public policies since the Reagan Administration years have exacerbated this problem. As Petersilia (2003a, p. 4) has recently pointed out, "dozens of laws were passed restricting the kinds of jobs for which ex-prisoners can be hired, easing the requirements for their parental rights to be terminated, restricting their access to welfare benefits and public housing, disqualifying them from a host of job training programs" (see also Jensen, in press). In addition, the ability to find and retain employment are key factors in forming bonds to the conventional society and desistance from criminal behavior (Elliott & Voss, 1974; Sampson & Laub, 1993).

Employment, and the lack thereof, is related to marriage. Studies cited by Wilson (1996, p. 96) found that 20% to 25% of the decline in marriage rates of African Americans is due to the joblessness of Black males. This is particularly problematic for young Black males. In addition, these studies were of general samples of African Americans and not specific to the low-income communities from which most drug prisoners are sentenced. The effect of the explosion in joblessness in inner cities combined with the obstacles faced by ex-prisoners finding employment can be expected to produce larger negative outcomes in these communities.

Research by Sampson (1995, p. 249) found that both the total sex ratios and the employment prospects of Black men had independent effects on the structure of Black families in cities in the United States: "this race-specific interaction clearly supports Wilson's (1987) hypothesis regarding the structural sources of black family disruption." In this earlier work, Wilson proposed that the ratio of employed men per 100 women of the same age and race influenced marital stability. With the decline in the number of economically stable Black men, Black female-headed households increased (Wilson, 1987). More specifically, Sampson (1995) also found strong independent effects of sex ratios and employment on family disruption among those families in poverty. That is, "the lower the sex ratio and the lower the male employment rate, the higher the rate of female-headed families with children in poverty" (Sampson, 1995, p. 250).

Furthermore, one of the strongest predictors of urban violence is family structure. With other factors controlled, "in cities where family disruption is high the rate of violence is also high" (Sampson, 1995, p. 249). Based on his earlier work, the author states that this causal connection appears to be based in patterns of community social ties and informal networks of social control (see Sampson & Groves, 1989; see also Hagan, 1994).

The causal chain between incarceration, joblessness, and weak social bonds is therefore long and complex. As stated by Sampson and Laub (1993),

> job stability and marital attachment in adulthood were significantly related to changes in adult crime—the stronger the adult ties to work and family, the less the crime ... We even found that strong marital attachment inhibits crime and deviance regardless of the spouse's own deviant behavior, and that job instability fosters crime regardless of heavy drinking. Moreover, social bonds to employment were directly influenced by State sanctions—incarceration as a juvenile and as an adult had negative effects on later job stability, which in turn was negatively related to continued involvement in crime over the life course. (p. 248)

Thus, the binge of imprisonment for drug offenses has substantial negative outcomes for society and inner-city African American communities in particular. The incarceration of large numbers of young Black men for drug offenses has created an artificially low unemployment rate in the United States in recent years.

In 2002 alone, nearly 600,000 people were released from prison. This puts hundreds of thousands of young Black men with the stigma of ex-convict back into primarily low-income urban communities each year (see Petersilia, 2003a). The obstacles they face in finding employment that provides a living wage and related marital stability should be focal points of public concern and social policy in the immediate future. As they currently exist, the punitive justice policies so popular in the United States today simply continue to fuel the social disorganization and decline of the most disadvantaged segments of our society.

HIV/AIDS—"INVISIBLE, EXTRAJUDICIAL EXECUTIONS?" (GREEN, 1996)

Two percent to 3% of state and federal prisoners are HIV-positive or have AIDS—a rate five times higher than that of the general population (Petersilia, 2003a). The number of confirmed AIDS cases among prisoners increased by nearly 400% between 1991 and 1997 (Bureau of Justice Statistics, 1999). Additionally, it is estimated that 22% of female and 13% of male inmates in New York City jails are HIV-positive (Aids in Prison Project, 1997). Marquart, Brewer, Mullings, and Crouch (1999) note that in the New York, California, and Texas prison systems, AIDS is now the leading cause of death. In 1997, about one in every five deaths of prisoners was attributable to AIDS-related causes (Bureau of Justice Statistics, 1999). The rate of mortality for HIV-infected prisoners is at least three times the rate of mortality of HIV-patients in non–prison communities (Center for HIV Information, 1997).

In addressing the issue of HIV in prisons, it is important to take into account the comparatively high rates of assault and sexual assault that can facilitate the spread of the virus. An earlier Federal Bureau of Prisons study reported that 30% of federal prison inmates engaged in homosexual activity while incarcerated (Nacci & Kane, 1984). Although no national studies of the extent of sexual assault in prisons have been conducted, based on projections from a number of studies, it is estimated that there were 530,000 male rape victims behind bars in the United States (Stop Prisoner Rape; www.igc.org/spr). A substantial proportion of these rapes occur in local and county jails, where over half the inmate population has not been convicted of an offense. There are, of course, other HIV-risk factors for prison inmates such as the frequent incidents of interpersonal violence in these settings involving lacerations and bites, which has been exacerbated by the double celling of inmates. The use of needles for tattooing and body piercing, and sharing of syringes for IV drug use in prisons are also of great concern.

Unfortunately, federal and state prison authorities have been slow to develop policies to deal with this crisis. In an international survey of 19 countries prepared for the World Health Organization, the United States was listed as one of four countries that did not have a national policy for HIV management in prison (Center for HIV Information, 1997). And although an increasing number of inmates in state and federal prisons are HIV-positive, the number of effective HIV prevention programs in these facilities is declining. In 1990, 96% of all state and federal prisons had AIDS education programs in at least one prison—by 1994, that rate had dropped to 75% ("HIV Prevention Programs," 1996). Green (1996), discussing the situation in California prisons and noting the disproportional concentration of HIV infection among minority inmates, asserts that

> considering the history of genocide in this country, imprisoning targeted groups in an epidemic situation and then withholding treatment and education to stop the spread of the diseases sounds like giving smallpox-contaminated blankets to the Native Americans.

Given recent history, it seems unlikely that state or federal governments will implement progressive policies such as making condoms, bleach, methadone, and sterile injection equipment available to prisoners, as the World Health Organization has suggested (Jurgens, 1996).

Although many Americans and policy makers currently view prisoners as unworthy of compassion, there is a far greater threat posed by the spread of HIV in prison populations. The overwhelming majority of prison inmates will be released at some time, and as Marquart et al. (1999) in a study of women prisoners in the state of Texas note,

> Recent drug control policies, grounded in deterrence and based on harsh legal penalties, have led to the incarceration of numerous offenders who are low criminal risks but represent major public health risks on release. Criminal justice policies penalizing drug users may be contributing to the spread of HIV infection in the wider society. (p. 82)

Are there any signs that any of this will end soon? It is perhaps notable that an overly optimistic and misleading press release from the Office of National Drug Control Policy (ONDCP) was titled "FY 2000 Drug Control Budget Builds on Success—Budget Provides $17.8 Billion for Demand and Supply Reduction." A perusal of the fine print of this press release reveals that, similar to drug control policy in the last two decades in the United States, two thirds of the money is devoted to supply reduction, the bulk of which is composed of additional monies for law enforcement. Only one third of the money is devoted to "demand reduction."

MEDICINAL MARIJUANA—REEFER MADNESS AGAIN

The ONDCP (1997), in its statement on the use of marijuana for medical purposes, asserted that state-level initiatives to allow the use of medical marijuana had

> sent a confusing message to our children that could not have come at a worse time. In recent years, we have seen drug use by our young people increase at an alarming rate. Among 8th graders, the use of illicit drugs, primarily marijuana, has tripled. This increase has been fueled by a measurable decrease in the proportion of young people who perceive marijuana to be a dangerous substance.

Aside from the fact that this statement conveniently neglects the reality that levels of illicit drug use by youth were considerably higher in the late 1970s, it is even more curious in the context of ONDCP's contention in the same document that the "foremost objective" of the office "is to create a national drug control strategy based on *science* rather than *ideology*" [italics added].

In critiquing California's medical marijuana legislation, President Clinton's "drug czar," General McCaffrey, noted that the wording of California's Proposition 215 led to a situation whereby "any other illness" would include "recalling forgotten memories, cough suppressants, and writer's cramp." McCaffrey continued, "this is not medicine. This is a Cheech and Chong show" (Mundell, 1998). In response to the

California initiative, the Clinton government threatened to prosecute doctors who prescribed marijuana to their patients.

Interestingly, as Grinspoon and Bakalar (1995) pointed out in an editorial published in the *Journal of the American Medical Association*, the Drug Enforcement Administration's (DEA's) own administrative law judge, Francis Young, asserted in 1988 that marijuana in its natural form fulfilled the legal requirements of currently accepted medical use in treatment in the United States. Young added that marijuana was "one of the safest therapeutically active substances known to man" (as cited in Grinspoon & Bakalar, 1995 p. 1875). Interestingly, Young's order that marijuana be reclassified as a Schedule II drug was overruled, not by any medical authority, but by the DEA itself.

There is also evidence that the National Institute of Drug Abuse was instrumental in suppressing a 1997 World Health Organization report suggesting that marijuana was far less harmful than alcohol and tobacco ("The report the WHO tried to hide," 1998). However, the evidence for marijuana's medical uses is mounting. The substance is effective in treatment of more than 100 separate illnesses or diseases (http://www.medicalmarijuana. org), with studies demonstrating marijuana's usefulness in reducing nausea and vomiting, stimulating appetite, promoting weight gain, and diminishing intraocular pressure associated with glaucoma (Zimmer & Morgan, 1997). And despite the contention of ONDCP and other federal drug agencies that similar effects are possible with synthetic tetrahydrocannabinal (THC) or Marinol, studies suggest that smoked marijuana is more effective because it delivers THC to the bloodstream more quickly. In addition, some evidence suggests that the psychoactive side effects of Marinol may actually be more intense than those that are associated with smoking marijuana (Zimmer & Morgan, 1997).

ONDCP and other federal drug agencies have also attempted to dismiss studies of marijuana's effectiveness by claiming that the research is lacking in scientific standards. However, as Grinspoon and Bakalar (1995) note, although it is certainly true that many of the studies examining medical marijuana are not consistent with FDA standards, this is primarily because of the bureaucratic, legal, and financial obstacles that are put in place by this same federal agency.

It appears as though federal drug agencies have a vested interest in keeping marijuana illegal. Since 1970, approximately 13.5 million Americans have been arrested for marijuana possession, and in 1999 alone, there were 708,480 marijuana-related arrests (Charbeneau, 1998; U.S. Department of Justice, n.d.). Despite popular belief then, there is little question that marijuana is the main focus of the drug warriors. It is worth noting, however, that the federal government's strict prohibitionist position with respect to marijuana is opposed by the American Public Health Association, the Federation of American Scientists, the Physicians' Association for AIDS Care, the Lymphoma Foundation of America, and national associations of prosecutors and criminal defense attorneys. *The New England Journal of Medicine* has supported marijuana's use as medicine, the *Journal of the American Medical Association* published the previously mentioned editorial by Grinspoon and Bakalar, which delivered essentially the same message (Morgan & Zimmer, 1997), and based on a review of the research the Senate Special Committee on Illegal Drugs (2002) in Canada recently concluded that cannabis can be a beneficial therapy for the treatment of specified medical conditions. Despite the fact that 11 states and the District of Columbia have passed legislation allowing for medicinal marijuana, the legal status of using the substance for these purposes is unclear given the federal resistance to recognize the new state policies.

THE WAR ON DRUGS AND DISENFRANCHISEMENT

One of the unanticipated consequences of the war on drugs is the disenfranchisement of a particular segment of society. Although most Americans will not be unduly disturbed by the prospect of convicted felons being unable to vote, the disproportionate impact of felony disenfranchisement on African Americans should be cause for concern.

Historically, the United States limited the right to vote to relatively few, primarily affluent White males, and excluded women, African Americans, and the poor. One other category, convicted felons, were unable to vote as a result of the United States's adopting the European practice of declaring convicted offenders "civilly dead" on conviction (Fellner & Mauer, 1998). The felony disenfranchisement laws gained some additional currency after the Civil War when White Southerners sought to limit Black suffrage with the aid of supposedly race-neutral laws (e.g., grandfather clauses).

Depending on state legislation, convicted felons may not lose the right to vote; or lose it while in prison, on probation, on parole, or even *for life*. Maine, for instance, does not disenfranchise convicted felons; Idaho disenfranchises incarcerated felons; California felons in prison or on parole; Georgia felons in prison, on parole, and on probation; and Alabama, similar to Georgia, also disenfranchises ex-felons (i.e., felons are disenfranchised *for life*) (Fellner & Mauer, 1998). The numbers of disenfranchised people are exceptionally large, but the proportions of certain categories of people are even more disturbing:

- 3.9 million adults are currently or permanently disenfranchised as a result of a felony conviction;
- Florida and Texas have each disenfranchised more than 600,000 people;
- 73% of the disenfranchised are not in prison but are on probation, on parole, or have completed their sentences;

- In Alabama and Florida, 31% of all Black men are permanently disenfranchised;
- 13% of all adult Black men are currently disenfranchised;
- 1.4 million Black men are disenfranchised compared to 4.6 million Black men who voted in 1996 (Fellner & Mauer, 1998).

An important study by Uggen and Manza (2002) recently concluded that felon disenfranchisement may have altered seven recent U.S. Senate elections and at least one presidential election.

Assuming that Democrats who might have been elected in the absence of felon disenfranchisement had held their seats as long as the Republicans who narrowly defeated them, we estimate that the Democratic Party would have gained parity in 1984 and held majority control of the U.S. Senate from 1986 to the present. ... In examining the presidential elections, we find that the Republican presidential victory of 2000 would have been reversed had just ex-felons been allowed to vote. (p. 794)

Unfortunately, if current trends continue, the situation will become worse. Mandatory minimum sentence laws, "three strikes" laws, and the war on drugs will increase the number of disenfranchised people and, most likely, increase the racial disparity in this practice. The long-term consequence of this will be the further attenuation of African American political power. More than a decade ago, Wilson (1987) spoke of *The Truly Disadvantaged*. Not only is work disappearing (see also Wilson, 1996), what little political clout existed has eroded. Urban areas have traditionally been strongholds of minority politicians and politicians sympathetic to minority issues. The disenfranchisement of some of their supporters will lead to a political restructuring of the city. In turn, this will lead to even fewer programs for these populations. Instead, politicians will likely heed the calls for more "law and order" emanating from the remaining electorate. And the vicious spiral will continue.

CONCLUSIONS

Few scholars who study the war on drugs are not aware of some of the problems this war entails for the criminal justice system. In fact, even professionals in the field echo some of the concerns of academicians. Former federal drug czar Barry McCaffrey spoke of "America's internal gulag" when referring to the seemingly ever-growing number of drug offenders in prisons ("Prison boom," 1999, p. 12). The irony of such a development must be overwhelming for Christie, should he be aware of McCaffrey's label.

Some positive developments are occurring at the state level, however. Since late 2000, Republican governors in at least seven states, including George Pataki in New York, Gary Johnson in New Mexico, and Dirk Kempthorne in Idaho, have called for placing more drug offenders into treatment and fewer in prison—although the previous year Governor Kempthorne advocated and passed longer sentences for methamphetamine offenses. Although these developments can be viewed in a positive light, it is important not to lose sight of the opposition of many criminal justice officials in the states where these changes have been suggested and of recent developments at the federal level.

In Arizona and California, citizen initiatives have passed that provide drug treatment instead of prison for persons convicted of first- and second-time drug possession offenses when no violent crime is present. Although these laws have faced criticism by prosecutors, police, and judges who assert that the law does not give criminal justice authorities enough power to force offenders into treatment, the research shows that these laws are diverting tens of thousands of persons convicted of possession from incarceration into treatment (www.drugpolicyalliance.com, www.prop36.org).

In the November 2002 elections, the voters of the District of Columbia passed a measure similar to those in Arizona and California. This initiative requires that persons convicted of drug possession for a nonviolent offense receive treatment instead of incarceration. The law contains no funding for implementation of this policy, however.

Recent appointments to key positions in the federal government by President George W. Bush indicate that the war may not yet be over. Former Senator John Ashcroft, appointed U.S. Attorney General, has supported revoking the driver's license of anyone arrested for marijuana possession, even if they were not driving at the time. He also supported evicting entire families from public housing if one of their members was suspected of using or selling drugs, even when the other family members were not involved. Ashcroft also opposes devoting funds to demand-side programs believing that a government that shifts resources to drug treatment and prevention programs instead of police and prisons "is a government that accommodates us at our lowest and least" (as quoted in Lindesmith Center, 2001). President Bush also appointed John Walters to the position of federal drug czar, leading Smith (2002, p. 121) to comment "Walters' appointment is the clearest sign yet that the Bush administration is committed to a punishment approach to the problems caused by illegal drugs." In 1996, Walters indicated that he opposed needle exchange programs on moral grounds (Smith, 2002); he also fervently opposes the decriminalization of marijuana. Walters actively campaigned against a marijuana initiative in the state of Nevada and in response to a proposal for decriminalization of marijuana in Canada, stated "If Canada wants to become the locus for that kind of activity, they're likely to pay a heavy price" (Bailey, 2003). As Stroup and Armentano (2002,

p. 223) suggest, "many of Mr. Walters more egregious claims about cannabis appear to have been lifted straight from the 1936 propaganda film [Reefer Madness]."

The rhetoric in recent federal documents might lead one to believe that there have been some changes, however. Witness, for example, the relative prominence that the prevention and treatment of drug abuse received in the 2001 Annual Report of the National Drug Control Policy,

> Preventing drug abuse in the first place is preferable to addressing the problem later through treatment and law enforcement. ... There are approximately five million drug abusers who need immediate treatment and who constitute a major portion of domestic demand. ... Accordingly, the *Strategy* focuses on treatment. Research clearly demonstrates that treatment works. ... Providing access to treatment for America's chronic drug abusers is a worthwhile endeavor. It is both compassionate public policy and sound investment (Office of National Drug Control Policy, 2001, pp. 4–6).

Unfortunately for the harm reduction effort, such rhetoric is offset by the reality of budgetary appropriations. An overview of the proportions of the budgets devoted to law enforcement and drug treatment during the decade of the 1990s indicates that there have not been major redistributions (Office of National Drug Control Policy, 2001, p. 119). Although there have been some increases in the percentage devoted to treatment, any declarations that the drug war is over are clearly premature.

However, it might be interesting to speculate how the end of the war on drugs would affect the consequences that we identified in this article. Although it seems highly improbable that we will witness such an event, it is theoretically possible that the war will be ended with the stroke of a few legislative, judicial, and executive pens. Even if this were to occur, such an event would not fundamentally change the adverse long-term consequences that have cumulated during the last 17 years. Only a comprehensive and vigorously enforced affirmative action–like program aimed at overcoming the negative consequences of the war would do so.

Incarceration provides one example. The mean time served for a federal drug sentence for a drug offense is 41 months. Even if the war ended today, the most recently admitted convicts would remain in prison an average of well over 3 years. The only escape from this situation would be large-scale pardons for drug offenders. Obviously this will not happen. Furthermore, the internal logic of prison expansion would also necessitate new "raw material" for the cell space that exists. If nothing else, states must pay off the long-term debts that have been encumbered for this unprecedented wave of prison construction. A new war on some other outlawed, or yet to be outlawed, behavior would likely be the end result.

Postconviction employment would continue to be problematic for ex-offenders. Given that the average time served is over 3 years and that employment difficulties are most pronounced for the first 3 to 4 years after release, employment difficulties would be with us for almost a decade after the end of the war on drugs. The problems associated with unemployment, such as marital instability and family violence would also exist, and their effects would be passed on to yet another generation.

All of the other negative consequences that we have identified in this study, the growth in HIV/AIDS rates, the prohibition of cannabis for medical uses, and the attenuation of the political power of targeted subordinate racial and ethnic groups, would also continue to exist. Whereas the end of the war might stop the further acceleration of the spread of HIV infection by not sending drug users to prisons, ex-inmates would still be infected and potentially spread the virus to their sexual partners and those with whom some will share needles. Similarly, ex-offenders would still be without franchise in many states, but there would be fewer newly disenfranchised felons and ex-felons. The only remedy for such adverse consequences would be the passage of legislation such as the Civic Participation and Rehabilitation Act of 1999. This bill, along with others not yet filed, could reverse some of these adverse consequences. For this to happen, though, powerful interest groups that lobby on behalf of offenders would have to emerge; a scenario that seems highly unlikely in the United States.

Most criminologists have paid little attention to the societal consequences of the war on drugs to date. We see this article as a wake-up call for the discipline. Social scientists interested in race relations, family issues, political participation, labor force issues, and health care policy have studied the areas we have identified as societal consequences of the war on drugs. Most criminologists, however, have limited their inquiries to Sutherland's traditional definition of criminology: the making of law, the breaking of law, and the societal response to the breaking of law. We would argue that criminologists cannot afford to ignore the societal consequences of the last dimension of Sutherland's definition. Doing so will make us "enablers." Limiting our studies to the making and breaking of law, and its societal responses, will reify the "drug problem" (or more broadly, "the crime problem") as nothing more than that. If we expand our inquiry, however, to the study of the societal consequences of public policies, we begin the process of challenging the assumptions underlying our (society's) proposed solutions.

REFERENCES

American Friends Service Committee. (1971). Struggle for justice: A report on crime and punishment in America. New York: Hill and Wang.

Bailey, E. (2003, February 2). The drug war refugees. *Los Angeles Times*. Retrieved from http://www.latimes.com

Beckett, K. (1995). Fetal rights and "crack moms": Pregnant women in the War on Drugs. *Contemporary Drug Problems*, *22*, 587–612.

Belenko, S. R. (1993). *Crack and the evolution of anti-drug policy*. Westport, CT: Greenwood.

Blumenson, E., & Nilsen, E. (1998). Policing for profit: The drug war's hidden economic agenda. *University of Chicago Law Review*, *65*, 35–114.

Blumstein, A., & Cohen, J. (1973). A theory of the stability of punishment. *Journal of Criminal Law and Criminology*, *64*, 198–207.

Bouley, E. E., Jr. (2001). The drug war in Latin America: Ten years in a quagmire. In J. Gerber & E. L. Jensen (Eds.), *Drug war, American style: The internationalization of failed policy and its alternatives* (pp. 169–195). New York: Garland.

Bullington, B. H., Krebs, C. P., & Rasmussen, D. W. (2000). Drug policy in the Czech Republic. In A. Springer & A. Uhl (Eds.), *Illicit drugs: Patterns of use—patterns of response* (pp. 73–88). Innsbruck, Austria: StudienVerlag.

Bureau of Justice Statistics. (n.d.a.). Retrieved from http://www.ojp.usdoj.gov/bjs

Bureau of Justice Statistics. (n.d.b). *Number of sentenced inmates incarcerated under state and federal jurisdictions per 100,000, 1980–1999*. Retrieved from http://www.ojp.usdoj.gov/glance/incrt.txt

Bureau of Justice Statistics. (1999, November). *HIV in prisons, 1997*. Washington, DC: U.S. Department of Justice.

Bureau of Justice Statistics. (2000a, April). *Prison and jail inmates at midyear 1999*. Washington, DC: U.S. Department of Justice.

Bureau of Justice Statistics. (2000b, August). *Prisoners in 1999*. Washington, DC: U.S. Department of Justice.

Butterfield, F. (2001, February 12). California lacks resources for law on drug offenders, officials say. *The New York Times*. Retrieved from http://www.nytimes.com

Center for HIV Information. (1997). Aids and HIV infection in prisoners. Retrieved from http://hivinsite.ucsf.edu/akb/1997/01pris

Charbeneau, T. (1998). *Might as well face it we're addicted to lies*. Retrieved from www.marijuananews.com

Christie, N. (2000). *Crime control as industry: Towards GULAGS, western style* (3rd ed.). New York: Routledge.

Coates, R. B., Miller, D. D., & Ohlin, L. E. (1978). *Diversity in a youth correctional system: Handling delinquents in Massachusetts*. Cambridge, MA: Ballinger.

Crowley, D. W. (1998). Drug testing in the Rehnquist era. In E. L. Jensen & J. Gerber (Eds.), *The new War on Drugs: Symbolic politics and criminal justice policy* (pp. 123–139). Cincinnati, OH: Anderson/Academy of Criminal Justice Sciences.

del Olmo, R. (1993). The geopolitics of narcotrafficking in Latin America. *Social Justice*, *20*, 1–23.

Denq, F., & Wang, H. (2001). The war on drugs in Taiwan: An American model. In J. Gerber & E. L. Jensen (Eds.), *Drug war, American style: The internationalization of failed policy and its alternatives* (pp. 149–167). New York: Garland.

Donzinger, S. (1996). *The real war on crime*. New York: Harper.

Donzinger, S. (1998). Fear, crime, and punishment in the United States. *Tikkun, 12*, 24–27.

Elliott, D.S. & Voss, H. L. (1974). *Delinquency and dropout*. Lexington, MA: Lexington.

Feldman, Lisa; Schiraldi, Vincent and Jason Ziedenberg. (2001) Too Little Too Late: President Clinton's Prison Legacy. *Center on Juvenile and Criminal Justice*. Retrieved from http://www.cjcj.org/pubs/clinton/clinton.html

Fellner, J. & Mauer, M. (1998). *Losing the vote: the impact of felony disenfranchisement laws in the United States*. Retrieved from www.hrw.org/reports98/vote

Garcia, A. F. (1997). Harm reduction at the supply side of the drug war: the case for Bolivia. In P.G. Erickson, D.M. Riley, Y.W. Cheung, & P. A. O'Hare (Eds.) *Harm reduction: a new direction for drug policies and programs* (pp. 99–115) Toronto, ON: The University of Toronto Press.

Green, C. (1996). *HIV+ and in prison: the shadow of death row*. Retrieved from www.igc.apc.org/justice

Greenberg, D. F. (1980). Penal sanctions in Poland: A test of alternative models. *Social Problems, 28*, 194–204.

Grinspoon, L., & Bakalar, J. (1995). Marijuana as medicine: A plea for reconsideration. *Journal of the American Medical Association, 273*, 1875–1876.

Hagan, J. (1994). *Crime and disrepute*. Thousand Oaks, CA: Pine Forge Press.

HIV prevention programs in prisons on the decline. (1996, May 16). *Reuters*. Retrieved from http://www.reuters.com

Inciardi, J. A., McBride, D. C., & Rivers, J. E. (1996). *Drug control and the courts*. Thousand Oaks, CA: Sage.

Irwin, J., & Austin, J. (2001). *It's about time: America's imprisonment binge* (3rd ed.). Belmont, CA: Wadsworth.

Jensen, E. L. (2000). The civil forfeiture of assets: Harms inherent within U.S. policy. In A. Springer & A. Uhl (Eds.), *Illicit drugs: Patterns of use—Patterns of response* (pp. 31–45). Innsbruck, Austria: StudienVerlag.

Jensen, E. L. (in press). Non-criminal sanctions for drug offenses in the U.S.A. In S. Scheerer (Ed.), *Drug prohibition regimes: International perspectives*. Onati, Spain: International Institute of the Sociology of Law.

Jensen, E. L., & Gerber, J. (1996). The civil forfeiture of assets and the War on Drugs: Expanding criminal sanctions while reducing due process protections. *Crime and Delinquency, 42*, 421–434.

Jensen, E. L., & Gerber, J. (1998). The social construction of drug problems: An historical overview. In E. L. Jensen & J. Gerber (Eds.), *The new war on drugs: Symbolic politics and criminal justice policy*. Cincinnati, OH: Anderson/Academy of Criminal Justice Sciences.

Julien, R. (1998, February 27). Lapeer supports thumb prison expansion. *Michigan Live* (Flint ed.). Retrieved from http://www.mlive.com

Jurgens, R. (1996). *HIV/AIDS in prison.* Canadian Aids Society. Ottawa: Health Canada.

Lindesmith Center. (2001, January 22). *Judiciary committee to vote on Ashcroft.* Retrieved from www.drugpolicy.org

Maguire, K., & Pastore, A. L. (Eds.). (1998). *Sourcebook of criminal justice statistics—1997.* Washington, DC: Government Printing Office.

Marquart, J., Brewer, V., Mullings, J., & Crouch, B. (1999). The implications of crime control policy on HIV/AIDS-related risk among women prisoners. *Crime and Delinquency, 45,* 82–98.

Mast, B. D., Benson, B. L., & Rasmussen, D. W. (2000). Entrepreneurial police and drug enforcement. *Public Choice, 104,* 285–308.

McDonald, P. (1997). The lockdown of higher education. *Westchester County Weekly.* Retrieved from http://www.westchesterweekly.com

Mundell, E.J. (1998, August 5). Legal expert supports medical marijuana. *Reuters.* Retrieved from http://www.reuters.com

Nacci, P., & Kane, T. (1982). *Sex and sexual aggression in federal prisons.* Washington, DC: Federal Bureau of Prisons.

National Institute of Justice. (1980). *American prisons and jails* (Vol. 1). Washington, DC: Government Printing Office.

Nevada secretary of state questions drug czar's failure to comply with law. (2002, December 5). *Drug Policy Alliance Newsletter.* Retrieved from http://actioncenter.drugpolicy.org/news

Office of National Drug Control Policy. (1997). *ONDCP statement on marijuana for medical purposes.* Washington, DC: Government Printing Office.

Office of National Drug Control Policy. (2001). *The national drug control strategy: 2001 Annual Report.* Washington, DC: Government Printing Office.

Overbeck, C. (1997). *Prison factories: Slave labor for the New World Order?* Retrieved from http://www.parascope.com/articles/0197/prison.html

Petersilia, J. (2003a, March/April). Prisoner reentry and criminological knowledge. *Criminologist,* pp. 1, 3, 4-5.

Petersilia, J. (2003b). *When prisoners come home: Parole and prisoner reentry.* New York: Oxford University Press.

President's Commission on Law Enforcement and Administration of Justice. (1967). *Task force report: Corrections.* Washington, DC: Government Printing Office.

Prison boom expected to go on for a generation, officials say. (1999, March 7). *Houston Chronicle,* p. 12A.

Quittner, J. (1998, April 22). The incarceration industry: Teeming prison rolls bode well for private jails. *Fox News.* Retrieved from http://www.iprnet.org/prison/news

The report the WHO tried to hide. (1998, February 21). *New Scientist.* Retrieved from http://www.newscientist.com

Robinson, M. (1998). *The new money machine*. Retrieved from http://accnt.ashcc.uky.edu

Rothman, D. (1971). *The discovery of the asylum: Social order and disorder in the new republic*. Boston: Little, Brown.

Rusche, G., & Kirchheimer, O. (1939). *Punishment and social structure*. New York: Columbia University Press.

Ryan, K. (1998). Globalizing the problem: The United States and international drug control. In E. L. Jensen & J. Gerber (Eds.), *The new War on Drugs: Symbolic politics and criminal justice policy* (pp. 141–156). Cincinnati, OH: Anderson/Academy of Criminal Justice Sciences.

Sagatun-Edwards, I. J. (1998). Crack babies, moral panic, and the criminalization of behavior during pregnancy. In E. L. Jensen & J. Gerber (Eds.), *The new War on Drugs: symbolic politics and criminal justice policy* (pp. 107–121). Cincinnati, OH: Anderson/Academy of Criminal Justice Sciences.

Sampson, R. J. (1995). Unemployment and imbalanced sex ratios: Race-specific consequences for family structure and crime. In M. B. Tucker & C. Mitchell-Kernan (Eds.), *The decline in marriage among African Americans: Causes, consequences, and policy implications* (pp. 229–254). New York: Russell Sage.

Sampson, R. J., & Groves, W. B. (1989). Community structure and crime: testing disruption. *American Journal of Sociology, 94,* 774–802.

Sampson, R. J., & Laub, J. H. (1993). *Crime in the making: Pathways and turning points through life*. Cambridge, MA: Harvard University Press.

Schlosser, E. (1998, December). The prison-industrial complex. *Atlantic Monthly*. Retrieved from http://www.theatlantic.com

Sellin, T. (1976). *Slavery and the penal system*. New York: Elsevier.

Senate Special Committee on Illegal Drugs. (2002, September). *Cannabis: Our position for a Canadian public policy* (Summary report).

Smith, A. (2002). America's lonely drug war. In M. Gray (Ed.), *Busted: Stone cowboys, narco-lords and Washington's War on Drugs* (pp. 121–124). New York: Thunder's Mouth Press/Nation Books.

Sourcebook of Criminal Statistics. (2001). Retrieved from http://albany.edu/sourcebook

Stroup, K., & Armentano, P. (2002). The problem is pot prohibition. In M. Gray (Ed.), *Busted: Stone cowboys, narco-lords and Washington's War on Drugs* (pp. 223–224). New York: Thunder's Mouth Press/Nation Books.

Sutton, J. R. (2000). Imprisonment and social classification in five common-law democracies, 1955–1985. *American Journal of Sociology, 106,* 350–386.

Uggen, C., & Manza, J. (2002) Democratic contraction? Political consequences of felon disfranchisement in the United States. *American Sociological Review, 67,* 777–803.

U.S. Department of Justice. (n.d). *Uniform Crime Reports*. Retrieved from http://www. ojp.usdoj.gov

Western, B., & Beckett K. (1999). How unregulated is the U.S. labor market? The penal system as a labor market institution. *American Journal of Sociology, 104,* 1030–1060.

Wilson, W. J. (1987). *The truly disadvantaged: The inner city, the underclass, and public policy*. Chicago: University of Chicago Press.

Wilson, W. J. (1996). *When work disappears: The world of the new urban poor.* New York: Vintage.

Wright, P. (1998). *Business behind bars.* Retrieved from http://www.speakeasy.org/wfp/29/prison1.html

Zimmer, L., & Morgan, J. P. (1997). *Marijuana myths, marijuana facts.* New York: Lindesmith Center.

Zimring, F. E., & Hawkins, G. (1991). *The scale of imprisonment.* Chicago: University of Chicago Press.

SUMMARY

The United States is one of the world leaders in both consumption of illicit drugs and in the prevalence of prescription drugs. Since the war on drugs was declared by Richard Nixon in the 1970s (both Ronald and Nancy Reagan championed this cause in the 1980s as well), the rate and number of drug deaths have increased exponentially.

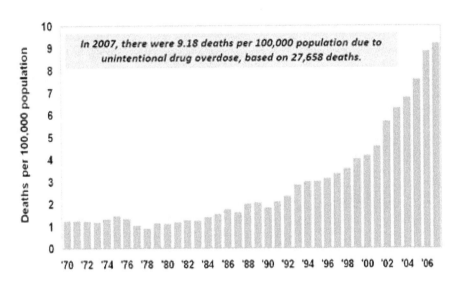

Source: Centers for Disease Control and Prevention. *Unintentional Drug Poisoning in the United States* (July 2010).

FIGURE 9.7   **Unintentional drug overdose deaths, United States, 1970–2007.**

In fact, 2017 marked a record high for drug deaths in the United States, with over seventy thousand. Prescription drugs are increasingly the cause of unintentional overdoses and were the plurality of such cases in the 2010s. The increases in drug deaths and incarceration that have followed the implementation of the war on drugs have led to recent social changes to the way in which we as a society think about drug laws and drug prohibition.

Image Credits

Fig. 9.1: Source: https://www.pewresearch.org/fact-tank/2018/10/08/americans-support-marijuana-legalization/.
Fig. 9.2: Source: https://commons.wikimedia.org/wiki/File:Drug_use_is_more_common_in_more_unequal_countries.jpg.
Fig. 9.3: Source: https://www.drugabuse.gov/related-topics/trends-statistics/overdose-death-rates.
Fig. 9.4: Source: https://www.drugabuse.gov/related-topics/trends-statistics/overdose-death-rates.
Fig. 9.5: Source: https://www.usnews.com/news/blogs/washington-whispers/2012/06/21/chart-what-the-dea-refuses-to-admit-about-drugs?google_editors_picks=true.
Fig. 9.6: Source: https://commons.wikimedia.org/wiki/File:HarmCausedByDrugsTable.svg.
Fig. 9.7: Source: http://www.nospinesurgery.com/blog/prescription-drug-abuse/.

Crime and Criminal Justice

CRIMINOLOGY TERMS

- **Crime**: The breaking of a formal written law; punished judicially.
- **Deviance**: The breaking or lack of conforming with existing societal norms; punished socially.
- **Felony**: Serious offenses with crimes punishable by more than a year in prison.
- **Misdemeanor**: Minor offenses.
- **Property crime**: Taking property without force; sometimes a felony, sometimes a misdemeanor.
- **Juvenile crime**: Crimes committed by those 7 to 17.
  - **Juvenile status offender**: Refers to someone who broke a law that only applies to those under 17.

Positivists versus Classicalists

Positivists: People are social and are not prone to act criminally unless some biological, psychological, or social factor is involved.

Classicalists: People make rational choices to commit crimes based on pleasure/pain calculations.

More resources:

Difference between Deviance and Crime: http://www.differencebetween.net/miscellaneous/legal-miscellaneous/difference-between-deviance-and-crime/

Functionalist Perspective

- **Anomie (Durkheim):** A state of normlessness, or little regulation from structure which leads to unguided (often criminal) behavior in an attempt to obtain societal goals (O-dog in *Menace II Society*).
  - **Theory of anomie:** Social instability caused by a wearing away of standards and ethics.
- **Strain theory (Merton)**: The idea that we are all socialized to attain the same goals and that being exposed to these goals without the ability to obtain them

causes strain; close to anomic stress but can be present in the face of structure and regulation (George Costanza in *Seinfeld*).
- **Merton**: Crime results because the pursuit of the American dream is blocked for some people. Crime is a response to some social factor.
- Durkheim's three functions of crime and deviance mark the boundaries of morality, promote social solidarity, and bring about needed change.[1]

Conflict Perspective

- Acts are not inherently criminal; society defines them as such.
- Law enforcement protects the interests of the powerful.
  - The wealthy create the laws that punish the poor while many illegal acts committed by the wealthy are often not considered crimes.
- Argues that the criminal justice system is intentionally unequal.
- Capitalism teaches people to be selfish and competitive, resulting in inequality.
- "The rich get rich, the poor get prison."

Symbolic Interactionist Perspective

- **Labeling theory** (Erikson): The audience labels what a crime is: "[D]eviance is a property conferred upon someone ... by witnesses."[2]
- More strongly considers race, gender, and culture.
  - People react to how they believe others view them.
  - People learn criminality through social interactions.
- **Shaming**: Process of expressing disapproval, which has the intent of invoking remorse; a deliberate effort to attach a negative meaning to a behavior.
  - Shaming is correlated with low crime rates.
  - **Stigmatized shame** is a permanent label given to an offender, which could actually increase the chances of reoffending because the guilty person is forever labeled.
  - **Reintegrative shaming** is an effort to bring an offender back into the community after punishment.

---

1   Émile Durkheim and George Simpson, *Émile Durkheim on The Division of Labor in Society* (New York: Macmillan, 1933); Hamlin, J. (2009) *The Normality of Crime.* Durkheim and Erikson, Department of Sociology and Anthropology. UMD

2   Howard Saul Becker, *Outsiders: Studies in the Sociology of Deviance* (London: Free Press of Glencoe, 1963), 9.

THEORIES OF CRIME

- **Critical/Marxist perspectives**: Capitalism produces a number of problems, including crime, and creates a surplus population, many of who are underclass.
- **Functionalist perspective**: Crime, and especially the crime control industry, is functional for capitalism and society.
- **Cultural deviance theories**: Criminal values and traditions emerge within communities most affected by social disorganization (e.g., Cohen's "culture of the gang" perspective). A high proportion of lowerclass youths (especially males) do poorly in school; poor school performance relates to delinquency; poor school performance stems from a conflict between dominant middleclass values of the school system and values of lowerclass youths; and most lowerclass male delinquency is committed in a gang (rather than individual) context, partly as a means of meeting some basic human needs, such as self-esteem and belonging.
- **Strain/anomie theory**: Cultural norms of "success" emphasize such goals as money, status, and power, while the means to obtain such success are not equally distributed. As a result of blocked opportunities, many among the disadvantaged resort to illegal means, which are more readily available.
  - Suggests there is a "dark side" to the American dream, which stems from a contradiction in American capitalism (Shelden); the same forces that promote progress and ambition also produce a lot of crime since there is such an incredible pressure to succeed "at any cost."
- **Social disorganization/social ecology**: Crime stems from certain community or neighborhood characteristics, such as poverty, dilapidated housing, high density, low mobility, and high rates of unemployment.
  - **Broken window theory**: Often credited with lowering the crime rate in NYC in the 70s, the idea that cleaning up graffiti, picking up trash, and generally making high-class areas look nicer reduces all crime, especially property crime.

Reading 10.1.

Crime Theory Tweets

by Justin W. Patchin

140 Character Summaries of Popular Criminological Theories
Justin W. Patchin, University of Wisconsin-Eau Claire (CRMJ 301)

THEORY	MAIN THEORIST(S)	SUMMARY
Classical school of criminology	Beccaria	Crime is inherently rewarding. People offend based on a free will choice. To prevent, must punish so potential benefit not worth it.
Positivist school of criminology	Lombroso	Born criminals. Crime caused by something beyond person's control (usually biological or psychological).
Social disorganization	Park & Burgess; Shaw & McKay; Sampson	High mobility areas result in inability of neighbors to organize in defense of common values. Physical disorder symbols of social breakdown.
Broken Windows	Wilson and Kelling	Criminal behavior thrives in areas where residents are apathetic toward their environment and neighbors (absence of collective efficacy).
General theory of crime	Gottfredson & Hirschi	Crime & deviance a result of low self-control. One's level of self-control stabile at age 8. Opportunity also important.
Social bonding theory	Hirschi	Our bond (attachment, commitment, involvement, belief) to parents & others restrains our innate desire to engage in deviance.
Strain theory (classic/anomie)	Merton	Pursuit of American Dream (wealth accumulation) is main cause of crime. Some will do whatever is necessary to acquire $$$.

Justin W. Patchin, "Crime Theory Tweets." Copyright © by Justin W. Patchin. Reprinted with permission.

THEORY	MAIN THEORIST(S)	SUMMARY
Strain theory	Cloward & Ohlin	Illegitimate means to achieve wealth are also inaccessible to some. Perception is that joining a gang increases opportunities.
Strain theory	Cohen	Some youth are unable to achieve middle-class standards so they supplant legit pursuits with desire to achieve status/respect among peers.
General strain theory	Agnew	Strain plus negative affect equals crime. 3 sources: inability to achieve; something valued removed; something painful introduced.
Differential association theory	Sutherland	We believe and behave in ways that are consistent with those in our lives who we value. Peers important.
Social learning theory	Akers	Criminal behaviors are learned in the same way that other behaviors are learned. Rewards, punishments, reinforcements, imitation.
Subcultural theories	Miller; Anderson; Wolfgang & Ferracuti	Certain groups have different values and incentives than dominant culture. Honor/respect esteemed over all else (even life and freedom).
Deterrence theory	Beccaria; Patternoster	People will refrain from criminal behavior if the cost is great enough. Penalty must be swift, certain, and sufficiently severe.
Rational choice theory	Clarke & Cornish	Potential criminals weigh possible costs versus possible benefits when deciding whether to offend. Behavior a function of opportunity.
Routine activities theory	Cohen & Felson	Crime occurs when motivated offender, suitable target, and lack of capable guardian converge.

THEORY	MAIN THEORIST(S)	SUMMARY
Labeling theory	Tannenbaum; Lemert	If society defines a person as a criminal, deviant, felon, or troublemaker, that person will organize life & behaviors around those titles.
Reintegrative shaming	Braithwaite	Shame is most important in understanding criminal's motives. When stigmatized by society, crime more likely. When reintegrated, less likely.
Feminist criminology theory	Adler; Simon	Patriarchy (male domination) main cause of crime. Gender socialization also important. Further liberation may increase female crime.
Conflict theory	Marx	There's conflict over values & scarce resources. Mediated by those who have power in a way that benefits them at the expense of others.
Developmental theory	Moffitt; Sampson & Laub	Different experiences over life course influence one's risk of offending. Risk highest in adolescence. Transitions important.
Control balance	Tittle	When one has excess of control over others or lack of control over their own circumstances, they're predisposed to crime.
Integrated theory	Elliott, Huizinga, & Ageton	Borrows ideas from various other perspectives and combines them in a way that makes sense and explains more crime.
General Theory of Crime	Agnew	Crime likely when constraints against it are low & motivations for it are high. Self, family, peers, work, & school domains important.

Factors Predictive of Criminal Acts

- Unemployment
- Education
- Social class
- Race
- Gender
- Neighborhood/Zip Code/Census Tract

Number of Prisoners

The United States has the highest percentage of its population in prison, as well as the highest raw total of prisoners. The prison population began to increase rapidly in the 1970s and is mostly related to the war on drugs and increasingly punitive sentences. The increase in prison population cannot be attributed to an increase in population, nor to an increase in the crime rate.

Note: Figures reflect most recent available data for each country. Territories are counted separately. Data accessed May 1, 2018.
Source: World Prison Brief, Institute for Criminal Policy Research.

PEW RESEARCH CENTER

FIGURE 10.1 US Incarcerates a larger share of its population than any other country.

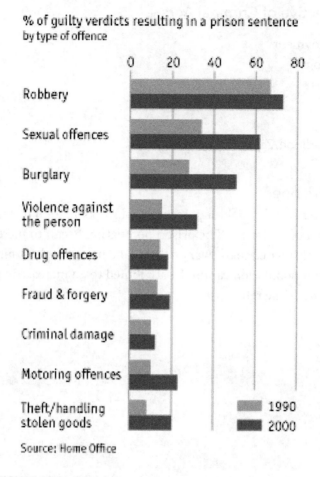

% of guilty verdicts resulting in a prison sentence by type of offence

FIGURE 10.2   Bang 'em up.

Reading 10.2.

2 Million Americans Behind Bars, but the Issue Gets Little Media Coverage

by Anonymous

They house a high proportion of mentally ill inmates. Violent-incident data from 99 state prisons from 2006 to 2012 show far more reports at facilities housing high numbers of mentally ill, violent offenders than at other prisons. Michele Deitch of the University of Texas says the data raise questions about the staff's ability to manage inmates and keep prisoners and officers safe.

Anonymous, "2 Million Americans Behind Bars, but the Issue Gets Little Media Coverage," *Corrections Forum*, vol. 22, no. 5, pp. 8,10. Copyright © 2013 by Criminal Justice Media, Inc. Reprinted with permission. Provided by ProQuest LLC. All rights reserved.

State officials say the numbers do not tell the whole story. They say state facilities are safe, and programs aimed at helping mentally ill inmates are working. "I think we do a very good job taking care of what we do here," said Barry Martin, a senior warden. The state is facing an increase in prisoners requiring psychiatric care, a trend seen nationwide in recent decades. The number of inmates treated for mental illness by the University of Texas Medical Branch, which provides most inmate care in Texas, grew from about 14,500 in August 2008 to nearly 17,900 in August 2012. More than 15 percent of the more than 151,000 inmates have been given a diagnosis of some form of mental illness.

2 MILLION AMERICANS BEHIND BARS, BUT THE ISSUE GETS LITTLE MEDIA COVERAGE
Nieman Reports

Attorney General Eric Holder says "too many Americans go to too many prisons for far too long, and for no truly good law enforcement reason," but Nieman Reports says that "despite the heavy toll that mass incarceration exacts every day and in countless ways on many American communities, families, and of course the incarcerated themselves, the topic attracts remarkably little consistent coverage in the mainstream media." David Fathi of the American Civil Liberties Union's National Prison Project has seen only a modest increase in news coverage of criminal justice reform despite his sense that the nation is starting to turn the corner on mass incarceration.

Crime and court reporters, still a staple of newsrooms everywhere, tend to see their role as ending after conviction. The number of reporters assigned to cover prisons and criminal justice, even part time, has dwindled due to decades of cuts, beat consolidation—and lack of interest. "They don't see this as an important beat," says Paul Wright, a former Washington state prison inmate who founded Prison Legal News in 1990, when he was behind bars. For news organizations to cover the issue properly, Wright says, they need reporters with background, and sources. "Normally well-intentioned or hard-nosed journalists, they tend to take statements by prison officials or government officials at face value, with no type of critical disbelief," he says.

CRITICS: PRIVATE PRISON FIRMS DEMAND "LOCKUP QUOTAS," "LOW-CRIME TAXES"
Tulsa World

A research group charges that private prison operators often have "lockup quotas" and "low-crime taxes" built into the language of their contracts. A group called In the Public Interest says that many contracts for private prison operators feature language guaranteeing 80 percent to 100 percent prison occupancy and forcing taxpayers to pay penalties for empty beds.

These practices result in taxpayers essentially paying more money to house inmates even when crime decreases, becoming a de facto low-crime tax, a report by the organization says. Lockup quotas in private prison contracts range between 80 and 100 percent. Arizona, Louisiana, Oklahoma and Virginia have the highest occupancy guarantee requirements, with quotas requiring between 95 and 100 percent occupancy. Former Oklahoma Department of Corrections Director Justin Jones said, "What corrections should not be is a turnkey for-profit machine, and that's exactly that we've turned them into when we guarantee occupancy, with no requirement to produce results."

Reading 10.3.

The New Jim Crow

How mass incarceration turns people of color into permanent second-class citizens

by Michelle Alexander

The first time I encountered the idea that our criminal-justice system functions much like a racial caste system, I dismissed the notion. It was more than 10 years ago in Oakland when I was rushing to catch the bus and spotted a bright orange sign stapled to a telephone pole. It screamed in large, bold print: "The Drag War is the New Jim Crow." I scanned the text of the flyer and then muttered something like. "Yeah, the criminal-justice system is racist in many ways, but making such an absurd comparison doesn't help. People will just think you're crazy." I then hopped on the bus and headed to my new job as director of the Racial Justice Project for the American Civil Liberties Union of Northern California.

What a difference a decade makes. After years of working on issues of racial profiling, police brutality, and drug-law enforcement in poor communities of color as well as working with former inmates struggling to "re-enter" a society that never seemed to have much use for them, I began to suspect that I was wrong about the criminal-justice system. It was not just another institution infected with racial bias but a different beast entirely. The activists who posted the sign on the telephone pole were not crazy, nor were the smattering of lawyers and advocates around the country who were beginning to connect the dots between our current system of mass incarceration and earlier forms of racial control. Quite belatedly, I came to see that mass incarceration in the United States has, in fact, emerged as a comprehensive and well-disguised system of racialized social control that functions in a manner strikingly similar to Jim Crow.

Michelle Alexander, "The New Jim Crow," *The American Prospect*, vol. 22, no. 1, pp. 19-21. Copyright © 2011 by The American Prospect. Reprinted with permission. Provided by ProQuest LLC. All rights reserved.

California Institution for Men, Chino, California

What has changed since the collapse of Jim Crow has less to do with the basic structure of our society than with the language we use to justify severe inequality. In the era of colorblindness, it is no longer socially permissible to use race, explicitly, as justification for discrimination, exclusion, or social contempt. Rather, we use our criminal-justice system to associate criminality with people of color and then engage in the prejudiced practices we supposedly left behind. Today, it is legal to discriminate against ex-offenders in ways it was once legal to discriminate against African Americans. Once you're labeled a felon, depending on the state you're in, the old forms of discrimination—employment discrimination, housing discrimination, denial of the right to vote, and exclusion from jury service—are suddenly legal. As a criminal, you have scarcely more rights and arguably less respect than a black man living in Alabama at the height of Jim Crow. We have not ended racial caste in America; we have merely redesigned it.

More than two million African Americans are currently under the control of the criminal-justice system—in prison or jail, on probation or parole. During the past few decades, millions more have cycled in and out of the system: indeed, nearly 70 percent of people released from prison are re-arrested within three years. Most people appreciate that millions of African Americans were locked into a second-class status during slavery and Jim Crow, and that these earlier systems of racial control created a legacy of political, social, and economic inequality that our nation is still struggling to overcome. Relatively few. however, seem to appreciate that millions of African

Americans are subject to a new system of control — mass incarceration—which also has a devastating effect on families and communities. The harm is greatly intensified when prisoners are released. As criminologist Jeremy Travis has observed. "In this brave new world, punishment for the original offense is no longer enough; one's debt to society is never paid."

The scale of incarceration-related discrimination is astonishing. Ex-offenders are routinely stripped of essential rights. Current felon-disenfranchisement laws bar 13 percent of African American men from casting a vote, thus making mass incarceration an effective tool of voter suppression—one reminiscent of the poll taxes and literacy tests of the Jim Crow era. Employers routinely discriminate against an applicant based on criminal history, as do land lords. In most states, it is also legal to make ex-drug offenders ineligible for food stamps. In some major urban areas, if you take into account prisoners—who are excluded from poverty and unemployment statistics, thus masking the severity of black disadvantage—more than half of working-age African American men have criminal records and are thus subject to legalized discrimination for the rest of their lives. In Chicago, for instance, nearly 80 percent of working-age African American men had criminal records in 2002. These men are permanently locked into an inferior, second-class status, or caste, by law and custom.

The official explanation for this is crime rates. Our prison population increased sevenfold in less than 30 years, going from about 300,000 to more than 2 million, supposedly due to rising crime in poor communities of color.

Crime rates, however, actually have little to do with incarceration rates. Crime rates have fluctuated during the past 30 years and today are at historical lows, but incarceration rates have consistently soared. Most sociologists and criminologists today will acknowledge that crime rates and incarceration rates have moved independently of each other; incarceration rates have skyrocketed regardless of whether crime has gone up or down in any particular community or in the nation as a whole.

What caused the unprecedented explosion in our prison population? It turns out that the activists who posted the sign on the telephone pole were right: The "war on drugs" is the single greatest contributor to mass incarceration in the United States. Drug convictions accounted for about two-thirds of the increase in the federal prison system and more than half of the increase in the state prison system between 1985 and 2000—the period of the U.S. penal system's most dramatic expansion.

Contrary to popular belief, the goal of this war is not to root out violent offenders or drug kingpins. In 2005, for example, four out of five drug arrests were for possession, while only one out five were for sales. A 2007 report from Sentencing Project found that most people in state prison for drug offenses had no history of violence or significant selling activity. Nearly 80 percent of the increase in drug arrests in the 1990s, when the drug war peaked, could be attributed to possession of marijuana, a substance less harmful than alcohol or tobacco and at least as prevalent in middle-class white communities and on college campuses as in poor communities of color.

The drug war, though, has been waged almost exclusively in poor communities of color, despite the fact that studies consistently indicate that people of all races use and sell illegal drugs at remarkably similar rates. This is not what one would guess by peeking inside our nation's prisons and jails, which are overflowing with black and brown drug offenders. In 2000, African Americans made up 80 percent to 90 percent of imprisoned drug offenders in some states.

The extraordinary racial disparities in our criminal-justice system would not exist today but for the complicity of the United States Supreme Court. In the failed war on drugs, our Fourth Amendment protections against unreasonable searches and seizures have been eviscerated. Stop-and-frisk operations in poor communities of color are now routine; the arbitrary and discriminatory police practices the framers aimed to prevent are now commonplace. Justice Thurgood Marshall, in a strident dissent in the 1989 case of Skinner v. Railway Labor Executive Association, felt compelled to remind the Court that there is "no drug exception" to the Fourth Amendment. His reminder was in vain. The Supreme Court had begun steadily unraveling Fourth Amendment protections against stops, interrogations, and seizures in bus stops, train stations, schools, workplaces, airports, and on sidewalks in a series of cases starting in the early 1.980s. These aggressive sweep tactics in poor communities of color are now as accepted as separate water fountains were several decades ago.

"Today, it's legal to discriminate against ex-offenders in many ways it was once legal to discriminate against African Americans."

If the system is as rife with conscious and unconscious bias, many people often ask, why aren't more lawsuits filed? Why not file class-action lawsuits challenging bias by the police or prosecutors? Doesn't the 14th Amendment guarantee equal protection of the law?

What many don't realize is that the Supreme Court has ruled that in the absence of conscious, intentional bias—tantamount to an admission or a racial slur—you can't present allegations of race discrimination in the criminal-justice system. These rulings have created a nearly insurmountable hurdle, as law-enforcement officials know better than to admit racial bias out loud, and much of the discrimination that pervades this system is rooted in unconscious racial stereotypes, or "hunches" about certain types of people that come down to race. Because these biases operate unconsciously, the only proof of bias is in the outcomes: how people of different races are treated. The Supreme Court, however, has ruled that no matter how severe the racial disparities, and no matter how overwhelming or compelling the statistical evidence may be, you must have proof of conscious, intentional bias to present a credible case of discrimination. In this way, the system of mass incarceration is now immunized from judicial scrutiny for racial bias, much as slavery and Jim Crow laws were once protected from constitutional challenge.

As a nation, we have managed to create a massive system of control that locks a significant percentage of our population—a group defined largely by race—into a permanent, second-class status. This is not the fault of one political party. It is not merely the fault of biased police, prosecutors, or judges. We have all been complicit in the emergence of mass incarceration in the United States. In the so-called era of colorblindness, we have become blind not so much to race as to the re-emergence of caste in America. We have turned away from those labeled "criminals." viewing them as "others" unworthy of our concern. Some of us have been complicit by remaining silent, even as we have a sneaking suspicion that something has gone horribly wrong. We must break that silence and awaken to the human-rights nightmare that is occurring on our watch.

We, as a nation, can do better than this.

WHY WE PUNISH

Understanding why a society punishes can go a long way toward understanding criminal justice in that society. It also relates to the methods and prevalence of punishments like incarceration and community service.

> **CRITICAL THINKING:** What narratives about punishment exist in our society?

Following are some of the basic social theories of punishment:

- **Retributivism** (more of a moral justification): The punishment in question is just because the offender deserves it.
  - *Lex talionis*: To restore the balance between offender and victim.

- **Social contract theory:** We make a contract to give up certain rights in order for other rights to be protected; when we break that contract, we deserve to have our rights taken away.
- **Grievance theory:** The offender has caused a grievance for the victim, and the punishment of the offender will satisfy the victim and make up for that grievance (although proposed as a form of retribution, it is questionable as to whether it really is retributivist in principle).

- **Utilitarian** (more of a social/structural justification): The punishment in question has some social benefit that outweighs the negative aspects of the punishment.
  - **General prevention**: General prevention uses the punishment of the offender to prevent others from committing crimes.
  - **Specific prevention**
    - "Imprisonment deters [the] individual from committing crime."[3] So, one reason for sending the offender to prison for a crime is to make him less likely to commit further crimes through fear of more imprisonment.
    - Prison is "to protect the public from certain offenders."[4]
  - Rehabilitation

More resources:

Once a Criminal, Always a Criminal?
https://www.cbsnews.com/news/once-a-criminal-always-a-criminal/

Prison Inmate: We Get Puppies, Ice cream and Flowers
https://www.youtube.com/watch?v=MauMi-CL7G9Y

Death Penalty

CRITICAL THINKING:
- Which country executes the most people?
- Which US state executes the most people?
- Is there a racial component?
- Is it a real deterrent?

- In a 1990 report, the non-partisan US General Accounting Office found "a pattern of evidence indicating racial disparities in the charging, sentencing, and imposition of the death penalty." The study concluded that a defendant was several times more likely to be sentenced to death if the murder victim was white. This

---

3   Martin Wright, *Making Good: Prisons, Punishment and Beyond* (UK: Waterside Press, 2008), 26.

4   Ibid.

has been confirmed by the findings of many other studies that, holding all other factors constant, the single most reliable predictor of whether someone will be sentenced to death is the race of the victim.[5]

- A report sponsored by the American Bar Association in 2007 concluded that one-third of African American death row inmates in Philadelphia would have received sentences of life imprisonment if they had not been African American.[6]
- A January 2003 study released by the University of Maryland concluded that race and geography are major factors in death penalty decisions. Specifically, prosecutors are more likely to seek a death sentence when the race of the victim is white and are less likely to seek a death sentence when the victim is African American.[7]
- A 2007 study of death sentences in Connecticut conducted by Yale University School of Law revealed that African American defendants receive the death penalty at three times the rate of white defendants in cases where the victims are white.[8]

Intersection with Race

As discussed in the chapter about race, the criminal justice system has a number of intersections with the social construct of race. Though racial disparities exist amongst other groups, and there are disparities that are not racial in nature, examining racial disparities among blacks in the American justice system can be very telling. LatinX individuals tend to have outcomes between those of Black Americans and Asians and/or white Americans. These disparities tend to exist at every level from the seemingly more benign (ie: being policed) to use of deadly force (ie: the killing of George Floyd). Moreover different demographic groups acknowledge this disparity at varying rates.

Blacks Are Overrepresented in Every Aspect of Criminal Justice

- They are more likely to have police called on them.
- They are more likely to be approached, stopped, and searched by police.

---

5   Lowell Dodge, "Death Penalty Sentencing: Research Indicates Pattern of Racial Disparities," February 26, 1990,

6   American Bar Association, "Evaluating Fairness and Accuracy in State Death Penalty Systems: The Pennsylvania Death Penalty Assessment Report Executive Summary, October, 2007,

7   Paternoster, R., Brame, R., Bacon, S., Ditchfield, A., Beckman, K., Frederique, N., et al. (2003). An Empirical Analysis of Maryland's Death Sentencing System With Respect to the Influence of Race and Legal Jurisdiction. University of Maryland, Department of Crimninology. College Park: Report to the Governor of Maryland.

8   John J. Donahue, III, Capital Punishment in Connecticut, 1973–2007: A Comprehensive Evaluation from 4686 Murders to One Execution," ; "Death Penalty and Race," Amnesty International, January 2003, https://www.amnestyusa.org/issues/death-penalty/death-penalty-facts/death-penalty-and-race/

- Black and Hispanic drivers are both are searched three times more often than whites.[9]
- Whites are 50 percent more likely to have contraband when searched.
- They are more likely to be arrested by police.
  - When African Americans or Latinos are stopped and questioned by police, the new research found that police arrested them in 82 to 85 percent of cases.
  - Non-Latino whites and Native Americans who were stopped and questioned by police were arrested about 70 percent of the time. And when police stopped and questioned Asians, about 60 percent of the encounters resulted in arrest.
- They are more likely to have escalated or violent encounters with police.
- Blacks are more likely to be given jail time for similar crimes as whites.
- Sentences for blacks are 25–40 percent longer for congruent crime as whites.
- They are more likely to be killed by police.
  - Controlling for population blacks are 2.5 times more likely to be killed. These disparities are greater among young people and unarmed people.

More resources:

Racial Stereotyping:
https://www.youtube.com/watch?v=8ABRI-WybBqM

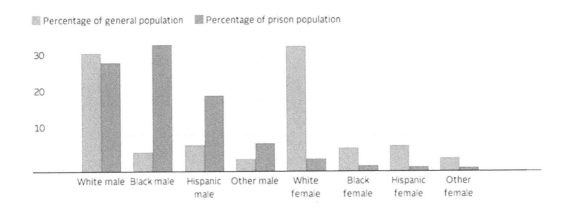

FIGURE 10.3   **Race and sex of general population versus prison population, 2012.**

---

9   Andrew Kahn and Chris Kirk, "What It's Like to Be Black in the Criminal Justice System," *Slate*, August 9, 2015, https://slate.com/news-and-politics/2015/08/racial-disparities-in-the-criminal-justice-system-eight-charts-illustrating-how-its-stacked-against-blacks.html

SUMMARY

While the crime rate of the United States has been dropping since the 1990s, the prison population continued to grow through the mid 2010s. The United States currently has the highest incarceration rate on Earth and has held that top spot for over two decades. While rehabilitation is part of the social narrative in America regarding punishment, as an outcome the United States has one of the worst recidivism rates in the world. Last, social factors like race matter. In the criminal justice system race matters in almost every aspect, from first police contact to sentencing, to death penalty. But as noteworthy is that race matters for the conference of deviance upon an individual.

Image Credits

Fig. 10.1: Source: https://www.pewresearch.org/fact-tank/2018/05/02/americas-incarceration-rate-is-at-a-two-decade-low/.
Fig. 10.2: Source: https://www.economist.com/britain/2002/03/21/prison-isnt-working.
Fig. 10.3: Source: https://makeupview.co/race-makeup-in-prison/.

Social Class

CRITICAL THINKING:
- What policies affect class/economic inequality?
- How do Americans talk about social class?
- Think back to Marx. How class conscious are Americans?

"The belief that the United States is a classless society or, alternatively, that most Americans are "middle class" persists ... despite pervasive socioeconomic stratification"

(Bullock, Wyche and Williams, 2001)

WHAT IS SOCIAL CLASS?

CRITICAL THINKING: There are multiple ways to categorize class. What are some?

Social class:

- A quick way to roughly refer to someone's standing or position in society.
- Takes into consideration wealth, income, occupation, power.
- Cultural (what you know) and social capital (who you know/who is in your social networks) and to a lesser extent prestige and residential location.
- We will use elite, middle/working, and impoverished (poor).
- SES (socioeconomic status), which is based on income, wealth, education, occupation, and related variables, is another way to measure class.

Stratification:

- Stratification denotes social inequality built into the structure of society (in our case capitalism).

- Denotes hierarchical differences in economic positions; that is, being higher is better or more valuable than being lower.
- Denotes a *system* that shapes opportunities for individuals.
- Can take many forms. We have a class system; other systems include slavery, caste, and serfdom.

In other words, a certain amount of inequality is inevitable and has a function (incentive to work, rewarding societal contributions, etc.).

CRITICAL THINKING: How much inequality is too much?

HOW EQUAL IS THE UNITED STATES?

Table 7: Income equality in selected countries

Country/Overall Rank	Gini Coefficient
1. Sweden	23.0
2. Norway	25.0
8. Austria	26.0
10. Germany	27.0
17. Denmark	29.0
25. Australia	30.5
34. Italy	32.0
35. Canada	32.1
37. France	32.7
42. Switzerland	33.7
43. United Kingdom	34.0
45. Egypt	34.4
56. India	36.8
61. Japan	38.1
68. Israel	39.2
81. China	41.5
82. Russia	42.3
90. Iran	44.5
93. United States	45.0
107. Mexico	48.2
125. Brazil	56.7
133. South Africa	65.0

Note: These figures reflect family/household income, not individual income.

Source: Central Intelligence Agency (2010).

FIGURE 11.1   The Gini coefficient has consistently been between 40 and 45 for the last 15 years.

More resources:

Gini in the Bottle:
https://www.economist.com/democracy-in-america/2013/11/26/gini-in-the-bottle

CRITICAL THINKING:

Is equality something we should aspire to?
- Why?
- Equality of opportunity?
- Equality of outcomes?
  - Race
  - Gender

ECONOMIC CHANGES THAT HAVE AFFECTED CLASS STRUCTURE

- Globalization
  - Outsourcing
  - Increase in availability of markets
  - Increase in connectedness of markets
- Technological advances
  - Automation
    - Less manufacturing
- Policy changes
  - Taxes
  - Legislation (e.g., labor laws, minimum wage laws)
- Structural changes
  - Cost of college
  - Percentage of jobs that require a high school or college degree

AMERICAN NARRATIVES ABOUT SOCIAL CLASS

- Think about American narratives about social class. What are they?
- Although there are many, the most prevailing narratives are the following:

1. Anyone can achieve anything.

   - Regardless of things like race, class, and gender.
   - This ability to achieve is mostly based on merit.

2. We are a highly mobile society.
   - Elevate/value rags-to-riches stories.
3. The "American Dream" is quite achievable.

When taken to their logical conclusions these narratives support/prop up a few ideas that permeate American society (and other societies with similar class narratives). Among these ideas is that those higher on the ladder usually have earned such a position, and those lower on the ladder tend to have made mistakes such as bad decision making, being lazy, or doing poorly at work. They also prop up the idea of a meritocracy. A meritocracy is a society where one's position in society is almost exclusively based on merit.

CRITICAL THINKING:	If we don't have a 100% meritocracy, what are positions in society also based on?

How Much Do Americans Value Equality?

In short, they value it quite a bit. Particularly, they value economic equality and equality of opportunity.

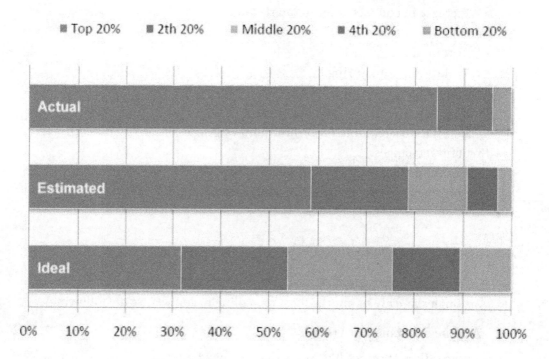

FIGURE 11.2 **Percent of wealth owned.**

FIGURE 11.3   Real versus imagined wealth distribution in the US.[1]

| CRITICAL THINKING: | How should equality versus mobility be weighed? Is America a mobile nation? |

More resources:

State Lawmakers Play a Major Role in Advancing the Quality of Americans' Lives: http://www.pewstates.org/news-room/video-library/economic-mobility-and-the-american-dream-85899378857

---

1   See also The Daily Conversation, "Wealth Inequality in America," March 6, 2013, https://www.youtube.com/watch?v=JTj9AcwkaKM.

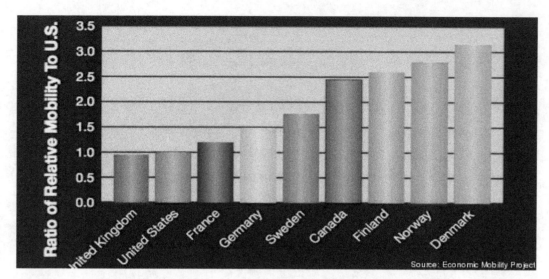

FIGURE 11.4 The US has less relative mobility than many industrialized nations.

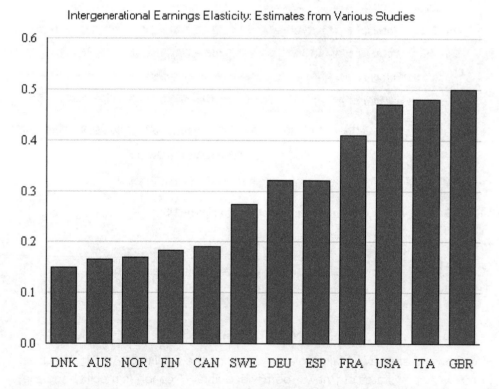

FIGURE 11.5 The strength of the link between individual and parental earnings varies across OECD countries.

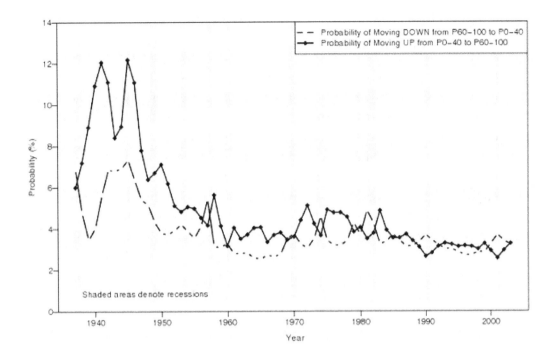

FIGURE 11.6   Downward and upward mobility.

Earnings Mobility of U.S. Households, 2001 to 2007					
	Income Quintile in 2007				
Quintile in 2001	Lowest	2nd	Middle	4th	Highest
Lowest 20%	56%	31%	8%	3%	2%
Second 20%	25%	39%	23%	10%	3%
Middle 20%	10%	17%	42%	24%	8%
Fourth 20%	4%	10%	20%	45%	21%
Highest 20%	5%	4%	7%	18%	66%
Fraction of Households That Left Their Income Quintile from 2001 to 2007					
	44%	61%	58%	55%	34%

FIGURE 11.7   Earnings mobility of US households, 2001 to 2007.

Tim Wise said the following about social mobility in the US:

"According to the available research, if your father's wages rank in the top fifth of all income earners in the country, you'll have nearly a 60 percent chance of surpassing your dad's status over time. On the other hand, if your father's earnings fall in the bottom fifth, the odds that you'll do better than him one day plummet to less than 5 percent. And not only is mobility itself limited, it appears to be diminishing relative to previous generations. As a recent study for the Boston Federal Reserve Bank discovered, among the nation's poorest families, the percentage that were able to climb simply to the next quintile (still far from well-off), fell from over half in the 1968–78 period, to only 46 percent in the period from 1993–2003. Additionally, the study found that poor families are 10 times more likely to remain poor than to move into the highest income quintile, while those who started out rich are 5 times more likely to remain there, as to fall into either of the lower two quintiles of earners."[2]

RSF *Russell Sage Foundation - Chartbook of Social Inequality*

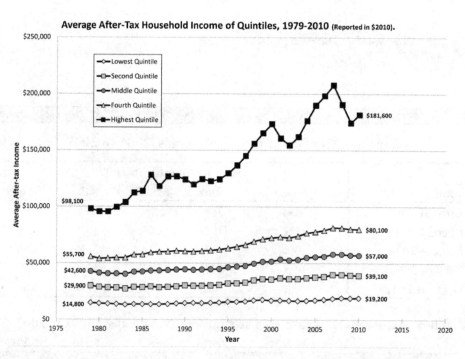

FIGURE 11.8 **Average after-tax household income of quintiles, 1979–2007.**

---

2   Tim Wise, "Getting What We Deserve? Wealth, Race, and Entitlement in America," September 26, 2011, http://www.timwise.org/2011/09/getting-what-we-deserve-wealth-race-and-entitlement-in-america/.

American mobility is hovering around an all-time recorded low. Particularly, it has become sticky at the ends, meaning that the poorest and richest Americans demonstrate the least mobility. This relates to the idea that social forces are strongest at the extremes.

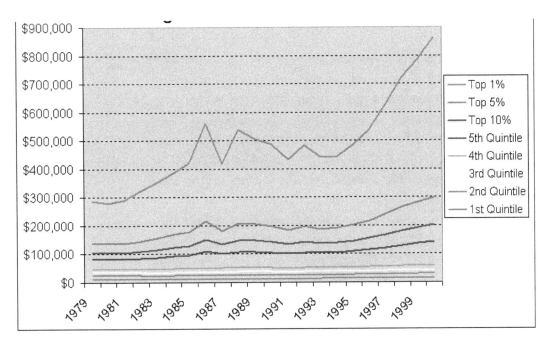

FIGURE 11.9   **Average after-tax income in 2000 dollars.**

Reading 11.1.

The New Inequality Debate

More mainstream economists now find that the income mal-distribution reflects the political sway of elites, not economic imperatives

by Robert Kuttner

More and more mainstream economists have lately discovered a phenomenon that their discipline too often assumes away. They have discovered power. And this fundamentally changes the nature of the debate about inequality.

In the usual economic model, markets are mostly efficient. Power is not relevant, because competition will generally thwart attempts to place a thumb on the market scale. Thus if the society is becoming more unequal it must be (a favorite verb form) because skills are receiving greater rewards, and the less-skilled are necessarily left

Robert Kuttner, "The New Inequality Debate," *The American Prospect*, vol. 27, no. 1, pp. 56-61. Copyright © 2016 by The American Prospect. Reprinted with permission. Provided by ProQuest LLC. All rights reserved.

behind; or because technology is appropriately displacing workers; or because in *a* global market, lower-wage nations can out-compete Americans; or because deregulation makes markets more efficient, with greater rewards to winners; or because new financial instruments add such efficiency to the economy that they justify billion-dollar paydays for their inventors.

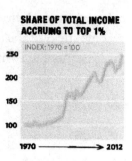

SHARE OF TOTAL INCOME ACCRUING TO TOP 1%

INDEX: 1970 = 100

250
200
150
100

1970 ——————▶ 2012

The top has pulled away, for beyond their contribution to the economy. Data source: Jason Furman and Peter Orszog, "A Firm-level Perspective on the Role of Rents in the Rise in Inequality"

Increasingly, however, influential orthodox economists are having serious second thoughts. What if market outcomes and the very rules of the market game reflect political power, not market efficiency? Indeed, what if gross inequality is not efficient, and there is a broad zone of indeterminate income distributions consistent with strong economic performance? What if greater liberalization of financial markets produced tens of trillions of costs to the economy, benefits that are hard to discern, and billion-dollar paydays for traders that don't comport with their contributions to general economic welfare? Evidence like this is piling up, and hard to ignore.

ANTHONY ATKINSON'S NEW BOOK, *Inequality: What Can Be Done?*, is both emblem and evidence of this shift in mainstream economic thinking. Atkinson, of the London School of Economics and Oxford's Nuffield College, is the dean of economists who study inequality. After an exhaustive compilation of data and trends, Atkinson bluntly attributes rising inequality directly or indirectly to "changes in the balance of power." Thus, he adds, "Measures to reduce inequality can be successful only if countervailing power is brought to bear."

Though it has not attracted the celebrity attention, in many respects Atkinson's work is more important than Thomas Piketty's path-breaking *Capital in the Twenty-First Century*, and is the perfect sequel. Where Piketty explained the tendency of wealth and income to concentrate, Atkinson digs deeper into what drove this shift and why conventional remedies will not reverse the trends. He has a far surer grasp than Piketty of the political dynamics that made possible the anomalous egalitarian era of the 30 glorious years after World War II.

In Atkinson's telling, the postwar social bargain drastically reduced inequality using several levers. Progressive taxes and welfare-state transfers were part of the story. Likewise a more highly regulated form of globalization. Worker and trade-union power resulted in a larger share of the total national product going to wage and salaries. Antitrust and some public ownership helped, too. All of these instruments, and more, have been reversed since about 1980—due mainly to a shift in political power. This shift increases the influence as well as the wealth of the rich, which leads to a self-reinforcing circle of more such policies, and more inequality.

In the labor market, the greater "flexibility" long promoted by many economists, Atkinson writes, has produced "a transfer of power from workers to employers. The growth of multi-national companies, and trade and capital-market liberalization, have strengthened the position of companies vis-à-vis customers, workers, and governments." Even technology, he adds, needs to be understood in terms of power. "Technological progress is not a neutral force but reflects social and economic decisions. Choices by firms, by individuals and by governments can influence the direction of technology and hence the distribution of income." He adds that inequality "is embedded in our social and economic structure, and a significant reduction requires us to examine all aspects of our society."

Isn't this account familiar? Yes, and no. Some further to the left have long made these arguments. But for most of the economics profession, widening inequality of earnings has been primarily a reflection of widening differentials in worker skills in the face of changes in technology that require more advanced workers. Therefore, the logical cure is better education and training. Lawrence Mishel and colleagues at the Economic Policy Institute have been challenging this account for years. But only lately has the mainstream conceded that the EPI view is substantially right. Three of the principal proponents of the view, Harvard's Lawrence Katz, MIT's David Autor, as well as *Prospect* co-founder Robert Reich, have walked back their previous embrace of the skills explanation, known in academia as skill-biased technological change, or SBTC.

As Paul Krugman recently wrote, "While one still encounters people invoking skill-biased technological change as an explanation of rising inequality and lagging wages—it's especially popular among moderate Republicans in denial about what's happened to their party and among 'third way' types lamenting the rise of Democratic populism—the truth is that SBTC has fared very badly over the past quarter-century, to the point where it no longer deserves to be taken seriously as an account of what ails us."

THIS REVISIONISM HAS huge implications for economic theory, for possible remedies, and for politics. If greater inequality does not reflect market efficiencies, then market distributions of income are not efficient. And policies that produce greater equality will, at worst, do no damage to economic growth—and quite possibly will improve it.

As an illustration of how pervasive was the previous consensus, consider a piece that the *Prospect* published in 1995 by Barry Bluestone, a well-known left-of-center

The Sleuth: Anthony Atkinson's new book provides the evidence.

economist. Bluestone's article, "The Inequality Express," invoked Agatha Christie's detective mystery *Murder on the Orient Express,* which contained the surprise twist that all of the suspects did it. Bluestone listed ten suspects on the Inequality Express: technology, trade, a shift from manufacturing to services, deregulation, declining unionization, downsizing, winner-take-all labor markets, capital mobility, immigration, and trade deficits. Each of these factors played apart, Bluestone concluded. They all did it.

Invoking another classic, Michael Young's essay "The Rise of the Meritocracy," Bluestone fretted that the new inequality was substantially earned. It was *meritocratic.* Better-equipped people simply commanded higher wages, while routine workers were swamped by outsourcing, offshoring, and technology. And if inequality is earned, it becomes much harder to justify tampering with it. Atkinson's list of causes is not all that different from Blue- stone's—but with one huge difference: Atkinson doubts that today's increased inequality is earned. Thus the obstacles to reversing it are not economic, but political.

Reich's influential 1991 book, *The Work of Nations, shared* the view that skills accounted for widening earnings disparities. In his new book, *Saving Capitalism: For the Many, Not the Few,* Reich recants. The real story, he writes, is a power-shift. Reich previewed those ideas in our Spring 2015 issue.

Reich's new work is the best statement since Karl Polanyi's 1944 masterwork, *The Great Transformation,* of how markets are creatures of government and politics rather than a default state of nature. As Reich writes, "Government doesn't 'intrude' on the 'free market.' It creates the market." (Polanyi likewise wrote, in a famous

The Seer: Joseph Stiglitz has been ahead of the curve for decades.

oxymoron, "Laissez-faire was planned.") Reich's latest book is a compendium of all the ways that political power by economic elites rigs the rules of how markets work—in favor not of efficiency, but of the rich and the powerful—increasing both inefficiency and inequality. With increased market power comes increased concentration of wealth, and still more concentration of both political and economic power.

More and more mainstream economists have been paying increasing attention to the connection between political power, market power, and the income distribution. As David Dayen wrote in a recent *Prospect* piece, anti-trust has ceased to be a meaningful brake on economic concentration, just as new business models have come up with new ways to exploit market power. Jason Furman, current chair of the Council of Economic Advisers, in a research paper with Peter Orszag, former head of the Office of Management and Budget, confirms that increasing numbers of firms enjoy monopoly or oligopoly profits not reduced by competition, as free-market theory would predict. Once, in the postwar era, when unions were stronger, oligopoly profits were shared with workers. Today, they go to CEOs, shareholders, and hedge fund operators.

Another emblem of the shift in mainstream economic thinking is the award of the 2014 Nobel Prize in Economics to the French economist Jean Tirole. The citation explicitly credited his contribution to "the science of taming powerful firms," recognizing that concentrated economic power undermines efficiency as well as equality.

A further example is revisionism of the relationship of inequality to consumption and debt, and the knock-on costs to economic efficiency. In traditional economic theory, mainstream economists ignored the role of income distribution in one's propensity to consume, as well as its macroeconomic effect. In recent decades, however, people with stagnant or declining earnings maintained consumption levels by running up consumer debt. A Federal Reserve substantially captured by bankers cooperated by lowering interest rates and blessing new, risky debt instruments like securities backed by subprime mortgages. What the British economist Colin Crouch termed "privatized Keynesianism" went abruptly into reverse when the crash of 2008 came, deepening the slump. Thus, widening inequality set off dynamics that resulted in an intensified collapse. In a new book, *Income Inequality: Why It Matters and Why Most Economists Didn't Notice*, Matthew Drennan explains how traditional theories of consumption, shared by relatively liberal economists such as Franco Modigliani and conservative Milton Friedman (both Nobelists), got the story wrong by leaving out the income distribution.

Still other examples include Joseph Stiglitz's latest book, *Rewriting the Rules of the American Economy.* He writes, "Today's inequality is not the result of the inevitable evolution of capitalism. Instead, the rules that govern the economy got us here." Stiglitz has always been something of an outlier, but enough of a mainstream economist to have won a Nobel and have served in senior posts in the Clinton administration and at the World Bank. At a festschrift conference for Stiglitz last October, people more mainstream than he, from Robert Solow to Jason Furman and Peter Orszag, paid tribute to the prescience of his work. "In Joe's honor," Furman and Orszag wrote, "we thought it appropriate to collaborate on a paper that explores two of his core interests: the rise in inequality and how the assumption of a perfectly competitive marketplace is often misguided."

At the festschrift, Solow, another eminently mainstream economist with a history of challenging received assumptions, observed that we would never solve the problem of extreme inequality without dealing with wages—an issue that is as much the consequence of power as of marginal productivity. Solow was coming back to his own roots. In 1990, he wrote a book titled *The Labor Market as a Social Institution,* challenging the idea that this is a market just like others, since workers are also human beings and "participants, on both sides, have well-developed notions of what is fair and what is not."

FOR PROGRESSIVES, WHO have assumed since Teddy Roosevelt that the state is the logical counterweight to the market, the new insights about the connection between political and economic inequality illuminate a huge practical problem. When large corporations and mega-banks capture the machinery of the state, regulation itself is undermined as remedy. The standard liberal story—that we need government to help tame the market for the benefit of ordinary citizens—loses credibility as well as veracity, since the plutocrats are inside the gates. This helps explain why right-wing populists have some credibility: Wall Street and Washington are all the same crowd.

Conservative economists, going back to public-choice theorists such as Gordon 'Tullock and James Buchanan, have long argued that regulatory capture by interest groups is inevitable; hence, the best policy is to minimize the role of the state altogether. This is why Atkinson is so refreshing. Not at all, he says; with a shift in political power, the state may yet be redeemed as an instrument of greater and more efficient equality.

Atkinson's book closes with a short manifesto of remedies. The good news: We could return the income distribution to something more like the one that prevailed during the postwar boom, a golden age both for income equality and for dynamic managed capitalism. His policy package calls for using "the whole of government" to reverse inequality on all fronts and "rebalancing power in the economy."

The inequality of earned income began creeping up in the late 1940s, Atkinson reports, but until the 1980s an expanding redistributive welfare state and the entry of women into the labor market were sufficient to keep inequality of final household income from rising. Since then, wage inequality has far outstripped redistributive capacity.

First, he proposes, we need a restoration of progressive taxation. Specifically, he calls for a top personal tax rate of 65 percent, higher than the current top rate but lower than the top rate in the Eisenhower era. Yet he also observes that inequality has become so extreme that more progressive taxes and more generous social transfers can no longer solve the inequality problem. That will take a drastic shift in primary income from wages, salaries, and capital.

To illustrate just how the shift in power from citizens to capitalists has made progressive taxation far more difficult politically, Atkinson quotes the current British Chancellor of the Exchequer, George Osborne, boasting to the 2014 Conservative Party Conference, "In a modern global economy where people can move their investment from one country to another at the touch of a button and companies can relocate jobs overnight—the economics of high taxation are a thing of the past." Standard economics interprets these shifts as expressions of economic efficiency. Atkinson explains them as shifts of power.

In addition to calling for stronger trade unions, Atkinson calls for reducing the unemployment rate to 2 percent, a goal that was achieved throughout Europe in the early postwar era, with guaranteed public employment as one of the strategies. To equalize wealth, he calls for the creation of public sovereign wealth funds, with the aim of "building up the net worth of the state by holding investments in companies and in property," and the payout of a universal capital endowment, or inheritance, to all citizens upon their reaching adulthood. That way, the wealth that allows the affluent to pass along inherited advantage to their children would be spread around.

He also has a wonderfully creative proposal to replace estate taxes with a "progressive lifetime capital receipts tax." At present, estate taxes (which cover less than half of 1 percent of estates) are paid by the donor's estate. Instead, Atkinson suggests, all gifts including bequests should simply be treated as income. They should incur taxes to be paid by the recipient, with the rate based on the income of the recipient, not the giver. Atkinson also calls for a different set of rules for globalization, consistent with a more equitable income distribution at home.

So after decades of market-loving economists helping to push politics to the center-right, we now have the anomalous spectacle of some influential economists being on the left edge of mainstream politics—a happy throwback to the prophetic role of John Maynard Keynes in the 1920s and 1930s. As Atkinson himself points out, most of these ideas are not especially radical compared with the norms and policies that were prevalent during the postwar era. The bad news: They are far to the left of what passes for mainstream politics today.

Nonetheless, the news that egalitarian policies are both attainable and salutary should be tonic for the liberal soul. It's also propitious that the unmistakable increase in inequality to levels that violate broadly shared norms of what's reasonable is a useful embarrassment to conservative economists and their political allies.

SINCE REAGAN, AMERICA has embraced much of the conservative package. Taxes are lower and less redistributive. Many benefits to the poor have been drastically cut. There is far less regulation, and the regulation that does operate is largely pro-corporate. Global trade is freer than ever and outsourcing easier. However, the basic growth trajectory has not changed and if anything is slightly slower than it was in the postwar decades. Financial deregulation caused growth to take a huge hit beginning in 2007, from which the economy is only now recovering. But inequality has soared. While some of it can be justified as meritocratic, billion-dollar hedge fund managers have few defenders and even some Republican presidential candidates want to increase their taxes.

> *"The good news: a more equal and dynamic economy is attainable. The sobering news: the remedies are to the left of Bernie Sanders"*

On the inequality conundrum, conservative economists divide four ways. Some are denialists. Rising inequality is simply a mirage if you make the right adjustments to the data. Scott Winship of the Manhattan Institute operates a small cottage industry purporting to demonstrate that if you correct for a variety of factors ranging from household size to counting health insurance as income, the statistical rise in inequality mostly vanishes.

A second group concedes increasing inequality but blames it on the deterioration of values. Marry everyone off and poverty largely disappears. The income distribution is indeed much flatter if you limit the sample to married couples. The trouble with this view is that it still has to reckon with immense and widening wage and salary inequality.

A third group, latter-day supply-siders, insist that if we really get government out of the way, then the poor as well as the rich will share in a burst of entrepreneurship. That, of course, has been the conservative story ever since Reagan, yet inequality keeps increasing.

"The new left-right policy consensus on incremental ways to reduce poverty is far too liberal for the republican congress."

And then there are the self-described "reformicons," who seek to define a conservative version of government anti-poverty policy, more or less in the spirit of Jack Kemp. Last year, a group of conservative intellectuals led by Yuval Levin, editor of *National Affairs,* and Peter Wehner, a former adviser to three Republican presidents, published a pamphlet titled "Room to Grow." The piece begins by frankly acknowledging trends that liberals usually emphasize—persistent poverty and reduced mobility, flat earnings for the broad middle class, a general sense of diminishing life horizons. The trouble with the reformicons, however, is the disconnect between their analysis and their remedies—which are mostly small-bore, such as the expanded use of tax credits. Nor do they address the policies that have produced grotesque inequality at the top.

MEANWHILE, BACK INSIDE the Capital Beltway, a group of center-left and center-right policy experts (mostly non-economists) have sought to reckon with power in a very different sense. They have been working for 14 months to see whether a

READING LIST

Inequality: What Can Be Done?
By Anthony B. Atkinson

Capital in the Twenty- First Century
By Thomas Piketty

Saving Capitalism: For the Many, Not the Few
By Robert B. Reich

Income Inequality: Why It Matters and Why Most Economists Didn't Notice
By Matthew P. Drennan

Rewriting the Rules of the American Economy: An Agenda for Growth and Shared Prosperity
By Joseph E. Stiglitz

new policy consensus is possible to reduce poverty. The group, under the auspices of the American Enterprise Institute (AEI) and the Brookings Institution, deliberately focused on poverty, not inequality, expressing a very different conception of political realism.

After a good deal of horse-trading and nearly breaking apart at several points, the group delivered an 85-page report in early December titled "Opportunity, Responsibility, and Security; A Consensus Plan for Reducing Poverty and Restoring the American Dream." The working group included anti-poverty scholars Lawrence Aber, Sheldon Danziger, and David Ellwood on the moderate left, and Stuart Butler, Ron Haskins, and Lawrence Mead on the right. Basically, the liberals in the group conceded more than they really wanted to in terms of blaming poverty on family structure, and the conservatives conceded more than they wanted in accepting that low and stagnant wages were a big part of the story.

The manifesto blends suggestions ranging from increasing work and the rewards for working, to promoting marriage and "delayed, responsible childbearing" as well as parenting education. The liberals on the panel did win some important concessions. Conservatives agreed to a higher minimum wage and major improvements in preschool and post-secondary education. The liberals beat back demands to attach onerous conditions to food stamps.

The price that the liberals paid was that the larger issue of the income distribution was not part of the discussion or the report. It focused on a relatively narrow stratum of the income distribution—the working poor and near-poor. The group largely ignored the struggles of the very poor, of the sort addressed in Kathryn Edin and H. Luke Shaefer's new book, $2.00 a Day: Living on Almost Nothing in America […]. Nor did the report engage the downward mobility and economic stress on the broad, working middle class. Nor did the group did address the extreme pulling-away of the top.

And unlike the Atkinson book, the panel did not discuss power. To read the report, one would think that cuts in outlays on the poor, the brutal slashing of welfare benefits in TANF, wage stagnation, and what the authors delicately termed "weakening" of "collective bargaining" just happened. The elephant in the room, in more senses than one, was the Republican war on the welfare state. This was never mentioned. Instead, there was the usual imputation of partisan symmetry to legislative blockage ("When one political party offers a proposal, the other usually disagrees…"), of the sort that Jacob Hacker and Paul Pierson so powerfully refuted in their book, Off Center, and in other research. The report also clings to the largely discredited story that low earnings are mainly a reflection of low skills.

Despite these omissions, a large majority of Americans would probably accept these policy ideas as a reasonable way of combating poverty, if they could just get a legislative hearing. I interviewed several members of the working group and they generally agreed that these policy proposals, if accepted, would probably reduce the rate of poverty in America by a few percentage points—no small achievement.

The aspiration of serving as a kind of role model for Congress, to show that sensible right and sensible left can agree on a core common program, is not a crazy idea. But as one of the panelists ruefully admitted, "these proposals do not stand a snowball's chance" of making it through the current Congress. Just as Atkinson's newly mainstream ideas are somewhere to the left of Senator Bernie Sanders's presidential campaign, the report of the Brookings-AEI working group is to the left of the entire Republican House—thus neatly proving Atkinson's point that it really is about power.

The conservatives in the group, looking over their shoulders at their political allies, demanded and got some changes that bordered on the absurd. The report is emphatic on the point that child-bearing should be delayed—but the report distances itself from the most effective form of contraception, long-acting reversible contraceptives (LARCs), the new generation of IUDs that are far safer and more effective than earlier ones, and which have dramatically reduced unwanted pregnancies. Why the distance? As the report tactfully puts it, some opponents of LARCs see them "as potentially a form of abortion." Yet the concessions by the liberals on the panel are unlikely to change a single Republican vote in Congress.

A report such as this one would nicely fit an era when there were still moderate Republicans in Congress. Indeed, the groundwork for the 1996 reform "ending welfare as we know it" was laid by similar left-right academic efforts. And because of the hard line of the Gingrich Congress, the welfare reform that Clinton signed, after vetoing two even worse versions, features a TANF block-grant design that is brutally punitive on people who really need help. Indeed, three subcabinet members who had designed the original Clinton welfare reform resigned in protest.

Conservatives organizing liberals to support center-right policies in the name of realism dates at least to the Reagan era. In 1987, AEI organized a similar working group that published a report titled "The New Consensus on Family and Welfare." The participants ranged from Charles Murray on the right to Robert Reischauer and Alice Rivlin on the moderate left. The recommendations, many of which parallel those of the latest report, are more Murray than Reischauer. The working groups on deficit reduction grew in the same soil of centrist policy intellectuals (including some of the same people) desperately seeking bipartisanship and mostly getting rolled by conservatives, culminating in the disastrous Bowles-Simpson Commission. That commission utterly failed to win popular support, but it created an elite policy consensus that combined with Republican political hardball to lock a Democratic administration into a decade of relentless budget cuts in domestic social programs, one that moots the calls for increased spending in the AEI-Brookings report.

The keynote speaker at the December 3 event unveiling the Brookings-AEI report was *New York Times* columnist David Brooks. That choice speaks volumes. Brooks is emblematic of the sort of moderate conservative who no longer exists in the Republican caucus.

If one can indulge optimism bordering on euphoria, it's possible to imagine a scenario in which Donald Trump wins the Republican nomination, Hillary Clinton is elected in a landslide, and the Senate goes narrowly Democratic, though the House is virtually certain to stay Republican. In those circumstances, some of the modest Brookings-AEI ideas might actually become law.

Paul Ryan, the new House Speaker, professes to care about poverty. His own anti-poverty program, unveiled when he was chair of the House Budget Committee, was more or less reformicon. It accepted that increased poverty was a problem, and he even made some policy proposals. But as critics noted at the time, Ryan's numbers didn't compute. They added up to massive cuts in existing outlays and largely precluded new ones.

However, it's possible that with a Democratic president, a Democratic Senate, and a Republican House with a reduced majority, some elements of the Brookings-AEI package might make it through Congress. At the same time, Republicans are still working to turn food stamps into a block grant, which would drastically cut benefits, and they have continued to try to kill the Affordable Care Act and slash other social outlays. If everything breaks right politically in 2016 (which is a big if), poverty could

The Speaker Paul Ryan professes to care about poverty, but his numbers don't compute.

be modestly reduced, especially for the working poor, but the larger problems of income inequality will continue to worsen.

SO WHICH GROUP REPRESENTS the greater realism? Is it the pursuit of incremental policy changes aimed at modest reductions in poverty? Or is it work like Atkinson's, acknowledging that a real improvement in the broader income distribution would require a sure grasp of power dynamics as well as policy changes well to the left of anything currently in mainstream debate?

I suppose you might say we need both. The AEI-Brookings effort seems more rooted in the near-term politics of the possible, though, as noted, the several members whom I interviewed don't believe that the current Republican Congress will touch even these toned-down ideas. The Atkinson analysis reflects a deeper understanding of the economic realities. Possibly, the AEI-Brookings effort will serve as a role model to a post-Tea Party generation of Republicans picking up the pieces from what could be a 2016 blowout, though if Trump self-destructs and Marco Rubio is the nominee, it's a whole other story. One must also hope that the work of Atkinson, Reich, Stiglitz, Solow, and others will energize a muscular progressive realism that pushes outward the politics of the possible.

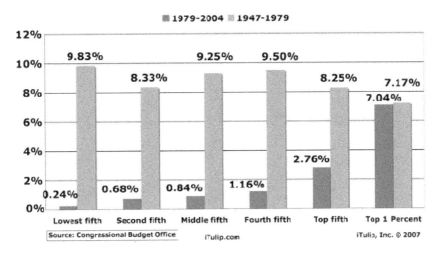

FIGURE 11.10 **Average annual income gains by quintile.**

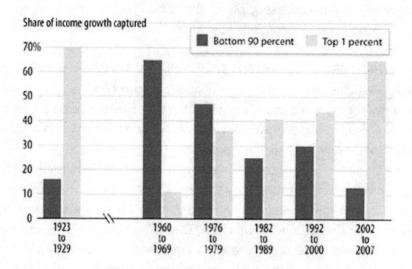

Source: CBPP calculations based on data from Piketty and Saez

FIGURE 11.11   **Share of nation's income gains going to top 1 percent at highest level since 1920s**

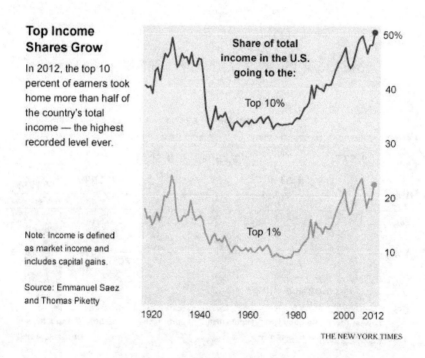

FIGURE 11.12   **Top income shares grow.**

Since the 1970s several policy changes, structural changes, global changes, changes in technology, and increasing globalization has led to a restructuring of the American class structure. What used to be the largest middle-class society in the world has become one of the most unequal rich countries. The gap from the elite to the middle class has grown in multiples; poor and middle-class families are increasing having similar qualitative experiences like living paycheck to paycheck, and the poor are moving out of poverty at a slower rate than in previous decades.

Additionally, income has not kept up with increases in productivity or with inflation for nearly forty years. Consequently, the relative income and buying power of the median American citizen has gone down.

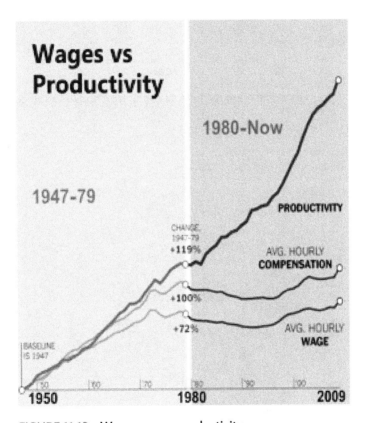

FIGURE 11.13 **Wages versus productivity.**

Another major change was to the United States tax structure. Note that income taxes maxed out well over 90 percent for almost two decades but were above 60 percent at the top marginal rate for nearly fifty years. Although there are political debates about whether taxes are too high or too low, we currently have very low tax rates in America from a historical perspective.

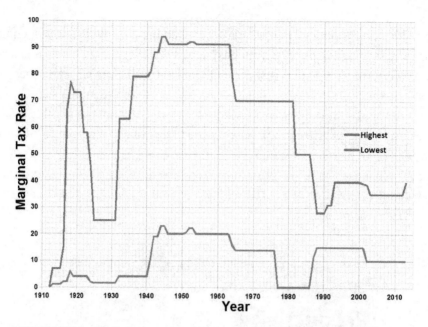

FIGURE 11.14 Historical marginal tax rate for highest and lowest income earners.

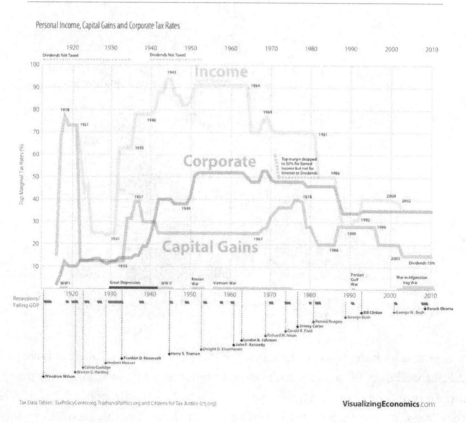

FIGURE 11.15 Top marginal tax rates: 1916–2010.

America's tax code is also less redistributive than that of other rich nations. Before taxes, the US is much more equal (relative to similar countries) than after taxes. This means that our tax code effectively benefits the rich (or hurts the poor) relatively more than those of other countries.

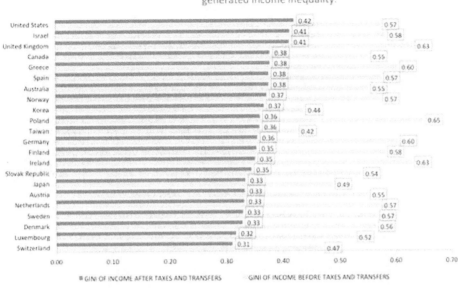

The U.S. government does less than many other rich countries to reduce market-generated income inequality.

Source: Author's calculations, 2013, based on LIS microdata, most recent datasets available (early to mid-2000s)

FIGURE 11.16 **Income inequality and redistribution.**

As a result, the United States is as unequal today in terms of wealth and income as it has been since social scientists and economists began keeping accurate data.

More resources:

Income Inequality Today May Be Higher Today Than in Any Other Era: https://www.washingtonpost.com/news/wonk/wp/2016/07/01/income-inequality-today-may-be-the-highest-since-the-nations-founding/

HYPER INEQUALITY AND WORLDWIDE INEQUALITY

In most ways America has never been so unequal in terms of social class. Most notably, the people at the very top have more than they have ever had. This is true both of American society and across the globe. For instance, the six Walton heirs (Walmart and Sam's Club) have owned more wealth than the bottom 40 percent of Americans (which is about 132 million people) for about five years.[3]

---

3   Molly Moorhead, "Bernie Sanders Says Walmart Heirs Own More Wealth Than Bottom 40 Percent of Americans," Politifact, July 31, 2012, https://www.politifact.com/factchecks/2012/jul/31/bernie-s/sanders-says-walmart-heirs-own-more-wealth-bottom-/

The richest three Americans surpassed the bottom 50 percent of Americans (about 165 million people) in wealth in 2017.[4]

And the richest forty to fifty people have more wealth than the bottom 50 percent of the world population (about 3.7 billion people).[5]

SUMMARY

Social class and where an individual falls in the social class hierarchy affect life chances and life outcomes quite a bit. Additionally, they also affect day-to-day lived experiences quite a bit. Changes in social class structure can have dramatic effects on the way a society operates and functions.

The American class structure has been changing rapidly since the 1970s, mostly trending toward more inequality. In fact, many sociologists now argue that America is currently in a phase of hyper inequality; and in terms of wealth distribution at the top, America is as unequal as it has ever been. The middle class is shrinking, and the elites are capturing more and more income and wealth yearly. The result is an increasingly disparate America, where there are vast differences in life experiences as one moves across the social class spectrum.

Image Credits

Fig. 11.1: Source: http://stconsultant.blogspot.com/2011/10/some-very-bad-news-for-america.html.
Fig. 11.2: Source: https://sdsuwriting.pbworks.com/w/file/fetch/71890982/ariely_wealth_distrib_DEBATE_GREAT.pdf.
Fig. 11.3: Source: https://sdsuwriting.pbworks.com/w/file/fetch/71890982/ariely_wealth_distrib_DEBATE_GREAT.pdf.
Fig. 11.4: Source: https://blog.wiziq.com/key-issues-with-american-public-schools-virtual-classrooms-solution/.
Fig. 11.5: Source: https://www.oecd.org/centrodemexico/medios/44582910.pdf.
Fig. 11.6: Source: https://www.businessinsider.in/21-Charts-On-US-Inequality-That-Everyone-Should-See/While-productivity-keeps-rising-inflation-adjusted-wages-have-been-flat-for-fifty-years-/slideshow/25959504.cms.
Fig. 11.7: Source: http://mjperry.blogspot.com/2011/10/income-mobility-is-more-important-than.html.
Fig. 11.8: Source: https://www.russellsage.org/research/chartbook/average-after-tax-household-income-quintile-1979-2010-reported-2010.
Fig. 11.9: Source: https://earthsharing.org/gilded-age-now/.
Fig. 11.10: Source: https://www.businessinsider.com/are-resentment-frustration-and-anger-the-defining-feature-of-the-new-american-2010-9.
Fig. 11.11: Source: https://www.cbpp.org/research/top-1-percent-of-americans-reaped-two-thirds-of-income-gains-in-last-economic-expansion.
Fig. 11.12: Source: https://www.washingtonpost.com/news/wonk/wp/2013/09/13/this-is-how-everyones-been-doing-since-the-financial-crisis/?utm_term=.3bfd2e9f12db.
Fig. 11.13: Source: https://www.maxkeiser.com/2016/03/what-killed-the-middle-class/.
Fig. 11.14: Copyright © Toobaz (CC BY-SA 4.0) at https://commons.wikimedia.org/wiki/File:USA_Historical_Marginal_Tax_Rate_for_Highest_and_Lowest_Income_Earners.svg.
Fig. 11.15: Source: http://visualizingeconomics.com/blog/2011/04/14/top-marginal-tax-rates-1916-2010.
Fig. 11.16: Source: https://www.economist.com/democracy-in-america/2013/11/26/gini-in-the-bottle.

4   Noah Kirsch, "The 3 Richest Americans Hold More Wealth Than Bottom 50% of the Country, Study Finds," Forbes, November 9, 2017, https://www.forbes.com/sites/noahkirsch/2017/11/09/the-3-richest-americans-hold-more-wealth-than-bottom-50-of-country-study-finds/#34b23ca13cf8

5   Larry Elliott, "Inequality Gap Widens as 42 People Hold Same Wealth as 3.7bn Poorest," The Guardian, January 21, 2018, https://www.theguardian.com/inequality/2018/jan/22/inequality-gap-widens-as-42-people-hold-same-wealth-as-37bn-poorest

CHAPTER 12

Society and Environment

ENVIRONMENTAL SOCIOLOGY VOCABULARY

- **Environmental sociology**: A field of study that examines the interactions between our physical world/environment and our social behaviors and social organizations.
  - http://www.sociology.com/2012/11/environmental-sociology/
  - http://link.springer.com/article/10.1007%2FBF02691936#page-1
- **Environmental justice**: The idea (which can also be labeled a movement) that all people and communities are entitled to be equally protected by laws and regulations.
- **Brownfields**: Abandoned or unused industrial sites whose redevelopment is made complicated by the potential of hazardous or dangerous substances.
- **Fracking**: Hydraulic fracturing; many scientists believe this is one of the most harmful and dangerous way to get energy, and as such this is a contentious political issue.
- **Climate change**: The idea that the climate of the earth is changing based on the actions of human beings

The following selection of articles discuss the relationship between society, individuals, and the environment.

Reading 12.1.

Glossary

by Michael Carolan

Abject poverty: Most severe state of poverty. Those living in this state cannot meet basic needs for food, water, shelter, sanitation, and health care.

Adaptation (climate change): Actions taken to adjust socioecological systems in response to existing or predicted climatic effects in order to reduce harmful effects.

Agrobiodiversity: All forms of life directly relevant to agriculture, including crops and livestock but also many other organisms, such as soil, fauna, weeds, pests, and predators.

Michael Carolan, "Glossary," *Society and the Environment: Pragmatic Solutions to Ecological Issues*, pp. 299-303. Copyright © 2016 by Taylor & Francis Group. Reprinted with permission.

Anaerobic decomposition: The breaking down of biodegradable material by microorganisms in an environment lacking oxygen.

Apolitical ecology: When conventional explanations do not fully account for the asymmetries in power that first created a problem materially and then later define it as a problem to be solved by the same system that gave birth to it.

Arable land: Land that can be cultivated to grow crops.

Biochar: Charcoal derived from a thermochemical decomposition of organic material at heightened temperatures in the absence of oxygen. Biochar is used to improve soil fertility and sequester carbon. Biochar oil and gas by-products can also be used as biofuels.

Biocultural diversity: Recognizes that cultural diversity does not merely parallel biological diversity but is profoundly interrelated with it.

Biodiversity hotspots: A biogeographic region with a significant reservoir of biodiversity that is under threat from humans.

Biofortification: The breeding and, increasingly, genetic engineering of plants with the aim of higher micronutrient content.

Biohazards: Environmental threats resulting from biological agents or conditions.

Biopiracy: The loss of biocultural diversity through legal and sometimes illegal means.

Birthrate: The ratio of live births to total population of a specified community, usually expressed per one thousand people per year.

"Bonding" social capital: Social ties that link people together who are primarily alike according to established characteristics.

"Bridging" social capital: Social ties that link people together across social cleavages.

Buyer power: An effect that results when a market has numerous sellers but only one buyer or a few.

Cap and trade: A scheme that involves the trading of a limited number of emission allowances. A regulatory authority establishes this limit, which is typically lower than the historical level of emissions.

Carbon credits: Units of carbon emissions that can be purchased or sold to meet compliance with carbon emission caps.

Carbon intensity: The amount of CO_2 emitted for each unit of economic output produced.

Carbon offsets: Reduction in emissions of carbon dioxide (or greenhouse gases more generally) in order to compensate for (offset) an emission released elsewhere.

Carbon tax: Tax on fossil fuels that seeks to reduce the emission of carbon dioxide.

Carrotmob: A type of consumer activism based on the idea of using carrots (or incentives) to reward businesses for engaging in socially or environmentally responsible practices.

Car sharing: A short-term (often by the hour) car rental model where the cars are scattered throughout a community to improve access rather than all being centrally housed at one location, as with traditional car rentals.

Clean coal: Defined by the coal industry as any technologies that improve the environmental performance of coal-based electricity plants, which include equipment that increases the operational efficiency of power plants as well as technologies that reduce emissions. Elsewhere, it refers to the CO_2 capture and (long-term) storage of emissions.

Climate change: A change in climate patterns that results from human activity like burning fossil fuels.

Climate change refugees: Populations that have been displaced as a result of climate change.

Coase theorem: When property rights are involved, parties naturally gravitate toward the most efficient and mutually beneficial outcome.

Collective coverage: Proportion of an area serviced by the municipal waste stream.

Commodity chain: The collective networks that encompass the beginning and end of a product's life cycle.

Community severance: The physical or social separation of an individual from the rest of the community.

Conspicuous consumption: The idea that we consume, at least in part, to display to others our social power and status.

Contingent valuation: A survey-based economic technique for placing a value on nonmarket resources.

Convention on Biological Diversity: An international, legally binding treaty that entered into force in 1993. The convention has three main goals: conservation of biological diversity, sustainable use of biological resources, and fair and equitable sharing of benefits arising from genetic resources.

Cornucopian: Someone who believes unending progress, economic growth, and material abundance can be had with advancements in technology.

Countermovements: A social movement that arises to explicitly oppose an existing social movement.

Cultural hotspots: A biogeographic region with a significant reservoir of cultural diversity that is under threat of extinction.

Daylighting: The practice of uncovering previously concealed natural amenities.

Dead zones: The name given to bodies of water with low levels of dissolved oxygen.

Decoupling: The ability for an economy to grow without corresponding increases in environmental pressure.

Demographic inertia: A well-documented demographic phenomenon relating to how a time lag is to be expected before the full effects of changes to a fertility rate are seen.

Demographic transition model: A model detailing the historical changes in birthrates and death rates for explaining rapid population growth. A country is said to have passed through the demographic transition when it moves from a condition of high birthrates and death rates (and a relatively small population) to low birthrates and death rates (and a relatively large population).

Desalinization: The removal of salt and other minerals from saline water.

Diminishing marginal utility: The more units of something we consume, the less added enjoyment we get from each additional unit.

Disability-adjusted life-years (DALYs): The sum of years of potential life lost from premature mortality and the years of productive life lost from disability.

Disease vectors: An organism, such as a mosquito or tick, that carries disease-causing microorganisms from one host to another.

Diversionary reframing: Diverting attention away from real problems by trying to reframe the debate as being about something else.

Down-cycling: The process of converting waste into new materials or products of lesser quality and decreased functionality.

Ecofeminism: An area of study that examines the historical (and present) links between the objectification of women and the objectification of nature.

Economism: The act of reducing the world to economic dimensions.

Ecosystem services: The processes by which the environment produces resources that we often take for granted but need for our survival, such as clean air and water, timber, habitat for fisheries, and pollination of native and agricultural plants.

Efficiency shifting: When money and resources saved through energy efficiency merely get shifted to and consumed by other goods and services.

Embodied energy: The sum total of the energy utilized throughout an entire product life cycle.

Energy intensity: The amount of energy required to produce each unit of the world's economic output.

Environmental racism: Racial discrimination in environmental policy making and enforcement of regulations and laws, in addition to the targeting of communities of color for toxic waste disposal and siting of polluting industries.

Environmental skepticism: A position that attempts to undermine knowledge claims supporting the argument that environmental problems are real and that they are the result of human activity.

Exponential growth: Constant growth in a system where the amount added is proportional to the amount present.

Ex situ: Sampling, transferring, and storage of a species in a place other than the original location in which it was found, like a zoo or seed bank.

Extended producer responsibility: Holding the manufacturer responsible for a product beyond the time of sale, thereby relieving consumers, governments, future generations, and the environment from the costs associated with landfilling and recycling hazardous materials.

Externality: Cost or benefit not transmitted through prices and incurred by a party who did not agree to the action causing the cost or benefit.

Family planning: Educational, social, and medical services that empower individuals to make choices around reproduction.

Food sovereignty: A movement and way of life that is diametrically opposed to the dominant view that presently dictates conventional food and agricultural policy.

Food system: The entire array of activities—from input production and distribution to on-farm activities, marketing, processing, wholesale, and retail—that connect seed (and gene) to the mouths of consumers.

Footprint shifting (life cycle): Making efficiency gains at one point in a commodity's life cycle while creating a larger environmental load at another point.

Fracking: A method of extracting natural gas from deep wells; also known as hydraulic fracturing.

Framing: Involves the social construction of social phenomena—by mass media, political or social movements, political leaders, or other actors and organizations—whereby symbols, words, or phrases are given distinct meanings with the aim of organizing people into social groups, e.g., social movements.

Full irrigation: The amount of water needed to achieve maximum yield.

Greenhouse effect: When a portion of the sun's radiation that enters the atmosphere is absorbed by the planet's atmosphere thanks to greenhouse gases like CO_2 rather than being reradiated back into space.

Greenhouse gases: Any gases in the atmosphere that absorb and emit radiation within the thermal infrared range.

Green revolution: A series of strategies developed during the mid- to late twentieth century to combat starvation by expanding the global production of staple food crops through crop breeding.

Habitat fragmentation: The emergence of discontinuities (or fragmentation) in an organism's preferred environment (or habitat).

Happy Life Years (HLYs): A measurement of the health of a nation found through multiplying life expectancy at birth by happiness score (on a scale of 0 to 1).

Heat island effect: Because concrete, tarmac, and other common construction materials absorb heat readily, built-up areas tend to be warmer than nearby rural areas.

Hypoxia: A state when oxygen concentrations in a body of water fall below the level necessary to sustain most animal life.

Indigenous knowledge: Knowledge unique to a given community, culture, or society.

Informal settlements: Unplanned housing constructed on land illegally or not in compliance with current building regulations, or both.

In situ: The management of a species at the location of discovery.

Intergovernmental Panel on Climate Change: Established by two UN organizations, the United Nations Environment Programme and the World Meteorological Organization, in 1988 to provide scientific assessments on issues relating to climate change. With the IPCC as the internationally accepted authority on the subject, the world's governments look to it as the official advisory body on climate change.

Irrigation efficiency: The ratio of water that evaporates to what saturates the soil.

Islandization (habitat): The breaking up of habitats without wildlife corridors to connect them.

Kyoto Protocol: An international treaty brokered by the UN, signed in 1997, that binds signatory nations to reduce their emissions of greenhouse gases. At Kyoto (where the agreement was first signed), nations agreed to cut their emissions of six greenhouse gases by an average of 5 percent overall, compared with 1990 levels, in what was termed the first commitment period, which was to end in 2012.

Landfill: A method of solid waste disposal where refuse is buried between layers of dirt.

Low-elevation coastal zones: Areas within ten meters of mean sea level.

Market concentration: The dominance of a particular market by a few large firms as a result of acquisition, mergers, and other processes.

Market environmentalism: A theory that emphasizes markets as a solution to environmental problems.

Maternal mortality ratio: The number of women who die from pregnancy-related causes while pregnant or within forty-two days of pregnancy termination per one hundred thousand live births.

Mechanical revolution: The gradual substitution of capital for labor in agriculture.

Megacities: Cities with more than ten million residents.

Memory banks: Spaces that preserve not only genetic material but the skills to grow and save seeds and prepare the fruits of those labors.

Micronutrient malnutrition: A condition that results from a diet lacking in sufficient quantities of micronutrients.

Mitigation: Making reductions in the concentration of greenhouse gases by reducing their sources, increasing sink capacity, or both.

Monocultures: An agricultural practice of producing a single plant species over a wide area for a number of consecutive years.

Mountaintop removal mining: Clearing upper-elevation forests (typically at the summit of mountains), stripping the ground of topsoil, and using explosives to break up rocks to expose underlying yet relatively shallow coal seams.

Municipal solid waste: All solid waste originating from homes, industries, businesses, demolition, land clearing, and construction.

Natural capital: Assets indispensable for human survival and economic activity provided by the ecosystem.

Naturalistic fallacy: When statements of fact are conflated with statements of value.

Neoliberalism: A set of economic practices grounded in the belief that human well-being is best advanced by limiting (if not eliminating) government and liberating individual entrepreneurial freedoms within legal and institutional frameworks that support strong private property rights, free markets, and free trade.

Neo-Malthusians: Those who advocate for the control of population growth.

Nongovernmental organization (NGO): Any legally constituted organization that operates independently from any government.

Nonpoint-source pollution: Pollution that is more diffuse, making the source harder to pinpoint.

Normal accidents: A failure that is inevitable, given the manner in which particular human and technological systems are organized.

One-child policy: First introduced in 1978, this policy restricts married urban couples in China to one child, though exceptions are allowed, such as for rural couples and certain ethnic minorities.

Open source seeds: Seeds that cannot be patented, licensed, or commodified in any way, even in those instances where they have been bred or genetically modified into something new.

Organic system (agriculture): A farm management system that seeks to enhance biodiversity while minimizing the use of off-farm inputs.

Pareto optimality standard: Deems a policy acceptable only if at least one individual is better off and no individuals are made worse off.

Pay-as-you-drive auto insurance: Insurance whose rate (but not coverage) is contingent on, among other things, the amount of miles driven.

Peasant-based movements: Social movements that began in the Global South and that centrally involve peasants. In this context "peasant" is not a pejorative term but one of empowerment.

Peer-to-peer renting: The process of one private individual renting an underused item of theirs to another individual.

Pigovian taxes: Taxes levied on companies that pollute or create excess social costs (called negative externalities).

Point-source pollution: Pollution with an identifiable source.

Political opportunity approach: Argues that success or failure of social movements is primarily affected by political opportunities.

Polycultures: Small, diverse farms that raise grains, fruits, vegetables, and livestock.

Popular epidemiology: A type of citizen science in which laypeople are involved and which requires a lower level of statistical confidence when claiming the existence of causal links.

Porter Hypothesis: Regulation spurs innovation, as it creates incentives for businesses to adjust to social and environmental realities.

Pronatal social norms: Individual attitudes and societal expectations that promote high fertility rates.

Resource mobilization framework: Emphasizes the ability of a movement's members to acquire resources and to mobilize people toward accomplishing the movement's goals.

Role strain: Tensions that emerge when expectations from holding multiple roles clash.

Salinization: The buildup of salt in soil and groundwater.

Sequestering CO_2: The act of removing CO_2 from the atmosphere and holding it in a sink.

Sink (greenhouse gas): A natural or artificial reservoir—like a forest—that holds and stores greenhouses gases for an indefinite period, thus preventing their accumulation in the atmosphere.

Social constructivism: An approach that focuses entirely on the sociologically dependent knowledge of a phenomenon rather than on any inherent qualities that the thing possesses itself.

Social norms: Standards of behavior shared by a social group.

Sociological ambivalence: Incompatible or contradictory normative expectations or attitudes, beliefs, and behavior that people have because of their holding multiple statuses or when a single status has contradictory expectations.

Sociological drivers: Real phenomena that can only be fully grasped with the help of social theory that underlie today's environmental problems.

Sociological imagination: A way of thinking that involves making connections between the particular and the general over time and across scales.

Species problem: The inherent ambiguity surrounding the use and definition of the species concept.

Street hierarchy: Eliminates connections between streets by funneling traffic up the hierarchy, from cul-de-sac streets to primary or secondary collector streets, arterial streets, and ultimately highways.

Strip-mining: The removal of soil and rock overlaying the mineral deposit.

Structure of agriculture: How farms, rural populations, and agribusiness firms are arranged to produce and distribute food and fiber.

Terminator technology: Genetically engineered seeds that produce sterile plants.

Tragedy of the commodity: Rather than being its savior, commodification of so-called natural capital contributes to the decline of biodiversity and ecosystem services.

Type I error: Concluding there is a causal link when there isn't one.

Type II error: Concluding there is not a causal link when there is one.

Uneconomic growth: Growth that costs us more than it benefits us.

Urban sprawl: The spreading of urban development into areas adjoining cities.

Vertical farming: The practice of farming "up," rather than "out."

Virtual water: Water used during the growing, making, or manufacturing of a given commodity.

Volatile organic compounds: Compounds that evaporate from housekeeping, maintenance, and building products made with organic chemicals.

Vulnerable road users: As defined by the WHO, this population includes pedestrians, cyclists, and users of motorized two-wheel vehicles.

Waste regimes: The realization that institutions, regulations, policy initiatives, and social conventions determine not only what is waste but also how waste is valued.

Water footprint: An indicator of freshwater use that looks at both direct and indirect water use by a consumer or producer.

Water privatization: The treatment of water like any other commodity and leaving questions of access and sanitation to market mechanisms.

Welfare economics: A branch of microeconomics that seeks to evaluate well-being, with the assumption that human well-being is wholly reducible to economic well-being.

Wildlife corridors: Areas of habitat connecting wildlife populations and larger islands of habitat.

Work-spend cycle: Where we work to spend, which in turn requires us to work more.

Worldview: A fundamental cognitive orientation shared by individuals within which is rooted the entirety of their knowledge.

Reading 12.2.

Toward an "Emergence" Model of Environment and Society: A Twilight Zone

by John Hannigan

On Boxing Day, 26 December 2004, a 'monster' tsunami slammed into coastal regions across the Indian Ocean bringing an almost unprecedented level of death and destruction. Triggered by an earthquake off the coast of Sumatra, the tsunami cut a wide swath impacting seventeen countries, most notably Indonesia, Thailand, Sri Lanka, India, Malaysia, Burma, the Maldives archipelago, Andaman and Nicobar Islands and the western coast of Africa. Even today, the final, official death toll is under constant revision, with recent estimates putting it in the order of 176,000 deaths. The highest loss of life was in the Indonesian district of Aceh on the northern tip of Sumatra. Meulaboh, the town nearest to the quake epicentre, was totally devastated—80 percent of its buildings were destroyed.

While those in the affected areas were no doubt too traumatised to engage in much reflection, academic and media commentators struggled to define the nature and meaning of the event. Was it a 'natural' environmental catastrophe on a massive scale or did it have some 'human' cause? A correspondent for the Financial Times stated quite plainly that 'the Indian Ocean tsunamis were caused by an underwater earthquake, and had nothing to do with global warming and climate change'; but, immediately qualified this by adding 'however, they may give a foretaste of some of the disasters that experts are predicting as a result of climate change' (Harvey 2004). Eco-activist Vandana Shiva (2005: 22–3) had a less nuanced view, warning readers of The Ecologist that the lesson from the tsunami was that this is a foretaste of what rising sea levels will look like if 'the rich North cannot afford to take action to reduce CO_2 emissions and work towards reducing the impact of climate change'.

Others noted that a contributing factor might have been over development, especially in the coastal tourist zones of Thailand. The International Tsunami Survey Team in Sri Lanka reported a number of instances where human development likely magnified the ease with which the tsunami penetrated ('ran up') inland. For example, one resort that had previously removed some of the sand dune seaward of its hotel suffered far greater damage (including destruction of the hotel) compared to neighbouring areas located behind unaltered dunes. And the Sumudra Devi, a passenger train, was derailed and overturned by the tsunami wave, killing more than 1,000 passengers in an area where substantial coral mining had occurred related to tourist development (Liu et al. 2005). In similar fashion, 900 fewer people were reported dead or missing in the Maldives, which regulates coral reef management,

John Hannigan, "Toward an "Emergence" Model of Environment and Society: A Twilight Zone," *Environmental Sociology: A Social Constructionist Perspective*. Copyright © 2008 by Taylor & Francis Group. Reprinted with permission.

than in Phuket, Thailand, where coastline coral and mangroves had been replaced by aquaculture and hotels ('Tsunami's impacts' 2005).

In the hours, days and months after impact, the tsunami generated a host of medical and social problems, some of which were beyond previous experience. Largely spared the water borne illnesses (hepatitis, typhoid, malaria) that health authorities feared would follow, thousands appear to have been stricken with 'tsunami lung', a disease caused by a mixture of bacteria in the saltwater and mud that the tsunami churned up and which people caught in the waves swallowed (Zamiska 2005). Oxfam reported that in the Indian state of Tamil Nadu the tsunami disproportionately took the lives of females and children (the males were out to sea on their fishing boats). This has drastically changed the demographic makeup of these fishing villages, thereby altering the social composition and responsibilities within individual families. One unexpected result here is that local authorities have announced a reversal of a government sponsored sterilisation programme, aimed at cutting population growth; surgery to reconnect a woman's Fallopian tubes will now be paid for by the state.

In Northern Sumatra, many residents have lost both their land and their personal identity. This has necessitated the formulation of new procedures. Thus, to reclaim your identity:

> First you need to find two people to whom you are not related who can vouch for you. Then you need to see the village or neighbourhood chief. Then you need to take his letter to the sub-district chief. Only then do you get an identity card. (Aglionby 2005)

As is typical in disaster situations, a whole range of volunteer initiatives and organisations have sprung up. Some are attached to existing NGOs such as Oxfam, Save the Children and the Red Cross, while others such as the Khao Luk Volunteer Centre in Thailand arose specifically in response to the situation.

It is common to observe the appearance of an 'altruistic community' in the first days of the emergency where existing conflicts and animosities are put aside and people reach out to help others in a spirit of cooperative reconstruction. In other cases, however, notably in technological disasters, we see the emergence of a corrosive community (Freudenburg and Jones 1991). Here, people are set against one another rather than bind together in a sense of common struggle and recovery; relations become caustic; and conflict predominates (Clarke 2003: 132). Even if this does not occur, pre-existing fault lines of ethnicity, class, race and gender often re-emerge after an initial grace period. At least two of the areas impacted by the tsunami, North Sumatra and northeast Sri Lanka, have been sites of rebel lion or civil war or both. In the immediate aftermath of the tragedy, some evidence of a truce was observed, but this is already beginning to erode. In Sri Lanka, for example, there have been disputes over distributing the nearly US$3 billion in promised foreign aid, culminating most recently in a Supreme Court-ordered freeze of the aid distribution agreement between the Government and the rebel Tamil Tigers (Goodspeed 2005).[1]

In the resort areas of Thailand, the imperatives of global tourism have created an especially uncertain situation. Recalling what he observed during the first days of the disaster, CBC television reporter Sasa Petracic noted that there was a dual response based on the identity of the victims. Tourist corpses were immediately refrigerated and a team of forensic technicians with laptop computers sprang into action, identifying the deceased and communicating with the next of kin abroad. By contrast, local Thai victims were collectively buried under a giant earth pile, later to be disinterred. Petracic remembered that the first business to be rebuilt at one of these resort towns was Starbucks. What this indicated was an awareness on the part of the Thai authorities that the international media coverage was concentrated, at least in part, on the fate of vacationers from Western nations.

On a visit to Khao Lak on Thailand's resort coast six months after the tsunami, another journalist, John Bussey (2005) observed a kind of twilight zone where the search for human remains continues, mourning is still in the early stages, and the economy is moribund. Some spas and luxury hotels have been rebuilt for foreign tourists who may not return in significant numbers. 'Sometimes it isn't clear', Bussey says, 'whether the region is rebuilding as a resort, or, for the time being, a memorial'.

How might the Indian Ocean tsunami and its effects most helpfully be conceptualised by environmental sociologists?

To begin, let us turn to Raymond Murphy's (2004) seminal treatment of another disaster, the ice storm that impacted parts of Quebec and Eastern Ontario in January 1998. Murphy uses the metaphor of a 'dance' to describe the interactive relationship between nature and society. Sometimes, nature takes the lead and humans react and improvise after nature's moves in this dance. Other times, humans take the lead and choreograph a response in anticipation of nature's moves. In the case of the ice storm, nature issued an extreme 'prompt' that was, at least initially, ignored or denied. To urban residents wholly dependent on a connection to the North American power grid, this was a catastrophe since their heat, light, electricity and even drinking water was dependent on the technology. By contrast, for the small, decentralised Amish communities in northern New York State who used wood stoves for their cooking and heating needs and milked cows by hand, the ice storm caused minimal problems. Murphy concludes that the ice storm disaster 'resulted not from freezing rain per se, but rather from the vulnerability of the infrastructure that modern society had constructed and upon which it had become dependent' (p. 257).

The tsunami case calls up some of the same points. For example, in the Andaman Islands 'stone age' tribal groups were unhurt, having fled the coast before the disaster. In the absence of a technologically sophisticated tsunami warning system, they were evidently alerted by the unusual flight behaviour of wild and domesticated animals that were observed to act in fearful, anxious or unusual ways days or hours before the onset of the wave (Sheldrake 2005). Further more, as has been noted, the extent of the damage and loss of human life was inflated by an ill-considered set of decisions in recent years to alter the natural ecology of the sand dunes, mangroves and coral reefs, all in the name of 'tourist development'. In such instances, nature's 'prompt' can and should inspire a process of environmental learning.

Perhaps because he is preoccupied with fleshing out the basic framework of a new 'constructionist realist' approach to environmental sociology, Murphy does not extend these important notions of prompts, improvisation and creative movement too much beyond the nature/society nexus. Yet, they have considerable applicability within a wide spectrum of environmental events, arenas and policy zones, including but by no means restricted to disaster episodes.

To capture these dynamics more fully, I am proposing an approach to environment and society that pivots on the concept of emergence.

Emergence denotes process, flow, adaptation and learning. In the physical and biological sciences, it is associated with what has come to be known as 'complexity theory'. In his book, Emergence, American cultural and technology commentator Steven Johnson (2001) says that emergence is what happens when an interconnected system of relatively simple elements self-organises to form a more intelligent, more adaptive higher-level behaviour. He illustrates this using the disparate cases of ant colonies, human immune systems, media events and urban neighbourhoods. Within the last decade, Johnson maintains, emergent complexity has entered a new phase in which self-organising systems are becoming the state of the art in software applications, video games and even music.

One recent social science adaptation of complexity theory can be found in the politics of international relations. Drawing on 'the science of complex systems', Harrison and Bryner (2004: 343–4) sketch out a theory of 'emergence processes' as applied to the production of international environmental policy. Complex systems, they explain, are emergent, dynamic and potentially nonlinear (disproportionately sensitive to small changes in internal and external conditions). This, they say, has several important implications.

First, international environmental policy should be seen as being not only the creation of states, but, rather, the product of a complex interaction of many related processes 'including the negotiated conclusions of authoritative scientific reports, international discourse between states, the emergent demands of interest groups and the public through domestic political processes, and the beliefs and preferences of governments and leaders' (p. 344). Second, scientific evidence can be a primary tool of persuasion and even individual scientists can make a difference. Third, social learning is possible, since international environmental policy is 'an emergent property of complex and dynamic processes' (p.345).

What all of these ideas of emergence have in common is a realisation that social organisation and the production of knowledge are fundamentally fluid, dynamic, and adaptive. There is also a strong suggestion that they percolate from the grassroots rather than pass from the top downwards. The case of the Indian Ocean tsunami offers an excellent opportunity to study emergence in action. With many existing certainties washed away, new actions and formations are possible, and in some cases, even necessary, at least for a while.

While conceptualised rather differently, emergence has a long, if not widely known, history in several areas of sociology. Although it never quite achieved paradigmatic status, emergence theory has been around for nearly half a century in the sociology of collective behaviour and social movements. In recent years, it has been recast as a significant but usually unacknowledged presence in cultural approaches to social movements, notably those relating to collective identity formation and social learning. From a policy perspective, emergence theory has been most influential in the sociology of disasters, most recently in relation to institutional and grassroots responses to the World Trade Center attacks.

An emergence framework can be a useful tool. One major advantage here is that it allows a range of phenomena—infectious diseases, ice storms and tsunamis, uncertainties and risks, scientific boundary organisations, environmental movements—to be conceptualised within the same framework. While it incorporates flow processes associated with globalisation (as in the Ali and Keil study of SARS), emergence theory is equally useful at the local level, for example in accounting for social interaction in the aftermath of disasters. Although it implies a 'bottom up' model of social learning, emergence theory is not explicitly prescriptive. Finally, as per the prediction of a researcher in the past, it allows a synthesis of the theoretical and the empirical in a more seamless manner than do other contemporary approaches, most notably actor-network theory.

DISCUSSION QUESTIONS

1   What are the elements that make up the concept of emergence?
2   Discuss some of the human elements that may have made the effects of the tsunami worse.

NOTE

1   In the rebel province of Aceh, by contrast, a peace settlement was tentatively announced in July 2005 between the Indonesian administration and the Acehnese government-in-exile in Sweden.

REFERENCES

Aglionby, J. (2005) '"Ghosts" seek their pre-tsunami past', *Guardian Weekly*, 24–30 June: 10.Bussey, J. (2005) 'Thailand tableau: rebuilt resorts, makeshift memorials', *The Wall Street Journal*, 23 June: A1.

Clarke, L. (2003) 'Conceptualizing responses to extreme events: the problem of panic and failing gracefully', *Research in Social Problems and Public Policy (Terrorism and Disaster: New Threats, New Ideas)*, Volume 11: 123–41.

Freudenburg, W. R. and Jones, T. R. (1991) 'Attitudes and stress in the presence of technological risk', *Social Forces*, 69(4): 1143–68.

Goodspeed, P. (2005) 'Violent clashes threaten tsunami relief', *National Post* (Toronto), 19 July: A14.

Harvey, F. (2004) 'Devastated environment will face long-term damage', *Financial Times* (London), 29 December: 2.

Harrison, N. E. and Bryner, G. C. (2004) 'Towards theory', in N. E. Harrison and G. C. Bryner (eds) *Science and Politics in the International Environment*, Lanham, MD: Rowman & Littlefield.

Johnson, S. (2001) *Emergence: The Connected Lives of Ants, Brains, Cities, and Software*, New York: Scribner.

Liu, P. L.-F., Lynett, P., Fernando, H., Jaffe, B. E., Fritz, H., Higman, B., Morton, R., Goff, J. and Synolakis, C. (2005) 'Observations by the International Tsunami Survey Team in Sri Lanka', *Science*, 308, 10 June: 159.

Murphy, R. (2004) 'Disaster or sustainability: the dance of human agents with nature's actants', *The Canadian Review of Sociology and Anthropology*, 41(3): 249–66.

Sheldrake, R. (2005) 'Listen to the animals: Why did so many animals escape December's tsunami?', *The Ecologist*, 35(2):18–20.

Shiva, V. (1990) 'Biodiversity, biotechnology and profit: the need for a People's Plan to protect biological diversity', *The Ecologist,* 20(2): 44–7.

Zamiska, N. (2005) '"Tsunami lung" strikes survivors; doctors fear widespread cases', *The Wall Street Journal*, 23 June: D2.

CLIMATE CHANGE AND GLOBAL WARMING

Climate change is an increasingly cited social problem and one that climate scientists generally predict will become worse. It is the job of sociologists to predict and monitor how these changes might affect society, as well as to monitor societies' behaviors and responses to climate change. While there is a consensus across most governments of the world, there are an innumerable number of approaches being taken by these nations. The United States is one of the few nations of the world that does not have such a consensus.

Political Disagreements

Of note, there are significantly more political disagreements on the issues of climate change and global warming in the United States than most other nations in the world. Though there are significant political disagreements, there is much less debate within the scientific community. Depending on how one counts, between 90 and 98 percent of peer-reviewed published climate papers form a consensus that human-induced global warming or climate change is an observable phenomenon today.

Multiple studies published in peer-reviewed scientific journals show that 97 percent or more of actively publishing climate scientists agree: Climate-warming trends over the past century are extremely likely due to human activities.[1]

More resources:

Scientific Consensus: Earth's Climate is Warming:
https://climate.nasa.gov/scientific-consensus/

The History of Earth's Temperature - BBC Environment:
https://www.youtube.com/watch?v=ztg-cK85EqPw

How Climate and the Environment Will Affect Society

It seems intuitive that our geography, climate, and physics world has a large impact on the development and maintenance of societies and cultures. Additionally, unlike social policies and social paradigms, climate change knows no borders or boundaries. In the same way that social structures both facilitate and constrain individuals and their social behaviors, the climate and physical world also operate as facilitators and constraints for society(ies). Concerns about climate change are likely to grow both in the Unites States and across the world. The following article addresses how this increasingly cited social problem might be dealt with.

More resources:

Towards a Global Environmental Sociology? Legacies, Trends and Future Directions:
https://www.ncbi.nlm.nih.gov/pmc/articles/PMC4396407/

I   "Climate Change: How Do We Know?," NASA, 2020, http://climate.nasa.gov/evidence/.

CONCLUSION

The condition of our immediate surroundings and our planet both affect not only our social lives as individuals but also the structures of the societies in which we live. Climate change, pollution, natural disasters, the outlay of the land, and more affect the way in which we live, the ways in which we work, and the policy decisions before nation-states and governments. In much the same way that individuals are bound by structure, societal possibilities are constrained by the physical world around us.

CHAPTER 13

Health Care

AS WE SAW earlier, health care is widely cited as an important social problem. This chapter will explore why it so often cited as a major social problem and what might contribute to the American health care system being seen as so problematic. The subdiscipline of sociology that focuses on the connection between health care and society, health outcomes, and so on is called medical sociology.

Medical sociological endeavors tend to follow two streams: sociology *in* medicine and sociology *of* medicine. In the former, sociologists work as applied investigators or technicians seeking to answer questions of interest to their sponsors, whether government agencies, foundations, hospitals, or medical schools. Depending on the ingenuity of the researcher, such work can make broader contributions than the particular task may suggest, but the emphasis is on information and application. This role is familiar, encompassing those who design and execute health surveys and who study such varied topics as access to care, use of services, satisfaction, risk factors in disease, health status determinants, and many more.

Sociology *of* medicine, in contrast, focuses on testing sociological hypotheses, using medicine as an arena for studying basic issues in social stratification, power and influence, social organization, socialization, and the broad context of social values. Work in this tradition explores such themes as how physicians control the work of other health occupations; how lower social status and gender affect health interactions; and how political and economic interests influence the structure of care, reimbursement, and the use of technology. At the organizational level, such studies commonly contrast rhetoric with reality, seeking to identify the motivations, incentives, and group interests that result in departures from public declarations and stated goals. Medical sociology has little theory of its own, depending on its parent discipline for its broader perspectives. Thus, the major points of emphasis that define sociology in general help focus the way generic questions about health and medicine are formulated.

The United States has the most expensive health care in the world. While it fairs very poorly compared to all countries when it comes to efficiency of spending, the US health care system is generally

More resources:

The Role of Sociology in Health Affairs: https://www.healthaffairs.org/doi/full/10.1377/hlthaff.9.1.85

average to above average in terms of most outcomes or metrics of health when making the same comparison. However, when compared to other rich nations the United States fairs poorly. For example, the United States ranks 43rd/195 countries in terms of life expectancy at just about 80 years old, but nearly every other wealthy advanced economy/OECD country ranks ahead. There has also been a slight decrease in life expectancy in America, where it has continued to increase in most countries across the world.

Source: National Center for Health Statistics • Get the data • Created with Datawrapper

FIGURE 13.1 **Average life expectancy in the US.**

More resources:

What's Behind High U.S. Health Care Costs: https://news.harvard.edu/gazette/story/2018/03/u-s-pays-more-for-health-care-with-worse-population-health-outcomes/

In addition to being an outlier in terms of cost of health care, the United States is an outlier in the world among rich countries in that it does not provide some form of universal healthcare coverage. In fact, of the 33 wealthiest nations it is the only nation that does not provide such coverage. How and why the United States remains so structurally different to countries with similar levels of wealth is almost a field unto itself.

DISPARITIES IN HEALTH CARE

There are also wide disparities in health and health outcomes across a number of social factors. People with less wealth and income, blacks, and Latinx are among the groups that are less likely to have health care insurance. There are also large gaps in the kinds of health care that people have, and wealthier and less marginalized populations are more likely to have "better" health care insurance as well. The following article examines some disparities along the lines of race and gender in more detail.

The following article looks at the specific issue of the disparity in the prevalence of asthma across races in the city of Fort Valley, Georgia. However, it is important to note that these sorts of disparities exist across a wide range of health metrics and outcomes and in a wide variety of geographic areas across the country.

More resources:

Racial/Ethnic and Gender Disparities in Health Care Use and Access: https://www.ncbi.nlm.nih.gov/pubmed/28480588

Reading 13.1.

Health disparities and factors that trigger asthma in African-American children in low-income communities in Fort Valley, Georgia

by Jasmine Williams and Saul Mofya

INTRODUCTION

Asthma is the most common chronic disease among United States children and the leading cause of childhood morbidity. The disease disproportionately burdens many socioeconomically disadvantaged communities, especially in urban cities (1). The Centers of Disease Control and Prevention (CDC) estimates that there are over 25.5 million people with asthma in the United States and approximately one third of these are children (1). Despite effective therapies, asthma prevalence, morbidity, and mortality among children is increasing in the United States, largely affecting minority and low-income groups. African-American and Latino children who live in low-socioeconomic-status within urban environments have been shown in some studies to be the most affected (2, 3).

Several studies have concluded that, as with many chronic conditions, disparities in asthma outcomes may be due to factors such as race, socioeconomic status (SES), housing , environmental exposure, low parental literacy, health insurance, quality of health care, and/or differing self-management strategies (2, 3). According to a study by researchers at John Hopkins University, African-Americans had more

Jasmine Williams and Saul Mofya, "Health Disparities and Factors That Trigger Asthma in African-american Children in Low-income Communities in Fort Valley, Georgia," *International Journal of Child Health and Human Development*, vol. 9, no. 4, pp. 465-473. Copyright © 2016 by Nova Science Publishers. Reprinted with permission. Provided by ProQuest LLC. All rights reserved.

severe symptoms than any other racial or ethnic group yet lacked the necessary information about avoiding asthma triggers (1). This study indicated that African-Americans were three to four times more likely than Caucasians to be hospitalized for asthma, and were four to six times more likely to die from this disease. They were also less likely to receive treatment, which contributes to the problem (1).

The purpose of this study was to assess health disparities and factors that trigger asthma in African-American children in low-income communities in Fort Valley, Georgia and to provide recommendations that may assist medical and public health professionals and other stakeholders to educate these communities.

METHODS
To assess health disparities and factors that trigger asthma in African-American children in low-income communities in Fort Valley, we conducted literature reviews which included the North Central Health District Peach County 2013 Health Status Report, Community Health Needs Assessment Peach Country 2015, the city-data of Fort Valley, GA, and several peer reviewed articles relating to our search.

RESULTS
Fort Valley is a city in Peach County, Georgia. The current total population for Peach County is 27,481, composed of predominantly Caucasians (47.26%) and African-Americans (46.5%) (4). However, the current population in the city of Fort Valley is estimated to be 10,000 people, 81% being African-Americans (5).

Asthma prevalence
According to the North Central Health District Peach County 2013 Health Status Report, from 2006–2010 in Peach County asthma accounted for 789 (1.3%) emergency department visits and had a hospital discharge rate of 154.9 per 100,000. Children ages 1–12 were most affected by asthma symptoms that led to an emergency department visit. The emergency department visit rates in Peach County due to asthma were much higher for African-Americans (974.9 per 100,000 people) and other races (489 per 100,000 people) compared to Caucasians (253.9 per 100,000 people) (6).

Socioeconomic status (SES)
The median household income in Fort Valley per year is $24,661; for the State of Georgia it is $49,604, while the national average is $53,046. Fort Valley has an unemployment rate (11.8%) which is above state 6.8% and the national average of 6.0%. It is estimated that 36% of the children live in poverty, more than 70% of the students are on free or reduced lunch, and 19% of the households are on food stamp/SNAP benefits (6).

Education status
Only 21.3% of our target population is functionally illiterate, with an average high school graduation rate of less than 60% (6).

Housing
The majorities of the housing units in the area were built in the 1960s and are in deplorable condition. Over 34% of housing units are classified as substandard because they have at least one of the following conditions: 1) lacking complete plumbing facilities, 2) lacking complete kitchen facilities, 3) having more than 1 occupant per room (4).

Health behaviors
Health behaviors such as poor diet, a lack of exercise, and tobacco smoking contribute to poor health status. 27.8% of the adults lack exercise, 34.6% are obese and 20.2% are current tobacco users (6). Half of the restaurants in the area are fast food establishments. Because current behaviors are determinants of future health, these indicators may predispose to future significant health issues, such as poor cardiovascular health and other complications of obesity such as diabetes (4, 6).

Health insurance
22.4% of the adults and 8.2% of children do not have health insurance (6).

Environmental exposure
Fort Valley tends to experience high temperatures and humidity, which are above the national average (5). These environmental factors are favorable for mold growth, which is one of the known triggering factors for asthma attacks. The area is ranked 14th in the nation as a city where people are at risk of year-round air particle pollution (5).

DISCUSSION
This study sought to determine health disparities and factors that trigger asthma in African-American children in low-income communities in Fort Valley, Georgia.

Socioeconomic status
Poverty has been directly and indirectly associated with health disparities and severity of illnesses. African-American populations with low SES, whether measured based on income or occupation have higher levels of illness than populations with higher income (2). Numerous studies have shown that mortality rates in almost every illness, including asthma, are higher in African-American populations with

low SES than those seen in Caucasians or other groups with higher SES (2, 3). From our literature review, the majority of African-American families in Fort Valley live in neighborhoods where 44% of families' income is below the Federal poverty level. This percentage is more than three times the national level (4).

Families and individuals with low SES are more likely to engage in high-risk behaviors associated with asthma exacerbations, such as smoking tobacco and illicit substances, eating fast foods more frequently or not exercising (6). In the United States, tobacco smoking and environmental tobacco smoking (Second hand tobacco exposure) vary widely by socioeconomic status and ethnicity (7). Current tobacco smoking in adults in Fort Valley is 20.2%, while the national rate is 18.1% (4, 6). Exposure of children or pregnant women to environmental tobacco smoke predisposes toward both earlier onset and increased severity of asthma. Maternal smoking in pregnancy may influence the development of the fetal respiratory system as well as lung function impairment in newborns (8). Several studies have concluded that maternal smoking in pregnancy increases the risk of asthma during the early part of the child's life. Smoking also contributes to low birth weight and preterm delivery, which are independent determinants of asthma (8). As for our study area, environmental tobacco smoking is a major concern as children are exposed both in homes and neighborhood communities. The need to start promoting and sensitizing the communities about the detrimental effect of tobacco smoking on the general health of the community should be a priority.

The prevalence of obesity and asthma in United States has increased drastically over the past 20 years (9). Epidemiologic studies have shown that obesity serves as a modifier for asthma risk (10). From our literature review, 27.8% of the adults lack exercise and 34.6% are obese (4, 6); this finding also may apply to the children in these communities. Lack of exercise and obesity can be attributed to health behaviors which are associated with low SES and poor diet. Notably, 50% of restaurant establishments in Fort Valley are fast foods. Eating excessive fast foods combined with a sedentary lifestyle predispose to obesity. Obese children are at an increased risk of experiencing severe asthma symptoms (11). There is a strong relationship between obesity and asthma, both of which show increasing prevalence.

According to asthma surveillance data from the Centers for Disease Control and Prevention (CDC), as recently as 2013, the prevalence of asthma in children in the United States was 8.3% and data from National Health and Nutrition Examination Survey (NHANES), put the prevalence of obesity in youth nearly 17%. It has been noted that both obesity and asthma affect certain minority and inner-city groups more than other populations (10, 11). In addition, it appears that even a little excess weight can directly affect lung function, particularly in minority children (11).

Childhood obesity can have complications for child's physical, social, and emotional well-being. Obese children are exposed to weight stigma and are vulnerable to psychological effects, such as depression, and social effects, such as isolation. Consequences of bias, such as isolation or social withdrawal, could contribute to the exacerbation of obesity through psychological vulnerabilities that increase the likelihood of over-eating and sedentary activity (3, 11).

Access to health care

Many African-American populations tend to access health care in fewer numbers compared to Caucasians. The reason varies from lack of health insurance to established beliefs and biases about interactions between African-Americans and their health care providers (12, 13). The predominant barriers include inability to pay for services, lack of health insurance, lack of transportation and child care, decreased understanding of treatment plans and inability to incorporate prescribed health plans into daily living patterns (2, 14). Furthermore, some African-American populations' cultural beliefs and health practices have a significant impact upon their well-being regardless of their income and educational levels (13).

Various health beliefs and practices can be observed among African-American groups, in part determined by their ages, socioeconomic levels and geographic locales. However, common cultural threads can be identified among many African-Americans. These commonalities include religious orientation, social support networks, and informal health care system (13). Religion is a central force within the lives of many African-Americans. Religion beliefs influence all aspects of many African-American families and communities' life, including work, education, recreation and health. Health is not viewed as made up of physiological and psychological components as defined within the traditional science oriented framework of health; rather, the beliefs of many African-American characterizes health as a continuum evolving around mind, body, and spirit (13). Many African-Americans are more likely to use prayer as a means of coping with worries than Caucasians peers, rather than seeking professional help, which is sorely limited anyway (13).

Support systems which are often utilized by African-Americans have a significant role in the lives of individuals. These support system include significant others who may or may not be related by blood or marriage. In times of crisis and stress, African-Americans are more likely to rely on the family network, both nuclear and extended than on outside traditional health and human service community agencies (13).

Informal health-care systems within the African-American community are often consulted. In the event of illness African-Americans are more likely to consult family members and friends than the professional health-care system (13).

Cultural values often influence the degree of adherence to health care treatment regimes. A number of studies have also shown that, in the African-American populations studied, at least a third of the patients would not take prescribed medicines due to cultural and health beliefs (13). In addition, lack of communication and understanding between patients and providers has also been a major contributing factor to asthma health disparities (14). Low literacy levels have been found within Fort Valley communities. In communities similar to Fort Valley, low literacy can contribute to misunderstanding information and directions provided by the physician. One study found that physicians seeing African-American patients would more likely control the conversation and talk to them less about their conditions compared to physicians seeing Caucasian patients (14). Health professionals need a particular skill set in order to provide culturally competent health care to minority patients, families and communities. Health professionals bemoan the lack of time, resources, and/or information to do so, yet they fail to recognize that these are the same reasons offered by patients who have difficulties managing a recommended therapeutic regimen.

Health insurance

We found that more than 8.2% of children and 22.4% of adults lack health insurance coverage (6). The percentage of children and adult lacking health insurance at national level is 7.5% and 15% respectively (4). More than 90% of children who have health insurance in Fort Valley have it with Medicaid or the State Children's Health Insurance Program. While Medicaid may improve access to care for low SES children who are otherwise uninsured, it does not ensure their access to the same locations and providers of care, nor the same continuity of care that children with private insurance receive (1). Choice among providers may be significantly limited in locations where the Medicaid provider payment rate is low compared to other insurers.

In Peach County, the emergency department visit rates due to asthma were much higher for African-American children, especially those between the ages of 1–12 years (6). Parents in these communities may only take their children to the emergency department when they show severe symptoms of an asthma exacerbation. These seek medical relief rather than treatment and control of the disease, perhaps due to the general complexities related to the health insurance enrollment process, lack of money to pay for medical services, and to some extent lack of transportation (14). Furthermore, complex enrollment rules and processes for initial enrollment and maintaining enrollment in Medicaid are commonly noted, compromising child participation in this program (2).

Housing structure

Housing-poor or substandard housing units are more likely to have above average exposure to indoor allergens, such as dust mites, rodent allergens, cockroach allergens, mold and mildew (8,12). In the Fort Valley area, most of the houses were built in the 1960s and are now in dilapidated condition, which contribute to indoor allergens.

Several epidemiological studies have linked substandard housing with an increased risk of chronic illness. Damp, cold, and moldy housing is associated with asthma and other chronic respiratory symptoms, even after potentially confounding factors such as income, socioeconomic status; smoking, crowding, and unemployment are controlled (16, 17). Water intrusion is a major contributor to problems with dampness. The dilapidated condition of many homes in Fort Valley area makes it likely that they have both interior and exterior leaks. Overcrowding and inadequate ventilation also increase interior moisture. Damp houses provide a nurturing environment for mites, roaches, respiratory viruses, and molds, all of which play a role in respiratory disease pathogenesis (12). Cross-sectional epidemiological studies have also established associations between damp and moldy housing and recurrent headaches, fever, nausea and vomiting, and sore throats (8, 18, 19).

Old, dirty carpeting, often found in substandard housing, is a significant reservoir for dust, allergens, and toxic chemicals (12). Exposure to these agents can result in allergic, respiratory, neurological, and hematologic illnesses. Pest infestations, through their association with asthma, provide another linkage between substandard housing and chronic illness (17). Cockroaches can cause allergic sensitization and have emerged as an important asthma trigger in inner-city neighborhoods (8). Children with asthma who are sensitized and exposed to cockroaches are at elevated risk for hospitalization (8). Mouse allergen also acts as a clinically important cause of allergy and asthma morbidity (8). Structural defects in substandard housing permit entry of cockroaches and rodents; leaking pipes and other sources of water provide them with water to drink. Inadequate food storage and disposal facilities provide pests with opportunities for obtaining food. Dead spaces in walls harbor pests and permit circulation among apartments in multiunit dwellings (17).

Minority children are significantly more likely to be exposed to indoor allergens as well as second hand smoke, which is a known contributor to asthma prevalence and morbidity (1). Our literature review indicted that 20.2% of the adults are current tobacco smokers (6). Unfortunately, most of these smokers also smoke indoors, exacerbating indoor air quality.

Environmental factors

A significant factor that contributes to asthma is air pollution. Air pollutants are associated with a high incidence of asthma attacks, as well as morbidity of respiratory illness (20). Fort Valley is ranked 14th in the nation as a city where people are at risk of year-round air particle pollution.

In Peach county (where Fort Valley is located), the average daily ambient Particulate Matter (PM2.5) is 11.9 µg/m³ with 5 days exceeding emissions standards while the national average PM2.5 is 10.7 µg/m³ with four days exceeding emissions standards (4). While the PM2.5 for Fort Valley is within acceptable range, individuals that are particularly sensitive to fine particle exposure (such as those with heart or lung disease, older adults, and children) can experience severe symptoms (20).

It is also important to understand that concentration of particulate matter in indoor air can differ substantially from outdoor concentrations. When substandard housing results in poor ventilation and low air exchange rates, contributions from indoor particulate sources such as cooking appliances and heaters can accumulate to dangerous levels (21).

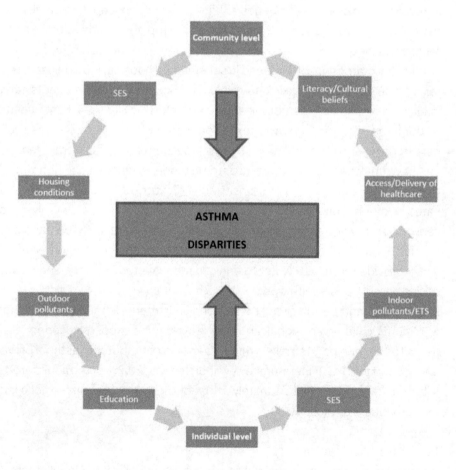

FIGURE 13.1.1 **Known determinants of asthma disparities.**

Other factors that may contribute to air pollution in the area include diesel exhaust from large trucks, cargo trains, and a school bus assembly plant, as well as agricultural pesticides. Diesel exhaust emissions contribute to the development and exacerbation of asthma, because of both the numerous chemical irritants and the large volume of small particulate matter (21). Peach County is one of the largest producers of peaches in Georgia, facilitated by the common place use of agricultural pesticides by farmers. Most of the pesticides are aerosols and can trigger allergies, asthma and respiratory irritation, especially in children and elderly. These pollutants have been known to increase airway obstruction, resulting in a greater number of children being hospitalized in these polluted areas (21).

The weather in the area also plays a major role in contributing to asthma exacerbations in the children. Fort Valley tends to experience hot and humid conditions in the summer months, with temperatures and humidity above the national average levels (5). The temperature ranges from 45-95 degree Fahrenheit, with humidity of 50 to 90% throughout the year. The national temperature and humidity ranges from 30-90 degree Fahrenheit and 40-80% respectively (5). Such environmental conditions, coupled with substandard or dilapidated housing units, encourage the growth of mold and mildew which are well known factors that triggers asthma (17, 22).

Figure 13.1.1 show the cycle of environmental health disparities and known determinants of asthma in Fort Valley. In order to break the cycle, several measures need to be considered. We suggested some of the important ways to break the cycle in the conclusion section of this article.

CONCLUSION

Our survey of the literature recognized factors which contribute to health disparities and asthma triggers in African-American children in low-income communities in Fort Valley. These factors include SES, (low literacy, health behaviors, limited access to health care, and lack of health insurance), dilapidated housing structures, and environmental exposure. Issues with SES include poverty, tobacco smoking, obesity, and increased risk of low quality health care due to problems, which originate from established beliefs and issues of communication between patient and provider. Environmental factors include indoor allergens, the condition of housing, weather conditions, and air pollution. One potential strategy to address these complex and compounding health issues is to forge a collaborative partnership between community leaders, medical, environmental, and public health professionals to promote asthma awareness in communities and schools.

The most important step to address the asthma disparities in Fort Valley would be to implement and enforce policies that increase access to healthcare for children and adults with asthma, regardless of their ethnicity or SES. This can be achieved through affordable health insurance with an easy enrollment system. If the enrollment system cannot be simplified, community-based enrollment programs should be implemented to help people to navigate through the complex health insurance system.

Access to high quality health care is essential. High quality health care involves culturally competent care, and ensures that patients receive high-quality, effective care irrespective of cultural background, language proficiency, socio-economic status and other factors that may be formed by a patient's race or ethnicity. Lack of cultural awareness can undermine the physician-patient relationship. Providers should ensure that patients receive effective, understandable, respectful care compatible with cultural and linguistic preferences. The recruiting of culturally diverse and culturally competent staff and practice leadership should be a common goal. High quality care also involves delivering patient-centered care which emphasizes respect for the patient, clear communication, shared decision making, and building of the physician-patient relationship.

Health status is influenced not only by access to health care but also by socio-economic determinants, such as income and availability of nutritious foods, environmental health of the community and access to early childhood education. Stakeholders and policymakers must also address these factors that play a part influencing the health of African-Americans and minority communities.

An individual's socioeconomic status, particularly income and education level, is among the many factors that significantly influence health. Lower-income individuals, regardless of race or ethnicity, are often in poorer health than those in higher income brackets. An individual's income may influence a number of other determinants of health status, such as one's access to educational opportunities, decent medical care, and affordable housing in a healthy community. A person's level of education also affects health status. Therefore, education is critical to increase the likelihood of employment and of better income that breaks the cycle.

Increased emphasis must be placed on reducing disparities in education if the health disparity gap is to be closed. Investments in early childhood education and after-school programs for underserved minorities should be made to ensure academic success later in life. Evidence shows that minority children who attended early childhood education program are less likely than those not to engage in high-risk activities, such as smoking and illicit drug use (23). In addition, children who regularly attended after-school programs have markedly increased academic performance compared with students who are unsupervised after school (23).

Physical fitness education is even more important, to combat the increasingly sedentary habits of young children. School and community based physical activities should be encouraged in these communities, such as swimming, marathon, cycling and several outdoor games.

A number of significant barriers impede the growth of African-Americans and other minority students in health professions. Among the greatest impediments faced by racial and ethnic minorities is unequal access to adequate educational opportunities and parental inability to access costly private-sector substitutes even if these are available. African-Americans and other minorities often are caught in the "Cycle of disadvantage and disability": often educated at schools with insufficient financial resources, less-qualified teaching staff, and fewer advanced courses, contributing to lower academic achievement. This lack of educational preparedness poses a challenge to students hoping to enter the medical professions. African-Americans and other minorities are disproportionately low-income and are often educated at schools with insufficient financial resources, less-qualified teaching staff, and fewer advanced courses. The need to improve educational opportunities for all children through local, state and federal funding should be a top priority if the health and education disparity gap is to be closed.

Public health education campaigns and programs targeting high-risk groups should be utilized to educate citizens about healthy living, the importance of prevention, and risk factors that contribute to preventable illness. These campaigns and programs should be community-driven to ensure that the materials and messages are tailored to the needs of the local population and reflect the culture of the community.

Efforts must be made to reduce the effect of environmental stressors that disproportionately threaten to harm the health and well-being of low-SES communities. An individual's environment can have a significant impact on his or her overall health status. Environmental dangers, such as poor air quality, mold growth or rampant lead contamination can harm the health of the community. Substandard housing is a likely contributor to the elevated rate of exposure to environmental stressors, as these homes are more likely to be located close to noxious land use such as industrial sites or hazardous dumping areas. Addressing health disparities that are the effect of environmental stressors is a complex and difficult task. However, more action needs to be taken to address, rectify and monitor the harmful effect of environmental stressors on minority communities.

In conclusion, methods that the families are capable of carrying out can also be taught to make communities health and safer. Activities such as fundraisers to raise money to renovate housing units which are dilapidated, community gardening and providing more family based program including nutrition and diet, exercise and smoking cessation are needed in order to lower asthma rates in low-income communities.

REFERENCES

1. Akinbami LJ, Moorman JE, Bailey C, Zahran HS, King M, Johnson CA, et al. Treads in asthma prevalence, health care use and mortality in the united States,2001–2010. NCHS Data Brief 2012;94:1–8.

2. Neeta TN, Oh SS, Nguyen EA, Martin M, Roth LA, Galanter J, et al. Socioeconomic status and childhood asthma in urban minority youths. The GALA II and SAGE II studies. Am J Respir Crit Care Med 2013; 188(10):1202–9.

3. Carroll K. Socioeconomic status, race/ethnicity and asthma in youth. Am J Respir Crit Care Med 2013; 188:1180–1.

4. Georgia Department of Health. Georgia, Peach County. Full health indicators report. Community health needs assessment. North Central Health District. Fort Valley, GA: Peach County Health Department, 2015.

5. Fort Valley, Georgia. City-Data.com. URL: www.city-data.com/city/Fort-Valley-Georgia.

6. Georgia Department of Public Health. 2013 North Central Health District, Peach County: Health status report. Fort Valley, GA: Georgia Department Public Health, 2014.

7. Kit BK, Simon AE, Brody DJ, Akinbami LJ. US prevalence and tread in tobacco smoke exposure among children and adolescents with asthma. Pediatrics 2013;131(3):407–14.

8. Kanchongkittiphon W, Gaffin JM, Phipatanakul W The indoor environment and inner-city childhood asthma. Asian Pac J Immunol 2014; 32:103–10.

9. Wang Y. Disparities in pediatric obesity in the United States. Am Soc Nutr Adv Nutr 2011;2:23–31.

10. Dooyema CA, Belay B, Foltz JL, Williams N, Blanck HM. The childhood obesity research demonstration project: A comprehensive community approach to reduce childhood obesity. Childhood Obes 2013;9(5): 454–9.

11. Quinto KB, Zuraw BL, Poon KY, Chen W, Schatz M, Christiansen SC. The association of obesity and asthma severity and control in children. J Allergy Clin Immunol 2011;128(5):964–9.

12. Holt EW, Theall KP, Rabito FA. Individual, housing and neighborhood correlates of asthma among young urban children. J Urban Hlth 2013;90: 116–29.

13. George M. Health beliefs, treatment preferences and complementary and alternative medicine for asthma, smoking and lung cancer self-management in diverse black communities. Patient Educ Couns 2012;89(3): 489–500.

14. Perry TT, Rettiganti M, Brown RH, Nick TG, Jones SM. Uncontrolled asthma and factors related to morbidity in an impoverished, rural environment. Ann Allergy Asthma Immunol 2012;108(4):254–9.

15. Cabana MD, Slish KK, Evans D, Mellins RB, Brown RW, Lin X, et al. Impact of physician asthma care education on patient outcomes. Pediatrics 2006;117(6): 2149–57.

16. Breysse J, Dixon S, Gregory J, Philby M, Jacobs DE, Krieger J. Effect of weatherization combined with community health worker in-home education on asthema control. Am J Publ Hlth 2014;104(1):57–64.

17. Turyk M, Banda E, Chisum G, Weems D Jr, Liu Y, Damitz M, et al. A multifaceted community-based asthma intervention in Chicago: effects of trigger reduction and self-management education on asthma morbidity. J Asthma 2013;50(7):727–36.

18. Strachan DP. Damp housing and childhood asthma: Validation of reporting of symptoms. BMJ 1988;297: 1223–6.

19. Institute of Medicine. Damp indoor spaces and health. Washington, DC: National Academies Press, 2004.

20. Lewis TC, Robins TG, Mentz GB, Zhang X, Mukherjee B, Lin X, et al. Air pollution and respiratory symptoms among children with asthma: Vulnerability by corticosteroid use and residence area. Sci Total Environ 2013;448:48–55.

21. Adamkiewicz G, Zota AR, Fabian MP, Chahine T, Julien R, Spengler JD, et al. Moving environmental justice indoors: Understanding structural influences on residential exposure patterns in low-income communities. Am J Publ Health 2011;101(Suppl 1): 238–45.

22. Meng YY, Babey SH, Wolstein J. Asthma-related school absenteeism and school concentration of low-income students in California. Prev Chronic Dis 2012; 9:1103–12.

23. American College of Physicians. Racial and ethnic disparities in health care. Philadelphia, PA: American College Physicians, 2010.

SUMMARY

The United States is an outlier in terms of health care cost among world nations and an outlier structurally among wealthy nations in not offering some form of universal coverage. While Americans spend the most in the world on health care, the health outcomes of Americans do not reflect that. There are also wide health disparities across a number of social dimensions, including race and wealth. Health care is also one of the most commonly cited social problems in social surveys and has increased in the frequency with which it is mentioned.

Image Credits

Fig. 13.1: Source: https://www.cnbc.com/2019/05/08/techs-next-big-disruption-could-be-delaying-death.html.

Family and Population

FAMILIES ARE EXTREMELY important in the socialization process. As such, the structures of families are something sociologists pay a great deal of attention to. As ideas and policies regarding sexuality and gender change, so too do structures and conceptions of families. Listed are a number of types of families, though this is not at all an exhaustive list.

TYPES OF FAMILIES

- **Nuclear family**: A social unit composed of two married adults and their children.
- **Family of orientation**: Family to which one was born.
- **Family of procreation**: A person, spouse, and their children.
- **Blended family**: Spouses and their children from former marriages live as a single nuclear family.
- **Binuclear family**: Divorced parents form separate households; children divide their time with each.
- **Cohabitating family**: A social unit composed of unmarried partners and their children.
- **Extended family:** Composed of two or more generations of kin that function as an independent social and economic unit.
- **Emerging and new families**: Family structures and types that are becoming increasingly common. They may have been discouraged by social policy or cultural ideas.

CHANGING FAMILY STRUCTURE

The ubiquitous prevalence of the married nuclear family began to change significantly in the 1970s and 1980s and has continued until present day. As emerging family types become more common, social norms and conceptions about families are likely to change as well. As these changes occur there has also been a more universal trend in the United States of marriage rates going down and the birth rate staying mostly

More resources:

New Families: Modern Couples as New Pioneers:
https://psycnet.apa.org/record/1998-07230-007

static since the 1980s after having been significantly higher in previous decades. The following article provides a more detailed discussion of these emerging families and the demographic trends related to families, respectively.

More resources:

Demographic Trends in the United States: A Review of Research in the 2000s:
https://www.ncbi.nlm.nih.gov/pmc/articles/PMC3293163/

HOW FAMILIES AFFECT US

The following article provides a deeper dive on the effect that families have on individuals. It is important to remember that family types not only affect individuals but are also predictive of social outcomes.

Reading 14.1.

The Influence of the Family

by Jay MacLeod

As the focal socializing agency, especially in the early years of a child's life, the family plays a crucial role in the process of social reproduction. In this [reading], we consider the particular circumstances of each boy's family and how the family influences his expectations for the future. In describing the families of these boys, we must be attentive to a number of factors, such as the presence of a father in the household, the occupational histories of parents and older siblings, and the length of the family's tenancy in public housing.

All families living in Clarendon Heights are lower class. For a family of four to qualify for federal housing projects, its annual income must not exceed $14,000; for state housing developments the limit is approximately $1,500 lower. These are, of course, the upper boundaries; the annual income of most families living in Clarendon Heights is well below the limit.

THE HALLWAY HANGERS' HOUSEHOLDS

Chris lives with his white mother and two younger sisters. Their father, who is black, moved out of the house a few years ago. "I kicked my father out," boasts Chris in

Jay MacLeod, "The Influence of the Family," *Ain't No Makin' It*, pp. 51-61. Copyright © 2008 by Taylor & Francis Group. Reprinted with permission.

a group interview. Chris also has two half brothers and one half sister who live on their own. His brothers work in unskilled, manual labor jobs; his sister is a part-time secretary. Chris seems to have free run of the household. His mother, a kind, friendly woman who has never married, has been pleading with Chris for two years to attend school regularly, but to no avail. Although she does not work regularly, for much of the year she babysits in her home for one and sometimes two young children from working-class families. In exchange for her labors (nine hours per day), she receives a small wage. Chris's family has lived in Clarendon Heights for sixteen years, prior to which his mother lived with her other children in private housing.

Boo-Boo also has lived in Clarendon Heights for his entire life. He and his older brother have a different father than his younger brother, Derek (a member of the Brothers), and his younger sister. Both fathers live out of state and very seldom venture to Clarendon Heights. Their mother, a high school dropout, has stable employment assembling computer and electronic parts in a nearby suburb. Boo-Boo's father, who graduated from high school, has been in the merchant marine "for a long, long time." Boo-Boo's older brother, Blade, has a drug dependency problem. He dropped out of high school a few years ago, recently has joined the army reserves and is struggling to acquire a General Equivalency Diploma (GED) so that he can join the army.

Stoney's mother's occupational history is a modest success story. She attended St. Mary's Catholic High School in the city but had to drop out during her freshman year to find work after her mother died. She subsequently earned a GED as well as a secretarial degree and has worked her way up to a supervisory position as secretary of a department in a state welfare office. Stoney's father's experience has been altogether different. Confined to the county house of correction a year and a half ago for passing a bad check, he broke out with only a month remaining on his sentence. With no place to go and unable to see his family, however, he subsequently turned himself in. After serving the remainder of his sentence plus some additional months for the escape, he has now found short-term work cleaning carpets. But like so many others from Clarendon Heights with a criminal record, Stoney's father probably will have a difficult time securing stable employment and is likely to end up back behind bars. Stoney's family moved to the Clarendon Heights neighborhood only three years ago; before that time they lived in Emerson Towers housing project, where Stoney's mother grew up. In contrast to the rest of the Hallway Hangers, Stoney's mother has a strong influence on him. A strict disciplinarian, she sets a nightly curfew for him, which he respects with diligence.

Frankie's family lived in the Heights for thirty years, and although his mother recently moved to another project in the city, Frankie spends nearly all of his time in the Clarendon Heights community. His mother and father both grew up in separate working-class neighborhoods in the city. Frankie's father attended City Tech for a few years before quitting school. He died when Frankie was seven years old. Frankie is the only Hallway Hanger whose mother graduated from high school; she currently works full-time at a camera factory. His sister also graduated from high school, but none of his seven brothers has earned a diploma. As mentioned earlier, all of Frankie's brothers have served time in prison; four of them presently are scattered around the state in various institutions. When out of prison, they find work in construction, landscaping, or painting. One of his brothers tends bar at the local pub, where recently he was shot trying to break up a fight. Most of Frankie's brothers work irregularly; at any given time, one or two may be unemployed.

Slick and Steve are the only members of the Hallway Hangers whose family has moved recently to public housing. Although their mother grew up only a few blocks from the Heights, the family lived in a neighboring city until they moved to Clarendon Heights about six years ago. Their father has never lived with the family, his background is hazy, and Steve's feelings about him are ambivalent. "I haven't seen that bastard for a long time. ... I think he got put away when he was a kid." Neither parent graduated from high school. "My mom quit in the ninth or tenth grade. She quit cuz she had to put money in the house. And, y'know, she was on her own by the time she was eighteen," declares Slick. Currently out of work due to ill health, their mother, an aggressive and strong-willed woman, usually is employed as a nurse's aide. Slick and Steve have a brother and sister, both younger.

Jinx, like Frankie, is part of a large family that has lived in Clarendon Heights for close to thirty years. Both of his parents grew up in the city and are currently employed full-time. His father has worked for the city maintenance department for nearly thirty years, while his mother has been employed at a hotel as a chambermaid for six or seven years. Neither parent graduated from high school, nor did five of his six older siblings, including his only sister. The one high school graduate is in the navy; of the other three brothers, one paints houses, one works in a factory assembling clothes racks, and one is unemployed, having himself completed a stint in the navy. Jinx's fifth brother died of natural causes at the age of sixteen. His sister recently obtained her own apartment in Clarendon Heights; she has a small daughter to look after and consequently does not work. Given that the largest apartment in Clarendon Heights contains only three bedrooms, Jinx's family must have been very cramped before his sister and her daughter moved out. Even now, six people live in the unit.

Shorty's family is even larger. He has ten older brothers and sisters, three of whom have graduated from high school.

Shorty: I got seven brothers. We lived here for thirteen years. ... I mean, we been through the riots and everything. My brother Joe had to quit school when he was sixteen years old, just because my father was an alcoholic. He had to go out and get a job. My [other] brother, he was a bikey; he had to sell pot. But Joe was out gettin' a job at sixteen to support all the kids. … He [went back to school and was subsequently employed as] a cop for two months; he got laid off. He was working at the weapons lab as a security guard. You ask him. He's our father. That's what he really is—he's our father. My father got put away for nine months. He didn't live with us for six years. Every fucking penny that my brother got he threw right into the family, right into the house. Cuz my mother can't work. She almost died three times; she has a brain tumor.

Aside from this account, information on Shorty's family is very sketchy, as he will very seldom speak about his home life. In a separate interview, however, Shorty did mention that with the exception of Joe, all the boys in his family have at one time or another been in the military service, as was his father.

Despite the difficulty inherent in generalizing about such diverse family histories, it is clear that the Hallway Hangers share certain family characteristics that may affect their aspirations. Foremost among these are the duration of these families' tenancy in public housing. With the exception of Slick and Steve, all the Hallway Hangers and their families have lived in the projects for many years: Shorty for thirteen years, Chris for sixteen, Boo-Boo's family for at least eighteen, Jinx's family for twenty-seven years, and Frankie's and Stoney's families for thirty years. Like most of the project residents, the educational attainment of these boys' parents and older brothers and sisters is very low; of their parents, only Boo-Boo's father and Frankie's mother graduated from high school. The sporadic employment record of family members is another common characteristic. For those who are able to find employment at all, it is typically menial, low paying, and unstable. Other less widespread commonalities between the families of these boys include the fathers' absence from the household, the large size of the families, and the numerous encounters of family members with the law.

THE BROTHERS' FAMILIES

Super's family has lived in public housing for eighteen years. The family moved to Clarendon Heights only five years ago but prior to that lived in a large housing project in a nearby city. Super's mother and father came to the North from South Carolina and Tennessee respectively in the early 1960s. Neither graduated from high school. Super's mother does not work; his father is a general laborer in construction but currently is unemployed, a typical predicament for low-level employees in the seasonal construction business. Super has two younger sisters and an older sister who attends a Catholic high school. Super has left home repeatedly, citing his parents' strict and inflexible disciplinary code as the reason. Although many parents in Clarendon Heights use force when disciplining their children, Super is the only boy who admits to being abused physically by his father.

Details about Mokey's home life are scarce. Mokey is not sure whether his parents graduated from high school. Apparently a heavy drinker, Mokey's father is a custodian in an office building in the commercial and financial district of the city. Although his father moved out of the house at least four years ago, Mokey frequently meets him at work to help with the evening cleanup, especially during the summer. His mother works part-time at a nearby day care center. He has a brother who is two years younger than he is and a five-year-old sister who has just entered kindergarten. His family lived in a very small public housing development before moving into Clarendon Heights.

James has lived in the Clarendon Heights community for his entire life. His mother, who is originally from Georgia, quit school when she was in the eighth grade. She is unemployed temporarily because she injured her shoulder about six months ago, but she usually works as a nurse's aide for the elderly. James's father graduated from high school and currently works in a factory that manufactures zippers and buttons. When asked if his father lives in the household, James shakes his head no but adds, "He didn't really move out. He comes and he goes." James's two younger sisters are excellent students, but his thirteen-year-old brother has a much more lackadaisical attitude toward his education. As noted previously, James's approach to school recently has undergone a dramatic change from ambivalence to commitment.

Craig's family came to this country from Haiti about eleven years ago and has lived in the Clarendon Heights neighborhood for six years. Although the educational system is somewhat different in Haiti, both his parents attained the rough equivalent of a high school diploma. His mother works part-time as a "homemaker"; she prepares meals, cleans, and performs other domestic chores for an elderly couple. Craig's father works as a janitor for an engineering company. Craig took pains to explain to me that his father has worked his way up to a supervisory role in the maintenance department.

Craig: I think he's a supervisor.

Jm: So what exactly does he do?

Craig: Before he used to do it himself—cleaning—but now he makes sure others do it.

Craig lives with his parents and six brothers and sisters. "Actually, I got four brothers and sisters, right? But since my father was messin' around, I got six brothers and sisters." The half siblings as well as his four full brothers and sisters all live in the household. His two older sisters have been very successful academically; there seems to be a supportive atmosphere for academic achievement in his home. His brother is in his second year at a technical college. One of the older sisters, who was a straight-A student in high school, is studying medicine at a local college.

Juan's family is also from the West Indies, in this case the Dominican Republic. His mother and father were divorced there, at which time Juan's mother came to the United States. Juan and his younger sister came to join her ten years ago; their three brothers preferred to remain in their home country. At some point, his mother remarried, and the family of four moved into Clarendon Heights in 1978. Juan's stepfather is presently unemployed.

Juan: He can't find a job.

Jm: What's his trade?

Juan: He used to work in a hotel, like in management—a boss. He decided to quit, and then he went to another hotel. Then the same thing happened: He decided to quit. Don't know why.

Juan's mother does not work either. Both his stepfather and mother graduated from high school in the Dominican Republic. He sorely misses his older brothers and hopes to return to his homeland in the near future.

Mike lives with his unmarried mother and grandmother. His father, an Italian immigrant, was a very successful professional wrestler, but Mike knows of him only from television. Mike has lived in public housing since he was two years old, first in Emerson Towers and, since 1977, in Clarendon Heights. His grandmother retired from her work in a local factory a few years ago. His mother, a high school dropout, has held a series of jobs. Most recently, she worked at Woolworth's and subsequently on the night shift at a large hotel. She found that job physically draining and currently is employed as a homemaker who takes care of elderly people. Neither woman has much success disciplining Mike; periodically, however, his uncle is brought in to help with the task, which Mike loathes. A navy veteran, Mike's uncle is the stereotypical tough, no-nonsense blue-collar worker. His uncle recounts stories of painful encounters with his own father when his self-discipline slipped perceptibly and threatens Mike with the same type of punishment.

Uncle: When my father said something, he meant it. When he said to be in at eleven o'clock, he meant eleven o'clock. I can remember being out with the boys one night and running all the way home—got in at 11:05. My old man was sitting there waiting for me. He looked at me, looked at the clock, and that was it. He knocked the shit out of me.

Mike: [*grimacing*] That's crazy. Jay, tell him that's crazy.

Uncle: It worked. And it'll work on you too. Damn right it will.

Indeed, the approach does have the desired effect, for now his mother exercises more control of Mike by threatening to summon his uncle.

In general terms, the Brothers' families are typical of lower-class households and are much like the families of the Hallway Hangers. Family structure is not of the conventional nuclear type; most are "broken homes." Educational achievement is low, and employment, for those who have a job, is typically in nondescript, uninteresting, unskilled work. There are, however, some differences between the families of the Brothers and of the Hallway Hangers in these areas. Whereas among the Hallway Hangers only Jinx's father lives regularly in the household, three of the Brothers have a male authority figure living with them. Nearly half the parents of the Brothers have graduated from high school; of the Hallway Hangers, only Boo-Boo and Frankie have a parent who has obtained a high school diploma. With the exception of Derek, all the Brothers are either the oldest male sibling or have older brothers and sisters whose educational achievement is significant; for the Hallway Hangers, on the other hand, it is more typical to find that an older sibling has been sent away to prison. In addition, all the Brothers' fathers work except Juan's, whereas among the Hallway Hangers, only Jinx's father works regularly. Moreover, the Hallway Hangers' families have lived in public housing for at least twenty years, and some are second-generation tenants (Stoney's, Jinx's, and Frankie's). The Brothers' families have lived in public housing for five to thirteen years (the exceptions are James, whose family has been in public housing for sixteen years, and Derek, who is Boo-Boo's brother). An even more pointed contrast arises when we consider how long the families of each peer group have lived in the Clarendon Heights neighborhood. Of the Hallway Hangers, only Steve's and Slick's family has moved to the area within the past twelve years. The opposite is true of the Brothers. Only James's family (and, of course, Derek's) has lived in Clarendon Heights for more than six years. In analyzing the feelings of hopelessness, immobility, and stagnation that plague the Hallway Hangers, this contrast will prove important.

The subjective side of these structural elements also shapes the boys' aspirations. Although rejection of parental authority is a common attribute of adolescent subcultures, the Hallway Hangers seem to respect the views of their parents, even though their parents do not play a large role in their lives. What we see in most cases is an unspoken but mutually accepted limitation of the parental role. At sixteen, seventeen, and eighteen years of age, these boys have gained a maturity from years of hard living on the street that is incommensurate with their chronological age. It appears that both they and their parents respect the notion that parental authority is incompatible with this maturity.

The boys' comments point to the limited role their parents play in their lives. In describing his mother's influence, Frankie says, "She wants me to do what I want to do." But, although she has little direct control of her son and does not exercise much authority, Frankie respects her wishes. He knew, for example, how badly she wanted one of her sons to graduate from high school. For reasons that will become clear [...], Frankie wanted to leave school. "The only reason I got my diploma wasn't for me; it was for my mother. My mother wanted a diploma." The limited influence Slick's mother had concerning the same issue is apparent from the following exchange.

(in a discussion with Slick and Shorty)

Jm: So did she [his mother] pressure you at all to stay in school when you decided to quit?

Slick: No. She wanted me to stay in high school, but at the time, things were tough, y'know?

Shorty: She knows his attitude is all right.

Slick: She knows what I want, and she's not gonna stop me from getting it my way.

This type of interaction is typical of the relationship between parent and son among the Hallway Hangers.

The respect these parents have for the autonomy of their sons extends to the way in which they influence their sons' occupational aspirations. When asked about the effect their parents have on their ambitions, the Hallway Hangers are unanimous in their declaration that such a determination is left up to them alone. Indeed, even Stoney's mother, the most authoritarian of the parents, does not feel it is her place to sway Stoney's aspirations. She thinks it inappropriate to foster high aspirations in her children, fearing that unrealistically high goals only will result in disappointment, frustration, and feelings of failure and inadequacy. "It's not like he's growing up in the suburbs somewhere. Sure, he could probably make it if everything went right for him, but lemme tell you, the chances aren't great. He's got his goals, and they're probably good, realistic ones. I personally think he should've stayed in school. I think he fucked up by dropping out. But he didn't think it was worth it, and what the hell, maybe it isn't."

Other parents also are hesitant to encourage hefty ambitions in their children; as the Hallway Hangers tell it, there is little stimulus from home to raise their aspirations.

Jm: What kind of work does your mother [do your parents] want you to do for a living?

(all in separate interviews)

Boo-boo: Anything. She doesn't really care, as long as I'm working.

Frankie: She don't fucking care. I mean, I'm sure she cares, but she don't push nothing on me.

Slick: She wants me to make a buck so I can move for myself.

Steve: Anything, man. Somethin'. I dunno. Just a fuckin' job.

Jinx: They don't talk about it. They hardly ever talk about it. Just as long as I'm not out of work. My mother hates when I'm unemployed.

If such an attitude is widespread among parents in Clarendon Heights, then the conventional sociological wisdom requires revision. The premise that lower-class parents project their frustrated ambitions onto their children in an attempt to reach their goals vicariously is a widely accepted notion among social psychologists and one to which Robert Merton alludes in his essay "Social Structure and Anomie." Citing work he and some colleagues undertook on the social organization of public housing developments, Merton reports that a substantial portion of both black and white parents on lower occupational levels want their children to have professional careers.[1] Before we challenge the sociological perspective on intergenerational mobility, however, we should consider the attitude of the Brothers' parents toward this issue.

In contrast to the Hallway Hangers, the Brothers' parents exercise a good deal of authority over them. All the Brothers have a relatively early curfew, which they conscientiously obey. They are expected to perform up to a certain standard at school, both in terms of academic achievement and discipline. Furthermore, they are expected to respect prohibitions against smoking cigarettes, drinking alcohol, and using drugs. Failure to meet expected standards of behavior invariably results in punishment. In these instances, the youth is confined to his family's apartment for specified times during the day. Sometimes one of the Brothers will be restricted to his room after school, occasionally for periods as lengthy as one month. By their obedience and consent to these restrictions the Brothers acknowledge the control their parents exercise. Comparable manifestations of parental authority are altogether absent among the Hallway Hangers. In fact, Craig explicitly made this point in comparing the differences in attitude and behavior between the Brothers and the Hallway Hangers. "I guess our parents are a lot tighter than their parents. Y'know, at least they tell us what to do and stuff. From the very beginning, ever since we were born, y'know, they'd always be telling us, 'Do this; do that.' Always disciplining us. As far as their parents go, I can't really say their parents are bad, but their parents aren't helping any."

Parental influence on the Brothers' aspirations accords with Merton's findings. James, for instance, feels that his parents project their own frustrated educational and occupational ambitions onto him.

> **James:** My father had to quit school when he had to go to work. But he went back to school. He was one of the top people in his class; he could've went to college. But he didn't have the money to go to college. He had to go to work. So now he wants us all to go to college.

> *(later in the same interview)*

> **Jm:** What do your mother and father want you to do for a living?

> **James:** They wanted me to be a lawyer when I was a little kid. They wanted me to grow up and be a lawyer.

James also attributes his dramatic turnaround in school performance to his father's influence.

> **Jm:** So how'd you get back on track, then? Why've you started working hard now? This year.

James: I decided I need to have good marks, so ...

Jm: Did anyone help you decide that or just ...

James: *Yeah.* My father.

Jm: Yeah?

James: He didn't hit me or anything; he just talked to me. Told me I wouldn't be able to go and do what I want to when school's over. Wouldn't be able to get no good job.

Other members of the Brothers indicate that similar processes are at work in their families.

Super: One thing I know they want me to do, they're always sayin' is finish school. They want me to go to college.

Jm: They want you to finish high school and college?

Super: Uh-huh. ... They want me to get a good job; I know that. And not no job with hard labor, y'know, standin' on my foot; they want me sittin' down, y'know, a good job, in an office.

Derek, Juan, and Craig also mention that their parents have high hopes for them. Craig's parents were the key figures in his decision to try becoming an architect. Juan's father wants him to get a job where "you can keep yourself clean." Derek's family nurtured hopes their son would enter a professional career. "They wanted me to be a lawyer. Ever since I went to Barnes Academy."

In addition to the Brothers' accounts, we have further evidence from the parents themselves. Mokey's mother, for instance, feels that her expectations heavily influence Mokey and undoubtedly will play a large part in whatever he decides to do. She insists that he pursue a career "which gives a successful future," such as management or ownership of a small business. She also believes that Mokey should "plan to be a success and reach the highest goal possible. The sky's the limit. That's what my mother told me, and that's what I tell my children. The sky is the limit."

Thus, the Brothers present a significant contrast to the Hallway Hangers with respect to their parents' influence in their lives. The Brothers' parents wield a substantial degree of authority, both in the present and in shaping their children's educational and occupational aspirations. These parents may be projecting their own unfulfilled occupational ambitions onto their children by nurturing in them high hopes for the future.

Some of the Brothers also have older siblings who serve as role models. Craig, Super, and James all have older brothers and sisters who have achieved at least moderate success in school. These three boys see that the path to academic achievement can be followed. Juan, Mokey, and Mike have no older siblings; they see a path that is as yet untried. In contrast, the Hallway Hangers, with the exception of Stoney and Slick, have older siblings who have failed in school; thus, the Hallway Hangers see a tortuous path that is difficult to negotiate. The Brothers all may not have older brothers and sisters who are high academic achievers, but, with the exception of Derek, at least they are not confronted exclusively with examples of academic failure, as most of the Hallway Hangers are. This difference between the two peer groups also has a significant impact on the boys' hopes for the future [...].

NOTE

1   Robert K. Merton, *Social Theory and Social Structure* (New York: Free Press, 1968), p. 213.

SOCIOLOGICAL PERSPECTIVES

Functionalism and the Family: The Family Satisfies Common Social Functions

- Socialization
  - Family is responsible for primary care and early learning.
- Birth; regulates sexual activity
  - Choosing mates and perpetuating population.
- Economic
  - Assigning assets.
  - Important economic production and consumption unit.
- Support and comfort
  - Help with problems.
- Social placement
  - Children inherit status and class of parents.

Family from the Conflict Perspective

- Power relationships
  - Men control wealth.
  - Norms require women to do most domestic chores.
- Perpetuation of social inequality
  - Family is a model of patriarchy that dominates society.

Symbolic Interactionism's Take on Family

- People construct their own families.
  - No two families are alike.
- Family is source of major roles and identity.
  - As new roles are learned, new concepts of reality are created.

More resources:

Fun with Charts: What Hans Rosling Can Tell us About Families and Population:
https://www.youtube.com/watch?v=hVimVzgtD6w
https://www.youtube.com/watch?v=jbkSRLYSojo
https://www.youtube.com/watch?v=fTznEIZRkLg

SUMMARY

Our families are very important social units. They are locations of the earliest socialization processes and social learning, serve as sources of knowledge about the world, and ultimately affect the social outcomes of their members.

As the structures of families change, so too do ideas about family. Conceptions about what a family is and what a family can be are changing. There are more interracial families, more families with LGBTQ parents, more step families, people getting married and having kids later, many more children being born outside of marriage, and changes in intergenerational livings. Over time these emerging types of families have generally become more socially accepted and more normative.

CHAPTER 15

Economy

ECONOMIC SOCIOLOGY IS the study of how the material conditions of life are produced and reproduced through social processes. The field of economic sociology can be separated into the sociology of markets and the sociology of consumption. The **sociology of markets** views markets as socially constructed arenas where repeated exchanges occur between buyers and sellers under a set of formal and informal rules governing relations between competitors, suppliers, and customers. Markets are dependent on governments, laws/policy, and cultural understandings that support market activity.

There are four bodies of work that provide different views on the mechanisms by which markets are organized: networks, institutions, political economy, and market devices and performativity.

The **sociology of consumption** situates consumption in the problem of what consuming things means to people. One core idea is that consumption is about how people constitute their lifestyles. Lifestyles can be constructed in emulation of other groups or instead by the competition between social groups for status. Another aspect of consumption is how morals and meanings affect what goods can be bought and sold. Scholars have explored why some products can and cannot be commoditized and how that has evolved over time. In other words, what people spend their money on, their purchasing and spending behavior, can tell us a lot about their lives, their values, and how they view society.

SOME PROBLEMATIC ASPECTS OF ECONOMIES

Potential economic social problems include the following:

- Inequality
- Poverty
- Hunger
- Unemployment
- Homelessness/affordable housing
- Wages and/or benefits
- Debt
- College tuition
- Corruption of markets/monopolies

CRITICAL THINKING: For whom is our economy functional?

THE US ECONOMY

The US economy is the largest in world history in terms of GDP. The United States, like most other nations of the world, uses a form of capitalism. America has mainly a service economy, which has transitioned from what used to be a manufacturing economy. Because of increasing globalization (the increasing linkage between the world) the internet, fast planes, cell phones, and so on we now have what many economists and sociologists call **global capitalism**. This entails competing against workers and with products and businesses from all over the world. This structural set of relations tends to drive down both wages and prices.

FROM MANUFACTURING TO SERVICE, FROM SERVICE TO KNOWLEDGE

The Industrial Revolution replaced family production in agrarian societies with market production. This made selling labor for wages exponentially more common and in turn started a process of urbanization, as workers no longer needed land to homestead. This process of industrialization lasted from the Industrial Revolution until about the 1960s.

De-industrialization was the systematic decline in production and manufacturing capabilities. Factories began to close in large numbers, and mass production began to be employed less. The industrial jobs like making cars or refrigerators that were lost began to be replaced by lower-wage service jobs.

The Service Revolution was the shift to an economy dominated by service and information occupations. The most common sorts of jobs in the service economy are fast-food worker, hospitality worker, retail sales, and cashier.[1]

The knowledge revolution refers to the potential undergoing transformation of the United States economy yet again. Most sociologists who study the economy have begun to come to a consensus that we are indeed undergoing a third large structural shift in

---

1   American Jobs, "Most Common Jobs in America," Ranker, June 14, 2019, https://www.ranker.com/list/most-common-jobs-in-america/american-jobs

economies. Many economists concur with this idea. We are beginning to see greater disparities in the economic lives of individuals of differing levels of education. Additionally, large swaths of the economy are now based on the ability to gather, understand, manipulate, and analyze data. For some this is the transition from a service-based economy to a knowledge economy.[2]

OTHER MAJOR ECONOMIC SHIFTS

- Elderly people are working in much larger numbers than before.
- Globalization has created competition not just between local workers but all workers.
- Other countries have developed better infrastructures since recovering from WW2, the fall of the USSR, and the decline of colonization.
- US manufacturing, particularly due to globalization, has dropped by more than half since 1965. Many more jobs are offshore outsourced.
- The US uses many more contingency workers than in the past. These workers are less likely to have long-term employment in one place or benefits like health care and pensions.

As the ability of goods, services, and people to flow across borders increases, and as technology fundamentally changes the manner in which production is done, longstanding economic understandings are increasingly unlikely to map onto the world. The following book excerpt discusses economic sociology in the context of rising globalization.

Reading 15.1.

Contemporary Economic Sociology: Globalization, Production, Inequality

by Fran Tonkiss

Here we will examine how we might analyze social and economic inequalities 'after' class. We turn first to debates that trace social and economic divisions in advanced economies not along class lines but around a range of factors including economic insecurity and forms of social exclusion. The discussion goes on to set these issues of inequality and insecurity in a global context, focusing on the links between poverty, inequality and economic growth.

---

2   Norton Sociology, "What Can Sociology Tell Us about the Economic Collapse and the Changing World Economy?," November 5, 2012, https://www.youtube.com/watch?v=9zmooAJmi5M&app=desktop

Fran Tonkiss, "Contemporary Economic Sociology: Globalization, Production, Inequality," *Contemporary Economic Sociology: Globalization, Production, Inequality.* Copyright © 2006 by Taylor & Francis Group. Reprinted with permission.

Recent approaches to economic inequality have seen a shift away from concepts of class—based on individuals' structural locations *within* an economic order—to notions of insecurity, as a condition where people have an uncertain or precarious relation to economic membership: that is, where they stand at least partly *outside* an economic order. Within European debates, this shift has been captured in the category of 'social exclusion', referring to the ways that economic and social marginality tend to overlap. In a US context, such arguments have been linked to theories of an impoverished 'underclass', a term used to denote the radical exclusion of vulnerable groups from the economic and social mainstream. In both cases, economic disparities stem not only from people's relative incomes, nor from their position within relations of production and work, but from their access to formal economic participation and their levels of social and economic protection. The argument in this [reading] is that current economic arrangements produce pronounced (if not entirely 'new') patterns of inequality, which continue to structure contemporary societies in quite systematic ways.

The latter part of the discussion takes up the issue of inequality in a global context. Here, lines of economic division are severe. The discussion focuses on large-scale analyses developed by researchers in major international agencies, examining the contentious relation between growth, poverty reduction and levels of inequality. The harsh disparities which characterize global economic relations can make theoretical and policy debates within advanced economies look almost trivial; however, the two parts of the discussion centre on common themes. The links between inequality, poverty and insecurity are critical to thinking about contemporary economic divisions in both national and international contexts. Degrees of inequality and of material deprivation vary sharply between the most and the least developed economies, but some of the key questions are the same. To what extent can poverty reduction be separated from decreasing inequality? Does it matter if the inequality gap widens so long as the poorest are protected? How does non-income poverty—exclusion, insecurity, incapacity—reinforce and reproduce economic and social divisions?

INEQUALITY 'AFTER' CLASS

The shift away from class that occurred within critical analysis from the 1980s was partly a response to changing forms of social and economic organization, but was also prompted by the claims of modes of inequality which sociology had been given to ignore or understate. An emphasis on class within social analysis had gone together with the relative neglect of inequality based on race or gender: racial or gender inequalities were frequently seen as secondary to class divisions, or appeared as effects of class structures. This conventional focus on class as the basis of social structure and the primary axis of social inequality has been roundly criticized for overlooking power relations which are not fundamentally about class, but rather centre on actual or ascribed identities of gender, race, culture, religion, or sexuality. Nancy Fraser (1995) has drawn a distinction in this respect between a 'social politics of equality', typically based on class, and a 'cultural politics of difference', associated with wider questions of identity. If class has been relegated from its primary analytic position, however, this does not mean that issues of economic inequality go away. Some of the most acute ways in which differences are socially marked, and personally and collectively experienced, are through economic structures. In this sense, criticisms of class from the standpoint of race or gender do not simply signal a move away from economic to cultural concerns, or from questions of inequality to those of identity. Inequality is still reproduced economically, and a focus on divisions other than class in fact can show up more severe economic disparities. Racial and ethnic differences frequently have been marked by forms of economic discrimination, domination and exploitation that are more vicious than class divisions, and which cannot be explained by recourse to class categories. So too, 'gender has exhibited far more pronounced inequalities of power and material rewards as well as offering more extreme examples of exploitation and brutal coercion than those occurring between classes' (Waters 2000: 49).

The critique of class therefore does not mean that economic inequality is no longer of analytic interest; in fact it can direct attention to starker forms of economic power and injustice. Too often, however, approaches to economic inequality have been seen as captive to a narrow 'distributive paradigm' that is over-determined by class, and which simply neglects forms of injustice which are not principally economic in character. Such an argument underlies a broad shift within social and political thought away from problems of inequality and redistribution and towards issues of difference and recognition.

In Anthony Giddens' (2000) work on *The Third Way and its Critics* the author seeks to make the claim that reducing poverty should take priority over reducing inequality. Giddens contends that the politics of the left has always conceived equality in terms of 'equality of outcomes'—the attempt to even up economic disparities, particularly through state intervention into market processes. Such a conception lies behind policies to redress social and economic inequalities by way of redistribution, both through welfare transfers and by narrowing inequalities of income and wealth via taxation.

The move away from equality of outcome towards equality of opportunity has gone together with a growing policy focus on investments in human capital—through education, skills training, childcare provision, and so on—in contrast to the redistribution of economic capital. Such strategies see people's capacities, including their skills and credentials, as determining their life chances in market societies. The answer for governments, then, is to help people to develop these capacities. Social and economic outcomes might be shaped by the development of opportunities, rather than through direct interventions at the level of 'who gets what'. The distinction between equality of opportunity and equality of outcomes is therefore a distinction between enabling capacities and engineering consequences. Some of this, to be sure, is little more than semantics. Giddens might stress the difference between equalities of opportunity and of outcome, but in practice British government policy of the late 1990s and early 2000s sought to intervene at the level of 'outcomes' as well as fostering people's life chances. A commitment to reducing poverty in any reasonable time-frame cannot wait for the slow feed of social mobility through enhanced opportunities.

A major rationale for such an emphasis on equality of opportunity is the argument that non-income poverty is as critical to individual life chances as income poverty. In this extended sense, poverty is defined not solely on the basis of income, but in terms of a lack of basic capacities or capabilities—health, education and literacy, reasonable housing conditions, safety—which allow individuals to participate in social membership and to make choices in respect of their own lives. We will revisit this approach to non-income poverty in thinking about global inequality; in the present context, it is linked with debates over social exclusion in advanced economies. The relation between poverty and social exclusion reproduces the distinction between economic outcomes and social opportunities which has characterized recent debates over inequality. While poverty is an economic category defined by material deprivation, exclusion refers to a broader sense of being shut out from full social and economic participation. It describes conditions of social deprivation which often overlap with, but are not simply identical to, economic disadvantage. This idea of social exclusion emerged from European policy debates of the 1980s, originating in France in particular, to refer to groups that stand in a marginal relation to core social and economic processes. In this way it does some of the same work as the notion of an 'underclass' in the United States, while aiming to avoid the latter's more negative connotations as well as its racial overtones.

Debates over the situation of an underclass in US society have been dogged by the conflation of economic, social and moral diagnoses. In an early work on the subject, Auletta (1982: xiii) noted that studies of poverty defined this excluded class in terms of 'behavioral, as well as income deficiencies'. The sociologist Herbert Gans concurs, arguing that the characterization of an underclass was based less on structural economic locations than on cultural or behavioral ascriptions (1995). In this sense it re-hashes earlier debates over a 'culture of poverty' amongst low-income groups, based on the reproduction of certain patterns of behavior and social and economic norms. Oscar Lewis' original work on impoverished families in Mexico, Puerto Rico and New York analyzed specific cultures of poverty as adaptive strategies developed in contexts of systematic discrimination and structural economic disadvantage; however the concept proved amenable to later arguments that material deprivation in wealthy societies was somehow due to a cultural problem with the poor themselves (Lewis 1959, 1966, 1996).

European debates over social exclusion generally sought to avoid the kinds of moral association that hung around the idea of an underclass; nevertheless some common themes are apparent. Policies to combat social exclusion in Britain from the late 1990s, for example, included community development initiatives on housing estates, as well as projects to lower rates of truancy and teenage pregnancy. Each of these elements features in Gans' round-up of the behavioral definition of an underclass in the US. These problems of social exclusion, however, were represented in the British context principally as barriers to individual opportunity rather than in terms of behavioral failures. An emphasis on such factors as housing environments and exclusion from education is based on the premise that economic inequalities are not reproduced solely through differentials in income levels, nor does income alone determine individuals' life chances. Rather, economic divisions are cross-cut with social conditions in limiting opportunities and stunting capacities.

Such an approach to equality—based on reducing poverty, enhancing opportunity, and combating social exclusion—raises a number of critical issues. For one thing, it is not clear just how 'new' any of this is. Recent arguments for widening social inclusion can be seen to rework, without always acknowledging, older arguments for the role of welfare provision in securing basic social rights and extending social citizenship (see Marshall 1950; Titmuss 1968). In this sense, the politics of welfare is not only about economic protections but also about social membership.

While no-one, to be sure, would argue with the goal of reducing poverty, it is less clear that poverty reduction and social inclusion can be so neatly separated from the goal of decreasing inequality. There is an argument to be made that the maintenance—and in some cases, the deepening—of economic inequalities is incompatible with efforts to widen social inclusion (see Phillips 1999). In this view, it is not simply absolute poverty but relative inequalities that undermine social cohesion and divide social groups. In contexts of entrenched inequality, the danger is that the stably employed and relatively secure come to identify with the better-off, detaching their own concerns from those of the unemployed or insecure. Economic divisions are compounded by social distance and moral disengagement. An approach to equality based on promoting opportunities at the level of the individual, however, tends to side-step this broader question of the relation between social inclusion and reducing inequality.

STRUCTURES OF INEQUALITY

Arguments that class categories are no longer the most obvious or accurate way to think about patterns of inequality do not mean that economic divisions are no longer structured in systematic ways. A number of recent analyses stratify contemporary societies around broad economic cleavages, based not simply on economic class locations but also on conditions of insecurity and exclusion. In this way they take up the critique of class-based models of inequality, recognizing that economic divisions are not solely organized around relations of production and work. The models considered below depict current patterns of stratification via broad schemes based on income, security and inclusion: the figures are approximate, therefore, but the lines of inequality they trace are more compelling.

Lash and Urry (1994) retain a class model to typify the economic divisions that are characteristic of advanced capitalist economies. One of the key challenges to conventional models of class has been the expansion of the service economy, and the related growth of the middle classes. The authors see this as a substantive shift in capitalist social structures, but argue that post-industrial economies produce both a mass middle-class grouping and also marked patterns of impoverishment, insecurity and exclusion. This is in large part due to the polarized nature of contemporary service industries, which generate both high-grade and very low-grade (poorly paid, insecure, unprotected and 'junk') jobs. They set out a basic model of social stratification along the following lines:

1   The top stratum is the relatively small capitalist class of owners. The rich, as ever, are always with us.

2   The mass class in advanced capitalist societies is the middle stratum of professional, managerial, administrative and service workers.

3   The working class, defined in conventional terms by their productive labor, is becoming smaller and is increasingly economically insecure. They are especially vulnerable to manufacturing downturns, downsizing, and the shift of productive jobs off-shore.

4   The bottom layer is occupied by a new lower class, defined by casual and insecure work (if any), social marginalization and poverty. This group tends to over-represent immigrant workers as well as women.

The interesting thing about this rather basic scheme is the depiction of a significant minority whose economic position is defined not by their work function but by their relative insecurity and exclusion from mainstream economic processes. Economic inequalities in this way are premised not only on relations of ownership and work, but on access to labor markets and security in work.

Indeed, Will Hutton (1995) sees insecurity as the central principle structuring contemporary economies. In his treatment of the 'thirty, thirty, forty society', Hutton jettisons the language of class to highlight patterns of relative economic security as the dividing line between different socioeconomic strata. Focusing on the British case, Hutton contends that the economy is broadly organized around:

1   Forty per cent who are stably employed and relatively secure: their work places are most likely to be covered by trade union agreements, they are more likely to have company or personal pensions and to have savings.

2   Thirty per cent who are relatively insecure: their work is casualized, their jobs are more likely to be unprotected, they may lack savings or pensions.

3   Thirty per cent are marginalized or excluded: this includes the unemployed or under-employed, those whose work is unprotected and low-paid, groups that live on state benefits or less.

Clearly this is a broad-brush depiction, and the figures are hit-or-miss. How the exact numbers carve up in such large-scale representations is less important than the lines of divisions these critics identify. In all cases, economic stratification does not simply follow income: rather, relative security becomes a key principle for understanding inequality. Structures of inequality are based on income and wealth but also on economic security, legal and welfare entitlement, and economic inclusion in society.

It is important to note, of course, that income and relative security will tend to overlap. Hutton points out that in increasingly flexible labor markets even very highly paid work can be insecure, but nonetheless the 'insecurity' of a freelance management consultant is not the same as that of casual cleaner. And while people's status within labor markets is crucial to their economic position, exclusion from the labor market altogether remains a primary source of inequality and insecurity.

While the framework of economic inclusion and exclusion, security and insecurity, can be applied to different international settings, the extremes of poverty and exclusion in the global system need to be considered in their own terms. It is to the question of global inequalities that the discussion now turns.

GLOBAL INEQUALITIES

The relation between poverty reduction and decreasing inequality is especially vexed in a global setting. In contexts of sheer deprivation and chronic hunger, reducing poverty is clearly the most immediate priority. It is less clear, however, how far poverty reduction can or should be linked with efforts to decrease inequality, both within and between nations. An important intervention in this debate is that made by the World Bank researchers Dollar and Kraay (2002), who emphasize the role of economic growth in poverty reduction. They contend that the recent period of globalization, dating from around 1980, has both promoted equality and decreased poverty. The authors track a long-term global trend towards greater inequality up to a peak in the 1970s; since 1980 growth has been more widely spread across the world economy; consequently the number of people living in absolute poverty has diminished. This is largely due to growth in China and India, which in 1980 included around one-third of the world's population but almost two-thirds of the world's poor.

For Dollar and Kraay economic growth is the key to taking people out of poverty, but to make a marked change to the global picture it is crucial that growth is not confined to those parts of the world that are already well-off. Poorer nations must have a share in economic growth, and the primary means to do this is through openness to international trade and investment. They are less interested, therefore, in nationalist or autarkic economic strategies than in the benefits to be gained from global integration. The authors argue that, during the period since 1980, the 'globalizers' amongst the less-developed countries have grown faster than 'non-globalizers' (and in many cases faster than developed economies). Those economies which have liberalized trade and attracted inward investment have seen the benefits in economic growth.

Such patterns are true not only for different national economies, but also for regions within national economies, as connected and 'disconnected' regions vary markedly in terms of growth. The problem of global inequality, then, is not so much that of growing inequality between the developed and the developing world, but of growing inequality within the developing world, based on varying access to global economic processes. Moreover, Dollar and Kraay argue that globalizing measures do not in themselves promote inequality; rather inequality within economies tends to reflect domestic policies on such matters as taxation, education, employment protection and welfare. It follows that ensuring the benefits of globalization—'spreading the wealth', as the authors put it—requires a policy mix which limits protectionist measures by rich nations, and promotes sound domestic governance in developing economies. Trade openness at the international level should be matched by policy interventions to narrow inequalities at the national level.

This analysis has been influential, but also controversial. Most simply it is seen as advocating a 'trickle-down' approach to economic growth—a criticism that does not exactly square with Dollar and Kraay's emphasis on the importance of domestic policy interventions in ensuring that economic benefits are spread. A more complex argument concerns the structural relation between poverty and inequality. How far can poverty reduction be separated from decreasing inequality? Should anti-poverty strategies centre on absolute poverty (the dollar a day measure) or relative poverty (degrees of inequality within societies)? There is evidence to suggest that more unequal economies do less well at translating economic growth into lower rates of poverty. The argument here is not simply a moral but an economic one: economic inequality can be seen not only as unjust but as inefficient. Inequities in land ownership, in access to productive assets, income and market opportunities can impede economic growth and prospects for inward investment. Cornia and Kiiski (2001: 37) argue that high levels of inequality represent a barrier to growth in numerous developing and transitional economies. If reducing poverty and decreasing inequality do not always go together, moreover, increases in both poverty and inequality often do—as shown by mounting poverty and inequality in the former states of the Soviet Union (see Oxfam 2003; UNDP 1999: 3, 2003: 37–8).

Dollar and Kraay's case centers on a sustained downward turn in *global* inequality—that is, in the disparity between rich and poor nations. Inequality cuts, however, in different ways. The UNDP (2003: 39) asserts that 'in recent decades there has unquestionably been a widening gap between the incomes of the very richest and the very poorest'. In the early years of the twenty-first century, the richest 5 per cent of the global population commanded 114 times the income of the poorest 5 per cent, while the top 1 per cent had as much as the bottom 57 per cent. Alongside these inequities in income levels may be set the unequal share of economic activity between nations. Richer nations continue to enjoy the lion's share of overall wealth, trade, investment and technology. By the end of the twentieth century, the fifth of the global population in the wealthiest countries had 86 per cent of world GDP to the bottom fifth's 1 per cent share; furthermore, the world's richest nations had 74 per cent of the world's telephone connections (and 91 per cent of its Internet users), while the bottom fifth had only 1.5 per cent (all figures UNDP 1999: 3).

Moving from the level of global inequality to that of national inequality adds to this picture. Dollar and Kraay state that levels of inequality within nations tend to decrease only very slowly. Slow reductions in domestic inequality are one thing, however; growing inequality is another. Over the critical period identified by Dollar and Kraay, from 1980 to the end of the 1990s—when global inequality and absolute poverty figures were both reducing—inequality increased markedly *within* transitional economies in the former Soviet bloc, as well as in such advanced capitalist countries as Japan, Sweden, the United Kingdom, the United States, Canada and Australia (Cornia and Kiiski 2001; UNDP 1999: 3). Looking more closely at specific countries and regions tends to interrupt this steady narrative of widening growth, diminishing poverty and decreasing inequality.

During the 1980s just four nations saw downturns in their human development index—a measure of life expectancies, levels of health and education, and basic living standards—while in the 1990s 21 nations witnessed such reversals (UNDP 2003: 34). This was in large part due to the HIV/AIDS crisis, but in the most severely affected nations the effects of the epidemic were compounded by a lack of economic growth, growing debt and falling commodity prices. In a large comparative review using data from 73 countries, representing 80 per cent of world population and 91 per cent of world GDP, Cornia and Kiiski adjudge that inequality increased during the 1980s and 1990s in 48 of the sample nations, and fell in just 9 (Cornia and Kiiski 2001).

POVERTY, INEQUALITY, INSECURITY: CHALLENGES FOR HUMAN DEVELOPMENT

These trends provided the backdrop to the United Nations Millennium Declaration of September 2000, endorsed by 189 member states. The Declaration made a collective commitment to efforts to reduce poverty, improve health, support environmental sustainability, promote peace and protect human rights. It is highly debatable how far advances have been made on any of these fronts, but progress in reducing poverty at least is measurable. The 'road map' for realizing this declaration is detailed in the form of eight Millennium Development Goals, the first of which is a goal to halve by 2015 the number of people living under the global poverty line of $1 per day (UNDP 2003: 15). A few years in, however, international agencies were projecting that the chances of reaching that goal varied markedly between regions and across nations: East Asia, Southeast Asia and South Asia had the best regional prospects, Latin America and the Caribbean were unlikely to meet the target, while sub-Saharan Africa was extremely unlikely to achieve it (see ILO UNDP 2003; World Bank 2005). At the national level dozens of countries were identified as priority cases, 'perilously off track to meet the Goals' (UNDP 2003: 15).

The emphasis in these analyses is on the linkage between economic growth and poverty reduction. On the one hand, this relationship can be quite straightforward: economic growth can reduce poverty by directly increasing household incomes. However, this is not an automatic effect of growth: it is more likely 'that economic growth reduces income poverty most when initial income inequality is narrow' (UNDP 2003: 17), while people can only share in economic growth where they have access to land and other assets, jobs, markets and credit. On the other hand, economic growth can also indirectly reduce poverty by increasing public revenues and allowing governments to invest in education, health and infrastructure. Such measures all promote skills and productivity levels, but they also have an impact on non-economic poverty. Anti-poverty measures may relate both to the distribution of private goods, and to the definition, distribution and quality of public goods: those goods held in common or public ownership, from water and air to hospitals or roads. This is to draw out the connection between income poverty and a broader 'human poverty' which limits people's capacities to make decisions in their communities and about their own lives due to poor health, sub-standard living environments or lack of education—that is, the lack of basic social and economic capabilities (UNDP 2003: 27).

Such arguments are indebted to Amartya Sen's work on inequality (see especially Sen 1992, 1999). Sen's core argument is that conventional approaches to inequality have focused too heavily on the distribution of commodities and capital, rather than on the share of capabilities or chances. He contends that strategies of economic development should aim to promote human capacities and not simply redistribute goods. Such capacities include individual human capital—knowledge, skills, abilities—but also shared forms of technical and informational capital—technology, information, intellectual goods. More broadly, a stress on capabilities takes in levels of health and education, standards of housing and environmental quality, community development and civil rights.

Leading debates on global equality emphasize the links between reducing poverty, decreasing inequality, and promoting human capacities. The distinction between economic and other forms of justice is in this sense a false one. The UN Development Goals are articulated as social and economic rights, and therefore tied up with wider human rights instruments and objectives. Moreover, problems of poverty and inequality are understood not merely in terms of income poverty, but also in respect of different kinds of insecurity. While uncertainties in employment conditions, labor market prospects and financial support are very significant in this context, insecurity is not confined to these economic forms. Rather, this problem can be defined in a number of ways (UNDP 1999):

1 Financial volatility and economic insecurity, including the immediate and longer-term effects of financial crises and economic downturns.
2 Job and income insecurity, linked to restructuring and job losses as well as to more general effects of casualization.
3 Health insecurity: the most obvious case is that of HIV/AIDS, but globalization also means that other epidemics have the potential to travel faster and wider than in the past.
4 Cultural insecurity, the effects of which extend from the extremes of cultural genocide to monocultural policy-making and global trends towards homogenization in media and cultural goods and images.
5 Personal insecurity, linked to crime and victimizaton—including problems of organized crime, sexual violence and sex traffic, vigilante and gun crime.
6 Environmental insecurity, a gathering crisis seen in depleted stocks, threats to biodiversity, and climate change.
7 Political and community insecurity, seen in war, civil conflict, state persecution and poor governance.

In all of these domains—from fears over personal safety to environmental degradation and organized violence—the costs of insecurity tend to be borne by the poorest groups in society. Situations of insecurity and risk in this way overlap with conditions of poverty, serving to reinforce existing structures of social and economic inequality.

CONCLUSION

Debates over inequality 'after' class in advanced capitalist societies have turned on a series of distinctions between economic and other forms of equality; between reducing poverty and narrowing inequalities; between income differentials, insecurity and exclusion. Setting these arguments in a more global context, however, tends to dissolve such lines of distinction. Inequality, poverty and insecurity interact in complex but legible ways to reproduce deep disparities both between and within nations. Furthermore, social and economic rights—those implied by politics to reduce poverty, promote human welfare and narrow inequalities—can be seen as continuous with wider cultural, political and human rights. To adopt the familiar maxim, famines do not happen in functioning democracies. This may be a truism, but it points to the fact that the stakes involved in arguments over inequality are much higher at a global level than they are in the most developed economies. In the latter setting, hair-splitting over equalities of opportunity as opposed to outcomes can appear as another of the luxuries of the better-off. It is fair to say that arguments over inequality are generally fraught by competing definitions, measures, focal points, and prescriptions. Still, there are more fundamental questions at issue than disputes over methodology or analysis. Sen (2002) criticizes the idea that technical measures of (increasing or decreasing) inequality or of (increasing or decreasing) income are the acid-test of economic growth, or indeed of globalization. They are neither easily comparable nor do they tend to be conclusive. The more relevant assessment, for Sen, is not the measure of existing distributions of wealth, but an evaluation of their *fairness* in comparison to alternative arrangements. Taking up a notion of justice as fairness in a global context is to underline the premise—of some politics and all economic sociology—that economic processes ultimately cannot be isolated from the social contexts within which they operate. Technical measures of economic inequality offer conflicting accounts of what nevertheless are objective conditions, but these real conditions are instituted through policy, structured by relations of power, and legitimized, reproduced or challenged by social actors.

DISCUSSION QUESTIONS

1   What is one concept that Tonkiss argues could be more useful in the 21st century than class? Why is this concept more useful than class?

2   Describe "non-income poverty."

3   What is the relationship between inequality and poverty at the national level? At the global level?

REFERENCES

Auletta, K. (1982) The Underclass. New York: Random House.

Cornia, G. A. and Kiiski, S. (2001) 'Trends in income distribution in the post-World War Two period: evidence and interpretation', UN/Wider Discussion Paper 2001/89. United Nations University, World Institute for Development Economics Research, Helsinki. http://www.wider.unu.edu/publications.

Dollar, D. and Kraay, A. (2002) 'Spreading the wealth', Foreign Affairs 81/1: 120–33.

Fraser, N. (1995) 'From redistribution to recognition? Dilemmas of justice in a "post-socialist" age', New Left Review 212: 68–93.

Gans, H. T. (1995) The War Against the Poor: The Underclass and Antipoverty Policy. New York: Basic Books.

Giddens, A. (1981) The Class Structure of the Advanced Societies (second edition). London: Hutchinson.

Hutton, W. (1995) 'The thirty, thirty, forty society', in The State We're In. London: Jonathan Cape, 105–10.

Lash, S. and Urry, J. (1994) Economies of Signs and Space. London: Sage.

Lewis, O. (1959) Five Families: Mexican Case Studies in the Culture of Poverty. New York: Basic Books.

Lewis, O. (1966) La Vida: A Puerto Rican Family in the Culture of Poverty—San Juan and New York. New York: Random House.

Lewis, O. (1996) [1966] 'The culture of poverty', in R. T. Le Gates and F. Stout (eds) The City Reader. London and New York: Routledge, 218–24.

Marshall, T. H. (1950) Citizenship and Social Class. Cambridge: Cambridge University Press.

Oxfam (2003) 'Growth with equity is good for the poor', in F. Lechner and J. Boli (eds) The Globalization Reader (second edition). Oxford: Blackwell, 183–9.

Phillips, A. (1999) 'Does economic inequality matter?', in Which Equalities Matter? Cambridge: Polity, 44–73.

Sen, A. (1992) Inequality Re-examined. Oxford: Clarendon Press.

Sen, A. (1999) Development as Freedom. New York: Alfred A. Knopf.

Sen, A. (2002) 'How to judge globalism', The American Prospect 13/1: 2–6. Titmuss, R. (1968) Commitment to Welfare. London: Allen and Unwin.

UNDP (1999) Human Development Report 1999: Globalization with a Human Face. New York: Oxford University Press.

UNDP (2003) Human Development Report 2003: Millennium Development Goals—A Compact Among Nations to End Poverty. New York: Oxford University Press.

Waters, M. (2000) 'Inequality after class', in K. Nash (ed.) Readings in Contemporary Political Sociology. Oxford: Blackwell, 43–62.

World Bank (2005) Global Monitoring Report 2005. Washington: World Bank.

COVID-19: AN EXAMPLE OF THE INTERSECTION OF SOCIETY AND THE ECONOMY

Generally, economies and the societies in which they operate are intimately intertwined. Social forces in a particular society are both caused by economic conditions as well as causally linked to economic change. Economies are both reflections of a society as well as primary drivers of social organization and social life. As national economies become more intertwined into what social scientists call a global economy, changes almost anywhere in the world can result in changes almost anywhere else.

Beginning in early 2020, many countries around the world underwent rapid social changes because of COVID-19. These social changes, such as social distancing, closing schools, and limiting gatherings, quickly resulted in massive economic upheaval, with increases in unemployment, decreases in employment prospects, and large fluctuations in stock markets. The economic hardships wrought by these economic changes in turn affect society quite a bit. Social morale is different because of the pandemic: Many social functions have been cancelled or delayed, shopping patterns have changed, living patterns have changed, daily routines have changed, education has changed, and so on. One can see how the economy (as an example of just one factor) and society are cyclically tied; taken a step further, education affects productivity and many other economic factors.

CONCLUSION

There have been many major economic shifts in the past fifty years or so. Globalization has affected markets, trade, and employment. Major changes around the globe have also dramatically affected the economies around the globe. What has remained consistent is the nature to which societies and economies are intimately tied, with major shifts in one dramatically affecting the other. One of the most recent examples of this is the COVID-19 pandemic.

While it has been the richest country in the world for nearly seventy years, the United States has undergone several economic transitions over that time. It has gone from an agrarian society in its colonial days to an industrial society, to a service economy, and is likely transitioning once again to a knowledge economy. The United States, like most nations, uses a form a capitalism, meaning that the ease of buying and selling goods in markets is highly valued, mostly voluntary, and relatively unrestricted. Lastly, within the United States there have been several specific changes, like the elderly working more often and longer, that also affect the overall economy of America.

CHAPTER 16

Conclusion

CONGRATULATIONS! YOU SHOULD now have a high level of understanding of social problems and hopefully enjoyed some of the material along the way. This anthology was designed to give a brief overview of what social problems are and how they are studied, sociological perspectives, sociological theories, and some of the commonly cited contemporary social problems. It is the job of sociologists to become experts in some or all of these areas, and hopefully the expertise of some of the authors included was able to come through.

While there are many social problems in America and across the globe, it is important to emphasize that there are wonderful aspects of society and humanity that are simply not the focus of this book.

The last fifty years have been a time of rising inequality within countries (although many nation-states have become more equal relative to each other) and across the globe. More and more wealth has become concentrated in the hands of very few people. The United States specifically is near its peak in recorded inequality and has also seen a marked decrease in mobility. Globalization and other forces have made work much more competitive, and the growth of median wages has slowed.

The last fifty years have also seen exponential increases in the prison population and drug deaths. The prison population peaked around 2.3 million in 2014, and the number of drug deaths reached an all-time high of over seventy thousand in 2017. Both figures increased despite the United States declaring and mostly maintaining a war on drugs since the 1970s.

Within the United States there are contemporary challenges to long standing paradigms about gender, sexuality, race, and families. Black Lives Matter and #MeToo are two such organizations/hashtags currently engaged in these sorts of challenges. Challenges to such longstanding and deeply held social beliefs and ideas are usually met with concerted push back, and how these challenges play out will have a large impact on American society. While inequalities still exist across all of these dimensions, in some arenas, like gay marriage, we have seen rapid changes to public opinion and public policy.

Health care is also an increasingly cited social problem; the United States is among the nations with the most expensive health care costs, yet health care outcomes among Americans does not rank nearly as high as such a level of spending would suggest. There are also disparities in health and health outcomes across social factors like race and income.

And the aforementioned problems all exist in a world in which societies across the globe are already having to deal with the ramifications of a changing climate. Dealing with a truly global issue may also affect the manner in which nation/societies interact with each other in addition to affecting nearly every nation individually as well.

With an increase in media consumption (up to about 12 hours a day, and higher for some groups) comes the increase in the ability to encounter and discuss social problems. And there have been a number of important and effective online social movements as a result. However, there is a downside to consuming so much media, and an especially pronounced downside to using social media for over 90 minutes.

We have also seen that if, how, and why something is labeled a social problem is related to a number of social factors and that the degree to which something is labeled a social problem can and does change over time. And that social factors like age and political affiliation can affect the manner and degree to which something is conceived as a social problem.

Although there is great variability in the types of social problems that were examined in this book, most social problems can be better understood with a working knowledge of sociology. They all relate to how individuals, social structures, social norms, and social institutions interact with one another and all can be analyzed through a social lens.

As a final takeaway, it is important to note that understanding social problems can give a great deal of insight into society itself. We learn about social problems not to be mired in despair or because the world is some terrible place of negativity, but because they are an important part of our social world. Learning about them can give us great insight into our societies, into our lives, and into ourselves. It is the recognition of and organization around social problems that lead to social change, social movements, and new social understandings.

Use your sociological tool belt and knowledge of social problems to help explore your social world and to gain better insights into society and social life.[1]

---

1 Please note that sociologists have been trained to go out into the world to study a wide variety of situations. One should never put themselves at risk to try and make a social observation.

CPSIA information can be obtained
at www.ICGtesting.com
Printed in the USA
LVHW060205310721
694167LV00005B/38